Lecture Notes in Computer Science 9337

Commenced Publication in 1973
Founding and Former Series Editors:
Gerhard Goos, Juris Hartmanis, and Jan van Leeuwen

More information about this series at http://www.springer.com/series/7408

Floor Koornneef · Coen van Gulijk (Eds.)

Computer Safety, Reliability, and Security

34th International Conference, SAFECOMP 2015
Delft, The Netherlands, September 23–25, 2015
Proceedings

 Springer

Editors
Floor Koornneef
University of Technology
Delft
The Netherlands

Coen van Gulijk
University of Huddersfield
Huddersfield
UK

ISSN 0302-9743   ISSN 1611-3349 (electronic)
Lecture Notes in Computer Science
ISBN 978-3-319-24254-5   ISBN 978-3-319-24255-2 (eBook)
DOI 10.1007/978-3-319-24255-2

Library of Congress Control Number: 2015948709

LNCS Sublibrary: SL2 – Programming and Software Engineering

Springer Cham Heidelberg New York Dordrecht London

Springer International Publishing AG Switzerland is part of Springer Science+Business Media
(www.springer.com)

Preface

With some pride, we present to you the proceedings of the 34th International Conference on Computer Safety, Reliability, and Security, SAFECOMP 2015, held at Delft University of Technology during 23–25 September 2015. SAFECOMP has become an excellent and high-quality platform for exchanging ideas between industry and academia about safety considerations in programmable industrial systems.

International collaboration constitutes an important success factor for conferences such as these. This volume contains contributions from Austria, Brazil, Finland, France, Germany, Iran, Ireland, Italy, the Netherlands, Spain, Sweden, UK, and USA. In the same spirit, the SAFECOMP Program Chair is shared by Delft University of Technology in the Netherlands and the University of Huddersfield in the UK.

The 34th edition of SAFECOMP focused on the challenges arising from networked multi-actor systems for delivery of mission-critical services. Such services are expanding rapidly in all domains of life. Society has, therefore, become very vulnerable to breaches in delivery of service, thus imposing serious risks to life and limb of people. This year's call for papers focused on assured connectivity. This put the emphasis on papers that focus on connectivity of systems and software applications to support that connectivity. Assured connectivity is important in the three major themes that emerged from the papers accepted for the conference: transport systems, medical systems, and security. The conference program was designed accordingly.

The conference started with a keynote address on communication networks by Andrey Nikishin, Director of Special Projects and Future Technologies of Kaspersky Lab. The subsequent sessions regarded automotive systems from various perspectives. Transport systems have always been heavily dependent on the safety of computer systems. The application of computers in safety-related critical systems is pivotal for the smooth operation of critical infrastructures. Though there is much emphasis on the ISO 26262 standard for road transport, human factors, technical systems, and flight systems are treated in this year's SAFECOMP.

The second day was devoted to medical technology systems and assurance. The keynote address is by Cor Kalkman, anesthesiologist at Utrecht University Medical Center. Medical systems are strongly interconnected and are critical almost by definition.

The theme of the third day was security and safety. The keynote address was by Eric Luiijf, principal consultant C(I)IP&Cyber Ops at TNO, the Netherlands, and it discussed industrial security. Protection from security attacks and cyber security are a necessity in today's systems, requiring attention and integration with safety critical systems. Here, the concept of an intelligent adversary in critical infrastructures adds complexity in the design of safe systems.

Some papers focus on the development of new methods rather than industry-related themes. These papers are placed in separate sessions, each of which is treated on a separate day: error detection on the first day, safety cases on the second, and programming and compiling on the third.

The reviewing and selection of papers is a careful process, which depends on the collaboration of many individuals. First of all it depends on authors willing to submit a paper to the evaluation process. This year 33 papers were accepted out of 104 submissions. We thank all authors for their submissions and would encourage all authors, particularly also the ones that were not accepted in SAFECOMP 2015, to consider SAFECOMP 2016 for publishing their papers. A team of 66 active International Program Committee members performed peer reviews, at least three per paper, and the International Program Committee decided on which papers to accept on April 15 at the University of Huddersfield. The quality and success of the SAFECOMP conference depends on the readiness and willingness to participate in the reviewing and selection process. We thank everyone for their efforts on this. EWICS TC7 has provided the stable background for SAFECOMP since its inception in 1979. We thank Francesca Saglietti, in her role as chair for EWICS TC7, for the continued support from EWICS TC7.

This conference was flanked by several workshops on safety and security considerations in programmable industrial systems and critical infrastructures. The acronyms for these workshops are: ASSURE, DECSoS, ISSE, ReSA4CI, and SASSUR. What these acronyms mean and the proceedings of these workshops can be found in LNCS volume 9338.

It has been the honor and pleasure of the program chairs to work with a team of such dedicated individuals. We thank the authors, the reviewers, the International Program Committee, EWICS TC7 members, and the Local Organizing Committee for their pleasant cooperation. We would also like to thank prior organizers of SAFECOMP, Andrea Bondavelli, Andrea Ceccarelli, Friedeman Bitsch, and Jérémie Guiochet, for sharing their experience. We also thank Saba Chockalingam and Yamin Huang for their contribution in formatting and completing the proceedings.

Last, but not least, we want to thank you, the participants at this year's SAFECOMP. We hope you enjoyed an interesting conference and a pleasant stay in Delft!

September 2015   Floor Koornneef
                                                      Coen van Gulijk

Organization

Committee

EWICS TC7 Chair

Francesca Saglietti   University of Erlangen-Nuremberg, Germany

General Chair

Pieter van Gelder   Delft University of Technology, the Netherlands

Program Co-chairs

Floor Koornneef   Delft University of Technology, the Netherlands
Coen van Gulijk   University of Huddersfield, UK

Workshop Chair

Frank Ortmeier   Otto-von-Guericke-Universität Magdeburg, Germany

Finance Chair

Erika van Verseveld   Delft University of Technology, the Netherlands

Publicity Chair

Sandra Koreman   schetsboek.com, the Netherlands

Local Organizing Chair

Genserik Reniers   Delft University of Technology, the Netherlands
Bas de Mol   Academic Medical Center, the Netherlands
Ginny Ruiter   Delft University of Technology, the Netherlands
Marie-Louise Verhangen   Delft University of Technology, the Netherlands
Larissa Mikhailovaa   LASEMN R&C, The Netherlands

International Program Committee

Stuart Anderson   University of Edinburgh, UK
Jan van den Berg   Delft University of Technology, the Netherlands
Friedemann Bitsch   Thales Transportation Systems GmbH, Germany
Peter Bishop   City University London and ADELARD, UK
Robin Bloomfield   ADELARD, London, UK
Sandro Bologna   Associazione Italiana Esperti in Infrastrutture Critiche
                                  (AIIC), Italy
Andrea Bondavalli   University of Florence, Italy

Jens Braband	Technische Universität Braunschweig, Germany
Francesco Brancati	Resiltech S.R.L., Italy
Frances Brazier	Delft University of Technology, the Netherlands
Nick Chozos	ADELARD, London, UK
Peter Daniel	EWICS, UK
Felicita Di Giandomenico	ISTI-CNR, Italy
Geoff Duke	LifeScan Scotland Ltd, UK
Sherman Eagles	SoftwareCPR, LLC, USA
Wolfgang Ehrenberger	Hochschule Fulda - University of Applied Sciences, Germany
Massimo Felici	HP Lab., UK
Roman Fiedler	AIT Austrian Institute of Technology, Austria
Francesco Flammini	Ansaldo STS, Italy, University Federico II of Naples, Italy
Pieter van Gelder	Delft University of Technology, the Netherlands
Janusz Górski	Gdansk University of Technology, Poland
Jérémie Guiochet	LAAS, CNRS, France
Coen van Gulijk	University of Huddersfield, UK
Wolfgang Halang	Fernuniversität Hagen, Germany
Maritta Heisel	University Duisburg-Essen, Germany
Chris Johnson	University of Glasgow, UK
Erland Johnson	Chalmers University, Stockholm, Sweden
Mohamed Kaaniche	LAAS, CNRS, France
Karama Kanoun	LAAS, CNRS, France
Johan Karlsson	Chalmers University of Technology, Sweden
Tim Kelly	University of York, UK
John Knight	University of Virginia, USA
Phil Koopman	Carnegie Mellon University, USA
Floor Koornneef	Delft University of Technology, the Netherlands
Peter Ladkin	Bielefeld University, Germany
Giuseppe Lami	ISTI-CNR, Italy
Søren Lindskov Hansen	Novonordisk A/S, Denmark
Bev Littlewood	City University London, UK
Eric Luiijf	TNO, the Netherlands
Meine van der Meulen	DNV/GL, Norway
Michele Minichino	ENEA, Italy
Bas de Mol	Academic Medical Center, the Netherlands
Gilles Motet	INSA Toulouse, France
Odd Nordland	SINTEF, Trondheim, Norway
Frank Ortmeier	Otto-von-Guericke Universität Magdeburg, Germany
Philippe Palanque	IRIT, France
Alberto Pasquini	Deep Blue, Italy
Michael Paulitsch	AIRBUS Group, Germany
Thomas Pfeiffenberger	Salzburg Research, Austria
Peter Popov	City University London, UK
Felix Redmill	Redmill Consultancy, London, UK

Genserik Reniers	Delft University of Technology, the Netherlands
Luigi Romano	University of Naples "Parthenope", Italy
Alexander Romanovosky	University of Newcastle, UK
Martin Rothfelder	Siemens, Germany
John Rushby	SRI International, USA
Francesca Saglietti	University of Erlangen-Nuremberg, Germany
Christoph Schmitz	Zühlke Engineering AG, Switzerland
Erwin Schoitsch	AIT Austrian Institute of Technology, Austria
Christel Seguin	ONERA, France
Amund Skavhaug	NTNU, Norway
Mark Sujan	University of Warwick, UK
Jos Trienekens	Eindhoven University of Technology, the Netherlands
Elena Troubistsyna	Åbo Akademi University, Finland
Martijn Warnier	Delft University of Technology, the Netherlands
Alex Zechner	ICS AG, Germany

Sub-reviewers

Victor Bandur	University of York, UK
Simon Foster	University of York, UK
Linas Laibinis	Åbo Akademi University, Finland
Inna Pereverzeva	TUCS, Finland
Thomas Santen	Microsoft, USA

Sponsors

EWICS TC7

Delft University of Technology

University of Huddersfield

Conference Partners

Austrian Association for Research
in IT

Austrian Institute of Technology

Advanced Research & Technology
for EMbedded Intelligence and
Systems

European Network of Clubs for
Reliability and Safety of Software

European Research Consortium for
Informatics and Mathematics
(ERCIM)

European Safety and Reliability
Association

VDE-ITG

ITG

Gesellschaft für Informatik e. V.

International Federation for
Information Processing

LAAS-CRNS

NASA

Austrian Computer Society

ResilTech

Safety Critical Systems Club

Verband Österreichischer Software Industrie

Invited Talks

Does IoT Stand for Internet of Threats and Other Stories

Andrey Nikishin

Kaspersky Lab, London, UK
a.nikishin@kaspersky.com

Story 1. Enterprise 4.0

They say history repeats itself and that holds true with revolutionary development. But when the scientific and technological revolutions occur, many old principles fade away for good – they don't answer to the new demands. Those that failed to attune are falling off the market irreversibly. The latest invention to spur a new industrial revolution is the Internet. While the Internet itself had been invented long ago, only quite recently has it become a part of production processes. It immediately gave birth to a new phenomenon – "Enterprise 4.0", an enterprise which uses cloud technologies, big data, etc., to improve its performance and output. Where Internet and Big Data can help? Let's retrofit the units with transducers, connect them to the Web, and allow them to deliver the data on the units' status to the analysis center. Based on practical experience and the data gathered from other units, it is decided whether maintenance is required. Some manufacturers do it that way: equip their hardware with the necessary transducers and controllers for performance improvement. But they forget that a revolution has occurred and times are different. One does not simply hook a pre-Internet unit to the Web without consequences. Quite recently all industrial equipment – hardware, connectivity protocols, etc. – were designed with safety in mind. If it is safely designed, it means that as long as safety procedures are maintained there won't be any failures, and neither people nor ecology will fall victim. Enterprise 4.0 acquired a new safety dimension – an information security. But the engineers who follow the "pre-Revolution" age design principles often overlook this. And the consequences may be (and sometimes are) pretty dire. How to avoid this?

Story 2. Privacy and IoT

There was one very interesting feature in one quite popular fitness bracelet among its functional – tracking of the number of burnt per day calories. In order to be more precise count is the number, the user can enter a kind of activity he or she doing – running, walking, swimming. Among the wide variety of activities there was making love. Also, the owner could share its achievement on Facebook or Twitter – how many calories he or she burnt today and how close to the target. Great idea, is not it? The idea looks great, but there was one more feature that spoils everything – share such information has been switch on by default. Imagine a wife or a husband who sees that a partner just had a sex with someone for 5 minutes. Here we come to a very important issue – the privacy of the data. What kind of information is private, and what is not? One's heart rhythm and pace, gas or electricity meter readings, route to work or the duration of one's sleep? How can we protect privacy in a world where coffee makers and refrigerators have their own Twitter account?

Story 3: Evolution of Malware

I am a happy person – I'm doing the same thing the last 20 years. The first computer virus I analysed was RCE2885 Yankee Doodle. I still remember myself sitting on the floor in front of 5 meter roll of paper, where was printed in the dump of the virus. For over 20 years of evolution malware have come a long way from the students' entertainment ("Look, I could write a virus and break down all the computers in a school or university"), to means of "earning" money, to the attributes of a modern spy, and even cyber weapon. 10-15 years ago, we even could not imagine that a computer program can physically damage any equipment. Now it has become a reality. Previously, the number of people who could write malicious software was the hundreds around the world, now it's thousands and millions. It would not be so bad if there were no extremists in the world. Should we wait for cyber Armageddon? What we need to do to prevent this from happening?

Medical Devices, Electronic Health Records and Assuring Patient Safety: Future Challenges?

Cor J. Kalkman

University Medical Center, Utrecht, The Netherlands
c.j.kalkman@umcutrecht.nl

Abstract. The patient safety movement was triggered by publications showing that modern health care is more unsafe than road travel and that more patients are killed annually by avoidable adverse events than by breast cancer [1]. As a result, an urgent need to improve patient safety has dominated international health care systems over the last decade. Some examples of safety issues that healthcare actively tries to address are: reducing the incidence of hospital-acquired infections, avoiding errors with patient identification (wrong patient, wrong procedure, wrong side), errors with drug prescription and administration (wrong drug, wrong dose, wrong route), recognizing deteriorating patients earlier to allow timely life-saving treatment, developing systems for rapid appropriate treatment for stroke and myocardial infarction and improving care for frail elderly patients with multiple diseases using many drugs. Addressing these issues has proven more difficult than anticipated and actual progress in patient safety has been frustratingly slow. [2] Root cause analysis of serious adverse events invariably points to problems with communication and orientation as the most important contributing factors. [3] Given that for centuries doctors used their - often illegible - handwriting to take notes and prescribe drugs, it is understandable that the advent of electronic health records (EHR) created huge anticipation for safer and improved work flows, as well as better connectivity between care givers - both within the hospital as between the hospital and general practitioners, nursing homes, rehabilitation facilities and pharmacies. By signing the *Health Information Technology for Economic and Clinical Health (HITECH) Act* in 2009 and incentivizing EHR adoption, the Obama administration made implementation of electronic health records an integral part of improving efficiency and safety of health care in the United States.

Cyber (In-)security of Industrial Control Systems: A Societal Challenge

Eric Luiijf

Netherlands Organization for Applied Scientific Research TNO
The Hague, The Netherlands
eric.luiijf@tno.nl

Abstract. Our society and its citizens increasingly depend on the undisturbed functioning of critical infrastructures (CI), their products and services. Many of the CI services as well as other organizations use Industrial Control Systems (ICS) to monitor and control their mission critical processes. Therefore, it is crucial that the functioning of ICS is well protected inter alia against cyber threats. The cyber threat areas to ICS comprise the lack of proper governance as well as cyber security aspects related to organizational, system and network management, technology and technical issues. Moreover, newer functionality entering organizations is often controlled by embedded ICS which hides itself from those that are responsible for cyber security. The immature cyber security posture of ICS and their connectivity with public networks pose a major risk to society. This article explores the threats, provide some examples of cyber incidents with ICS, and will discuss the ICS security challenges to our societies.

Contents

Invited Talks

Medical Devices, Electronic Health Records and Assuring Patient Safety:
Future Challenges? 3
  Cor J. Kalkman

Cyber (In-)security of Industrial Control Systems: A Societal Challenge. 7
  Eric Luiijf

Flight Systems

Modeling Guidelines and Usage Analysis Towards Applying HiP-HOPS
Method to Airborne Electrical Systems 19
  Carolina D. Villela, Humberto H. Sano, and Juliana M. Bezerra

The Formal Derivation of Mode Logic for Autonomous Satellite Flight
Formation 29
  *Anton Tarasyuk, Inna Pereverzeva, Elena Troubitsyna,
  and Timo Latvala*

Automotive Embedded Systems

Simulation of Automotive Security Threat Warnings to Analyze Driver
Interpretations and Emotional Transitions.......................... 47
  Robert Altschaffel, Tobias Hoppe, Sven Kuhlmann, and Jana Dittmann

Improving Dependability of Vision-Based Advanced Driver Assistance
Systems Using Navigation Data and Checkpoint Recognition 59
  *Ayhan Mehmed, Sasikumar Punnekkat, Wilfried Steiner,
  Giacomo Spampinato, and Martin Lettner*

Safely Using the AUTOSAR End-to-End Protection Library............. 74
  Thomas Arts and Stefano Tonetta

A Structured Validation and Verification Method for Automotive Systems
Considering the OEM/Supplier Interface 90
  *Kristian Beckers, Isabelle Côté, Thomas Frese, Denis Hatebur,
  and Maritta Heisel*

Automotive Software

Model-Based Analysis for Safety Critical Software   111
  Stefan Gulan, Jens Harnisch, Sven Johr, Roberto Kretschmer,
  Stefan Rieger, and Rafael Zalman

Integrated Safety Analysis Using Systems-Theoretic Process Analysis
and Software Model Checking   121
  Asim Abdulkhaleq and Stefan Wagner

Back-to-Back Fault Injection Testing in Model-Based Development   135
  Peter Folkesson, Fatemeh Ayatolahi, Behrooz Sangchoolie,
  Jonny Vinter, Mafijul Islam, and Johan Karlsson

Error Detection

Understanding the Effects of Data Corruption on Application Behavior
Based on Data Characteristics.   151
  Georgios Stefanakis, Vijay Nagarajan, and Marcelo Cintra

A Multi-layer Anomaly Detector for Dynamic Service-Based Systems.   166
  Andrea Ceccarelli, Tommaso Zoppi, Massimiliano Itria,
  and Andrea Bondavalli

Medical Safety Cases

Safety Case Driven Development for Medical Devices.   183
  Alejandra Ruiz, Paulo Barbosa, Yang Medeiros, and Huascar Espinoza

Towards an International Security Case Framework for Networked Medical
Devices   197
  Anita Finnegan and Fergal McCaffery

Medical Systems

Systems-Theoretic Safety Assessment of Robotic Telesurgical Systems   213
  Homa Alemzadeh, Daniel Chen, Andrew Lewis, Zbigniew Kalbarczyk,
  Jaishankar Raman, Nancy Leveson, and Ravishankar Iyer

Towards Assurance for Plug & Play Medical Systems.   228
  Andrew L. King, Lu Feng, Sam Procter, Sanjian Chen,
  Oleg Sokolsky, John Hatcliff, and Insup Lee

Risk Classification of Data Transfer in Medical Systems   243
  Dagmar Rosenbrand, Rob de Weerd, Lex Bothe,
  and Jan Jaap Baalbergen

Requirement Engineering for Functional Alarm System for Interoperable
Medical Devices 252
Krishna K. Venkatasubramanian, Eugene Y. Vasserman, Vasiliki Sfyrla,
Oleg Sokolsky, and Insup Lee

Architectures and Testing

The Safety Requirements Decomposition Pattern. 269
Pablo Oliveira Antonino, Mario Trapp, Paulo Barbosa,
Edmar C. Gurjão, and Jeferson Rosário

Automatic Architecture Hardening Using Safety Patterns 283
Kevin Delmas, Rémi Delmas, and Claire Pagetti

Modeling the Impact of Testing on Diverse Programs 297
Peter Bishop

Safety Cases

A Model for Safety Case Confidence Assessment 313
Jérémie Guiochet, Quynh Anh Do Hoang, and Mohamed Kaaniche

Towards a Formal Basis for Modular Safety Cases 328
Ewen Denney and Ganesh Pai

Security Attacks

Quantifying Risks to Data Assets Using Formal Metrics in Embedded
System Design 347
Maria Vasilevskaya and Simin Nadjm-Tehrani

ISA^{2}R: Improving Software Attack and Analysis Resilience
via Compiler-Level Software Diversity 362
Rafael Fedler, Sebastian Banescu, and Alexander Pretschner

Cyber Security and Integration

Barriers to the Use of Intrusion Detection Systems in Safety-Critical
Applications 375
Chris W. Johnson

Stochastic Modeling of Safety and Security of the e-Motor,
an ASIL-D Device 385
Peter T. Popov

Organisational, Political and Technical Barriers to the Integration of Safety
and Cyber-Security Incident Reporting Systems   400
  Chris W. Johnson

A Comprehensive Safety, Security, and Serviceability Assessment Method. . .   410
  Georg Macher, Andrea Höller, Harald Sporer, Eric Armengaud,
  and Christian Kreiner

Programming and Compiling

Source-Code-to-Object-Code Traceability Analysis for Avionics Software:
Don't Trust Your Compiler   427
  Jörg Brauer, Markus Dahlweid, Tobias Pankrath, and Jan Peleska

Automated Generation of Buffer Overflow Quick Fixes Using Symbolic
Execution and SMT   441
  Paul Muntean, Vasantha Kommanapalli, Andreas Ibing,
  and Claudia Eckert

A Software-Based Error Detection Technique for Monitoring the Program
Execution of RTUs in SCADA.   457
  Navid Rajabpour and Yasser Sedaghat

Real-World Types and Their Application   471
  Jian Xiang, John Knight, and Kevin Sullivan

Author Index   485

Invited Talks

Medical Devices, Electronic Health Records and Assuring Patient Safety: Future Challenges?

Cor J. Kalkman[(✉)]

University Medical Center, Utrecht, The Netherlands
c.j.kalkman@umcutrecht.nl

Abstract. The patient safety movement was triggered by publications showing that modern health care is more unsafe than road travel and that more patients are killed annually by avoidable adverse events than by breast cancer [1]. As a result, an urgent need to improve patient safety has dominated international health care systems over the last decade. Some examples of safety issues that healthcare actively tries to address are: reducing the incidence of hospital-acquired infections, avoiding errors with patient identification (wrong patient, wrong procedure, wrong side), errors with drug prescription and administration (wrong drug, wrong dose, wrong route), recognizing deteriorating patients earlier to allow timely life-saving treatment, developing systems for rapid appropriate treatment for stroke and myocardial infarction and improving care for frail elderly patients with multiple diseases using many drugs. Addressing these issues has proven more difficult than anticipated and actual progress in patient safety has been frustratingly slow. Reference [2] Root cause analysis of serious adverse events invariably points to problems with communication and orientation as the most important contributing factors. Reference [3] Given that for centuries doctors used their - often illegible - handwriting to take notes and prescribe drugs, it is understandable that the advent of electronic health records (EHR) created huge anticipation for safer and improved work flows, as well as better connectivity between care givers - both within the hospital as between the hospital and general practitioners, nursing homes, rehabilitation facilities and pharmacies. By signing the *Health Information Technology for Economic and Clinical Health (HITECH) Act* in 2009 and incentivizing EHR adoption, the Obama administration made implementation of electronic health records an integral part of improving efficiency and safety of health care in the United States.

1 EHR Promises and Problems

There is little doubt about the benefits of making the transition from paper-based documentation to the digital domain. When a hospital implements an EHR, many safety problems are immediately solved. No longer will patients suffer avoidable harm from illegible doctors' notes and prescriptions, and there are no more dangerous delays due to 'lost' X-rays. Every note and lab result is now properly time-stamped and the writer can always be traced. EHRs also create unique new problems, such as over-worked residents copying and pasting entire blocks of text from earlier notes,

F. Koornneef and C. van Gulijk (Eds.): SAFECOMP 2015, LNCS 9337, pp. 3–6, 2015.
DOI: 10.1007/978-3-319-24255-2_1

sometimes accidentally copying older physiological measurements to the new date. At least in theory, the EHR can utilize real-time clinical decision support by scanning continuously for possible patient deterioration. However, for this to work reliably, doctors and nurses would need to enter structured data. Unfortunately, structured data entry is counterintuitive for most health care professionals, who typically use a fluid, narrative driven documentation style. One possible solution – often requested by doctors – uses Natural Language Processing techniques to create a medically knowledgeable agent that understands our hasty error-riddled typing and distills diagnoses, treatments and contemplations from the narrative. The resulting output would be a structured abstract of the doctor's typing that only needs to verified and accepted, perhaps after a some fine-tuning and editing. In the background each diagnosis could then be coded in a universal ontology system as SNOMED-CT. Reference [4] The clinical realization of such advanced software is still far away and will not come from the large monolithic EHR vendors, but more likely from innovative startups. Here is huge obstacle, however: many vendors will not allow third parties to read from and write into their databases, often quoting 'safety' or 'security' as reasons for denying access. In a strong worded article in the *New England of Medicine* Mandle and Kohane posited that : "…EHR vendors propagate the myth that health IT is qualitatively different from industrial and consumer products in order to protect their prices and market share and block new entrants…". Reference [5] The result of the current status is that health IT lags decades behind consumer IT, where disruptive innovation continually challenges and replaces the status quo, much to the benefit of consumers.

2 Connectivity and Medical Devices

Although almost everybody concurs that connectivity is vital to health care IT, it is currently almost impossible to exchange patient data electronically between the hospital and general practitioners, rehabilitation facilities or nursing homes. Costly local custom-made communication interfaces for every distinct pair of programs that need to exchange data are the norm rather than the exception. Therefore connectivity remains the biggest hurdle for realizing the full potential of EHR. I believe that an open market, open standards, generic software and tight security protocols are the answer.

Increasingly, EHR's are interfaced with medical devices that perform measurements on the patient. Examples are ECG machines, blood pressure meters, pulse oximeters, anesthesia machines, ICU ventilators, X-ray machines. When interfacing such measurement equipment the goal is to obtain error-free timely readings from the device and store them as properly time-stamped measurements in the EHR. This can be trickier than it would seem at first sight. First, the device needs to be coupled with the correct patient, a process that requires, for example, barcode scanning both the patient and the device, followed by explicitly linking them for the duration of the measurement. Alternatively devices could be linked to the patient and labeled as such for the entire duration of hospitalization.

One of the most ubiquitous medical devices is the infusion pump, used to deliver fluids and drugs to patients, most often through the intravenous route. These devices are extremely useful, but also a source of many adverse events, some of which can be lethal. Examples are: wrong drug, inadvertent overdose, inadvertent low dose, inadvertent interruption of infusion and wrong route (for example, intravenous infusion of a drug used for epidural analgesia). There is pressure on manufacturers to make infusion pumps less bulky, which has resulted in smaller displays with poor user ergonomics. Errors in setting the correct infusion rate are therefore frequent. Given the high number of reported incidents with infusion pumps in 2010, the FDA started an infusion pump improvement   initiative   (http://www.fda.gov/MedicalDevices/ProductsandMedical Procedures/GeneralHospitalDevicesandSupplies/InfusionPumps/ucm202501.htm).

There is a role for software engineers and device manufacturers to improve on this situation by connecting all infusion pumps to the EHR, so that settings and current mode of operation are known and can be read remotely. This would allow infusion pumps to be remotely monitored by doctors, nurses and clinical decision support rules and prevent potentially devastating adverse drug events such as infusion of drugs at a rate one order of magnitude higher than prescribed (e.g., 40.0 ml/h instead of 4.0 ml/h). One further step to improve safety would be to build monitoring for inappropriate infusion rates into clinical decision support systems.

3   eHealth and Home Monitoring

There is an increasing trend to decrease length of stay in the hospital, to avoid hospitalization whenever possible and to monitor patients with chronic conditions such as heart failure or chronic obstructive lung disease at home. In this situation 'safe' connectivity becomes an even bigger challenge, as the patient's data are no longer generated within the confines of the hospital. Currently, this kind of home monitoring requires patients to enter health data such as weight and self-measured heart rate and blood pressure into a secure web page or smartphone app. In the future 'wearable' technology will allow continuous and simultaneous remote monitoring of multiple physiological parameters. This calls for innovative solutions to secure safe uninterrupted data transmission. It will also need to allow for dropouts caused by radio interference or a patient moving too far from his/her base station connected to the internet. For example: how long can the signal be stored locally on the wearable device so that data transmission may 'catch up' later - when in range of the base station again? Such decisions obviously will depend on the particular monitoring goals. If the goal is home monitoring for a chronic condition such as heart failure, it may be acceptable to 'catch up' with the data as long as one hour later. However, if the goal is to alert family members and emergency services to a potentially lethal event such as ventricular arrhythmia, then such a period of data loss would be entirely unacceptable. In such a scenario an alert needs to be generated as soon as data transmission fails.

4   The Tension Between Patient Privacy and Patient Safety

Many patients fear intrusions of their privacy, especially as more of their private health data are stored in various databases and shared by care providers over the Internet. Solid data security is of utmost importance, but it is important to realize that there is an inherent tension between data security and patient safety. One obvious example would be long, overly complex login procedures that waste health care workers' time and may result in valuable minutes lost during emergencies. Blocking unauthorized access sometimes also hinders legitimate access. Herein lies a challenge for software engineers and human factors specialists to improve the user experience for health care workers while at the same time improving data security. One of the more interesting potential solutions is the move away from monolithic institution-based EHRs to patient owned 'private' electronic health records (PHR). Full-scale adoption of the PHR would be a paradigm shift, beacuase as owners of their medical record, patients would no longer have any difficulty to access their doctor's notes, images and lab results. Instead, they will 'allow' theirs doctors to read from and or write into their personal health record. Such personal systems could be stored securely on servers of any party that the patient trusts. This would be a game changer for interoperability issues, because the PHR now defines the common data format and the patients themselves control read or write access for every possible professional involved in their health care.

5   Conclusion

While health care systems around the world are in rapid transition and struggle to improve quality at reduced costs, health care IT lags behind. Monolithic legacy-based EHR systems have hindered adoption of new technology based on open standards, often in the name of safety or privacy. Government-mandated use of open standards and the entry of innovative players in the field may be needed to reverse this situation. The medical device market and software community can play a huge role by developing, implementing and endorsing high-quality open communication standards.

References

1. Institute of Medicine: To Err is Human: Building a Safer Health System (2000)
2. Landrigan, C.P., Parry, G.J., Bones, C.B., Hackbarth, A.D., Goldmann, D.A., Sharek, P.J.: Temporal trends in rates of patient harm resulting from medical care. N. Engl. J. Med. **363**, 2124–2134 (2010)
3. Brown, J.P.: Closing the communication loop: using readback/hearback to support patient safety. Jt. Comm. J Qual. Saf. **30**, 460–464 (2004)
4. Gobbel, G.T., Reeves, R., Jayaramaraja, S., Giuse, D., Speroff, T., Brown, S.H., Elkin, P.L., Matheny, M.E.: Development and evaluation of RapTAT: a machine learning system for concept mapping of phrases from medical narratives. J. Biomed. Inform. **48**, 54–65 (2014)
5. Mandl, K.D., Kohane, I.S.: Escaping the EHR trap–the future of health IT. N. Engl. J. Med. **366**, 2240–2242 (2012)

Cyber (In-)security of Industrial Control Systems: A Societal Challenge

Eric Luiijf[(✉)]

Netherlands Organisation for Applied Scientific Research TNO,
P.O. Box 96864, The Hague, The Netherlands
eric.luiijf@tno.nl

Abstract. Our society and its citizens increasingly depend on the undisturbed functioning of critical infrastructures (CI), their products and services. Many of the CI services as well as other organizations use Industrial Control Systems (ICS) to monitor and control their mission-critical processes. Therefore, it is crucial that the functioning of ICS is well protected inter alia against cyber threats. The cyber threat areas to ICS comprise the lack of proper governance as well as cyber security aspects related to organizational, system and network management, technology and technical issues. Moreover, newer functionality entering organizations is often controlled by embedded ICS which hide itself from those that are responsible for cyber security. The immature cyber security posture of ICS and their connectivity with public networks pose a major risk to society. This article explores the threats, provide some examples of cyber incidents with ICS, and will discuss the ICS security challenges to our societies.

Keywords: Critical infrastructure · Cyber security · Cyber resilience · ICS · Industrial Control Systems · Supervisory Control and Data Acquisition · SCADA

1 Introduction

Our society and citizens increasingly depend on the undisturbed functioning of critical infrastructures (CI), their products and services. Despite national differences, most national definitions of CI have alike elements, see e.g. the CIPedia© website definitions of critical infrastructure by a manifold of nations [2]. The EU definition of CI is 'An asset, system or part thereof located in Member States which is essential for the maintenance of vital societal functions, health, safety, security, economic or social well-being of people, and the disruption or destruction of which would have a significant impact in a Member State as a result of the failure to maintain those functions' [3]. Examples of CI sectors are energy (power, oil, gas), transport (road, air, rail, ship, pipeline), drinking water, waste water, water management, financial services, and public administration [2]. Many of the mission-critical processes that are crucial to deliver CI

© Springer International Publishing Switzerland 2015
F. Koornneef and C. van Gulijk (Eds.): SAFECOMP 2015, LNCS 9337, pp. 7–15, 2015.
DOI: 10.1007/978-3-319-24255-2_2

services in a reliable fashion rely on the correct functioning of Industrial Control Systems (ICS) 24/7. Any failure of ICS, cyber-initiated ones in particular, may both cause mission-critical processes of organizations to fail and may result in safety risk to people and or the environment. Therefore, the cyber security and cyber resilience of ICS is of utmost importance to our society as a whole, to CI operators, and many other public and private organizations. Nevertheless, organizations, manufacturers and system integrators collaboratively have failed to a large extent to address the cyber threats to ICS which stem from the lack of proper governance as well as organizational, system and network management, technology and technical issues [1].

Apart from the monitoring and control of crucial CI processes such as the power grid, ICS monitor and control processes in many other small to large organizations. ICS may be as small as a single programmable logic controller (PLC) automating and controlling a very simple process. Often such ICS are embedded in acquired functionality by the organization. As will be discussed below, such ICS hide itself from proper information security governance as the acquired function falls under the responsibility of unconscious insecure management and operators. Moreover, the physical ICS components are put in a closet or hidden within a piece of equipment which has wireless connectivity. The result is that the cyber safety and security risk related to the ICS-controlled processes is unmanaged.

Unnoticed we are surrounded by ICS controlled and monitored services which allow the well-functioning of our society. ICS make our lives easy. An illustrative example of the pervasive penetration of ICS in our daily live can be found in 'Good Morning with ICS' [8].

As the societal impact may be high, collective action is needed by all stakeholders to address the ICS cyber security challenges in order to mitigate the risk to society, our safety, health and environment. The next sections will discuss the risk aspects and need for governance in more detail.

2   Definitions

A *critical infrastructure* (CI) consists of those assets and parts there of which are essential for the maintenance of critical societal functions, including the supply chain, health, safety, security, economy or social well-being of people [3].

Cyber resilience is defined as the ability of systems and organizations to withstand cyber events, measured by the combination of mean time to failure and mean time to recovery [14].

Cyber security is defined as the safeguards and actions that can be used to protect the cyber domain, both in the civilian and military fields, from those threats that are associated with or that may harm its interdependent networks and information infrastructure [4].

3 Paradigm Changes to ICS

3.1 From Closed to too Open Environments

ICS were traditionally designed around process reliability and safety [12]. For long, cyber security was not a design consideration for ICS because:

1. ICS were based on specialized hardware, proprietary code and protocol standards. Only specialists knew about how to use and tweak ICS. Nobody else, including hackers, would be interested in ICS, their protocols and telecommunication means.
2. ICS are operated as a closed environment without any external connection.
3. ICS operate only in benign environments without hackers or malware. Manufacturers therefore had no reason for creating secure and robust ICS protocols and to stress-test ICS protocol implementations.
4. The end-users of ICS did not ask for cyber secure ICS; they only asked for new functionality and user friendly interfaces.

The aforementioned paradigm shift took place due to the take up of the fast innovation cycles in information and communication technologies (ICT) in general and in ICS networking. All basic assumptions mentioned above about the security by obscurity and benign environments of ICS have been flawed by those developments, as outlined by [8] at pp. 23–24:

1. ICS applications increasingly operate on commercial off-the-shelf (COTS) hardware, common operating systems such as Windows and Unix, and use the TCP/IP suite of protocols for communications. ICS applications moved to open source environments. ICS control apps can be found on smart phones and are probably migrating to smart watches right now.
2. ICS knowledge and documentation is widely available on the Internet.
3. ICS networks are either directly or indirectly connected to public networks such as the Internet to reduce communication costs and to control processes from home locations.
4. ICS have fallen victim to disgruntled insiders. Hackers have become very interested in ICS as is shown by the number of ICS-related talks at Black Hat and Def Con® hacking conventions. Moreover, ICS security testing frameworks for the MetaSploit toolset are publicly available [8].

3.2 Hide in Functionality but Connected to Internet

Functionality acquired under the responsibility of a non-IT department is 'since history' controlled and monitored by process automation. However, gradually process automation with switches and relays have been replaced 'under the hood' by ICS which in the last years evolves to ICS that is largely based on common commercial-off-the-shelf information and communication technologies. Small but powerful ICS can be found at the road site, above the ceiling, in vehicles and behind innocent looking display panels. The management and operators of 'functionality' still think in terms of the old on/off switches and a knob to crank up the flow of the controlled process. The fact that there is ICS operating between the display with the switch or knob, and the monitored and controlled the actuator, motor or valve, etcetera, is not recognized. The notion of ICS and information and communication technologies with a potential high cyber security risk is only subconsciously present [6]. The responsible department for, e.g. the city waste water processing, traffic control, speed and observation cameras, and ferry operations allows the connection of the embedded ICS to public networks for remote management and third party maintenance in an unsecured fashion. The Industrial Risk Assessment Map (IRAM) project by the Freie Universität Berlin, Germany used the Shodan search engine [13] to globally locate ICS connected to the Internet. They mapped the discovered ICS on a geographical map of the globe. Project SHINE (SHodan INtelligence Extraction), which ran from 2012 till October 2014, did the same and found 2.2 million of Internet-connected ICS devices [11], many of them located in European nations.

According to incidents that became publicly known, hackers and malware took control of non-CI ICS which monitor and control municipal waste water systems, tropical swimming paradise pumps, the heating, ventilation and air conditioning of a hospital, a wind power farm, the building automation system of the Salvation Army, airport baggage system, robots in a car manufacturing plant, a milk processing plant, municipal street light systems, and even quiesced a large ship at the North Sea.

4   Lack of Governance of ICS Security

4.1   The Executive Level

Governance of ICS security should start at the executive level which manages the risk to the business objectives of the organization and protects the public and private shareholder interests [8]. They understand how to make business plans and earn money from for instance transport of gas, passenger transport by metro or the mass-production of innovative electronic equipment. As most top level management has no affection with technology, a gap exists with respect to executive level interest in ICS controlled production processes. For IT- and ICT-departments it is already hard to get the attention of the executive level; for most ICS departments that is even harder. When asked about cyber security of ICS, the assignment of responsibilities is clear to the executive level: cyber security is a responsibility of 'IT'. At the same time, it is not uncommon that IT departments do not understand ICS which for most IT-departments is equivalent to 'grease, pumps and motors'. IT reboots and upgrades systems and routers when necessary, even during the lunch break. Why is the process-responsible department not able to accept a router upgrade which may take ten minutes to half an hour?

On the other hand, the responsible department for process automation and ICS does not understand the ICT domain, their issues, threats and vulnerabilities. The reason is obvious: most process engineers are not educated in IT and cyber security. Their main focus is on process efficiency and improvements. It is therefore not surprising that the cyber security of ICS does not get the proper attention in organizations. No risk analysis takes place, no security auditing of ICS, no analysis of firewall logging, and so on. In short: organizational leadership and an integrated ICT-ICS approach are missing.

At the same time, as already was made clear by the European Workshop on Industrial Computer Systems Reliability, Safety and Security (EWICS) in 2003, the then ISO/IEC 17999 standard, now ISO/IEC 27000-series, lack proper controls and support for the 24/7 ICS environment. Organizations trying to close the ICS cyber security gap using these information security standards experience trouble when trying to implement the controls in the 24/7 environment with often legacy ICS. The International Society of Automation (ISA) tries to close this gap by developing international standards for the ICS domain as outlined by [8] on pages 43–45.

5   ICS Technology

5.1   Aging, Legacy and too New ICS Technology

Despite the move of ICS to common ICT, replacement plans and the financial depreciation of hardware often still follows the old technology investment and replacement cycles of the controlled processes, that is ten years or even longer. Although the support for Windows XP ended April 8th, 2014, one can still find 486 computer running Windows XP (or even older operating systems) and an ICS application on top of that controlling for instance a MRI scanner. Many years old ICS equipment may have, considered from the current point of view, only limited CPU power and memory. Their performance is often just enough to control the process. No capacity is left for running an anti-malware package or a cryptographic algorithm.

Replacing all ICS at once is often infeasible, meaning that organizations need to operate new ICS with at the same time legacy ICS in their networks. Newer security capabilities can not be switched on as they break the interaction with legacy ICS. Careful planning to deal with legacy is required, see for some good practices [10]. At the same time, new 'plug compatible' ICS components may have on-board chip sets with a mail and web server. Easy for system engineers to deep dive in a user friendly way into the ICS component input and output states or getting an emailed alarm message. However, when the component is installed without configuring or blocking such a functionality, the services are by default accessible to unauthorized persons when they manage to get access to the network which is often the case in smaller organizations or when embedded ICS gets internetted.

5.2   Weak and Insecure ICS Protocols

ICS protocols such as Modbus moved from serial communication to implementations which also run the same protocol on top of TCP/IP. Unfortunately both the protocols and the protocol implementations were developed with a benign closed network environment in mind. This weakness comes to the fore when a system or network manager of the IT-department starts a network scan or puts the network to a load test. Connected ICS may crash or become unresponsive; according to tests by CERN the larger part of ICS may fail [9]. Just one byte too much may cause a ping-of-death reaction as happened years ago in the Internet. Internet protocols have become well-tested and robust. ICS components controlling dangerous or mission-critical processes, however, not.

5.3   Insecure ICS by Design

ICS are packaged insecure by design. During installation one is not required to change the default factory password(s). Sometimes they even cannot be changed when it concerns a legacy system or when the manufacturer has a policy of security-by-obscurity with hard-wired passwords. Stuxnet made use of such a weakness in Siemens ICS. Nevertheless, new ICS versions still show hidden functionalities and hard-wired passwords as is exposed by, for instance, ICS-CERT bulletins [5]. There is a lack of security documentation for ICS, or when available, one has to be very persistent to find it at the end of a manual hidden on a DVD that can be found in the same box as for instance a PLC.

5.4   Common TCP-IP Based Connectivity

ICS networks are coupled directly or indirectly to the Internet, some exceptions excluded. Firewalls are sometimes hard to configure to control ICS protocols. the business side, however, wants to have information from the processes and require ICS connectivity. Process and system engineers want to have 24/7 access to ICS from home to deal with alarm and maintenance situations. Third parties that support the ICS and process operations want to have such an access possibility as well. If not supplied, they create it themselves as was found when the safety panel of a nuclear power plant went down due to a virus. The risk of malware or hackers to obtain access to ICS is high as has been demonstrated by many cyber security incidents with ICS; some of them are listed in [8].

6   ICS Maintenance and Operations

Maintaining a proper cyber security posture in the ICS environment is not easy. Apart from the governance and organizational issues discussed above, topics like password management, keeping anti-malware software current, and timely patching are major challenges for organizations knowingly operating ICS [8].

Passwords are often not individual user but group passwords with indefinite or at least many months lifetime. When someone leaves the ICS department, the very well-known passwords are not changed.

When organization care for ICS security - which is not the case for the unconscious insecure operated functionality in for instance elevators, access control systems, and HVAC-systems - malware signatures may be updated once in a number of weeks. Patching requires an agreement by the system integrator or the manufacturer which already may take long. Then one has to plan, test and apply the patch. As a result, the window of exposure of the ICS domain and therefore mission-critical processes to malware and hackers is quite long.

7   Third Parties

Third parties often have access to the ICS domain of organizations for both online and remote maintenance and support. They are a risk to the organizations unless the mutual trust level is high, procedures are followed, and regular audits take place. However, with the 24/7 around the globe support, the risk is that authentication information is known around the globe. The support organization wants to keep its operation as simple as possible using the same or similar passwords 'nationwide', e.g. supportBE, supportNL. Guess what the password is for Spain or Indonesia. It is hard to convince such organizations that they need to use a strong special password for their client which does not include the organization name, nation and equivalent simplicity.

Moreover, third party support engineers may bring equipment to the inside and connect that to the ICS network bypassing all cyber security measures and procedures (if any): a perfect entry path for malware in the ICS domain.

8   Conclusion: Long and Short Term Actions

As discussed above, the potential impact of cyber-related disturbances of ICS to the society may be high. Many of these challenges have to be overcome by both end-users, system integrators and ICS manufacturers at the long run:

1. executive management leadership (see [8,14]),
2. proper governance of ICS: the right level of attention, established security policies and procedures, financial means to keep ICS up-to-date and secure, and raising security awareness,
3. organizational, procedural and technical measures,
4. development of good practice standards for ICS,
5. development of secure-by-design and secure-out-of-the-box ICS,
6. proper education and workforce development (see [8]),
7. supporting cyber security oversight by the CI regulator,
8. government support to raise ICS security awareness in all CI sectors and all ICS using organizations,
9. government to stimulate information exchange(s) on security information while avoiding the pitfalls discussed in [6].

At the same time, end-user of ICS, system integrators and manufacturers have to act now. Increase the cyber resilience of ICS monitoring and controlling mission-critical processes by:

1. give ICS cyber security instruction and require change of passwords at the end of a system acceptance test (SAT),
2. introduce proper password management (individual; decent expiration interval with a grace period),
3. audit firewall logs and network connectivity on a regular basis,
4. stress test ICS network components or network parts before they are connected to the production network,
5. disconnect the engineering test system(s) from the daily operations,
6. follow ICS-CERT and alike threat, vulnerability and intelligence resources and or become member of a sectoral ISAC ([7]),
7. being - last but not least - vigilant.

References

1. Bruce, R., Dynes, S., Brechbuhl, H., Brown, B., Goetz, E., Verhoest, P., Luiijf, E., Helmus, S.: International Policy Framework for Protecting Critical Information Infrastructure: A Discussion Paper Outlining Key Policy Issues, TNO report 33680, TNO, The Netherlands and Tuck School of Business/Center for Digital Strategies at Dartmouth, USA (2005). http://www.ists.dartmouth.edu/library/158.pdf
2. CIPediaMain Page. http://www.cipedia.eu
3. EC: European Council Directive 2008/114/EC of 8 December 2008 on the identification and designation of European critical infrastructures and the assessment of the need to improve their protection, OJ 2008 L 345/77, Brussels, Belgium (2008). http://eur-lex.europa.eu/LexUriServ/LexUriServ.do?uri=OJ:L:2008:345:0075:0082:EN:PDF
4. EC: Joint Communication to the European Parliament, the Council, the European Economic and Social Committee and the Committee of the Regions - Cybersecurity Strategy of the European Union: An Open, Safe and Secure Cyberspace, Brussels, Belgium (2013). http://ec.europa.eu/dgs/home-affairs/e-library/documents/policies/organized-crime-and-human-trafficking/cybercrime/docs/join_2013_1_en.pdf
5. ICS-CERT. https://ics-cert.us-cert.gov
6. Luiijf, E.: Why are we so unconsciously insecure? Int. J. Crit. Infrastruct. Prot. 6(3–4), 179–181 (2013). doi:10.1016/j.ijcip.2013.10.003. http://www.sciencedirect.com/science/article/pii/S1874548213000486
7. Luiijf, E., Kernkamp, A.: Sharing Cyber Security Information. TNO, The Hague (2015). http://www.tno.nl/info-share
8. Luiijf, E., te Paske, B.J.: Cyber Security of Industrial Control Systems. TNO, The Hague (2015). http://www.tno.nl/ICS-security
9. Lüders, S.: Control Systems under attack? In: 10th ICALEPCS Int. Conf. on Accelerator and Large Expt. Physics Control Systems, CERN, Geneva (2005). https://accelconf.web.cern.ch/accelconf/ica05/proceedings/pdf/O5_008.pdf
10. Oosterink, M.: Security of legacy process control systems: moving towards secure process control systems (whitepaper). CPNI.NL, The Hague, Netherlands (2012). http://publications.tno.nl/publication/102819/5psRPC/oosterlink-2012-security.pdf
11. Radvanosky, R., Brodsky, J.: Project Shine (SHodan INtelligence Extraction) Findings Report (2014). http://www.slideshare.net/BobRadvanovsky/project-shine-findings-report-dated-1oct2014

12. Russel, J.: A Brief History of SCADA/EMS (2015). http://scadahistory.com/
13. Shodan search engine. http://www.shodanhq.com
14. World Economic Forum: Risk and Responsibility in a Hyperconnected World (WEF principles), Geneva, Switzerland (2014). http://www.weforum.org/reports/risk-and-responsibility-hyperconnected-world-pathways-global-cyber-resilience

Flight Systems

Modeling Guidelines and Usage Analysis Towards Applying HiP-HOPS Method to Airborne Electrical Systems

Carolina D. Villela[1]([⊠]), Humberto H. Sano[1], and Juliana M. Bezerra[2]

[1] EMBRAER S.A., São José dos Campos, Brazil
cduartevi@gmail.com, humberto.sano@embraer.com.br
[2] Computer Science Division, Instituto Tecnológico de Aeronáutica,
S José dos Campos, Brazil
juliana@ita.br

Abstract. Aircraft development process requires safety assessment to ensure aircraft continued airworthiness by guaranteeing that hazards related to aircraft functions are properly addressed. Safety analyses require increasingly more reliable and efficient solutions, particularly for complex and highly integrated aircraft systems. Fault Tree Analysis (FTA) is a safety technique broadly applied in aerospace industry. The generation of fault trees can be facilitated by using the HiP-HOPS method proposed by Dr. Yiannis Papadopoulos. HiP-HOPS supports semi-automatically generation of fault trees based on system architectural model and annotations regarding system failure modes. In this paper, we investigate the usage of HiP-HOPS method in airborne electrical systems. We propose modeling guidelines, in order to help engineers and analysts to build system models more suitable to the application of HiP-HOPS. We apply both HiP-HOPS and guidelines in a case study and evaluate HiP-HOPS applicability using criteria as acceptability, suitability and practicality.

Keywords: Hip-HOPS · Fault Tree Analysis · Failure analysis · Safety analysis · Electrical system

1 Introduction

An aircraft system is a combination of parts that correlate to each other, being items or subsystems, organized to perform specific functions. Systems' safety is extremely important as it dictates whether the systems accomplish their tasks successfully and whether they fail in any hazardous way. Nevertheless, systems components' inter-relationship is of concern due to its complexity. The resulting system behavior is a consequence of the integration of more than one part through their physical interfaces, and through its functions. This integration involves the combination and interconnections of different kinds of safety critical systems [1, 2]. Among the critical systems present in an aircraft, the electrical system is an important one. It is gaining greater importance with the advent of more electric aircrafts, which means that the aircraft functions are more dependent on the proper behavior of the electrical system. Essential functions of the aircraft rely on this system, once the loss of some functions could lead to many deficiencies, degrading the aircraft airworthiness [3, 4].

© Springer International Publishing Switzerland 2015
F. Koornneef and C. van Gulijk (Eds.): SAFECOMP 2015, LNCS 9337, pp. 19–28, 2015.
DOI: 10.1007/978-3-319-24255-2_3

To show compliance with safety requirements and cover all the necessary safety assessment, engineers employ safety analysis methodologies such as Fault Tree Analysis (FTA) [5]. It is a technique recommended by the Aerospace Recommended Practice (ARP) [6], which supports engineers to find design and operational weaknesses in complex and integrated systems, as well as to identify safety improvements. This practice demands meticulous analyses, becoming time consuming when applied and further demands rework on the safety analysis results, when reusing, improving or reviewing the system. Based on the difficulties and great efforts of engineers to handle the analysis, it is interesting to consider alternative ways of working with FTA.

HiP-HOPS (Hierarchically Performed Hazards Origin and Propagation Studies) [7, 8] is a method to semi-automatically generate fault tree from system models annotated with fault conditions. This approach can both reduce development costs and improve the quality of the safety analysis, especially in the context of Model-based Design [9]. For instance, it allows modifying the system design during the development period by accomplishing design and safety goals according to the generated fault tree, in a way to bring safety to the final system.

Our objective is to investigate the use of HiP-HOPS method in airborne electrical systems. We propose modeling guidelines that suggest a way of modeling the system foreseeing the method application. We then apply both HiP-HOPS and proposed guidelines in a case study representative of a real-life aircraft electrical system and analyze the method usage through criteria examination.

The paper is organized as follows. In the next section, we discuss the HiP-HOPS foundations. Later, in Sect. 3, we propose the modeling guidelines to support HiP-HOPS usage. In Sect. 4, we present a case study as well as the usage analysis. A discussion about the benefits and limitations of our proposal, the conclusions and future work are presented in the last section.

2 HiP-HOPS Foundations

The HiP-HOPS method uses the architectural model of a system to annotate each component failure logics. It describes how the component can internally fail based on the FMEA [10] of the component, and how it reacts to a failure received at its inputs. This way, it is possible to determine the component's output as a combination of these two events, expressed as logical equations known as the component's annotations. The architectural model also offers the information of the architecture of the system; therefore, components' connections and dependencies between the components are also characterized. The system's topology and component's failure propagation logic are then obtained to generate the fault tree to the desired top event. For instance, take the following lamp system. The system model, the components annotations and the generated fault tree are described in Fig. 1 and Eqs. (1)–(4).

Lamp: Omission-out = RUPTURE_OF_FILAMENT OR Omission-in   (1)

Switch: Omission-out = SWITCH_FAILURE OR Omission-in1 AND
Omission-in2   (2)

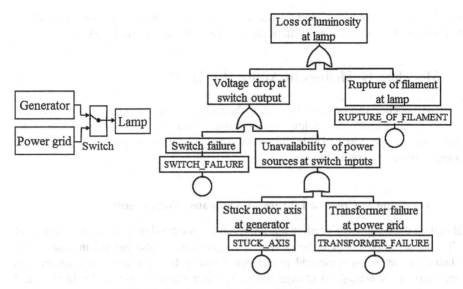

Fig. 1. Lamp system and system Fault Tree

Generator: $\text{Omission-out} = \text{STUCK\_AXIS}$ (3)

Power grid: $\text{Omission-out} = \text{TRANSFORMER\_FAILURE}$ (4)

The internal failure modes are described to each component: rupture of filament for the lamp failure, switch failure for the switch, stuck axis for the generator failure mode and transformer failure to the power grid failure mode.

HiP-HOPS method was implemented in distinct study cases; predominantly in aircraft brake systems [11, 12] and automotive matter [8, 13]. Papadopoulos [8] used the HiP-HOPS method to create a monitoring mechanism of critical systems, and discusses innumerous conceptual modeling problems. Further researches about HiP-HOPS method applied in airborne systems, especially in electrical systems, have not yet been much explored to know whether the method can be applied to make the tree generation more effective in such context.

Other approaches have been proposed to identify fault conditions in a system. For instance, Kehren et al. [14] use a formal language (AltaRica) to assess models. They do not adopt the Fault Tree Analysis; instead, they propose the use of model-checkers to assess qualitative requirements by performing exhaustive simulation on the system model. Joshi et al. [15] understand that keeping the system model and the fault model separated is important to aid models' evolution, and to reduce errors and unnecessary clutter. They apply exploratory analysis using model checkers. Lisagor [16] is concerned about modern large-scale and complex safety-critical systems. He identifies model-based safety assessment methods and unifies existing techniques through a single Metamodel. Mortada et al. [17] use a new version of AltaRica language, which claims to solve two issues: the difficulty to handle systems with instant feedback's loop, and the trouble in constructing the model's structure. They use the new version of the language in a simple electrical system and examine the results by compiling the model into Fault Trees and into Markov chains. In our work, we explore the potential of HiP-HOPS method to support safety analysis in airborne electrical systems.

3   Modeling Guidelines to Apply HiP-HOPS

System modeling can be made foreseeing the method application in a way to make the model more suitable to retrieve better results from the method. With that goal, guidelines are proposed to help the model development. Such guidelines support the application of the method to come along.

3.1   Guideline 1: Create a Library of Annotated Components

Based on the component's failure modes, it can be annotated only once, and a library of all system components can be created. The guideline is also helpful in case of the library's components reuse and model maintenance. If any change or adjustment is necessary, it is enough to change the component characteristic in the library, and updates in every component in the model based on that library are automatically done.

$$
\text{Omission-onA = ELS\_CTT\_OPN OR Omission-posCoil OR} \\
\text{Omission-negCoil OR Omission-A} \tag{5}
$$

$$
\text{Omission-A = ELS\_CTT\_OPN OR Omission-posCoil OR} \\
\text{Omission-negCoil OR Omission-onA} \tag{6}
$$

Figure 2 exemplifies the contactor annotated with its failure propagation and also its internal failure modes, including contactor failure in open position (ELS_CTT_OPN) or in closed position (ELS_CTT_CLD).

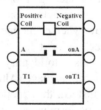

Fig. 2. Library component contactor: model and annotations

3.2   Guideline 2: Support Annotation Customization

In Fig. 3, we introduce a generic electrical system with its energy flow in order to use it as an example of annotation customization applicability hereafter. In this system, each generator (GEN1 and GEN2) powers each bus (DC Bus 1 and DC Bus 2) on normal operation. GLC1 (Generator Line Contactor) and GLC2 are closed, and BTC (Bus Tie Contactor) is opened. When necessary, BTC closes and power flows from one bus to another. It only happens when either GLC1 or GLC2 is opened. The system model is composed by this DC Power portion, by the logics involved to control the contactor maneuvers and by the pilot's command switches. These logics and all the components are used in the annotation customization.

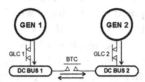

Fig. 3. Example of basic electrical system with its energy flow

To help the library usage, it is important to make each component adaptable accordingly to its functionality. Based on the use of each component in the system, some parts of it can work in different manners, especially when it is about flow of energy and flow of information. Accordingly to the flow direction, it is possible to use a customized component, which is composed of a subset of the annotations previously stated. Considering the equations for the annotation of a generic contactor, described in the Guideline 1, each equation is selected or not. For GLC1, accordingly to this component's single way of energy flowing, only one equation between Eqs. (5) and (6) is selected, leading to the customized component annotation.

3.3   Guideline 3: Define the System's Modes of Operation

The possible operation modes of the system define the ways energy and information can flow on it. It is important to have the annotations based on the scenarios on which the components are operating as the developed fault tree depends on it. Failing to comply with this guideline can lead to erroneous fault trees of the system.

In the example shown in Fig. 3, one operation mode is the single generator mode with generator 1 operative and generator 2 off. In this mode of operation, energy flows from DC Bus 1 to DC Bus 2. This way, a DC Bus 1 failure can lead to a DC Bus 2 failure. The other way around is not true, i.e. a failure in DC Bus 2 will not lead to a failure in DC Bus 1 for this mode of operation. The fault tree for this mode of operation has to be consistent with these facts, so, the annotations must reflect these character-istics. Accordingly to the energy flow the previously annotations are judged and the component is customized, as supported by Guideline 2.

3.4   Guideline 4: Group Components by Its Function

When building a system model, it is suggested to segregate system power from its logics and from system manual commands. It avoids situations where the under-standing of the system's operation, internal dependencies, as well as the role of each component in the system is affected. For the example of the simple electrical system, the power portion (DC Power) is one big block with the contactors, the buses and the generators of the system. The contactors logic is distributed inside small blocks connected to the power portion (BTC Logic, GLC1 Logic and GLC2 Logic). Possible pilot commands are grouped together also segregated from the other parts of the system.

It is also suggested to segregate parts of a component based on each part function. Segregating its parts leads to a cleaner design, easier to be deduced and understood. For instance, consider a relay, composed of the coils, at which the component is energized, and four sets of auxiliary contacts. The use of this component in the system can be segregated, for example, two sets of contacts would be used in the GLC1 logic group and the other two sets would be used in the GLC2 logic group. It means that each set of auxiliary contact is used for different purposes, in different parts of the system.

3.5   Guideline 5: Model Considering the Common Mode Effects

When assessing the system, the common mode effects should not to be forgotten. The common mode failure involves the simultaneous failure of two or more components due to a single fault. In our case, when disassembling one component into more than one part, it is important to guarantee that when the component fail, all its part that are affected will fail as well. It is also important to guarantee that, when the input of one part fails, the other affected parts will in fact act as affected.

Despite being represented in different parts of the design, as suggested in Guideline 4, the parts of the exemplified relay are still the same component. Thus, the common mode effect is to be considered when assessing this component's failure modes and failure effects; therefore, if one of the coils fails, or receive a failed input, the effect must be taken into account to every contact that is part of this relay.

3.6   Guideline 6: Avoid Loops

There is one situation that must be avoided for any fault tree construction, that situation is the loop. Take as an example the electric system in Fig. 4 and its Emergency Bus Contactor (EBC). The contactor allows the energy from DC Bus to source the Emergency Bus of the system. The contactor activation logic (EBC) is fed by a relay, which is sourced by the emergency bus (EMER BUS), the same energy bus that this contactor allows to be sourced. It means that, to propagate a fault, the EBC depends on the relay to propagate this fault, which depends on the Emergency Bus to propagate this fault, which depends on the EBC to propagate this fault, and the loop is done.

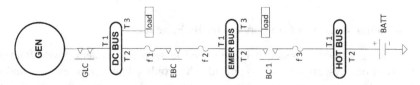

Fig. 4. Electrical system composed by three buses and EBC activation logic

It is necessary to strike this loop out, and the way of doing so is to skip one of these fault propagation annotations. One of the blocks will have one annotation intentionally missing, which will avoid the loop in the fault tree generated. This lack will not hide fault propagation, as in the tree it will only avoid a component to fail because of its own failure.

3.7   Guideline 7: Design Models with Incremental Complexity

It is suggested to break the complete system in sections of reduced modeling complexity when building the model and annotating each component. After having a first section modeled, fully working and the fault tree of this part completed, go to the next section, until having all sections modeled. This way, when a problem is found, it is easier to correct the model or the annotation. It is also easier to check the generated fault tree and to make some modification, if necessary.

Take the electrical system example in Fig. 4. The system design and its annotations shall be configured first in the main part, where only the generator powers the DC Bus. At each step, the components are annotated and a fault tree is generated in order to ensure that all annotations are correctly defined. Then, the information and energy propagated are annotated in the components feeding the Emergency Bus when the generator is on. At last, the other kind of source is included, so the battery is taken into account and its contribution powering the buses is also considered in the annotations. This way, there is no accumulation of adjustments and corrections to be made.

4   Usage Analysis of HiP-HOPS with Modeling Guidelines

To investigate the HiP-HOPS method, we use a general aircraft electrical system as a case study (Fig. 5). Based on that, the method capability is evaluated according to the criteria: acceptability, suitability and practicality. By acceptability, we mean to evaluate the fault tree generated and analyze if it is coherent with what is expected to the system. Suitability considers the evaluation of adequacy in replacing the manual method. Practicality reasons about convenience and easiness of applying the method.

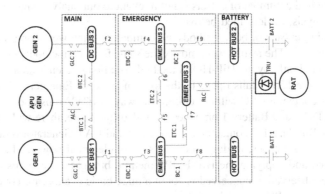

Fig. 5. Electrical system diagram

4.1 Scenario

The electrical system (Fig. 5) is mainly composed of two main DC Generators (GEN1 and GEN2), an Auxiliary Power Unit (APU) Generator, and two main DC Buses. These components are connected through the contactors GLC (Generator Line Contactor), ALC (APU Generator Line Contactor) and BTC (Bus Tie Contactor).

Emergency part is composed of three Emergency Buses. They are powered either by the two DC Buses from the main part or by the two Hot Buses and the RAT (Ram Air Turbine). The contactors connecting these components are the EBC (Emergency Bus Contactor), ETC (Emergency Transfer Contactor), BC (Battery Contactor), and RLC (RAT Line Contactor). The TRU (Transformer Rectifier Unit) converts RAT generated power and delivers this power to the DC system. Battery part is composed of two Hot Buses, which are used to interface the Batteries (BATT1 and BATT2). The batteries are powered by the Hot Buses through the Emergency Buses connected to them, or the batteries source the Emergency Buses through the Hot Buses temporarily, until the RAT deploys and takes on the powering task.

The HiP-HOPS method was applied in the electrical system case study following all the guidelines. The steps applying the method will not be herein described due to space limitations. Having the system model prepared to generate the fault tree, the desired top event is chosen and the fault tree is created. This fault tree created based on the system model and on the components annotation is the result of this work and is now evaluated.

4.2 Evaluating Acceptability, Suitability and Practicality of HiP-HOPS

In order to compare the results and verify the HiP-HOPS acceptability, a manually created Fault Tree made by other engineers is used. The comparison is made to the top event "Loss of all electrical power", which is a critical case usually assessed as it involves the loss of every energy bus. In our case, it is determined by the combination of the loss of all energy sourcing: Generator 1, Generator 2, Batteries and RAT. For the energy sourcing, APU Generator is not considered. The comparison is accomplished through the cutsets generated by both approaches: HiP-HOPS and manual. In the HiP-HOPS method, 700 cutsets were generated and, in the manual method, 128 cutsets. The difference in the number of cutsets is not relevant to our analysis since we focus on qualitative analysis, as described below.

The resulting cutsets of both methods are compared. They were composed of three or four basic events. The results were mostly the same for both methods, except for two cases encountered only by the HiP-HOPS method. The first of then is about a four basic events case where ETC2 fails open. In the system logic, if Emergency Bus 1 is not energized, the contactor RLC will not close. This way, if ETC2 fails open in a scenario where DC 1, DC 2 and Battery 1 branches are failed (therefore, there will be no power to Emergency Bus 1), RLC contactor will not close and RAT Generator power will not reach the emergency buses, leading to the loss of all electrical power. This fact is not easily observed and applying the HiP-HOPS method brought the benefits of this perception. Other observation conceived is about a three basic events case concerning the APU. Even though APU is not taken into account as energy source, any possible failure in the APU branch must be taken into account as it can affect the system operation. In the system logic, it is necessary to have Generator 1, Generator 2 and APU Generator branches disabled in order to activate the RLC contactor. It was detected by the HiP-HOPS method that a failure occurring in ALC contactor (ALC failing closed) leads to RLC not closing. Therefore, in a scenario where DC1 and DC2 branches are failed, ALC contactor failing closed will lead as well to the loss of all electrical power.

The time spent creating the fault trees using HiP-HOPS has some considerations as there is a time consumed developing the model with the annotations. In the other hand, when annotations are completed, the Fault Tree is easily created for any chosen top event. The manually creation of the Fault Tree demands time for each desired top event. Regarding fault tree organization, when creating the fault tree manually, some cuts or interpretations are made, so the fault tree can be cleaner and smaller. The HiP-HOPS method creates the fault tree with all the possibilities described in annotations, leading to a more detailed fault free.

Applying the HiP-HOPS method is not a trivial task. However, when the user follows the guidelines, this task becomes easier. As the experience with the annotations increases, the method gets more intuitive. As the library becomes more complete, the time effort to generate a fault tree based on the model decreases. In the HiP-HOPS method, once the system is completely designed and annotated, it is ready to generate all the fault trees desired. In the manual method, each fault tree needs to be created independently, leading to more work, low rate of reuse and more chances of making mistakes. For instance, considering the system used in the case study, the manual method took 40 h against 16 h of HiP-HOPS to generate the fault tree.

5 Conclusions

In this work, we investigate the capability of the HIP-HOPs method to be adopted by a safety assessment process in airborne systems, specifically in electrical system. Firstly, we propose recommendations to support the model development since its beginning. The recommendations aid the safety analyst to follow guaranteed steps, which in turn lead to a more mature process and to achieve better results. It is recommended to invest time in building the component's library as it will favor the work not only for one fault tree generation, but for as many fault trees as necessary to the designed system. Moreover, owning the annotated library will help the development of other systems in the future, as the library itself will be ready.

We developed a case study, where we applied the HiP-HOPS method and the proposed recommendations. Based on the case study results, HiP-HOPS was considered to be acceptable, as it confirmedly conduces to correct results. The method also proved to be practical to be used as it brings convincing benefits related to time spending (during model development and maintenance), as well to fault tree completeness. The method is also relatively easy to learn and keep in usage. The reuse of component library greatly adds the practicality of applying the method. There were no constraints that would impede the method adoption; on the contrary, distinct advantages were presented.

As future work, we plan to apply both HiP-HOPS and recommendations in other case studies, in a way to bring confidence to our first results. The proposed guidelines were suggested based on the electrical system context. We believe it can be adapted and applied to other contexts different from electrical; however, further investigations are required in this trend.

References

1. Knight, J.C.: Safety critical systems: challenges and directions. In: 24rd International Conference on Software Engineering, pp. 547–550. IEEE, Orlando (2002)
2. Belcastro, C.M.: Aircraft loss-of-control: analysis and requirements for future safety-critical systems and their validation. In: 8th Asian Control Conference (ASCC) on Dynamic System & Control, pp. 399–406. IEEE, Hampton (2011)
3. Code of Federal Regulations: Federal Aviation Regulations (FARs), Part 25—Airworthiness Standards: Transport Category Airplanes
4. Society of Automotive Engineers (SAE): ARP 4754 / ED-79: Certification Considerations for Highly-Integrated or Complex Aircraft Systems. SAE International/EUROCAE, Warrendale, PA, (1996)
5. U.S. Nuclear Regulatory Commission: Fault Tree Handbook. Systems and Reliability Research. Office of Nuclear Regulatory Research, Washington, D.C. 20555
6. Society of Automotive Engineers (SAE): ARP 4761: Guidelines and Methods for Conducting the Safety Assessment Process on Civil Airborne Systems and Equipment, Warrendale (1996)
7. Papadopoulos, Y., McDermid, J.A.: Hierarchically performed hazard origin and propagation studies. In: Felici, M., Kanoun, K., Pasquini, A. (eds.) SAFECOMP 1999. LNCS, vol. 1698, pp. 139–152. Springer, Heidelberg (1999)
8. Papadopoulos, Y.: Safety-directed system monitoring using safety cases. DPhil thesis, The University of York, Department of Computer Science (2000)
9. Society of Automotive Engineers (SAE): ARP 4761: "Model Based Safety Analysis" ARP 4761 associated appendix, Warrendale (1996)
10. United States Department of Defense: MIL-STD-1629A: Procedures for Performing a Failure Mode Effects and Criticality Analysis, Washington, D.C. (1980)
11. Papadopoulos, Y.; Maruhn, M.: Model-based synthesis of fault trees from Matlab-Simulink models. In: The International Conference on Dependable Systems and Networks, pp. 77–82. IEEE, Goteborg (2001)
12. Adachi, M., et al.: An approach to optimization of fault tolerant architectures using HiP-HOPS. Softw. Pract. Experience $41(11)$, 1303–1327 (2011). Published online in Wiley Online Library (wileyonlinelibrary.com)
13. Papadopoulos, Y.: et al.: Automatic allocation of safety integrity levels. In: 1ST workshop on Critical Automotive applications: Robustness & Safety, New York, pp. 7–10 (2010)
14. Kehren, C., et al.: Advanced simulation capabilities for multi-systems with Altarica. In: International System Safety Conference (2004)
15. Joshi, A., et al.: A proposal for model-based safety analysis. In: 24th IEEE on Digital Avionics Systems Conference, Washington, DC (2005)
16. Lisagor, O.: Failure logic modelling: a pragmatic approach. Thesis (Doctor of Philosophy) - Department of Computer Science, University of York, York, p. 348 (2010)
17. Mortada, H., Prosvirnova, T., Rauzy, A.: Safety assessment of an electrical system with AltaRica 3.0. In: Ortmeier, F., Rauzy, A. (eds.) IMBSA 2014. LNCS, vol. 8822, pp. 181–194. Springer, Heidelberg (2014)

The Formal Derivation of Mode Logic for Autonomous Satellite Flight Formation

Anton Tarasyuk[1], Inna Pereverzeva[1,2][✉], Elena Troubitsyna[1],
and Timo Latvala[3]

[1] Åbo Akademi University, Turku, Finland
{anton.tarasyuk,inna.pereverzeva,elena.troubitsyna}@abo.fi
[2] Turku Centre for Computer Science, Turku, Finland
[3] Space Systems Finland, Espoo, Finland
timo.latvala@ssf.fi

Abstract. Satellite formation flying is an example of an autonomous distributed system that relies on complex coordinated mode transitions to accomplish its mission. While the technology promises significant economical and scientific benefits, it also poses a major verification challenge since testing the system on the ground is impossible. In this paper, we experiment with formal modelling and proof-based verification to derive mode logic for autonomous flight formation. We rely on refinement in Event-B and proof-based verification to create a detailed specification of the autonomic actions implementing the coordinated mode transitions. By decomposing system-level model, we derive the interfaces of the satellites and guarantee that their communication supports correct mode transitions despite unreliability of the communication channel. We argue that a formal systems approach advocated in this paper constitutes a solid basis for designing complex autonomic systems.

Keywords: Autonomous flight formation · Formal modelling · Event-B · Refinement · Formal verification

1 Introduction

Nowadays the space industry puts increasingly strong emphasis on novel distributed satellite technology – formation flying. The most recent development in the field – autonomic formation flying – allows multiple satellites autonomously position themselves into a formation, efficiently maintain the formation and change it according to the mission and system requirements [4]. The satellites should function in a coordinated manner to guarantee safety (collision avoidance) and integrity (maintaining proximity) of the formation. Currently, the space industry is experimenting with the novel development and verification technologies that guarantee correctness and safety of autonomic flight formation.

The dynamic behaviour of the formation is defined in terms of modes – mutually exclusive sets of system behaviour [12]. The mode transition logic is complex because the mode transition conditions are defined by a variety of

© Springer International Publishing Switzerland 2015
F. Koornneef and C. van Gulijk (Eds.): SAFECOMP 2015, LNCS 9337, pp. 29–43, 2015.
DOI: 10.1007/978-3-319-24255-2_4

unpredictable factors – the relative position of the satellites, their health and environmental disturbances. The main challenge is to guarantee that, despite highly non-deterministic environment and the absence of the centralised control, the satellites perform mode transitions in a coordinated manner.

To address this challenge, we undertake a formal development of autonomous formation flying in Event-B. Event-B [1] is a state-based approach to correct-by-construction system development. It supports system-level reasoning about properties and behaviour. In particular, it allows us to define system invariants and verify them over all execution scenarios. The main development technique – refinement – supports stepwise construction and verification of complex specifications. We start the development by creating a high-level abstract specification, which is incrementally augmented with the detailed representation of requirements. Each refinement step is accompanied by proofs. When a sufficient level of details is reached, by relying on the modularisation extension [8,16], we can decompose the obtained specification into a number of independent components, i.e., arrive at the distributed architecture.

Event-B has an industrial strength automated tool support – Rodin platform [17]. The platform provides the developers with an integrated engineering environment, which supports modelling in Event-B as well as verification by proofs and model checking. Reliance on a common Event-B model to perform two types of verification helps us to address different aspects of system behaviour: model checking facilitates verification of dynamic properties of the inter-satellite communication, while proofs support reasoning about invariant properties of mode transition logic.

A combination of abstraction, refinement, proofs and decomposition as well as mature tool support makes Event-B a powerful framework for reasoning about behaviour of distributed systems. Development of Event-B and Rodin platform have been significantly advanced in the Deploy project [6]. Space Systems Finland has participated in the project and built a strong in-house expertise in formal modelling. Moreover, it has been encouraging the development of new features of Event-B, such as modularisation support, and validating them in practice. The company continues experimenting with the use of formal techniques in development of high assurance systems. In particular, this work builds on our previous experience in modelling of a reconfigurable on-board satellite system [21] as well as an attitude and orbit control system [10].

In this paper, we define the general patterns for ensuring coordinated mode transitions in the distributed autonomous systems. We analyse the inter-satellite communication, impact of failures and the mechanisms of losing and regaining the coordination. These patterns are integrated into the development of the overall formation flying specification. We start from an abstract model of the entire system, gradually introduce the details of the mode transitions, describe communication between the satellites, and finally decompose the system into independent sub-systems (i.e., satellites) and the communication link between them. Such an approach allows us to define precisely the properties that should hold at the different stages of mode transitions. We believe that the proposed approach offers a powerful technique for formal development and verification of autonomous distributed systems.

2 Satellite Flight Formation

Formation flying is a novel technology for a future generation of space missions. It offers benefits from both economical and technological perspectives. To perform a specific mission it is usually more cost-effective to compose a system from a number of simpler satellites rather than to develop a single dedicated spacecraft. Moreover, formation flying is easier to manage from the fault tolerance point of view – a failed satellite can be replaces by a similar one without the need to abort the entire mission. Finally, relatively small and simple satellites with specific functionalities are faster to develop and easier to maintain.

A few European missions have already exercised formation flying on low earth orbit, e.g., PRISMA [15] and TANDEM [3] missions. However, due to high gravity on lower orbits, it is unfeasible to establish precise relative positioning of satellites in the formation and therefore to perform sophisticated scientific observations. To overcome these limitations, the European Space Agency is currently developing PROBA-3 [4,14] mission (to be launched in 2017) that should demonstrate autonomous formation flying on the highly elliptical orbits. In this paper, we use the currently adopted configuration of the PROBA-3 mission.

The purpose of the PROBA-3 mission is to obtain the pictures of the inner solar corona. The mission consists of two satellites – the Coronagraph Spacecraft and Occulter Spacecraft. In simple non-technical terms, the Coronagraph is responsible for detecting sun position and taking pictures, while the Occulter should provide the shadow. To actually take the pictures, the spacecraft should maintain close proximity to each other (with relative distance from 25 to 250 m), which is achievable only in the low gravity region of the elliptical orbit.

Traditionally, in the space sector, the global system behaviour is specified in terms of modes – the mutually exclusive sets of system behaviour [12] – defined according to the mission and system requirements. The PROBA-3 mission has the following modes: STACK, MANUAL, OPERATIONAL and PARKING. The scheme of possible mode transitions is given in Fig. 1. The STACK mode is the initial mode where spacecraft are not yet separated. MANUAL is the safest mode that used for formation commissioning and during error recovery. OPERATIONAL and PARKING are "active" modes, at which the formation flying is performed. They are highly autonomous modes.

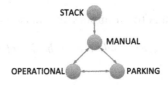

Fig. 1. System modes

The mode transition scheme given in Fig. 1 looks fairly simple. However, system autonomy and unreliability of the communication channel posses a significant challenge to coordination of the mode transitions. In the next section, we will investigate this problem in detail and derive the requirements guaranteeing correct implementation of the coordination.

3 Coordinated Mode Transitions in Autonomous Systems

Mode-rich distributed systems typically have the hierarchical architecture [9]. There is a dedicated component, called a Leader, that triggers mode transitions by broadcasting the id of the next target mode to all components in the system. The other spacecraft(s) is called the Follower. Essentially, after receiving the mode transition command from the Leader, the Follower performs the actions required to execute mode transition.

To make the decisions about mode transitions, the Leader should have the knowledge of the global state, i.e., its own state, the state of the Follower and the environment. In the case of the centralised or ground-coordinated distributed systems, such knowledge is always available. However, in case of the autonomous systems, due to the communication failure, the Leader might lack the knowledge of the Follower state. The active autonomous modes OPERATIONAL and PARKING require the maintenance of the close spacecraft proximity. Therefore, in the off-nominal situations of communication failure or relative position failure, the Leader has an incomplete knowledge of the global state and cannot make safe decision about the active mode transition, i.e., collision avoidance cannot be guaranteed under such uncertainty. This leads us to the first requirement imposed on the mode logic:

R1: The Leader can trigger transition to OPERATIONAL and PARKING modes only in the nominal situations.

To guarantee safety, in the off-nominal situations, we should merely take care of avoiding a collision, i.e., put the spacecraft at the safe distance from each other. In other words:

R2: In case of relative positioning failure, the Leader should trigger the MANUAL mode.
R3: In case of communication failure, the Leader and the Follower should enter the MANUAL mode. This is a self-triggered mode transition, i.e., the Leader and the Follower perform it independently upon detection of failure.

The requirement R3 leads to an important safety design constraint R4:

R4. Communication failures should always be detectable within the predefined time bound.

Now we have to address two problems: how to restore the coordination, and how to ensure that the communication failures are always detected.

Essentially, in the autonomous flight formation, failures result in the loss of the situation awareness that should be regained to restore coordination. Since the formation has the elliptical trajectory, each round includes the perigee phase (low gravity region of the orbit), where GPS measurement and mission ground control are available. The intervention of the ground control is required to restore the coordination between the spacecraft. Since there are no other means to restore the coordination, failure to restore coordination by the ground control implies failure of the entire mission. This observation implies our next requirement:

R5. In the MANUAL mode in the perigee phase the ground control should control both the Leader and the Follower to restore coordination between them. Upon successful completion of this, the control is passed to the Leader and a transition to an active mode PARKING or OPERATIONAL becomes enabled.

Communication is a critical aspect in ensuring coordination and safety of the autonomous formation flying. The spacecraft communicate with each other to coordinate not only mode transitions but also orbital manoeuvring. The orbital manoeuvring is structured by four phases: the perigee phase, the apogee phase (high gravity region of the orbit) and the intermediate preparation phases. The phase transitions are performed according to the predefined logic.

According to *R4*, we should ensure that communication failures can be promptly detected by each spacecraft. Eventual but slow detection might cause a collision. This rules out the asynchronous communication and implies the following requirements:

R6: Communication should be periodic.
R7. Communication timeouts are set for sending and receiving messages during each communication period. No communication during the timeout is treated (by a spacecraft) as a failure of the communication link.

The analysis presented above shows that ensuring correctness of coordinated mode transitions in autonomous formation flying is a challenging engineering task. To approach it in a systematic rigorous way, in the next section we present our modelling framework – Event-B.

4 Modelling and Refinement in Event-B

Event-B is a state-based formal approach that promotes the correct-by-construction development paradigm and formal verification by theorem proving. In Event-B, a system model is specified using the notion of an *abstract state machine* [1]. An abstract state machine encapsulates the model state, represented as a collection of variables, and defines operations on the state, i.e., it describes the dynamic behaviour of a modelled system. The important system properties to be preserved are defined as model invariants. A machine usually has the accompanying component, called context. A context may include user-defined carrier sets, constants and their properties (defined as model axioms).

The dynamic behaviour of the system is defined by a collection of atomic *events*. Generally, an event has the following form:

$$e \; \widehat{=} \; \textbf{any } a \textbf{ where } G_e \textbf{ then } R_e \textbf{ end},$$

where e is the event's name, a is the list of local variables, and (the event *guard*) G_e is a predicate over the model state. The body of an event is defined by a *multiple* (possibly non deterministic) assignment to the system variables. In Event-B, this assignment is semantically defined as the next-state relation R_e. The event guard defines the conditions under which the event is *enabled*, i.e., its body can be executed. If several events are enabled at the same time, any of them can be chosen for execution nondeterministically.

Event-B employs a top-down refinement-based approach to system development. A development starts from an abstract specification thatnondeterministically models the most essential functional system behaviour. In a sequence of refinement steps, we gradually reduce non determinism and introduce detailed design decisions. In particular, we can add new events, refine old events as well as replace abstract variables by their concrete counterparts.

The consistency of Event-B models – verification of model well-formedness, invariant preservation as well as correctness of refinement steps – is demonstrated by discharging the relevant proof obligations. The Rodin platform [17] provides tool support for modelling and verification. In particular, it automatically generates all required proof obligations and attempts to discharge them. When the proof obligations cannot be discharged automatically, the user can attempt to prove them interactively using a collection of available proof tactics. Moreover, a user can also rely on verification by model checking supported by ProB plug-in.

Recently the Event-B language and the tool support have been extended with a possibility to define *modules*. Modules are components containing groups of callable atomic operations [8,16]. Modules can have their own (external and internal) state and invariant properties. An important characteristic of modules is that they can be developed separately and, when needed, composed with the main system. Since decomposition is a special kind of refinement, such a model transformation is also a correctness-preserving step that has to be proven.

A module description consists of two parts – *module interface* and *module body*. A module interface is a separate Event-B component that consists of the external module variables, the module invariants, and a collection of module operations, characterised by their pre- and postconditions. In addition, a module interface may contain a group of standard Event-B events. These events model autonomous module thread of control, expressed in terms of their effect on the external module variables. In other words, they describe how the module external variables may change between operation calls. A formal development of a module starts with the deciding on its interface. Once an interface is defined, it cannot be changed in any manner during the development. This ensures that a module body may be constructed independently from a system model that relies on the module interface. A *module body* is an Event-B machine. It implements the interface by providing a concrete behaviour for each of the interface operations. To guarantee that each interface operation has a suitable implementation, a set of additional proof obligations is generated.

A general strategy of a distributed system development in Event-B is to start from an abstract centralised specification and incrementally augment it with design-specific details. When a suitable level of details is achieved, certain events of the specification are replaced by the calls of the interface operations. The variables become distributed across the modules. As a result, a monolithic specification is decomposed into the separate modules and communication mechanisms are introduced explicitly. In the next section, we demonstrate how to use such a general refinement strategy to model the mode logic of the autonomous flight formation.

5   Modelling Satellite Flight Formation in Event-B

In this section, we outline the overall Event-B development of formation flying and discuss the most challenging aspects. The full Event-B development can be found in [20].

Abstract Specification. The outline of the initial model FFS_abs is shown in Fig. 2. It abstractly represents the Leader's mode transitions as well as failure occurrence and handling. The variable $cur\_mode\_leader \in$ MODES represents the current mode of the leader spacecraft, while the variable $prev\_mode\_leader \in$ MODES stores its previous mode. Here the set MODES = {STACK, MANUAL, OPERATIONAL, PARKING} contains all system modes that can be entered by the satellites.

The events StackSeparation, ModeTransitionManual and ModeTransition-Autonomous model all possible mode transitions (i.e., entering a target mode) of the Leader. The satellite might also maintain the current mode as modelled by the event RemainCurrentMode. This event will be further refined by the events modelling the manoeuvres within the currently active mode, i.e., by the phase transitions. The mode transition rules (defined in Fig. 1) are specified as the model invariant properties, where the auxiliary function $nextMode$ defines all possible successor modes for any system mode.

The failure detection is modelled by the event FormationFailureDetection that assigns value TRUE to the flag *failure*. This will enable the event ModeTransition-Manual, i.e., according to the requirements *R2* and *R3* trigger transition to the Manual mode. In this paper, we keep an abstract representation of the failure detection and recovery procedures.

First Refinement: Modelling Follower Behaviour. Our first refinement step introduces the similar data structures and events for the Follower spacecraft. At this stage, we do not constrain mode transitions, i.e., there is no coordination

```
Machine FFS_abs
Variables cur_mode_leader, prev_mode_leader, failure
Invariants cur_mode_leader ∈ MODES ∧ prev_mode_leader ∈ MODES ∧ failure ∈ BOOL ∧
   cur_mode_leader ≠ STACK ⇒ cur_mode_leader ∈ nextMode(prev_mode_leader) ...
Events
StackSeparation ...                    // spacecraft separation
ModeTransitionManual ...               // transition to MANUAL mode
ModeTransitionAutonomous ≙            // autonomous mode transition
   any mode
   when cur_mode_leader ∈ {OPERATIONAL, PARKING} ∧
        mode ∈ nextMode(cur_mode_leader) ∧ failure = TRUE ⇒ mode = MANUAL
   then cur_mode_leader, prev_mode_leader := mode, cur_mode_leader     end
RemainCurrentMode ...                  // spacecraft remains in the current mode
FormationFailureDetection ≙           // failure detection
   when cur_mode_leader ∈ {OPERATIONAL, PARKING} ∧ failure = FALSE
   then failure := TRUE     end
FormationFailureHandling ...  // failure handling in MANUAL mode
```

Fig. 2. Satellite flight formation: initial model

between the satellites. It will be introduced upon modelling the inter-satellite communication link in the next refinement.

Modelling Mode-level Communication. Modelling and verification of the communication mechanism is the central part of our development. In our second refinement step, we focus on modelling the *mode-level* communication – the high level communication between satellites – used to coordinate the transitions between the modes of the formation.

To trigger mode transitions in the nominal conditions (according to *R1*) the Leader sends the unique id of the target mode to the Follower via the inter-satellite communication link. Upon delivery of the message, the Follower performs transition into the requested mode and sends the acknowledgement to the Leader. Upon receiving the acknowledgement, the Leader also makes the transition to the new target mode. Essentially, our communication is a simple version of the sliding window protocol with the one-place buffers. However, our communication is *two-layered* – it is split into the higher-level mode communication and the lower-level phase communication – which makes proof-based verification of correctness challenging.

According to the *R6* and *R7* the communication between the satellites is periodic and has the predefined maximal delay. This requirements allow us to fulfil the *R4*, i.e., ensure detection of failures. In our models, we could have represented the communication failure as a non-deterministic change of the inter-satellite link status as it is typically done in Event-B modelling. However, we have chosen another approach and decided to model the link failure as an explicit notification that is delivered to both satellites. This approach closely resembles the timeout mechanism used to detect communication failures. Moreover, it facilitates specification of invariant properties of the inter-satellite communication.

To model communication according to the defined requirements, we introduce the models of one-place incoming and outgoing buffers for each of the satellites:

– *modeOutgoing*: leader's outgoing buffer for target mode

LeaveOperationalMode $\hat{=}$
  any $mode\_id$
  where $cur\_mode\_leader = \text{OPERATIONAL} \wedge cur\_mode\_follower = \text{OPERATIONAL} \wedge$
          $modeOutgoing = \varnothing \wedge modeDeliveryReport = \varnothing$
          $mode\_id \in \{\text{PK}, \text{MAN}\} \wedge failure = \text{FALSE} \wedge \dots$
  then $modeOutgoing := \{mode\_id\}$ **end**
ModeCommunicationLink $\hat{=}$
  any msg
  where $modeOutgoing \neq \varnothing \wedge msg \in modeOutgoing \cup \{\text{LOST}\}$
  then $modeOutgoing, modeDeliveryReport, modeIncoming := \varnothing, \{msg\}, \{msg\}$ **end**
EnterParkingModeLeader $\hat{=}$
  refines ModeTransitionManualLeader, ModeTransitionAutonomousLeader
  when $(cur\_mode\_leader = \text{MANUAL} \vee cur\_mode\_leader = \text{OPERATIONAL}) \wedge$
         $modeDeliveryReport = \{\text{PK}\}$
  with $mode = \text{PARKING}$
  then $cur\_mode\_leader, prev\_mode\_leader := \text{PARKING}, cur\_mode\_leader$
         $modeDeliveryReport := \varnothing$ **end**
EnterParkingModeFollower $\hat{=}$
  refines ModeTransitionManualFollower, ModeTransitionAutonomousFollower
  when $(cur\_mode\_follower = \text{MANUAL} \vee cur\_mode\_follower = \text{OPERATIONAL}) \wedge$
         $modeIncoming = \{\text{PK}\}$
  with $mode = \text{PARKING}$
  then $cur\_mode\_follower, prev\_mode\_follower := \text{PARKING}, cur\_mode\_follower$
         $modeIncoming := \varnothing$ **end**

Fig. 3. Flight formation: second refinement

- *modeIncoming*: follower's incoming buffer for target mode
- *modeDeliveryReport*: leader's acknowledgment delivery buffer

To demonstrate communication during the mode transition, in Fig. 3 we show several events representing the transition to the PARKING mode. The event LeaveOperationalMode models initiating a mode transition by the Leader while being in the OPERATIONAL mode. In this case, two transitions are enabled – either to the PARKING or to the MANUAL mode. At this stage the choice between them is modelled nondeterministically ($mode\_id \in \{\text{PK}, \text{MAN}\}$). The mode-level communication link is modelled by the event ModeCommunicationLink that can either deliver the issued instructions, i.e., the next mode id stored in the *modeOutgoing* buffer, or "deliver" the LOST message, that abstractly models detection of a communication failure by the time-out. Finally, two events EnterParkingModeLeader and EnterParkingModeFollower represent transition into the PARKING mode by the leading and the following satellites correspondingly. Transitions to other modes are modelled in the similar way.

In case a satellite receives LOST message, it independently initiates the transition into the MANUAL mode (according to the requirement *R3*). The events modelling off-nominal conditions can be found in the full development [20].

Note that at this stage we still rely on the availability of the global knowledge, i.e., we are not yet ready to decompose the system into a distributed model. Indeed, to guarantee correctness of the coordination, we explicitly allow the Leader to assess the current mode of the Follower before it schedules the next mode transition (see the second guard of LeaveOperationalMode). This modelling trick helps us to postulate important properties of the coordination. In the later refinement step, we abandon this abstraction and refine the global state representation into the model of a distributed state space. The Leader will rely solely on the communication to assess state of the Follower.

Formal development in Event-B allows us to formulate and verify a number of the *mode consistency* properties. They are defined and proved as system invariants. For example,

$$cur\_mode\_leader \neq cur\_mode\_follower \Rightarrow$$
$$cur\_mode\_leader = prev\_mode\_follower \vee$$
$$cur\_mode\_follower = prev\_mode\_leader \quad (1)$$
$$modeOutgoing \neq \varnothing \Rightarrow cur\_mode\_leader = cur\_mode\_follower \quad (2)$$

Property (1) stipulates that the satellites can be *at most one* mode transition ahead (or behind) each other. Moreover, the divergence can be only in the case, when the satellites are actually performing the transition to the next mode (one satellite has already made a transition and another is still in process of doing it). In case, when the Leader's outgoing buffer is not empty (i.e., it is ready to initiate a mode transition), the satellites are in the *same mode* (as defined by property (2)).

We can also formally define the connection between the formation modes and the state of the inter-satellite link, i.e., the values of the satellite buffers as shown by properties (3) and (4):

$$modeIncoming = \{PK\} \wedge cur\_mode\_leader = PARKING \Rightarrow$$
$$prev\_mode\_leader = cur\_mode\_follower$$
$$(3)$$
$$modeIncoming = \{PK\} \wedge cur\_mode\_leader \neq PARKING \Rightarrow$$
$$cur\_mode\_leader = cur\_mode\_follower \quad (4)$$

In the similar way, properties (5) and (6) below describe relationships between the Leader's acknowledgement buffer and the current Follower mode.

$$modeDeliveryReport = \{PK\} \wedge cur\_mode\_follower = PARKING \Rightarrow$$
$$prev\_mode\_follower = cur\_mode\_leader$$
$$(5)$$
$$modeDeliveryReport = \{PK\} \wedge cur\_mode\_follower \neq PARKING \Rightarrow$$
$$cur\_mode\_leader = cur\_mode\_follower \quad (6)$$
$$failure = TRUE \wedge modeOutgoing \neq \varnothing \Rightarrow modeOutgoing = \{MAN\} \quad (7)$$

Property (7) describes dependency between the communication failure and the leader's outgoing buffer. In case, when a failure has been detected, the Leader can only command transition to the MANUAL mode. The properties describing dependency between the communication failure and other buffers are formulated in the similar way. In total, we have formulated and proved more than 40 invariant properties of mode-level communication.

Modelling Phase-level Communication. In the OPERATIONAL and PARKING modes the designed orbital routine for the nominal operation consists of four different phases. The phase-level communication is used to coordinate the transitions between the phases. Our third refinement step described in [20] focuses on modelling it. The phase-level communication is more complex than the mode-level communication. To ensure synchronisation and safety of orbital manoeuvring, not only the Follower but also the Leader sends the acknowledgements of the phase-transition message delivery. The modelling style is similar to the previous step. Modelling the fine-grained phase-level communication resulted in a complex specification that contains a hierarchy of properties ensuring consistency not only at level of mode-logic but also at the level of phases. At this refinement step we formulated and proved more than 70 logical properties described the phase-level communication.

Modelling Communication With the Ground. As described in Sect. 3 (requirement *R5*), the ground control should intervene when the spacecraft have lost the coordination. The ground control generates and sends telecommands to the leading satellite. A telecommand might consist of the next target mode and a number of orbits to be performed (if the target mode is OPERATIONAL).

Decomposition. As a result of the previous refinement steps, we have arrived at a detailed centralised model of the flight formation system. In the final refinement step, we employ decomposition approach provided by the Modularisation plug-in and derive a distributed architecture of the flight formation mode logic. We decompose centralised model into two independent components representing the satellites and the communication link. A graphical representation of the system after decomposition refinement is given in Fig. 4. The previous, more abstract model is refined by a machine CommLink and two modules for satellites – Leader and Follower. To enable two-way communication between the spacecraft, the generic interfaces of the modules Leader and Follower describe a collection of externally callable operations. The machine CommLink, that models all types of communication, invokes these operations in the bodies of its events.

The machine CommLink imports two module interfaces – Leader and Follower. The events ModeCommunicationLink, LeaderFollowerPhaseComm, FollowerLeader-PhaseComm, ManualTC and FailureTC are refined by the communication link events. The rest of the events (e.g., mode transitions) are now becoming a part of the autonomous processes of the Leader and Follower modules. Thus, the events modelling the behaviour of the Leader satellite are now refined by the Leader's interface events, while the events related to the follower satellite are refined by the corresponding events of the Follower's interface. Similarly, the variables of abstract model are now refined by the variables of Leader and Follower modules.

Discussion. The presented development focuses on studying the coordination aspect of mode transitions. The further refinement steps can be performed to

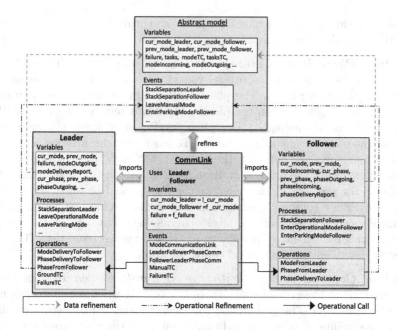

Fig. 4. The decomposition refinement

model the internal architecture and detailed behaviour of each spacecraft. The properties of coordination were formulated as model invariants that are related to the high-level requirements informally defined in Sect. 3.

To verify correctness of the models we discharged more than 2200 proof obligations. Around 86 % of them have been proved automatically by the Rodin platform and the rest have been proved manually in the Rodin interactive proving environment. Most of the manual proofs were related to proving the invariants describing the mode/phase consistency properties as well as logical connections between the formation modes and the state of the inter-satellite link. However, some of the manually proved POs were identical (as some mode/phase transitions are identical up to the variable/constant names) and the corresponding proofs were reused. Moreover, a significant amount of manually proved POs were promptly discharged by calling a single external prover (e.g., predicate prover or SMT-prover). Thus, actual amount of manually proved POs was less that 10% of the total amount, which is a very good result for such a complex model.

The considered formation of two satellites is inspired by a PROBA-3 mission. However, the created model of inter-satellite communication is rather generic and can be used to model formations with similar architecture. For instance, it can be adopted for modelling formations with an arbitrary number of follower satellites by using support for decomposition into an an indexed collection of modules.

6   Conclusion and Related Work

In this paper, we have presented a formal development and verification of autonomous formation flying in Event-B. We have proposed a novel approach to modelling unreliable asynchronous communication in Event-B. We formally define requirements that ensure coordinated mode transitions of autonomic flight formation. The Rodin platform was used to automate modelling and verification efforts. The framework has demonstrated a good scalability and provided us with a suitable basis for designing such a complex distributed system. We believe that the following aspects were critical for the success of the development. The first aspect is support for refinement and decomposition. It allowed us to start from a centralised succinct system model and derive complex and tangled communication mechanism gradually in a correctness preserving way. The second aspect, is a support for highly iterative development provided by the Rodin platform. Proofs provided us with an immediate feedback on our models and helped to spot many intricate interdependencies between modes, phases and effects of faults. Finally, our experience has also shown that it is essential to combine proving with model animation and model checking [11] because they help to validate the model and prevent introducing deadlocks in intertwined communication. For instance, we used ProB model checker to validate invariants, i.e. check that requirements are correctly represented by the logical formulae.

In our modelling we focused on verifying consistency of mode logic in presence of satellite and communication failures. The autonomy of satellites required complex handshaking schemes to ensure proper coordination between them. As a future work, it would be interesting to extend the proposed approach to modelling multiple satellite formation and explore the properties of autonomic coordination in such complex multi-party environment.

Event-B follows top-down refinement strategy that allowed us to formulate system-level properties defining mode consistency conditions. An alternative approach is to rely on high-level programming paradigms to facilitate the design of the decentralized control. In particular, it would be interesting to compare the approach proposed in this paper, with the actor-based design approach [2].

In our previous work [10] we have studied development of centralised mode-rich systems. We have demonstrated how to derive a specification of an Attitude and Orbit Control System – a generic system of satellites by refinement in Event-B. However, due to centralised nature of the system, the model was much simpler with smaller set of properties. The development presented in current paper, is much more complex. The resultant model contains a large set of invariants describing in details the relationships not only between modes and phases but also the effect of failures at different stages of communication.

The application of Event-B formalism to describe safety layered architectures for Unmanned Aerial Vehicle (UAV) control system has been presented in [5]. The authors unfold the system architecture by a refinement, while in our work we rely on refinement technique to model and derive complex and tangled communication mechanism for mode transitions.

Formal validation of the mode logic and, in particular, fault tolerance mechanisms of satellite software has been studied by Rugina et al. [19]. They have investigated different combinations of simulation and model checking. The similar approach that relies on collaborative modelling and simulation was also used to validate the spacecraft's functional behaviour and command/control FDIR [18]. Though the authors combine model checking with simulation while we combine proofs and model checking, they draw the similar conclusions: a combination of different techniques as well as reliance on abstraction are required to model such complex systems as satellites.

The work [7] reports on modelling and analysis effort of a satellite platform using the COMPASS toolset that is based solely on model checking. The work aims at combining different safety analysis techniques and modelling to verify correctness, safety and dependability of a single satellite. A quantitative evaluation of dependability of navigation of satellite systems using probabilistic model checking is presented in [13]. In our work, we aimed at studying logical aspects of the impact of failures on system behaviour.

Webster et al. [22] adopted the agent concept to verify decision-making aspects of Autonomous Unmanned Aircraft control. Specifically, they choose the particular Rules of the Air and verified that the behaviour of the system does not violate them. Verification is performed using agent model checker AJPF. This is an interesting approach for verification and can be seen as complementing our work. In our approach, formal development helps not only verify but also identify the properties of the system.

Acknowledgements. This work is supported by Cyber Trust program http://www. digile.fi/cybertrust.

References

1. Abrial, J.R.: Modeling in Event-B. Cambridge University Press, Cambridge (2010)
2. Agha, G.A., Kim, W.: Actors: a unifying model for parallel and distributed computing. J. Syst. Archit. **45**(15), 1263–1277 (1999)
3. Buckreuss, S., Werninghaus, R., Pitz, W.: German satellite mission TerraSAR-X. In: Radar Conference 2008, pp. 1–5. IEEE (2008)
4. Castellanic, L.T., Llorente, S., Fernandez, J.M., Ruiz, M., Mestreau-Garreau, A., Cropp, A., Santovincenzo, A.: PROBA-3 mission. In: SFFMT 2013 (2013)
5. Chaudemar, J.C., Bensana, E., Seguin, C.: Model based safety analysis for an unmanned aerial system. In: Dependable Robots in Human Environments (2010)
6. DEPLOY: IST FP7 IP Project. http://www.deploy-project.eu/
7. Esteve, M., Katoen, J., Nguyen, V.Y., Postma, B., Yushtein, Y.: Formal correctness, safety, dependability, and performance analysis of a satellite. In: ICSE 2012, pp. 1022–1031. IEEE (2012)
8. Iliasov, A., Troubitsyna, E., Laibinis, L., Romanovsky, A., Varpaaniemi, K., Ilic, D., Latvala, T.: Supporting reuse in Event B development: modularisation approach. In: Frappier, M., Glässer, U., Khurshid, S., Laleau, R., Reeves, S. (eds.) ABZ 2010. LNCS, vol. 5977, pp. 174–188. Springer, Heidelberg (2010)

9. Iliasov, A., Troubitsyna, E., Laibinis, L., Romanovsky, A., Varpaaniemi, K., Väisänen, P., Ilic, D., Latvala, T.: Verifying mode consistency for on-board satellite software. In: Schoitsch, E. (ed.) SAFECOMP 2010. LNCS, vol. 6351, pp. 126–141. Springer, Heidelberg (2010)

10. Iliasov, A., Troubitsyna, E., Laibinis, L., Romanovsky, A., Varpaaniemi, K., Ilic, D., Latvala, T.: Developing mode-rich satellite software by refinement in Event-B. Sci. Comput. Program. **78**(7), 884–905 (2013)

11. Leuschel, M., Butler, M.: ProB: an automated analysis toolset for the B method. Int. J. Softw. Tools Technol. Transf. **10**(2), 185–203 (2008)

12. Leveson, N., Pinnel, L.D., Sandys, S.D., Koga, S., Reese, J.D.: Analyzing software specifications for mode confusion potential. In: Human Error and System Development, pp. 132–146 (1997)

13. Peng, Z., Lu, Y., Miller, A., Zhao, T., Johnson, C.: Formal specification and quantitative analysis of a constellation of navigation satellites. CoRR abs/1402.5599 (2014)

14. Peters, T.V., Brancob, J., Escorial, D., Castellani, L.T., Cropp, A.: Mission analysis for PROBA-3 nominal operations. Acta Astronautica **102**, 296–310 (2014)

15. Prisma Satellites. http://www.prismasatellites.se/

16. Rodin: Modularisation plug-in. http://wiki.event-b.org/index.php/Modularisation_Plug-in

17. Rodin: Event-B platform. http://www.event-b.org/

18. Rugina, A., Leorato, C., Tremolizzo, E.: Advanced validation of overall spacecraft behaviour concept using a collaborative modelling and simulation approach. In: WETICE 2012, pp. 262–267. IEEE Computer Society (2012)

19. Rugina, A.E., Blanquart, J.P., Soumagne, R.: Validating failure detection isolation and recovery strategies using timed automata. In: EWDC 2009 (2009)

20. Tarasyuk, A., Pereverzeva, I., Troubitsyna, E., Latvala, T.: The formal derivation of mode logic for autonomous satellite flight formation. Technical Report 1137, Turku Centre for Computer Science (2015)

21. Tarasyuk, A., Pereverzeva, I., Troubitsyna, E., Latvala, T., Nummila, L.: Formal development and assessment of a reconfigurable on-board satellite system. In: Ortmeier, F., Lipaczewski, M. (eds.) SAFECOMP 2012. LNCS, vol. 7612, pp. 210–222. Springer, Heidelberg (2012)

22. Webster, M., Fisher, M., Cameron, N., Jump, M.: Formal methods for the certification of autonomous unmanned aircraft systems. In: Flammini, F., Bologna, S., Vittorini, V. (eds.) SAFECOMP 2011. LNCS, vol. 6894, pp. 228–242. Springer, Heidelberg (2011)

Automotive Embedded Systems

Simulation of Automotive Security Threat Warnings to Analyze Driver Interpretations and Emotional Transitions

Robert Altschaffel[✉], Tobias Hoppe, Sven Kuhlmann,
and Jana Dittmann

Otto-von-Guericke University, Magdeburg, Germany
{robert.altschaffel, tobias.hoppe, sven.tuchscheerer,
jana.dittmann}@iti.cs.uni-magdeburg.de

Abstract. With the evolution of cars into complex electronic-mechanical systems and related increasing relevance of electronic manipulation and malicious attacks on automotive IT, Security warnings are becoming also more important. This paper presents the findings regarding the potential effect of IT security warnings in vehicles. Different warning approaches were designed and analyzed in driving simulator tests, based upon three representative IT security threats and three variations of the information quantity and recommended action. The potential effect of these warnings was measured using three scenarios, including the simulated consequences, e.g. sudden swerve of vehicle. We analyzed the implications on drivers reaction, task performance, thoughts and emotions to derive the stress level. We found a positive effect of given recommendations due to the lack of security awareness in automotive IT, accompanied by a high variety of warnings cause interpretations. Especially without given recommendation a higher rate of ignorance was observed, leading to accidents.

Keywords: Human aspects in safety-critical systems design and analysis · Safety & security interactions · Automotive security and safety interplay

1 Motivation: The Role of Drivers in Automotive Safety/Security

Automotive systems have evolved into complex, networked systems tied together by a networking architecture. While this allows for more comfort and safety and added functionalities, it also increases the systems complexity and can introduce new external safety and security threats. Tampering with vehicle IT (be it constructive or destructive) always risks escalation into a safety incident. Based on prior work from us where we demonstrated real IT attacks on several automotive subsystems [1, 2], such common automotive vulnerabilities have also been illustrated later on full cars by [3, 4]. The spectrum of observed results leads up influencing the brakes, the steering wheel or disabling the engine by specially crafted CAN bus commands. As these practical analyses have substantiated, unforeseen IT incidents (like intentional, IT-based attacks) may also bear severe safety implications.

© Springer International Publishing Switzerland 2015
F. Koornneef and C. van Gulijk (Eds.): SAFECOMP 2015, LNCS 9337, pp. 47–58, 2015.
DOI: 10.1007/978-3-319-24255-2_5

In conventional IT network security concepts, intrusion detection systems (IDS) constantly monitor the system and log suspicious behaviour. Any indication of an active IT attack is then reported to system administration or computer emergency response teams (CERTs) for assessment and, if necessary, countermeasure implementation. Unlike these trained specialists, however, the average owner of an automotive system lacks the expertise in network security to fulfil that role. While intrusion detection could also be applied to automotive system security [5, 6] with central monitoring by the manufacturer (assuming privacy concerns are addressed), the users of the cars – especially the drivers – may not be completely excluded.

In case of automotive IT security incidents - especially in a running car which might have safety critical impacts - the driver should be involved. If an attack that cannot be mitigated by the system is detected the driver could be notified about the incident or actively prompted to perform a reaction. These reactions may range from an immediate stop of the car to driving on with a later visit at a service station. For more details on possible automotive intrusion responses see [7] or [8].

This paper approaches another important aspect: the drivers emotional responses to automotive safety and security measures. As shown in [9] emotional and affective driver state play an important role in road safety enhancement. Therefore we analyzed strategies to take into account factors like stress level and distraction and determine safety incident responses accordingly. Related to this approach we also researched the acquisition of stress level using biometric data, such as EEG signals or electrical conductance of the skin. In other work this has been done, for example, by the correlation of EEG signal representation to observed - and self reported stress level using emotional video sequences, watched by the subjects [10]. Our approach utilises a driving simulator where the test drivers are confronted with several security incident scenarios and security warnings. We combined three methods to capture their emotional state and reactions, think-aloud-tests, recorded video of the facial expression and thermal cameras.

This article is structured as follows:

- In Sect. 2, selected basics are introduced.
- In Sect. 3 the concept and the setup for the tests are presented and the test execution is described.
- In Sect. 4 the evaluation procedure and the test results are described.
- In Sect. 5 the evaluation methods and the findings from the emotion and emotion transition with the recorded thermal images are presented.
- Section 6 closes the paper with a summary and an outlook.

2   Basics

This section provides relevant basics for our work and understanding of the performed tests and its results.

2.1   Think-Aloud-Tests

Think-aloud-tests are a well known technique to gather thoughts and feelings committed by a person [11]. In the beginning of the experiment the test persons are instructed to speak out loud their thoughts and the feelings during a certain phase of the experiment or the whole time. In general this is a simple task but in practice and over a long time this task is likely to be forgotten by a test person. Thus the experiment leader has to remind the test person from time to time about this task. Due to this the opinions about such tests differ in recent literature. One of the key problems considered in relation to think-aloud-test is, that thinking aloud is seen as an unnatural process which could change the demands of a task [12]. This could imply for instance that the test persons believe that they have to fulfil certain expectations which could lead to a distortion of the results. We took this into account and instructed the test person before the test that there is no judgement of the committed thoughts and feelings and reminded them if they forgot the task.

2.2 Driving Simulator

Driving simulator studies are a commonly used research tool to analyze vehicle-driver interactions. The simulated environment needs to be as plausible as possible to allow the acquisition of reliable and valid data to be applicable to real driving scenarios. This includes physical controls (steering wheel, dashboard) and environment (seats, car body etc.) to avoid "simulator sickness", a type of motion sickness caused by the disparity between the moving simulated environment and the still body of the simulator hardware. Our custom-built simulator environment, which we used as the hardware component of our simulator setup, consists of electronic control units (ECU) and a dashboard of a VW Passat B6. It can trigger various instruments, such as the speed meter, and also sports a Logitech force-feedback steering wheel and pedals. The simulated environment is displayed in front of the vehicle via video projector on a transparent screen. On the software side, our simulator used the Java-based, open source driving simulation software OpenDS 2.0 [13] for the generation of our test driving environments.

3 Concept, Test Setup and Execution

To investigate the reaction of test drivers and their driving performance we introduced a tailored driving simulator study.

We use three different scenarios for this study: City (S1), Highway (S2) and Lane-Change (S3). In each of these scenarios we simulate an IT security incident. In detail these scenarios were:

- S1 - City Scenario: The driver is tasked to drive to a target destination. The driver does not know the city beforehand so he needs to rely on directions given by the navigation system. The navigation system itself gives these instructions using voice. During this scenario the navigation system is manipulated by an attacker and gives wrong directions. After roughly 3½ min this leads to the navigation system instructing the driver to turn 180° on a straight road in multiple repetitions.
- S2 – Highway Scenario: The task in this scenario is to reach the end of a populated highway road. The driver is asked to imagine *"...to be in a hurry"* which is

supported by a clock on his HUD running down. In this scenario a malicious attacker is manipulating the steering of the car. At minute 0:37 this leads the car to steer strongly aside in an unpredictable manner.

- S3 – Lane-Change: This scenario is a reaction test to measure the speed of reaction of the driver. The test is set on a straight highway with five lanes. Above the lanes are bridges with traffic guiding panels. When the vehicle is approaching a bridge, one of the panels will either display a red x or a green o. The red x prompts the driver to brake, while the green o prompts the driver to switch lanes to the lane above which the symbol is displayed. A tone is prompting the driver to return back to the central lane after each test. In total the driver is asked to brake or change lanes ten times each. In this scenario the hands-free is manipulated by an attacker. A warning at minute 3:37 informs the driver of this incident. In contrast to the other scenarios this one commences until the end of the track is reached after five minutes.

Depending on the scenario, the drivers were informed of the incidents using different types of warnings:

- W1 – Warning Icon: A warning icon was displayed on the HUD to inform the driver of the incident
- W2 – Warning Icon + Text: A warning icon was displayed on the HUD to inform the driver of the incident. Furthermore a text was displayed on the HUD to give a more detailed information in the style of "malicious software detected within the navigation system" (example from S1)
- W3 – Warning Icon + Text + Voice: In addition to the warnings given in W2 the driver is informed using a voice message reading the warning of the text aloud.
- W4 – Warning Icon + Text + Voice + Recommendation for conduct: In addition to W3 the text and the voice warning both contain a recommendation for conduct. In the case of S1 this is "visit a nearby maintenance station".

For scenario S3 all of these warnings have been used. For the scenarios S1 and S2 only W3 and W4 were used.

The tests themselves took between 30 and 40 min for each of the tests persons. The setup started with an introductory interview to determine if the tests person owns a car and how familiar he is with modern car IT systems. The driver had a few minutes to familiarise with the simulator afterwards using the city track, before the three test scenarios started. We varied the sequence of the different scenarios between the different test persons. During the individual tests the drivers were recorded using a standard web camera and a thermal camera. In addition, the reactions of the drivers were noted. The tests ended with a second interview concerning the drivers thoughts about their performance during the tests, the helpfulness of the warnings and the reasons for the various incidents.

3.1 Emotional Transitions

Besides monitoring the driver reactions in general, a second research question covers the aspect if future cars could automatically detect emotional transitions of the driver.

Such events could be included into the human machine interaction in order to address such psychological effects.

In order to find first indications about how this might become possible in future, we analyzed the potential of thermal cameras. These can record thermal reactions e.g. within the drivers face which could be linked to his emotional stage. To do this, our driving simulator was equipped with two cameras, a conventional web camera and an infrared-based thermal camera. During the above-mentioned driving simulator experiment, the test subjects were filmed enabling a later evaluation of the recorded video material.

4 Test Evaluation

Following the tests, an exhaustive evaluation has taken place to evaluate the results. During this evaluation, the potential effect of various factors towards the variables and between different variables has been examined.

4.1 Recommendation of Conduct and Understanding of the Warning

This subsection evaluates the findings regarding the implication of using a recommendation of conduct (W4) instead of just informing the driver of an incident (W3). Data for this evaluation is taken from S1 (City) and S2 (Highway) and is displayed in Tables 1 and 2, respectively.

Table 1. Recommendation of conduct and understanding of the warning in S1

	No recommendation (W3)	Recommendation (W4)
Warning not understood	1	1
Warning understood	9	9

Table 2. Recommendation of conduct and understanding of the warning in S2

	No recommendation (W3)	Recommendation (W4)
Warning not understood	2	4
Warning understood	8	6

We performed a chi^2-test on these nominal values to determine if both factors are independent of each other. For S1 we calculated P = 1, 0 which means that in the City-scenario a recommendation of conduct has no measurable effect on the understanding of the warning by the respective drivers. In the Highway-scenario (S2) the calculation yielded P = 0.248. This is pointing to a probable effect of recommendation of conduct on the driver behaviour. In this case a recommendation of conduct had a negative influence on the understanding, though. We suppose the reason for this is the added confusion during the already challenging Highway-scenario.

4.2   Recommendation of Conduct and Quality of Reaction

In this subsection we evaluate the potential of giving a recommendation of conduct (W4) against only informing the driver about the incident (W3) on the quality of the reaction. The quality of reaction was judged by the drivers and by the investigator. The drivers rated themselves ranging 0 to 4 with 4 denouncing the best possible reaction.
    The investigators used the following scale:

- R1 – risky: The driver either ignores or misses the warning and commences without any reaction.
- R2 – cautious: The driver is insecure which leads to a late reaction or he hesitates before taking any action at all.
- R3 – optimal: The driver reacts in a calm way to the incident and minimizes the risk of an accident, depending also on the type of incident (e.g. ESP brake function vs. navigation system).

The data recorded from scenario S1 can be seen in the Tables 3 and 4, while Tables 5 and 6 cover scenario S2.

Table 3. Recommendation of conduct and quality of reaction (self-perceived) in S1

	No recommendation (W3)	Recommendation (W4)
Self rating 0–1	2	4
Self rating 2–4	8	6

Table 4. Recommendation of conduct and quality of reaction (investigator) in S1

	No recommendation (W3)	Recommendation (W4)
risky/cautious reaction (R1 + R2)	6	9
optimal reaction (R3)	4	1

Table 5. Recommendation of conduct and quality of reaction (self-perceived) in S2

	No recommendation (W3)	Recommendation (W4)
Self-rating 0–1	5	4
Self-rating 2–4	5	6

Table 6. Recommendation of conduct and quality of reaction (investigator) in S2

	No recommendation (W3)	Recommendation (W4)
Risky/cautious reaction (R1 + R2)	9	7
Optimal reaction (R3)	1	3

For the city-scenario S1, Tables 3 and 4 show a decrease of the quality of reaction with the addition of a recommendation of conduct in the warning. Using a chi^2-test again we calculated a $P = 0.248$ for the recommendation of conduct and the quality of reaction as perceived by the driver being independent and $P = 0.142$ taking into account the type of warning and the quality of reaction as perceived by the investigator. We hence conclude that a recommendation of conduct has a significant implication on the reaction quality in the scenario S1 based on the recorded data.

Tables 5 and 6 show the relevance of different warnings in the highway scenario (S2). Here the quality of reaction improves when a recommendation of conduct is given. The calculated P for the self-observed quality of reaction is P = 0.467 which allows no statement if these two values are independent. For the investigator-judged quality of reaction P = 0.215 which shows that there is a probable influence of the inclusion of a recommendation of conduct to the quality of reaction.

While a recommendation of conduct shows a tendency of a negative effect on S1 a positive effect in S2 seems probable. We presume the reason for this in the fact that in scenario S1 drivers were mostly confused about the nonsensical orders given by the navigation system so the added recommendation only added to their confusion. This might be made even more severe by the fact that the warning message used the same voice than the navigation assistant. Additionally the recommendation was to ignore the commands from the navigation system which also collides with the general intent of a warning that typically requires an action, not ignoring something. In scenario S2 however, where a quick reaction was needed to prevent an accident, the drivers seemed to rely on the commendation of conduct.

4.3   Self-perceived and Investigator-Perceived Quality of Reaction

We also examined if the self-perceived and investigator-perceived quality of reaction were coherent. Therefore we examined the data taken from S1 and S2 as shown in Tables 7 and 8.

Table 7. Self-perceived and investigator-perceived quality of reaction in S1

	Self-rating 0–1	Self-rating 2	Self-rating 3
Risky reaction (R1)	3	5	1
Cautious reaction (R2)	3	3	0
Optimal reaction (R3)	0	4	1

Table 8. Self-perceived and investigator-perceived quality of reaction in S2

	Self-rating 0–1	Self-rating 2	Self-rating 3
Risky reaction (R1)	8	4	1
Cautious reaction (R2)	0	2	1
Optimal reaction (R3)	1	1	2

Table 7 shows some coherence between self-perceived and investigator-perceived quality of reaction in the city-scenario S1. Drivers who reacted optimal (R3) judge themselves with a 2 or 3, while only 1 driver who reacted not optimal (R1 and R2) judges himself with a 3. We conducted a chi^2-test to examine if these two variables are independent. The calculation yields P = 0.183 which shows that these two variables are probable dependable and therefore coherent to each other.

For the highway-scenario S2, Table 8 also suggests coherence between self-perceived and investigator-perceived quality of reaction. Risky (R1) drivers rate themselves especially low in this scenario, which might be influenced by the fact that driving on led to accidents in this case, while a risky reaction in general did not lead to an accident in S1. A chi^2-test confirms this coherence with P = 0.178.

4.4   Warning Understood and Quality of Reaction

We expected a great influence from the understanding of the warning on the quality of reaction of the driver. Tables 9 and 10 show the results of our tests.

Table 9. Warning understood and self-perceived quality of reaction in S1

	Warning not understood	Warning understood
Risky reaction (R1)	1	8
Cautious reaction (R2)	0	6
Optimal reaction (R3)	0	5

Table 10. Warning understood and self-perceived quality of reaction in S2

	Warning not understood	Warning understood
Risky reaction (R1)	4	9
Cautious reaction (R2)	1	2
Optimal reaction (R3)	1	3

Table 9 shows for the City Scenario S1 that only one test person noted the warning was not understood. Hence a dependency between these two variables is highly unlikely. However, the understanding of the warning seems to have no positive effect on the quality of reaction. This can be explained by the fact that the tests person where asked if they understood the warning afterwards which might be inaccurate or that the drivers got overconfident after they understood the warning and deemed the situation as low-risk. However, a chi^2-test was performed yielding P = 0.283.

In the more complex Highway scenario S2, there is a slight tendency towards a better quality of reaction after an understanding of the warning. The chi^2-test yields P = 0.439 which shows that a real dependency is improbable, though.

4.5   Lane Change Test

In the Lane Change test scenario S3 the warnings were given at minute 3:37. At this point of time the driver was tasked to brake for the sixth time. In order to evaluate the reaction times we exclude the reaction times of the first brake test due to the habituation to the task. We then combine the reaction times of brake task 2−6 and 8−10 in the "No Warning" factor. The reaction times in the brake task 7 are the "Warning was given" factorial group. Reaction times above 9990 ms are defined as a missed reaction and labelled as error. Additionally an outlier analysis was performed. As a result one person in the "No warning" condition was identified as an outlier and excluded from the further statistical tests. Thus the values of 19 ("No Warning") and 18 ("Warning") test drivers were taken into account. As a first indicator we calculated the mean values and the 95 % confidence intervals of the reaction times and identified a difference in the mean values (see Fig. 1). Then we performed a multivariate variance analysis with repetition (using SPSS Statistics V12). We found significant higher reaction times in the warning condition (F171,34, df = 16, p = 0,00). The corrected Eta-squared ($\eta2$) was calculated and points with 0,99 to a high effect size, the statistical power of 1 to a reliable result.

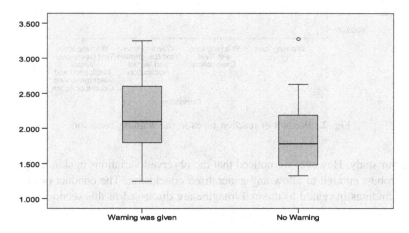

Fig. 1. Boxplot of reaction times in the warning vs. no warning condition

In the warning condition we used four different types of warnings, W1-W4 as introduced in Sect. 4. Therefore we analysed also the reaction times between these different types of warnings with a univariate, one factorial variance analysis. We observed no significant differences in the mean reaction time for braking, as visible in Fig. 2.

A small effect can be observed in the last warning condition, as the reaction times are a little bit faster with the recommended course of action.

We also analysed the errors in the lane change test (defined as a missing reaction). We did not find a significant difference in the distribution of the errors in the lane change test, as there are 2 errors in the first brake task, 1 in the second and third, 0 in the fourth, 3 in the fifth and seventh, 1 in eight and 0 in ninth. In the warning trial we observed 2 missing reactions.

5 Emotion Detection with Thermal Images

The following section gives a brief overview on thermal image recordings taking during our study. We intend to use these thermal images as a new approach to measure the psychophysical condition of the driver. In particular the skin temperature was used

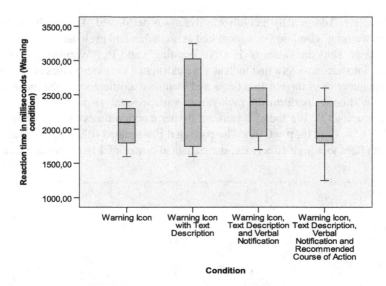

Fig. 2. Boxplot of reaction times in the warning condition

during our study. However we noticed that the observed variations in skin temperature are not robust enough to allow any generalised conclusion. The conduct or our study and the findings in regard to thermal imagine are discussed in this section.

5.1   Measurement, Observed Results and Interpretation

In the first step video material recorded by the thermal camera was analyzed in order to yield a first estimation on the suitability of thermal video recordings for the detection of emotional transitions.

As a reference measure we recorded regular web-cam video streams. These were used for visual emotion detection based on the face expressions by three independent trained persons. For 19 test subjects[1] the perceived emotions were tagged in a written protocol.

Afterwards we compared relevant locations in both, synchronized video streams. We discovered that stress and cognitive effort lead to a slight increase of temperature in some cases. This increase was located in the forehead region and measured 0.2 degree Celsius. The increase might be caused by the cognitive component of the driving tasks. The forehead region is associated with the frontal lobe. The frontal lobe is located at the front of the brain and is one of the four major lobes of the cerebral cortex in the brain. The major part of the frontal lobe is the Motorcortex which steers movement actions. It also involves the ability to project future consequences resulting from current actions and the choice between appropriate and false actions. Hence the pre frontal cortex

---

[1] For the first test person the thermal video was lost due to an error discovered in the recording software.

regulates the cognitive processes that are necessary for the given driving tasks [14]. Therefore the increase of temperature in the forehead region might be evocated by the activated blood supply as a consequence of the cognitive stress in the different incident situations, which was reported by the test persons in the interview after the experiment.

As stated above we found only very small effects which are not statistically significant. Due to a delay of several seconds up to minutes between the increased demand level and the resulting stress level thermal imaging seems not applicable for short term emotion transition measurement in automotive scenarios. Nevertheless, the authors recommend to investigate this revealed effect, by maximising the experimental variance e.g. in different domains like clinical psychology or [13].

6 Summary and Outlook

In the course of this work a driving simulator study has been conducted to investigate on the potential effect of different types of warnings on the reaction of drivers. Both the quality and the quickness of the reaction have been examined. We found that a warning with an added recommendation of conduct (W4) can decrease the risk of an accident in scenarios where a quick reaction is needed (S2). On the other hand, such warnings seem to confuse drivers during less critical incidents (S2). We propose therefore that such a recommendation of conduct is only used in very critical scenarios.

Furthermore we examined the potential effect of warnings on the reaction time of drivers. We observed prolonged times for the warning condition in general. This stands against research results of other studies that find a positive effect on reaction times. It can be explained by the type of warning. While those studies that find a positive effect have a direct relation between the type of warning and endangering situation (e.g. collision warning) we used a warning that could not be directly mapped on a safety relevant action. In fact the security relevant incident required attention and, depending on the type of warning, cognitive task load to interpret the warning. This was additionally intensified by the IT security domain, which is unfamiliar to drivers accompanied by missing IT-security awareness in cars. Critically considered, the findings are preliminary based on a first, small test set and further work should consider more test persons in further varying conditions.

Acknowledgements. We thank our students in the team AUTOalert and EmotionTransition for supporting these research activities with their contributions in our Multimedia Systems Project lecture in winter term 2014/2015.

This work was partly (performing the tests and evaluation of the results, emotional aspects and resilience linked analysis) supported by German Research Foundation, project ORCHideas (DFG GZ: 863/4-1).

This work was also partly (definition of the scenarios derived from the high level project requirements) supported by European Research Foundation, project SAVELEC (Safe control of non cooperative vehicles through electromagnetic means, FP7- SEC-2011, Grant Agreement Number 285202).

References

1. Hoppe, T., Kiltz, S., Dittmann, J.: Security threats to automotive CAN networks – practical examples and selected short-term countermeasures. In: Harrison, M.D., Sujan, M.-A. (eds.) SAFECOMP 2008. LNCS, vol. 5219, pp. 235–248. Springer, Heidelberg (2008)
2. Hoppe, T., Kiltz, S., Dittmann, J.: Automotive IT-security as a challenge: basic attacks from the black box perspective on the example of privacy threats. In: Buth, B., Rabe, G., Seyfarth, T. (eds.) SAFECOMP 2009. LNCS, vol. 5775, pp. 145–158. Springer, Heidelberg (2009)
3. Koscher, K., Czeskis, A., Roesner, F., Patel, S., Kohno, T., Checkoway, S., McCoy, D., Kantor, B., Anderson, D., Shacham, H., Savage, S.: Experimental security analysis of a modern automobile. In: The IEEE Symposium on Security and Privacy, Oakland, CA, 16−19 May 2010
4. Miller, C, Valasek, C.: Adventures in automotive networks and control units. In: DEF CON 21 Hacking Conference, 1–4 August 2013, Las Vegas, USA (2013). http://illmatics.com/car_hacking.pdf. Accessed 20 January 2015
5. Larson, U.E., Nilsson, D.K., Jonsson, E.: An approach to specification-based attack detection for in-vehicle networks. In: Proceedings of the IEEE Intelligent Vehicles Symposium, Eindhoven, The Netherlands, 4–6 June 2008, pp. 830–835. IEEE Xplore, 978-1-424-42568-6 (2008)
6. Müter, M., Groll, A.: Attack detection for in-vehicle networks. In: 25. VDI/VW Gemeinschaftstagung – Automotive Security, Ingolstadt, Germany, 19. Oktober 2009. VDI Wissensforum, Verein Deutscher Ingenieure (VDI) (2009)
7. Hoppe, T., Kiltz, S., Dittmann, J.: Applying intrusion detection to automotive IT – early insights and remaining challenges. J. Inf. Assur. Secur. (JIAS) 4(3), 226–235 (2009)
8. Müter, M., Hoppe, T., Dittmann, J.: Decision model for automotive intrusion detection systems. In: Automotive - Safety & Security 2010, pp. 103−116. Shaker Verlag, Aachen (2010). ISBN 978-3-8322-9172-3
9. Han, I.S., Han, W.-S.: Application of biologically inspired visual information processing in affective driver status monitoring. In: The 24th International Technical Conference on the Enhanced Safety of Vehicles (ESV), Gothenburg, Sweden, 8–11 June 2015
10. Soleymani, M., Esfeden, S.A., Fu, Y., Pantic, M.: Analysis of EEG signals and facial expressions for continuous emotion detection, IEEE Transactions on Affective Computing, May 2015
11. Nielsen, J., Clemmensen, T., Yssing, C.: Getting access to what goes on in peoples heads? - Reflections on the think-aloud technique. In: Proceedings of the Second Nordic Conference on Human-Computer Interaction, pp. 101−110 (2002)
12. McDonald, S., Edwards, H.M., Zhao, T.: Exploring think alouds in usability testing: An international survey. IEEE Trans. Prof. Commun. 55, 2–19 (2012). cited on Page 55 and 56
13. OpenDS: Open Source Driving Simulator (2015). Project web site at http://www.opends.eu/
14. Kimberg, D.Y., Farah, M.J.: A unified account of cognitive impairments following frontal lobe damage: the role of working memory in complex, organized behavior. J. Exp. Psychol. Gen. 122(4), 411–428 (1993)

Improving Dependability of Vision-Based Advanced Driver Assistance Systems Using Navigation Data and Checkpoint Recognition

Ayhan Mehmed[1(✉)], Sasikumar Punnekkat[2], Wilfried Steiner[1],
Giacomo Spampinato[2], and Martin Lettner[1]

[1] TTTech Computertechnik AG, Vienna, Austria
{ayhan.mehmed,wilfried.steiner}@tttech.com
martin.lettner@tttech-automotive.com
[2] Mälardalen University, Västerås, Sweden
{sasikumar.punnekkat,giacomo.spampinato}@mdh.se

Abstract. Advanced Driver Assistance Systems (ADAS), like adaptive cruise control, collision avoidance, and, ultimately, autonomous driving are increasingly evolving into safety-critical systems. These ADAS frequently rely on proper function of Computer-Vision Systems (CVS), which is hard to assess in a timely manner, due to their sensitivity to the variety of illumination conditions (e.g. weather conditions, sun brightness). On the other hand, self-awareness information is available in the vehicle, such as maps and localization data (e.g. GPS).

This paper studies how the combination of diverse environmental information can improve the overall vision-based ADAS reliability. To this extent we present a concept of a Computer-Vision Monitor (CVM) that identifies predefined landmarks in the vehicles surrounding, based on digital maps and localization data, and that checks whether the CVS correctly identifies said landmarks. We formalize and assess the reliability improvement of our solution by means of a fault-tree analysis.

Keywords: Computer-vision system · Computer-vision monitor · Latent failures · External environmental disturbances · Fault tree analysis

1 Introduction

With approximately 1.24 million deaths and another 20 to 50 million of non-fatal injuries on the world's road in 2010, road traffic injuries are estimated to be the eighth leading cause of death nowadays [1]. Additionally to the human tragedies, the cost of dealing with the consequences of these road traffic crashes runs to billions of dollars.

Among the strategies which are proven to reduce road traffic injuries like reducing the urban speed limits, reducing drunken driving and increasing seat-belt use is the strategy of providing new passive and active vehicle safety systems.

© Springer International Publishing Switzerland 2015
F. Koornneef and C. van Gulijk (Eds.): SAFECOMP 2015, LNCS 9337, pp. 59–73, 2015.
DOI: 10.1007/978-3-319-24255-2_6

Today, there is a strong development focus on active safety systems ranging from Anti-lock Breaking Systems (ABS), Electronic Stability Control (ESC), Emergency Brake Assistant (EBA) to complex Advanced Driver Assistance Systems (ADAS) with accident prediction and avoidance capabilities [2]. Such systems are increasing the traffic safety either by informing the driver about the current situation (e.g. night vision, traffic sign detection, pedestrian recognition), by warning the driver with regard to hazards (e.g. obstacle and collision warning, lane departure warning, blind spot detection), or by selective control of actuators (e.g. Adaptive Cruise Control (ACC), adaptive headlights, pedestrian protection, collision avoidance) [3].

To perform functions, such as those listed above, ADAS rely heavily on environment perception. Examples for the most widely used sensors are ultrasonic sensors, Long and Short Range Radars (LRR, SRR), Light Detection and Ranging sensors (LiDAR) and video cameras (vision systems). Video cameras have an important role in ADAS, because of their ability to give more detailed representation of the environment than the other sensors. Therefore, special attention should be paid to vision systems which are used in safety-related and safety-critical systems. Furthermore, an automotive vision system also integrates Electronic Controller Units (ECUs) and a communication subsystem connecting the cameras to the ECUs and the ECUs to each other. Thus, automotive systems in general and Computer-Vision Systems (CVSs) in particular become quite complex. The safety standard ISO 26262 has been introduced for automotive Electrical/Electronic (E/E) systems to address the potential risk of malfunction for automotive systems [4], and ensuring correct functionality of ADAS becomes mandatory from a qualification perspective.

One way to satisfy the safety standards is by designing systems to be dependable. According to Laprie [5], dependability is the ability of the system to deliver service that can justifiably be trusted. It encompasses the concept of reliability, availability, safety, maintainability, integrity and confidentiality which are measures used to quantify the dependability [5,6]. Fault tolerance and fault prevention are among the means capable of achieving dependable systems. While fault prevention techniques prevent the occurrence of Hardware Failures (HF) and Software Errors (SE) by selecting high-quality components, design rules, etc., fault-tolerance techniques handle HF and SE, when they occur by fault masking and reconfiguration techniques (fault detection, location, containment and recovery). Fault masking simply "hides" the faults by using available redundancy. In case a given redundant component fails, the failure is mitigated by using majority voting. Therefore faults are contained or in other words the effect of faults does not propagate throughout a system, and stays local [6]. A drawback of this approach is that if faults are only "hidden" and fault detection is not used, the faulty components will not be detected, the available redundancy is going to decrease and the system will not be aware of that - a process called redundancy attrition [7]. Thus in real fault-tolerant system, it is common to use a combination of fault masking and fault detection. Fault detection can be accomplished through dedicated hardware circuitry, software code and test methods. Some of these various failure detection methods are referred as monitors [8].

One assumption is that the monitor provides 100 % diagnostic coverage of the item performing a given function and a monitor verification operation ("scrub") verifies (with 100 % diagnostic coverage) that the monitor is fully operational. Unfortunately, real life monitors, firstly (i) may fail before the component fails, allowing the failure to spread and secondly (ii) may not provide 100 % diagnostic coverage. Both cases are known as latent failures - faults whose presence is neither detected by a monitor, nor perceived by the driver within a time interval, after which it will contribute to a failure ([9] - part 1). The remainder of this paper will use the terms monitor and internal monitor interchangeably, where in both cases referring to monitors implemented locally in the CVS.

In this paper we are introducing a novel concept of Computer-Vision Monitor (CVM), whose aim will be to detect latent failures (i) by verifying that the internal monitors of the CVS are fully operational ("scrub") and (ii) by detecting failures which are not in the diagnostic coverage of the internal monitors. Furthermore, the paper demonstrates in a step-by-step manner, how to perform reliability analysis of ADAS with and without CVM and proposes a solution, how to include the issue of detecting a special case of latent failures (leading directly to a hazard in a very short time) to the fault tree analysis.

The paper is organized as follows. In Sect. 2, the problem statement and the chosen ADAS scenario are presented. The CVM concept is introduced in Sect. 3, followed by Sect. 4, where reliability analysis of the proposed solution will be done. Conclusions and future work will be presented in Sect. 5.

2   Problem Statement

In the field of vision-based ADAS, latent failures, resulting from not full diagnostic coverage, very often are consequences of External Environmental Disturbances (EED). A typical example in the automotive environment is the illumination, which can be barely controlled, due to weather conditions, different sun position and brightness, and artificial light (headlights, street lamps). The situation, such as direct sun light for instance, highly affects the image acquisition and processing, thereby, decreasing the abilities of computer vision algorithms to interpret the environment correctly, which in turn might lead to wrong decisions and actions of the system. A solution for that issue could be the fast Automatic Exposure Control (AEC), which ensures, that the right amount of light is perceived from the camera.

As regards to the effects of the bad weather conditions, various image enhancement methods are used to improve the dependability of CVS. Image de-weathering is used in [10] to remove the weather effects from images. Image based fog detection and visibility estimation is presented in [11]. Raindrop detection and removal techniques can be seen in [12].

Furthermore, often used in ADAS is the competitive (redundant) sensor fusion, where different types of sensors deliver measurements of the same property. An example for ACC where safe distance to the front vehicle is measured by four different sensors (LRR, SRR, CVS, LiDAR) is given in [13]. The main idea of using different types of sensors to measure the same property is that the sensors will fail in different environmental conditions, but less likely in the same.

Even though, there are particular solutions, such as AEC for direct sunlight and image enhancement methods against the effect of bad environmental conditions, the diversity of EED scenarios are difficult to be covered exhaustively.

As far as to the competitive sensor fusion, it must be emphasized, however, that this example is not the only way of realization of ACC or any other ADAS functions. In case of pedestrian detection for instance LiDARs and vision sensors are used collaboratively, where the first one is ensuring the detection and tracking and the second one is responsible for the classification of the object in the ROI (Region of Interest) [14]. In another example of ACC, active sensors (radar and LiDARs) and vision sensors do not exchange information between each other, but the data from each one is used for different functions of the ADAS. In that case the active sensor is used to detect obstacles and to provide directly the distance to the obstacle, while the camera is used to support the other ACC related functions, such as lane detection and traffic sign recognition [15].

In this paper we are interested in improving the dependability (in particularly the reliability attribute) of vision-based systems. Thus, the reminder of this paper is focused on a scenario, where ADAS relies only on vision for given functions, such as pedestrian detection and tracking, obstacle detection, lane and traffic sign recognition, night vision - each of which can be used in autonomous vehicles (Fig. 1).

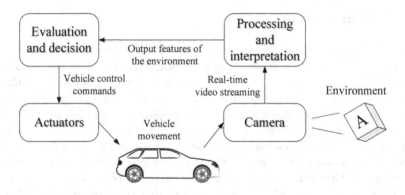

Fig. 1. High-level overview of vision-based ADAS.

Figure 1 depicts an exemplary control system of an autonomous vehicle. The environment is captured by the camera and the information is transmitted to the processing and interpretation subsystem. After processing the image and extracting the useful data, the information is given to the evaluation and decision subsystem. According to the features of the environment, as well as on the implemented logic, the evaluation and decision subsystem generates the vehicle control commands, which in turn are executed by the actuators.

3   The Computer-Vision Monitor (CVM) Concept

Current research in the field of digital maps, GPS and intelligent vehicles is focused on mainly two areas. On the one hand GPS-based systems combined with data from laser scanners, cameras, on board sensors are used to localize the precise position and orientation (especially in the urban areas, where the accuracy of the GPS alone is limited and unreliable) of the vehicle, using knowledge regarding mapped landmarks (traffic signs, lanes, traffic lights, etc.) on a digital map [16,17]. On the other hand data from digital maps and vehicle position, direction and speed are fused in order to improve the success rate of vehicle camera traffic sign recognition [18,19].

While the research shown above focus on a precise localization of vehicles and improving success rate of traffic sign recognition using pre-mapped landmarks and various sensory systems, we propose a complementary approach using the same resources. Labeling the precise position of the traffic infrastructure objects, such as traffic signs, road markings, traffic lights, etc. as checkpoints on a detailed digital map can be used to identify the correct functionality of CVS (Fig. 2).

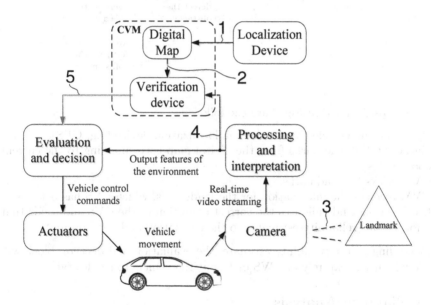

Fig. 2. Conceptional view of vision-based ADAS with CVM.

Our approach is to place new landmarks to the road or use the already implemented road infrastructure on the road, as landmarks in digital maps. Knowing their exact position in the digital map, the ability of the vision system to find a given traffic sign will be verified. According to the results from the CVS, whether the traffic sign is found or not, the correct operation of the computer vision system will be assessed.

Table 1. Example system level FHA.

Function failure ref.	Function	Phase	Failure condition	Failure effect	Classification
F_1	Lane departure warning	Highway	Inability to detect the road lanes	Driver is not informed upon leaving the lane	S2
F_2	Traffic sign recognition	Highway/Urban	Inability to detect the traffic sign	Vehicle does not stop on a "STOP" sign	S3
F_3	Blind spot detection	Highway/Urban	Inability to detect the car in the blind spot area	Driver is not informed of a car in the blind spot area	S2
F_4	Pedestrian protection	Urban	Inability to detect the pedestrian	Vehicle does not decrease the speed to protect the pedestrian	S3
F_5	Collision avoidance	Highway/Urban	Inability to detect the obstacle	Vehicle does not decrease the speed in order to avoid or mitigate the collision	S3

The steps depicted in Fig. 2 are the following:

1. Receiving the vehicle coordinates via localization device (e.g. GPS),
2. Gathering the landmarks from the digital map corresponding to the current coordinates,
3. CVS checks for landmarks,
4. CVM receives the information for the landmarks, which CVS has detected,
5. CVM verifies and validates the correct operation of the CVS and sends that information (reliability estimate) to the evaluation and decision unit.

According to the reliability estimate, the evaluation and decision block will decide whether it can rely on CVS or to put the vehicle to a safe state.

4   Reliability Analysis

In this section, we use a simplified Functional Hazard Analysis (FHA) and Fault Tree Analysis (FTA) in order to analyze the reliability of the vision-based ADAS with and without the proposed CVM. Furthermore in the future, both, FHA and FTA could be used in a safety assessment process.

4.1   Functional Hazard Analysis

FHA is an approach which identifies and classifies the failure conditions related to a given function, according to their severity. An example of a system level

FHA, according to [8], for the vision-based ADAS is depicted in Table 1. The columns in the table include the reference of the failure, function name and the phase in which it is used, as well as its probable failure condition and effects, followed by classification of the failure by its severity.

The classification of the failures was made according to ISO26262 standard ([9] - part 3), where the severity classes range from S0 to S3 (Table 2).

Table 2. ISO-26262 severity classes [9].

Class	S0	S1	S2	S3
Description	No injuries	Light and moderate injuries	Severe and life-threatening injuries (survival probable)	Life-threatening injuries (survival uncertain), fatal injuries

In this example, we assume, that a failure of the CVS may lead to a life-threatening or fatal injury. Therefore the reminder of the paper will assume that each CVS failure not detected by the monitor might lead to high-level severity class.

4.2   FTA for Vision-Based ADAS

FTA is a deductive (top down) approach, which is used to (i) determine what single failures or combination of failures can exist at the lower levels, that might cause each failure condition in the FHA and (ii) to evaluate qualitatively or quantitatively the probability of the top-level event. The level of details of the Fault Tree (FT) is dependent upon the overall knowledge and experience, and requires consultation of numerous specialists. Figure 3 presents a high-level FT of a vision-based ADAS, where the internal monitor has only 90 % coverage of the function F_i failures and the monitor might fail before the failure in F_i occurs.

The variables depicted in the Fig. 3 are as follows:

- λ_f - Function F_i failure rate per hour,
- λ_m - Monitor failure rate per hour,
- $travel\_time$ - time of travel of the vehicle,
- t_f - Function F_i exposure time,
- t_m - Monitor exposure time,
- D_{λ_f} - percentage of function F_i failures detectable by the monitor,
- L_{λ_f} - percentage of function F_i failures not detectable by the monitor.

The FT shown in Fig. 3 has the following main events:

- Event E_1:
  - The internal monitor has only 90 % (D_{λ_f}) coverage of the function F_i failures.

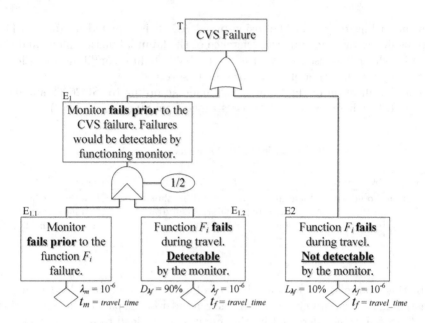

Fig. 3. High-level FT for vision-based ADAS.

- The internal monitor might fail prior to the function F_i failure of the CVS and there is no monitor verification. Thus, t_m is equal to *travel_time*, addressing the need for "scrubbing".
- Event E_2:
  - Presents the rest of the failures which are not detectable from the monitor ($L_{\lambda_f} = 10\%$). Thereby, addressing the latent failures, resulting from not full diagnostic coverage (Sect. 2).

Having the approximate failure rates and exposure times, the probability of each primary event in the FT can be calculated according to Eq. 1:

$$P_f = 1 - e^{\lambda_f t} \tag{1}$$

In case when $\lambda_f t < 0.1$, the equation can be simplified to:

$$P_f = \lambda_f t \tag{2}$$

Thus, the top level event failure probability can be calculated as:

$$P_f^{Top} = E_1 + E_2$$

where:

$$E_1 = \frac{1}{2}E_{1.1}E_{1.2} = \frac{1}{2}\lambda_m t_m D_{\lambda_f}\lambda_f t_f$$

$$E_2 = L_{\lambda_f}\lambda_f t_f \tag{3}$$

The probability of elements failing in a certain sequence (monitor fails prior to the function F_i failure) is included via multiplication by $\frac{1}{2}$. For illustration purposes, we assume a failure rate of 10^{-6} per hour for both λ_f and λ_m, which is about the best a component can be constructed and analyzed by means of testing. Monitor exposure time t_m and function exposure time t_f are equal to the *travel_time*. Within this paper we assume maximum travel time of two hours. Given the values, the top level event probability is $P_f^{Top} = 2 \times 10^{-7}$.

4.3 FTA for Vision-Based ADAS with CVM

Figure 4, presents a high-level FT of vision-based ADAS with CVM, where CVM is able to detect 5 % out of 10 % of the non-detectable by the internal monitor function F_i failures and 95 % of the monitor failures. The new variables depicted in FT are as follows:

- T_{CVM} - CVM diagnostic test interval,
- P_{cvm} - The probability, that CVM will fail to detect the function F_i latent failures within the sufficient time, required to put the vehicle in a safe state,
- D_{λ_f} - percentage of function F_i failures detectable by the monitor,
- $L_{\lambda f1}$ - percentage of function F_i failures not detectable by the monitor, but detectable by the CVM,
- $L_{\lambda f2}$ - percentage of function F_i failures neither detectable by the monitor, nor by CVM,
- D_{λ_m} - percentage of monitor failures detectable by CVM,
- L_{λ_m} - percentage of monitor failures not detectable by CVM.

The main events of the fault tree depicted in Fig. 4 are as follows:

- Event E_1:
    - The internal monitor has 90 % (D_{λ_f}) coverage of the function F_i failures, but monitor fails prior to the function F_i failure.
    - CVM has 95 % (D_{λ_m}) diagnostic coverage of the monitor failures. Therefore, monitor exposure time (t_m) for failures detectable by CVM is equal to the time interval in which CVM diagnoses the monitor (T_{CVM}).
- Event E_2:
    - The internal monitor has 90 % (D_{λ_f}) coverage of the function F_i failures, but monitor fails prior to the function F_i failure.
    - CVM does not have coverage on 5 % (L_{λ_m}) of the monitor failures. Therefore, monitor exposure time (t_m) for failures not detectable by CVM is equal to the *travel_time*.
- Event E_3:
    - CVM is able to detect 5 % ($L_{\lambda f1}$) out of 10 % of the function F_i failures, which are not detectable from the internal monitor. This percentages are taken as an example. Sensitivity analysis with different diagnostic coverage will be performed later in the paper.
    - Probability (P_{cvm}) that CVM will fail to detect function F_i latent failure within the sufficient time, required to put the vehicle to a safe state, also effects the event E_3 probability. P_{cvm} will be estimated in Sect. 4.3.1.

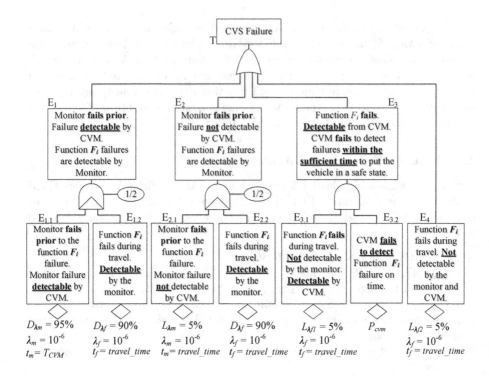

Fig. 4. High-level FT for vision-based ADAS with CVM.

- Event E_4:
  - Presents the rest 5% ($L_{\lambda f2}$) of the failures which are neither detectable by the internal monitor, nor by CVM.

4.3.1 CVM Failure Probability

Latent failures can persist for a time interval which is either greater or shorter than the time of travel. Latent failure in CVS, used to keep the vehicle on the road for instance, will lead directly to a hazard in short time. In that case, the time interval in which a failure remains latent (not perceived) is comparable to the time interval before the hazardous event can take place. In ISO26262, this interval is referred as Fault Tolerant Time Interval (T_{FTTI}), (Fig. 5).

The rest of the variables depicted in Fig. 5 are the diagnostic test interval (T_{DTI}), which is the amount of time between executions of diagnostic test by a safety mechanism (monitor) and the fault reaction time (T_{FRT}) which is the time-span from the detection of fault to reaching to the safe state.

We assume that the diagnostic test interval (T_{DTI}), for failures, not in the diagnostic coverage of the internal monitor, but in the diagnostic coverage of CVM, is equal to the time interval in which CVM diagnoses the system (T_{CVM}):

$$T_{DTI} = T_{CVM} \qquad (4)$$

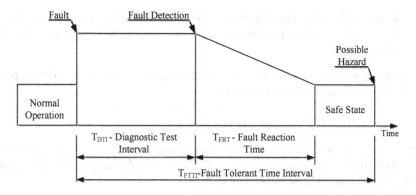

Fig. 5. Fault reaction time and fault tolerant time interval (source: [9] - part 1).

If T_{CVM} is greater than T_{FTTI}, CVM might fail to detect the failure within the sufficient time, required to put the vehicle to a safe state (T_{FRT}) or even to miss the latent failure. Therefore to guarantee that the latent failure will be detected and the vehicle will enter to a safe state, the difference between T_{FTTI} and T_{CVM} should be less than T_{FRT}:

$$T_{FTTI} - T_{CVM} < T_{FRT} \qquad (5)$$

This is an essential issue for systems in which latent failures lead to hazards in very short time. Because our system is such, the probability (P_{cvm}), that the CVM will fail to detect function F_i latent failures within the sufficient time required to put the vehicle to a safe state has to be estimated and included properly in the FTA. This estimation is made according to ISO 26262 - part 3:

$$P_{cvm} = \lambda_f \delta T \qquad (6)$$

where:

- δ - rate of occurrence of the hazardous event.
  For non-autonomous vehicles this rate could vary from occurs less often than once a year to occurs during almost every travel. For the scenario we have chosen, the rate occurrence for fully autonomous vehicle is considered as each time when the system does not get correct information from CVS about the environment for 10 ms. Thus, $\delta = 10$ ms.
- T - the duration of time that the failure is not perceived.
  Failure might be perceived in two ways - (i) by leading to a hazard and (ii) by being detected from a safety mechanism. Therefore T could be taken from one of the two cases:
    1. T is equal to the time between latent failure occurs and leads to possible hazard. This interval of time is also referred as Fault Tolerant Time Interval (T_{FTTI}).

2. T is equal to the time between latent failure occurs and its presence is detected by a safety mechanism. Also referred as Diagnostic Test Interval (T_{DTI}), (Fig. 5).

According to Eqs. 4 and 6, the probability that CVM will fail to detect function F_i failure within sufficient time is:

$$P_{cvm} = \lambda_f \delta T_{CVM} \tag{7}$$

Having $\lambda_f = 10^{-6}$ and $\delta = 10\,\mathrm{ms}$ as constant values, the only variable is T_{CVM}. Within this paper we assume a maximum travel time of two hours. Thus, we consider T_{CVM} to vary from 1 ms to 7200 s.

4.3.2   CVS Failure Probability

Top level event probability for the vision-based ADAS with CVM is equal to:

$$P_f^{Top} = E_1 + E_2 + E_3 + E_4$$

$$where:$$

$$E_1 = \frac{1}{2}E_{1.1}E_{1.2} = \frac{1}{2}D_{\lambda_m}\lambda_m t_m D_{\lambda_f}\lambda_f t_f$$
$$E_2 = \frac{1}{2}E_{2.1}E_{2.2} = \frac{1}{2}L_{\lambda_m}\lambda_m t_m D_{\lambda_f}\lambda_f t_f \tag{8}$$
$$E_3 = E_{3.1}E3.2 = L_{\lambda f1}\lambda_f t_f P_{cvm}$$
$$E_4 = L_{\lambda f2}\lambda_f t_f$$

Top level event probability for the current FT depends (i) on the diagnostic test interval (T_{CVM}) and (ii) on the percentage of the latent failures CVM may detect. Therefore sensitivity analysis on different diagnostic coverages $L_{\lambda f1}$ will be performed. Sensitivity analysis on D_{λ_m} is not done, due to the fact that its weight on the top level event probability is very low.

Figure 6 depicts the top level event probability (P_f^{Top}) results for different diagnostic coverage percentages of CVM ($L_{\lambda f1}$) and diagnostic test interval (T_{CVM}) ranging from 1 ms to 7200 s.

Results from Fig. 6 show that depending on the diagnostic coverage of CVM and on the diagnostic test interval, the failure probability of top level event (P_f^{Top}) can be decreased up to 10^{-13} when the CVM has full coverage of the latent failures ($L_{\lambda f1} = 10\,\%$) and diagnostic test interval of 1 ms.

However, diagnostic test interval of $1ms$ is difficult to be achieved. Therefore Fig. 7 presents top level event probability (P_f^{Top}) results for different diagnostic coverage percentages of CVM ($L_{\lambda f1}$) and T_{CVM} ranging from 1 s to 300 s.

The results from Fig. 7 show that, when T_{CVM} is under 50 s and $L_{\lambda f1} = 10\,\%$, P_f^{Top} decreases to less than 10^{-9}. In the case when the T_{CVM} is 1 s and CVM has full diagnostic coverage ($L_{\lambda f1} = 10\,\%$), the top level event failure probability is 2.01×10^{-11}, which is sufficient for safety-critical functions.

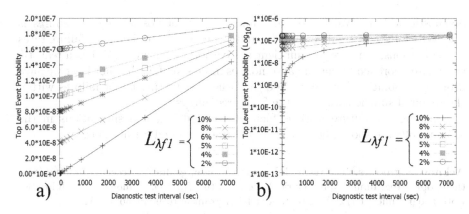

Fig. 6. (a): P_f^{Top} results for different $L_{\lambda f1}$ and T_{CVM} ranging from 1 ms to 7200 s. (b): Logarithmic scale (log_{10}) of P_f^{Top}.

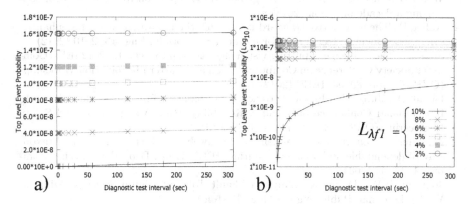

Fig. 7. (a): P_f^{Top} results for different $L_{\lambda f1}$ and T_{CVM} ranging from 1 s to 300 s. (b): Logarithmic scale (log_{10}) of P_f^{Top}.

5   Conclusions and Future Work

Autonomous vehicles are no longer a distant future goal. Top vehicle producers invest serious amount of resources in research, development and testing in the said area. When it comes to the need of collecting detailed information for the environment, vision systems are inevitable part of the autonomous vehicles. Therefore, the vision-based systems have to be dependable enough in order to be used for vehicle safety-critical functions.

In this paper we have proposed a concept of CVM which combines environmental information to enhance the reliability of CVS in ADAS. Using FT and sensitivity analysis, we have shown, that the proposed CVM can contribute to improving the overall reliability of the in-vehicle computer-vision system, by achieving top level event probability of failure of 2.01×10^{-11}, given that the diagnostic test interval is $1sec$ and full coverage of possible latent failures is achieved. This is certainly optimistic and a consequence of idealized failure rates and conditions, but gives us sufficient motivation to consider CVM as a realistic candidate approach to making automobiles more safe. Last but not least we have proposed a solution how to include the issue of detecting latent failures within the required sufficient time, to the fault tree analysis.

Ongoing and future work is focused on modeling and simulations in the Möbius software tool in order to validate the presented estimations.

Acknowledgments. The research leading to these results has received funding from the People Programme (Marie Curie Actions) of the European Union's Seventh Framework Programme FP7/2007–2013/under REA grant agreement no. 607727.

References

1. World Health Organization: WHO global status report on road safety 2013: supporting a decade of action (2013)
2. Kafka, P.: The automotive standard ISO 26262, the innovative driver for enhanced safety assessment & technology for motor cars. Procedia Eng. **45**, 2–10 (2012)
3. Stein, F.: The challenge of putting vision algorithms into a car. In: 2012 IEEE Computer Society Conference on Computer Vision and Pattern Recognition Workshops (CVPRW), pp. 89–94. IEEE (2012)
4. Ismail, A., Jung, W.: Research trends in automotive functional safety. In: 2013 International Conference on Quality, Reliability, Risk, Maintenance, and Safety Engineering (QR2MSE), pp. 1–4. IEEE (2013)
5. Avizienis, A., Laprie, J.C., Randell, B., Landwehr, C.: Basic concepts and taxonomy of dependable and secure computing. IEEE Trans. Dependable Secure Comput. **1**, 11–33 (2004)
6. Johnson, B.W.: Design & Analysis of Fault Tolerant Digital Systems. Addison-Wesley Longman Publishing Co., Inc., Boston (1988)
7. Proenza, J.: RCMBnet: a distributed hardware and firmware support for software fault tolerance. Ph.D. thesis, Department of Mathematics and Informatics. Universitat de les Illes Balears (UIB) (2007)
8. SAE ARP4761: Guidelines and methods for conducting the safety assessment process on civil airborne systems and equipment. SAE International (1996)
9. CD ISO: 26262, road vehicles-functional safety. International Standard ISO/FDIS (2011)
10. Aponso, A.C., Krishnarajah, N.: A hybrid approach for a vision based driver assistance system with de-weathering. In: 2012 IEEE Southwest Symposium on Image Analysis and Interpretation (SSIAI), pp. 105–108. IEEE (2012)
11. Negru, M., Nedevschi, S.: Image based fog detection and visibility estimation for driving assistance systems. In: 2013 IEEE International Conference on Intelligent Computer Communication and Processing (ICCP), pp. 163–168. IEEE (2013)
12. Wahab, M.H.A., Su, C.H., Zakaria, N., Salam, R.A.: Review on raindrop detection and removal in weather degraded images. In: 2013 5th International Conference on Computer Science and Information Technology (CSIT), pp. 82–88. IEEE (2013)
13. Ghahroudi, M.R., Sabzevari, R.: Multisensor data fusion strategies for advanced driver assistance systems. Sensor and Data Fusion, pp. 141–166. In-Teh, Croatia, (2009)

14. Premebida, C., Monteiro, G., Nunes, U., Peixoto, P.: A LiDAR and vision-based approach for pedestrian and vehicle detection and tracking. In: Intelligent Transportation Systems Conference, ITSC 2007, pp. 1044–1049. IEEE (2007)
15. Panciroli, M.: Vision-based ACC. In: Eskandarian, A. (ed.) Handbook of Intelligent Vehicles, pp. 1061–1069. Springer, London (2012)
16. Schindler, A.: Vehicle self-localization with high-precision digital maps. In: Intelligent Vehicles Symposium (IV), pp. 141–146. IEEE (2013)
17. Vu, A., Ramanandan, A., Chen, A., Farrell, J.A., Barth, M.: Real-time computer vision/DGPS-aided inertial navigation system for lane-level vehicle navigation. IEEE Trans. Intell. Transp. Syst. **13**, 899–913 (2012)
18. Peker, A.U., Tosun, O., Akin, H.L., Acarman, T.: Fusion of map matching and traffic sign recognition. In: 2014 IVS Proceedings, pp. 867–872. IEEE (2014)
19. Jamshidi, H., Lukaszewicz, T., Kashi, A., Berghuvud, A., Zepernick, H., Khatibi, S.: Fusion of digital map traffic signs and camera-detected signs. In: 2011 5th International Conference on Signal Processing and Communication Systems (ICSPCS), pp. 1–7. IEEE (2011)

Safely Using the AUTOSAR End-to-End Protection Library

Thomas Arts[1] and Stefano Tonetta[2]([⊠])

[1] QuviQ, Gothenburg, Sweden
thomas.arts@quviq.com
[2] FBK, Trento, Italy
tonettas@fbk.eu

Abstract. The AUTOSAR End-to-End library is used to protect data. On the producer side a counter and checksum are added, such that on the consumer side it can be detected whether there was a communication failure. For optimal bus utilisation, it is a common solution that a producer publishes data that is read by many consumers. If the data also needs to be protected, this results in an End-to-Many-Ends solution.

In this paper, we analyse the impact of an End-to-Many-Ends solution on the safety guarantees of the AUTOSAR End-to-End Protection. In particular with focus on the problem that arises when the consumers read the messages with a periodicity that differs from the producer. It turns out that this common situation severely reduces the safety guarantees these standard components offer. In this report we analyze these reductions on different architectures.

Keywords: Verification · Formal methods · AUTOSAR · E2E Protection · Communication failures

1 Introduction

A modern car may deploy around a hundred Electronic Control Units (ECUs) communicating over several networks. These ECUs provide different functions that range from driving support to entertainment. Safety functions such as braking and airbag control can be located at different physical ECUs so that safety-critical data is communicated over a network. For this reason, the ISO26262 standard [1] prescribes to implement measures to detect communication faults such as loss or corruption of messages.

The AUTOSAR standard [2] is a detailed architectural description of software components for the automotive industry. AUTOSAR caters for a common set of the communication fault models by offering a solution called *End-to-End (E2E) Protection* [3] and is specified as a library with functions to protect a data item and to check it at the other end of the communication. In short, it adds a counter and identifier to the data, computes a checksum and sends the data and checksum over the bus instead of the raw data. At the other end, the checksum

© Springer International Publishing Switzerland 2015
F. Koornneef and C. van Gulijk (Eds.): SAFECOMP 2015, LNCS 9337, pp. 74–89, 2015.
DOI: 10.1007/978-3-319-24255-2_7

is used to see if the data got corrupted and if not, the data is compared to an earlier value to see if it can be trusted. By addressing a number of fault models once and for all with a library, the AUTOSAR software developers know what they can use when they are faced with specific safety requirements.

For optimal bus utilization, a common design choice is that a producer publishes data that can be read by many consumers. If the data also needs to be protected, then the standard solution would be to send the same data many times using the End-to-End-Protection, which increases the cost of bus resources. Alternatively, all consumers should be reading as fast as the fastest consumers, which implies higher hardware cost. In both cases, increased cost is the price of safety caused by the End-to-Many-Ends protection challenge.

In this paper, we analyse the impact of using the End-to-End Protection Library to address the End-to-Many-Ends challenge. In particular we concentrate on the realistic situation in which different consumers are scheduled with different periods depending on their cost and safety criticality. For example, an ABS function may have to read the speed sensor data more frequently than cruise control or the speedometer on the driver panel. We specify a formal model of a receiver and sender using the AUTOSAR End-to-End Protection for message communication, where sender and receiver(s) run with different periods. We show that running with different periods reduces the safety guarantees that these standard components offer. We make these reductions explicit and analyse the consequences in a number of different configurations.

The main contribution of this paper is that we address the challenge observed in the standard [3, p. 10]:

> Moreover, the appropriate usage of the E2E Library alone is not sufficient to achieve a safe E2E communication according to ASIL D requirements. Solely the user is responsible to demonstrate that the selected profile provides sufficient error detection capabilities for the considered network (e.g. by evaluation hardware failure rates, bit error rates, number of nodes in the network, repetition rate of messages and the usage of a gateway).

We contribute with a method accompanied by a toolset to help automotive engineers to demonstrate that their overall solution can be delivered with ASIL D level safety. That is, not only the profile, but even the use of the library in a certain context with certain safety goals. We demonstrate this by modelling a realistic system with a C implementation of about 20000 lines of C code.

The conclusion is that with different periodicities, many implementations become unsafe and have to be discarded. But, we are able to compute certain combinations of profiles and periodicities that do guarantee safety. This allows the OEMs to implement safe systems cheaper.

The paper is organised as follows. In Sect. 2, we give an overview of AUTOSAR, of the ISO26262 requirements for safe communication, and of the AUTOSAR End-to-End Protection from communication failures. In Sect. 3, we briefly describe the formal techniques used in the paper. In Sect. 4, we give an account of the formal model and analysis of different configurations on the safety guarantees. In Sect. 5, we compare with the related work and in Sect. 6 we conclude and provide future directions.

2   AUTOSAR E2E Protection

2.1   ISO26262 Requirements and AUTOSAR E2E Protection Measures

In order to implement effective measures against communication loss the ISO26262 standards prescribe to take into account a series of possible communication faults, such as: loss of peer to peer communication; unintended message repetition due to the same message being unintentionally sent again; message loss during transmission; insertion of messages due to receiver unintentionally receiving an additional message, which is interpreted to have correct source and destination addresses; etc.

AUTOSAR is a software standard for the automotive industry providing the specification of the basic software components, such as several protocol stacks, memory management, communication routing, etc. The AUTOSAR platform offers a variety of components to provide functionality, for example a component for E2E data protection that encodes and decodes a message in a standard way so that corruption or message loss can be detected. More specifically, the faults described in ISO26262 are represented in AUTOSAR by the following fault models:

- Repetition: a message is received more than once.
- Deletion: a message or parts of it have been removed from the communication stream.
- Insertion: an additional message or parts of it have been inserted into the communication stream.
- Incorrect sequence: the messages of a communication stream are received in an incorrect order.
- Corruption: the corruption data of a message or parts of it occurred.
- Delay: a message is received too late.
- addressing faults: a message is sent to the wrong destination.

The protection measure provided by the AUTOSAR E2E library consists of using:

1. a counter modulo N ($N = 14$ in Profile 1) increased by one at every sent message;
2. a checksum provided by the AUTOSAR CRC library;
3. data ID to verify the identity of each transmitted safety-related data element.

In particular, the repetition, deletion, insertion, and incorrect sequence are addressed by the counter, corruption by the CRC checksum, addressing faults by the data ID. In addition to this, the real-time properties of AUTOSAR in combination with periodically sending messages enable detection of not receiving new data on the bus. Timeouts are therefore represented by either no new data available or by receiving new data with the same counter as the previously received valid data.

In [4], we formalise the assumptions and guarantees of the E2E components. Moreover, the AUTOSAR state machine implementing the check on the message counter has been formalised both in Erlang [5] to be used with model-based testing techniques provided by QuickCheck [6,7] and in SMV, the input language of the NuSMV model checker [8] and its extension nuXmv [9]. This formal model can be reused in the component-based approach provided by OCRA [10] in different architectural solutions.

2.2 The Impact of Different Periodicity

In this paper we consider the problem of using the End-to-End library for consumers that read with different periodicity. In fact, for optimal bus utilisation a common solution is that a producer publishes data that can be read by many consumers, which may run with different periodicity.

A typical example of such data is the speed of the vehicle. The wheel controller produces this data. The brakes, ABS, cruise control and dashboard, as well as the stereo and the navigation software may use that data. Even an airbag and parking brake read the speed of the vehicle, since there are regulations that an airbag may not inflate at low speed and a parking brake must automatically disconnect when driving faster than a certain speed.

All data consumers have different safety demands, the brakes and ABS normally need to have a more accurate and frequent view of the vehicle speed than the stereo or even cruise-control need. Instead of overloading the wheel ECU by sending the speed information End-to-End to each consumer individual, it is common to publish the information and have many consumers read it. This reduces the computation demand on the wheel ECU as well as that it utilizes the bus better.

At the same time, speed data is of such kind that corruption or loosing such messages may be harmful. Using the End-to-End protection library, seems a safe choice. When doing so, we create a problem. The wheel needs to publish the data with a certain speed, regulated by the consumer that needs the data with the highest speed to operate safely. For example, brakes and ABS need the current speed with a high frequency. They will read incoming speed data say every 5 ms. Therefore, the wheel will have to send it every 5 ms.

The stereo or parking brake need the speed rarely. It would be sufficient if they read the speed once every 50 ms or even slower than that. They could better use their cycles for doing other things than reading the speed. But if they look at the speed every 50 ms, then the counter will jump 10 steps since the previous read. Since the counter also is computed modulo 14, strange counter values will be observed. As a consequence, the slower reader may conclude that all incoming speed data is invalid.

For the parking brake, there is a safety demand on the speed data, thus simply ignoring the counter and checksum would be hard to defend in the safety argumentation.

3   Background Techniques

3.1   Model Checking

In model checking, a system is described in terms of states and transitions. A system's state provides an instantaneous picture of the system in a particular execution state. It is determined by the values of the data variables, the control location, the messages in transit and so on. We denote by V the set of variables that represent all this information. Therefore, a state is an assignment to the variables in V. We denote by S the set of all states. We denote by I the set of initial states (thus, $I \subseteq S$). From one state, the system can transit to another state. Usually, a transition is labelled with a set of events, which determine the cause of the transition (e.g., a write into memory, the reception of a message, a fault). We denote by E the set of events and by $A \subseteq 2^E$ the set of actions. Formally, a transition is a triple $\langle s, a, s' \rangle$ (also denoted by $s \xrightarrow{a} s'$) where s and s' are states and a is an action. We denote the set of transitions by T.

The behaviour or trace execution of a system is a sequence $\sigma = s_0 \xrightarrow{a_1} s_1 \xrightarrow{a_2} s_2 \xrightarrow{a_2} \ldots$ of consecutive transitions in T starting from an initial state $s_0 \in I$. Given a system M, we denote by $L(M)$ the set of behaviours of M. A property P is a set of behaviours determining which ones are good, i.e., σ satisfies the property P iff $\sigma \in P$. A property for example may be the set of behaviours in which a variable x never decreases. The model checking problem consists of deciding if all behaviours of a system M satisfy a property P, i.e., $L(M) \subseteq P$.

We have used the SMV [11] language to describe the transition system and LTL [12] to describe the properties. SMV describes initial states and transitions by means of symbolic formulas. LTL is a temporal logic that can express the temporal relationship between events occurring along the trace execution of the system.

3.2   Component-Based Design

In component-based design, the system consists of components interacting through event and data ports. Each component has an interface description and an internal implementation. The interface defines the boundary with the component environment in terms of input and output ports. The input ports are controlled by the environment, while the output ports are controlled by the component implementation. The implementation can be described either by a behavioural model or by the composition of other subcomponents. In the second case, the behaviour is determined by the composition of the behaviours of the subcomponents.

In this setting, a basic component can be seen as a system whose variables and events are divided into input, output and internal respectively variables and events. As for a composite component, the connections defined by the decomposition introduce some relationship among the inputs and outputs of the composite component and its subcomponents. For example, the input of a subcomponent can coincide with the input of the composite component or with the output of another subcomponent. The state (and thus the behaviour) of the composite component is therefore the combination of local states of the subcomponents that are compliant with the relationship defined by the connection.

We used the OCRA [10] language for describing components, their interfaces and how they are connected, while SMV was used to describe the behaviour of the basic components. The composition is synchronous, in the sense that there is an implicit clock and all components may execute simultaneously at every tick of this clock.

4 Analysis of End-to-End Protection Safety Guarantees

4.1 Modelling

System Overview. We consider a sender and a receiver equipped with AUTOSAR E2E Protection Mechanism. They are scheduled by a scheduler with different fixed periods. The length of each period is called the cycle time; the shorter the cycle time, the more frequent a signal is sent or received. Sender and receiver communicate by means of a bus. These components are part of a large system of around 20,000 lines of C code. The complete system is not detailed in the model but the interference of other components is abstracted into a fault model that feeds the bus with fault signals: the bus behaves correctly unless it receives a fault signal. The fault model includes data loss and corruption faults. An overall picture of the components is shown in Fig. 1.

The system architecture, namely the component interfaces and their interconnections, have been specified in OCRA, while the behaviour of the components has been specified in SMV. OCRA is used to compose the components in a

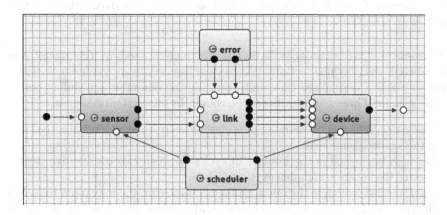

Fig. 1. System components and their connections

monolithic SMV behavioural model according to the composition defined by the system architecture. The picture in Fig. 1 is obtained with the visualisation of AF3 [13] and the OCRA plugin.

All component ports and local variables have a bounded domain. The size of the model depends on the configuration of the fault model, in particular on the domain of the local counters. We considered different configuration, but the system has at most 56 bits (so, potentially 2^{56} states). In some cases, we prove certain properties for any possible value of the sender and receiver periods. In these cases, the periods are unbounded integers and the system has an infinite number of states.

Fault Model. In this paper, we consider three types of faults, namely the deletion and the corruption of a message, where we corrupt either over a longer time, or just one message. In case of deletion, the receiver will see there is no data available on the communication link. In case of corruption, the CRC function will inform the receiver that the message has been corrupted. In both cases, the message is lost and if the receiver will later manage to read the message, then the associated counter will be greater than the one sent when the fault happened.

The reason to consider both corruption over a longer time and a corruption on a sporadic message is that we are in the first place interested in safety in the event of several possible faults and in the second place that those faults are defined differently. A period of message corruption is also known as a burst, where there is some electrical disturbance for a longer time. A sporadic message corruption is also known as a bit flip and is a quite rare behaviour that finds its origin in the hardware implementation, rather than the outside world.

The fault model has three parameters to control the strength of the assumptions on faults. More specifically, in the model, we can specify the minimum time between two deletions, the minimum fault-free time between two corruptions, and the maximum duration of the burst causing message deletion. The behavioral model uses one counter for each of these three quantities. Note that realistic values are domain specific, but that our method is generally applicable for the values chosen in this paper as well as for values derived from a hazard analysis in a real case.

Parameters. We summarise here the parameters used in the model and described in the previous sections. The system has overall six parameters. Recall that a cycle is a normalised time unit, typically the minimum scheduling period in the system. Three parameters can be chosen by the system designer:

- *SenderPer*, which is the number of cycles between two consecutive activations of the sender component;
- *ReceiverPer*, which is the number of cycles between two consecutive activations of the receiver component;
- *MaxDeltaInit*, which is the initial value for *MaxDelta*, the maximum tolerated difference in the counter between two valid received messages (in this paper we fixed this to 7).

The interesting issue is the difference between sender and receiver frequency, i.e., how many times faster or slower the producer is with respect to its consumers. Having all consumers equally fast as the fastest producer in the system is expensive. The *MaxDeltaInit* is user configurable and a software switch. *MaxDelta* can be increased up to 14, but cannot be larger than 14 without choosing a different profile[1].

Three parameters are assumptions on the fault model. These typically originate from domain expert experience and can only be modified by different hardware/software solutions for used components. We assume here that the bus can loose or corrupt messages because of electric bursts and make assumptions on the length of the burst and on how many cycles after the burst have fail free communication[2]. Note that a burst is normally measured in milliseconds and that faster networks therefore may experience longer bursts. Another assumption is that sometimes the bus hardware will cause a bit flip in the submitted data. This only happens sporadically and the parameter is used to indicate how many messages there are between such bit flips. The burst and bit flips happen independently of each other.

– *MinBurstInt*, which is the minimum interval between two consecutive bursts and therefore between two deletion faults;
– *MinBitflipInt*, which is the minimum number of messages between two consecutive bit flips in the bus;
– *MaxBurstDur*, which is the maximum duration of a burst and therefore the maximum number of consecutive steps with a potential corruption fault;

4.2   Verification Problem

The verification problem we are interested in is stated as follows: given the six parameters as input, how many cycles after an event has happened can we guarantee a reaction? More specifically, given a value for each model parameter described in the previous section, can we find the minimum number of cycles *Delay* such that we can guarantee that in every execution the delay between the trigger and the reaction is less than *Delay*? The verification must take into account the combination of the nominal delay of the communication, the occurrence of faults, and the initialisation of the E2E Protection check. In fact, as discussed in Sect. 2.1, the receiver may discard a first valid message to initialise the E2E Protection mechanism.

We set up an experimental evaluation to answer the above question automatically. For each configuration of the model described in the previous section, we automatically generate the input for the NuSMV model checker. We check whether a minimum delay can be guaranteed with the following LTL property:

---

[1] The standard for Profile 1 makes it impossible to distinguish dropping 14 messages from dropping none.
[2] Minimal 1 fail free cycle between two bursts, otherwise it is the same burst, but of a longer period.

$$(MaxDeltaInit \geq n \wedge (\mathbf{G} \; (trigger \rightarrow \mathbf{X}trigger)))$$
$$\rightarrow \mathbf{G} \; (collision \rightarrow \mathbf{F} \; (reaction))$$

The formula expresses that if *MaxDeltaInit* is greater than n and if a trigger is continuously active, then any trigger is followed by a reaction. Note that, as shown in [4], the system satisfies the property only under the assumption that the MaxDeltaCounter, i.e. the tolerated difference in the counters of consecutive received messages, is greater than a certain value and that the trigger event is continuously active. For example, in the airbag example described in [4], the trigger event is a collision and the reaction event is the inflation of the airbag.

If the above property holds, since all variables are bounded, we know that there exists a minimum guaranteed delay[3]. Therefore, we verify the following LTL property for increasing value of n until finding the minimum delay:

$$(MaxDeltaCounterInit \geq n \wedge (\mathbf{G} \; (trigger \rightarrow \mathbf{X}trigger)))$$
$$\rightarrow \mathbf{G} \; (collision \rightarrow \mathbf{X}^m(reaction))$$

The property is the same as the previous one apart from the operator $\mathbf{X}^m$, which means that the reaction is active m cycles after the trigger. Since in our model the reaction remains true when activated, the property means that the delay can be at most m.

4.3   A Concrete Safety Case

In a concrete case[4], one gets a specific safety goal. For example, one should react within 50 ms after detection of an event. Suppose that the involved hardware has a max burst time of 25 ms and that you may assume that a minimum of 15 ms non-burst in-between two consecutive bursts. Moreover, bit flips occur only once out of 5 received messages. A lot of parameters are therewith set. The question is: how do we need to schedule the sender and the receiver?

In order to make sure you do get a message in the non-burst time, you need to send and receive a message at least each 15 ms (1 cycle = 15 ms). If you want, for example, to run the sender faster, on a 5 ms cycle you need to have the slowest schedule still run within 15 ms, thus sender 1, receiver 3 (1 cycle = 5 ms). You can also make both sender and receiver faster, such that you can send two or three messages in the gap without burst. Note that in general, the more frequent you schedule the messages, the more expensive it gets.

We know that End-to-End protection needs to receive the same value twice with different counters. If so, the message is considered correct. Thus, intuitively one would guess that if we can send the message twice in 15 ms, then we would be rather safe. If we can receive 3 messages in 15 ms we would even be able to tolerate one bit flip!

---

[3] All the results and scripts to reproduce them are available at https://es.fbk.eu/people/tonetta/tests/safecomp15.

[4] The presented method is applicable to any concrete case, we present a case that closely resembles our understanding of car software.

In Table 1 we show a sample of our data. The first row shows a 15 ms cycle, which means that only once every 15 ms the sender and receiver are scheduled. Given the above parameters, we know that a burst can take 25 ms, which is almost 2 cycles. After that, we get one cycle (and a bit more) in which no corruption will occur. Not surprisingly we cannot guarantee the safety goal with such a slow schedule. We need to schedule more frequently.

Table 1. Results for a concrete safety case

Sender period	Receiver period	Cycle time	Max burst	Min burst	Bit flip	Meet goal	Result
1	1	15 ms	2	1	*	4 cycles	Impossible
1	1	10 ms	3	1	*	5 cycles	Impossible
1	1	10 ms	3	2	5	5 cycles	Guaranteed 9 cycles, too late and stronger assumption min burst
1	1	8 ms	3	3	5	6 cycles	Guaranteed 6 cycles, but stronger assumption min burst
1	2	5 ms	5	3	*	10 cycles	Impossible
2	1	5 ms	5	3	*	10 cycles	Impossible
1	1	5 ms	5	3	2	10 cycles	Guaranteed in 9 cycles

We try with a 10 ms cycle, which means a burst takes 2 to 3 cycles. To be sure, one should assume 3. The time between two bursts is one and a half cycle, we try for both 1 and 2 cycles as minimum between two bursts. With this more frequent scheduler, we can actually get a message over to the other side, but only in the case we strengthen the assumption on the time between bursts then a response is guaranteed and we would need 9 cycles to get there! That is, if it is guaranteed that when the same data is transmitted 9 times in a row, then we know on the receiver side what the data is. Since 9 cycles corresponds to 90 ms in this case, we are 40 ms late according to the safety goal.

Note that the 9 cycles are due to the fact that we also have bit flips. We look at combined fault models. If we first have a burst, then one valid message, then a bit flip, followed by yet another burst, we are pretty unlucky, but this could happen. Therefore, we need 9 cycles and a guarantee that we only have a bit flip each 5th transmission. With a more frequent bit flip rate, we would not meet our goal.

The fourth row shows a more frequent schedule, instead of 10 ms we schedule each 8 ms. The advantage is that 25 and 15 are closer to multiples of 8 than multiples of 10. Therefore, we can extend the non-burst interval in order to be able to meet the goal, without that, it would be impossible. Nevertheless, changing the non-burst interval from 20 ms to 24 ms is something that the original safety assumptions do not allow. In other words, we cannot guarantee the safety goal.

In the fifth, sixth and seventh row, we use an even faster schedule. But only increasing either the sender or the receiver schedule is insufficient. There is no solution at all in those cases, not even if we would allow more than 10 cycles delay. However, when both sender and receiver are scheduled each 5 ms, the solution is valid. It is guaranteed that we meet the deadline in 45 ms (9 cycles), given a burst of 25 ms (5 cycles) and a bit flip possible every other message (may occur even more often than our assumption).

Table 1 demonstrates a particular case in which increasing the frequency in which sending and receiving is scheduled helps to meet a safety goal. It also demonstrated that the relative speed between sender and receiver is important; sending faster than receiving and the other way around does not work for that example. Both sender and receiver needed to be scheduled more frequently.

In Table 2 we present data for a different engineering challenge. If we have a working solution that meets the safety demands, can we then replace one of the schedules by a faster schedule? In other words, would it matter that the wheel ECU is replaced by an ECU that sends speed twice as many times as before? Not completely surprising, it turns out to matter.

Table 2. Results for different sender/receiver speed

Sender period	Receiver period	Cycle time	Max burst	Min burst	Bit flip	Meet goal	Result
1	1	10 ms	3	2	5	10 cycles	Guaranteed in 9 cycles
1	2	5 ms	6	4	5	20 cycles	Guaranteed in 20 cycles
2	1	5 ms	6	4	5	20 cycles	Guaranteed in 22 cycles, too late
1	5	2 ms	15	10	5	50 cycles	Guaranteed in 48 cycles
5	1	2 ms	15	10	5	50 cycles	Guaranteed in 60 cycles, too late
1	1	8 ms	3	3	5	10 cycles	Guaranteed in 6 cycles
1	2	4 ms	6	6	5	20 cycles	Guaranteed in 13 cycles
2	1	4 ms	6	6	5	20 cycles	Guaranteed in 14 cycles

In the first row of Table 2 we revisit a sender and receiver with a cycle time of 10 ms with a maximum burst of 30 ms and a minimum burst of 20 ms. We again assume at most each 5th message to have a corruption due to a bit flip, similar to the third row of Table 1. However, we now need to meet a deadline of 100 ms, instead of 50 ms, which this configuration does. In fact, a reaction is guarantee within 9 cycles or 90 ms.

In the second row, we replace the sender by another one that is twice as fast. The cycle time therewith changes to 5 ms and the receiver still receives each

10 ms. The safety goal is guaranteed to be met, but it takes 20 cycles, or 100 ms. This is worse than having a sender that is twice as slow.

In the third row, we schedule the receiver twice as frequent. We now miss the deadline! The safety goal is not fulfilled. This may feel counter intuitive. The brakes are dependent on the speed data. We read it twice as often, and therewith we break our safety goal. Note that this may feel like a contrived example, to read messages faster than we produce them. However, the point here is to demonstrate that something that seems harmless from a top-level view, i.e., re-using a well functioning ECU consuming speed data in a different car, may have safety consequences.

Row four and five demonstrate that even when we schedule either sender or receiver five times faster than the other, we loose. In one case we meet the safety goal, but only have a guarantee of 96 ms compared to 90 ms in the slower case. In the case of a fast receiver, the response is actually 20 % slower than our safety goal demands.

The last three rows in the table show that when we have stronger assumptions on the minimum burst time, i.e., we can send at least 3 messages without burst, then we still pay a price for safety. With a faster sender or receiver, instead of 48 ms, we can guarantee 52 ms and 56 ms respectively.

Both tables in this section demonstrate that scheduling safety critical tasks when using End-to-End protection is a delicate matter. The standard worst-case execution time is orthogonal to the challenge of getting the relative schedules of sender and receiver in line with the safety goals one needs to meet. Scheduling sender or receiver more frequent is definitely no sufficient solution when it comes to meeting safety goals. The method set out in Sect. 4.2 provides the safety engineer a way to create the data needed for a safety analysis and to demonstrate correct use of the End-to-End Protection library in the End-to-Many-End case.

4.4 Scalability Evaluation

The purpose of the approach is to support a specific case as discussed in the previous section. We also evaluated the approach on a large set of configurations to test the scalability and validate the results. We considered and verified more than 20000 configurations. With the default BDD-based algorithm of NuSMV, all configurations were verified in reasonable time (from a 1.3 to 62.4 s, with a median of 10.6 and a mean of 12.7 s, using one core on a 2.93 GHz Intel machine with 8 GB of memory).

4.5 Analysis of Impossible Cases

In this section, we investigate how we can extend the setting considering unbounded integers as parameters using infinite-state model checking and the limits thereof.

As shown above, in some cases, we obtain a negative result (i.e., that there is no bound for the delay) for any value of a parameter. For example, if *MinBurstInt* and *MinBitflipInt* are both 1, at every clock cycle the message can be lost or corrupted. Therefore, the receiver is not guaranteed to receive any message. In order to better understand the limitations, the designer may wonder if this is true for a particular choice of the sender/receiver periods or holds for any other parameter value.

However, with the above setting, we can only prove the negative result for a finite number of configurations. Therefore, we extended the model also with unbounded integer values for sender and receiver periods and prove that with the above fault model there is no bound for any values of these parameters. In order to do so, we have first to switch to infinite-state model checking: we use nuXmv and, in particular, the algorithm that combines IC3, predicate abstraction, and K-liveness [9]. Unfortunately, this is not sufficient because nuXmv can only prove either universal or existential properties, while we want to prove that for every value of periods and any bound, there exists a trace with a larger delay. So, instead of proving the bounded reaction, we consider the special case in which the error model alternates deletion faults and corruption faults one after the other, and prove that no reaction is possible at all.

Although, the example was really simple and a manual modification of the verification problem was needed, the exercise shows that it is in principle possible to prove some results in the infinite-state case.

4.6 Discussion

In our verification we have assumed that the sender sends the same message from the start of the event to at least the deadline for the safety goal. In some cases, such as for the airbag example [4], it is natural that a collision message is repeatedly send and does not change, certainly not within a few milliseconds. However, the speed of the car may vary a bit over time, even when time is measured in milliseconds.

In order to analyse safety goals that depend on the speed of the car, we would need to add to the fault model how often the speed may change within a certain interval. But note that if the speed is measured in meter per second in integer values, changing one unit in 50 ms would require quite some horse power![5]

We have assumed only two independent faults, a burst and a bit flip. The length of a burst can be quite long, probably longer than the times we used in our example. In reality, it is probably even impossible to guarantee that a burst is shorter than a deadline in a safety goal. In such cases, other arguments must be used for bursts and the model can be used for the other fault models. At the same time, bit flips are happening less frequent than we assumed in this paper. This does not influence the results, since it is relative to the non-burst time and our findings show that with any less frequent bit flip, the same deadlines are met.

---

[5] A very fast car can accelerate 0.65 m in 50 ms. Reducing speed can go much faster, but at that moment, most safety functions do not need the speed data any more.

There are additional fault models that we did not consider. The actual values we have chosen in this paper are not so relevant, we contribute with a method that can determine whether safety goals can be met when using the End-to-End protection library.

We have assumed that writing the message to the bus and reading it from the bus are much faster than the actual computation of the message. Even if the frequency is 2 ms we have assumed that the sender can perform all necessary sensor reading, checksum computation and message assembly within those 2 ms. It depends on the case one has at hand whether this is realistic. Our methodology allows an easy solution for adding additional delays on either end.

5   Related Work

The safety guarantees provided by the E2E Protection library has been studied also in other papers. We build on the work presented in [4], where we focus on the formalisation of the assumptions in order to guarantee a safe communication with the E2E Protection mechanism; in this paper, we extend the approach by enriching the fault model with parameters to control the assumptions and we focus on the impact of different frequency of the components on the communication delay. In [14], the fault detection capabilities of the CRC used by the E2E Protection library is analysed; in this paper, we use an ideal abstraction of the CRC that always detects a bit flip in the message, but we focus on the interaction with the counter mechanism and the frequency of components and we analysed the impact on the communication delay.

The analysis of the delay on the End-to-End communication is somehow related to the analysis performed by Worst-Case Execution Time (WCET) analysis techniques. However, WCET typically focuses on the structure of a program code with some assumptions on the underlying hardware; instead, here we focus on the impact of components frequency on the system-level delay taking into account a formal model of faults.

6   Conclusions and Future Work

In this paper we presented a method for computing safety guarantees in a system design using the AUTOSAR End-to-End protection library. The method is based upon a formal component-based model of the system. Although we present a specific safety case, the method is general and can be applied to different cases as well. In the formal methods area it is often a problem to scale from a small system to a large one, but with our experiments we have shows that this method scales well.

It turns out that computing configurations for which certain safety goals are met is a delicate matter. Our method and tool support help in identifying good sets of parameters such that safety goals are met. We also can show how certain other sets of parameters violate a safety goal. In particular, we have shown that scheduling sender and receiver with different frequencies is a serious challenge for safety, which should not be compromised by a wish from car manufacturers to keep the cost low.

When using the End-to-End Protection library without using the results presented in our paper, the engineers have only two safe choices: either all consumers should be reading equally fast as the producer, which implies all hardware to be able to meet high performance goals; or, in systems with different periodicity of producers and consumers, one should use the bus to send the same value several times to different consumers, thus, putting higher demand on bus utilization. In both cases an increased cost is necessary for the purpose of safety. However, with our method, one can find cases in which several consumers receive the same produced signal with different periods for sender and receiver and nevertheless meet the safety goals; cheap and safe!

Future Directions. In the future, we will investigate alternative solutions to allow a safe utilization of the E2E Protection library with different components speeds and we will consider the integration of the methodology in a certification case requiring ASIL D. For this purpose, we will investigate how to extend the method to take into account probabilistic fault models and other independent safety mechanisms. From the formal methods point of view we will investigate extensions of parameter synthesis techniques such as [15] for temporal logics to automatically synthesise the relationship among parameters for which the bounded delay is guaranteed.

Acknowledgements. We thank Martin Skoglund for useful input on realistic values for the safety case parameters. The research leading to these results has received funding from the ARTEMIS JU for the nSafeCer project under grant agreement n° 295373 and from National funding.

References

1. ISO 26262: Road vehicles Functional safety (2011)
2. AUTOSAR: Software architecture specification www.autosar.org
3. AUTOSAR. In: Specification of SW-C End-to-End Communication ProtectionLibrary. AUTOSAR consortium (2008–2013)
4. Arts, T., Dorigatti, M., Tonetta, S.: Making implicit safety requirements explicit. In: Bondavalli, A., Di Giandomenico, F. (eds.) SAFECOMP 2014. LNCS, vol. 8666, pp. 81–92. Springer, Heidelberg (2014)
5. Armstrong, J.: A history of Erlang. In: HOPL, pp. 1–26 (2007)
6. Arts, T., Hughes, J., Johansson, J., Wiger, U.: Testing telecoms software with Quviq QuickCheck. In: ACM SIGPLAN Workshop on Erlang (2006)
7. Arts, T., Hughes, J., Norell, U., Svensson, H.: Testing AUTOSAR software with QuickCheck. In: Proceedings of TAIC Part 2015 (2015)
8. Cimatti, A., Clarke, E., Giunchiglia, E., Giunchiglia, F., Pistore, M., Roveri, M., Sebastiani, R., Tacchella, A.: NuSMV 2: an opensource tool for symbolic model checking. In: Brinksma, E., Larsen, K.G. (eds.) CAV 2002. LNCS, vol. 2404, pp. 359–364. Springer, Heidelberg (2002)

9. Cavada, R., Cimatti, A., Dorigatti, M., Griggio, A., Mariotti, A., Micheli, A., Mover, S., Roveri, M., Tonetta, S.: The NUXMV symbolic model checker. In: Biere, A., Bloem, R. (eds.) CAV 2014. LNCS, vol. 8559, pp. 334–342. Springer, Heidelberg (2014)

10. Cimatti, A., Dorigatti, M., Tonetta, S.: OCRA: a tool for checking the refinement of temporal contracts. In: ASE, pp. 702–705 (2013)

11. McMillan, K.L.: Symbolic Model Checking. Kluwer Academic, Dordrecht (1993)

12. Pnueli, A.: The temporal logic of programs. In: FOCS, pp. 46–57 (1977)

13. Broy, M., Huber, F., Schätz, B.: AutoFocus - Ein Werkzeugprototyp zur Entwicklung eingebetteter Systeme. Inform. Forsch. Entwickl. 14(3), 121–134 (1999)

14. Forest, T., Jochim, M.: On the fault detection capabilities of AUTOSAR's end-to-end communication protection CRC's. In: SAE (2011)

15. Cimatti, A., Griggio, A., Mover, S., Tonetta, S.: Parameter synthesis with IC3. In: FMCAD, pp. 165–168 (2013)

A Structured Validation and Verification Method for Automotive Systems Considering the OEM/Supplier Interface

Kristian Beckers[2], Isabelle Côté[2], Thomas Frese[3],
Denis Hatebur[1,2(✉)], and Maritta Heisel[1]

[1] paluno - The Ruhr Institute for Software Technology – University Duisburg-Essen,
Essen, Germany
{maritta.heisel,denis.hatebur}@uni-due.de

[2] Institut Für technische Systeme GmbH, Dortmund, Germany
{k.beckers,i.cote,d.hatebur}@itesys.de

[3] Ford Werke GmbH, Cologne, Germany
tfrese@ford.com

Abstract. The released ISO 26262 standard for automotive systems requires several validation and verification activities. These validation and verification activities have to be planned and performed jointly by the OEMs and the suppliers. In this paper, we present a systematic, structured and model-based method to plan the required validation and verification activities and collect the results. Planning and the documentation of performed activities are represented by a UML notation extended with stereotypes. The UML model supports the creation of the artifacts required by ISO 26262, enables document generation and a rigorous check of several constraints expressed in OCL. We illustrate our method using the example of an electronic steering column lock system.

Keywords: Safety management · Verification · Validation · ISO 26262 · Automotive · UML · OCL · UML4PF · V&V

1 Introduction

Developing and constructing road vehicles has become a complex task due to the increase of features, such as adaptive cruise control or lane keeping assist functions. The safety aspects of these features have to be taken into account during the product development. Another fact is that most of these complex systems are distributed. Distributing the system amongst the different parties involved means that the overall system is broken down into several components and/or subsystems provided by different suppliers. This raises the complexity for the manufacturer (OEM), who has to organize the necessary V&V activities.

With the release of ISO 26262 - Road vehicles – Functional safety in November 2011 [1], the automotive sector benefited from a consistent functional safety process for developing and constructing electric/electronic (E/E) systems. ISO 26262 addresses all levels of development, including definition of

© Springer International Publishing Switzerland 2015
F. Koornneef and C. van Gulijk (Eds.): SAFECOMP 2015, LNCS 9337, pp. 90–108, 2015.
DOI: 10.1007/978-3-319-24255-2_8

functions/features, systems engineering as well as details of software and hardware development.

The standard should be applicable to different scenarios for establishing this process, including e.g., the OEM and any number of suppliers for the distributed systems.

Usually, the OEM division responsible for the development of the system creates the logical architecture and then distributes requirements to different divisions within the OEM responsible for the components. These divisions receive all requirements from systems in which their component is involved in, integrate the requirements and cascade the requirements to the component suppliers. They do the implementation and supply pieces of hardware and software that then have to be integrated into the vehicle.

This distribution includes several challenges: For the requirement engineering, it has to be determined who has to provide which content at which level of detail. Some of the requirements engineering (RE) has to be done by the OEM and the supplementary RE has to be added by the suppliers. For the verification and validation (V&V), the OEM division responsible for the overall system has to ensure that the V&V tasks are defined and cascaded to the other divisions and the suppliers. Some aspects can only be validated on vehicle level by the OEM division responsible for the system (e.g. the overall behavior of the system), some aspects can be validated on component level by the divisions responsible for the components (e.g. the behavior of the component) and other aspects can only be validated using internal interfaces of the component by the suppliers. When the V&V is performed, the results of the V&V activities at suppliers side and within the different OEM divisions needs to be fed back and collected in an appropriate way to support the creation of the safety case. In addition, heterogeneous and concurrent engineering processes, methods and tools exists within the affected parties which need to be harmonized. Communication between OEM and divisions/suppliers has to be organized via requirements as well as verification and validation documents.

Note that verification and validation are not always clearly distinguished in ISO 26262. Examples are part 3 Sect. 8.4.5 Verification of the functional safety concept where a note mentions, that the same methods can be applied for verification and validation or part 4, Sect. 6 "Specification of the technical safety requirements", where verification and validation are addressed in the same subsection. Another example, found in part 3 Sect. 7.4.5, defines the verification of the hazard analysis, which is according to the definition of the terms in part 1 – more a validation activity. Therefore, we do not distinguish between verification and validation actions and always talk about V&V and use the more general term "verification" throughout our paper.

In this paper, we propose a structured method based on UML models supported by a tool for the V&V activities. This work is part of a larger model-based safety requirements engineering approach in support of ISO 2626 as described in Sect. 3. The papers referenced there also include V&V in the early development steps, i.e., the V&V of functional safety requirements regarding the safety goals and technical safety requirements regarding the functional safety requirements. This paper addresses the V&V activities in later development steps after handing-over requirements to the divisions and supplier(s). The advantage of a UML model-based approach is that the different artifacts are explicitly connected instead of having loosely coupled documents. On this overall model, consistency checks can be performed. These consistency checks can be specified with the Object Constraint Language (OCL) from the Object Management Group (OMG) [2].

Our paper is organized as follows: Background to our work is presented in Sect. 2, which is the ISO 26262 standard. We give an overview on our functional safety framework in Sect. 3. Section 4 outlines the tool support. Our case study is introduced in Sect. 5. Our method including the application on the case study is presented in Sect. 6. This section also describes our UML profile, which can be used to express all relevant ISO 26262 artifacts. Section 7 presents related work, while Sect. 8 concludes the paper and gives directions for future work.

2   ISO 26262

ISO 26262 is a risk-based functional safety standard intended to be applied to safety-related systems that include one or more E/E systems and that are installed in series productions of passenger cars with a max gross weight of up to 3500 kg. It addresses possible hazards caused by malfunctions of E/E safety-related systems, including the interaction of these systems. ISO 26262 was derived from the generic functional safety standard IEC 61508 [3] and is aligned with the automotive safety life-cycle including specification, design, implementation, integration, verification, validation, configuration, production, operation, service, decommissioning, and management. ISO 26262 provides an automotive-specific risk-based approach for determining risk classes that describe the necessary risk reduction for achieving an acceptable residual risk, called *automotive safety integrity level (ASIL)*. The possible ASILs are *QM, ASIL A, ASIL B, ASIL C*, and *ASIL D*. The ASIL requiring the highest risk reduction is called ASIL D. For functions with ASIL A, ASIL B, or ASIL C, fewer V&V requirements are given in ISO 26262. In case of a QM rating, the normal quality measures applied in the automotive industry are sufficient.

Regarding the OEM-supplier interface, ISO 26262 Part 8 requires an appropriate definition (e.g. by using a development interface agreement), but as the application of the standard should be possible in different project scenarios, the standard does not predefine a dedicated split of technical responsibilities.

3   Functional Safety Framework

The Ford Integrated process for Functional Safety (FIFS) consists of templates, examples and guidelines in Microsoft Word and Microsoft Excel. These templates, examples and guidelines were developed and improved (using project feedback) since 2009. They were applied in more than 20 projects and cover

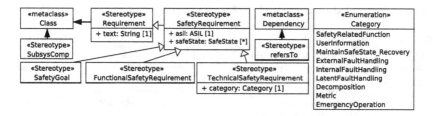

Fig. 1. Profile Part concerning Requirements and Components

all parts of ISO 26262 being relevant for an OEM who does not develop software and hardware. If the templates are applied according to the guidelines, ISO 26262 compliant (work) products are developed. The method is based on practical experience in the automotive domain.

Within the V-model applied in ISO 26262, the first step of requirements engineering is to perform a hazard analysis and risk assessment for the system under consideration. Output of this step is given by the safety goals, describing the highest level of safety requirements. In the functional safety concept (FSC), the safety goals from the hazard analysis are broken down into functional safety requirements. These functional safety requirements are mapped to subsystems or components.

The task of the subsequent step is to split the functional safety requirements up into technical safety requirements. Within our approach, the technical safety requirement categories *SafetyRelatedFunction*, *UserInformation*, *MaintainSafeState_Recovery*, *ExternalFaultHandling*, *LatentFaultHandling*, *Decomposition*, and *Metric* are used.

With these functional safety requirements and technical safety requirements, the requirement activities of the OEM are finalized within the setup chosen for our method. The technical safety requirements are cascaded to the other OEM divisions and finally to the suppliers as described in Sect. 1 and the V&V phase is started.

The method presented in this paper supports the planning and performing of V&V activities as well as the documentation of their results (see Sect. 6). It is embedded in the overall functional safety process according to ISO 26262. The created documentation is an essential part for the subsequent steps that result in the safety case. The safety case is the argument that the safety requirements for an item are complete and satisfied by evidence compiled from documents of all ISO 26262 safety activities during the whole lifecycle. It represents the key argument for the Functional Safety Assessment and product release and concludes the ISO 26262 development process.

Aiming at tool support, we started to develop a UML profile and a set of OCL constraints to support the development activities.

Table 1. Derived Technical Safety Requirements

ID	Requirement	Purpose	Category
ESCL-T-S-Req01000	SSM (Speed Sensor Module) shall measure vehicle speed and shall send vehicle speed signal with quality factor every 20 ms protected with checksum	Vehicle speed signal is used to determine that the vehicle is at standstill, which is one of the conditions that allow steering column locking	Safety Related Function
ESCL-T-S-Req01010	SSM shall detect faults (including sensor faults) leading to an erroneous vehicle speed information < PERMITT-TED_LOCKING_SPEED with a tolerance of 2 km/h	For Safety Goal 01, valid vehicle speed is one information to detect if ESCL locking is allowed. Therefore faults of vehicle speed shall be detected	Internal Fault Handling
ESCL-T-S-Req01040	SSM shall fulfill the specified target value for PMHF	Metric Requirement for Safety Related Function	Metric

The whole approach was presented on the automotive industry conferences VDA Automotive SYS Conference[1], Baden-Baden Spezial 2012[2] and Safetronic 2014[3]. The Electronic Steering Column Lock case study is used in all papers and presentations.

In these papers, we introduced (among others) the following stereotypes (see Fig. 1):

– To represent the system to be built the stereotype ≪*Item*≫ is introduced,
– Relevant entities in the environment of the item are called domains (≪*domain*≫),
– Requirements (≪*Requirement*≫) extending UML classes with the an attribute for the requirement text,
– safety requirements (≪*SafetyRequirement*≫) being special requirements with attributes for the ASIL and the safe state,
– safety goals (≪*SafetyGoal*≫) as a top-level requirement being a special safety requirement,
– functional safety requirements (≪*FunctionalSafetyRequirement*≫), also being special safety requirements, systematically derived from the safety goals,
– technical safety requirements (≪*TechnicalSafetyRequirement*≫), also being special safety requirements, systematically derived from the functional safety requirements and being the input for the supplier,
– components or subsystems (≪*CompSubsystem*≫) extending UML classes, and

---

[1] Presentation on 2012-06-18/20, 2012, Berlin: http://vda-qmc.de/en/software-processes/vda-automotive-sys/.

[2] 2012-10-10/11, Baden-Baden: http://www.vdi.de/technik/fachthemen/fahrzeug-und-verkehrstechnik/artikel/pressegespraech-auf-der-vdi-tagung-baden-baden-spezial-2012/.

[3] 2014-11-11/12 Stuttgart: https://www.hanser-tagungen.de/web/index.asp?task=001\&vid=201402241659596.

– to show the relation between technical safety requirements and components or subsystems, the ≪*refersTo*≫-dependency was created.

4 Tool Support

We use a tool called UML4PF, developed at the University of Duisburg-Essen, and integrated support for the method to create a safety requirements specification as described in Sect. 6 into it. UML4PF is based on the Eclipse platform [4] together with its plug-ins EMF [5] and OCL [2]. Our UML-profile is conceived as an Eclipse plug-in, extending the EMF meta-model. The OCL constraints are integrated directly into the profile. Thus, it is possible to automatically check the constraints using the validation mechanisms provided by Eclipse.

After the developer has drawn some diagram(s) using an EMF-based editor, for example Papyrus UML [6] and applied our stereotypes, UML4PF provides him or her with the following functionality: it checks if the developed model is valid and consistent by using our OCL constraints described in Table 5. It returns the location of invalid parts of the model, and generates documentation that can be used for the manual validation and review activities.

5 Case Study

Our case study is an electronic steering column lock (ESCL) system, which was introduced as case study in several presentations and papers (see Sect. 3).

The item definition, the hazard analysis and risk assessment, the safety goals, the functional safety requirements, and the technical safety requirements exist as input.

In this paper, we choose the safety goal SG01 "*Locking the steering column when vehicle is moving shall be prevented*" as an example from which the following functional safety requirement is derived: ESCL-F-S-Req 01: "*The steering column shall only be locked if the physical vehicle speed information is valid (correct and in time) and the absolute value is lower than permitted locking speed. Invalid vehicle speed information shall be detected.*" From this functional safety requirement, the technical safety requirements of different categories given in Table 1 were derived representing the implementation of the respective functional safety requirement in the speed sensing module (SSM).

6 V&V Method and Case Study

We propose a method for planning and documenting performed V&V activities. The V&V methods need to address the following ISO 26262 topics: For all technical and functional safety requirements, a link to an analysis (e.g. FMEA or fault tree analysis (FTA)) is required. For each functional and technical safety requirement, the correctness and the completeness of the detailed V&V method (e.g. a test case in a test specification) needs to be assessed and it needs to be

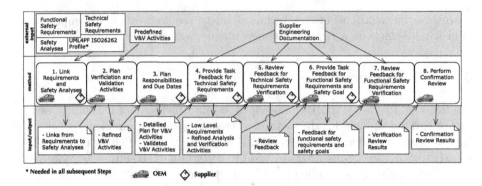

Fig. 2. V&V Method considering the OEM/Supplier Interface

checked that the results of the V&V fulfill the acceptance criteria. From OEM perspective, it has to be ensured that the suppliers have derived and implemented appropriate hardware (HW) and software (SW) requirements for each technical safety requirement. This includes the application of the processes and methods as required by ISO 26262. Checking these processes and methods is an additional V&V step for the OEM. Additionally, the calculation of the HW metrics on safety goal level is required by ISO 26262, based on the input values provided by the suppliers. Details on metric calculation and corresponding V&V are provided in [7].

Within our method, we structure the *V&V activities* as follows: An *engineering activity* (e.g. derivation of HW and SW requirements by the supplier(s), or engineering V&V activities like analyses or testing). An *engineering activity feedback* (e.g. a reference to the derivation of HW and SW requirements, analyses or test cases). A *safety V&V activity* to check if the task feedback is appropriate (e.g. review if the derivation of the HW and SW is sufficiently justified, review if the applied analyses are according to ISO 26262, review if all safety aspects of a requirement are covered by test cases). A *safety V&V activity feedback* to document the results of the V&V activity.

Our method includes matching the ISO 26262 topics to the different V&V activities. Figure 2 depicts an overview of our method consisting of eight steps in which we highlight for each activity the contribution of the OEM and its supplier(s). Each step is described in the subsequent paragraphs. We illustrate the application of these steps with functional safety requirements and the exemplary technical safety requirements introduced in Sect. 5.

Step 1. Link Requirements and Safety Analyses. As input for this step, we need the functional and technical safety requirements, and the safety analyses, as well as our UML-profile. As the OEM is responsible for the overall system, he provides the majority of information for this step and requests specific information from involved suppliers. The suppliers are reacting upon demand of the OEM. ISO 26262 [1, Part 4:7.4.3.1] requires that the safety analyses are

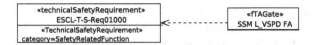

Fig. 3. Safety Analysis Linked to Requirements

consistent to functional as well as technical safety requirements. To ensure this, a mapping is created in this step: Each functional and technical safety requirement is linked to some part of the safety analyses, i.e., a line item of a Failure Mode and Effect Analysis (FMEA) [8] or a gate or event of a Fault Tree Analysis (FTA) [9]. The output is generated from the input by systematically comparing the elements contained in the analyses with the functional and technical safety requirements. Whenever an element in the analyses is found that is also addressed by a requirement, we establish a link between the element and the requirement. The UML4PF ISO 26262 profile provides appropriate stereotypes to support this step. We introduce the stereotype ≪*addressedBy*≫, which extends the UML dependency. This dependency points from the analysis element to the corresponding requirement. Additionally, the FTA or FMEA elements need to be imported to the model. They can be represented by UML classes with the stereotype ≪*FTAGate*≫, ≪*FTAEvent*≫, or ≪*FMEALineItem*≫. UML4PF offers us the opportunity to run some automated checks, e.g. it is possible to check that all technical and functional safety requirements address an element of an analysis (see condition 1C01RA in Table 5[4]), and vice-versa (see condition 1C02AR in Table 5), and the stereotype ≪*addressedBy*≫ points from an analysis element (class with the stereotype ≪*FTAGate*≫, ≪*FTAEvent*≫, or ≪*FMEALineItem*≫ to a functional or technical safety requirement (see condition 1M03AR in Table 5). In the case study, the analysis used for the SSM is the fault tree analysis created during the system design phase. The analysis is systematically reviewed to identify the elements representing the functional and technical requirements: For example, the technical safety requirement ESCL-T-S-Req01000 is represented by a gate block in the FTA (SSM L_VSPD FA), describing that the SSC transmits a vehicle speed less than the permitted speed threshold even the real speed is higher or equal to the threshold. This is represented by using the UML class for ≪*FTAGates*≫ and the stereotype ≪*addressedBy*≫ in the class diagram. With the tool support, it is checked that all functional safety requirements and technical safety requirements are connected to an analysis element with the stereotype ≪*addressedBy*≫. The result of this step is depicted in Fig. 3.

Step 2. Plan V & V Activities. As input for this step, we use the safety goals, the functional safety requirements, and the technical safety require-

---

[4] The first number refers to the step in the procedure, C is for consistency checks, M is for checks considering correct modeling, G is for generation expressions; the next number is the number of the check within the step, and the last characters are an abbreviation of the description.

ments with their categories and the components that realize these requirements. For each safety requirement certain V&V activities are necessary to
fulfill different ISO 26262 requirements. An essential part of our method
is a set of pre-defined V&V-activities (see Table 2). Taking project experience into account, we have defined these activities in a way that the ISO
26262 requirements ([1, Part 4, 6.4.2.2] for ≪*InternalFaultHandlingVaV*≫,
[1, Part 4, 6.4.2.2] for ≪*LatentFaultHandlingVaV*≫, [1, Part 4, 7.4.3.4/5]
for ≪*PMHFVaV*≫, [1, Part 6, 9.4] for ≪*HW_SWDerivationVaV*≫,
[1, Part 6, 10.4] for ≪*HW_SWVerificationVaV*≫, [1, Part 4, 8.4.3/4]
for ≪*SRSVerificationSpecVaV*≫, and [1, Part 4, 8.4.3/4] for ≪*SRS-
VerificationResultVaV*≫) can be fulfilled. For example for technical safety
requirements of category "SafetyRelatedFunction", we propose the following
V&V activities:

- ≪*HW_SW DerivationVaV*≫: The engineering activity is the derivation of
  detailed HW and SW requirements for each technical safety requirement. The
  engineering activity feedback is a reference to HW and SW requirements and
  the corresponding safety analysis, the safety V&V activity is the review of
  this feedback.
- ≪*HW_SWVerificationVaV*≫: The engineering activity is the verification of
  the implemented HW and SW requirements. The engineering activity feedback
  is the reference to the component level verification measures, consisting of e.g.
  component test specifications and analyses and as safety V&V activity the
  review of this feedback.
- ≪*VerificationSpecificationVaV*≫: The engineering activity is the creation
  of a test case for the technical safety requirement. The engineering activity
  feedback is a reference to the test case, e.g. as part of a test specification, and
  the safety V&V activity is the review of this feedback.
- ≪*SRSVerificationResultVaV*≫: The engineering activity is the execution
  and documentation of the verification. The engineering activity feedback is the
  reference to the test report containing the results of the test case as feedback
  and the safety V&V activity is the review of this feedback.

This step is usually performed by the OEM. The purpose of this step is to
ensure that all safety related aspects of each safety requirement are covered by
V&V activities. The input is used to plan which V&V activities have to be performed. The V&V activities are specific depending on the verified requirement.
In Table 2, we show which activities are necessary for the different requirement
categories. Tables 3 and 4 show all pre-defined details for the activities to be
performed, as well as review criteria.

    In this step, we create classes with the stereotypes from the second col-
umn given in Table 2. Additionally, we create dependencies with the stereotype
≪*verifies*≫ from the classes with a stereotype derived from ≪*VaV*≫ to the
corresponding requirement. The tool can generate the aforementioned classes
and dependencies (see 2G01DR in Table 5). It can be checked that the stereotype
≪*VaVActivity*≫ is not used directly. Instead only its specialized stereotypes

Table 2. V&V activities depending on the verified safety requirement type/category

Requirement Category and ASIL	V&V activities
≪*SafetyGoal*≫ with ASIL C-D	≪*SG_HW_Metric*≫
≪*FunctionalSafetyRequirement*≫ (or derived) with QM	has to be handled according to normal automotive processes
≪*FunctionalSafetyRequirement*≫ (or derived) with ASIL A-D	≪*FSCVerificationSpecVaV*≫, ≪*FSCVerifiactionResultVaV*≫
≪*TechnicalSafetyRequirement*≫ (or derived) with QM	has to be handled according to normal automotive processes
≪*SafetyRelatedFunction*≫ or ≪*Decomposition*≫ or ≪*EmergencyOperationRequirement*≫ or ≪*UserInformation*≫ or ≪*MaintainSafeStateRecovery*≫ with ASIL A-D	≪*HW_SWDerivationVaV*≫, ≪*HW_SWVerificationVaV*≫, ≪*VerificationSpecificationVaV*≫), (≪*SRSVerificationResultVaV*≫)
≪*InternalFaultHandling*≫ with ASIL A-D	≪*InternalFaultHandlingVaV*≫, ≪*HW_SWDerivationVaV*≫, ≪*HW_SWVerificationVaV*≫, ≪*VerificationSpecificationVaV*≫, ≪*SRSVerificationResultVaV*≫
≪*ExternalFaultHandling*≫ with ASIL A-D	≪*HW_SWDerivationVaV*≫, ≪*HW_SWVerificationVaV*≫, ≪*VerificationSpecVaV*≫, ≪*SRSVerificationResultVaV*≫
≪*LatentFaultHandling*≫ with ASIL A-D	≪*LatentFaultHandlingVaV*≫, ≪*HW_SWDerivationVaV*≫, ≪*HW_SWVerificationVaV*≫, ≪*SRSVerificationSpecVaV*≫, ≪*SRSVerificationResultVaV*≫
≪*Metric*≫ with ASIL C-D	≪*PMHFVaV*≫, ≪*SRSVerificationSpecVaV*≫
≪*SafetyRelatedFunction*≫ with ASIL A-D	≪*HW_SWDerivationVaV*≫, ≪*HW_SWVerificationVaV*≫, ≪*SRSVerificationSpecVaV*≫, ≪*SRSVerificationResultVaV*≫

(see condition 2M02NV in Table 5) have been applied. For example, the technical safety requirement of category SafetyRelatedFunction gets the V&V activities as described in Sect. 6. Figure 5 shows the results for the example requirements selected for the case study.

Step 3. Plan Responsibilities and Due Dates. As input for this step, we use the output of Step 2. We can distinguish between different V&V activities. V&V activities referring to functional safety requirements can usually be performed by the OEM. For V&V activities referring to technical safety requirements, OEM and supplier(s) have to plan which activity is performed by the supplier and which activity is performed by the OEM. If the OEM does not

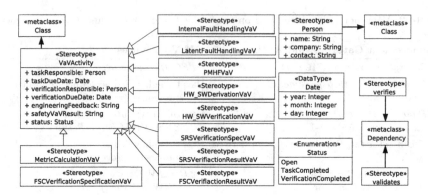

Fig. 4. Profile Part concerning V&V activities

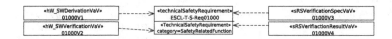

Fig. 5. Planned V&V Activities for T-S-Req01000 of the ESCL Example

develop hardware and software, the related activities are usually performed by the supplier(s). Project experience shows that the verification of the suppliers' activities is often done by the OEM. To reach the overall project milestones, it is necessary to assign responsible persons and define due dates for the activities. For the relevant activities, the responsible person to provide the feedback and the responsible person to verify this feedback shall be assigned. Additionally, a time to complete the task shall be defined. The V&V activities are specific depending on the verified requirement. In this step, we set the properties taskResponsible, taskDueDate, verificationResponsible, and verificationDueDate for the different V&V activities being a sub-type of ($\ll VaV\,Activity\gg$) (see center of Fig. 4). This enables us to check whether the attributes taskResponsible, taskDue-Date, verificationResponsible, and verificationDueDate are set and not empty (see condition 3M01AS in Table 5). The specification of the test case for the technical safety requirement ESCL-T-S-Req01000 is done by the engineers responsible for the SSM component development at the suppliers side. The review of the test case is done by the OEM, the responsible person is the safety consultant of the ESCL development project. For $\ll Verification SpecVaV\gg$, the properties taskResponsible and verificationResponsible are set and the necessary information (name, company, contact data) is provided accordingly. In addition, the properties taskDueDate and verificationDueDate are set and the due dates for the creation of the test case and the review of the test case are defined (see Fig. 7). The same procedure is applied to all V&V tasks.

Step 4. Provide Engineering Activity Feedback for Technical Safety Requirements. Input for this step is the documentation of engineering activities from OEM and supplier(s), including the derivation of lower level

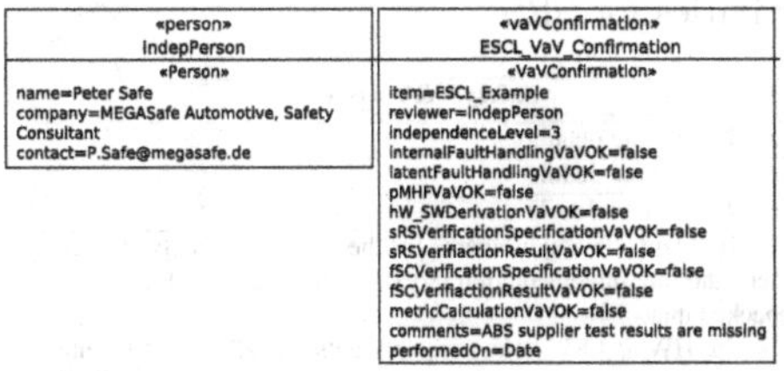

«person» IndepPerson	«vaVConfirmation» ESCL_VaV_Confirmation
«Person» name=Peter Safe company=MEGASafe Automotive, Safety Consultant contact=P.Safe@megasafe.de	«VaVConfirmation» item=ESCL_Example reviewer=indepPerson independenceLevel=3 internalFaultHandlingVaVOK=false latentFaultHandlingVaVOK=false pMHFVaVOK=false hW_SWDerivationVaVOK=false sRSVerificationSpecificationVaVOK=false sRSVerifiactionResultVaVOK=false fSCVerificationSpecificationVaVOK=false fSCVerifiactionResultVaVOK=false metricCalculationVaVOK=false comments=ABS supplier test results are missing performedOn=Date

«person» SupplierEngineer	«sRSVerificationSpecVaV» 01000V3
«Person» name=Marianne Holzapfel company=SSM Ltd contact=mholz13@ssm.com	«SRSVerificationSpecVaV» taskResponsible=SupplierEngineer taskDueDate=Date verificationResponsible=SafetyConsultant verificationDueDate=Date engineeringFeedback="Testplan SSM v12.02.pdf, section 4.2 safetyVaVResult=The test case is appropriate. status=VerificationCompleted
«person» SafetyConsultant	
«Person» name=Tim Safemaster company=OEM, Technical Specialist contact=tsafemas@ford.com	

Fig. 6. V&V Confirmation Review of ESCL Example

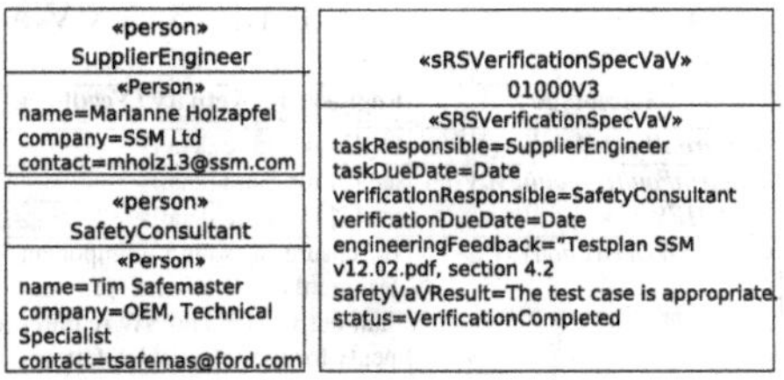

Fig. 7. V&V Activities for SRS of ESCL Example, Steps 3 and 4

requirements, their analyses, and their verification activities and the output of all previous steps. For this step, the supplier(s) provide necessary information to complete the requirements and V&V activities on HW and SW level. The OEM divisions or supplier(s) provide test specification, test results and safety analyses. Purpose of this step is to collect information according to the engineering activities as specified in Table 3. The output of this step is the feedback on the engineering activities (see Table 3) for all technical safety requirements. In this step, we set the attribute engineeringFeedback in the classes with the stereotypes $\ll InternalFaultHandlingVaV\gg$, $\ll LatentFaultHandlingVaV\gg$, $\ll HW\_SWDerivation\ VaV\gg$, $\ll PMHFVaV\gg$, $\ll HW\_SW\ VerificationVaV\gg$, $\ll SRSVerificationSpecVaV\gg$, $\ll SRSVerificationResultVaV\gg$, $\ll FSCVerificationSpecVaV\gg$, and $\ll FSCVerification\ ResultVaV\gg$ (see Fig. 4). Depending on the stereotype assigned to the technical safety requirement, the information or a reference to this information should be provided by the OEM or the supplier(s) as described in Table 3, column 'Feedback'.

It can be checked that the attribute engineeringFeedback is set and not empty (see condition 4M01AS in Table 5). After the tasks are performed, the task feedback is inserted by the persons assigned to the task. For the selected example, the supplier engineer creates a test case for the component SSM, covering ESCL-T-S- Req01000. This test case is part of the test specification "Testplan_SSM_v12.02.pdf", therefore the engineer provides this information, including a reference to the document section containing the test case. For $\ll VerificationSpecVaV\gg$, the attribute engineeringFeedback is set and the received information is inserted (see Fig. 7).

Step 5. Safety V&V for Technical Safety Requirements. Input for this step is the engineering activity feedback of the OEM or supplier from Step 4 and the output of all previous steps. A different engineer from the OEM and in some cases from the supplier reviews the included or referenced information. For all technical safety requirements, the ISO 26262 [1, Part 4, 6.4.6] requires a verification review. Output of this step is the safety V&V activity result. It is checked if all requirements given in column "Safety V&V Activity" for the stereotype of the V&V activity assigned to the technical safety requirement in Table 3 are fulfilled. In this step, we set the attribute safetyVaVResult of the classes with the stereotypes $\ll InternalFaultHandlingVaV\gg$, $\ll LatentFaultHandlingVaV\gg$,

Table 3. V&V activities for SRS

Stereotype	Engineering Activity / Feedback	Safety V&V Activity
≪*InternalFaultHandlingVaV*≫	see [7] for more details	see [7] for more details
≪*LatentFaultHandlingVaV*≫	see [7] for more details	see [7] for more details
≪*PMHFVaV*≫	see [7] for more details	see [7] for more details
≪*HW_SWDerivationVaV*≫	To ensure a sound component design, the component provider shall derive HW and SW requirements for the technical safety requirement. A reference to this information should be inserted.	The HW and SW requirements for the Technical Safety Requirement and the implementation process shall be assessed. It shall be checked that: – the HW and SW safety requirements, the HW and SW interface requirements and the Component Design are correctly derived from the Technical Safety Requirement, – a Safety Analysis (e.g. FTA) to determine faults leading to the violation of the Technical Safety Requirement is complete (e.g. inputs) and correct (e.g. logic), and – the HW/SW Design (including internal and external interfaces) is appropriate and corresponds to Safety Analysis . To achieve this, the component provider provides input and the OEM reviews a sample to assess the component provider processes and safety analyses.
≪*HW_SWVerificationVaV*≫	The component provider shall verify the implementation of the HW and SW requirements in the component. A reference to the verification documentation (e.g. review reports, analyses, test cases) should be inserted.	The V&V of the component shall be assessed. It shall be checked that – ... see [7] for more details
≪*SRSVerificationSpecVaV*≫	A verification specification for the technical safety requirement shall be generated (including activity and acceptance criteria considering parameters that can be identified) in order to verify the correct implementation of the Technical Safety Requirement (e.g. Fault insertion, Safety Function testing, review of the implementation). A reference to the verification specification should be provided .	The V&V of the component shall be assessed. It shall be checked that – the test specification to verify the effectiveness and the failure coverage of the safety mechanisms are correct and complete, – the stated failure rates (e.g. in FMEDA) are justified by robustness testing specified in a qualification plan for the HW components and the test results are documented (optional for phase 1), and – the HW metrics calculation (e.g. by FMEDA or FTA) as defined in ISO 26262 Part 5 (provide evidence that the target values, specified in the Safety Requirement Specification, are fulfilled by the design) is correct and complete. To achieve this, the component provider provides input and the OEM reviews a sample to assess the component verification and metric calculation (e.g. FTA, FMEDA).
≪*SRSVerificationResultVaV*≫	The verification shall be executed as specified and the results shall be documented. A reference to verification results shall be given.	The verification results from the V&V activities (e.g. test cases) shall be assessed and validated. This can be done by a technical review of the V&V specification.

≪*HW_SW DerivationVaV*≫, ≪*PMHFVaV*≫, ≪*HW_SWVerification VaV*≫, ≪*SRSVerificationSpecVaV*≫, and ≪*SRSVerificationResult VaV*≫ (see Fig. 4). It can be checked that the attribute verificationReviewResult is set and not empty (see condition 5M01AS in Table 5). For the selected example, the OEM Safety Consultant reviews the referenced test case and checks it against ESCL-T-S- Req01000. The review result is, that the test case is correctly defined and addresses all safety relevant aspects of the technical safety requirement. For ≪*VerificationSpecVaV*≫, the attribute safetyVaVResult is set to "Test case is appropriate" and the information is inserted. Finally, the property status is set to "VerificationCompleted" (see Fig. 7).

Step 6. Provide Engineering Activity Feedback for Functional Safety Requirements and Safety Goals. Input for this step is the documentation of engieering activity of the supplier or OEM and the output of all previous

Table 4. V&V activities for FSC

Stereotype	Engineering Activity / Feedback	Safety V&V Activity
≪SG_HW_Metric≫	HW metrics shall be calculated on safety goal level by the OEM.	Result and conclusions of the HW metrics calculation on safety goal level shall be assessed and validated. It is checked if the quantitative metrics (calculated on Safety Goal level) fulfill the ASIL related requirements and is correctly calculated by a technical review of the safety analyses
≪$FSCVerificationSpecVaV$≫	A verification specification shall be created, e.g. a test specification. This verification specification shall include a unique identification of the verified work product, a reference to the verification plan, specification of verification including all relevant parameters, the configuration of the verification environment and verification tools together with calibration data. The OEM shall provide a reference to the verification specification for the referenced functional safety requirement.	The correctness and the completeness of the verification specification shall be assessed and validated by a technical review and the result shall be documented
≪$FSCVerificationResultVaV$≫	The verification shall be performed and the results shall be documented. This documentation shall include an unambiguous statement whether the verification passed or failed, including the rationale for failure and possible suggestions for changes in the verified work product. The OEM shall provide a reference to the verification result for the referenced functional safety requirement.	It shall be checked that the results of the performed verification activity fulfill the specified acceptance criteria. This can be done by checking the corresponding and referenced verification report

steps. For this step, usually the OEM documents or references the required information. Purpose of this step is to collect information according to the engineering activities as specified in Table 4. We specified these activities in a way that the ISO 26262 requirements ([1, Part 4, 7.4.3] for ≪SG_HW_Metric≫, [1, Part 4, 8.4.3/4] for ≪$FSCVerificationSpecVaV$≫, and [1, Part 4, 8.4.3/4] for ≪$FSCVerificationResultVaV$≫) can be fulfilled. The output of this step is the feedback on the engineering activities given in Table 4 for all functional safety requirements and safety goals. In this step, we set the attribute engineeringFeedback of the classes with the stereotypes ≪SG_HW_Metric≫, ≪$FSCVerificationSpecVaV$≫, and ≪$FSCVerifiactionResultVaV$≫ (see Fig. 4). Depending on the stereotype assigned to the functional safety requirement or safety goal, the information or a reference to this information should be provided as described in Table 4. It can be checked that the attribute engineeringFeedback is set and not empty (see condition 6M01AS in Table 5). Step 6 is performed for the functional safety requirements in the same manner as Step 4 for the technical safety requirement example.

Step 7. Safety V&V for Functional Safety Requirements. Input for this step is the engineering activity feedback referenced in Step 6 and the output of all previous steps. A different engineer from the OEM and in some cases from the supplier reviews the included or referenced information. For all functional safety requirement, the ISO 26262 [1, Part 3, 8.4.5] requires a verification review. Output of this step is the safety V&V activity result. It is checked if all requirements

given in column "Safety V&V Activity" for the stereotype of the V&V activity
assigned to the functional safety requirement or safety goal in Table 4 are fulfilled.
In this step, we set the attribute safetyVaVResult of the classes with the stereotypes
$\ll InternalFaultHandlingVaV \gg$, $\ll LatentFaultHandlingVaV \gg$, $\ll HW_-$
$SWDerivationVaV \gg$, $\ll PMHFVaV \gg$, $\ll HW\_SWVerificationVaV \gg$,
$\ll SRSVerificationSpecVaV \gg$, and $\ll SRSVerificationResultVaV \gg$ (see
Fig. 4).

It can be checked that the attribute safetyVaVResult is set and not empty (see
condition 7M01AS in Table 5). Step 7 is performed for the functional safety
requirements in the same manner as Step 5 for the technical safety requirement
example.

Step 8. Perform Confirmation Review. ISO 26262 requires to perform a
confirmation review of the V&V activities. Input for this step is the output of
all previous steps. This step is usually performed by the OEM. ISO 26262 [1,
Part2,6.4.7] requires a confirmation review by a person independent from the
division responsible for the development of the system. We provide a detailed
checklist (addressing all ISO 26262 requirements) to support this review. The
output is the confirmation that the V&V activities are preformed according to
ISO 26262. To perform this step, an independent person checks the V&V activities regarding the ISO 26262 requirements. In this step, we set the attributes
in a class with the stereotype $\ll VaVConfirmation \gg$. The person performing
the review and his/her independence level according to ISO 26262 (1='different person', 2='different team', 3='different company or organization') is set to
the corresponding attributes reviewer and independenceLevel. The person doing the
confirmation review checks the following:

- HW metrics values have been calculated, documented and assessed for each
  safety goal.
- Verification methods have been specified and verified for all functional safety
  requirements.
- The verifications have been performed and results have been checked for all
  functional safety requirements.
- The component providers have provided the information to complete the technical safety requirements and these information have been validated.
- The HW and SW requirements (derived by the component providers) have
  been documented and checked.
- The verification of the HW and SW requirements (performed by the component providers) have been documented and checked.
- Verification methods for the technical safety requirements have been generated, validated and assessed (including activity and acceptance criteria).
- The verifications have been performed and results have been checked for all
  technical safety requirements.

The reviewer sets the corresponding attributes to true or false. If a statement
cannot be confirmed, a comment is given. Additionally, the date of the review is
set. It can be checked that if one of the attributes is false, the attribute comment

Table 5. Validation Conditions (excerpt)

Step	ID	Condition
1	1C01RA	All technical and functional safety requirement address an element of an analysis
1	1C02AR	All elements of the analyses are addressed by technical and functional safety requirement
1	1M03AR	The stereotype ≪*addressedBy*≫ points from a an analysis element (class with the stereotype ≪*FTAGate*≫, ≪*FTAEvent*≫, or ≪*FMEALineItem*≫) to a functional or technical safety requirement
2	2G01DR	Generate these classes and dependencies as described in Table 2
2	2M02NV	The stereotype ≪*VaVActivity*≫ is not directly used
3	3M01AS	The attributes taskResponsible, taskDueDate, verificationResponsible, and verificationDueDate are set and not empty

is set (see condition 7C01CO in Table 5), that all attributes are set (see condition 7C02AT), and that for each item a V&V confirmation is performed (see condition 7M03VV). Additionally, overviews of the performed V&V activities can be generated to support the confirmation review (see condition 7G0GVV).

The confirmation review by an independent person is performed after all previous steps are completed.

For the selected example, an external safety consultant reviews the V&V report and sets all attributes in the class with the stereotype ≪*VaVConfirmation*≫ as shown in Fig. 6. As the Safety Consultant is from an independent company, the attribute independenceLevel is set to 3. For this element of our case study, all boolean attributes are set to true except HW_SWVerificationVaVOK and SRSVerificationResultVaVOK since the SSM supplier has not provided test results from the detailed HW and SW testing and from the testing of the technical safety requirement. The attribute comment is set accordingly. Finally, the attribute date is set to the date of the confirmation review. If the corresponding attributes are set to "false", the problem needs to be addressed and the confirmation review will be repeated. When all V&V activities are completed, the corresponding attributes are set to "true" and the confirmation review is passed, the creation of the V&V report is closed and the functional safety process proceeds with its next step, the creation of the safety case. Herein the V&V report is used as an input document.

This step concludes our method. All the created documentation is an essential part for the subsequent steps that result in the safety case.

7   Related Work

We are not aware of any publication about a model-based structured validation and verification of automotive systems with a focus on the OEM-supplier interface for automotive systems equipped with integrity checks. Maropoulos et al. [10] presented a survey of industrial verification and validation efforts. The report presents evidence that verification and validation of products and processes is vital for complex products and in particular modelling and planning of such methods are an ongoing research challenge. Sinz et al. [11] used formal methods to validate automotive product configuration data. In contrast to our work, their method specifically focuses on detecting inconsistencies in product configurations of vehicles to support business decisions. Instead we focus on technical verification and validation efforts. Bringman et al. [12] described the impact model-driven design has in the automotive industry and showed how models can be used to derive test cases during different steps of the automotive product lifecycle. In contrast to our work Bringman et al. focus exclusively on model-based testing of automotive systems. Dubois et al. [13] presented a method for model-based validation and verification efforts to check if the final product matches initial requirements. In contrast to our work Dubois et al. focus on using UML-based models to create test cases for more detailed implementation models in e.g. SIMULINK. Montevechi et al. [14] focuses on the simulation of processes in the automotive industry. Their methodology builds simulation models to analyse which combinations of variables can lead to problems. Within the automotive industry, different activities are started to extend the safety processes with model-based system engineering aspects, mainly focusing on architecture description[5] and semiautomatic safety analyses [15].

8   Conclusions and Future Work

Our method has been applied to several Ford of Europe projects. However, the formal validation conditions and tool support was not used in these projects and was developed as contribution for this paper. We are confident that this contribution will ensure the same consistency and correctness of future verification &validation with less effort than the manual approach currently used. The main contributions of our approach are:

Structured Method helping to

- ensure consistency between the safety requirements, safety analyses and safety V&V,
- define a complete set of V&V activities, including reviews, analyses, simulations and tests by using pre-defined V&V activities based on the category of the requirement,
- allocate the V&V activities between OEM and the involved suppliers,
- define due dates,
- collect and assess the V&V results for all requirements, and
- provide input to the safety case

---

[5] Electronics Architecture and Software Technology - Architecture Description Language, http://www.east-adl.info/.

UML Profile for **expressing all elements** relevant for an ISO 26262-compliant safety verification and validation, including traceability to the functional and technical safety requirements and the safety analyses.

OCL Checks concerning consistency and completeness of the V&V activities. Thus, we provide a **computer-aided technique** to discover errors in the V&V activities caused by inconsistencies or errors in one or more (UML) diagrams.

The V&V report including the supplier interface in practice is currently document-based using spreadsheet-processing tools from Microsoft Office. We propose to conduct the analysis on UML models and to create tables from the models for the V&V report. Thus, we use a model-based approach, but the suppliers will receive the same type of documentation they are used to. In the future, we will extend the approach to Safety Analysis and Safety Management. Currently, Ford is implementing tool support in NoMagic's MagicDraw. Ford is also creating import and export functionalily for their current templates and is developing an interface to requirements management tools.

Acknowledgments. The authors thank Nelufar Ulfat-Bunyadi and the anonymous reviers for their valuable feedback on the paper.

References

1. International Organization for Standardization (ISO): Road Vehicles - Functional Safety. ISO 26262 (2011)
2. UML Revision Task Force: OMG Object Constraint Language: Reference (2010)
3. International Electrotechnical Commission (IEC): Functional safety of electrical/electronic/programmable electronic safety-relevant systems. IEC 61508 (2000)
4. Eclipse Foundation: Eclipse - Development Platform (2011). http://www.eclipse.org/
5. Eclipse Foundation: Eclipse Modeling Framework Project (EMF) (2012). http://www.eclipse.org/modeling/emf/
6. Atos Origin: Papyrus UML Modelling Tool (2011). http://www.papyrusuml.org/
7. Beckers, K., Côté, I., Frese, T., Hatebur, D., Heisel, M.: A structured validation and verification method for automotive systems considering the oem/supplier interface technical report. Technical report (2015). https://www.uni-due.de/imperia/md/content/swe/papers/vav2015tr.pdf
8. Safety Management System and Safety Culture Working Group (SMS WG): Guidance on hazard identification. Technical report (2009)
9. Leveson, N.: Safeware: System Safety and Computers. Addison-Wesley, Reading (1995)
10. Maropoulos, P.G., Ceglarek, D.: Design verification and validation in product lifecycle. CIRP Ann. Manuf. Technol. **59**, 740–759 (2010)
11. Sinz, C., Kaiser, A., Küchlin, W.: Formal methods for the validation of automotive product configuration data. Artif. Intell. Eng. Des. Anal. Manuf. **17**, 75–97 (2003)
12. Bringmann, E., Kramer, A.: Model-based testing of automotive systems. In: 2008 1st International Conference on Software Testing, Verification, and Validation, pp. 485–493 (2008)

13. Dubois, H., Peraldi-Frati, M., Lakhal, F.: A model for requirements traceability in a heterogeneous model-based design process: application to automotive embedded systems. In: Proceedings of ICECCS, pp. 233–242 (2010)
14. Montevechi, J.A.B., de Pinho, A.F., Leal, F., Marins, F.A.S.: Application of design of experiments on the simulation of a process in an automotive industry. In: Proceedings of WSC, WSC 2007, pp. 1601–1609. IEEE Press (2007)
15. Rasmus, A., Dominik, D., Kai, H., Sören, K., Thomas, K., Jean-Pascal, S., Mario, T.: Integration of component fault trees into the UML. In: Juergen, D., Arnor, S. (eds.) MODELS 2010. LNCS, vol. 6627, pp. 312–327. Springer, Heidelberg (2011)

Automotive Software

Model-Based Analysis for Safety Critical Software

Stefan Gulan[1]($\boxtimes$), Jens Harnisch[2], Sven Johr[1], Roberto Kretschmer[1],
Stefan Rieger[1], and Rafael Zalman[2]

[1] TWT GmbH Science and Innovation, Ernsthaldenstr. 17,
70565 Stuttgart, Germany
{stefan.gulan,sven.johr,roberto.kretschmer,stefan.rieger}@twt-gmbh.de
[2] Infineon Technologies AG, Am Campeon 1-12, 85579 Neubiberg, Germany
{jens.harnisch,rafael.zalman}@infineon.com

Abstract. Safety-relevant software developed within the automotive domain is subject to the safety standard ISO 26262. In particular, a supplier must show that implemented safety mechanisms sufficiently address relevant failure modes. This involves complex and costly testing procedures.

We introduce an early analysis approach for safety mechanisms implemented in safety-relevant software by combining model checking and model-based testing. Model checking is applied to verify the correctness of an abstract amodel of the system under test. The verified model is then used to automatically generate tests for the verification of the implemented Safety Elements. The approach has been evaluated in an industrial case study, addressing Analogue Digital Converters as part of the motor control within a hybrid electric vehicle. The results suggest that our approach allows to create high quality test suites. In addition, the test model helps to reduce misunderstandings due to imprecise specification of safety mechanisms.

Keywords: Safety analysis · Functional safety · ISO 26262 · AUTOSAR · Formal methods · Model checking · Model-based testing

1 Introduction

A key challenge in the development of safety critical embedded software (SW) in the automotive domain is the testing of safety mechanisms (SM) with respect to hardware (HW) and software faults. The relevant safety standard ISO 26262 defines SMs as technical solutions to detect faults or control failures in order to achieve or maintain a safe state [1]. State of the art testing of SM for HW specific software, involves to show the necessity and sufficiency of SMs by injecting faults in the running system, consisting of the target microcontroller and the implemented SW. This raises the particular challenge that faults have to be injected in the target HW itself, which requires complex and costly fault injection processes. One reason is the laborious specification of tests and test protocols as

© Springer International Publishing Switzerland 2015
F. Koornneef and C. van Gulijk (Eds.): SAFECOMP 2015, LNCS 9337, pp. 111–120, 2015.
DOI: 10.1007/978-3-319-24255-2_9

well as the iteration of these development artefacts in all development phases. For SW implemented in SMs, the possible faults are systematic in nature, which are usually already part of specification refinements. Hence, a verification of the implementation against its specification is deemed to be ineffective.

The present study is concerned with an early analysis of SMs implemented in the driver SW. The goal is to find design errors of SMs already in the requirement specification phase of the ISO 26262 compliant development process. Our approach is based on two methodologies: (1) model checking and (2) model-based testing (MBT). Model checking is applied to ensure that no errors have been introduced in the abstract model of the system under test (SUT). The MBT component uses the abstract model to automatically generate a test suite to verify the SW implementation. Our approach was applied to a real life use case: an analogue-digital converter (ADC) driver SW developed as a part of the microcontroller abstraction layer (MCAL) of the AUTOSAR SW stack [2]. The ADC driver is developed by a supplier as a Safety Element out of Context (SEooC). Thus, the ADC driver itself implements only the technical possibilities to employ certain SMs. It is ultimately the responsibility of the user, i.e. the application SW, to realise the SMs based on these possibilities. The challenge for the SEooC supplier is to show the ability of the SW to work safely in its context.

Several other studies have been conducted on the subject of a model-based safety analysis using formal methods. Most of these studies focus on fault tolerant systems. Only few target the automotive domain. Bruns and Sutherland present an algebraic approach to model checking of fault tolerant systems [7]. However, their work is focused on the verification of communication protocols. [9] aim at the verification of fault-tolerance in systems formalised as finite state machines (FSMs). Fault descriptions are used to build observer and saboteur FSMs to model faults and verify safety properties. In contrast to our work, the authors focus on HW system models. [12] introduce the notion of model-based safety analysis. They propose the utilisation of a single model for safety analysis and systems engineering. In contrast, we advocate the use of a separate test model for design verification and the automatic creation of test cases used for system verification. Because SW faults are systematic by nature, we consider our approach to be better suited to find such flaws, as it targets an early SW design validation. The authors of [6] introduce a method for model-based integration testing ahead of system development based on formal models which is applied to a laser-scanner system. Their work addresses primarily system integration, while we focus on low-level software and safety aspects. Hänsel et al. describe an approach for test-case generation from networks of timed automata applied to an anti-lock braking system [8]. They encounter resource problems when generating test cases with the tool UPPAAL CoVer [10, 11] and develop an evolutionary algorithm. Later, Hänsel describes a concept for an improved method that is still to be implemented and evaluated. In contrast, our approach – also using UPPAAL CoVer – has not exposed any such problems yet, most likely due to the higher abstraction level enabling an application in early system design.

2   ADC Use Case

Hybrid Electric Vehicle. As use case a motor control is considered, as used for example within a hybrid electric vehicle (HEV), depicted in Fig. 1. The AURIX microcontroller generates a PWM signal with the help of its generic time module (GTM) peripheral that is dedicated to signal generation and capturing. The PWM is fed from the GTM via some external driver chips towards the PMSM (permanent magnet synchronous motor). However, for generating the proper motor control signal, it is crucial to have information about the current position of the motor rotor which is mechanically connected to a resolver generating this information. The resolver signal is fed into the Delta-Sigma ADC (DS-ADCs) of the microcontroller, where a digital signal of the current rotor position is generated. If the rotor position is not calculated properly, this may lead to the incorrect generation of motor control signals, thermal issues may arise, the electric motor may break completely and cause accidents. The complete HEV system has to meet safety requirements up to ASIL-D. The DS-ADCs, converting the analogue signal from the resolver into a digital signal, are controlled by an AUTOSAR MCAL driver. In our use case, one signal is fed into two different ADC channels. This redundancy provides a certain safety against malfunction of the ADC peripheral on the microcontroller. It needs to be checked from the application on the core of the microcontroller, whether the two ADC channels generate equal values after each conversion. Of course, it would be even safer to duplicate wiring of the resolver, or even duplicate the resolver itself.

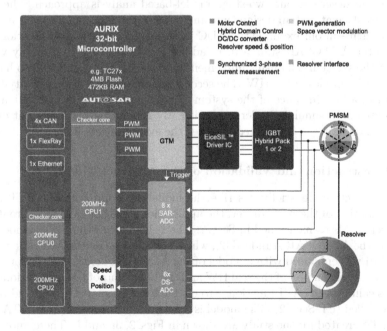

Fig. 1. Electric motor control with the help of a resolver

Failure Modes and Safety Mechanisms. Here, we use the ISO 26262 terminology that defines a *fault model* as a representation of a failure mode, which is the manner in which an item fails. In our case, the item is either the driver SW, the application SW or the ADC HW. As HW failure modes we consider: (1) an alteration of data in the result registers of the ADC due to a HW fault; (2) the reading of a wrong channel value by the HW; (3) a failure of the shared converter HW part such that the conversion does not work correctly.

Similarly several SW faults, due to design flaws are considered: (1) data corruption due to control problems, e.g. an erroneous manipulation of the result buffer, which is the internal memory space that the ADC driver uses to store the conversion data; (2) errors in the configuration of the HW setup; and (3) improper setting of a control flag, which is normally set on conversion completion, which yields old data or no data at all in the result buffer.

To handle the before mentioned failure modes the following safety mechanisms are considered: (1) comparison of the conversion result between two redundant channels, i.e. the conversion is realised by independent HW instances (referred to as redundant channel SM); (2) a check of configuration values for correctness during initialisation, by recalculating the configuration from the static configuration stored (correctly) in flash memory; and (3) a check of a separate end-of-conversion flag.

3   Analysis Approach

This section describes our two-stage model-based analysis approach. The first part takes place at system design time and enables validation of abstract models of the system—in our example the ADC in Sect. 1—against its specification—in our case the AUTOSAR standard. In addition, it is possible to formally verify whether the safety mechanisms implemented in the SUT are sufficient to handle different fault modes of the HW. The second and main verification activity takes place when a first instance of the system's implementation is available that can be executed on a simulated microcontroller. By generating test cases out of the abstract model, it can be verified whether the system meets its specification.

3.1   Construction and Validation of the Abstract Model

In this subsection we briefly describe the modelling approach. The SUT is an implementation of the ADC driver, the application SW that calls driver routines and several SMs as mentioned in Sect. 2. The behaviour of the SUT is modelled based on the AUTOSAR standard [2], which specifies the driver API. The model of the API was enhanced with a model of the ADC HW, i.e. the conversion units are based an abstraction of the real HW and the behaviour of the application SW, which is calling ADC API functions. To enable a safety analysis, SMs and faults were modelled (c.f. Sect. 2). The model is a network of timed automata (TA) [4]. Several TA created for the study are shown in Figs. 2, 3a and b. These automata synchronize via messages, shown as transition labels with a trailing symbol '!'

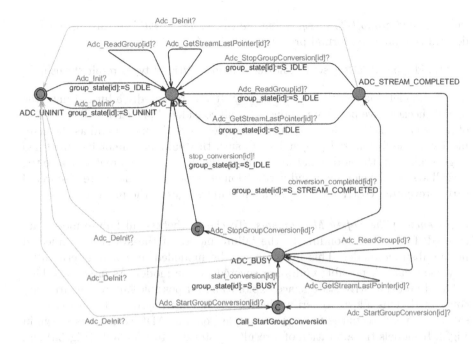

Fig. 2. Model of the channel group SW triggered, one-shot, single access conversion.

or '?'. More precisely, we used the modelling language of the UPPAAL tool, which implements networks of enhanced TA [5]. UPPAAL allows to quickly develop prototypes graphically, which can be explored using the included simulator. The model in Fig. 2 is derived from an UML statechart given in the AUTOSAR specification [2] for the one shot, SW triggered, single access conversion mode.

Validation of the Abstract Model. To ensure validity and consistency of our abstract model, we established an approach in three steps: (1) a diverse modelling approach, (2) model reviews by domain experts and (3) model checking of the model against formal properties. The first step was realised by the development of two models by two individual formal method experts. These two models were created independently based on the same specification. It was then checked that both models converge, i.e. that both models exhibit the same behaviour. This check was based on mutual model reviews. Differences in the modelled behaviour indicated understanding issues and were also used to guide discussions with domain experts. The latter reviewed the converged model by examining the UPPAAL graphical representation and sequence diagrams produced by UPPAAL. Step three was based on the derivation of a set of temporal properties from the requirements of the AUTOSAR standard. In addition to function specific requirements, the general behaviour of the application SW calling the driver API, was specified. For instance, requirement SWS_Adc_00384 states: '*The ADC modules environment shall ensure that a conversion has been completed for the requested group before requesting the conversion result.*' In this instance we derived the following formal property in UPPAAL-TCTL[1]:

$$\forall(i : id\_type) \; AdcUser\_sw(i).Call\_ReadGroup \rightsquigarrow \forall(j : id\_type) \; result\_status[j]$$

The model was constructed iteratively: It was repeatedly adjusted until the model checker gave positive responses for all considered properties. The number of necessary iterations depends on the complexity of the model and as the complexity of the formalized properties. As such this number cannot be quantified in general. Still, the additional iterations in the design phase greatly reduce the overall system development and verification effort as design flaws are discovered early preventing costly reiterations in the later stages of the process.

Sufficiency of the Safety Mechanisms. To check whether all failure modes are covered, faults corresponding to the failure modes of the system are injected in the abstract model. This injection can be modelled in a non-deterministic way such that all possible faults are covered by the model. As model checking is based on exhaustive state space exploration, all possible failure scenarios are considered. This allows to verify whether the modified system always reaches a safe state, i.e. detects the fault. An example from our ADC scenario is shown in Fig. 3. It models the alteration of a result register due to HW fault (Fig. 3a) and the comparison of independent results as a safety mechanism (Fig. 3b). In this example we abstracted from the actual data types and used Booleans instead, as for the conversion results only their equality is of importance for the SM.

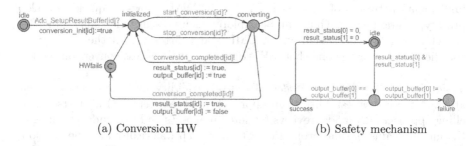

(a) Conversion HW   (b) Safety mechanism

Fig. 3. Test model of a conversion HW unit with a model of the safety mechanism

3.2   Model-Based Testing Approach

The abstract model in Sect. 3.1 was used for model-based testing as visualised in Fig. 4. For reactive embedded systems, like the ADC driver, the events that trigger the transition-sequence correspond to calls of the ADC API. This allows to generate test-cases, i.e. sequences of function-calls, by identifying them with

---

[1] Here, $\rightsquigarrow$ is the *response* operator. $\varphi \rightsquigarrow \psi$ for UPPAAL-TCTL formulae φ and ψ means: whenever φ is fulfilled at a certain moment in time, ψ must be true at a later point in time. This is the UPPAAL-equivalent of the CTL formula $\mathbf{AG}(\varphi \rightarrow \mathbf{AF}\psi)$.

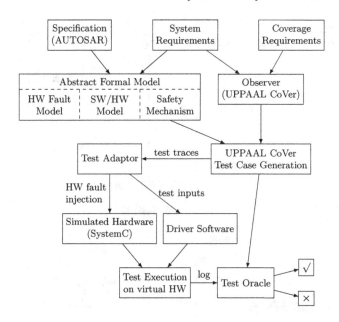

Fig. 4. Process view of the model-based testing approach

feasible paths of the state machine model. There is a methodical overlap of model-based test case generation with model checking: both methods rely on enumerating paths of state-machine models: While model-based test generation aims at explicitly outputting many paths in general (to execute them as tests), model checking only explicitly outputs few paths with respect to specific properties (namely counterexamples, that show the violation of some property). As it turns out, model checkers can emulate model-based test generators. The crucial point is to enforce sets of counterexamples that might be utilised as a test suite. This is commonly realised using an observer (automaton) which is runs in parallel with model automaton. States of the observer encode properties of the initial model that are relevant for tests. The model checker is then asked to verify that the encoding state of the observer is *un*reachable. Consequently, a counterexample rejecting that property consists of a path on the initial state machine that shows the behaviour under observation.

For the UPPAAL model checker, the CoVer tool [10,11] implements this method. It generates traces that cover both HW and SW. In particular, traces may contain HW faults that result from injecting faults on the simulated HW executing the driver SW, which in turn is driven by inputs derived from the generated trace. A test execution log is then compared against its expected outcome by the test oracle. The verdict 'pass' is attached only if the final state of a test trace (execution log) is a safe state, otherwise 'fail'.

Matching of abstract and concrete traces is non-trivial as described in Sect. 4. An example UPPAAL trace for the ADC use case is shown in Fig. 5 including the following information: (1) CG1 and CG2 show the behaviour of two channel

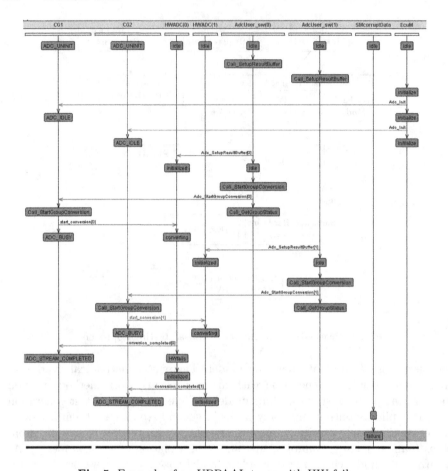

Fig. 5. Example of an UPPAAL trace with HW failure.

groups (channel groups facilitate the control of the ADC peripheral with very little overhead); (2) HWADC(1) and HWADC(2) denote the status of the two ADC peripherals; (3) AdcUser_sw(0) and AdcUser_sw(1) denote the order in which the MCAL driver functions are being called from application SW; (4) EcuM refers to the status of the complete Electronic Control Unit (ECU); and (4) SMcorruptData denotes the SW part of the SM redundant channel.

4   Testing the C Implementation on Simulated Hardware

An application running on top of the ADC MCAL driver, comparing the conversion results from two ADC channels was executed on a SystemC simulator, featuring cycle approximate behaviour of the microcontroller silicon. The SystemC simulator is built upon the CoMET simulation framework from Synopsys, and features the cores, all buses and memories and almost all peripherals of the AURIX microcontroller. The SystemC simulator is tested with the same test bench as the

```
1  /Top/TC27x/TriCore0/VpmCtrl Target: MCAL driver: entering Adc_SetupResultBuffer()
2  /Top/TC27x/TriCore0/VpmCtrl Target: MCAL driver: leaving Adc_SetupResultBuffer()
3  /Top/TC27x/TriCore0/VpmCtrl Target: MCAL driver: entering Adc_SetupResultBuffer()
4  /Top/TC27x/TriCore0/VpmCtrl Target: MCAL driver: leaving Adc_SetupResultBuffer()
5  /Top/TC27x/TriCore0/VpmCtrl Target: MCAL driver: entering Adc_StartGroupConversion()
6  /Top/TC27x/TriCore0/VpmCtrl Target: MCAL driver: leaving Adc_StartGroupConversion()
7  /Top/TC27x/TriCore0/VpmCtrl Target: MCAL driver: entering Adc_StartGroupConversion()
8  /Top/TC27x/TriCore0/VpmCtrl Target: MCAL driver: leaving Adc_StartGroupConversion()
9  /Top/TC27x/TriCore0/VpmCtrl Target: MCAL driver: entering Adc_GetGroupStatus()
```

Fig. 6. Trace from C-code, simulated on the SystemC simulator.

RTL model, from which the final silicon is derived, and with additional directed tests. It was easy to add debug output with additional information about the status of the application, the MCAL driver and the microcontroller. The trace information generated from the simulator was compared against the trace generated within UPPAAL, to check whether the C-implementation behaves the same way as the model in UPPAAL.

The matching trace generated from the C-implementation, which was executed on the SystemC simulator, is shown in Fig. 6. It corresponds to the API-calls AdcUser_sw(0) and AdcUser_sw(1) from the UPPAAL trace. For example, the call Adc_SetupResultBuffer() in the simulation run corresponds to Call_SetupResultBuffer() from the UPPAAL trace. The trace from the simulated HW is much more complex and not shown here.

It turns out that for efficiently matching a large number of traces or long traces some automatic means are needed. The identifiers would need to be generated automatically to assure uniqueness, and would have to be used within the UPPALL model, the C-code and the HW model in the same manner. Automatic trace matching based on unique identifiers was not performed within the project yet; however, can be considered as a major learning experience.

5   Conclusion

We have presented an approach for early analysis of safety mechanisms in safety-relevant applications, demonstrated by its application to an AUTOSAR ADC driver part of a hybrid electric vehicle's motor control. In particular, by building an abstract model of both hardware and software including fault models for the relevant failure modes of the system, we were able to verify whether the implementation actually conforms to the AUTOSAR specification and the functional system requirements by systematically generating high quality test suites.

Being based on model checkers, the approach is prone to the well-known problem of combinatorial state-space explosion. Since the models specified in AUTOSAR and those of the considered faults and safety mechanism are comparatively small, we did not run into serious problems. Still, scalability is an issue that might require evaluation for bigger models.

The conformance of the system's design with respect to the relevant standards – in our case AUTOSAR – is proven on a high level of abstraction before an implementation is actually available and thus enables an early validation. The effect of design changes can be evaluated with a relatively low degree of effort at this stage. Furthermore, our approach enables fault injection on both, software and hardware components, based on the test traces generated from the abstract model. Hardware fault injection of course requires that the hardware is available as a simulation model, for example, based on SystemC. While there are also several means for fault injection directly in the hardware, those means are usually limited to very selected use cases as they make the final product more complex and expensive.

Future work will focus on increasing the degree of automation and the seamless chaining of tools. The automation of test-suite generation, fault injection and test execution is particularly desirable. This requires additional work to achieve a fully automatic matching of traces from the abstract model and the log data of concrete test executions.

Acknowledgement. This work was funded by the German Federal Ministry of Education and Research and the European Union in the context of the European VeTeSS project [3] (ARTEMIS Joint Undertaking, Grant No. 295311).

References

1. ISO/DIS 26262-1 - Road vehicles Functional safety Part 1 Glossary. Technical report, Geneva, Switzerland, July 2009
2. Specification of ADC Driver. Technical report (2011). http://www.autosar. org/fileadmin/files/releases/4-0/software-architecture/peripherals/standard/ AUTOSAR_SWS_ADCDriver.pdf
3. VeTeSS - Verification and Testing to support functional Safety Standards (2012). http://vetess.eu/
4. Alur, R., Dill, D.L.: A theory of timed automata. Theor. Comput. Sci. **126**(2), 183–235 (1994)
5. Behrmann, G., David, A., Larsen, K.G.: A tutorial on UPPAAL 4.0 (2006). http:// www.it.uu.se/research/group/darts/papers/texts/new-tutorial.pdf
6. Braspenning, N., van de Mortel-Fronczak, J.M., Rooda, J.E.: A model-based integration and testing method to reduce system development effort. Electron. Notes Theor. Comput. Sci. **164**(4), 13–28 (2006)
7. Bruns, G., Sutherland, I.: Model checking and fault tolerance. In: Johnson, M. (ed.) AMAST 1997. LNCS, vol. 1349, pp. 45–59. Springer, Heidelberg (1997)
8. Hänsel, J., Rose, D., Herber, P., Glesner, S.: An evolutionary algorithm for the generation of timed test traces for embedded real-time systems. In: 2011 IEEE Fourth International Conference on Software Testing, Verification and Validation (ICST), pp. 170–179, March 2011
9. Hazelhurst, S., Arlat, J.: Specifying and verifying fault tolerant hardware. In: Proceedings of the Designing Correct Circuits (2002)
10. Hessel, A.: Model-based test case generation for real-time systems. Acta Universitatis Upsaliensis (2007)
11. Hessel, A., Pettersson, P.: COVER - a real-time test case generation tool. In: 19th IFIP International Conference on Testing of Communicating Systems (2007)
12. Joshi, A., Miller, S.P., Whalen, M., Heimdahl, M.P.: A proposal for model-based safety analysis. In: Digital Avionics Systems, vol. 2, pp. 13-pp. IEEE (2005)

Integrated Safety Analysis Using Systems-Theoretic Process Analysis and Software Model Checking

Asim Abdulkhaleq[✉] and Stefan Wagner

Institute of Software Technology, University of Stuttgart,
Universitätsstraße 38, 70569 Stuttgart, Germany
{Asim.Abdulkhaleq,Stefan.Wagner}@informatik.uni-stuttgart.de

Abstract. Safety-critical systems are becoming increasingly more complex and reliant on software. The increase in complexity and software renders ensuring the safety of such systems increasingly difficult. Formal verification approaches can be used to prove the correctness of software; however, even perfectly correct software could lead to an accident. The difficulty is in defining appropriate safety requirements. STPA (Systems-Theoretic Process Analysis) is a modern safety analysis approach which aims to identify the potential hazardous causes in complex systems. Model checking is an efficient technique to verify software against its requirements. In this paper, we propose an approach that integrates safety analysis and verification activities to demonstrate how a systematic combination between these approaches can help safety and software engineers to derive the software safety requirements and verify them to recognize software risks. We illustrate the proposed approach by the example of the adaptive cruise control system.

Keywords: STPA · Software safety · SPIN · Safety verification · Modex

1 Introduction

Software has become a crucial part of modern safety-critical systems, and the amount of software in such systems is increasing. An unforeseen behaviour of software may result in catastrophic consequences such as injury or loss of human life, damaged property or environmental disturbances. In the last ten years, the number of accidents and losses related to software flaws has increased. The Toyota Prius and the General Motors airbag are two recent software problems in the automotive domain. Many standards to describe safety engineering were introduced such as Software System Safety Handbook [2] and Functional Safety in Automotive ISO-26262 [3]. Safety engineering, as described in these safety-related standards, is an engineering discipline to identify system hazards and prevent systems from transitioning to unsafe (hazardous) states. Developing safe software for safety-critical systems involves a clear understanding how the software contributes to an accident. Indeed, the accidents with systems are caused by

© Springer International Publishing Switzerland 2015
F. Koornneef and C. van Gulijk (Eds.): SAFECOMP 2015, LNCS 9337, pp. 121–134, 2015.
DOI: 10.1007/978-3-319-24255-2_10

software flaws, software specification errors and uncontrolled interaction between different components which form the system rather than failures of single component [1]. Many safety analysis techniques have been developed, however, they do not adequately address these hazardous types [1]. A recent countermeasure is to advance safety analysis techniques by system and control theory instead of reliability theory. STPA (System-Theoretic Process Analysis) [1] is a modern safety analysis technique built based on the STAMP accident model by Leveson to treat safety as a control problem rather than a component failure problem. STPA has been developed to cope with complex systems to identify potential hazardous behaviours that could lead to accidents. To assure that these behaviours cannot happen, safety verification involves demonstrating whether the software fulfils those safety requirements and will not result in a hazardous state. Formal verification techniques are used to prove the correctness of software and check whether the software satisfies its requirements. Model checking [9] is a well-established formal verification technique to verify whether embedded software of safety-critical systems meets the requirements through exhaustive exploration of the state space of the software.

Problem Statement. Safety is a system level property and, hence, needs to be analysed on the system level. Yet, we also need to verify the software components to ensure the whole system's safety. Therefore, there is a gap between system-level safety constraints and software safety requirements. Ensuring the safe operation of software involves that software must deal with hazardous behaviours which are identified by safety analysis at an early stage. Moreover, software must fully satisfy the corresponding safety requirements which constrain the software from these behaviours that violate the safety of the whole system. STPA has been developed to cope with complex systems to develop detailed safety requirements that prevent the occurrence of the potential hazardous behaviours. However, its subject is the system, not software. Although, verification approaches are used to assert the functional correctness of software, ensuring that might not be enough to ensure the safe operation of software.

Research Objectives. The objective of this research is to fill this gap by investigating the possibility of integrating STPA with model checking to allow safety and software engineers a seamless safety analysis and verification. This, in turn, shall help them to reduce the associated software risks to a low acceptable level.

Contribution. The main contribution of this research is the method to derive software safety requirements at the system level and to verify them at the code level. We provide four major contributions: (1) We develop an algorithm based on STPA to derive the software safety requirements at the system level. (2) We show how to map the output of STPA directly to formal specifications in Linear Temporal Logic (LTL) [4]. (3) We explore how to extract the input model for the SPIN model checker [8] directly from actual code of software. (4) We show how to verify STPA output with SPIN and generate the safety verification report.

2   Background

STPA [1] has been developed by Leveson with the purpose of identifying hazardous scenarios that could lead to accidents and generating detailed safety requirements which must be implemented in the design to prevent the occurrence of these unsafe scenarios in the system. STPA is a top-down process, like FTA (Fault Tree Analysis), but STPA addresses more types of hazards of components and their interactions like design errors, software flaws and component interaction failures. One of the advantages of STPA is that it can be applied at any stage of the system development process. We can also apply STPA like other traditional techniques to an existing system design. STPA is performed by four main steps: (1) Before conducting an STPA analysis, the safety analysts should establish fundamentals of the analysis (e.g. accidents, the associated hazards) and construct the control structure diagram. (2) For each control action in the control diagram, the safety analysts must identify the potentially unsafe control actions of the system that could lead to a hazardous state. A hazardous (unsafe) control action is a control action that violates system safety constraints. (3) Use the identified hazardous control actions to create safety requirements and constraints. (4) Determine how each potentially hazardous control action, identified in step 2, could occur by augmenting the control structure diagram with a process model.

Software model checking is an automatic technique based on a verification model which explore all possible software states in a brute-force manner to prove properties of their execution [9]. The model checking process involves the target software to be formally modelled in the input language of a model checker and specifications (properties) to be formalized in a temporal logic. Many safety-critical software systems are being written in ANSI-C. Therefore, there exist a number of software model checker tools which are used to verify code written in Schlich et al. [10] conducted a comparison and evaluation of existing model checking tools for C code. This comparison showed that the SPIN model checker, a general-purpose model checker, uses an efficient algorithm to reduce the state explosion problem. Moreover, SPIN accepts PROMELA code as input which is similar to C code that can be automatically extracted from C code by using Modex [7]. In this work, we chose the SPIN model checker to integrate with STPA according to the following reasons: (1) SPIN allows fragments of C code to be embedded within the PROMELA model. (2) SPIN supports to verify properties in LTL. (3) SPIN has been proven to be flexible enough for a number of applications (e.g. verifying multi-threaded C programs [11]).

3   Integrated Application of STPA and Model Checking

In this section, we will describe a novel approach that combines the safety-related activities of safety analysis and verification during the development process of safety-critical software. Figure 1 shows an overview of our approach which is divided into three kinds of activities: (1) deriving software safety requirements

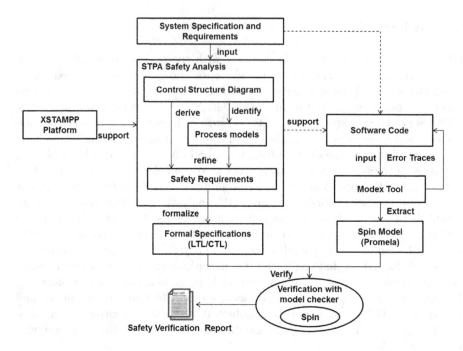

Fig. 1. Overview of the integrated application of STPA and software model checking

using STPA; (2) formalizing of safety requirements and (3) verifying software against its safety requirements at the code level.

The proposed approach can be applied at an early stage of development or on existing software. The initial input of the approach is the system design specification and requirements which include the general software specification. From the system specification, the safety control structure diagram of system must be constructed which includes the main subsystems that interact with software. The software is the controller in the control structure diagram. This diagram will be used to guide the procedure of identifying software safety requirements based on STPA. A result of this step is a list of the potential hazardous scenarios that could lead to the accidents, corresponding software safety constraints and a list of the process models and their variables. The process models describe the states of software (only critical states which are relevant to the safety of the control actions) and their variables describe the software communication, inputs and outputs. The process model variables are important to understand how a hazardous behaviour could occur. Moreover, they also can be used to derive the implementation specification of software along with the safety-related specification. The process model variables in the next step will be used to refine the informal textual safety requirements to be easily translated into a formal specification in LTL. The SPIN model checker is used to check whether the software implementation conforms to the safety requirements which are formalized in LTL. The input model of SPIN is generated directly from the software code by using Modex. If the model does not hold a property, a counterexample will be generated which describes an execution path that the model fails to fulfil a certain requirement. In the following we describe in more detail the three major activities:

Step 1: Deriving Software Safety Requirements at the System Level: The input to this step are the analysis fundamentals which should be identified before performing this step from the system specification such as the system Accidents (AC), the associated Hazards (HA) and the Control Structure Diagram (CSD) (for an example, see Fig. 2). Based on the STPA procedure and an extended approach to STPA [12], we developed an algorithm to identify software safety requirements at the system level. For each software controller in the control structure diagram, its software safety requirements can be derived by performing the following steps:

1.1 Identify all software Control Actions (CA) that can lead to one or more of the defined hazards (HA).
1.2 Evaluate each CA with four general types of hazardous behaviours to identify the Unsafe Control Actions (UCAs): (1) a control action required for safety is not provided, (2) an unsafe action is provided, (3) a potentially safe control action is provided too early, too late or out of sequence and (4) a safe control action is stopped too soon or continued too long.
1.3 Translate the identified UCAs into informal textual Software Safety Requirements (SSR).
1.4 Identify the process model and its variables and include them into the software controller in the control structure diagram to understand how each UCA could occur.
1.5 Identify the combinations of the process model variables for each unsafe control action. Each combination should be evaluated within two contexts (C_i = **Providing CA** or **Not Providing CA**) to determine whether the control action is hazardous in that context or not. A control action CA could be considered as hazardous in context C if only a combination of process variables related to CA lead to a system-level hazard H $\in$ HA.
1.6 Use the results of the step 1.5 to refine and construct the software safety requirements from the context table by using Boolean operators AND and OR for each context.

The output of this step is a list of the corresponding software safety requirements. Each Software Safety Requirement (SSR_{ij}) corresponds to an unsafe control action UCA_{ij} which will be expressed formally as follows, where i is the number of the control action and j is the number of the unsafe control behaviour of a control action (UCA):

Definition 1. *Let* $PMV_{i,j} = \bigcup(\mathcal{P}_{i,1} \ldots \mathcal{P}_{i,n})$ *be a set of the process model variable values which are related to a control action* CA_i *that could lead to the hazard* $H \in HA$ *within the context* $C_1 = \{providing\}$ *or within the context* $C_2 = \{Notproviding\}$ *of* CA_i, *where n is the maximum number of relevant variables and* Ω *is the occurrence of the combination of* $PMV_{i,j}$ *values. Then the* SSR_{ij} *can be expressed formally as follow:*

$$SSR_{i,j} = (\Omega\, PMV_{i,j} \rightarrow CA_i) \vee SSR_{i,j} = (\Omega\, PMV_{i,j} \rightarrow \neg CA_i)$$

This means that the control action CA_i must (or mustn't) be provided in the occurrence Ω of the combination $PMV_{i,j}$ values.

To support the safety analysts in performing this step, we have developed a tool called XSTAMPP [6]. XSTAMPP is an open-source platform designed specifically to support safety engineers in editing the fundamentals of analysis, drawing the control structure diagram, the process model and its variables and documenting the unsafe control actions and the safety requirements.

Step 2: Formalising Software Safety Requirements: Once the corresponding software safety requirements have been identified and expressed by Boolean operators, these requirements can be easily mapped into a formal specification in LTL to be able to verify them by model checking. An LTL formula can be defined over a set of atomic propositions, Boolean operators ($\neg, \vee, \wedge, \leftrightarrow, \rightarrow, true, false$) and temporal operators ($\bigcirc$ next, $\square$ always, $\lozenge$ eventually, $\mathcal{U}$ until, $\mathcal{R}$ release). A safety requirement (property) ensures something bad (hazardous behaviour) never happens during the execution.

Definition 2. *Let SSR_{ij} be a software safety requirement which must always be true for all execution paths of a software. Then an LTL formula φ of SSR_{ij} can be expressed as follows: $\varphi = \square(SSR_{ij}), where\ SSR_{ij} = (PMV_{i,j} \rightarrow (CA_i)) \vee SSR_{ij} = (PMV_{i,j} \rightarrow (\neg CA_i)).$*

This formula means: The occurrence of $PMV_{i,j}$ always implies ($\rightarrow$), that the software must (or mustn't) provide the control action CA_i. Based on the above definitions, the software safety requirements identified by safety analysis activities can be easily translated into LTL. This step can be fully automated by converting Boolean expressions of the hazardous combinations of process model variables into LTL.

Step 3: Software Safety Verification at the Code Level: This step aims at verifying whether the software satisfies the software safety requirements which we derived and specified in LTL. This step is divided into two sub-steps: (1) Extracting the input model of the SPIN model checker from software code and (2) using SPIN to verify the software safety requirements and generating the safety verification report.

Step 3.1: Extracting the Input Model: To verify software with a model checker, the software has to be translated into the input language of the model checker. SPIN involves an input model that is written in PROMELA code which is similar to C code. The PROMELA model can be extracted automatically by using Modex [7]. Modex translates the basic control structures (e.g. IF-ELSE, and control loops) into corresponding PROMELA control structures and inserts the others C statements as embedded C code into the PROMELA model with the primitive $c\_code\{\dots\}$. However, a few errors might be obtained in the generated SPIN model due to the limitations of Modex which should be traced manually (e.g. enumeration data structures).

Step 3.2: Verifying Software Safety Requirements via SPIN: Once the SPIN model has been extracted from software code and safety requirements have been expressed in temporal logic, the verification activities with the SPIN model checker can be performed. This step aims at verifying if the SPIN model of the software conforms to the software safety requirements identified in step 1. SPIN provides a C program which automatically examines all software behaviours to decide if the SPIN model of the software satisfies the given properties. The current version of SPIN supports two ways to verify safety requirements that are written in LTL: (1) specify LTL formulae inline, as part of a verification model and SPIN will convert it in the background into a never claim or (2) convert a LTL formula into a never claim and include it into the verification model. However, use of the inline LTL formulae is restricted by the scope of the LTL variables which must be globally declared. Never claims are used to verify safety properties and express that behaviours should never occur. Never claims accept directly to include the code variables which are expressed in the primitive $c\_expr\{\dots\}$. SPIN supports automatically converting LTL formula into never claims. The activities of this step are fully automated. However, there still is a manual intervention required to trace the defects in the actual source code.

4   Illustrative Example: Adaptive Cruise Control System

We demonstrate our proposed approach by the software controller of the Adaptive Cruise Control (ACC) system. ACC is a well-known automotive system which has strong safety requirements. ACC [17] is an advanced version of the cruise control which allows a vehicle's cruise control autonomously adapt the vehicle's speed to the traffic environment. The operation of an ACC is based on a long range forward-radar sensor which is attached to the front of the vehicle to detect whether there is a vehicle moving in the ACC vehicle's path. When the radar sensor detects a foregoing slow moving vehicle in the path, the ACC system will adapt the speed of ACC vehicle automatically (slow down or accelerate) and control the distance between the ACC vehicle and the target vehicle. If the road is free and the radar sensor detects that the target vehicle is no longer in the path, then the ACC will automatically return back the vehicle speed to its pre-set speed. In the following, we discuss briefly the application of the proposed approach. All materials, safety analysis results, Simulink and SPIN models, and C source code of the ACC software controller are freely available in a Github project[1].

4.1   Deriving Safety Requirements of the ACC Software Controller

Following the algorithm which is described in Sect. 3, step 1, we derived the software safety requirements of the ACC controller. We used the existing ACC specification requirements and design models described in [17] as input to this step. We also used XSTAMPP [6] to document the safety analysis results. We first established the fundamentals of analysis as follows:

---

[1] https://github.com/asimabdulkhaleq/STPA-and-Software-Model-Checking.

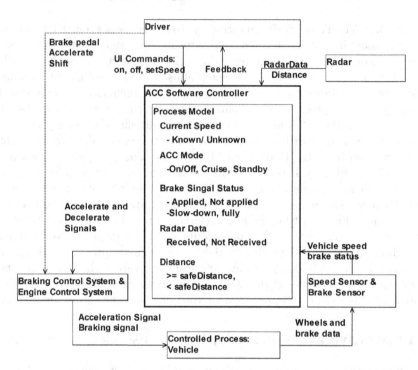

Fig. 2. The control structure diagram and process model variables of ACC controller

System-level Accidents: For example, the accident that the ACC controller software can lead or contribute to is: **AC-1:** *ACC vehicle crashes with front vehicle while ACC status is active.*

System-level Hazards: The related software-hazards which can lead to the accident **AC-1** are:

- **H-1:** *ACC software does not maintain safe distance from nearby vehicle.*
- **H-2:** *An unintended acceleration when the ahead vehicle is too close.*

Control Structure Diagram: The control structure diagram (Fig. 2) shows the main interconnecting components of the ACC system at a high level such as the ACC software controller, the engine control system and the brake control system as actuators, the driver as a human controller and the vehicle as the physical controlled process. The ACC software controller receives the data from the radar sensor and processes the data to determine if a vehicle is present. The ACC software controller will send the information to the engine control system and the brake control system to control the clearance between the ACC vehicle and the target vehicle. Based on this diagram, we identified the unsafe control actions as follows:

Software Control Actions (1.1): The ACC controller has three control actions: *accelerate signal*, *decelerate signal* and *receiving radar data*. Each control action in the control structure diagram should be documented in the unsafe control action table (Table 1) based on the four general hazardous types.

Table 1. Examples of potentially unsafe control actions of the ACC software controller

Control action	Not providing causes hazard	Providing causes hazard	Wrong timing or order causes hazard	Stopped too soon or Applied too long
Accelerate signal	**UCA-1.1:** The ACC Controller does not provide accelerate signal when the target vehicle is no longer in the lane. [**H-1**]	**UCA-1.2:** The ACC controller provides an unintended acceleration signal when distance to the target vehicle is too close. [**H-1**] [**H-2**]	**UCA-1.3:** The ACC controller provides the acceleration signal before a safe distance to the target vehicle is reached. [**H-1**] [**H-2**]	**UCA-1.4:** The ACC controller provides the acceleration signal too long so that it exceeds the desired speed of the vehicle. [**H-2**]

Unsafe Control Actions (1.2): Table 1 shows examples of the potential unsafe control actions of the ACC controller. Each item in Table 1 will be evaluated to check whether it leads to hazardous causes or not. If the item is hazardous, the safety analyst should assign an associated hazard from the system-level hazards (HA). If an item is not hazardous, he/she should write *Not-Hazardous.*

High-level Safety Requirements (1.3): Each unsafe control action in Table 1 will be translated into informal textual safety requirements. Table 2 shows the corresponding safety requirements for the unsafe control actions.

Process Model Variables (1.4): To understand how each unsafe control action identified in Table 1 could occur, we identify the process model variables of the ACC software controller that have an effect on the safety of each control action to identify the unsafe scenarios. Figure 2 shows an example of the critical process model, its variables and values of the ACC software controller. The

Table 2. Examples of corresponding software safety requirements at the system level

Related UCAs	Corresponding safety constraints
UCA-1.1	**SSR1.1**-ACC controller should provide acceleration signal when the target vehicle is no longer in the lane
UCA-1.2	**SSR1.2**-ACC controller should not increase the speed when the distance to the target vehicle is too close
UCA-1.3	**SSR1.3**-ACC controller should not provide the acceleration signal speed before a safe distance is reached
UCA-1.4	**SSR1.4**-ACC controller should not increase the speed beyond the value of the speed set by the driver

ACC controller has several process model variables in which the ACC system can migrate from one state to another such as *current speed, ACC mode, brake single status, front distance and radar data.*

Hazardous Contexts (1.5): After identifying the process model variables, the potential unsafe scenarios of each control action in Table 1 can be identified by examining each combination set of relevant values of the process model variables (context) to determine whether the control action in this context will be hazardous or not. Table 3 shows examples of the context table of providing the three control actions *accelerate signal, decelerate signal and radar data.* The relevant process model variables are *Distance to the lead vehicle (2 values),the ACC mode (off, standby, cruise)* and *current speed of vehicle (2 values).* We identified 22 unsafe scenarios. 13 unsafe scenarios in the context of **providing** the three control actions: *acceleration signal* (6 scenarios), *deceleration signal* (6 scenarios) and *radarData* (1 scenario); 9 unsafe scenarios in the context of **not providing** these three control actions *acceleration signal* (4 scenarios), *deceleration signal* (4 scenarios) and *radarData* (1 scenario).

Refined ACC Software Safety Requirements (1.6): Once each unsafe control action in the different contexts (e.g. providing or not providing) has been evaluated, the potential hazardous scenarios can be identified and mapped into the software safety requirements to prevent the software to transit into these unsafe scenarios. We constructed 22 corresponding safety requirements to the unsafe scenarios of the ACC controller software. For example, as shown in Table 3, an unsafe scenario in the context $C_1 = \{providing\}$ of control action $CA_1 = \{acceleration\ signal\}$ can be expressed as follows: The relevant values of process model variables are: $P_{1,1} = \{distance <= safe\ distance\}$, $P_{1,2} = \{current\ speed >= desired\ speed\}$ and $P_{1,3} = \{ACC\ mode == cruise\}$. The set of combination values of this hazardous scenario can be combined with the logic operator $\land$ as $PMV_{1,1} = (P_{1,1} \land P_{1,2} \land P_{1,3})$. This unsafe scenario simply means **UCA-1.1:** *ACC software controller provides* acceleration signal *while the front distance to target vehicle is shorter than safe distance and the speed of vehicle is larger than the desired speed and ACC in the cruise mode.* The refined software safety requirement (**SSR-1.1**) of this hazardous scenario can be written as follow: $SSR_{1,1} = \Box((\Omega\ PMV_{1,1}) \rightarrow \neg (CA_1))$. That means *the ACC controller must always not provide the acceleration signal when the $PMV_{1,1}$ happens.*

4.2 Formalisation Software Safety Requirements

Based on Definition 2, we map the software safety requirements derived by STPA at the system level into formal specification in LTL. Examples of formal specifications of software safety requirements in LTL are:

$SSR_{1,1} = []$ ((distance <= safe distance && speed >= desired speed && ACCMode ==*cruise*) −> !(accelerationSignal))
$SSR_{1,2} = []$ ((distance >= safe distance && speed <= desired speed && ACCMode ==*cruise*) −> (accelerationSignal))
$SSR_{1,3} = []$ ((distance <= safe distance && speed <= desired speed

Table 3. Examples of the context table of providing the control actions

Control actions	Process model variables			Is it a hazardous control action?
Accelerate	**Distance**	**Current speed**	**ACC mode**	**Providing**
	Distance <= safe distance	speed >= Desired speed	cruise	Yes
	Distance >= safe distance	speed <= Desired speed	cruise	No
	Distance <= safe distance	speed <= Desired speed	cruise	Yes
Decelerate	Distance >= safe distance	doesn't Matter	cruise	Yes

&& ACCMode == $cruise$) $->$!(accelerationSignal))

$SSR_{2,1}$ = [] ((distance <= safe distance && ACCMode == cruise) $->$ (deccelerationSignal))

$SSR_{3,1}$ = [] (ACCMode==$cruise$ $->$ (radarData ==Received))

4.3   Verifying Software Safety Requirements Using SPIN

To execute the verification activities, we built a Simulink model for the ACC. Based on this model, we developed a software program written in ANSI-C which simulates the ACC software controller in the ACC system. Our prototype includes four main components: radar monitoring unit, ACC input configuration, ACC controller and PID controller. The radar monitoring unit processes the speed data of the front vehicle and the ACC software controller will control the current speed of the vehicle based on the radar data. The PID controller calculates an error value of the difference between the actual speed and desired speed. The main method of the C code runs three threads *run_simulator, move_car* to move the host vehicle and control the current speed of the vehicle and *rada_unit_sensor* to monitor the data of the target vehicle which is generated randomly. The program contains 412 lines of C code. To verify our software program, we first generated the PROMELA model by using Modex 2.7. A few errors were in the generated PROMELA Model such as Modex does not include the C library *math.h* into the model. We traced all errors in the generated model to make it work correctly in SPIN. We ran SPIN 6.4.3 using a depth of the search tree of more than 10^4 on a 64 bit Ubuntu 14.04 Linux PC that was equipped with an Intel Core i7-2640M CPU with 2.80 GHz, 8 GB main memory and a hard disk with a capacity 700 GB. The SPIN model succeeded in verifying our software program within *1.38e + 03* s and no further errors were obtained. SPIN consumed *1.1* gigabyte to store *7,642,219* states and performed *13333010* transitions.

To verify the derived safety requirements, we generated automatically the never claims for all LTL formulae by using the SPIN command line option. Next, we included these never claims into the PROMELA model and ran SPIN to verify them one-by-one. Table 4 shows examples of the verification results of the software safety requirements with depth of search, number of different states found in the model, number of transitions performed during depth-first search, total of memory needed for states and total time in second. The results in Table 4 show that the safety requirements SSR 1.1, SSR 1.2 and SSR 2.2 are satisfied while SSR 2.1 is incomplete because not all parts of the model were exercised. SSR 3.1 is refuted and a counterexample is yielded. To analyse the counterexample, we ran SPIN to perform a guided simulation using the trail file on the verification model. An example of SPIN result for this counterexample is shown as follows:

```
spin: trail ends after 5 steps
#processes: 10
5: proc 9 (p_main:1) model:701 (state 4)
5: proc 8 (p_runSimulator:1) model:623 (state 7)
5: proc 7 (p_radarSensorUnit:1) model:604 (state 7)
...
10 processes created
Exit-Status 0
```

The results show that the SSR3.1 fails because the radar unit monitor does not always provide *radarData* to the ACC software controller when ACC is in the cruise mode. This situation will cause an accident if there is a vehicle in the lane and the distance to a forward vehicle is too small. To eliminate this counterexample, we constrained the radar unit by checking the status of the ACC system before providing the data of the target vehicle.

5   Related Work

There exist a number of considerable and interesting works on integrating model checkers with traditional safety analysis approaches such as FTA and FMEA. We will discuss the most related work:

Shariva and Papadopoulos [15] proposed an approach that combines the new Symbolic Model Verifier (NuSMV) model checker [16] with the Hierarchically Performed Hazard Origin and Propagation Studies (HiP-HOPS) safety analysis technique which automatically constructs fault trees and FMEA from a system model. They showed how such a combination between these approaches can help to verify the design of a system at an early stage in the design phase of a safety critical system. They translated the model of Hip-HOPS into an abstract state machine model. Next, they converted manually the abstract state machine model of a brake-wire system into an SMV Model to be verified by NuSMV. It is the closest to our preliminary work [14] in its use of the NuSMV model checker with safety analysis technique. However, its verification is focused on verifying the system requirements based on the high-level abstract model converted from the model Hip-HOPS at the system level. We differentiated our work here from this work by identifying the hazardous behaviours of software control actions at the system level and verifying the software against the corresponding safety requirements which constrain the software from these unsafe behaviours. We are not aware of any other work that integrates STPA safety analysis with a model checker with the purpose of identifying safety requirements of software at the system level and verifying them at the code level.

Table 4. Examples of the verification results of software safety requirements

SSR	#Depth	#States stored	#Transitions	#Time (s)	#Memory usage (GB)	Results
SSR1.1	4964	9584017	16196785	1.5e + 03	1.02	Satisfied
SSR1.2	9999	8851830	15413578	1.4e + 03	0.91	Satisfied
SSR2.1	484	157289	294864	22.7	0.16	Incomplete
SSR3.1	5	2	2	0.2	0.02	Fails

Our earlier work [5] reported a case study of applying STPA to a well-known example of a safety-critical system in the automotive domain: *Adaptive Cruise Control (ACC) system*. This case study was based on an existing case study of applying safety cases to the ACC system with MAN Truck & Bus AG [13]. We also in [14] proposed a safety verification methodology based on STPA safety analysis. We applied STPA to vehicle cruise control software to identify the software safety requirements at the system level. We used NuSMV [16] to verify these requirements based on SMV model constructed manually from software specification. The approach is effective in identifying software safety requirements and verifying them based on an abstract model, but we could not ensure that the SMV model match exactly the software implementation. In this work, we investigated the possibility of verifying the software safety requirements based on the model extracted directly from the source code of software.

6   Conclusions and Future Work

In this paper, we proposed an approach that integrates the modern safety analysis approach STPA with software model checking to enable a safety engineer to verify software based on a verification model extracted automatically from code against the software safety requirements derived at the system level. The proposed approach exploits the advantages of applying STPA to software at the system level to identify potentially unsafe control actions of software and derive the corresponding safety requirements that prevent software to provide unsafe control action. The approach also exploits the benefits of using Modex to extract the verification model directly from actual code and using SPIN to verify the results of STPA based on this model. One of the key benefits of the proposed methodology is that it can be iterated until the satisfactory software code that fulfils software safety requirements is reached. Our approach is a general approach which can be applied to any software of embedded systems; however, we believe that our approach can especially be adapted to use in the ISO 26262-part 6 in support of the automotive software safety requirements section 6-6 and verification of software safety requirements section 6-11. The limitation of the proposed approach is that there are still manual interventions required to be performed by safety analyst, especially in using SPIN and Modex. Therefore, we are exploring the automation of the proposed approach and plan to provide a plug-in tool called *STPA-Verifier* which will be integrated with our extensible platform XSTAMPP as future work to enable safety analyst performing STPA and verifying the STPA results with SPIN. Furthermore, we plan to conduct a case study with realistic software that simulates ACC adaptive control system to investigate the effectiveness of applying the proposed methodology to real safety-critical software.

Acknowledgments. The authors would like to thank Mr. Ebrahim Ameen, Robert Bosch Softtec GmBH and Mr. Hossam Yahia, Group Electronics Expertise Services, Valeo, for their valuable suggestions and comments.

References

1. Leveson, N.G.: Engineering a Safer World: Systems Thinking Applied to Safety. Engineering Systems. MIT Press, Cambridge (2011)
2. NASA-GB- 8719.13: NASA Software Safety Guidebook (2004)
3. ISO26262: Road vehicles - Functional safety. International Standard (2011)
4. Pnueli, A.: The temporal logic of programs. In: 18th Annual Symposium on Foundations of Computer Science, 31 October 1977–2 November 1977, pp. 46–57 (1977)
5. Abdulkhaleq, A., Wagner. S.: Experiences with applying STPA to software-intensive systems in the automotive domain. In: STAMP Conference. MIT (2013)
6. Abdulkhaleq, A., Wagner, S.: XSTAMPP: an eXtensible STAMP platform as tool support for safety engineering. In: STAMP Conference. MIT (2015)
7. Holzmann, G.J., Ruys, T.C.: Effective bug hunting with spin and modex. In: Godefroid, P. (ed.) SPIN 2005. LNCS, vol. 3639, p. 24. Springer, Heidelberg (2005)
8. Holzmann, G.J.: The model checker SPIN. IEEE Trans. Softw. Eng. **23**(5), 279–295 (1997)
9. Baier, C., Katoen, J.P.: Principles of Model Checking (Representation and Mind Series). The MIT Press, Cambridge (2008)
10. Schlich, B., Kowalewski, S.: Model checking C source code for embedded systems. Int. J. Softw. Tools Technol. Transf. **11**(3), 187–202 (2009)
11. Zaks, A., Joshi, R.: Verifying multi-threaded C programs with SPIN. In: Havelund, K., Majumdar, R. (eds.) SPIN 2008. LNCS, vol. 5156, pp. 325–342. Springer, Heidelberg (2008)
12. Thomas, J.: Extending and Automating a Systems-Theoretic Hazard Analysis for Requirements Generation and Analysis. Massachusetts Institute of Technology, Cambridge (2013)
13. Wagner, S., Schätz, B., Puchner, S., Kock, P.: A case study on safety cases in the automotive domain: modules, patterns, and models. In: Proceedings of IEEE 21st International Symposium on Software Reliability Engineering, pp. 269–278 (2010)
14. Abdulkhaleq, A., Wagner, S.: A software safety verification method based on system-theoretic process analysis. In: Bondavalli, A., Ceccarelli, A., Ortmeier, F. (eds.) SAFECOMP 2014. LNCS, vol. 8696, pp. 401–412. Springer, Heidelberg (2014)
15. Sharvia, S., Papadopoulos, Y.: Integrating model checking with HiP-HOPS in model-based safety analysis. Reliab. Eng. Syst. Saf. **135**, 64–80 (2015)
16. Cimatti, A., Clarke, E., Giunchiglia, F., Roveri, M.: NUSMV: a new symbolic model checker. Int. J. Softw. Tools Technol. Transfer **2**(4), 410–425 (2000)
17. SAE: Society of Automotive Engineering, Adaptive Cruise Control Operating Characteristics and User Interface, SAE J2399 (2003)

Back-to-Back Fault Injection Testing
in Model-Based Development

Peter Folkesson[1(✉)], Fatemeh Ayatolahi[2], Behrooz Sangchoolie[2],
Jonny Vinter[1], Mafijul Islam[3], and Johan Karlsson[2]

[1] SP Technical Research Institute of Sweden, Boras, Sweden
{peter.folkesson,jonny.vinter}@sp.se
[2] Department of Computer Science & Engineering,
Chalmers University of Technology, Gothenburg, Sweden
{fatemeh.ayatolahi,behrooz.sangchoolie,
johan}@chalmers.se
[3] Advanced Technology and Research,
Volvo Group Trucks Technology, Volvo AB, Gothenburg, Sweden
mafijul.islam@volvo.com

Abstract. Today, embedded systems across industrial domains (e.g., avionics, automotive) are representatives of software-intensive systems with increasing reliance on software and growing complexity. It has become critically important to verify software in a time, resource and cost effective manner. Furthermore, industrial domains are striving to comply with the requirements of relevant safety standards. This paper proposes a novel workflow along with tool support to evaluate robustness of software in model-based development environment, assuming different abstraction levels of representing software. We then show the effectiveness of our technique, on a brake-by-wire application, by performing back-to-back fault injection testing between two different abstraction levels using MODIFI for the Simulink model and GOOFI-2 for the generated code running on the target microcontroller. Our proposed method and tool support facilitates not only verifying software during early phases of the development lifecycle but also fulfilling back-to-back testing requirements of ISO 26262 [1] when using model-based development.

Keywords: Fault-injection · Back-to-back testing · Model-based development · Embedded systems · Functional safety · Soft errors

1 Introduction

Contemporary and emerging embedded systems across industrial domains are representative of software-intensive systems. With increasing reliance on software to realize functionalities and growing complexity of electrical and/or electronic (E/E) systems, it has become more important than ever before to develop novel techniques to design, implement and verify software in a time, resource and cost effective manner. At the same time, one of the key challenges is to comply with the safety requirements in the context of the E/E systems because safety is a first-order requirement in a number of industrial domains, for example, automotive and avionics that develop safety-related systems.

© Springer International Publishing Switzerland 2015
F. Koornneef and C. van Gulijk (Eds.): SAFECOMP 2015, LNCS 9337, pp. 135–148, 2015.
DOI: 10.1007/978-3-319-24255-2_11

In response to the challenges, safety standards have been developed for all industrial domains to specify requirements and processes that shall be applied during the development of safety-related systems. Consequently, industries are constantly striving for complying with the requirements of the relevant safety standards. The automotive industry is no exception and appropriately, ISO 26262 [1], a functional safety standard, has been introduced for road vehicles. The standard provides requirements on an automotive safety lifecycle of the E/E systems within road vehicles. Particularly, Part 6 (product development at the software level) of the ISO 26262 specifies requirements and methods that shall be applied to demonstrate that software achieve robustness and confidence in the absence of unintended functionality [2]. Accordingly, fault injection testing is stated as a highly recommended method for unit testing and integration testing of software [2]. This paper proposes a novel workflow along with tool support to evaluate robustness of software by performing fault injection testing, assuming different abstraction levels of software representation.

Apart from the push from the safety standards, model-based development is be-coming increasingly popular while developing safety-related software. Such development paradigm, among other benefits, facilitates verifying software as early as possible in the development lifecycle. In model-based development, requirements are translated into executable models (e.g., Simulink models) used for generating production code (e.g., object code). The verification activities then can be performed both at the model level during early development phases and at the generated code level at the later phases. Finally, back-to-back comparison can potentially be performed to assess whether two different representations (executable model and generated object code) of the same application are equivalent. In this regard, we propose a model-based workflow and evaluate the effectiveness of back-to-back testing by performing fault injection testing between the two different abstraction levels.

In this paper, we propose a workflow for fault injection based back-to-back testing to evaluate robustness of software in a model-based development environment. We assess the effectiveness of our workflow experimentally by performing back-to-back fault injection testing at two different abstraction levels – Simulink model representation of software and the generated code running on target hardware. We apply our technique to a brake-by-wire (BBW) application use case from automotive domain and use two tools to perform fault injection testing – MODIFI on a Simulink model of the BBW application and GOOFI-2 for the generated code running on the target microcontroller.

The experimental results support our claim that the proposed method and tool support facilitate not only verifying dependability requirements for software during early phases of the development lifecycle but also fulfilling the back-to-back testing requirements of ISO 26262 when developing safety-related software using model-based development.

The remainder of this paper is organized as follows. In Sect. 2, we describe the background and related work to model-based design and different fault injection techniques. Section 3 describes the proposed workflow for back-to-back fault injection testing in model-based development. The experimental setup is explained in Sect. 4 including tool descriptions, use case, and fault model. The results of the back-to-back comparison are studied in Sect. 5. Finally, we provide conclusions in Sect. 6.

2 Related Work

Model-based design using tools such as Simulink [3] and TargetLink [4] is increasingly used for the development of safety-related software for avionics and automotive applications. Reference workflows for model-based development of safety-related software are described in some studies [5–7]. Figure 1 shows an overview of such a workflow. Here, requirements are translated into an executable model, which is refined into models that are used for generating production code, e.g. using tools such as Embedded Coder [8] or TargetLink. An advantage of model-based testing is that verification activities can be performed in early phases of the development, before the actual physical system or prototype is available, and that there is no need to handle the requirements separately since they can be included directly in the model. In later phases, a back-to-back comparison [9] is used to test that the behaviour of the gen-erated object code and the model is equivalent. The Simulink model and a system executing the generated object code are tested with the same inputs, and the generated outputs are compared to check that the two versions behave in a similar way.

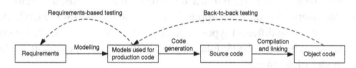

Fig. 1. A general workflow for model-based development of safety-related software

Fault injection is a way to accelerate the occurrences of faults for measuring the dependability and thoroughly testing the fault tolerance mechanisms of a system [10]. It is a highly recommended assessment method in the ISO 26262 standard [1]. Fault injection can be performed at different abstraction levels for application at different stages of the design cycle. In early stages, model level fault injection (MLFI) tech-niques are suitable while hardware level fault injection (HLFI) can be used later when the actual physical system or prototype is available.

In MLFI, faults are injected in hardware-, software- or system models. Faults can be injected in hardware models, e.g. VHDL specifications [11, 12], at a development phase when no physical prototype is available. Fault injection in hardware models is usually denoted as simulation-based fault injection. Faults may also be injected into either software models, where they may, for example, result in data errors, or system models where they can emulate faulty sensors, actuators or sub systems etc. [13, 14]. The FISCADE tool [13] is a fault injection plugin to the SCADE [15] simulator for developing code for avionic and automotive systems which could be applied in the same context as the MODIFI tool [14] used in this study. A tool chain resembling the workflow presented in this paper is the Honeywell Integrated Lifecycle Tools & Environment (HiLiTE) [16] which focus on testing rather than fault injection. In addition to generating tests to be executed on flight code, HiLiTE has been applied by control engineers for detecting and removing design defects during early design phases. The HiLiTE tool chain has been qualified according to the avionic standard RTCA

DO-178B [17] and shown to be a very cost effective approach for verifying avionic system software developed using MATLAB Simulink models.

In HLFI, faults are injected into actual physical systems or prototypes. The faults are injected using some additional hardware or software (or both). Examples of techniques using additional hardware include pin-level fault injection [18, 19], radiation-based fault injection [20], and injection of faults using built-in debug or test logic of circuits [21, 22]. Using additional software to inject faults is often referred to as software-implemented fault injection (SWIFI) [23, 24].

A back-to-back comparison was performed in a previous study using MLFI and HLFI showing that effects from data errors are similar if experiments leading to exceptions are excluded [25].

3 Workflow for Back-to-Back Fault Injection Testing in Model-Based Development

In this section, we describe a workflow for testing fault handling with respect to hardware faults affecting the system under test (SUT) in model-based development and present how the workflow may be applied in the context of ISO 26262. Activated hardware faults can cause different types of errors, such as data errors, timing errors and control flow errors, which can be simulated directly in an implementation model (e.g. a behavioural model of software).

Figure 2 shows a conceptual view of fault injection testing in model-based development. The *implementation model* can be a model of software, hardware or system. *Test cases* (fault injection experiments) are generated for the implementation model and the real target system (*SUT*) while the *test case specification* defines the input values (stimulus) to be used for each experiment. *Model level fault injection (MLFI)* is performed by the function developer (or equivalent role) using an MLFI tool capable of inserting faults in the implementation model during execution. The aim is to exercise and evaluate fault handling mechanisms in the model and in an iterative manner find dependability flaws, which can be corrected. Consequently, new tests can be carried out using an improved implementation model. This fulfils the ISO 26262 objective of demonstrating that software achieves robustness; and evaluating the effectiveness of the error detection and handling mechanisms (see Clause 9.4.3 in Part 6 of ISO 26262). *Requirements* are used by the tool to have a guideline for pass/fail. Each fault injection experiment is compared with a golden run (fault-free run) to reveal erroneous behavior and the safety requirements are used to reveal safety violations.

The function model verifier (or equivalent role) then generates code from the implementation model (Simulink or equivalent) and uses *hardware level fault injection (HLFI)* to perform fault injection experiments on the SUT with the same workload, but with a subset of the faultload. Then the *back-to-back fault injection results (B2B FI results)* from MLFI and HLFI are compared to check that they are equivalent (e.g., see Clause 10.4.3 in Part 6 of ISO 26262). The results of the fault injection tests and back-to-back comparison may then provide input to the work product "9.5.3 Software verification report" of ISO 26262 Part 6.

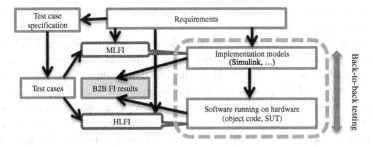

Fig. 2. Back-to-back (B2B) fault injection testing at model level and hardware level

Clause 9.4.6 in Part 6 of ISO 26262 [2] states that the test environment for software unit testing shall correspond to the target environment. For model-based development, testing can be performed on a model but the tests must be followed by a back-to-back comparison between the model and the object code to ensure that the behaviour of the model and the generated code is equivalent with respect to the test objectives. For fault injection testing in model-based development, this means that model level fault injection (e.g. on a Simulink model) needs to be followed by fault injection testing on the generated code at the hardware level.

4   Experimental Setup

We define a fault injection *experiment* to be the injection of one fault and the monitoring of its impact on the program. A fault injection *campaign* is a set of fault injection experiments using the same fault model on a given workload. And a *workload* is a program running with a given input. See Sect. 4.3 for a description of the *faultload* used in our experiments.

4.1   Tools

MODIFI [14] is an MLFI tool for dependability assessment of software developed as Simulink models. Using this tool, non-functional properties such as error detection coverage of fault tolerance mechanisms can be tested using Simulink models complementing HLFI tests on the target system. This method makes it possible to perform functional as well as non-functional testing in early phases of the development within the same environment used for developing the software.

MODIFI injects faults by adding separate blocks modelling the faults between the connected blocks of the model and supports a wide range of fault models and can easily be extended with new fault models. In this study, fault models for single bit-flip errors are used. The single bit-flip fault model is commonly used to emulate the effects of transient hardware faults. MODIFI also supports fault models for sensors, implemented based on the failure modes specified in Annex D in Part 5 of the ISO 26262 standard. Although the standard does not provide a generic fault model for sensors, it lists typical failure modes for sensors that should be investigated when diagnostic coverage is evaluated: out-of-range, stuck in range, offsets, and oscillations. In addition, MODIFI supports stuck-at and gain faults.

We use the GOOFI-2 (Generic Object-Oriented Fault Injection) tool [21] to conduct HLFI experiments. GOOFI-2 defines faults as time-location pairs according to a fault-free execution of a workload. Here the location is one of the target locations shown in Table 1 and the time is an instruction inside the execution trace. The time granularity is based on the execution of machine instructions, i.e. errors are only injected between the executions of two machine instructions. In addition, we employ Barbosa et al.'s *inject-on-read* technique [26] to only target live registers and memory words from the target locations. This reduces experiments that would not have an observable impact on the program. Note that the authors do not make any presumptions about the type of errors represented by the ones injected using this technique. Using the inject-on-read technique, faults are only injected in a target location just before the location is read by an instruction.

Table 1. GOOFI-2 fault injection locations

Instruction Set Architecture Registers (ISA registers)			Memory Segments
General purpose registers			Stack
Floating point registers			Data
Program counter register			Sdata
Miscellaneous registers	Condition Register		Bss
	Link Register		Sbss
	Integer Exception Register		

Figure 3 shows an overview of the two tools. MODIFI presented on the left and GOOFI-2 on the right. MODIFI's GUI is implemented using Java, and the fault injection engine is developed as MATLAB m-code. Campaign configurations and results from fault injection experiments are stored in an SQL database designed for storing generic fault injection data (i.e., not tailor-made specifically for MODIFI). A separate analysis tool retrieves desired results from the database and presents them in various formats. GOOFI-2 uses a Nexus [27] port to inject faults into the instruction set architecture registers and memory words of a PowerPC-based microcontroller from Freescale (MPC565). Nexus is a standard on-chip debug interface, which offers access to processor's resources. Experiments are controlled by GOOFI-2 using the winIDEA development environment [28] in conjunction with the iC3000 debugger [29]. GOOFI-2 also stores the acquired data of each experiment into an SQL database, which can later on be used to classify the outcome of the experiments.

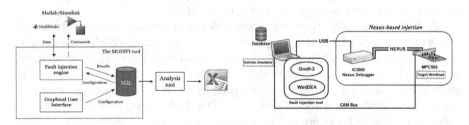

Fig. 3. Overview of the tools: *Left*: MODIFI, *Right:* Goofi

4.2   Brake-By-Wire (BBW) Use Case

A four-wheel brake-by-wire (BBW) application is used for our fault injection based B2B testing. Such a BBW system can be developed using five ECUs (Electronic Control Units) connected to a bus. Each wheel has one corresponding ECU, and the central brake controller is located on the brake pedal ECU. The system has the following interfaces: brake pedal, for driver input of requested brake torque; vehicle speed sensor, for measuring longitudinal speed of the vehicle; wheel speed sensors, for measuring wheel rotation; and brake actuators, for controlling the brake torque of each wheel. The overall functionalities of the BBW application are as follows:

- The brake pedal, connected to the central ECU, provides driver input for the required brake torque. The brake torque calculator computes the driver required torque and sends the value to the global brake controller function.
- The global brake controller then decides the requested torque on each wheel. Each of the requested brake torque values for the individual wheels is sent, together with the current measured vehicle speed, and wheel rotation to the wheel ECUs.
- Based on the torque request received, current vehicle speed and wheel rotation, the local brake-function decides appropriate braking force to apply to the wheel.

The structural decomposition of the BBW in line with ISO 26262 [1] is depicted in Fig. 4. Different software components (SWCs) perform different functionalities to fulfil certain functional safety requirements. For example, "Global Brake Controller" (software) is allocated to "Brake Pedal ECU" (system) and calculates the requested brake torque for each wheel. It takes the driver requested brake force as input and distributes the requested brake force as output to each wheel. As a result, any failure at the software level ("Brake Control") may propagate to the system level (e.g., "Rear Right Wheel ECU"). Eventually, this may cause violation of functional safety requirements (e.g., the determined brake force shall be distributed proportionally across the wheel brakes that are under direct control of the item) and thus violation of safety goals.

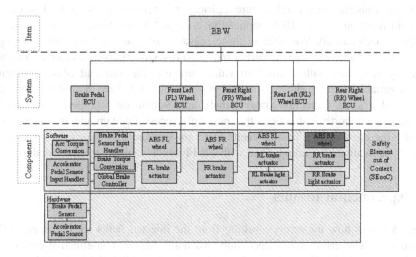

Fig. 4. Structural decomposition of the BBW in line with ISO 26262.

In our study, we use a Simulink model of the mentioned BBW application for fault injection experiments using MODIFI and one ECU (running the ABS RR wheel software) for fault injection experiments using GOOFI-2. The C code is generated from the Simulink model and compiled for execution on an ECU, in our case, an MPC565 microcontroller.

4.3   Fault Model and Fault Locations

In this paper, bit-flip errors are injected using the well-established single bit-flip model, which has been studied in the literature for decades. The single bit-flip model has been a valid engineering approximation to mimic errors that originate from both transistor-level faults and direct hits into instruction set architecture registers and memory segments. Ideally, the fault model to adopt for this evaluation should account for single and multiple bit errors. However, for simplifying the comparison between the model level and hardware level fault injection results, we only focused on single bit-flip errors. Moreover, in an earlier study [30], we concluded that it is unlikely that double-bit errors (a variation of multiple bit flips) would expose weaknesses that are not revealed by single-bit errors.

The *ABS_RR_Wheel* block of the BBW model (see Sect. 4.2) was targeted in three separate fault injection campaigns using MODIFI. All data locations in the block accessible for bit-flip faults were targeted for fault injection. This corresponds to sixteen 64-bit data values and one 8-bit value, resulting in 1032 possible locations. The *ABS_RR_Wheel* block was also equipped with a plausibility check mechanism combined with a substitute value mechanism. Here faults are injected in seventeen 64-bit values and one 8-bit value resulting in 1096 fault locations. Faults were injected during one iteration of the control loop corresponding to two time steps in the implementation model. Since faults were injected in both time steps, the corresponding number of faults injected in each campaign was 2064 and 2192, respectively.

In GOOFI-2, we run the code on the target microcontroller and inject bit-flip errors in all bits of instruction set architecture registers and memory segments used by one of the main functions of the BBW application; *ABS_RR_Wheel* (with and without error handling mechanisms). We refer to these registers and memory segments as *target locations* (see Table 1). Here the data and sdata segments contain variables that are explicitly initialized with a non-zero value, whereas the bss and sbss segments contain variables that are either initialized to zero or not initialized at all. Moreover, the sbss and sdata segments contain small data, which are data items that can be accessed using shorter instructions that may only access a certain address range. Note that, for the back-to-back testing, faults were not injected into the code segment of memory to facilitate the comparison with MLFI which cannot access the code.

5   Experimental Results

Figure 5 shows how the errors resulting from the injected faults are classified in the experiments. The errors are divided into two main classes, non-effective errors and effective errors. Non-effective errors are errors which are either latent (i.e., the output produced by the system is correct and no error detection mechanism has been triggered, but differences between the fault injected and fault free system states can be observed at the end of the experiment) or overwritten (i.e., no difference between the fault injected and fault free system states can be observed at the end of the experiment) while effective errors are errors which are either detected by an error detection mechanism or non-covered, i.e., causing silent data corruptions (SDC). The detected errors are further classified as errors detected by hardware error detection mechanisms (DHW) (e.g., CPU exceptions), software error detection mechanisms (DSW) (e.g., plausibility checks) and timeouts.

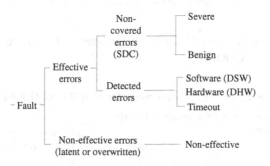

Fig. 5. Error/Outcome classification

The BBW model contains eleven output signals: *BrakeTorqueRR, BrakeTorqueRL, BrakeTorqueFR, BrakeTorqueFL, VehSpdEst, DriverReqTorque, WheelRotationRR, WheelRotationRL, WheelRotationFR, WheelRotationFL, VehSpdReal*. A non-covered error is produced when at least one of the values of these outputs is different from the fault free output during the observed time interval. The non-covered errors are further classified according to how severely they affect the system behaviour. The output signal *VehSpdEst*, which denotes the estimated speed of the vehicle, is used for classifying the severity. Non-covered errors are classified as severe when the *VehSpdEst* signal has a difference of more than ±10 km/h from the fault free value anytime during the observed time interval, while the errors are classified as benign when any of the observed signals differ from the fault free values, but the *VehSpdEst* signal is within ±10 km/h from the fault free value. Here the choice of ±10 km/h is only for the sake of performing the back-to-back fault injection testing, and in reality, this number should be selected from the safety requirements of the system under test.

5.1   Results of the Back-to-Back Comparison

The observed simulation time for the fault injection experiments on the BBW model is 30 s, corresponding to 3000 control loop iterations. Figure 6 shows the *VehSpdEst* signal (estimated vehicle speed) during the observed time interval in the fault free scenario. The vehicle is accelerated to a speed of ~75 km/h and at approximately 19.5 s of simulated time the braking of the vehicle starts. Faults were injected during iteration 2014 (corresponding to the interval between 20.125 and 20.13 s) as indicated by the vertical line in the figure.

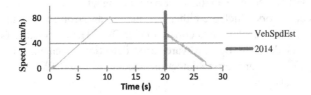

Fig. 6. Fault free *VehSpdEst* values and chosen fault injection time (iteration)

Table 2 shows the number of bit-flip faults injected and the outcome classifications for both MODIFI and GOOFI-2.

Table 2. Outcome classifications for MODIFI and GOOFI-2

Fault injection level	Campaign (workflow step)	Faults	Non-effective	Effective						Fault injection effort (time)
				SDC		Detected				
				Severe	Benign	DSW	DHW	Timeout		
MLFI (MODIFI)	RR (1)	2064	1635 79.2 %	**42** **2.0 %**	387 18.8 %	0 0 %	0 0 %	0 0 %		10 s/fault
	RR_EHM (2)	2192	1701 77.6 %	**14** **0.6 %**	388 17.7 %	89 4.1 %	0 0 %	0 0 %		10 s/fault
HLFI (GOOFI-2)	RR_EHM (3)	9731	4554 46.8 %	**7** **0.1 %**	551 5.7 %	99 1 %	4369 44.9 %	151 1.6 %		30 s/fault
HLFI (GOOFI-2)	*RR*	*8700*	*4070 46.8 %*	*23* *0.3 %*	*527 6.1 %*	*0 0 %*	*3960 45.5 %*	*120 1.4 %*		*30 s/fault*

Step 1: We perform experiments on *ABS_RR_Wheel* block at model level using MODIFI (see *RR* campaign in Table 2). This set of experiments helps us identify *sensitive locations* of the application that cause severe failures. An analysis of the target locations for the severe failures shows that all 42 failures originated from errors in the requested or calculated torque signals. Since the values of these signals are between 0.0 and 1000.0 in the simulations and represented as 64-bit (IEEE 754) floating point numbers, bit-flip faults injected into the exponential bits and most significant bits of the mantissa may result in large numbers causing a peak in the calculated torque value, which is the output of the *ABS_RR_Wheel* block. Consequently, the estimated velocity is affected more than 10 km/h for 6 iterations (2019 to 2024). Therefore, we improve the model by adding a plausibility check on the calculated torque to avoid unacceptably large numbers.

Figure 7 shows the *ABS_RR_Wheel* block of the BBW model which is extended with a plausibility check error detection mechanism, detecting values outside the range of 0.0–2000.0 on the calculated torque, combined with a value substitution mechanism setting the output to 0.0 and 2000.0, respectively upon detection. The error handling mechanism is implemented using a Simulink Saturation function block in the model.

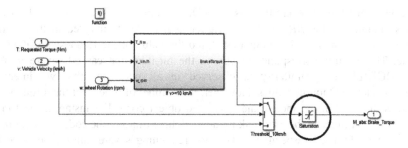

Fig. 7. *ABS_RR_Wheel* block of BBW model with error handling mechanism implemented as a saturation function block added on the output (encircled)

Step 2: We performed a new set of experiments using MODIFI on the *ABS_RR_Wheel* block equipped with the Saturation function block (Campaign *RR_EHM* in Table 2). For these experiments, the plausibility check detected 89 errors (which are transformed to a benign outcome by the value substitution mechanism). The results from these experiments suggest an improvement when using the proposed error handling mechanism, as the number of severe failures is reduced from 42 to 14. This process of model level redesign and testing can be continued iteratively until the system requirements are fulfilled.

Step 3: We performed back-to-back fault injection testing by executing the program on the MPC565 microcontroller using GOOFI-2. This way, we can compare the results obtained by MODIFI with the ones generated by GOOFI-2 to check that identical results are obtained for identical faults. GOOFI-2 injected faults during execution of the object code for the *ABS_RR_Wheel* block including code for the plausibility check and the saturation block shown in Fig. 7. Note that the injected faults were selected from the complete faultload available for GOOFI-2 (except the code segment, see Sect. 4.3) to investigate the additional results obtainable at hardware level. In order to perform back-to-back testing according to the proposed workflow, a subset corresponding to the faultload available for MODIFI should be selected. We have manually identified the faults causing severe failures for this comparison but did not derive the complete subset due to the size and complexity of the generated object code. Instead we suggest implementing an automatic tool for this process.

The results show that 99 errors are detected by the plausibility check for GOOFI-2 compared to 89 errors for MODIFI (see *RR_EHM* campaign in Table 2). Seven severe failures were obtained for GOOFI-2 compared to 14 for MODIFI. The severe failures are the results of faults injected in the output of the saturation block and the equivalent object code.

To verify the effectiveness of our approach, we also performed back-to-back fault injection testing by executing the original unmodified code for the *ABS_RR_Wheel* block on the MPC565 microcontroller using GOOFI-2 (results in italics in Table 2). The results show that the number of severe failures obtained is reduced from 23 to 7 for GOOFI-2 when the error handling mechanism is applied compared to a corresponding reduction from 42 to 14 severe failures for MODIFI. For GOOFI-2, 21 of the 23 severe failures obtained in the *RR* campaign originated from faults injected in the floating point registers or memory locations that stored the value of the Requested/Calculated Torque. These faults correspond directly to the bit-flips that caused severe failures using MODIFI. This similarity is observed in all occasions that we inject in requested/calculated torque values. However, the number of times that the torque value is read is different in the model and generated object code. For instance, the torque value is read six times in the Simulink model and three times in the code resulting in 42 and 21 severe failures, respectively. The two remaining severe failures obtained for GOOFI-2 originated from errors injected in the program counter.

In addition to faults in the program counter, there are other faults that are only injected when using GOOFI-2. Examples of these faults are registers and memory locations holding an address to somewhere in the memory. E.g, as shown in Table 2, DHW and Timeout outcomes are 0 for MODIFI. Since the greater part of the DHWs and Timeouts are the results of errors in address values, e.g., more than 80 % of the DHWs and 100 % of Timeouts are originated from errors in the program counter register, link register, or general purpose registers that store addresses. These outcomes are not measured in MODIFI given that there is no hardware exception at model level and we do not have address values as target locations.

In brief, designing error handling mechanisms based on MODIFI results would cover many of the severe failures whenever the failure is originated from errors in signal values, however, there are also target locations which are not accessible or considered in MODIFI, which should be taken into account by performing fault injection experiments using GOOFI-2. However, being able to improve the model in a way that the number of severe failures is reduced (due to errors in signals) before the actual hardware is available to do the testing is of great benefit, while back-to-back testing is needed to verify the model level design at the hardware level and further improve the design. It is worth mentioning that we also performed campaigns on different time stamps (iterations 1957, 1984, 2014, 2040) to examine the dependency of the results on the time of fault injection. We observe that the outcome distribution is very similar and specifically the number of severe failures is independent of time (23 and 42 severe failures were obtained for all iterations for GOOFI-2 and MODIFI, respectively).

6   Conclusions and Future Work

We have proposed a back-to-back fault injection testing workflow for model-based development. The workflow can be applied in the context of ISO 26262 and provides a guideline for performing back-to-back testing using fault injection on different levels of abstraction. The effectiveness of the proposed workflow is assessed experimentally by using the MODIFI tool on a Simulink model of a BBW application and the GOOFI-2 tool for the generated code running on a target microcontroller to perform model level- and hardware level fault injection respectively.

Although we only performed fault injection experiments using a limited workload, our experimental results indicate that MODIFI may be used to identify most of the severe failures in an early stage of the development. Therefore, it should be possible to improve the robustness of the application by using error handling mechanisms implemented at the model level before the physical system or prototype is available.

We used GOOFI-2 to perform hardware level fault injection to verify model level behavior and proposed error handling according to the workflow. Although, we did not derive the complete subset of hardware level faults corresponding to model level faults due to the complexity of the generated object code, the results indicate that the outcome is the same when using identical fault sets at the model and hardware levels.

These results support our claim that the proposed method and tool support facilitate not only verifying dependability requirements for software during early phases of the development lifecycle but also fulfilling the back-to-back testing requirements of ISO 26262 when developing safety-related software using model-based development.

As part of our future work, we plan to improve the suggested workflow and analyse it further using additional fault injection tools and workloads.

Acknowledgements. We would like to thank Daniel Skarin for valuable input to the proposed workflow and for his work with the implementation of the BBW application for GOOFI-2. We would also like to thank Fredrik Bernin and Johan Haraldsson from Volvo AB for their support with the BBW application model and code generation. This work was partly funded by the ARTEMIS Joint Undertaking research project VeTeSS under grant agreement no. 295311 and the national research project BeSafe funded by Vinnova (Swedish Governmental Agency for Innovation Systems) within the Vehicle Development Program (Diary number: 2010-02114).

References

1. ISO 26262:2011, Road vehicles — Functional safety
2. ISO 26262-6:2011, Road vehicles — Functional safety — Part 6: Product development at the software level
3. The Mathworks, Inc. http://www.mathworks.se/products/simulink/. Accessed March 2015
4. dSPACE. http://www.dspace.com/en/pub/home/products/sw/pcgs/targetli.cfm. Accessed March 2015
5. Conrad, M.: Testing-based translation validation of generated code in the context of IEC 61508. Formal Methods Syst. Des. **35**(3), 389–401 (2009)
6. Conrad, M.: Verification and Validation According to ISO 26262: A Workflow to Facilitate the Development of High-Integrity Software (2012)
7. Beine, M.: A model-based reference workflow for the development of safety-critical software. In: Embedded Real Time Software and Systems (2010)
8. The Mathworks, Inc. http://www.mathworks.se/products/embedded-coder/. Accessed March 2015
9. Vouk, M.A.: Back-to-back testing. Inf. Softw. Technol. **32**(1), 34–45 (1990)
10. Iyer, R.K.: Experimental evaluation. In: Special Issue of Proceedings Twenty-Fifth International Symposium on Fault-Tolerant Computing (1995)
11. Jenn, E., Arlat, J., Rimen, M., Ohlsson, J., Karlsson, J.: Fault injection into VHDL models: the MEFISTO tool. In: Proceedings of the 24th International Symposium on Fault Tolerant Computing, pp. 66–75 (1994)
12. Certitude Functional Qualification Tool from Synopsys. https://www.synopsys.com/TOOLS/VERIFICATION/FUNCTIONALVERIFICATION/Pages/certitude-ds.aspx. Accessed March 2015

13. Vinter, J., Bromander, L., Raistrick, P., Edler, H.: FISCADE - a fault injection tool for SCADE models. In: Proceedings of the 3rd IET Conference on Automotive Electronics, pp. 1–9 (2007)

14. Svenningsson, R., Vinter, J., Eriksson, H., Törngren, M.: MODIFI: a MODel-implemented fault injection tool. In: Schoitsch, E. (ed.) SAFECOMP 2010. LNCS, vol. 6351, pp. 210–222. Springer, Heidelberg (2010)

15. Esterel Technologies. http://www.estereltechnologies.com/products/scade-suite/. Accessed June 2015

16. Bhatt, D., Madl, G., Oglesby, D., Schloegl, K.: Towards scalable verification of commercial avionics software. In: AIAA Infotech@Aerospace, April 2010

17. RTCA: DO-178B: Software Considerations in Airborne Systems and Equipment Certification. Radio Technical Commission for Aeronautics, RTCA Inc., Washington, D.C. (1992)

18. Madeira, H., Rela, M.Z., Moreira, F., Silva, J.G.: RIFLE: a general purpose pin-level fault injector. In: Proceedings of the 1st European Dependable Computing Conference, pp. 199–216 (1994)

19. Arlat, J., Crouzet, Y., Karlsson, J., Folkesson, P., Fuchs, E., Leber, G.: Comparison of physical and software implemented fault injection techniques. IEEE Trans. Comput. **52**(8), 115–1133 (2003)

20. Karlsson, J., Liden, P., Dahlgren, P., Johansson, R., Gunneflo, U.: Using heavy-ion radiation to validate fault-handling mechanisms. IEEE Micro **14**(1), 8–23 (1994)

21. Skarin, D., Barbosa, R., Karlsson, J.: GOOFI-2: a tool for experimental dependability assessment. In: 40th International Conference on Dependable Systems and Networks (2010)

22. Rebaudengo, M., Reorda, M.: Evaluating the fault tolerance capabilities of embedded systems via BDM. In: Proceedings of the 17th IEEE VLSI Test Symposium, pp. 452–457 (1999)

23. Costa, D., Madeira, H., Carreira, J., Silva, J.: Xception: software fault injection and monitoring in processor functional units. In: Benso, A., Prinetto, P. (eds.) Fault Injection Techniques and Tools for Embedded Systems Reliability Evaluation. Frontiers in Electronic Testing, vol. 23, pp. 125–139 (2003)

24. Han, S., Shin, K.G., Rosenberg, H.A.: DOCTOR: an integrated software fault injection environment for distributed real-time systems. In: Proceedings of 1995 IEEE International Computer Performance and Dependability Symposium, pp. 204–213 (1995)

25. Svenningsson, R., Eriksson, H., Vinter, J., Törngren, M.: Model-implemented fault injection for hardware fault simulation. Paper presented at MoDeVVa 2010, Oslo, Norway, 3 October 2010

26. Barbosa, R., Vinter, J., Folkesson, P., Karlsson, J.M.: Assembly-level pre-injection analysis for improving fault injection efficiency. In: Dal Cin, M., Kaâniche, M., Pataricza, A. (eds.) EDCC 2005. LNCS, vol. 3463, pp. 246–262. Springer, Heidelberg (2005)

27. Nexus 5001™ Forum, IEEE-ISTO (1999). http://www.nexus5001.org/. Accessed March 2015

28. winIDEA – iSystem's Integrated Development Environment. http://www.isystem.com/products/software/winidea. Accessed March 2015

29. iC3000 debugger. http://www.isystem.com/products/11-products/89-ic3000-activeemulator. Accessed March 2015

30. Ayatolahi, F., Sangchoolie, B., Johansson, R., Karlsson, J.: A study of the impact of single bit-flip and double bit-flip errors on program execution. In: Bitsch, F., Guiochet, J., Kaâniche, M. (eds.) SAFECOMP. LNCS, vol. 8153, pp. 265–276. Springer, Heidelberg (2013)

Error Detection

Understanding the Effects of Data Corruption on Application Behavior Based on Data Characteristics

Georgios Stefanakis[1]($\boxtimes$), Vijay Nagarajan[1], and Marcelo Cintra[2]

[1] University of Edinburgh, Edinburgh, UK
{g.stefanakis,vijay.nagarajan}@ed.ac.uk
[2] Intel, Braunschweig, Germany
marcelo.cintra@intel.com

Abstract. In this paper, the results of an experimental study on the error sensitivities of application data are presented. We develop a portable software-implemented fault-injection (SWIFI) tool that, on top of performing single-bit flip fault injections and capturing their effects on application behavior, is also data-level aware and tracks the corrupted application data to report their high-level characteristics (usage type, size, user, memory space location). After extensive testing of NPB-serial (7.8M fault injections), we are able to characterize the sensitivities of data based on their high-level characteristics. Moreover, we conclude that application data are error sensitive in parts; depending on their type, they have distinct and wide less-sensitive bit ranges either at the MSBs or LSBs. Among other uses, such insight could drive the development of sensitivity-aware protection mechanisms of application data.

Keywords: Data-level error sensitivity · Bit-level error sensitivity · Software-implemented fault injection

1 Introduction

Reliability challenges have long been present in all parts of a system due to occurrences of anomalous physical conditions known as *hardware faults* [1]. Depending on the fault characteristics (location, type, timing, duration), the executing workload and the underlying hardware, faults can either (a) get masked by various levels of fault-masking effects (logic, architecture, application level) and result in a correct execution with no visible effects or (b) not get masked and result either in an observable execution upset (application crash, stall or delay) or an unobservable output corruption (Silent Data Corruption - SDC).

Motivated by the aforementioned fact, in this paper we study the effects of hardware-induced data corruption on application behavior in relation to the *high-level characteristics of the corrupted data* and the executing workload. Our purpose is to identify the error sensitivities and notice their variation for different data characteristics (usage type, size, user, memory space location) and also

© Springer International Publishing Switzerland 2015
F. Koornneef and C. van Gulijk (Eds.): SAFECOMP 2015, LNCS 9337, pp. 151–165, 2015.
DOI: 10.1007/978-3-319-24255-2_12

for different bit locations within the data; we define error sensitivity as the probability of a hardware fault in that data (or bit) to result in an SDC.

To do so, we employ software-implemented fault injection (SWIFI) to model transient single-bit faults in memory locations during application execution in an unprotected system and capture the corruption effect on the execution. Our focus is on gaining detailed error-sensitivity insight of the data accessed by an application. Therefore our SWIFI tool is *data-level aware*. Given an application binary, without need of its source code, our tool can finely control the location of the corruption in the application's memory space without further intruding the application behavior. Once a fault is injected at runtime, without need for binary file modifications per test, it tracks the corrupted data to classify them according to their use by the application. Meanwhile it monitors the execution's state and outcome to report back many diagnostics regarding the corruption characteristics/effects. As we monitor until completion, all fault-masking effects and corruption outcomes are captured.

SWIFI is commonly used in the literature mainly for system-level dependability assessment of reliability mechanisms [2–6]. Other works that study error sensitivities usually operate at a higher hardware level [7] or agnostic to the corrupted data characteristics [8] or to the exact corrupted bit. Instead, here we employ SWIFI to gain detailed error sensitivity insight at *application data level* and at a *per-bit granularity*. Thus, the main value of our study stems from the data-level awareness of the tests and the extensive set of tests performed. In general, there are many possible uses of the obtained error sensitivity insight. E.g., it can be used (a) to increase the protection of more sensitive data under SW-level fault-tolerant mechanisms, (b) to drive unequal protection of data words by assigning stronger protection to more sensitive bit ranges under HW-level fault-tolerant mechanisms, (c) to drive a sensitivity-aware SW-level modification of applications, (d) to reduce the testing space of dependability assessment, etc.

In this paper, we make the following main contributions:

(a) We establish a portable instrumentation-based SWIFI framework that can perform extensive tests on target binaries for a *data-level aware* study of the exact effects of data corruption on application behavior.

(b) After performing extensive (7.8M) fault-injection tests, we observe the error sensitivity of application data of the NPB-serial benchmarks based on the data characteristics, along with the variation among different bit locations of the data. We conclude that data are sensitive in parts; data holding output-related values have continuous less-sensitive bit ranges at their LSBs and memory addressing data at their MSBs. E.g., up to 32 LSBs of floating-point data in CG (Conjugate Gradient) each have <1 % probability to cause an SDC if corrupted.

2   SWIFI Framework

In this section we present our instrumentation-based SWIFI framework that can perform extensive *data-level aware* fault injections and can track the corrupted data to report their high-level characteristics.

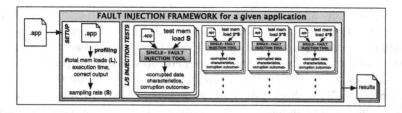

Fig. 1. Overview of our proposed data-level aware framework to capture the application behavior under corruption through extensive injection tests.

Our proposed **SWIFI framework** (Fig. 1) operates as follows: First, a fault-free run of the target binary is profiled to obtain (a) its expected correct output (for SDC detection), (b) its normal execution time under instrumentation by our tool (for delayed/stalled execution detection) and (c) its total number of memory load accesses (for deciding the sample rate to drive the tests uniformly over the test space). Then a *single-fault injection tool* is repeatedly invoked on a clean instance of the target application, each time corrupting a different memory load access. Once all tests complete, the extensive reported results are aggregated to relate the corruption outcome to the corrupted data characteristics (Sect. 4).

The **single-fault injection tool** performs and monitors the fault-injection tests. In each test, just before a specified memory load access (*fault trigger*), a random bit of the accessed data is flipped to emulate a single-bit transient fault in the accessed memory location (*injected fault model*). Then the rest of the execution is *monitored* to *report* the exact end-to-end corruption effects. On top of that, the corrupted data are *tracked* to classify their high-level characteristics and, thus, report more corrupted data characteristics (Table 1). All these are performed by special software that emulates the behavior of expected hardware faults during application operation only (and not the kernel's).

Fault Trigger: First, the application-under-test is instrumented until the execution reaches a specified memory load access to be corrupted. Using the memory load access as a fault trigger acts as both a spatial and a temporal trigger to invoke the injection routine just before the load operation. This trigger captures all possible times that a transient fault could occur and all possible live memory locations that could get corrupted. Thus it simplifies driving where/when to inject a fault by just selecting a load access, without relying on external events.

Fault Injection and Fault Model: Once the trigger is reached, the injection routine is invoked in a manner similar to a software trap. The chosen injected fault model emulates *single-bit transient faults in memory locations* by randomly flipping a bit of the data just before their access. The now-corrupted value is stored at the same memory location, without further intruding the application's original behavior, to avoid activating any reliability mechanisms of the system.

Due to our focus on data-level error sensitivity, the chosen fault model suffices without a need for precise realistic hardware fault models. Moreover, due to using instrumentation-based SWIFI, the fault model does not need to be adapted per target system but only to have the necessary high-level characteristics (type, duration, location). In particular, we chose a bit-flip *fault type* to ensure that data will always be corrupted at every test. The inject-before-load policy enforces emulation of transient faults as the injected corruption will not persist after the corrupted location is overwritten. Modeling transient *fault duration* fits better our purposes as they affect only a single memory object. Finally, the injected *fault's location* is in main memory as a natural fit for a data-aware investigation.

The goal of our tool is mainly to observe how corruption in application data would affect the application's behavior. For our purposes corrupting data loaded from memory using an inject-before-load policy assists to cover as many as possible data used by an application while avoiding unnecessarily testing dead memory locations. This does not cover the entirety of application data; e.g. temporary data in registers that are never stored/loaded to/from memory or memory data never accessed. Despite faults are emulated only in memory, the fault model can translate to emulate faults occurring in other functional units too without revising the model and the injection policy. E.g., a fault in a register could be effectively emulated in a test where its value is stored in memory and then loaded but fault injected. Injecting directly faults all over the processor would be out of scope of this SW-implemented methodology.

Monitoring, Data Tracking and Reporting: After the injection, the rest of the execution is still instrumented to monitor/report the effects of the corruption. As the instrumentation/analysis operates in a different virtual memory space to provide instrumentation transparency, the original binary observes the same addresses and values as it would in an uninstrumented execution [9]. Therefore, the original binary behavior is not changed, apart from the injected corruption, to ensure the non-intrusiveness of our injection tool.

Due to the chosen fault trigger, fault model and instrumentation-based injection we can perform data-level aware fault injection. Once the memory location is corrupted and loaded, we track it as an application variable to get its high-level characteristics. More precisely, at fault injection time, the tool tries to finely identify as many characteristics of the corrupted data as possible (Table 1). Attributes such as their location in the memory address space (global, heap or stack), size and user (system or user data) can be identified immediately.

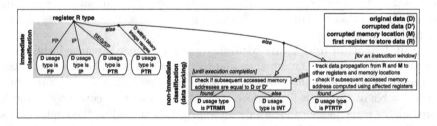

Fig. 2. Decision tree used by the single-fault injection tool to classify the corrupted application data according to their first use by the application.

Table 1. Reported corruption characteristics and corruption effects

Characteristics of corrupted data	
Injected bit-flip location, Memory address of corrupted data	
Memory space location: global, heap or stack	
Size:	1, 2, 4, 8 or 16 bytes
User:	System library data or application-space (user) data
Usage type:	**FP**: Floating-Point data (immediate classification)
	IP: Instruction Pointer (immediate classification)
	PTR: memory addressing data (immediate classification)
	PTRMR: mem. addressing data (classification by checking subsequent Mem. References)
	PTRTP: memory addressing data (classification by data tracking through Taint Propagation until first use as memory addressing data within an instruction window)
	INT: INTeger data (if none of the above)
Corruption effects	
Total number of executed instructions	
Execution outcome:	**Correct output**
	Delayed correct output: when the total execution time is a set amount of times more than the normal uncorrupted execution time
	Application crash
	Application stall: due to excessive total executed instructions (or execution time)
	Silent data corruption (SDC): wrong output

Classifying the type of the corrupted data according to their use by the application (Fig. 2) can be either immediate or it may require tracking the data through the execution until a first meaningful use (i.e., to determine if they are used for addressing memory or not). To elaborate, at fault injection we can identify the first register (R) where the corrupted data (D') are stored. If it is an FP register, the instruction counter or a segment/stack pointer register, we can classify immediately the corrupted data as floating-point (FP), instruction pointer (IP) or memory addressing data (PTR) respectively.

If the data usage type cannot be determined immediately, data tracking and close monitoring of the execution is used. The corrupted (and the uncorrupted) value is checked against all subsequent accessed effective memory addresses to check if these values are used for memory addressing (PTRMR). Meanwhile, we use dynamic taint analysis [10] to track the data propagation from the first register (R) to hold the corrupted data and from the corrupted memory location (M). After every instruction, we track the corruption propagation to other registers and memory locations. This continues until a register whose contents have been affected by the original corruption is used for computing a memory address. If this happens within a specified instruction window, then the original corrupted data are reported as memory addressing data (PTRTP). If none of the above occur by the end of execution, the corrupted data are reported as INT.

We report memory addressing data as three separate categories, not only because they are identified by different means, but because they represent different usage cases. PTRs are memory addressing data that when loaded from memory have immediately the semantics of a pointer and are to be used as pointers. PTRTPs are memory addressing data that are identified through Taint Propagation analysis and are used to eventually compute a memory address; e.g. a loop counter that is used as memory offset. PTRMRs are identified by checking subsequent Memory References and are not immediately used as pointers.

After the injection, apart from the above, the tool keeps monitoring closely the execution to capture all possible corruption effects. The execution time is monitored to detect application stalls or delayed executions, the output is checked for correctness or SDCs, and fatal signals are caught to detect crashes. Once the execution completes (or stops due to a crash or stall), the tool reports back all the captured corruption characteristics and corruption effects (Table 1).

3   Experimental Setup

The proposed SWIFI framework was implemented as a set of scripts and dynamic binary instrumentation Pin tools [9]. Using Pin's instrumentation enabled the portability, transparency and efficiency properties of our tools. The full set of the ten workloads of the NAS Parallel Benchmarks [11] (64-bit, NPB-serial version 3.3.1, input class size S, gcc 4.4.6 -o3, Linux kernel 2.6.32) was extensively tested by our framework on a x86-64 computer cluster.

Before commencing with the individual fault-injection tests, the benchmarks were profiled (Table 2) to obtain their total memory load accesses and their normal uncorrupted execution time under instrumentation. The number of total memory loads indicated the test space size. Given that it ranged from 4.7M to 914.9M, summing up to a cumulative total of 2.28 billion, testing every bit of every memory load access would be impractical and unreasonable. Instead we set sample rates per benchmark (Table 2) to uniformly distribute our fault-injection tests over the test space of possible memory load accesses to corrupt. Moreover, in every test the bit-flip was randomly injected within the tested data to ensure an equal distribution of tested bits. The chosen sample rates ranged from 1/5 to 1/2947 to uniformly test each benchmark in approximately the same total time on the available computer cluster, where the embarrassingly parallel nature of the tests was exploited for a faster completion of the experiments (less than a week). The test space sampling brought the total number of performed fault-injection tests to 7.8M for the full benchmark suite (ranging from 310.4K to 1.33M for individual benchmarks). Despite the test space sampling, compared to related fault-injection based works, we performed significantly more extensive fault-injection tests that, coupled with the detailed collected test results, enabled us to thoroughly elaborate on them, as we discuss in the next section.

Table 2. Profiling information for the tested NPB-serial benchmarks

Bench-mark	Total memory loads (M)	Execution time (sec)	Sample rate	Memory loads tested (K)	Test space coverage (%)
BT	187.5	20.7	1/234	801.6	0.43
CG	111.9	22.7	1/153	731.3	0.65
DC	33.1	21.9	1/43	769.9	2.33
EP	778.2	52.3	1/2461	316.2	0.04
FT	112.0	31.9	1/216	518.5	0.46
IS	4.7	3.4	1/5	959.3	20.00
LU	62.9	16.5	1/62	1015.6	1.61
MG	10.6	13.7	1/8	1335.0	12.50
SP	66.9	15.3	1/62	1079.3	1.61
UA	914.9	53.3	1/2947	310.4	0.03
Total	2283.1	-	-	7837.6	0.34

4 Experimental Results and Discussion

In this section, we study the results to gain insight and elaborate on the varying error sensitivities of application data based on their high-level characteristics.

Application-Level Error-Sensitivity Variations: Fig. 3 shows the breakdown of the exact end-to-end corruption effects on the tested benchmarks. This breakdown reconfirms that hardware faults have varying effects on application behavior. Out of the 7.8M performed fault-injection tests on NPB-serial, 61.1 % resulted in correct execution. As for the rest outcomes, 23.5 % of the total tests resulted in SDCs, 15 % in application crashes, 0.3 % in application stalls and less than 0.1 % in delayed correct executions. More importantly the number of tests that corrupted silently the output varied per benchmark; the reported occurrences of SDCs ranged from 5.8 % (DC) up to 37.9 % (IS). This indicates that applications have different inherent error-sensitivity characteristics mostly attributed to their data-level sensitivity and their data access patterns.

Data-Level Error-Sensitivity Variations: Due to the data-level awareness of the fault-injection tests, we can study how the error sensitivity of application data varies in relation to their high-level characteristics. For this purpose we introduce the *experiment-based Data Vulnerability Factor* (eDVF) that we calculate using our testing results and we define as the statistical probability of a corruption in specified data categories to result in an SDC.

Figure 4 shows the eDVF variation over the tested applications for the various high-level data characteristics that our fault-injection framework can identify. Generally most eDVFs are around 0.2, with limited exceptions going as high as 0.83, and quite a few being less than 0.05. This points that application data sensitivity can be characterized according to their characteristics. In a few cases, eDVFs are down to zero due to no reported SDC outcomes or due to absence of the particular data categories in the specific benchmark; in any case indicating them as less error-sensitive data for the application in question.

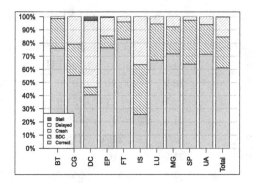

Fig. 3. Breakdown of corruption outcomes per tested NPB-serial benchmark and in total over all performed injection tests.

System library data (Fig. 4(c)) are less sensitive almost consistently across all benchmarks as they tend not to be output related and if corrupted tend to get masked or cause crashes. On the contrary, in some benchmarks, there is a trend of longer data being more vulnerable (Fig. 4(b)), as longer data often hold output-related values and thus if corrupted are more likely to corrupt the output too. As for the usage type eDVFs (Fig. 4(d)), there is no benchmark wide observation to be made. Despite that, they can be used in a per-application basis to rank the data sensitivities according to their type. Moreover, given the application's data access patterns, they can explain the total application error sensitivity.

Given the volume of our tests, our study captures the varying error sensitivities of application data per application with a high statistical confidence. As there are numerous combinations of data characteristics, only the variations per single data characteristics were presented here. Since the results of our experiments allow to compute the eDVFs for *combined* data characteristics, the application data error sensitivities can also be investigated more closely.

Per-Bit Data-Level Error-Sensitivity Variations: Moving down to per-bit investigation we can get more consistent error-sensitivity insight. Figures 5 and 6 show how the per-bit error sensitivity varies among application data usage-type categories (see Table 1), while it shows common location patterns per each category across most of the tested applications. For given combinations of usage types and data sizes, the more-sensitive bits tend to concentrate in continuous bit ranges either at the MSBs (Fig. 5(a) and (b)) or at the LSBs (Figs. 5(c) through 6(c)) for most of the tested benchmarks, while the remaining bit ranges have generally near-zero eDVF per bit. All these suggest that we can clearly identify bit ranges within particular application data with distinct sensitivity levels to confidently conclude that application data are sensitive in parts.

More precisely, for the tested floating-point data (FP-8B, Fig. 5(a)) the less-sensitive bit ranges are located at their LSBs across most of the tested benchmarks, while moving towards the MSBs the per-bit eDVF increases steadily. When considering as less-sensitive bits those with per-bit eDVF less than 0.01, the less-sensitive bit-range width varies from 20 LSBs for SP up to 32 LSBs for

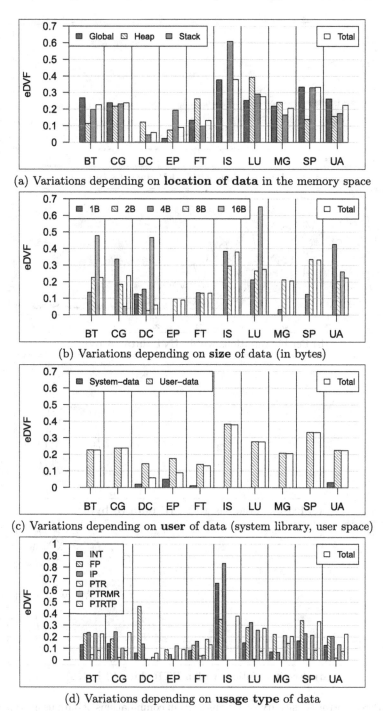

(a) Variations depending on **location of data** in the memory space

(b) Variations depending on **size** of data (in bytes)

(c) Variations depending on **user** of data (system library, user space)

(d) Variations depending on **usage type** of data

Fig. 4. Error-sensitivity variations of application data per tested NPB-serial benchmark depending on different high-level characteristics. *Total* indicates the reported SDCs for a given benchmark regardless of data characteristics.

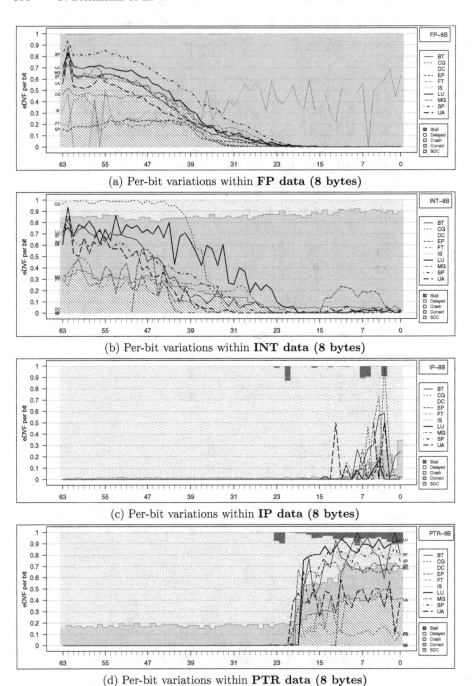

(a) Per-bit variations within **FP** data (**8 bytes**)

(b) Per-bit variations within **INT** data (**8 bytes**)

(c) Per-bit variations within **IP** data (**8 bytes**)

(d) Per-bit variations within **PTR** data (**8 bytes**)

Fig. 5. Per-bit error-sensitivity variations (within combinations of data usage types and sizes) per tested NPB-serial benchmark. *Background bars* show the per-bit breakdown of corruption outcomes in total over all benchmarks.

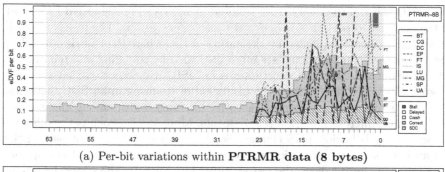

(a) Per-bit variations within **PTRMR data (8 bytes)**

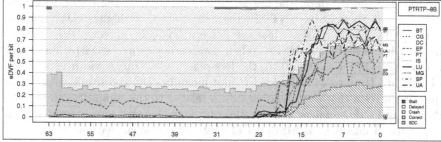

(b) Per-bit variations within **PTRTP data (8 bytes)**

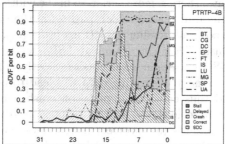

(c) Per-bit variations within **PTRTP data (4 bytes)**

Fig. 6. Same as Fig. 5.

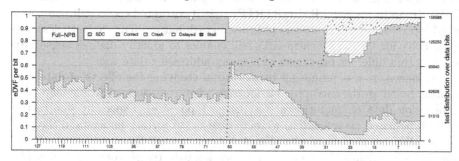

Fig. 7. Per-bit error-sensitivity variations (and breakdown of rest corruption outcomes) in total over all benchmarks, regardless of data usage type and size. *Dotted line* shows the number of times each bit was tested.

CG, while many of these bits never resulted in an SDC. For the tested FPs, most of the non-SDC observed outcomes were correct executions. The observed sensitivity variations are explained by the nature of FPs where their LSBs only affect the accuracy of computations, are often discarded by rounding and tend not to affect the output. Moving to corruptions in MSBs it is expected that the data upset is intensified and as such the likelihood of resulting in an SDC increases. This also explains the varying less-sensitive bit-range width among applications as they have different precision requirements. Moreover it explains the different FP-sensitivity behavior in IS (Integer Sorting), where FPs are not part of the output but control the execution and are more likely to cause output corruption.

Similar to the FP data, the less-sensitive bit ranges in the tested INT data are located at their LSBs (INT-8B, Fig. 5(b)) but show higher eDVF per bit than their FP counterparts, while the pattern holds for higher eDVFs per bit when moving towards the MSBs. When considering as less-sensitive bits those with per-bit eDVF less than 0.10, the less-sensitive bit-range width varies from 24 LSBs for LU up to 43 LSBs for EP (not including DC and IS). This common behavior suggests that data holding values related to the computation, as both FPs and INTs do, tend to corrupt the output when they are corrupted at a greater magnitude (i.e., at MSBs). INTs can also be separated into distinct bit ranges with different sensitivity levels. Though, as they are used in many different application specific ways, there is more variation in the width of the less-sensitive ranges and not a common increasing eDVF pattern in the more-sensitive ones.

Moving on to memory addressing data (Figs. 5(c)-6(c)), we notice a reversal of the per-bit sensitivities; corruption at LSBs tends to result in SDCs and corruption at MSBs in application crashes mostly. This is because corruptions in MSBs of memory addressing data will lead to pointers into invalid memory locations and thus cause an application crash. On the contrary, corruptions in LSBs are more likely to lead to pointers into valid memory locations with undesired contents (or incorrect instructions) and thus corrupt the application output (or the instruction flow) but without causing an immediate crash. This is why the sensitive bit-range width of IP data is narrower than the PTR/PTRMR/PTRTP ones that are similar. The application program space is narrower compared to the data memory space and, thus, there are less bits in IPs (than in PTR/PTRMR/PTRTP) that if corrupted could still point to a valid location and not cause an application crash but an SDC. Nevertheless, the clear behavior for most benchmarks still enables to identify distinct sensitivity levels within different bit ranges of memory addressing data too.

As shown, it was promising to move into studying the effects of data corruption based on the corrupted bit location when considering specific high-level application data characteristics (i.e., usage type, size). Especially due to the usage-type-based classification, we were able to (a) further understand the previous eDVF usage-type results (Fig. 4(d)) and (b) get more consistent results among most benchmarks regarding the location patterns of more-sensitive application data parts. What changes across benchmarks is the less-sensitive bit-range width and the sensitivity intensity levels of the rest. For more detailed insight the eDVF per-bit variation can also be analyzed for *combined* data characteristics. As we can now identify clear bit ranges within particular application data with distinct sensitivity levels, the bit-level insight can be used instead of the higher-level eDVFs to characterize application data sensitivities more accurately.

Similar analysis could be performed for each of the other identified high-level characteristics of the corrupted data (i.e., location, user) or for the total per-bit eDVFs for all tested benchmarks combined (Fig. 7). Such analysis though does not provide the same clear insight, as the per usage type analysis, because the per-bit variation depends mostly on how the data-under-consideration are used.

5 Related Work

Various analytical and experimental techniques have been proposed usually for dependability assessment of systems and reliability mechanisms. Analytical techniques model the behavior of HW structures under the presence of faults usually through slow microarchitectural analysis [7]. An alternative is to use experimental techniques, such as experimental verification, error logging or full-system simulation under simulated faults. As these are also slow, the experimental approach of **fault injection** has been used instead to test real systems under realistic faults. Fault injection can be HW [3,4,12] or SW implemented [2–6,13,14]. In HW-implemented injection, faults are injected physically by electromagnetic interference and radiation [12] or through the circuit pins [3,4]. Although these inject real hardware faults that can reach all locations, they lack flexibility and are difficult to operate and control. Moreover, they suffer from low portability as they target specific systems, require special purpose dedicated hardware to access the tested hardware and may damage the tested system. On the contrary, **SW-implemented fault injection** (SWIFI) overcomes most of these drawbacks by injecting realistic faults using software methods. SWIFI achieves higher properties of repeatability, controllability (in space and time), reproducibility, non-intrusiveness and efficacy [12]. Generally, in SWIFI, transient faults are injected by adding traps or replacing instructions, either at pre-runtime or at runtime. Pre-runtime injection methods mutate the application, i.e., by substituting instructions and program data [14] or by source code mutation [13]. Runtime injection methods most commonly corrupt memory or register contents using time-based, path-based or stress-based triggers, while they inject faults by direct program memory image corruption [6], dynamic process control structure corruption using debugging registers [2,4,5], forcing execution of pre-loaded routines using software traps [3,13] or hardware breakpoints [3,4].

Varying Error Sensitivities: Many approaches have implied a sensitivity classification of hardware parts albeit without a formal exploration [15,16]. Similarly, other approaches implied a data sensitivity classification based on cache access patterns [17]. Moving to higher abstraction levels is promising to observe the varying effects of faults [4,13]. Similar variations are implied in approaches where code segments [18,19] or individual instructions [20] are marked as critical. More formally, a reliability-aware analysis can be used to detect statistically-vulnerable code segments [21] and instructions [20,22]. The same applies for data-level sensitivities, where it has been implied that not all data are equally sensitive, i.e., by marking data segments as non-critical if they only affect the output of multimedia workloads [23], or as approximate if their preciseness is not required [24]. More formally, analysis can further elaborate on the criticality of data, e.g., by profiling data according to their liveliness [22], or by detecting sensitive bit ranges [25] within data with known value ranges. For the same purpose, finely-controlled fault injection and execution monitoring can be used for more insight on the corruption effects in a per-bit manner [8].

6   Conclusion

In this paper we developed an instrumentation-based SWIFI tool that is data-level aware and tracks application data in order to gain detailed error-sensitivity insight at application data level. We showed through a set of extensive fault-injection experiments on NPB-serial that we can analyze the exact effects of data corruption on application behavior based on the high-level characteristics of the corrupted data (usage type, size, user, memory space location). This not only enabled to capture the varying sensitivities of data given their characteristics but also to identify less-sensitive bit ranges within data. Among many potential future uses, the gained insight could motivate the development of sensitivity-aware protection mechanisms trading-off between protection cost and fault coverage.

Acknowledgements. We thank the reviewers for their valuable comments and suggestions. This work is supported by EPSRC grant EP/M00113X/1 to the University of Edinburgh.

References

1. Sorin, D.J.: Fault tolerant computer architecture. Synth. Lect. Comput. Archit. **4**, 1–104 (2009)
2. Kanawati, G., et al.: FERRARI: a flexible software-based fault and error injection system. Trans. Comput. **44**(2), 248–260 (1995)
3. Skarin, D., et al.: GOOFI-2: a tool for experimental dependability assessment. In: DSN (2010)
4. Stott, D., et al.: NFTAPE: a framework for assessing dependability in distributed systems with lightweight fault injectors. In: IPDS (2000)
5. Carreira, J., et al.: Xception: a technique for the experimental evaluation of dependability in modern computers. Trans. Softw. Eng. **24**(2), 125–136 (1998)
6. Segall, Z., et al.: FIAT-fault injection based automated testing environment. In: FTCS (1988)
7. Mukherjee, S.S., et al.: A systematic methodology to compute the architectural vulnerability factors for a high-performance microprocessor. In: MICRO (2003)
8. Ayatolahi, F., Sangchoolie, B., Johansson, R., Karlsson, J.: A study of the impact of single bit-flip and double bit-flip errors on program execution. In: Bitsch, F., Guiochet, J., Kaâniche, M. (eds.) SAFECOMP. LNCS, vol. 8153, pp. 265–276. Springer, Heidelberg (2013)

9. Luk, C.K., et al.: Pin: Building customized program analysis tools with dynamic instrumentation. In: PLDI (2005)
10. Zhu, Y., et al.: Privacy scope: a precise information flow tracking system for finding application leaks. Technical report (2009)
11. Bailey, D., et al.: The NAS parallel benchmarks. Intern J. High Perform. Comput. Appl. **5**(3), 63–73 (1991)
12. Arlat, J., et al.: Comparison of physical and software-implemented fault injection techniques. Trans. Comput. **52**(9), 1115–1133 (2003)
13. Hiller, M., et al.: PROPANE: an environment for examining the propagation of errors in software. In: ISSTA (2002)
14. Gerardin, J.P.: The DEF-Injecto test instrument, assistance in the design of reliable and safe systems. Comput. Ind. **11**(4), 311–319 (1989)
15. Greskamp, B., et al.: BlueShift: designing processors for timing speculation from the ground up. In: HPCA (2009)
16. Ernst, D., et al.: Razor: a low-power pipeline based on circuit-level timing speculation. In: MICRO (2003)
17. Zhang, W., et al.: Performance, energy, and reliability tradeoffs in replicating hot cache lines. In: CASES (2003)
18. de Kruijf, M., et al.: Relax: an architectural framework for software recovery of hardware faults. In: ISCA (2010)
19. Reis, G.A., et al.: SWIFT: software implemented fault tolerance. In: CGO (2005)
20. Borodin, D., et al.: Instruction-level fault tolerance configurability. J. Sig. Process. Syst. **57**(1), 89–105 (2009)
21. Feng, S., et al.: Shoestring: probabilistic soft error reliability on the cheap. In: ASPLOS (2010)
22. Mehrara, M., Austin, T.: Exploiting selective placement for low-cost memory protection. TACO **5**(3), 1–24 (2008)
23. Lee, K., et al.: Partially protected caches to reduce failures due to soft errors in multimedia applications. Trans. VLSI Syst. **17**(9), 1343–1347 (2009)
24. Sampson, A., et al.: EnerJ: approximate data types for safe and general low-power computation. In: PLDI (2011)
25. Chang, J., et al.: Automatic instruction-level software-only recovery. In: DSN (2006)

A Multi-layer Anomaly Detector for Dynamic Service-Based Systems

Andrea Ceccarelli[1], Tommaso Zoppi[1(✉)], Massimiliano Itria[2],
and Andrea Bondavalli[1]

[1] University of Florence, Viale Morgagni 65, Florence, Italy
{andrea.ceccarelli,tommaso.zoppi,bondavalli}@unifi.it
[2] Resiltech s.r.l, Piazza Nilde Iotti, 25, Pontedera (PI), Italy
massimiliano.itria@resiltech.com

Abstract. Revealing anomalies to support error detection in complex systems is a promising approach when traditional detection mechanisms (e.g., based on event logs, probes and heartbeats) are considered inadequate or not applicable. The detection capability of such complex system can be enhanced observing different layers to achieve richer information that describes the system status. Relying on an algorithm for statistical anomaly detection, in this paper we present the definition and implementation of an anomaly detector able to monitor data acquired from multiple layers, namely the Operating system and the Application Server, of a remote physical or virtual node. As case study, such monitoring system is applied to a node of the Secure! crisis management service-based system. Results show the monitor performance, the intrusiveness of the probes, and ultimately the improved detection capability achieved observing data from the different layers.

Keywords: Anomalies · Monitor · Complex event processor · Service oriented architecture · Secure!

1 Introduction

Large-scale software systems as for example Service Oriented Architectures (SOAs) or cyber-physical infrastructures in general are composed of several different components, software layers and services. These systems are characterized by a dynamic and evolutionary behavior, which leads to changes in part of the system, as well as their services and connections. Recent trends show the increasing introduction in these systems of safety-critical requirements, as for example in crisis management systems where rescue personnel on-the-field is remotely guided [12]. Although it is often mandatory to deploy monitoring solutions of the system and its services to timely detect failures, the complexity of software (and of the fault model), and the dynamic and evolutionary behavior of the whole system, make the definition and instrumentation of an effective monitoring solution an open challenge [1, 18, 20].

Amongst the possible monitoring approaches, in this paper we focus on anomaly detection, which refers to the problem of finding patterns in data that do not conform to the expected behavior [6]. Such patterns are changes in the indicators characterizing the

© Springer International Publishing Switzerland 2015
F. Koornneef and C. van Gulijk (Eds.): SAFECOMP 2015, LNCS 9337, pp. 166–180, 2015.
DOI: 10.1007/978-3-319-24255-2_13

behavior of the system caused by specific and non-random factors. For example, pattern changes can be due to a system overload, or to the activation of faults. Thus, anomaly detectors may be able to infer the status of a service without directly observing it, but observing the "surroundings". This has been proven relevant and useful for dynamic software and systems which are subject to frequent, possibly abrupt changes, or when the instrumentation of the target services with the required probes is unfeasible [17]. In these situations, timely detection of anomalies will allow activating reaction strategies and ultimately contribute to improve the system safety.

The approach that we present in this paper consists in shifting the observation perspective from the services at the application layer to the underlying layers, specifically in our instantiation of the monitor we selected the Application Server (AS) and the Operating System (OS). This paper proposes the design and the implementation of a monitoring solution for physically or virtually distributed systems and applications, also applicable to cloud environments and SOAs, which processes data coming from such underlying layers to indirectly observe the services running on the user layer by revealing anomalies that infer their status.

In the case study, the monitoring system is exercised to observe services of the Secure! [5] crisis management system, a safety-critical Service Oriented Architecture, where the services are owned and managed by different entities and are deployed on different (virtual) nodes. The services may also incur in frequent updates and removal, or even new services may be introduced, together with modification to their orchestration. Thus, while instrumenting with probes and monitoring each service is unfeasible, the opportunity to observe the underlying layers (AS and OS) is offered. Results measures the performance of the CEP under different load, the intrusiveness of the probes, and through software error injection it is observed that a more accurate detection of failure is offered thanks to the combined usage of AS and OS.

Summarizing, the main contributions of this paper lie in: (i) describe a monitoring approach to infer the status of the applications by observing the underlying layers; (ii) define, implement and execute on a target system a CEP-based anomaly detector for remote virtual or physical nodes; (iii) prove via software error injection that the detection capability of the algorithm is enhanced by considering multiple layers; (iv) assess the whole solution on the Secure! case study, showing performance and probes intrusiveness. The rest of the paper is organized as follows. Section 2 presents the state of the art on CEP and anomaly detection monitoring, Sect. 3 discusses the motivations and overall architecture of a multi-layer monitor for anomaly detection, Sect. 4 contains details of our instantiation of the monitor, Sect. 5 describes a case study with details on experiments and results and Sect. 6 concludes the paper.

2 State of the Art on CEP Monitors and Anomaly Detection

CEP systems are widely applied to manage stream of data, in different fields and applications, as business process management, financial services, and also dependability and security monitoring, especially for complex, large scale systems where large amounts of information is generated. Focusing on dependability (and security) monitoring, we report on relevant examples that have been considered as references to structure our work. In [15, 16] the high flexibility allowed by CEP queries is used for anomaly detection in critical infrastructures. In particular, [15] proposes a Security Information and Event Management (SIEM) framework where the event correlation engine is able to parallelize arbitrary rules expressed as CEP queries. In [16] authors propose a CEP approach for on-line detection and diagnosis, which allows to detect intrusions by collecting diverse information at several architectural layers as well as perform complex event correlation. In our work, we will use CEP technologies to efficiently apply rules on the data received from the different probes.

Anomaly detection is largely used as a possible approach for timely detection of errors or attacks [6, 17]. Remote applications are considered in [18], where the authors use temporal and combinatorial rules, obtained from protocol specifications and system administrators to reveal anomalies; different systems or part of the system can be observed for anomaly detection. Also remote services are observed for anomaly detection purposes in [19], where data mining techniques are exploited adopting static algorithms, although this makes the monitoring system not easily adaptable to the overall system changes. The ability to retrieve data from different system layers is exploited in [23], where the authors extend the mobile anomaly detection technique based on the observation of MAC layer by considering also routing and application layer. Also in [24] the authors give a new multi-layer anomaly detection perspective about intrusion detection in wireless networks aimed to identify the attacks that cannot be blocked using information coming only from the lower levels of the network protocol stack, basically the MAC layer.

Regarding statistical anomaly detection, the work in [7] proposes a detection framework to reveal anomalies in the OS behavior. For each observed OS-layer indicator, the framework uses the *Statistical-Predictor Safety Margin* (SPS, [2]) algorithm, which computes a prediction of the behavior of an indicator, based on a statistical analysis of the past observations. The prediction produces an interval, given by a minimum and a maximum value, in which the value of the indicator is expected to fall. If the value of the indicator is outside the interval, SPS signal that an anomaly is suspected for such indicator. Our monitoring system includes the first running implementation of the algorithm in [2].

3   Motivations and Overview of a Multi-Layer Anomaly Detector

As mentioned before, the dynamic and evolutionary characteristics of SOA systems call for monitoring solutions which are as much independent as possible from the services running on the application layer, in order to *not*: (i) require information on the services, (ii) need to instrument the services with monitoring probes, (iii) be forced to reconfigure the monitoring system each time services are updated, added or removed. A possible approach to address such issues is moving the observation perspective from the application layer to the underlying layers (e.g., operating system, application server, network protocols [24], databases [25]).

Our multi-layer monitoring solution is organized in two parts. The first part is composed of the probes inserted in the different layers of the nodes (that we call

Machine) to be monitored. These can be virtual or physical nodes. The probes should be easily pluggable into the nodes and it should be possible to configure them, e.g., deactivate them or change the data acquisition rate. Probes should not interfere with the services executing at the application layer. The probes periodically send the data they observe to a centralized *Monitor*, which collects the values and relying on a Complex Event Processing (CEP, [3]) applies the selected anomaly detection algorithm.

4   AS and OS Cross-Layer Monitoring Solution

In our instantiation, the probes are inserted in the OS and AS of the Machines.. The Monitor collects data from all Machines, and executes an anomaly detection algorithm integrated with a CEP correlator in order to detect anomalies. The adopted anomaly detection algorithm is the Statistical-Predictor Safety Margin (SPS, [2]), already applied exclusively to the OS layer and validated with offline analysis in [7].

Machines are instrumented with probes required to collect the value of indicators at both Application Server (AS) and Operating System (OS) layers with the aim to provide a complete vision of the state of the monitored machines, because they embrace different aspects of the behavior of both operating system and application.

The Machines transmit the observed data to the Monitor; once the monitor receives a set of values, it applies the SPS [2] algorithm that is able to update the thresholds of the observed indicators at runtime, in order to match the temporal evolution of the system or to satisfy changes in the application environment. This allow to build a monitoring system that does not require to study at pre-deployment the expected workload and services, and that is able to match possible variations in the services running on the observed Machines. The CEP correlator module is realized using the *Esper* tool [3], that is an open-source software based on *Event Stream Processing* techniques. It can process huge amounts of data in real-time or near real-time by means of SQL-like queries called rules. If the result of data processing performed by SPS matches the Esper rules, our monitoring system raises an *Alert* to signal an anomaly to a target *Operating Center* (that is not discussed in this paper), where the alerts are evaluated and it is decided if an intervention is required.

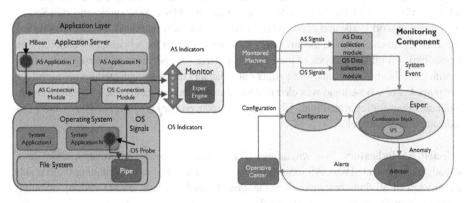

Fig. 1. Logical architecture of a Machine.   **Fig. 2.** Structure of the Monitor.

4.1   The Machines and the Observed Probes

We describe the architecture of each Machine and its probes with the help of Fig. 1. On each Machine, probes are installed to observe AS and OS indicators. AS probes are collected relying on the *Java Management Extensions* (*JMX*, [4]). JMX gets the values of the observed indicators by means of some Java objects called *Managed Beans* (*MBeans* [9]). For instance, MBeans allows the runtime extraction of information on execution time, number of activations, risen exceptions, application errors, amount of data exchanged between services. Each MBean maps onto an AS indicator to be extracted, creating a significant set available to external modules. In our study we consider a Machine equipped with AS Apache Tomcat 7 and Tomcat MBean server to get information about indicators related to Tomcat and JVM. In order to monitor AS indicators, each Machine includes the AS Connection Module that interfaces the MBean Server and the Monitor. The collected data are forwarded to the AS Connection Module which is in charge of transmission to the Monitor.

Probes that observe the OS indicators are located in kernel modules. Indicators from OS are retrieved in our implementation using System Tap [10] on Linux CentOS 6 and transmitted to the OS Connection Module via pipe. System Tap exploits the modularity of the Linux kernel design to produce a kernel module that once loaded has visibility on kernel structures. The System Tap compiler produces a kernel module which directly accesses kernel internal data. OS indicators generate signals for the next upper layers. OS indicators provide the monitoring module with information about the current status of the system.

Indicators from both AS and OS layers are collected on each Machine and sent to the Monitor through dedicated socket, transmitting block of data at configurable time intervals; data are transmitted periodically in blocks, instead than as soon as they are detected by the probes, to reduce the overhead on the Machine. The time interval between two data transmissions can be tuned depending on the desired resolution of the observations; in our selected configuration, the whole set of indicators is read and transmitted each second. Also, to reduce the impact on the observed system, AS and OS probes write their data without any rearrangement, which is left to the Monitor.

Since the many indicators available (about 1300 only for Tomcat), we selected a filtered subset of them. To perform such selection, aimed to exclude indicators that do not provide relevant information on the status of the node, we exercised the case study described in Sect. 5 with different workloads, and executed repeated runs for each workload logging each time a subset of all indicators (given the amount of indicators, logging the whole set for each run was unfeasible). An offline analysis of the values collected, together with an investigation of the meanings of the indicators, allowed to filter out indicators that were static values not useful for our purposes or whose trend was clearly unpredictable and especially showing considerable different values for replicated runs. Ultimately, we reduced our list to a set of 20 AS and 9 OS indicators discussed below.

Selected AS indicators. *Java threadings (2 indicators).* Provides information about Java threads management. These AS indicators report the amount of current running threads and the amount of all threads started since the *Java Virtual Machine* (JVM) started, including daemons, non-daemons and ended threads.

Managers (4 indicators). Provides information about HTTP sessions: rate of sessions creation and expiration during the execution of a certain workload, or the sessions that have been rejected because the maximum limit has been reached.

Memory pools (2 indicators). Provides information about memory allocation. The JVM sees different kinds of memory for different usages. We consider *Code Cache*, *Eden Space* and *Perm Gen* memory space as the most significant for our monitor. *Code cache* is non-heap memory used to compile and store native code. *Eden space* is heap memory used to allocate the major part of Java objects. *Perm Gen (Permanent Generation)* is non-heap memory used to manage class and method reflection.

Memories (3 indicators). Provides information about heap/non heap memory management performed by the JVM.

Requests (5 indicators). Provides information about management of HTTP requests.

Operating_systems (4 indicators). In spite of its name, those are still AS probes, because provide information about the OS tools required by the JVM at the AS layer.

Selected OS indicators. *Disk_in_throughput, Disk_out_throughput* are the number of data written/read on the hard-disk. *Disk_read_timeout, Disk_write_timeout* are the number of read/write timeouts of a syscall. *Net_in_throughput, Net_out_throughput* are the amount of data sent/received on the network. *Process_exit* is the number of processes that reached a *System.exit()* function. *Sched_threshold* is the number of timeout experimented by a thread or a process since its last scheduling and *Syscall_error_code* represents the number of terminated system calls.

4.2   The Monitor

A description of the Monitor is shown in Fig. 2. For each machine, AS and OS indicators are intercepted by the receiving sockets of their respective Connection Modules. The Data Collection Modules reads AS and OS data coming from the observed Machine, in order to manage data from two different layers: this logical division has the purpose to facilitate possible further extensions to include additional layers. Since AS and OS probes write their data without any rearrangement, the AS and OS Data Collection modules are responsible for parsing, organizing and arranging data. As output of such modules, the OS and AS indicators are aggregated in a unique Java object called System Event (see Fig. 2), composed of the values of the different indicators for a specific machine. The System Event is passed as input to the Esper CEP.

The Combination Block and the SPS module. For each System Event, Esper invokes the Combination Block, which for each constituent indicator computes the SPS algorithm and, if an anomaly is suspected by the indicator, notifies an alert to the caller module. Note that each indicator in the combination block is matched to a weight which represents the relevance of such indicator in the anomaly detection process. In other words, some indicators have more discontinuous trends with respect to others and then are particularly prone to false alarms, as for example the *SystemCpuLoad*: these indicators are weighted less with respect to others which in general are less prone to false alarms (e.g., *Http_ErrorRate,* in group *Requests*).

The Combination Block collects all SPS outputs for all indicators of a System Event, and then execute a weighted sum of the whole set of alerts; if the resulting score is above a given threshold, an *anomaly* alert is transmitted to the Advisor module and from there to the Operative Center. Such threshold can be configured by the Operative Center via the Configurator, together with the configuration parameters of SPS, the name and number of indicators that are part of the System Event, and the weight assigned to the different indicators. In particular, the Combination Block needs to maintain the history of past values for each indicator in order to allow SPS to make a prediction on the basis of the history of observations; the length of such history is specified in the SPS configuration parameters.

The Esper correlator. The Esper correlator is the module that allows to implement the monitoring system by means of rules on the value returned by the Combination Block or on some indicator values. More in detail, a rule is a statement that specifies a condition on some indicators monitored by the system. The Esper correlator allows to find out whether the AS and OS signals indicate anomalous events. The Esper engine allows to store rules about the system behavior: once the Combination Block makes data available, Esper performs an online evaluation of rules that detect anomalies.

Esper rules are written in *Event Programming Language* (*EPL*, [3]). EPL syntax is very similar to SQL and provides sum, average, join and other useful functions to assure high adaptability of our system to any kind of monitoring. Also, it makes possible to implement temporal conditions on data incoming from the SPS modules. If an anomaly is detected, Esper outputs the set of anomalous events and it alerts the operating center, providing some details related to anomalies (involved Machine, timestamp …). In our implementation, EPL rules are stored an XML file. In the following we provide an example of an EPL rule specified in XML.

```
<Rules createDate="11-09-2013" purpose="monitoring test" command="store
and enable" name="SPS test">
  <rule EPL="select*from pattern[ [every(systemEvent)
  where systemEvent.combinationBlock() > 10" >
  </rule>
</Rules>
```

The field "rule" states that every time the weighted sum of the combination block is greater than 10, an alarm is raised. The *store and enable* command states that the received rules have to be stored in the Esper rule repository. Esper was selected for our monitor as it offers the following benefits: (i) EPL monitoring rules can be modified without any changes in the implementation of the Monitor internals, (ii) such rules can be modified at run-time, and (iii) being Esper totally developed in Java, its integration with the other components of the monitoring system was facilitated.

5 Experiments Execution and Results

After discussing the design and implementation of our monitoring system, we present its evaluation in the context of the *Secure!* Crisis management system aimed to (i) understand and assess the intrusiveness of the probes on the different machines, (ii) define the performance of the Monitor in terms of being able to sustain a different number of machines, and (iii) show the detection capability of our multi-layer approach. We note that the results related to point (i) and (ii) are closely related to the hardware settings of the monitor and the machines; these can generally be improved by using more powerful systems with higher network bandwidth. However we believe that this analysis is relevant to be reported here to show the applicability of our monitoring solution in the *Secure!* system. All the virtual machines mentioned in this section execute on the rack server with 3 processors Intel Xeon E5-2620@ 2.00 GHz available at *Resiltech s.r.l.* premises. In addition to the considerations shown below, the data that constitute the results are freely available in [14].

5.1 Case Study: The Secure! Machine and the Monitor

The Secure! system [5] is a Decision Support System (DSS, [12]) for emergency management that exploits information retrieved from a large quantity and several types of data sources available in a target geographical area, in order to detect critical situations and command the corresponding reactions including guiding rescue teams or delivering emergency information to the population via the Secure! *app*. Input data to Secure! may come from the following sources: (i) social media as for example Twitter [13], (ii) web sites, (iii) mobile devices and their embedded sensors as camera, microphone and GPS, (iv) sensor networks available in the infrastructures (e.g., surveillance cameras, proximity sensors). Data is received, collected, homogenized, correlated and aggregated in order to produce a *situation* for the DSS system that is ultimately shown to operators in a control room which take the appropriate decisions. While the Secure! project is currently ongoing, the foreseen final prototype will be composed of different virtual machines in charge of the different services. While all the virtual machines will have the same configuration in terms of operating system, application server and security solutions, virtual machines and services are owned by different partners and may change due to updates, reconfigurations, or modification of their orchestration.

Regarding the current Secure! prototype available at *Resiltech s.r.l.* premises, it is one of the four virtual nodes that will compose the final Secure! system, which several services running on it. This node corresponds to our Machine that is a virtual machine equipped with 3 GB RAM and 2 virtual cores (allocated on one other physical core of the rack server), running the Liferay [8] portal 6.1.2 Community Edition on Tomcat 7.0.40 with the Secure! services and CentOS 6, appropriately instrumented with the monitoring probes. The Liferay framework is at the basis of the development of the Secure! system, whose core is based on the instantiation of new Liferay services.

We exercise different workloads to simulate the behavior of a Secure! user. Due to the high number of services offered by the prototype, the actions performed by the workload during execution are very heterogeneous (e.g., file transmission and storage, creation of events ...). The Monitor has been implemented on a virtual machine running Linux CentOS 6 with kernel 2.6.32, with assigned 2 GB RAM and a single virtual core (1 physical core of the rack server is dedicated to it).

29 indicators re read once per second and their values are transmitted to the Monitor. We selected this monitoring resolution as it resulted adequate for the anomaly detection algorithm in use, as discussed in [2, 7].

5.2   Evaluation of Probes Intrusiveness

The objective of this study is a quantitative estimation of the intrusiveness [21, 22] of the probes on a Machine, both in terms of system load and network utilization. To reach this purpose we performed experiments to observe the status of the Machine with and without probes. This requires developing the following measuring instruments. The Machine is equipped with a module that every second gets some information about system parameters using the *top* UNIX function; system parameters that we collect are CPU usage, RAM /swap usage, buffer size, system usage per task.

An additional virtual machine is specifically created to control the experiments and collect the results. Such *controller* is able to execute a workload on the Machine to stimulate Liferay services and also collect values from the Machine, e.g., the outputs of the probes is sent to the controller instead of the Monitor. On such controller, the packet sniffer Wireshark [11] executes, collecting packet traffic data coming from the Machine. Note that the introduction of *top* and Wireshark doesn't affect the quality of the analysis: the packet sniffer Wireshark is not located on the target system machine and the *top* command is launched in every test, including those without probes active, introducing a systematic error which is considered equal in all experiments.

To generate the workloads, first of all a cyclic sequence of invocations of Secure! SOAP (*Simple Object Access Protocol*) services are composed. This allowed us to create four different workloads that differ in the delays between subsequent invocations of the services. The duration of the four workloads is approximately 400 s; each of them generates different amount of loads on the Machine, ranging from a very low load (1 invocation every 3.2 s), to higher loads (1 invocation per second in average). Note that the values above are comprehensive of the waiting time for the completion of the execution of the call, which is a rather long time for some services as these devoted to file transmission.

The following experiments are planned and executed: for each of the 4 workloads above, 5 runs with probes active and 5 runs with deactivated probes are executed for a total of 40 runs. Results related to the memory utilization are visible in Fig. 3, which shows the average results for each workload including standard deviation, matching the execution in presence and absence of active probes.

Data related to system utilization allows us to understand how probe processes affects the memory utilization (about 5 % RAM on the Machine, that corresponds to about 150 MB, see the difference between the grey and earl gray bars in Fig. 3), while no significant alteration are identified for the CPU consumption and consequently not shown for brevity. The number of active tasks differs by 15 ones: these are the tasks required to execute the JMX and System Tap for the available set of indicators.

Relevant differences for the execution with and without active probes can be observed regarding the network usage, which is affected by data generated by the probes (figure is not shown for brevity). For example, for the workload with the lowest load, the amount of bytes exchanged without probes is significantly less than those exchanged with active probes. The other three workloads produce network traffic, like remote calls or file transfer, that pile up on the traffic generated by the probes as it is evident from the figures. The additional invocations do not alter the amount of data transmitted by the probes; this is as expected, although it cannot be verified graphically in the figures mostly due to data aggregation at lower stack layers.

5.3 Evaluation of the Monitor Performance

This task is aimed to measure monitor's ability to process data under different loads, where the load is determined by (i) the number of connected machines, and (ii) the number of indicators processed in the Combination Block. The estimation of these quantities aims to find the threshold beyond which the monitor is not able to answer in due time, i.e., the load is so high that the input data keeps queuing in the monitor. Given the limited possibility to instantiate additional Machines on our rack server, to generate the load on the Monitor we created several identical data flows, originating from a unique machine. This was considered a reasonable alternative to have different Machines sending data. Every second, each data flow outputs the values of its indicators as if it was collected via JMX and System Tap.

We want to point out that the elaboration time of a single data block received from a single machine is fundamentally the same regardless of its content, because the amount of data sent every time depends only on the number of indicators observed and not on their value. In addition to this, we have focused our experiments on the evaluation of the number of connected machines rather than the number of indicators sent by the probes. In fact, the number of indicators may be modified given the analysis of the Machine and the coverage and accuracy offered by SPS, possibly reducing the number of indicators to be observed. For the purpose to capture data on system

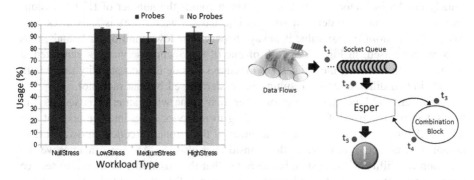

Fig. 3. Memory utilization differences.   **Fig. 4.** Position of time instants in exam.

resource usage, as in the previous experiments, *top* is executing on the Monitor. We also added instructions to the Java source code to timestamp some quantities that allow us to understand which module uses more resources with a growing number of connected data flows (Fig. 4). Getting this data every time a block is analyzed by the Monitor consists in 5 *Java getTime()* invocations, that negligibly increases the load without changing the normal behavior of the system.

Experiments are executed in which a different number of data flows are submitted to the Monitor; each experiment is repeated 5 times. The CPU usage of the monitor sharply rises up, while the RAM has a limited growth, about 1 % of difference between tests with 1 and 7 data flows activate. We measured the overall delay t_5 - t_1 for data flows submitted concurrently to the monitor (Table 1). It resulted that up to 5 data flows, such delay is close to 0 for the whole duration of the experiment, meaning that all data is processed with minimal and stable waiting time. As we can see in Table 1, the processing time grows linearly with respect to the number of data flows i.e., the number of machines; if the number of data flows is above 5, the queuing delay increases, growing more and more as time passes; this would lead first to long queuing time and ultimately to a queue exceeding the allowed queue limit, thus resulting inapplicable in practice. This limit is adequate for the *Secure!* prototype, that is currently in its integration phase, because as specified before it will be composed of 4 Machines.

In the same table we can note that most of the time spent by the monitor is due to the Combination Block (t_4-t_3) activity: while other contributes remain constant (with decreasing percentages), the time spent from this module, that calls SPS for each indicator in exam, rises according to the number of connected Machines. To scale our Monitor for systems with more machines, we can consider that (i) the resources assigned to the Monitor can be raised, (ii) more Monitors can execute in parallel, observing different systems (i.e., multiple virtual machines on a unique rack server), and (iii), a further reduction of the indicators can be defined, and data acquired more sparingly.

5.4   SPS Behavior and Detection Capability

Figure 5 illustrates the transient behavior of SPS when applied to a single indicator, namely the AS indicator *SessionCounter* which counts the number of HTTP sessions created. In Fig. 5a, a golden run with no injected software errors is shown: as time passes, the *SessionCounter* value is always between the lower and upper bounds, thus no alerts are raised. In Fig. 5b a crash of one of the Secure! services is generated at second 200. In this case, the indicator is measured outside the acceptability range built by SPS in two different cases, resulting in an alert raised by that indicator.

To understand how these indicators alter their value when an error is activated in the system we insert a software error leading to a service hang into the code of one service. A timer is set to enable the execution of the erroneous code at a defined time instant. Our objective is to show that considering also the AS, we can improve the detection capability of the system (to be noted that the possibility of detecting service crashes or hangs using the OS indicators was shown in [7]). It should also be noted that

Table 1. Monitor processing times varying the number of connected machines

Machines	Processing time $t_5 - t_1$		Blocks contribution(%)			
	value	Std	queue $t_2 - t_1$	Esper $t_3 - t_2$	comb. block $t_4 - t_3$	alert $t_5 - t_4$
1	178	8,62	0,19	0.38	94,56	4,88
2	382	24,09	0,00	0,17	97,21	2,62
3	526	9,61	0,00	0,06	98,03	1,84
4	688	15,72	0,10	0,05	38,40	1,45
5	856	12,29	0,00	0,12	98,95	0,93
6	994	31,80	0,06	0,10	99,09	0,80
7	1134	3,61	0,00	0,09	99,18	0,68

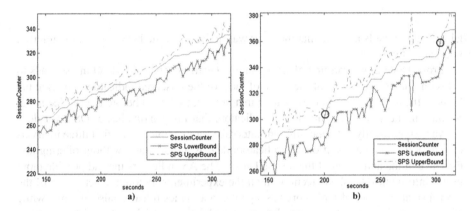

Fig. 5. a) Golden run and b) faulty execution for the HTTP SessionCounter indicator.

the hang we introduced made the service unavailable without generating any notification on the log files of the AS and OS. The expectation in order to detect an anomaly is that after the manifestation of the error, a high number of indicators present a behavior similar to Fig. 5b. We also expect that anomalies are not detected all at the same time, when the error is first activated, but that for some indicators they may be detected at a later stage (e.g., the failure of a service may cause an alteration of the indicator *SessionCounter* only after some seconds that the service is actually failed).

In Table 2 we reported the number of indicators which raised alarms in different time slots during the execution of four experiments: runs 1a and 1b relate to tests with a hang in the service that manages the calendar, while 2a and 2b are characterized by a hang error in the service that manages the file storage. For each run we consider 280 s of workload; the first 120 s are not shown because it is the transient time required by the SPS algorithm to acquire data on the behavior of the indicators and start its prediction [2]. In each run, the error activates at second 160. We aggregate the results considering intervals of 40 s, because of the nature of the hangs we inject: they first manifest at a defined time instant (when the errors activate) but additional time is needed such that their effects can be seen on some of the indicators. For each line in the

Table 2. Alerts raised by the indicators for each interval of time; in grey, the slot of 40 s which follows the injection instants.

		Time Intervals				
Run	**Type**	0 120	120 160	160 200	200 240	240 280
1a	AS	*Transient Phase (120 sec.)*	8	12	9	3
	OS		7	7	7	2
1b	AS		2	6	6	3
	OS		0	3	1	1
2a	AS		2	5	7	0
	OS		1	4	5	0
2b	AS		5	14	11	0
	OS		4	6	6	0

table, the grey cells indicate that the error was activated at the beginning of the referred interval of time.

From Table 2, we can first observe that the heterogeneous workload in use leads to a discontinuous evolutions of the value of most of the observed indicators; this is at the basis of the high number of false alarms that are detected even before the service hang. Second, in most cases the number of indicators that raise anomalies at OS layer does not vary significantly between different intervals: for example, in the first three intervals of run 1a the same amount of OS indicators detects an anomaly, without offering any evidence of the activation of the injected error. The AS indicators instead provide more useful information for the detection; in all the experiments, before the activation of the error a small number of indicators has signaled anomalies (clearly false alarms), while after the service hang a higher number of AS indicators is raising alerts. This suggests that while an accurate tuning process of the SPS parameters is necessary to improve the quality of the detection response, the combined use of information from OS and AS indicators looks a promising approach to enhance the detection capability.

We notice the different behavior of the system depending on the injected error. The service hanged in the runs 1a, 1b alters the behavior of the system with no significant consequences on the whole execution. In fact the failure of the targeted service does not immediately lead to a manifest failure of the whole system, but it could generate inconsistences in the data set that may be at the origin of system degradation at a later stage. In the other two experiments, instead, the error halts the entire system. This is highlighted by the absence of detection in the last reported slot. The whole application hangs until the recovery mechanisms of Tomcat restart the corrupted service allowing the system to resume its execution although at the cost of possible data inconsistencies.

6 Conclusions and Future Works

This paper presented the design, development and assessment of a monitor for anomaly detection. Our solution is based on a CEP monitor that acquires information on both the OS and the AS, and executes the SPS algorithm to identify anomalies. The solution has been exercised on the Secure! system, and it is intended to become a component of the whole Secure! framework as the Secure! project progresses.

Fine tuning of SPS parameters is a long task that is outside the scope of this work, which focuses on presenting and exercising the monitoring system. As future works, we are planning to exploit the Secure! service to further assess the monitoring solution with an appropriate testing campaign. In particular, a further clarification on which indicator works better than others for detection purposes is needed, in order to identify the minimum subset of useful indicators and weight them appropriately.

Acknowledgements. This work has been partially supported by the European Project FP7-PEOPLE-2013-IRSES DEVASSES, the Regional Project POR-CREO 2007-2013 Secure!, and the TENACE PRIN Project (n. 20103P34XC) funded by the Italian Ministry of Education, University and Research.

References

1. Cinque, M., Cotroneo, D., Della Corte, R., Pecchia, A.: Assessing direct monitoring techniques to analyze failures of critical industrial systems. In: ISSRE 2014, pp. 212–222 (2014)
2. Bondavalli, A., Brancati, F., Ceccarelli, A.: Safe estimation of time uncertainty of local clocks. In: ISPCS, pp. 1–6 (2009)
3. Esper Team and EsperTech Inc. "Esper Reference version 4.9.0", Technical report (2012)
4. Oracle corporation., Java Management Extensions (JMX) Technology (2014). http://www.oracle.com. Accessed on 5 March 2015
5. Secure! project. http://secure.eng.it/. Accessed on 5 March 2015
6. IEEE. 1044-2009 - standard classification for software anomalies (2009)
7. Bovenzi, A., Brancati, F., Russo, S., Bondavalli, A.: An OS-level Framework for Anomaly Detection in Complex Software Systems. IEEE Transactions on Dependable and Secure Computing (in press)
8. Liferay. http://www.liferay.com. Accessed on 5 March 2015
9. Oracle Corp. Lesson: Introducing MBeans. https://docs.oracle.com. Accessed on 5 March 2015
10. System Tap. https://sourceware.org/systemtap/. Accessed on 5 March 2015
11. Wireshark. https://www.wireshark.org/. Accessed on 5 March 2015
12. Eom, S.B., Lee, S.M., Kim, E.B., Somarajan, C.: A survey of decision support system applications. Journal of the Operational Research Society, pp. 109–120 (1998)
13. Cameron, M.A., Power, R., Robinson, B., Yin, J.: Emergency situation awareness from twitter for crisis management. In: Proceedings of the 21st International Conference companion on World Wide Web, pp. 695–698 (2012)
14. https://rclserver.dsi.unifi.it/owncloud/public.php?service=files&t=e41b704d5d546f7e14808ed36a94b9e7 (web site)
15. Vianello, V., et al.: A Scalable SIEM correlation engine and its application to the olympic games IT infrastructure. In Proceeding of International Conference on Availability, Reliability and Security (2013)
16. Ficco, M., Romano, L.: A generic intrusion detection and diagnoser system based on complex event processing. CCP **2011**, 275–284 (2011)

17. Cherkasova, L., et al.: Anomaly application change or workload change? towards automated detection of application performance anomaly and change. DSN **2008**, 452–461 (2008)
18. Khanna, G., Varadharajan, P., Bagchi, S.: Automated online monitoring of distributed applications through external monitors. IEEE TDSC **3**(2), 115–129 (2006)
19. Lee, W., Stolfo, S.J.: Data mining approaches for intrusion detection, In: Proceedings of the 7th conference on USENIX Security Symposium, vol. 7, pp. 7–21 (1998)
20. Duchi, F., Antunes, N., Ceccarelli, A., Vella, G., Rossi, F., Bondavalli, A.: Cost-effective testing for critical off-the-shelf services. In: Bondavalli, A., Ceccarelli, A., Ortmeier, F. (eds.) SAFECOMP 2014. LNCS, vol. 8696, pp. 231–242. Springer, Heidelberg (2014)
21. Bondavalli, A., Ceccarelli, A., Falai, L., Vadursi, M.: Foundations of measurement theory applied to the evaluation of dependability attributes. In: DSN 2007, pp. 522–531 (2007)
22. Bondavalli, A., Ceccarelli, A., Falai, L., Vadursi, M.: A new approach and a related tool for dependability measurements on distributed systems. IEEE Trans. Instrum. Meas. **59**(4), 820–831 (2010)
23. Bose, S., Bharathimurugan, S., Kannan, A.: Multi-layer integrated anomaly intrusion detection system for mobile AdHoc networks. In: International Conference on Signal Processing, Communications and Networking, ICSCN 2007. IEEE (2007)
24. Yongguang, Z., Lee, W.: Intrusion detection in wireless ad-hoc networks. In: Proceedings of the 6th annual international conference on Mobile computing and networking. ACM (2000)
25. Kamra, A., Terzi, E., Bertino, E.: Detecting anomalous access patterns in relational databases. VLDB J. **17**(5), 1063–1077 (2008)

Medical Safety Cases

Safety Case Driven Development
for Medical Devices

Alejandra Ruiz[1]([⊠]), Paulo Barbosa[2], Yang Medeiros[2],
and Huascar Espinoza[1]

[1] ICT-European Software Institute, Tecnalia, Parque Tecnológico Ed. 700,
Derio, Spain
{alejandra.ruiz,huascar.espinoza}@tecnalia.com
[2] Núcleo de Tencologias Estratégicas em Saúde – NUTES,
Universidade Estadual da Paraíba, Campina Grande, PB, Brazil
{paulo.barbosa,yang.medeiros}@nutes.uepb.edu.br

Abstract. Medical devices are safety-critical systems that must comply with standards during their development process because of their intrinsic potential of producing harms. Although the existing trend of an increasing complexity of medical hardware and software components, very little has done in order to apply more mature safety practices already present on other industrial scenarios. This paper proposes a methodology to enhance the Model-Based System Engineering (MBSE) state-of-art practices from the safety perspective, encouraging the use of safety cases and providing guidance on how to show the correspondent traceability for the development artifacts. We illustrate our methodology and its usage in the context of an industrial Automated External Defibrillator (AED). We suggest that medical device industry could learn from other domains and adapt its development to take into account the hazards and risks along the development, providing more sophisticated justification, as, for example, the impact of design decisions.

Keywords: Safety case · Medical device · Software development methodology · Automated external defibrillators

1 Context

Safety-critical systems are defined as those which in case of an accident, people or the environment might be put in danger [22]. Different safety-related standards in practice provide guidelines for systems developers. One of the main challenges is that the use of new technologies will be increasingly important for the future and complying with these standards should prevent innovation from being stifled, while still tackling the expected safety objectives. In order to cope with that, those standards and guidelines tend to be sometimes ambiguous and open to multiple interpretations. While those interpretations leave the door open to new ideas, technologies, methods, they also make it difficult for authorities and companies to share the same views. We are talking about the ambiguities resulting from openness to new technologies.

© Springer International Publishing Switzerland 2015
F. Koornneef and C. van Gulijk (Eds.): SAFECOMP 2015, LNCS 9337, pp. 183–196, 2015.
DOI: 10.1007/978-3-319-24255-2_14

In the context of medical devices, new functionalities and the increasing contents of software and hardware components from different manufacturers requires focus on interface, reuse and integration issues. By increasing this technological complexity, we also observe an increase of systematic and random failures. Medical device malfunctions cause hundreds of thousands of incidents and thousands of serious injuries and deaths annually, with these numbers increasing year after year. According to [1–3], it is estimated that medical device malfunctions cause more than 400,000 incidents and 7,000 deaths every year in Europe and the US alone. Safety assurance and certification practices for medical devices must be improved in order to better ensure system safety and to gain more confidence about the safe operation of these systems.

There is a need for better safety assurance and certification practices. Incidents have occurred as a result of inadequate quality assurance practices, impact analysis, and documentation review [4]. Shortcomings in industrial practices have been identified as a culprit for deficiencies in the identification of safety risks [5], traceability management [6] and safety assessment [7].

A study of past medical device failures [4] identified important issues in safety evidence information, having to do with deficiencies in system requirements, verification and validation procedures and results, and impact analysis. One of the main overall problems noted in the study is the lack of detail in safety evidence information (e.g., about its characteristics and the relationship between different pieces of evidence). Specific issues in traceability information have further been reported in [6], including lack of knowledge regarding the artefacts to trace, trace granularity not being clearly defined, redundant traceability information, and important links missing.

A safety case can be defined as a mean to "communicate a clear, comprehensive and defensible argument that a system is acceptably safe to operate in a particular context" [8]. It is an assurance case addressing safety. In fact, a safety case is becoming a requirement on different standards from different domains. For example, lately, the automotive functional safety standard ISO 26262 includes the safety case creation as a requirement for compliance [9].

Safety cases on the heath domain and medical devices in particular are not widely spread. The most notable efforts come from the Generic Infusion Pump project[1] with the safety case for a GPCA pump, becoming a guide for other infusion pumps through the derivation of patterns. Authors in [5, 10] have reported about the start of usage of safety cases on the healthcare system. From [11] we can extract some of the safety assurance case benefits for the application on medical devices:

- Provides a framework and a vehicle to stimulate critical thinking;
- Ensures the completeness of risk identification and risk controls;
- Provides rationale for the validity of risk acceptance;
- Logically documents and connects safety critical information in an easily and understandable manner;
- Communicates safety critical information effectively to internal and external stakeholders.

---

[1] http://rtg.cis.upenn.edu/medical/assurance_cases.html.

The paper is structured as follows. Section 2 defines the purpose of this work and the challenge it faces. Section 3 details the methodology to incorporate safety case development activities over the V model. Section 4 instantiates the methodology with a case study over an industrial medical device. Section 5 discusses the main achieved results and lessons learned. Finally, Sect. 6 points the final remarks and further developments.

2 Objective

This paper focus on the main challenge that medical device industry is facing, *i.e.*, how to deal with the increasing complexity of the systems which directly affects the safety integrity. Similar challenges have been faced by other industries such as automotive or avionics domains. In automotive industry, for example, we have seen mature standardization through ISO 26262 (a functional safety standard for road vehicles) due to concerns such as the growing of ECUs, CANs, LINs, signals and messages. In medical device industry, we are facing the same problems, but without the same interest for supporting solutions. Taking as example a sample Automated External Defibrillator (AED), we should mention there are specific microcontrollers for performing each one of the following functions: (i) analyzing the ECG signal to drive decision processes; (ii) filtering the ECG signal according to several parameters; (iii) modulating frequency signals; (iv) user interface; (v) monitoring the electrical shock and ensuring accurate deliver of energy; (vi) monitoring the electrodes in order to ensure patient safety, among others. Even so, very few multi-core technologies have been used in this domain, as far as we have investigated in the medical instrumentation literature.

We aim at defining a methodology for a safety-oriented software development that will be later on integrated onto hardware. The system software and hardware shall comply with safety standards and we shall ensure the safety of the product. In this sense, we aim at bringing the safety case theory onto medical devices focusing on the software architecture as the main driver. We provide guidance through industrial examples on how to trace the safety requirements and safety related properties for software compliance and integration. In the scope of this paper, we use the Goal Structuring Notation (GSN) [12] as the graphical notation for representing the argumentation on the safety case.

3 Methodology

We present a twofold methodology where safety concerns drive design decisions and, at the same time, we aim at complying with the standard ISO 14971 [14], which is the standard related to risk management on medical devices. As we are addressing the use of Model Based System Engineering (MBSE), the conformance with IEC 62304 standard [13], which is the medical device software – software life cycle processes standard, also needs to be addressed.

For this industry, it is still unclear how safety concerns affect the development of each phase. That is our main justification to introduce the idea of the safety case driven development. We have inspired on the automotive functional safety standard ISO

26262, which proposes a V cycle for system development (including such activities as requirements specification, design, implementation, integration, verification, validation, and configuration). On the automotive domain, a safety case is developed along the lifecycle with the aim at communicating in a clear, comprehensive and defensive argument (supported by evidence) that the system is free of unreasonable risk to operate in a given context. Figure 1 presents an overview of the proposed methodology where the safety case is created along the system development.

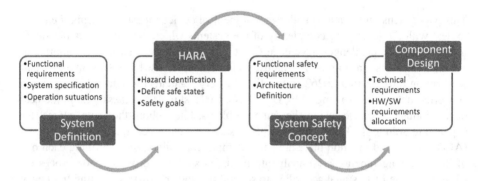

Fig. 1. Safety case driven process for system design

In our approach, safety-related activities progress along the development and provide contexts and outputs to be gathered and used on the safety case:

1. At the *System Definition* phase, we need to specify the functionalities of our system as well as the context in use. This will produce inputs for the context and situations of the use of the medical device that will be introduced into the safety case.
2. At the *Hazard Analysis and Risk Assessments (HARA)* phase, we focus on the identification of possible hazards. This will serve as an input for including functional safety requirements into the requirements list.
3. At the *System Safety Concept* phase, we provide a link with the system architecture as a specification in which safety mechanism and patterns will be put in place in the system so as to fulfill the functional safety requirements at high level.
4. At the *Component Design* phase, we should iterate at the same time with the hardware and the software where we should derive the functional safety requirements and decisions made for the system safety concept definition into more technical requirements. These technical requirements will also be allocated either into hardware, software or both.

Figure 2 shows the arguments decomposition as well as the decomposition process. The context of operation arguments are extracted from the *System Definition* phase. On the *HARA* phase we will gather the arguments related to hazard identification and the safety goals that will serve for linking with the next phase arguments, *i.e.*, the *System Safety Concept*. On this phase, we collect arguments about the functional safety requirements and link them with the decisions made regarding which mechanism we

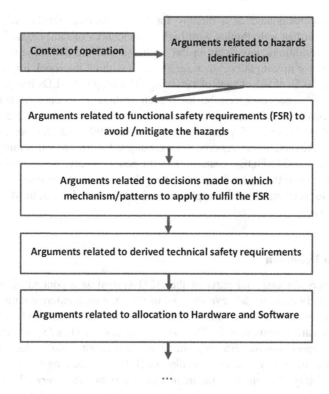

Fig. 2. Safety case decomposition structure

will apply to fulfill those requirements. Finally, on the *Component Design* phase, we should trace the previous requirements with the derived technical requirements and how they are allocated to hardware and software.

4   Use Case

In this section, we explore a running example to demonstrate how the proposed methodology is employed over the development of the medical device *Automated External Defibrillator* (AED), a current research trend inside NUTES. NUTES is part of an initiative for promoting the technological development of Brazil, where the Brazilian Health Ministry has started some technological transfer projects from well-consolidated manufacturers to institutes for science and technologies in order to retain the know-how of manufacturing medical devices inside the country. In this context, the NUTES project is in charge of receiving and improving methodologies for manufacturing AEDs from the Lifemed[2] and providing new improvements.

---

[2] lifemed.com.br.

AEDs are consolidated as a therapy for the ventricular fibrillation/tachycardia, which are the cardiac arrhythmias with highest incidences of fatal cases. In the treatment of such conditions, any delay in the application of the defibrillator shock is an important issue for investigation, since each minute without the shock implies in a loss among 7 % to 10 % of the chance of surviving. The usage of AEDs has gained much more popularity, since they can be used even without a specialized rescuer team available. According to [21], more than 1000 cardiac arrests deaths were connected to the failures of AEDs over 15 years, between January 1993 and October 2008, in the United States. Adverse event reports were catalogued in the Manufacturer and User Device Experience (MAUDE) database. Due to patient safety, both the development and the validation of the technologies for these devices follow rigorous standards.

The next subsections show the application of the methodology defined in Fig. 1 for the AED use case.

4.1   System Definition

Figure 3 depicts the essential parts of the AED system as a context diagram. Considering the safety case, we achieve the goal of showing each external entity, the main functional unities and their interaction with the system. The main input variable to be received is the cardiac pulses of the *Patient*. A module defined as *Signal Analyzer* uses sophisticated algorithms for detecting the signal complexity and to decide if a defibrillator pulse is necessary in case of fibrillation. If it is the case, the *Shock Generator* is in the responsibility of controlling the main output variable, the *energy*, by providing it in the *Biphasic Truncated Exponential* waveform to the *Patient* chest through the *Pads*.

Figure 4 describes the main AED use cases of our interest, which is the chosen scope addressed in this safety case construction running example. These use cases will be referred when assembling the safety case for the context specification.

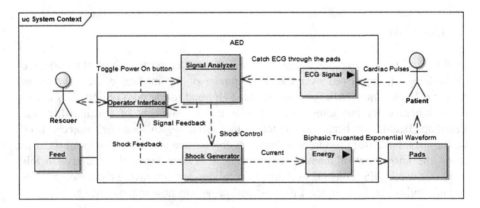

Fig. 3. AED system blocks diagram

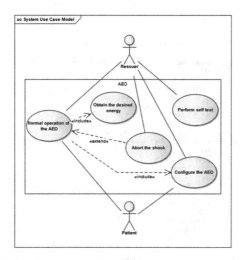

Fig. 4. AED use case model

4.2 Hazard Decomposition

In the scope of this work, we focus on a hazard named *Overshocking*. Figure 5 presents a trace of a specific tool for Enterprise Architect[3] as an add-in for managing development in the context of this research in order to manage architectural elements according to the Risk Management Process described in ISO 14971 [14] standard medical devices and its specific technical report IEC/TR 80002 [15]. Therefore, we see that the main variable to be controlled in the *Overshocking* hazard is energy. The investigated scenario where the hazard is present is *Normal operation of the AED* use case, activating the alternative scenario *Failure to deliver the shock*, since the hazardous situation is having the *Pads* connected to the *Patient*. IEC 62304 on clause 7.3.3 [13] requests us to trace the hazard to the situation and to the item, and later on to the risk mitigation measures put in place. The identified harm is *Skin damage*, affecting the *Patient* chest.

At this stage, we are able to start the safety case construction where the first arguments on the context of operation and arguments referring to hazard identification. By defining safety goals, we mean to insert all information possible about hazard. For example, we have *software safety class* for the *Overshocking* hazard in the category C.

After an effective hazard analysis that should involve systems engineering artifacts, such as the use cases, we proceed with the specification of exception cases, as shown in Fig. 6. The goal is to improve system reliability with the hazard concerns. Finally, we also define safe states at this phase, when defining scenarios and alternative flows. For example, we defined that system must restart and clear all memories after all procedures for verification suggested by exception cases as shown in Fig. 7 for the *Failure to Deliver the Shock* exception case.

---

[3] sparxsystems.com.

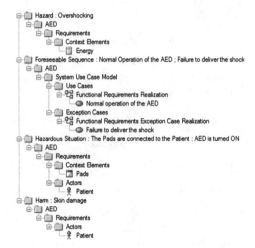

Fig. 5. Hazard *Overshocking* from AED tracing to system engineering artifacts

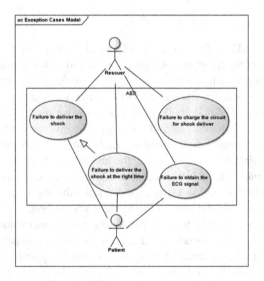

Fig. 6. AED exception cases model

4.3 System Safety Concept

In this phase we have to derive the safety goals into functional safety requirements. Figure 8 describes mitigation procedures that interact with software and hardware components that were identified. These mitigation procedures are the input for the next safety case iteration, which is the decomposition of the safety goals into functional safety requirements. We have created templates for hazard description like the one shown on Table 1, in order to serve as guidelines for functional safety requirements elicitation.

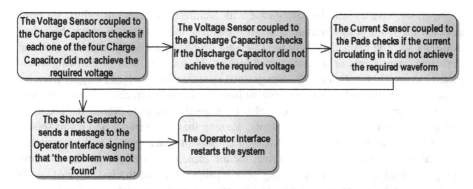

Fig. 7. Failure *to Deliver the Shock* state machine specification to a safe state

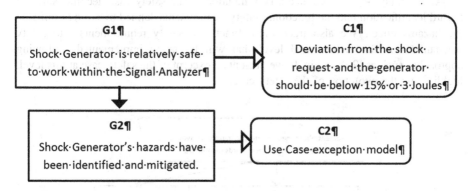

Fig. 8. Safety case at HARA phase

Table 1. Hazard description

Hazard	Overshocking
Cause	The energy delivered is over 15 % or 3 Joules the estimated one
Safety requirements	The delivered energy cannot vary more than 15 % or 3 Joules
Fault categories	Class C: Death or SERIOUS INJURY is possible
Alarm	Deviation is over or equal 14 %
Warning	Deviation is over or equal 10 %
Information	Deviation is over or equal 7 %
Failure mode	When an alarm is triggered, we go to the safe state which is do not deliver any energy at all and reset all the variables and parameters to the default state.
Failure distribution	If we capture the desired energy with a deviation, we send the deviation as entrance for the algorithm to process the quantity of energy to be delivered; we send a command to deliver the energy with a deviation; we will also send the deviation as an entrance to the monitoring function and we deviation might not be detected. (fail in all those software units)

Next, we have to link the safety case with architectural decisions. Thus, we have modeled the main design decisions about the safety mechanisms to cover the safety requirements. The main causes for the *Overshocking* hazard were identified as wearing electronic components or an unexpected loss of the software control throwing unexpected values. This motivates new fine grained specifications such as charging rates for capacitors; specific peak values; or specific frequencies over semiconductors switching. These fine grained specifications can also be refined as fault tolerance requirements such as indication of wear of components, warning that maintenance and repair should be provided; coupling of new amortization circuits in order to deal with unexpected peak values; or coupling of new circuits for the management of periods for avoiding extrapolation of time limits for issuing peak tensions. Finally, the last layer of specification will require specific sensors and actuators for efficient detections and actions over all hazardous conditions.

At this time, we also produce a new iteration of the safety case decomposing the hazard identification into the functional safety requirements defined to avoid or mitigate the hazards effect. We also trace these functional safety requirements into safety mechanisms at the architectural level that will be lately implemented, following approaches such as [20]. In Fig. 9, we present an excerpt of the safety case at this level, highlighting the evolution of the safety case.

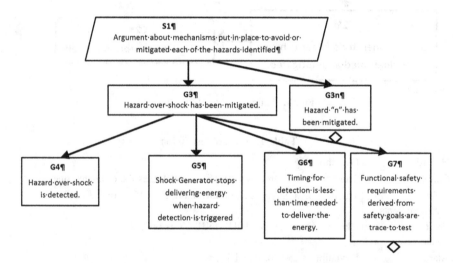

Fig. 9. Excerpt of AED safety case at system safety concept level

4.4   Component Design

The proposed approach focuses on traceability and the suggested solution shall explicitly demonstrate the mapping from *System Goals* to *Electronic Components*, in case of a hardware mitigation solution, or to a *Software Component*, in case of a software mitigation solution. It is at this phase where most of the design decisions were taken and needs to be traced.

In order to discuss a specific concern, we start by discussing some traceability and design decisions over the software component inside the *Signal Analyzer* block, since it is essential do decide whether the patient needs a shock, and automatically decide what the parameters of the shockable-energy are. Focusing on one of the claims, which are still under development from the safety case shown on previous section, we see that among other issues, we decided to implement a data error detection mechanism. In order to do so, we have implemented the *ErrorHandler* component. This component has the responsibility of avoiding problems that could interfere in the correct decision of applying the shock, such as signal propagation discrepancies, influences of harmonics, floating point corrections, among others. We took a design decision with the component realization modeling for the Process ECG component according to the *Pipes and Filters* design pattern for safety purposes. In this sense, we divided each specific phase of the ECG signal processing into filters and throughout this process, information concerning errors and flaws are collected and processed in the *Error-Handler* module for activating safe states.

Finally, in Fig. 10, we show how the safety activities influenced the system's design solution in a codesign scenario. A specific excerpt of the design concerning the hazard *Overshocking* is shown in the upper part of the figure as a traceability model. In the end of the trace, we have 4 components. Two of these components are for detection, as *Voltage and Current Sensors*. The other two are actual mitigation components, as a *Snubber* for controlling frequency switching of the semiconductors near the transformer and a *Charge Controller* to close the loop in the secondary of the transformer in order to correct voltage peaks. These components are mapped to the bottom part of the figure as Simulink model and are realized in the component implementation phase.

5 Brief Discussion

In this section, we provide a discussion about the main efforts from the system designer viewpoint according to the development of a safety case. In our opinion, the metrics to define the main suitability and improvements of the methodology come from the care when dealing with traceability between safety engineering and safety engineering artifacts can be assigned to the availability of solutions and patterns to do that in the current state of MBSE approaches. This could be observed in all the phases when building the safety case.

For example, currently we have very good approaches for system definition and document software and system architectures. Approaches based on ISO 42010 [16], Architecture Tradeoff Analysis Method (ATAM) [17], Software Architecture Analysis Method (SAAM) [18], Active Reviews for Intermediate Design (ARID) [18], Views and Perspectives [19], among others, are suitable to address the main issues when defining a system architecture with concerns that are able to fill well what is required by the safety case. All these approaches can be easily supported by UML/SysML modeling tools, such as Enterprise Architect, by following good design practices.

At the *HARA* phase, we have defined a domain specific solution to trace hazard analysis and risk assessment artifacts from ISO 14971, such as *Foreseeable Sequence*,

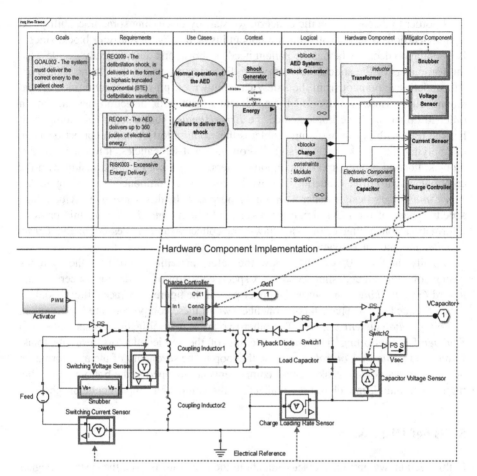

Fig. 10. Traceability from system engineering artifacts towards mitigation components

Hazardous Situation and *Harm* to system engineering artifacts such as *Context Elements*, *Actors*, *Subsystems*, *Use Cases*, among others.

For the *safety concept*, focusing on the *Overshocking* hazard, we were able to specify and show conformance of a bunch of mitigation procedures in a qualitative way. During the safety requirements decomposition, we have showed the early detection of need for error handlers for software components and sensors (e.g. for voltage and current), controllers (e.g. for charge) and suppressors (e.g. *Snubber*). The main metrics at this phase can be checked with analytic models, built, for example, in powerful platforms such as Matlab/Simulink, ISOGRAPH, among others, allowing later realization with more feasible and validated safety constraints.

Finally, during the *component realization* phase, the safety case focuses on the measures that the design shall reflect in order to prove to be safe. Criteria such as requirements coverage, design decisions being impacted or even efforts on the design realization are important testimonials before starting the validation phase, where tests shall provide for each design phase following the V model discipline.

6 Conclusions and Future Work

In this paper, we have demonstrated the main benefits of a methodology for safety-critical system development based on MBSE that is driven by the construction of safety cases. The main activities were explained following an example-driven approach, through a case study on an industrial medical device. This explanation provided a clear traceability between system design main phases in a tool integrated way. Furthermore, several trends continue under investigation, intending to provide a tool chain integration, where compliance management tools will be able to exchange information between design environments, testing tools and safety cases. For the main features, we are adapting GSN tools for new concepts still unexplored, such as decomposition and traceability to safety requirements, architectural elements and a bunch of operation between safety cases in order to provide fusions between safety specifications.

As future work, we shall follow the compliance with the complete V model and directions on each phase of validation part will be provided. One of the most challenging parts that we aim to continue researching is on the component composition perspective. Different suppliers could come up with different developments that will compose the system. Finally, we also plan to incorporate modular safety cases applications to this approach. Modular safety cases are described on the extension B1 of the GSN standard.

References

1. Alemzadeh, A., Iyer, R.K., Kalbarczyk, Z., Raman, F.: Analysis of safety-critical computer failures in medical devices. IEEE Secur. Priv. **11**(4), 14–26 (2013)
2. MHRA: Report on Devices Adverse Incidents in 2010 (2011). http://www.mhra.gov.uk/home/groups/dts-bs/documents/publication/con129234.pdf
3. The Boston Consulting Group: EU Medical Device Approval Safety Assessment: A comparative analysis of medical device recalls 2005–2009 (2011). http://www.eucomed.org/uploads/Press%20Releases/BCG%20study%20report.pdf
4. Wallace, D.R., Kuhn, D.R.: Failure modes in medical device software: an analysis of 15 years of recall data. Int. J. Reliab. Qual. Saf. Eng. **8**(4), 351–371 (2001)
5. The Health Foundation: Supplements to: Using safety cases in industry and healthcare (2012). http://www.health.org.uk/public/cms/75/76/313/3847/Using%20safety%20cases%20in%20industry%20and%20healthcare_supplements.pdf?realName=yjOYNa.pdf
6. Mäder, P., Jones, P.L., Zhang, Y., Cleland-Huang, J.: Strategic Traceability for Safety-Critical Projects. IEEE Softw. **30**(3), 58–66 (2013)
7. Eucomed: Towards a regulation that guarantees patient safety, ensures patient access and keeps innovation in Europe (2013). http://www.eucomed.org/uploads/Modules/Publications/20130130_2013_eucomed_detailed_position_on_proposal_mdd_revision.pdf
8. Kelly, T.: Arguing Safety - A Systematic Approach to Managing Safety Cases. Ph.d. thesis, Department of Computer Science, The University of York (1998)
9. ISO 26262 International Organization for Standardization (ISO), "ISO/DIS 26262: Road vehicles - functional safety," (2011)

10. Bloomfield, R., Chozos, N., Embrey, D., Henderson, J., Kelly, T., Koornneef, F., Pasquini, A., Pozzi, S., Sujan, M.-A.: A Pragmatic Review of the Use of Safety Cases in Industry–Lessons and Prerequisites for their Application in Healthcare (2011)
11. Eagles, S., Wu, F.: Safety Assurance Cases for Medical Devices. In: AAMI 2014, Biomedical Instrumentation & Technology, February 2014
12. GSN Community Standard. Version.: Origin Consulting GSN Community Standard Version 1 (2011)
13. International Electrotechnical Commission Medical device software – Software life cycle processes. INTERNATIONAL IEC STANDARD 62304 First edition 2006-05. International Electrotechnical Commission (2006). Accessed 2 June 2012
14. ISO 14971 - medical devices – application of risk management to medical devices. Technical report, International Organization for Standardization (2010)
15. IEC/TR 80002-1:2009: Medical Device Software Part 1: Guidance on the application of ISO 14971 to medical device software. ISO, Switzerland (2009)
16. ISO/IEC 42010 (IEEE Std) 1471-2000: Systems and Software engineering- Recomended practice for architectural description of software-intensive systems, ISO/IEC/(IEEE), p. 23
17. Rick, K., Mark, K., Paul, C: ATAM: Method for Architecture Evaluation, Software Engineering Institute, Carnegie Mellon University, Pittsburgh, Pennsylvania, Technical report CMU/SEI-2000-TR-004 (2000). http://resources.sei.cmu.edu/library/asset-view.cfm? AssetID=5177
18. Dobrica, L., Niemelä, E.: A survey on software architecture analysis methods. IEEE Trans. Softw. Eng. 28(7), 638–653 (2002)
19. Rozanski, N., Woods, E.: Software Systems Architecture: Working with Stakeholders Using Viewpoints and Perspectives. Addison-Wesley Professional, Reading (2005)
20. Antonino, P., Trapp, M..: Improving consistency checks between safety concepts and view based architecture design. In: Proceedings of 12th International Probabilistic Safety Assessment and Management Conference, PSAM 2014, Honolulu, Hawaii, USA, 22–27 June 2014
21. DeLuca Jr., L., et al.: Analysis of automated external defibrillator device failures reported to the food and drug administration. Annals Emerg. Med. 59(2), 103–111 (2012)
22. Knight, J.C.: Safety critical systems: challenges and directions. In: Proceedings of the 24th International Conference on Software Engineering, ICSE 2002, pp. 547–550, 25 May 2002

Towards an International Security Case Framework for Networked Medical Devices

Anita Finnegan[⊠] and Fergal McCaffery

Regulated Software Research Centre,
Dundalk Institute of Technology, Dundalk, Ireland
{anita.finnegan, fergal.mccaffery}@dkit.ie

Abstract. Medical devices (MDs) are becoming increasingly networked. Given, that safety is the most significant factor within then MD industry and the radical shift in MDs design to enable them to be networked, it would make sense that strong security requirements associated with networking of a device should be put in place to protect such devices from becoming increasingly vulnerable to security risks. However, this is not the case. Networked MDs may be at risk. In an attempt to reduce this risk to the MD industry there are a number of upcoming regulatory changes, which will affect the development of networked MDs, how they are regulated and how they are managed in operation. Consequently, an industry-wide issue exists as there is currently no standardised way to assist organisations to satisfy such security related requirements. This paper describes ongoing research for the development of an innovative framework to improve the overall security practices adopted during MD development, in operation and through to retirement.

Keywords: Networked medical devices · Medical device security assurance · Medical device cybersecurity · Assurance case · Security case · Security capabilities

1 Introduction

In 2011, at the Black Hat Security Conference in Las Vegas, a diabetic security researcher hacked his own insulin pump during his presentation [1]. This was the first of many high profile showcases and such events subsequently raised a lot of concern within the Medical Device (MD) domain. In 2012, the US Government Accountability Office (GAO) conducted an inquiry into the Food and Drug Administration's (FDAs) assessment of medical devices (MDs). The resultant outcome, detailing the FDA's lack of consideration for both intentional and non-intentional security vulnerabilities during the Premarket Approval (PMA) and 510 k assessments, was published in August 2012 [2]. It is now apparent that MD security is becoming more stringently regulated following the publication of FDAs Guidance document for Cybersecurity in Medical Devices [3]. As a result of this guidance, medical device manufacturers (MDMs) will now be required to include, at a minimum, the following documentation for premarket submissions (in relation to cybersecurity of MDs):

© Springer International Publishing Switzerland 2015
F. Koornneef and C. van Gulijk (Eds.): SAFECOMP 2015, LNCS 9337, pp. 197–209, 2015.
DOI: 10.1007/978-3-319-24255-2_15

"Hazard analysis, mitigations, and design considerations pertaining to intentional and unintentional cybersecurity risks associated with your device, including:

(a) A specific list of all cybersecurity risks that were considered in the design of your device;
(b) A specific list and justification for all cybersecurity controls that were established for your device;
(c) A traceability matrix that links your actual cybersecurity controls to the cybersecurity risks that were considered".

These requirements will affect development procedures for MDs that are intended to be placed on a network, how they are regulated and how they are managed during operation. This presents an issue as there is currently no standardized way to assist organizations to satisfy new security related requirements [2].

This paper discusses the development of a security assurance case (henceforth security case) framework which can be adopted by both MDMs and Healthcare Delivery Organisations (HDOs) to improve overall security practices during MD development, whilst in operation and through to retirement.

2   Solution Overview

Assurance cases are structured, evidence based arguments used to demonstrate confidence that a system holds a particular critical property [4]. Assurance cases were originally used to address safety concerns for systems. However, the uses of assurance cases have been widely adopted and now address other critical properties such as dependability, reliability and security across a range of safety critical domains such as automotive, railway, defence, aviation etc. An assurance case is called a security case when used to argue the security of a system. Similarly they are referred to as safety cases when arguing safety. In this framework, the objective of the security case argument is to demonstrate confidence in the establishment of security capabilities (as outlined in IEC/TR 80001-2-2) [5]. This particular approach was taken as it is tremendously difficult, if not impossible, to argue that a system is secure beyond all doubt [6, 7]. Therefore, a more obtainable goal to argue that a number of security capabilities have been adequately established using a risk based approach has been adopted [4]. A security argument pattern is used in this work using the Goal structure notation (GSN) [8].

IEC/TR 80001-2-2 [5] aims to promote the communication of security controls, needs and risks of MDs which are intended to be incorporated into IT networks, between MDMs, IT vendors and HDOs [9] through the use of an informative set of high-level security capabilities. The security capabilities, of which there are 19 (Table 1), are the foundation upon which this security pattern has been developed. In addition to IEC/TR 80001-2-2, this research also leverages on a number of other industry-generic security standards (NIST SP-800-53 [10], ISO/IEC 15408-2 [11], ISO/IEC 15408-3 [12], ISO/IEC 27002 [13], ISO 27799 [14], IEC 62443-3-3 [15]). Each of these standards provides families of security controls that can be utilized to establish the security capabilities and hence, inform part of the security pattern.

Table 1. IEC/TR 80001-2-2 security capabilities

Code	Security Capability	Code	Security Capability
ALOF	Automatic logoff	MDLP	Malware protection/detection
AUDT	Audit controls	NAUT	Node authentication
AUTH	Authorization	PAUT	Person authentication
CNFS	Configuration of security features	PLOK	Physical locks on device
CSUP	Cyber security product upgrades	SGUD	Security guides
DTBK	Data backup/disaster recovery	SAHD	System & application hardening
IGAU	Health data integrity & authenticity	DIDT	Health data de-identification
STCF	Health data storage & confidentiality	TXCF	Transmission confidentiality
TXIG	Transmission integrity	EMRG	Emergency access
RDMP	Third-party components in product lifecycle		

3   Approach

This section outlines the research method for developing the security case and the approach to developing the components of the pattern with the inclusion of mappings informing a component of the pattern.

3.1   Method

Action design research [16] (ADR) is a combination of design research (DR) and action research (AR) that provides guidance for the building, intervention and evaluation of an IT artifact as a research strategy. "It focuses on the building, intervention, and evaluation of an artefact that reflects not only the theoretical precursors and intent of the researchers but also the influence of users and on-going use in context" [16]. Given the nature of this research in developing a security risk management solution (involving input from a number of stakeholders from standards communities, HDO's, MDMs etc.) and the versatile nature of security threats and vulnerabilities, this approach to developing the framework was considered to be the most appropriate. There are four stages involved in applying ADR [16]. These are: (1) Problem formulation, (2) Building, intervention and evaluation, (3) Reflection and learning and (4) Formalization of learning.

The objective of the problem formulation stage (done by performing a literature review) was also to establish and refine the scope of the work. The following research objectives (ROs) were developed as a result:

- **RO.1:** Perform a literature review to investigate the problem area and guide the study;
- **RO.2:** Establish the approach and structure for the security case;
- **RO.3:** Develop the argument patterns for the security case;
- **RO.4:** Identify mappings between the components of the security case;
- **RO.5:** Validate the security case.

The focus of the remainder of this paper relates to RO.2 through to RO.5. Stage 2 of ADR, is called "Building, Intervention, and Evaluation" (BIE) and is based upon the findings and output from Stage 1 to provide a platform to develop the initial design. This was an iterative stage where the BIE cycles were executed in order to allow the IT artifact and the organizational context to intersect. Practitioners involved in the BIE cycle include the ISO/TC215 JWG7 standards community, a private US based HDO and an additional focus group made up of both security and assurance case experts.

The remainder of this section discusses the work carried out to achieve RO.2 (Establish the approach and structure for the security case), RO.3 (Develop the argument patterns for the security case) and RO.4 (Identify mappings between the components of the security case).

3.2   Security Case and Pattern Development

Using a combination of techniques established in risk management and security-risk management literature and standards (informed by the LR), a structured method for the presentation of the components of the security case was developed. As previously stated, the purpose of the security case is to demonstrate confidence in the establishment of the security capabilities from IEC/TR 80001-2-2 which heavily influenced the layout of the security case components. Therefore, the top level claim for the security case will be claiming that all required security capabilities have been acceptably established meaning; IEC/TR 80001-2-2 has been adequately applied.

The security capabilities were selected for this research due to the fact that this technical report, IEC/TR 80001-2-2 is the only security specific document that contains security requirements for networked medical devices. Furthermore, FDA's cybersecurity guidance [17] recommends the use of this technical report to guide the security risk assessment activities for medical devices.

Although assurance cases are already in use in the medical device industry (a safety case is required for FDA a PMA and 510 k approval for infusion pump MDMs), the process for development has proven challenging for MDMs [18]. The reason for this is due to the lack of guidance for developing safety cases, the time and resources required to develop a safety case and also the lack of instruction regarding what constitutes as "enough" in terms of evidence gathered. Because of these challenges it was decided to focus the security case in terms of applying a specific re-useable argument pattern to argue specific security capabilities. The use of the argument pattern is applied to each of the security capabilities. It employs a risk based approach similar to common safety risk assessment practices as MDMs already have in place.

Figure 1 shows the top level argument for the security case. The meaning of GSN symbols and pattern adornments can be found in the GSN Standard [8]. The top goal, IEC 80001-2-2 security capabilities successfully established for device [#], is supported by a number of context references. This information is included in the security case to support the development of the security case. Gathering and storing this information in one location along with the risk analysis is intended to inform the development, maintenance and updating of the security case. For the purposes of post-market surveillance or in the event of an incident concerning a medical device, supporting information such as this is useful for root cause analysis purposes. It is also useful in a case where a reader/assessor is reviewing the security case in order to determine the adequacy of the evidence gathered. The information should influence the choice of security capabilities to be established. Including reference to the risk control policy will drive risk reduction activities detailed in the argument pattern.

Once the generic structure and purpose of the security case had been established, an argument pattern was developed using the outputs from RO.2 and RO.3.

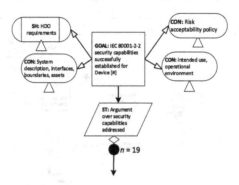

Fig. 1. Security case top level argument

3.3 Security Pattern

The argument pattern developed adapts two approaches known as the (1) goal based approach and (2) the standards and guidelines approach. The goal-based approach uses arguments and evidence to support a particular critical property (i.e. safety, security, reliability) of a system in a "top down" approach. This research focuses on security as the critical property arguing over a specific set of security capabilities. The developed argument pattern contains the steps a developer would use in carrying out a risk assessment and so, the approach of the argument pattern incorporates a number of security risk management standards and guidelines [19, 20]. Table 2 presents the pattern which is applied to each of the security capabilities. The entire security case is made up of the top level argument (Fig. 1) and the pattern applied 19 times.

3.4 Security Controls/Security Capability Mapping

A key part of this research was to conduct a mapping to identify security controls from a selection of security related standards that could be used to help establish each of the 19 security capabilities outlined in IEC/TR 80001-2-2. The security controls identified with the work are intended to inform the security case in particular, the relationship between G3 and G7 outlined in Table 2.

The first step in conducting the security mapping was to identify the most appropriate security related standards. Initially, the criterion for selecting the standards for the mapping was based on popularity of use and level of security rigour in terms of the

Table 2. Pattern

	Security Capability Argument Pattern
Pattern Name	
Author	Anita Finnegan
Intent	This pattern provides a framework for arguing security capabilities. Security capabilities that can be defeated (in the given context) are sufficiently instantiated following a risk reducing pattern.
AKA	IEC/TR 80001-2-2 Security Case
Structure	
G1	For each security capability, a *claim* to specifically address each one should be included.
CON1	G1 *inContextOf* IEC/TR 80001-2-2 reference security capability
G2 **or** G3	Either G3 or G4 child-*goal* should be developed here. The black diamond represents optionality (G3 or G4).
J1	The reason security capability [#] has not been selected should be included as a justification for the *goal* G2.
J2	A security capability is required where the capability protects a documented asset. This should be included as a justification for the *goal* G3 and further development of the security

(Continued)

Table 2. (*Continued*)

Pattern Name	Security Capability Argument Pattern
ST1	*Strategy* to argue over all threats/vulnerabilities that can defeat security capability [#].
CON2	For security capability [#], include (or instantiate) all defeating threats/vulnerabilities identified.
A1	ST1 relies on the assumption that risk identification was carried out. Instantiate with details of completion.
G4	*Claim* that no unacceptable risks remain for security capability [#].
Sn1	Where no unacceptable risks exist, evidence should be provided to support this. (n=0).In order to provide confidence in this assertion (G4), solution (Sn1) should be instantiated. Records of threat/vulnerability log should be included to indicate no remaining unacceptable risks. For all remaining risks requiring risk reduction, G6 should be developed.
G5	Where unacceptable risk remains, what threats/vulnerabilities require risk reduction? Each threat/vulnerability presenting unacceptable risk should be explicitly stated here to be addressed in the following sub-goals. When developing the security case there may be a number of claims in parallel to this depending on the number of threats and vulnerabilities requiring risk treatment. This is indicated by the arrow with a black dot and n>0.
CON3	What is the associated consequence of this? Details of consequence associated with identified threats/vulnerabilities (and unacceptable risk) should be included (or instantiated) *inContextOf* G5.
ST2	Change the *strategy* to argue over the security controls. The strategy of the argument should change to address risk control measures for threat/vulnerability [#].
G6	What security controls reduce the risk associated with threat/vulnerability [#]? For each mitigating security control(s), assert that the security control has been implemented.
CON4	Identify the source for the selected security control. Include (or instantiate) the source of the security control selected e.g. IEC/TR 80001-2-8 clause [#].
Sn2	Provide evidence of the correct implementation of security control [#].
G7	Does the security control [#] introduce new threats/vulnerabilities? Claim to show that no new threats remain.
Sn3 **OR** G4	Where no new threats/vulnerabilities are introduced provide evidence of this in the threat/vulnerability/risk log **OR** Where new threats/vulnerabilities have been introduced with the implementation of security control [#] revert back to follow the process from G4.

range of security controls and associated requirements to apply a particular security control. The set of standards selected was then validated for appropriateness by four experts in the security domain. The standards agreed upon include (1) ISO/IEC 27001, (2) ISO 27799, (3) ISO/IEC 15408-2, (4) ISO/IEC 15408-3, (5) NIST 800-53 and (5) IEC 62443-3-3. A total of 863 security controls across all 6 security standards were identified as security capability controls. However, many security controls were mapped to multiple security capabilities and therefore, in total, for all security capabilities, 1225 controls were included in the mappings. The security capabilities with the most mapped security controls included: (1) Malware detection/protection, (2) Node authentication and (3) Security Guides. The security capabilities with the least number of security controls included: (1) Automatic log off, (2) Health data de-identification and (3) Health data storage confidentiality.

The process in which the mappings were conducted from standard to standard is outlined in Fig. 2. An example of a mapping for the security capability "Automatic log off" is presented below in Table 3.

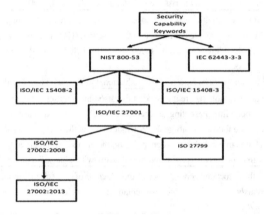

Fig. 2. Workflow for mapping

Table 3. Automatic log off mapping to security controls

Standard	Ref	Control
SP 800-53	AC-1	Access Control Policy and Management
	AC-11	Session Lock
	AC-12	Session termination
	IA-11	Re-authentication
ISO/IEC 15408-2	FTA_SSL	Session Locking and Termination
	FMT_SAE	Security Attribute Expiration
	FIA_UAU	User Authentication
ISO/IEC 27002	5.1.1	Policies for information security
	5.1.2	Review of the Information Security Policy
	9.1.1	Access control policy
	9.4.2	Secure Log-On Procedures
	11.2.8	Unattended user equipment
	11.2.9	Clear desk and clear screen policy
	18.2.2	Compliance with Security Policies and Standards
ISO 27799	7.2.1	Information Security Policy Document
	7.2.2	Review of the Information Security Policy
	7.8.1.2	Access Control Policy
	7.8.3	Unattended User Equipment
	7.8.3	Clear desk and Clear Screen Policy

4 Results

This section discusses the work done to date in relation to the evaluation of the security pattern and the security mappings. As with action design research (ADR), the security case was developed initially outside of an authentic setting i.e. a medical device manufacturer. As part of the BIE cycle, this work has been evaluated by experts as an iterative process throughout the research. This has guided the enhancement and refinement of the work to date. As part of the "expert evaluation" a number of channels were utilized to validate the work.

The security pattern was presented to a HDO for feedback in 2013. The HDO is a non-for-profit health system in the US that includes four hospitals on five campuses, dozens of outpatient clinics, thousands of affiliated physicians, home health and hospice care. A questionnaire was developed by the researcher to obtain constructive feedback on the potential use and benefit of the security case for HDOs. Due to restrictions in terms of space the transcript of the interview cannot be included here, however, in summary; feedback from the HDO respondent reported the security case pattern to be helpful in terms of the management of security risk practices. The respondent noted that the information on the security case would be a key element to evaluating all changes on a network containing MDs as well as during assessments in the event of network problems or events *(e.g., "Was this threat missed in the security case?" or "Was the control properly managed?", etc.).* Another expressed advantage of the security case is that it would enable concrete and standardised communication between the various stakeholders (HDOs, IT vendors, MDMs).

Additionally, the security case work was invited as a New Work Item Proposal (NWIP) for the International Standards Committee ISO/TC215, JWG7 as a new work item with ISO/IEC. The purpose of this security case TR is to provide guidance to MDMs, IT vendors and HDOs for developing, interpreting and updating security cases (using GSN) for networked medical devices. This will contribute to RO.5 (validation) with expert evaluation from the International Standards Community during the drafting process. This work was raised as a NWIP [21] in May 2014. The TR (IEC/TR 80001-2-9) has since been approved by the committee members and undergone one round of comments and a subsequent revision.

The work conducted in identifying security controls required to establish security capabilities was also proposed as a New Work Item Proposal (NWIP) with the International Standards Committee ISO/TC215, JWG7. Developing the mappings as a TR (IEC/TR 80001-2-8) with the International Standards Committee again provided expert evaluation for the research and hence, contributed to the overall validation of the work (RO.5). As part of this review process, the security mappings have been circulated to all members of the International JWG7 Standards Community. Members of this committee include experts from both industry (HDOs and MDMs) and academia. During this time, members were given the opportunity to comment on the mappings until such a time as the members agree to publish the work as a working TR.To date, there have been three rounds of comments and subsequent revisions to the TR and it is expected that this will be published and available to the healthcare domain in late 2015.

As the expertise required to evaluate the mappings was very specialized, a separate evaluation was conducted in parallel to the standard community's work. For this, a group of security experts, competent in the use of the selected security standards, carried out an additional technical review of the mappings. Each expert focused their review on security standard for all security capabilities. The work carried out here also resulted in a number of changes to the mappings.

Table 4 presents the summary of changes to the number of security controls mapped to each of the security capabilities throughout the duration of this research.

Table 4. Security control mapping – summary of evaluations

Code	# Pre-review	# Post-review	#Additional	#Removed	Difference
ALOF	22	24	2	0	+2
AUDT	45	47	2	0	+2
AUTH	33	38	5	0	+5
CNFS	38	41	5	2	+3
CSUP	34	34	3	3	0
DIDT	17	22	6	1	+5
DTBK	17	18	2	1	+1
EMRG	25	26	9	8	+1
IGAU	38	37	2	3	−1
MLDP	86	83	2	5	−3
NAUT	80	76	2	4	−7
PAUT	71	68	0	3	−3
PLOK	42	44	3	1	+2
RDMP	46	42	1	5	−4
SAHD	57	56	1	2	−1
SGUD	73	70	5	3	−3
STCF	20	27	10	3	+7
TXCF	35	36	4	3	+1
TXIG	27	23	0	4	−4

5 Future Work

In order to validate the work done to date, a pilot is currently being conducted with an Irish medical device manufacturer. This is a critical phase when applying ADR to a research project as this allows for the observation and analysis of the framework in an authentic setting. The results, of which, will allow for the researcher to adjust the framework and draw from it, a generic set of design principles applicable to a broader set of problems and/or settings.

This phase is a highly participatory process relying on the commitment of the manufacturer to guide the framework to an advanced, adaptive framework. The following describes the phases of industry evaluation.

Stage 1 of the Pilot- Training – Completed. Training was provided to two developers (familiar with the development project for the selected device), a risk manager and a project manager from the MDM prior to conducting the industry evaluation. The aim of this training was to provide the pilot participants with adequate knowledge to enable the creation of a single thread security case and its inherent components.

Stage 2 of the Pilot – Security Pattern Development Trial – Completed. The input required for this stage of the pilot was a detailed description of the selected medical device including its intended use. During this stage the participants selected 2 security capabilities (automatic log off and node authentication) that most closely matched the security features of their medical device. Independently, the two developers then developed the security case threads for the two security capabilities. This activity was performed over a number of days by the two developers without the researcher being present.

Stage 3 - Results Gathering – Session 1 – June 2015. The input required for this stage of the pilot is the completed security case patterns from stage 3 (for each security capability) from each of the participants. This will be conducted in a two part feedback session/focus group. The purpose of the first session is to gather the core information from each of the participants in relation to the: participants' level of skill/experience in conducting security risk assessments; participants' involvement in the actual product development; ease of the process using the components of the pattern; accuracy and coverage of the security control mappings; potential to re-use strands of the pattern linking cybersecurity threats to vulnerabilities and controls.

Stage 4 - Results Gathering – Session 2. This stage will involve two developers, the risk manager, the researcher and the project manager. The inputs to this stage will be the two completed security case patterns and the original security risk analysis artifact for the product. This second focus group session will be conducted to analyze the accuracy of the objective evidence gathered by the developers during the trial and to assess how the security pattern informed the internal approval/sign-off procedure. The core information gathered during this session will relate to the: readability of the security pattern; level of detail contained in the pattern; accuracy of objective evidence; potential to re-use strands of the pattern linking cybersecurity threats to vulnerabilities and controls; time required assessing the security pattern; comparative analysis of the original security risk analysis compared to security pattern outputs; and security pattern output compared to the FDA cybersecurity documentation requirements.

6 Conclusion

Due to the nature of security and its evolving threat profile, it is difficult to assert that a MD is secure, or will remain secure in any given context. Therefore, the approach taken in this research is to demonstrate confidence in the establishment of a set of security capabilities. These security capabilities include a broad category of security controls required to manage risks to confidentiality, integrity, availability and accountability of MDs.

The objective of this research is to develop a solution for both MDMs and HDOs to manage MD security assurance. A key component of this research is based upon the two international TRs that are currently being developed by the researcher. It should be noted that, because there are number of these TRs, one of the key objectives is to integrate the guidance from each of these reports into a single end-to-end framework. The purpose of this is to enable organisations to seamlessly implement them in a standardised and structured sequence.

Developing security cases for use by MDMs to demonstrate security capabilities, with the inclusion of security patterns, will assist MDMs in gathering the appropriate evidence to provide confidence in the security of their MDs. This will provide MDMs with a mechanism to address particular security threats or vulnerabilities in a repeatable and assured manner while also producing the artefacts as recommended in FDAs cybersecurity guidance. Likewise, using these security cases will equip HDOs with an effective way to manage, monitor and maintain the security of MDs to better assure the overall security of the healthcare network. Another advantage for HDOs is that through the supply and use of security cases, HDOs will better understand the security capability of a MD and therefore will better understand the requirements to maintain this.

Acknowledgments. This research is supported by the Science Foundation Ireland (SFI) Principal Investigator Programme, grant number 08/IN.1/I2030 (the funding of this project was awarded by Science Foundation Ireland under a co-funding initiative by the Irish Government and European Regional Development Fund), and supported in part by Lero - the Irish Software Engineering Research Centre (http://www.lero.ie) grant 10/CE/I1855.

References

1. Radcliffe, J.: Hacking medical devices for fun and insulin: breaking the human SCADA system. In: Black Hat Conference Presentation Slides (2011)
2. Government Accountability Office: Medical Devices, FDA Should Expland Its Consideration of Information Security for Certain Types of Devices, GAO, Editor (2012)
3. FDA and CDRH: Content of Premarket Submissions for Management of Cybersecurity in Medical Devices, in Draft Guidance for Industry and Food and Drug Administration Staff (2013)
4. Finnegan, A., McCaffery, F.: A security argument pattern for medical device assurance cases. In: ASSURE 2014, Naples, Italy. IEEE (2014)
5. IEC: TR 80001-2-2 - Application of risk management for IT-networks incorporating medical devices - Guidance for the disclosure and communication of medical device security needs, risks and controls, International Electrotechnical Committee, p. 30 (2011)
6. Kelly, T., Weaver, R.: The goal structuring notation – a safety argument notation (2004)
7. Bloomfield, R., Bishop, P.: Safety and assurance cases: past, present and possible future - an Adelard perspective. In: Dale, C., Anderson, T. (eds.) Making Systems Safer, pp. 51–67. Springer, London (2010)
8. Consulting (York) Ltd.: GSN Community Standard Version 1 (2011)
9. Finnegan, A., McCaffery, F., Coleman, G.: A process assessment model for security assurance of networked medical devices. In: Woronowicz, T., Rout, T., O'Connor, R.V., Dorling, A. (eds.) SPICE 2013. CCIS, vol. 349, pp. 25–36. Springer, Heidelberg (2013)
10. NIST: SP 800-53 R4 - Recommended Security Controls for Federal Information Systems and Organisations, U.S.D.o. Commerce, Editor (2013)
11. ISO/IEC: 15408-2 Information Technology - Security Techniques - Evaluation Criteria for IT Security, in Security Functional Components (2008)

12. ISO/IEC: 15408-3 Information Technology - Security Techniques - Evaluation Criteria for IT Security, in Security Assurance Components (2008)
13. ISO/IEC: 27002:2013 Information Technology - Security Techniques - Code of Practice for Information Security Management (2013)
14. ISO: EN ISO 27799:2008 Health informatics. Information security management in health using ISO/IEC 27002 (2008)
15. IEC: 62443-3-3 Ed 1.0 – Security for industrial automation and control systems -Network and system security – System security requirements and security assurance levels (2013)
16. Sein, M.K., et al.: Action design research. Mis Q. **35**(1), 37–56 (2011)
17. FDA and CDRH: Content of Premarket Submissions for Management of Cybersecurity in Medical Devices, in Guidance for Industry and Food and Drug Administration Staff (2014)
18. Federici, T.: RE: Docket No. FDA-2010-D-0194: Agency Information Collection Activities; Submission for Office of Management and Budget Review; Comment Request; Draft Guidance for Industry and FDA Staff; Total Product Life Cycle: Infusion Pump—Premarket Notification Submissions, T.a.R. Affairs, Editor 2014: AdvaMed
19. ISO/IEC: 27005 Information Technology - Security Techniques - Information Security Risk Managment (2011)
20. ISO: 14971- Medical devices - Application of risk management to medical devices (2007)
21. IEC/WD: 80001-2-9 - Application of risk management for IT networks incorporating medical devices – Part 2-8: Application guidance - Guidance for use of security assurance cases to demonstrate confidence in IEC/TR 80001-2-2 security capabilities. Lead Author: Finnegan, A. (in press)

Medical Systems

Systems-Theoretic Safety Assessment of Robotic Telesurgical Systems

Homa Alemzadeh[1](✉), Daniel Chen[1], Andrew Lewis[2],
Zbigniew Kalbarczyk[1], Jaishankar Raman[3], Nancy Leveson[4],
and Ravishankar Iyer[1]

[1] University of Illinois at Urbana-Champaign, Urbana, IL 61801, USA
{alemzadl,dchen8,kalbarcz,rkiyer}@illinois.edu
[2] Applied Dexterity, Seattle, WA 98195, USA
andrew@applieddexterity.com
[3] Rush University Medical Center, Chicago, IL 60612, USA
jai_raman@rush.edu
[4] Massachusetts Institute of Technology, Cambridge, MA 02139, USA
leveson@mit.edu

Abstract. Robotic surgical systems are among the most complex medical cyber-physical systems on the market. Despite significant improvements in design of those systems through the years, there have been ongoing occurrences of safety incidents that negatively impact patients during procedures. This paper presents an approach for systems-theoretic safety assessment of robotic telesurgical systems using software-implemented fault injection. We used a systems-theoretic hazard analysis technique (STPA) to identify the potential safety hazard scenarios and their contributing causes in RAVEN II, an open-source telerobotic surgical platform. We integrated the robot control software with a software-implemented fault injection engine that measures the resilience of system to the identified hazard scenarios by automatically inserting faults into different parts of the software. Representative hazard scenarios from real robotic surgery incidents reported to the U.S. Food and Drug Administration (FDA) MAUDE database were used to demonstrate the feasibility of the proposed approach for safety-based design of robotic telesurgical systems.

Keywords: Hazard analysis · System safety · STAMP · STPA · Fault injection · Robotic surgery · Telerobotics · FDA MAUDE database

1 Introduction

In an analysis of over 10,000 adverse events related to robotic surgical systems, reported between 2000–2013 to the U.S. FDA MAUDE database [1], we showed that 9,382 (88.3 %) of the reported events involved device and instrument malfunctions. Those events had significant negative patient impacts, occasionally leading to deaths and injuries or causing procedure interruptions to troubleshoot system problems. In particular, out of 536 system errors detected during procedures, 488 (91 %) led the surgical teams to manually restart the system (43 % of 488), convert the procedure (61.5 %), or reschedule it to a later date (24.8 %). (Note that these categories are not

© Springer International Publishing Switzerland 2015
F. Koornneef and C. van Gulijk (Eds.): SAFECOMP 2015, LNCS 9337, pp. 213–227, 2015.
DOI: 10.1007/978-3-319-24255-2_16

mutually exclusive. In some cases after several system resets, the procedure was converted or rescheduled.) [2]. This data shows the importance of designing robust safety features in robotic surgical systems and verifying the effectiveness of detection and recovery mechanisms in order to prevent similar safety hazards in the future.

The international safety standards (e.g. ISO 14971 for medical devices and ISO 26262 for automobiles) recommend identifying potential safety hazards and defining safety requirements to implement mechanisms that can detect and mitigate hazards. The standards also emphasize the importance of fault injection testing as a means to validate the robustness of safety mechanisms in presence of faults and abnormal conditions [3].

However, traditional hazard analysis techniques primarily focus on the failures of individual components or human errors in the system. Other potential causal factors, such as complex software errors and unsafe component interactions, are often not thoroughly considered during the analysis. Systems-theoretic hazard analysis techniques such as STPA (Systems-Theoretic Process Analysis) [4] overcome this limitation by modeling accidents as complex dynamic processes resulting from inadequate control mechanisms that violate safety constraints. It is shown that STPA can identify additional causes for accidents that are not detected by FTA and FMEA techniques [4, 5].

Software-implemented fault injection (SWIFI) [6, 7] is a common technique for validating the effectiveness of fault-tolerance mechanisms by studying the behavior of the system in presence of faults. The effects of software or hardware faults are emulated by randomly changing code or data at different software locations. However, with the increasing size of software in today's complex systems, it is a challenging task to define specific fault types and locations that can effectively emulate realistic fault scenarios.

In this work, we took a systems-theoretic approach to empirically validate the robustness of safety mechanisms in robotic telesurgical systems by identifying the critical locations within the system to target software fault injection. More specifically, we used the potential causes of safety violations identified by STPA to define types and locations of faults to be injected in robot control software in order to evaluate the system under realistic hazard scenarios. As a case study, we used RAVEN II robot, an open-source platform for research in telerobotic surgery [8]. We developed a software fault injection framework that mimics the control flaws identified during hazard analysis by automatically injecting faults into robot control software modules. We evaluated the feasibility of the proposed approach using examples of real adverse events from the FDA MAUDE database, which resemble the hazard scenarios identified in our analysis.

2   Background

2.1   RAVEN II Robotic Surgical Platform

The RAVEN II robot is an open-source platform for research in tele-operative robotic surgery [8]. Figure 1 depicts a typical configuration of a robotic telesurgery system, composed of a master console, communication channel, and a RAVEN II surgical robot, including software and hardware components. The **master console** provides the means for the surgeon to issue commands to the robot using foot pedals and master tool manipulators. The desired position and orientation of robotic arms, foot pedal status, and robot control mode are transferred between the master and slave robot over the network using the Interoperable Teleoperation Protocol (ITP), a protocol based on the UDP packet structure [9]. RAVEN II **control software** receives the user command packets, translates them into motor commands, and sends them to the **control hardware**, which enables the movement of robotic arms and instruments.

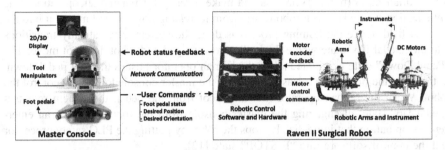

Fig. 1. Robotic Telesurgery using RAVEN II Surgical Platform (modified from [10, 11])

Figure 2 shows the main hardware and software modules in the RAVEN II control system. The control software runs on top of the Robotic Operating System (ROS) middleware and real-time (RT-Preempt) Linux kernel and communicates with the motor controllers and a Programmable Logic Controller (PLC) through custom USB interface boards. The PLC controls the brakes. The motor controllers send movement commands to the motors. There are three main threads running in parallel in the RAVEN control software: (1) the **network layer thread** which receives the command packets from the master controller over network; (2) the **control thread** where the robot's kinematics and control computations are performed; and (3) the **console thread** which provides an interface for setting the control modes and displaying robot's status to user.

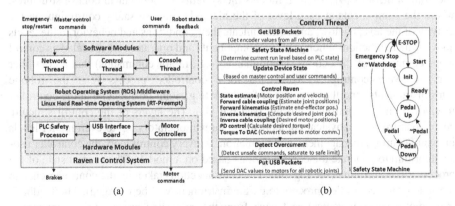

Fig. 2. RAVEN II control system: (a) Software and hardware modules [8, 11], (b) Computation steps in the control thread when in the Cartesian space mode and the safety state machine [11]

Both the control software and the PLC operate in a state machine that consists of four states: (a) emergency stop ("E-STOP"), (b) initialization ("Init"), (c) foot pedal released ("Pedal Up"), and (d) foot pedal pressed ("Pedal Down"), as shown in the Fig. 2b. The control software's state is synced with the PLC state every 1 ms through the USB interface boards. At power-up, both software and PLC are at "E-STOP" state, the motor brakes are engaged, and motor controllers are stopped. As a safety mechanism, the robot has a physical start button which should be pressed in order to start the robot initialization (homing) process and make it ready for manual teleoperation. The initialization state takes each robotic arm from its resting position and moves it into the surgical field. Once the homing process is done the system automatically transitions into the "Pedal Up" state where the brakes are engaged and robot does not move. The "Pedal Down" state is initiated when the human operator pushes the foot pedal down. In this state the brakes are released, allowing the master console to directly control the robot. When the human operator lifts their foot from the pedal, the system re-enters "Pedal Up" state, disengaging the master console from the robot. There is an emergency stop button that immediately stops the robot by putting the PLC safety processor and the control software into "E-STOP" state [12].

The control software detects and corrects any unsafe motor commands (e.g., electrical currents directed to the motor controllers exceeding a safe limit) using *overdriveDetect* function. During normal operation, the software continuously sends a square-wave watchdog signal to the PLC through the USB boards. Upon detecting an instant over-current command by *overdriveDetect* function, the control software stops sending the watchdog signal. The watchdog timer implemented in the PLC safety processor monitors the periodic watchdog signal from the software and upon loss of the signal immediately puts the system into the emergency stop ("E-STOP") state.

2.2   Systems-Theoretic Hazard Analysis Using STPA

STPA is a hazard analysis technique based on the STAMP (Systems-Theoretic Accident Model and Processes) accident causality model which is driven by concepts in systems and control theories [4]. STAMP models the systems as hierarchical control structures, where the components at each level of the hierarchy impose safety constraints on the activity of the levels below, and communicate their conditions and behavior to the levels above. The interactions among system components and operators are modeled as control loops composed of the actions or commands (e.g., motor commands) that a controller (e.g., software controller) takes/sends to a controlled process (e.g. the robotic arms/instruments) and the response or feedback (e.g., joint positions) that the controller receives from the controlled process (see Fig. 3a). The layers of the control structure could span from the physical components to human operators, up to even higher levels in manufacturing, management, and regulation. In every control loop, the controller uses an algorithm to generate the control actions based on a model of the current state of the process it is controlling (see Fig. 3b). The control actions taken by the controller change the state of the controlled process (e.g., the instrument will be engaged). The feedback (e.g., motor encoder values) sent back from the controlled process (e.g., motor controllers) update the process model used (e.g. current joint status) by the controller.

STPA starts by defining the accidents to be considered, the hazards associated with those accidents, and the safety requirements (constraints) for the system. Then unsafe control actions in each loop of control structure are identified and the potential causes for unsafe controls are determined by considering any potential flaws in the inputs, control algorithm, process model, outputs, or feedback received by the controller [4].

3 Systems-Theoretic Safety Validation Using Fault Injection

We used systems-theoretic hazard analysis using STPA to identify the safety hazards of a typical robotic telesurgical system and the potential causal factors that might lead to safety violation in RAVEN II system. Then we validated the robustness of the safety mechanisms of RAVEN II to the safety hazard scenarios identified using STPA by simulating their causal factors using software-implemented fault injection.

3.1 Safety Hazards and Unsafe Control Actions

First, based on the review of almost 1,500 accident reports from the FDA MAUDE database and specification of RAVEN II system functionality, we classified the accidents in robotic surgical systems into three types: patient deaths (A-1); patient injuries during procedure or serious complications experienced after procedure (A-2); and costly damage to surgical system or instruments (A-3). We also identified three main system hazards or set of system conditions that could lead to these accidents (Table 1).

Table 1. Accidents and safety hazards in robotic surgical systems

Accidents
A-1. Patient expires during or after the procedure.
A-2. Patient is injured during procedure or experiences complications after the procedure.
A-3. Surgical system or instruments are damaged or lost.
Safety Hazards
H-1. Robot arms/instruments move to an unintended location (H1-1), or with an unintended velocity (H1-2), or at unintended time (H1-3).
H-2. Robotic arms or instruments are subjected to collision or unintended stress.
H-3. Robotic system becomes unavailable or unresponsive during procedure.

We then modeled the hierarchical safety control structure of the system, as shown in Fig. 3. Software and hardware control loops (outlined by dashed lines in Fig. 3a) are further refined in Fig. 3b to illustrate details of the interactions among the software and hardware controllers. Next, we identified the set of system conditions under which the control actions could possibly be unsafe and lead to hazardous system states. The following unsafe scenarios were specifically considered: (i) a required control action was not performed, (ii) a control action was performed in a wrong state, leading to a hazard, (iii) a control action was performed at an incorrect time, (iv) a control action was performed for an incorrect duration, (v) a control action was provided, but not followed by the controlled process [4]. For example, in software control loop shown in Fig. 3b any flaws (marked with ✎) in the master console inputs, the incorrect feedback from the motor controllers or hardware control, and the flaws in the process model of software or output generated by the control algorithm can be considered as a potential causal factor. Table 2 shows the potentially unsafe control actions and their corresponding possible causal factors for the software and hardware control loops.

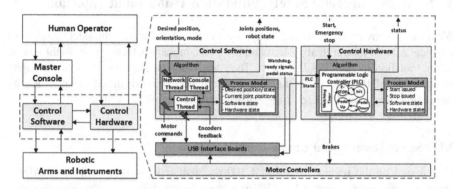

Fig. 3. (a) Hierarchical control structure of RAVEN II system, (b) Software and hardware control loops, including control algorithms, process models, control actions, and feedback.

As shown in the next section, the identified causal factors in combination with the knowledge of software structure provide the scope for performing directed fault injection experiments. They can define the location within each software module to inject, the variables within each function to target, and the conditions to trigger the injections.

3.2 Safety Hazard Injection Framework

To evaluate the safety mechanisms of robotic surgical system, we developed a Safety Hazard Injection Framework, which consists of seven modules for retrieving hazard scenarios, generating fault injection campaign, selecting fault injection strategy, conducting fault injection experiment, and collecting data, all in an automated fashion. Figure 4 shows the overall architecture of these modules and how they interface with each other and with the RAVEN II control software and hardware. A detailed description of each module is provided below.

Injection Controller. The Injection Controller is responsible for starting, stopping and automating the fault injection campaign. It communicates with other modules in the Safety Hazard Injection Framework through sockets or by direct invocation. In a normal campaign execution, it first accesses the Safety Hazard Scenario Library to retrieve the list of hazard scenarios. Second, the controller calls the Fault Injection Strategies to generate the fault injection parameters that could cause each hazard scenario. Next, it runs the user input generator module and calls the appropriate

Table 2. Potential unsafe control actions and causal factors for safety hazards in RAVEN II

Control	Potentially Unsafe Control Actions		Safety Hazards	Possible Causal Factors
	Control Action (Type)	Context (System Condition)		
Software Control	Motor command (provided)	User desired joint position does not match user desired position	H1-1	- Incorrect console inputs - Faulty control algorithm - Incorrect process model (desired positions, joint positions, runlevel) - Faulty USB communication - Arms/Instruments malfunctions
		User desired joint position is at a large distance from the current joint position (unintended jump)	H1-2	
		Left and right arm end-effector positions are very close (unintended collision)	H2	
		Software State = E-STOP or Software State = Pedal Up, PLC State = Pedal Down	H1 H2	- Missing/incorrect input from PLC - Faulty control algorithm - Incorrect process model (desired positions, joint positions, runlevel) - Missing/incorrect watchdog signal or output to PLC - Faulty USB communication
		Software State = Pedal Down, PLC State = Pedal Up or PLC State = Init	H3	
		Software State = Not E-STOP, PLC State = E-STOP	H3	
	Motor command (not followed)	Software State = Pedal Down or Software State = Init	H3	- Faulty USB communication - Mechanical malfunctions (e.g. broken instruments or cables)
Hardware Control	Brake (provided)	Stop not pressed and Software not stopped/pedal up	H3	- Missing/incorrect watchdog signal or output from software - Faulty USB communication
	Brake (not provided)	Stop pressed or Software is stopped	H1 H2	
	Brake (not followed)		H1 H2	- Mechanical malfunctions (e.g. broken instruments or cables)

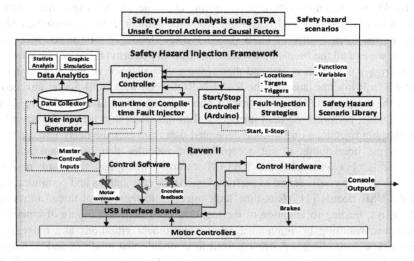

Fig. 4. Safety Hazard Injection Framework integrated with the RAVEN II Surgical Platform

Fault-Injector and robotic software to conduct a fault injection experiment. At the end of each injection run, the injection parameters and data are collected and written to the Data Collector.

Safety Hazard Scenario Library. The safety Hazard Scenario Library contains the safety hazard scenarios identified during the hazard analysis using STPA. Each hazard scenario includes a possible unsafe control action that might happen in the system and a list of potential causal factors. An example unsafe control action would be a motor command is provided by the control software when *there is a mismatch between the software state and hardware state of the robot* (rows 4–6 in Table 2). *Faulty USB communication* is an example causal factor that might lead to such unsafe control action.

Fault Injection Strategies. Based on the causal factors involved in each safety hazard scenario, the analysis of RAVEN source code, and software/hardware architecture, the Fault Injection Strategies module retrieves information on software functions which can most likely result in the hazard scenario, as well as the key variables in those functions and their normal operating ranges. This information is translated to the parameters to be used by the fault injection engine for simulating potential causal factors and validating whether they lead to the unsafe control or the safety hazards in the system. The fault injection parameters include the *location* in the software function, the *trigger* or condition under which the fault should be injected and the *target* variables to be modified by the injection.

User Input Generator. User input generator emulates master console functionality by generating input packets based on a previously collected trajectory of robotic movements made by a human operator and sends them to the RAVEN II control software.

Fault Injectors. The Fault Injectors perform the fault injection during robot operation. We developed both compile-time and run-time fault injectors with minimum changes to the RAVEN software and hardware. Run-time fault injector is implemented by extending the functionality of GDB (GNU Project Debugger for Linux). More specifically, we extend the *breakpoint* feature in GDB to perform fault injection when the desired *trigger* condition is met and then resume the execution of the target program. Run-time fault-injector launches the RAVEN ROS node with GDB Server attached to it, then the extended GDB is run from a remote process and after connecting to the RAVEN node, performs the fault injections. Run-time fault injector has the advantage of performing injections on run-time generated data; however the delay introduced by the run-time breakpoints is not acceptable for modules that have hard real-time requirements. For example, the RAVEN control thread has the hard real-time requirement of one millisecond to perform kinematics calculations and communication with the USB boards [11]. Run-time fault injection to the control thread introduces small delays, leading to violation of the real-time constraint and failure of kinematics calculations, resulting in unintended robotic instrument vibrations and movements. Compile-time fault injector is implemented as a module that modifies and recompiles the fault injection conditions into the source code. The main advantage is negligible timing overhead (small compile and build times), which is acceptable for modules with hard real-time requirements. We use compile-time injector to inject faults into the control thread.

Start/Stop Controller. To perform automated fault injection experiments without manual user intervention, we added a hardware mechanism to automatically start and stop the RAVEN system. We connected the start input of the PLC to the output of a relay switch controlled by an Arduino microcontroller (http://www.arduino.cc/) which receives start signals from the Injection Controller. After each injection, the controller stops the system by shutting down the RAVEN ROS node. The next injection gets started by automatically launching the software and sending the start signal to the Arduino relay controller to start the PLC and homing process.

Data Collection and Analysis. For each fault injection run, the fault injection parameters, surgical robot's trajectory, and detected errors are collected and sent to a MySQL server on a remote machine (Data Collector). These data are later queried for statistical analysis or graphics simulation.

4 Experimental Results

In our experiments, we simulated 45 scenarios (corresponding to the causal factors shown in Table 2) by injecting faults into 25 locations within 13 software functions of the network and control threads of RAVEN II robot, while running a pre-collected trajectory of a surgical movement. We ran a total of 2,146 fault injection experiments on the RAVEN robot. However, the majority of the faults (e.g., injected values within the range of variables) were not manifested in the system, or their effect was not logged completely by the data collection process due to system hangs/crashes (e.g., hardware "E-STOP") caused by the faults. Table 3 shows examples of scenarios where the faults were manifested in the system. For each scenario, we conducted multiple runs (in total 368 fault injections) to get confidence in reproducibility of the manifested/observed system behavior and manually collected the results. In each case we analyzed the system behavior both during the homing process (which system is being initialized and user manipulation has not started yet) and after the homing. The third column in the table shows the number of experiments done for each scenario and the last column corresponds to the scenario ID. A complete list of causal scenarios is available at [13].

In this section, we discuss our findings from the conducted fault injection experiments, including the causes for undetected hazards and the hazard scenarios that were mitigated by the safety mechanisms. The next section shows representative incident reports from the MAUDE database, which resemble the safety hazard scenarios identified here.

4.1 Undetected Safety Hazards

In what follows we describe the scenarios in which the injected faults led to hazards that were not detected or mitigated by the safety mechanisms in the system.

Unintended Robotic Movement (H1). We found a total of six scenarios where the faults in the console inputs, control algorithm, or the communication between the control software and hardware led to robotic arms/instruments making movements to an unintended position (H1-1) or with an unintended velocity (H1-2).

i. Out of range values injected permanently into the position, orientation, and foot pedal status inputs received from the master console (in *network_process* function) did not have any impact on the system during the homing process. However, after homing and in "Pedal Down" state, these injections led to kinematics calculations failures, small jumps, or stopping the robot. If the injected values passed the safe limits, movement was stopped by the overdrive detector and E-STOP was raised.

ii. Intermittent injection of out-of-range values into the master console inputs occasionally caused small instrument jumps or stopping the PLC when the faults were injected at very high frequency (e.g., at every other cycle).

iii. Injecting a random constant torque value to the joints current commands sent from the control software to the motor controllers (in *TorqueToDAC* function) caused very abrupt jumps of robotic arms, which resulted in the breakage of cables on the arms.

iv. Faulty estimation of motor velocities by the control algorithm (in *stateEstimate* function) caused unintended rotation and movement of instruments. In one case, upon intermittent injection of zero velocity, the instruments unexpectedly overshot the home position and collided with the surgical field floor during homing process.

v. Intermittent faulty packets received by the USB interface function (*getUSBPacket*) from the PLC caused the software control to assume that PLC is in "E-STOP" state, while PLC was in "Init" state. During homing process, this fault led the software and PLC to switch back and forth from "Init" to "E-STOP" state, causing failure of synchronization between left and right arms. Therefore, the robotic system got stuck in the initialization process and never moved to "Pedal Up". After homing, depending on the frequency of the intermittent faults, either the robot completely stopped or PLC applied brakes repeatedly to the motors.

vi. Injecting faults into the packets sent to the motor controllers through the USB interface function (*putUSBPacket*) did not impact the behavior of the system during the homing process, but led to abrupt jumps of robotic arms, resulting in cable breaks. A video recording of this scenario is available at [13].

Unintended Collision or Mechanical Stress (H2). The last four scenarios discussed above (iii – vi) also involved mechanical stress on the robot due to hanging in the homing process, repeating initialization steps, applying brakes over and over again, abrupt jumps of robotic arms, colliding with the surgical field floor, or breaking cables. The robotic system also became unresponsive or unavailable (H3) for almost an hour while repairing each broken cable. Due to the risk of damage to the robot, we repeated these specific injections only a few times.

Unresponsive Robotic System (H3). The majority of undetected safety hazards were due to faults injected in the USB communication or communication between software and PLC (17 scenarios [13]), leading the robotic system to not start the homing process, stop movement, become unresponsive to the received console packets, or become unavailable due to mechanical issues. Table 3 shows examples of these scenarios (vii, viii).

In case of transient or intermittent faults (e.g., in input console packets or USB packets), restarting the system can resolve the E-STOP conditions. However, permanent faults (e.g., a loose or disconnected USB cable causing incorrect information sent from PLC to software, or a DAC malfunction causing incorrect values sent to the motors, simulated as stuck at software faults here) cannot be recovered from even after multiple restarts and by hanging in E-STOP state the robotic system becomes unavailable (H3).

4.2 Mitigated Safety Hazards

Out of 23 scenarios related to corruption of the console inputs and the control algorithm, only 6 caused the unintended movements (depending on the robot configuration), collision, or cable damage. All these cases where related to intermittent faults (out of range absolute values) injected into the console inputs (tool positions and orientation or foot pedal) in a periodic manner or to applying constant velocity/torque values to the motors. All other scenarios either did not have any impact (3 cases), were detected by the *overdriveDetect* function and mitigated by forcing a hardware "E-STOP" (9 cases) (see scenario ix in Table 3), or only caused the system to hang in "Pedal Up" or "E-STOP" with no potential harm (4 cases).

5 Discussion

5.1 Related Safety Incidents from FDA MAUDE Database

Table 4 shows representative incident reports from the FDA MAUDE database, related to the da Vinci surgical system (the leading surgical robot for minimally invasive surgery available on the market) [14]. In these examples, similar hazard scenarios studied in this paper (including master console malfunctions and communication failures between the controller and robotic parts) occurred during real robotic procedures. These failures led either to non-intuitive movement of instruments or system errors that could not be cleared even by multiple system restarts.

In cases of instruments moving of their own accord or getting stuck due to malfunctions, the consequences may range from minor, where there are just short delays or system resets for troubleshooting the problem, to major, where the instruments may impale or impinge on a bodily structure, causing perforation or bleeding. Tearing or perforation of tissues can cause long-term complications and even death. Conversion of procedure to non-robotic approaches is a recovery mechanism to ensure survival of the patients. However, lack of tactile feedback can be a major issue in extracting malfunctioning instruments safely from patient's body.

This study demonstrated the value of software-implemented fault injection for simulation of safety hazard scenarios, which might help surgeons recognize complications and act promptly to prevent similar incidents in the future.

Table 3. Example scenarios simulated by fault injection and the observed system behavior

Potential Causal Factor	Injected Software Fault *Target Function*: Variables [Fault Type, Values]	No.	Observed System Behavior	Hazard	ID
Incorrect console inputs	*network_process*: Position and Orientations [Stuck At Out of Range]	20	During Homing: No impact After Homing in Pedal Down: IK-failure, small jumps, no movements with no E-STOP, E-STOP	H1 H3	i
	network_process: Foot Pedal Status [Stuck At 0, StuckAt 1]	20	During Homing: No impact After Homing: Does not start movement if Stuck At 0, No impact if Stuck at 1.		
	network_process: Position and Orientations [Intermittent Out of Range every10, 100, 500 packets]	40	Homing: No impact After Homing in Pedal Down: IK-failure, No movement, small jumps with no E-STOP, or E-STOP depending on robot configuration	H1 H3	ii
	network_process: Foot Pedal Status [Intermittent 0/1 Flip every 30,100,3000 cycles]	20	Pedal Down: Movement stops or small jumps PLC stops at very high flipping rate (e.g. every other cycle)		
Faulty control algorithm	*TorqueToDAC*: Joints Current Commands [Stuck At -1000]	1	Abrupt jump of both robotic arms, Cables on both left and right arms broke	H1 H2 H3	iii
	stateEstimate: Motor Velocity [Stuck At 0, -1, 1000]	5	During Homing: Unintended rotation, E-STOP After Homing: No Impact	H2	
	stateEstimate: Motor Velocity [Intermittent 0 injection every 100, 3000 cycles]	5	During Homing: Unintended tool movement, hard collision of instrument to the floor After Homing in Pedal Down: No impact	H1 H2 H3	iv
	stateEstimate: Motor Position [Stuck At or Intermittent]	10	Detected and mitigated by (*overdriveDetect*) Raised E-STOP Error and Stopped	NA	ix
Faulty USB communication	*getUSBPacket*: PLC State [Stuck At 0]	12	Homing: Does not start initialization, software assumes hardware is in E-STOP After Homing: E-STOP, software assumes hardware is in E-STOP, goes to E-STOP, stops sending watchdog, causing hardware to really stop.	H3	vii
	getUSBPacket: PLC State [Intermittent 0 injection]	10	Homing: Repeats the homing process over and over again due to synchronization failure between two arms. After Homing: Hardware completely stops or brakes are engaged/disengaged repeatedly	H2 H3	v
	putUSBPacket: Joints Current Commands [Stuck At Random Value]	5	During Homing: No Impact. After Homing: Abrupt jump of robotic arms and cable breaks, Software E-STOP	H1 H2 H3	vi
Incorrect output to PLC	*updateAtmelOutputs*: Output to PLC [Stuck At 0, 1, 3]	16	Does not start the initialization process or stops after homing because hardware goes to E-STOP and gets stuck there	H3	viii

Table 4. Relevant incident reports on da Vinci surgical system from FDA MAUDE database

Report # (Year)	Summary Event Description from the Report	Potential Causal Factors (ID in Table 3)	Observed Behavior (Hazard)	Patient Impact
2120175 (2011)	During a hysterectomy procedure, the left master controller did not have full control of the maryland bipolar forceps instrument, resulting in non-intuitive motion and causing a small bleed on the patient's uterine tube.	Master console calibration issue (i)	Non-intuitive movement (H2)	Small bleed on patient's uterine tube
2663924 (2012) 2589307 (2012)	Approximately 3.5 hours into a pancreatectomy procedure, multiple instances of non-recoverable system error code #23 was experienced and the surgeon was unable to control the patient side manipulator (psm) arms.	Communication failure between master console and robot (i)	Non-recoverable system error (H3)	Converted to open surgery after 3.5 hours

5.2 Vulnerabilities in Safety Mechanisms and Mitigation of Safety Hazards

We discovered the following vulnerabilities in the safety mechanisms of RAVEN II robot which contributed to the simulated safety hazards:

(a) Lack of monitoring mechanisms for the initialization (homing) process.
(b) No safety mechanisms for monitoring the USB board communications.
(c) No hardware detection mechanisms for monitoring unsafe motor commands.
(d) No feedback from the motor controllers and brakes to the PLC

The initial specifications of the RAVEN robot [12] included the requirements for the PLC to monitor the robotic hardware through feedback received from the motors and brakes. However, we found that those monitoring mechanisms are not included in the current implementation of the robot. Also, separate software and hardware mechanisms for monitoring the activities of USB interface boards are needed in the future.

The following robust safety mechanisms had a major role in mitigating safety hazards in RAVEN II, by preventing unintended movements and possible system damage:

(a) Robot movements cannot start without a start signal provided by the user.
(b) PLC engages the brakes upon loss of watchdog ("E-STOP") or foot pedal signals from software ("Pedal Up"); and software only sends the pedal signal to the PLC when the foot pedal is pressed and it is not in "E-STOP" or "Init" state.
(c) Software checks the status of PLC on every cycle (1 ms interval) to immediately follow the state transitions of the robotic hardware.

6 Related Work

Software-implemented fault injection (SWIFI) [6, 7] has been used for evaluating the dependability of different computing systems, including operating systems [15], smart power grids [16], and SaS cloud platforms [17]. International safety standards, such as NASA Software Safety Guidebook and functional safety standard for automobiles (ISO 26262), recommend using fault injection for validation of safety-critical software [3]. However, medical devices safety standard (ISO 14971) does not consider fault injection testing for validation of medical software [18]. Only one study showed the use of software simulation fault injection for testing the UML model of software for a pacemaker [19]. In this work, we developed a software fault injection framework that targets the critical locations in a real medical cyber-physical system to validate the robustness of the system safety mechanisms during design and implementation phases.

STPA was previously used for hazard analysis and safety-based design in safety-critical domains such as aviation [20], medical devices [5, 21], and automotive systems. Most previous studies used STPA only to derive the high-level safety constraints and identify the unsafe interactions that should be eliminated or controlled during the design process. However, here we further used the causal factors identified by the STPA analysis to identify the types and locations of faults to be injected into software to empirically assess the system's safety under realistic hazard scenarios.

7 Conclusions

This paper presents a framework for validating the robustness of safety mechanisms in robotic telesurgical systems. A systems-theoretic hazard analysis technique, STPA, was used to determine the safety hazard scenarios and their potential causes, in robotic surgical systems. A software-implemented fault injection framework was developed to simulate hazard scenarios by emulating the impact of intermittent and permanent faults in the robotic control software and hardware of the RAVEN II robot.

Software-implemented fault injection directed by the systems theoretic hazard analysis enables us to: (i) identify the safety hazard scenarios and determine their potential causes; (ii) trace propagation of faults in the system and discover the vulnerabilities in system safety mechanisms; (iii) determine strategic placement of new detectors that can mitigate the propagation of causal factors into safety hazards; (iv) provide useful feedback to the system developers on how to improve the safety mechanisms in the next-generation of devices. In particular, the identified hazard scenarios and the propagation paths from causal factors to safety hazards can be used for design of hazard prediction and mitigation mechanisms in the system. The proposed software fault injection framework can be also used for simulating realistic safety-hazard scenarios experienced in the field during robotic surgical training.

Acknowledgements. A non-restricted grant from Infosys and a faculty award from IBM partially supported this work. Our special thanks to Blake Hannaford and researchers at the University of Washington Biorobotics Lab for access to a RAVEN II robot. We also thank Frances Baker and Carol Bosley for their editing of the paper.

References

1. MAUDE: Manufacturer and User Facility Device Experience, U.S. Food and Drug Administration. http://www.accessdata.fda.gov/scripts/cdrh/cfdocs/cfMAUDE/search.CFM

2. Alemzadeh, H., et al.: Adverse events in robotic surgery: a retrospective study of 14 years of FDA data. Technical report (2015). http://arxiv.org/abs/1507.03518v2

3. Cotroneo, D., Natella, R.: Fault injection for software certification. IEEE Secur. Priv. **11**(4), 38–45 (2013)

4. Leveson, N.: Engineering a Safer World: Systems Thinking Applied to Safety. MIT Press, New York (2011)

5. Balgos, V.: A systems theoretic application to design for the safety of medical devices. SDM Master's Thesis, Engineering Systems Division, MIT, Cambridge (2012)

6. Hsueh, M.C., Tsai, T.K., Iyer, R.K.: Fault injection techniques and tools. Computer **30**(4), 75–82 (1997)

7. Arlat, J., et al.: Fault injection for dependability validation: a methodology and some applications. IEEE Trans. Softw. Eng. **16**(2), 166–182 (1990)

8. Hannaford, B., et al.: RAVEN-II: an open platform for surgical robotics research. IEEE Trans. Biomed. Eng. **60**(4), 954–959 (2013)

9. King, H.H., et al.: Plugfest 2009: global interoperability in telerobotics and telemedicine. In: IEEE International Conference on Robotic Automation (ICRA), pp. 1733–1738. IEEE Press (2010)

10. Robotic Surgery Simulator (RoSS), Simulated Surgical Systems. http://www.simulatedsurgicals.com/

11. RAVEN II Source Code, University of Washington. http://astro.ee.washington.edu/raven2docs/

12. Lum, E., et al.: The RAVEN: Design and validation of a telesurgery system. Int. J. Robot. Res. **28**(9), 1183–1197 (2009)

13. Safety Assessment of RAVEN II Robot. http://web.engr.illinois.edu/~alemzad1/papers/RAVEN.html

14. The da Vinci® Surgical System. http://www.intuitivesurgical.com/products/davinci_surgical_system/

15. Chen, D., et al.: Error behavior comparison of multiple computing systems: a case study using Linux on Pentium, Solaris on SPARC, and AIX on POWER. In: 14th IEEE Pacific Rim International Symposium on Dependable Computing (PRDC 2008). IEEE Press (2008)

16. Faza, A., Sedigh, S., McMillin, B.: Integrated cyber-physical fault injection for reliability analysis of the smart grid. In: Schoitsch, E. (ed.) SAFECOMP 2010. LNCS, vol. 6351, pp. 277–290. Springer, Heidelberg (2010)

17. Di Martino, C., et al.: Analysis and diagnosis of SLA violations in a production SaaS cloud. In: 25th International Symposium on Software Reliability Engineering (ISSRE), pp.178–188. IEEE Press (2014)

18. Park, J.D., et al.: Method of fault injection for medical device based on ISO 26262. In: 18th IEEE International Symposium on Consumer Electronics (ISCE 2014), pp. 1–2. IEEE Press (2014)

19. Majikes, J.J., et al.: Literature review of testing techniques for medical device software. In: 4th Medical Cyber-Physical Systems Workshop (MCPS 2013). ACM Press (2013)

20. Ishimatsu, T., et al.: Hazard analysis of complex spacecraft using systems-theoretic process analysis. J. Spacecraft Rockets **51**(2), 509–522 (2014)

21. Antoine, B.: Systems Theoretic Hazard Analysis (STPA) applied to the risk review of complex systems: an example from the medical device industry. Ph.D. Dissertion, Massachusetts Institute of Technology (2013)

Towards Assurance for Plug & Play Medical Systems

Andrew L. King[1]([✉]), Lu Feng[1], Sam Procter[2], Sanjian Chen[1],
Oleg Sokolsky[1], John Hatcliff[2], and Insup Lee[1]

[1] University of Pennsylvania, Philadelphia, USA
{kingand,lufeng,sanjian,sokolsky,lee}@cis.upenn.edu
[2] Kansas State University, Manhattan, USA
{samprocter,hatcliff}@k-state.edu

Abstract. Traditional safety-critical systems are designed and integrated by a systems integrator. The system integrator can asses the safety of the completed system before it is deployed. In medicine, there is a desire to transition from the traditional approach to a new model wherein a user can combine various devices post-hoc to create a new composite system that addresses a specific clinical scenario. Ensuring the safety of these systems is challenging: Safety is a property of systems that arises from the interaction of system components and it's not possible to asses overall system safety by assessing a single component in isolation. It is unlikely that end-users will have the engineering expertise or resources to perform safety assessments each time they create a new composite system. In this paper we describe a platform-oriented approach to providing assurance for plug & play medical systems as well as an associated assurance argument pattern.

Keywords: Medical device interoperability · Safety assurance · Compositional safety

1 Introduction and Motivation

Traditionally, safety-critical systems have been designed and integrated as monolithic units before they are delivered to the customer. Typically, a prime contractor manages development of the system from design through final systems integration. Because the prime contractor manages the entire development process, they are in a unique position to assess the completed product for safety: They know what components comprise the system, how those components interact (*e.g.*, as verified via integration testing), the intended use of the system and the system-level safety requirements. Very often in regulated domains, such as aviation and medical systems, the prime contractor must also construct an assurance case which is an argument that the system satisfies its safety requirements.

In medicine, clinicians currently deliver therapy by manually coordinating collections of independently developed devices. Now that many devices marketed today already include some form of network connectivity (serial ports,

© Springer International Publishing Switzerland 2015
F. Koornneef and C. van Gulijk (Eds.): SAFECOMP 2015, LNCS 9337, pp. 228–242, 2015.
DOI: 10.1007/978-3-319-24255-2_17

Ethernet, 802.11 or Bluetooth wireless) clinicians are recognizing the potential to automate device coordination via external control applications [8]. Ideally, future medical devices would support plug & play protocols which would allow clinicians to construct networks of medical devices that automatically interoperate to automate life-critical clinical workflows [7]. The integration model for plug & play systems would differ from traditional systems because they would not be supplied or integrated by a single vendor. Instead, a Health Delivery Organization (HDO) would purchase interoperable devices, infrastructure (*i.e.,* computational platforms) and software applications implementing clinical algorithms (*i.e.,* "apps") from a variety of different vendors. Specific medical systems would then be assembled from devices on-hand to address a particular clinical need. While practical use of such systems is still in the future, there are emerging interoperability standards [19] and prototype implementations that aim to support this vision [16,18]. In this paper, we study the problem of constructing safety assurance arguments for plug & play medical systems intended to provide life-critical therapy (*i.e.,* where failure of the system could result in death or serious injury - see the example in Sect. 2). We describe how the plug & play integration paradigm has serious implications for safety assurance and propose an approach for constructing an assurance argument for such systems.

Plug & play medical systems will be assembled by their (non-technical) users which means that there will not be a single entity with technical competency (*e.g.,* prime contractor) positioned to assess the safety of a specific combination of devices. The lack of a traditional prime contractor poses a challenge to ensuring the safety of these systems for two reasons: First, safety is a property of systems that arises from the interactions between system components [17]. Second, what constitutes safe inter-device interactions will vary considerably between different clinical scenarios. It is critical to ensure that interactions between devices are predictable *and* that those interactions satisfy the safety requirements of the given clinical scenario. Since it will not be known specifically which devices will be assembled into the composite system *a priori*, traditional methods of assessing safety cannot be used.

A number of efforts in academia, industry, and standards groups have studied different aspects and implications of plug & play medical systems. Nearly all of the prior work has assumed that plug & play medical systems would exist within a "platform-oriented ecosphere" similiar to what exists in different segments of the consumer electronics industry (*e.g.,* USB peripherals for personal computers or "apps" for smart-phones). In the consumer-electronics industry these ecospheres ensure *interoperability* between components in the ecosphere. For example, one can reasonably expect a consumer operating system to seamlessly interoperate with a new USB keyboard or that an "app" downloaded from an official "app store" will be able to access and use smartphone hardware.

We believe that, in addition to supporting interoperability, a platform-oriented ecosphere for plug & play medical systems could be designed to ensure safety. Such an ecosphere would need to establish certification processes and criteria such that system-safety assurance obligations can be appropriately divided between the different system component manufacturers and ecosphere stakeholders.

The premise of our work is that to establish safety of a plug & play system, *application vendors* should be the ones to produce system-level safety arguments. This is because the application vendors will know what clinical scenario their application is targeting (*i.e.*, its *intended use*) and therefore know the system-level safety requirements. These arguments would have to leverage both safety of individual devices and the assurances provided by the platform ecosphere. Our goal is to establish a sound way of combining component and ecosphere assurances into an assurance case for the application.

There are two contributions of this paper. First, we propose a platform-oriented ecosphere with specific certification processes designed to support the assurance of plug & play medical systems. The second contribution is an assurance argument pattern that exploits the design of our proposed ecosphere. Vendors would use the pattern to construct application assurance cases. We illustrate the use of this pattern by instantiating it for a particular medical system use-case.

The organization of this paper is as follows: In Sect. 2 we describe an example clinician proposed safety-critical medical control system as a use-case for plug & play medical systems. Section 3 gives an overview of our proposed ecopshere and how that ecosphere should be managed. Section 4 contains the assurance argument pattern and its instantiation for an application that implements the system of Sect. 2. We give an overview of related work in Sect. 5 and conclude with some ideas for future work in Sect. 6.

2   Motivating Example: Clinical Scenario: Patient Controlled Analgesia

One common method used to control patient pain in clinical settings is Patient Controlled Analgesia (PCA). PCA therapy provides consistent control of pain by allowing patients to self-administer doses of an opioid. Typically, a patient is attached to a special infusion pump equipped with a "bolus trigger." When the patient presses the trigger, the pump will deliver a predetermined amount of opioid to the patient. Evidence from systematic reviews of randomized controlled clinical trials indicate that the use of IV PCA leads to better pain relief, improved patient outcomes (e.g., reduction in pulmonary complications) and increased patient satisfaction compared with conventional nurse administered parenteral opioids [13].

One major opioid side effect is respiratory depression. Respiratory depression increases progressively with dose. If respiratory depression increases to the point that the patient's ability to take in oxygen is compromised it is called respiratory distress and serious injury or death can result. In theory, properly configured PCA provides some protection from overdose because it is inherently self-limiting: Patients will usually lose consciousness before respiratory depression reaches dangerous levels which prevents them from requesting further doses and causing an overdose. Additionally, modern PCA-pumps allow clinicians to set limits on the total amount infused per hour as well as lockout intervals between boluses.

Despite these protections, PCA therapy is associated with a large number of adverse events: There were over 9500 cases of PCA related errors voluntarily reported to the Institude of Safe Medicine between 2000 and 2004 alone [11] and there continues to be cases of severe respiratory complications due to PCA [6]. Patients undergoing PCA therapy can still receive overdoses if the pump is misconfigured, if the pump configurer overestimates the maximum dose a patient can receive, if the wrong concentration of drug is loaded into the pump, or if someone other than the patient presses the bolus trigger (known as PCA-by-proxy).

2.1   A Fail-Safe Device Coordination Protocol

Previously Arney *et al.* [3] developed a fail-safe device coordination protocol designed to prevent overdose resulting from PCA therapy. The control-loop of the system is illustrated in Fig. 1 and consists of a network-connected PCA pump, pulse-oximeter, and a supervisory controller. The pulse-oximeter periodically transmits measurements of the patient's blood oxygen saturation (SpO_2) to the controller. The controller maintains a "worst-case" model of patient opioid pharmokinetics. This

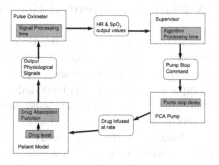

Fig. 1. Control loop with sources of timing delays [3].

model relates opioid concentration levels to SpO_2 and respiratory depression. This model allows the controller to use SpO_2 to infer the patient's level of respiratory depression. Using the inferred level of respiratory depression, the controller will calculate a control decision and transmit that decision to the PCA pump.

Arney *et al.*'s control-loop is fail-safe in the sense that failures of omission (*e.g.,* dropped messages in the network) will not result in an overdose. Failsafety is accomplished using a ticket-based control strategy. Instead of simply sending the pump activation or deactivation commands, the controller sends a timed-ticket. This ticket encodes the maximum amount of time (called Δt_{safe}) the pump can continuously run without pushing the patient into respiratory distress.

The calculation of Δt_{safe} must take into account the maximum timing delays present in each stage of the control loop (see Fig. 1). Pulse-oximeters use a sliding-window averaging algorithm to calculate SpO_2 from raw sensor data. The size of the window and processing time ensures that the SpO_2 measurement is delayed from the "real" SpO_2 value by several seconds. The network adds delay between both the pulse-oximeter and the controller and between the controller and the PCA pump. The controller introduces some delay because it takes time to calculate the ticket. Finally, there will be a delay from the moment the pump's ticket timer times out and the moment the pump stops because it will take time for the physical pump mechanism to cease infusion.

Arney *et al.* modeled their coordination protocol as a network of communicating Timed Automata [1]: Each component (including network links) illustrated in Fig. 1 were modeled as Timed Automata. Each source of delay was modeled and the network was allowed to arbitrarily drop messages. SpO_2 was used as a proxy for respiratory distress: The patient model included a state variable representing the patient's current SpO_2 value. The value of the variable was periodically calculated via a pharmokinetic model that relates drug concentration in the patient to respiratory rate and SpO_2. The UPPAAL model checker [5] was used to verify that the patient will not experience overdose.

3   A Platform-Oriented Ecosphere

We believe that a platform-oriented ecosphere of medical components, if appropriately designed, could be used to ensure the safety of plug & play medical systems. In this paper, we define an *ecosphere* as set of devices, software applications and computational platforms intended to interact with one another using standardized plug & play interoperability protocols; the stakeholders that organize, manufacture, and use these products; as well as the explicitly defined processes that are followed to develop, certify, and use these products.

Our proposed ecosphere contains three categories of interoperable system components. The component categories are *device*, *application*, and *platform*. Devices expose a logical interface that acts like an API which applications can use to control or receive data from the device. Applications implement the clinical algorithms used to address a specific clinical scenario. Applications are not just executable code; they have a requirements specification which declares what interfaces compatible devices must implement and a QoS specification that declares timing requirements (*e.g.,* periods and deadlines on program execution). Each platform consists of a network, computational resources (CPU, RAM, *etc.*), real-time operating system and *platform services*. The platform's job is to act as a trusted base to enforce the correct assembly of on-demand systems: When the Health Delivery Organization (HDO) plugs a device into the platform the device will upload its interface specification. Then, when the HDO staff tries to launch an application with a set of selected devices the platform will (1) check if those devices' interfaces are compatible with the application requirements and (2) verify that the application's requested QoS can be guaranteed. If either 1 or 2 is false the platform will prevent application launch.

There are a number of *actors* that participate in our vision of the ecosphere. Each actor has different responsibilities and assurance obligations:

– *The Ecosphere Standards Consortium* consists of representives of the other actors and follows a consensus process to define ecosphere standards: The connectivity protocols used by each component to exchange data, the logical interfaces devices can implement, what it means for a device to be compatible with an application, and the compliance requirements that each type of component (applications, devices, and platforms) must satisfy before that component can be certified as a member of the ecosphere. We emphasize that the consortium does not explicitly define specific systems - rather it establishes constraints on the architecture and interfaces of such systems and their sub-components.

- *The Device Vendor* designs, manufactures, and markets their devices. Before their device can be admitted to the ecosystem they must provide assurance (*e.g.,* via an assurance case) that their device satisfies the ecosphere compliance requirements for all interfaces the device claims it implements.

- *The Application Vendor* is responsible for providing assurance that their application is safe when instantiated with compatible devices. Application vendors play a role analogous to "system integrators" in conventional systems: They define the overall system function, and reason about overall system safety. However, the distinction is that they define the system using a software application and requirements/assumptions on the devices and platforms. They do not specify a single system but a family of possible system instances that satisfy the functional and safety goals of the clinical scenario. Thus, the integration is "virtual": they do not integrate specific physical devices and platforms but specifications of devices and platforms where each such specification represents a set of compliant components.

- *The Platform Vendor* must provide assurance that their platform will correctly perform its responsibilities. Because the platform is the trusted base for each system these responsibilities include correctly executing application code, correctly implementing the ecosphere device-application compatibility check and providing adequate system security.

- *The Certification Authority* polices component membership in the ecosphere: The certification authority only grants certification to components that satisfy the ecosphere compliance requirements. When a component becomes certified the authority will sign the component with a digital certificate. If postmarket surveillance reveals that a component has a previously undetected problem resulting in non-compliance, the certification authority can revoke the certificate associated with that component's make and model. The digital certificate enables the platforms to use cryptographic methods to verify whether or not applications or devices have been certified. [10] contains an overview of how cryptographic methods can be used to establish trust and how the platform acts as a trusted base for this process.

- *The HDO* does not have assurance responsibilities *per se* (*i.e.,* they are not required to provide assurance to any other ecosphere actor) however, they must still use the application as intended. If the HDO uses an application in an unintended way (*i.e.,* off-label use) then the (safety) assurances provided by the Application Vendor for that application are not guaranteed to apply.

The ecosphere assurance and compliance obligations (combined with the runtime checks performed by the platform) create a series of "gating functions" that prevent the HDO from assembling potentially unsafe combinations of devices and applications. Figure 2 illustrates the relationship between the ecosphere actors, ecosphere components, the gating functions and the final physical instantiation

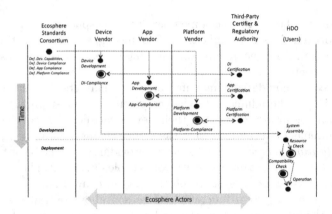

Fig. 2. Ecosphere actors, their interactions and certification activities.

of a system. The unringed circles indicate steps in development or assembly of the physical system. Lines indicate interactions between the actors. The ringed circles indicate completion of one of the primary assurance steps and represent the gates. First the Ecosphere Standards Consortium must establish the ecosphere standards and component compliance requirements. Once the standards have been defined the component manufacturers can design their respective components. The certification authority enforces the first set of gates: components are only allowed into the ecosphere if they satisfy their respective compliance requirements. The final set of gates are enforced by the platform: The platform will only let the application run if it is being paired with compatible and compliant (*i.e.,* certified) devices and if the platform can guarantee that the application's QoS requirements will be met.

A Note on Interfaces, Compatibility, and Device Compliance: For the purposes of this paper we imagine that device and application interfaces are analogous to software interfaces from programming languages like Java: When an application specifies that it requires a device interface it is much the same as declaring a field variable in a Java class to have an interface-type: Any object that implements that interface can be substituted for that variable. Compatibility checking between devices and applications thus amounts to checking if the device implements the required interface(s). A device is compliant with an interface if it satisfies the Consortium defined compliance requirements for that interface type. Consider the PCA pump from the motivating example. The Ecosphere Consortium could define a standardized interface for PCA pumps called "void InfusionTimedTicket(x)" which applications could use to send a timed ticket to the pump. The Consortium would then define the behavior a PCA pump must have in order to comply with that interface. In this case, the pump should correctly implement the ticket timer and cease infusion after some mandated amount of time.

A Note on Platform Assurance and Compliance: A compliant platform must correctly implement compatibility checking and resource management. Ideally, applications would be portable across platforms in the ecosphere. This means that the Consortium would also standardize an execution model for the applications (*i.e.,* application byte code format, semantics, and available APIs). A compliant platform must then also correctly implement the standard model of execution. Different applications will have different levels of criticality: Applications with low criticality do not pose serious consequences in the event of failure while failure of a high-criticality application may result in catastrophic consequences. Because the application is totally dependent on the platform to function correctly, the assurance requirements for each platform should be at least as stringent as the assurance requirements for the most critical application that will be admitted to the ecosphere. While the specifics of these requirements are well beyond the scope of this paper, we can imagine that the Consortium could mandate that all Platform Vendors follow guidance that would result in levels of assurance similar to that of DO-178C Level A [12].

4 The Platform Argument Pattern

Each plug & play application defines a *set* of possible systems: One for each allowed combination of devices and platform with the application. The multitude of potential systems implied by a single application presents a challenge for both the application developer and Certification Authority. The application vendor will need to devise an assurance argument that explains why all these possible combinations are safe. Practically, it won't be possible for the vendor to analyze or test each combination individually because the number of possible combinations would prohibitively large. Additionally, new components (*i.e.,* platforms & devices) may be admitted to the ecosphere *after* the application is certified. Because the application vendor will not be able to directly analyze all possible device combinations they will have to use some form of model-based reasoning: They would analyze their application for safety using models as proxies for the concrete devices. In theory, as long as the models capture the range of behavior allowed by the different ecosphere gating functions (*i.e.,* the compliance/certification checks and the platform compatibily checks) then safety conclusions derived from the model-based reasoning should hold for any allowed instantiation of the application.

Of course, in practice, it is generally impossible to capture *all* the allowed behavior of a physical system in a model. If an application vendor is using model-based reasoning to support safety-claims they should justify *why* the models they used are *adequate*. In our context, adequacy depends on the intended use of the application (*i.e.,* the meaning of adequate will vary from application to application) *as well as* the assurances on each component provided by the ecosphere itself. To this end we propose an assurance argument pattern that requires application vendors to make model adequacy arguments explicit. Our hope is that it can help both application vendors and the Certification Authority to quickly identify assurance deficits or other fallacious reasoning in application assurance arguments, especially those related to model-based reasoning. The remainder of this section is organized as follows: First we define the terms the pattern uses. Then we introduce and explain the platform argument pattern. Lastly, we instantiate the pattern to make a mock assurance case for an application implementing the PCA coordination protocol from Sect. 2.

4.1 Pattern Terms

Figure 3 maps out the terms used in the pattern. Our terms make an explicit distinction between models[1] and physical embodiments. We ultimately care about the physical embodiments but we are left with the models to analyze. The rows correspond to the different types of ecosphere components (with the addition of a row for the environment and instantiated system). The columns separate out different abstractions for each of the component categories: The specifications refer to the actual specification artifacts created by either the application developer or device manufacturer, the models are semantic (*i.e.*, analyzable) objects created by the application developer based on the specifications. The last column (physical embodiments) represent the physical object that correspond to the models and specifications.

		Model	Specification	Physical Embodiment
Devices		-	$DI_1,\ldots,DI_l$	$D_1,\ldots,D_l$
App	Algorithm	A^m	A	$P(A)$
	Interface	AI_j^m	AI_j	$\mathbb{D}_j = \{D_i \mid DI_i \simeq AI_j\}$
Platform		-	-	P
Environment		E^m	-	E
System		$A^m \parallel_{j=1}^n AI_j^m \parallel E^m$	$A \parallel_{j=1}^n AI_j$	$\{P(A) \parallel_{j=1}^n D_j \parallel E \mid D_j \in \mathbb{D}_j\}$

Fig. 3. Pattern terms: the relationship between models, specifications, and physical embodiments.

Each entity in Fig. 3 is defined as follows: The l devices admitted to the ecosphere are $D_1,\ldots,D_l$. Each D_i is compliant with its interface DI_i, Each application consists of an A and set of AI_j. The A is the algorithm of the application and represents executable code. Since these applications are typically real-time we assume any QoS specifications in the application are contained within A. The AI_js represent the application's required device interfaces (If the application uses n devices then $1 \leq j \leq n$). The physical emobodiment of each AI_j is the set of devices that implement the interface AI_j (we use $\simeq$ to represent

---

[1] Through out this section we adopt a formal notation that might lead some readers to believe that when we use the term "model" we are explicitly refering to formal models (*i.e.*, ones that could be analyzed by a model-checker). This is not the case. We are using "model" in a very general sense and a model could range from an informal "mental model" to an executable model that could be simulated to a formal model that could be analyzed by a model-checker.

the compatibility relation). The AI_j^m are models created by the application developer and are intended to capture all the behaviors of the devices that implement the AI_js. Since A is a program, it has no physical embodiment until it is executed on a platform, therefore $P(A)$ represents platform P executing A. The device interfaces of an application are syntactic objects. They don't have explicit semantics but they do imply a set of behaviors (i.e., the union of the behaviors of all the compliant devices that are compatible with that interface). Each platform is represented by a P. E represents the environment where the application will be deployed and E^m is the model of that environment. The last row are the system entities. $A^m \|_{j=1}^n AI_j^m \| E^m$ is the model of the system. It is the composition of the application model, the device models, and the environment model (We borrow the parallel composition operator, $\|$, from process algebras to denote the combination of two or more components running together). $A \|_{j=1}^n AI_j$ (i.e., the application) represents a specification of the system. $\{P(A) \|_{j=1}^n D_j \| E \mid D_j \in \mathbb{D}_j\}$ is the set of possible physical systems specified by the application (one system for each compatible combination of application and device(s)).

4.2 The Pattern

Figure 4 is a specification of the argument pattern using Goal Structured Notation (GSN) [14]. The top level goal (**G:AllSat**) states that all instantiantions of the application must satisfy some property ϕ in a specified environment. Assurance for this claim is argued via the platform argument strategy (**S:PlatArg**). The strategy must always be applied in at least two contexts: One referencing the models used in the model-based reasoning and the other referencing the ecosphere assurance and compliance requirements. **S:PlatArg** requires adequate

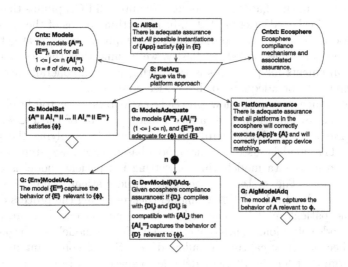

Fig. 4. The argument pattern for application assurance.

assurance for three sub goals. The first goal (**G:ModelSat**) is the model-based reasoning step. The argument application vendor must argue that the chosen models satisfy ϕ. The remaining two goals explicitly relate the models used in **G:ModelSat** to the possible physical systems via the ecosphere assurance and compliance requirements. **G:ModelsAdequate** asks the developer to argue why the models chosen in **G:ModelSat** capture all the possible (relevant) behaviors allowed by the application's specification. Typically, the arguments for the adequacy of the environment, application, and devices models will all take on a different character so the pattern separates the arguments for each as a different sub-goal (Note the multiplicity on the **G: DevModel{N}Adq.** that forces a sub-goal for each device model). **G:PlatformAssurance** asks the developer to argue why the minimum level of assurance provided by any ecosphere compliant platform is sufficient to support the application: The application developer relies on the platform to correctly execute their application and ensure that the application is only instantiated with compatible devices. If a platform fails to do either of these correctly, then ϕ could be violated even if sound models were used in **G:ModelSat**.

4.3   An Example Assurance Argument

Figure 5 shows an example assurance argument for an application implementing the PCA device coordination protocol of Sect. 2. We assume that the application specifies two required interfaces ("void InfusionTimedTicket(x)" and "float getSpO2()"). We also assume that the application code was auto-generated from Arney *et al.*'s controller timed automata model via the TIMES tool [2]. The application would have a QoS specification that requires that all network delays are bounded by 500 ms and that the controller will take no more than 200 ms to generate a ticket after it receives a fresh SpO_2 reading. We assume for the purposes of this argument that the Consortium requires all PCA pumps that comply with void InfusionTimedTicket(x) halt infusion within 100 ms of the ticket expiring. We also assume that any pulse-oximeter compliant with "float getSpO2()" have an averaging time ≤ 2000 ms. Lastly, we assume that the ecosphere compliance requirements for platforms is very stringent (*i.e.*, generally accepted by domain experts to be adequate for life-critical systems).

The assurance argument now proceeds as follows: The top-level goal **G: NoOverinfusion** claims that all allowed instantiations of the **PCAapp** prevent over-infusion. **G: NoOverinfusion** is argued by applying the platform argument. The models used in the model-based reasoning step are Arney *et al.*'s timed automata models (in this setting the patient model is the environment model). The system is shown to avoid patient overdose states by verifying its models in the UPPAAL model-checker (using the process described in [3]). The patient model is claimed to be sound because it is an accepted textbook model of opioid pharmokinetics. The device models are argued to be adequate because they capture all allowed behavior of compliant devices (we elide the argument for the PCA model due to space constraints). For example, the model of the pulse-oximeter assumes that all pulse-oximeters compliant with

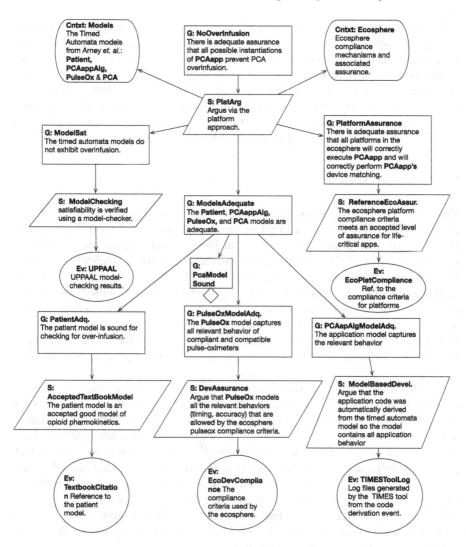

Fig. 5. Assurance case fragment for the PCA-Control Application

"float getSpO2()" exhibit an averaging time ≤2000 ms. This is the exact range of timing behavior captured in Arney *et al.*'s pulse-oximeter model. The application model is argued to be sound because the TIMES tool generated the executable code from the model. Finally, all platforms are argued to have adequate levels of assurance for **PCAapp** because ecosphere platform compliance requires a stringent level of assurance generally accepted to be adequate for life-critical systems.

Of course, just because a developer is able to instantiate the pattern does not mean their system is safe or their argument is good. The Certification Authority or any other reviewer may or may not accept the argument. For example, they could employ a domain expert in opiod pharmokinetics who judges that the text-book pharmokinetic model used in the analysis is not adequate or too simplistic. Or perhaps the application vendor had erroneously interpreted the compliance requirements for pulse-oximeters implementing "float **getSpO2**()" and some compliant pulse-oximeters may in fact have an averaging time >2000 ms (in which case the app's ticket calculation would be wrong). The point is that, by making the soundness argument explicit it helps both the application vendor and Certification Authority more quickly identify assurance deficits.

5   Related Work

The study of assurance and ecospheres for plug & play systems is relatively new. ASTM F2761 [19] is a standard that defines the Integrated Clinical Environment (ICE) out of work started at the Medical Device Plug & Play Interoperability Program at CIMIT [7]. ASTM F2761 abstractly defines a medical application platform and alludes to how the platform could support an ecosphere of plug & play medical devices. More recently, [9] described how a medical application platform would facilitate the safe integration of applications and medical devices drawn from an ecosphere of interoperable componets. OpenICE [18] and the MDCF [16] are both prototype medical application platforms and have been used to inform both academic and industry research on plug & play medical systems.

While, as far as we know there has not been any work on assurance arguments for plug & play systems, there has been some work on assurance arguments for model-based development [4]. The authors of [4] describe an assurance argument pattern for systems developed using a model-based development process. Like our proposed pattern, their pattern requires that the argument preparer to first prove a propery using a model, and then justify the use of that model. Their pattern does not address the peculiarities of model based reasoning for plug & play systems. There has been some interesting work on modular certification [20] and compositional safety arguments [15]. These works are primarily concerned with argument reuse but introduce some concepts that may be applicable to providing assurance for plug & play systems.

6   Conclusions and Future Work

This paper described two contributions. First, we proposed a platform-oriented ecosphere designed to support the assurance of plug & play medical systems. Second, we described an assurance argument pattern that exploits the design of this ecosphere. The key challenge we sought to address is that, unlike traditional systems, plug & play systems do not fully exist until they are assembled by their users. Our approach leverages a specially managed ecosphere of components that enables application vendors to constrain which combinations of devices can be used with their application. This puts the application developer to be in the unique position of being able to use model-based reasoning to predict the possible behaviors of the allowed instatiations of their application. Our proposed assurance argument pattern explicitly links the model-based reasoning performed by the vendor to assurances provided by the ecosphere. We illustrated the use of this pattern via a small case-study of a closed-loop medical system. For future work we would like to apply this approach to a more involved case-study. One objective of this case-study could be to submit a mock-submission to a regulatory agency (*e.g.,* the FDA) and then report on the feedback received. It would also be interesting to explore how approaches for argument reuse (*e.g.,* [20] or [15]) could be incorporated into our proposal.

Acknowledgements. This research was supported in part by NSF CNS-1035715, NSF CPS 1239324, NIH 1U01EB012470-01, and DGIST Research and Development Program of the Ministry of Science, ICT and Future Planning of Korea (CPS Global Center).

References

1. Alur, R., Dill, D.L.: A theory of timed automata. Theor. Comput. Sci. **126**(2), 183–235 (1994)
2. Amnell, T., Fersman, E., Mokrushin, L., Pettersson, P., Yi, W.: TIMES - a tool for modelling and implementation of embedded systems. In: Katoen, J.-P., Stevens, P. (eds.) TACAS 2002. LNCS, vol. 2280, pp. 460–464. Springer, Heidelberg (2002)
3. Arney, D., Pajic, M., Goldman, J.M., Lee, I., Mangharam, R., Sokolsky, O.: Toward patient safety in closed-loop medical device systems. In: Proceedings of the 1st ACM/IEEE International Conference on Cyber-Physical Systems, pp. 139–148. ACM (2010)
4. Ayoub, A., Kim, B.G., Lee, I., Sokolsky, O.: A safety case pattern for model-based development approach. In: Goodloe, A.E., Person, S. (eds.) NFM 2012. LNCS, vol. 7226, pp. 141–146. Springer, Heidelberg (2012)
5. Behrmann, G., David, A., Larsen, K.G., Hakansson, J., Petterson, P., Yi, W., Hendriks, M.: Uppaal 4.0. In: 2006 Third International Conference on Quantitative Evaluation of Systems, QEST 2006, pp. 125–126. IEEE (2006)
6. Bonner, J., McClymont, W.: Respiratory arrest in an obstetric patient using remifentanil patient-controlled analgesia*. Anaesthesia **67**(5), 538–540 (2012)
7. Goldman, J.: Advancing the adoption of medical device plug-and-play interoperability to improve patient safety and healthcare efficiency. Medical Device "Plug-and-Play" Interoperability Program, Technical report (2000)
8. Goldman, J.M.: Getting connected to save lives. Biomed. Instrum. Tech. **39**(3), 174–174 (2005)
9. Hatcliff, J., King, A., Lee, I., MacDonald, A., Fernando, A., Robkin, M., Vasserman, E., Weininger, S., Goldman, J.M.: Rationale and architecture principles for medical application platforms. In: 2012 IEEE/ACM Third International Conference on Cyber-Physical Systems (ICCPS), pp. 3–12. IEEE (2012)
10. Hatcliff, J., Vasserman, E., Weininger, S., Goldman, J.: An overview of regulatory and trust issues for the integrated clinical environment. In: Proceedings of HCMDSS 2011 (2011)

11. Hicks, R.W., Sikirica, V., Nelson, W., Schein, J.R., Cousins, D.D.: Medication errors involving patient-controlled analgesia. Am. J. Health Syst. Pharm. **65**(5), 429–440 (2008)
12. Hilderman, V., Baghi, T.: Avionics certification: a complete guide to DO-178 (software), DO-254 (hardware). Avionics Communications (2007)
13. Hudcova, J., McNicol, E.D., Quah, C.S., Lau, J., Carr, D.B.: Patient controlled opioid analgesia versus conventional opioid analgesia for postoperative pain. The Cochrane Library
14. Kelly, T., Weaver, R.: The goal structuring notation-a safety argument notation. In: Dependable Systems and Networks Workshop on Assurance Cases (2004)
15. Kelly, T.P.: Concepts and principles of compositional safety case construction (2001)
16. King, A., Procter, S., Andresen, D., Hatcliff, J., Warren, S., Spees, W., Jetley, R., Jones, P., Weininger, S.: An open test bed for medical device integration and coordination. In: 31st International Conference on Software Engineering-Companion, ICSE-Companion 2009, vol. 2009, pp. 141–151.IEEE (2009)
17. Leveson, N.: A new accident model for engineering safer systems. Saf. Sci. **42**(4), 237–270 (2004)
18. Plourde, J., Arney, D., Goldman, J.M.: Openice: An open, interoperable platform for medical cyber-physical systems. In: 2014 ACM/IEEE International Conference on Cyber-Physical Systems (ICCPS), pp. 221–221. IEEE (2014)
19. Quigley, P.: F2761 and the integrated clinical environment. Stand. News **37**(5), 20 (2009)
20. Rushby, J.: Modular certification. Technical report, SRI CSL, September 2001

Risk Classification of Data Transfer in Medical Systems

Dagmar Rosenbrand[1]([⊠]), Rob de Weerd[2], Lex Bothe[1], and Jan Jaap Baalbergen[1]

[1] Instrumentele Zaken, Leiden University Medical Center, Leiden, The Netherlands
{d.m.rosenbrand,a.l.j.bothe,j.j.baalbergen}@lumc.nl
[2] Directoraat ICT, Leiden University Medical Center, Leiden, The Netherlands
r.de_weerd@lumc.nl

Abstract. Nowadays, the hospital IT network is increasingly used to transport data between medical devices and information systems. The increase in network integration and the importance of the transported data results in high dependency on the IT network in the clinical setting. Until now, risk classification methods focused on two individual components of a medical system: medical devices and medical software. In this paper, we present a tool to classify patient safety risks of data transfer in medical systems by indicating the dependency on the IT network. The new method shifts the focus from separate components to the intended use of the entire system. It supports communication about risks and enables us to link risk analysis techniques and safety measures to the classification. The tool can be used in the design phase and is the start of a risk management process to secure safe use of a medical system.

Keywords: Patient safety · Medical systems · Medical devices · IT network integration · Safety critical systems · Risk classification · Data transfer · IEC80001-1

1 Introduction

For a long time, medical devices have been used in healthcare to assist healthcare givers with patient care. Conventionally, these medical devices were either standalone devices or communicated with other medical devices using a dedicated local network or a direct link. Currently, medical devices are more and more integrated in the hospital IT network to transport data from these devices to other locations in the hospital or to register important information in the hospital information system. This information is not only for registration purposes but is increasingly used to make decisions for diagnosis or treatment. Consequently, the IT network transfers both data for office and clinical purposes. Moreover, for multiple applications the hospital IT network is connected to the internet which generates new vulnerabilities for data transport over the IT network.

The integration of medical devices in the IT network results in complex medical systems with accompanying risks. We use the definition of medical systems as medical

© Springer International Publishing Switzerland 2015
F. Koornneef and C. van Gulijk (Eds.): SAFECOMP 2015, LNCS 9337, pp. 243–251, 2015.
DOI: 10.1007/978-3-319-24255-2_18

devices incorporated in the IT network and (optionally) coupled to hospital information systems. The IT network is an extra component in these systems compared with the conventional standalone medical devices. Data can be transferred over the wired or over the wireless network. The IT mobility trend increases the demands on the wireless IT network and the connections to workplaces outside the hospital.

Articles in newspapers address the risk of network failure in clinical settings and point out the high dependency on (wireless) data transport, e.g. [1]. The high dependency on information technology often results in chaos for users and organizations when the systems become unavailable [2–4] because standard workflows have been adapted to these new technologies and fallback procedures may be lacking. Another new risk is the possibility for hackers to interrupt data transfer or even change the settings of medical devices through their (wireless) network connections [5–10].

In most cases, only the individual components of a medical system are evaluated in a risk analysis, such as those delivered by the individual vendors of the medical devices. It is important to check if the risk analyses performed by individual vendors and the taken risk mitigations are appropriate. Moreover, usually different departments in the hospital are responsible for the separate components. The organization Himss performed a survey on the effectiveness of risk management programs in hospitals [11]. They state that effective risk management is absolutely critical to identify major technology-related risks and to secure patient safety with the increasingly integrated complex technologies. Among other conclusions, they frequently found a separate application of risk management techniques to IT and medical devices. This is sufficient for systems that are clearly identified as either IT or biomedical but is not sufficient for medical systems composed of medical devices, IT applications and (often crucial) data transfer over the IT network. Therefore, risk evaluation and risk management of an entire medical system is needed by multidisciplinary teams and the already determined risk mitigations should be checked for the composed system.

Medical devices are classified by the Medical Device Directive 93/42/EEC Annex IX (MDD) [12]. This classification is introduced because it is financially not feasible and necessary to subject all medical devices to the most rigorous conformity assessment. Eighteen rules are formulated to classify non-invasive, invasive and active devices according to their level of potential hazard to the patient inherent to the intended purpose of the medical device ("the use for which the device is intended according to the data supplied by the manufacturer on the labelling, in the instructions and/or in promotional materials"). Examples of safety criteria used for the risk evaluation are the duration of contact with the body, degree of invasiveness (causing for instance risk of infection), the monitoring of vital physiological parameters, administration or modification of blood, body liquids or other liquids for infusion, and the exchange of energy or radiation. More information about this classification method is available in the Medical Devices Guidance Document (MEDDEV 2.4/1 Rev.9 [13]).

Medical software is also defined as medical device and thereby classified by the MDD. The Dutch organization Nictiz published a whitepaper in 2013 to clarify this classification of medical software [14]. The MDD method is used for classifying the separate system components, but not the system, including data transfer, as a whole.

In 2011, the International Electrotechnical Commission (IEC) published a standard IEC 80001-1: Application of risk management for IT networks incorporating medical devices [15]. This standard is addressed to responsible organizations, the manufacturers of medical devices and providers of other information technology components and describes the need for risk analysis, risk management and change management of the IT network. Three key properties are defined for the IT-network: Safety, Effectiveness and Data and system security (the latter can be split up in Confidentiality, Integrity and Availability as described in the NEN7510 [16]). Although the standard describes the necessity of risk management it does not describe in detail how healthcare organizations should accomplish this. However, the IEC80001-1 emphasizes the need for risk management of the IT network and indicates the strong influence incorporated medical devices and IT network components have on each other.

The healthcare organization is responsible for safe use of the medical system composed of all the different components. Until now, the classification methods were focused on the individual components. With the addition of the IT network as an important, and not yet classified, component the need for a different classification method becomes evident. The intended use of the whole medical system is important to determine the risk of the components and the system as a whole. For instance, if a system is used to monitor the vital signs of patients from a distance (central nurse station or even outside the hospital) and patient care processes are adapted to this technology, the MDD classification of the telemonitors is not enough to determine appropriate risk management for the system. The monitor sends the patient data to the central nurse station by means of the IT network. If this network traffic is interrupted, the impact on the clinical situation is high. The organization of patient care is highly dependent on the availability of the IT network and thus the data transfer from telemonitor to central station is a critical component of the safety critical system.

The high risk data transfer necessitates certain requirements on the IT network, the organization of patient care and the management of the whole medical system in addition to the requirements that were already imposed on both the telemonitor and the nurse central station.

This paper describes a classification method to objectively score the risk level of data transfer over the IT network. This method mainly focusses on the availability of the IT network for data transfer in medical systems and the consequences for patient safety in case of failures. Applying this method to designs of medical systems gives an impression of the dependency on the IT network in the clinical setting and the accompanying risk levels.

2 Tool

To be able to classify risks of data transfer, a classification tool is developed comparable to the before mentioned MDD classification [12, 13]. Answering six questions results in the appropriate risk class for data transfer, see the flowchart in Fig. 1.

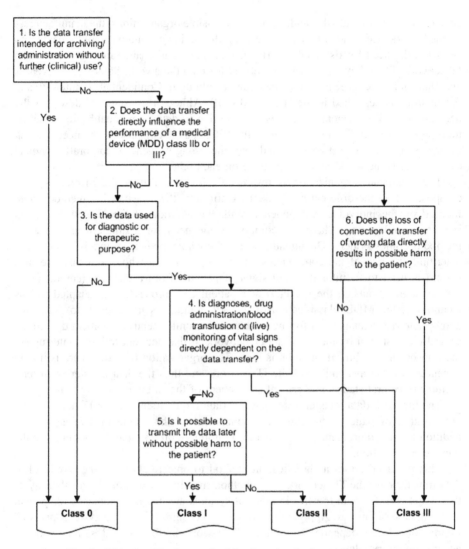

Fig. 1. Risk classification method for data transfer in medical systems

Below, a clarification with examples is given for the six questions stated in the flowchart.

1. Data transfer is intended for archiving or administration when, for instance, information about the use of a medical device is registered in a registry, or information about the operation of a device is documented in the information system of the medical technology department.
2. The performance of a high risk medical device (classified according to the MDD as class IIb or III) is influenced by data transport if the operation according to the intended use is changed by the transported data: for example, a pacemaker with

settings adjusted wirelessly via a laptop, or radiotherapy equipment with the radiation plan sent from computer to the equipment. Also, the performance of a nurse central station is affected if, due to interruption of the network, no vital signs are sent from the monitor to the central station.

3. All data transfer for diagnostic or therapeutic purposes is classified as class I, II or III. Data transfer for other purposes (e.g., education, registration, science) is classified as class 0.

4. If the diagnosis, administration of drug, transfusion of blood or live monitoring is directly dependent on the data transfer, it will be classified as class III data transfer. In this case, the medical professionals are highly dependent on the IT network availability in this clinical setting and loss of network connection necessitates fallback scenarios (both technical and organizational, e.g. adjustments of patient care processes)

5. Many medical devices do not totally depend on the data transfer to other components of the medical system. For instance, images are sent from an ultrasound scanner to a database for storage and further analysis. The actual diagnosis is in some clinical settings done directly during the exam by using the display of the medical device. Transportation of the images to the database is not necessarily done the same day so the availability of network communication is not critical.

6. If a high risk medical device is controlled by network traffic and this is done with erroneous data, this could directly harm the patient. In addition, the loss of network connection could seriously harm the patient if monitoring or diagnosis is disturbed while needed immediately. If this is the case, the data transfer is classified as class III data transfer.

The determined class defines the dependency on data transfer over the IT network in the clinical setting of the medical system. Class III is high risk network traffic and the loss of connection could have high impact on the clinical situation. Class I is low risk network traffic which means that loss of connection will result in loss of efficiency but will not directly result in risks for patient safety. Class 0 is even lower risk data transfer because this transport is only intended for storage or scientific/educational purposes.

Table 1 lists a couple of medical systems scored with our new classification method. The example of telemonitoring is scored as class III data transfer because monitoring of vital signs is directly dependent on the data transfer from telemonitor to nurse central station. The intended use of the nurse central station is the monitoring of vital signs of the patients at a distance which is impossible in case of interruption of network traffic. Question 1 is answered with "no" because data is not only used for archiving or administration, question 2 is answered with "yes" because no data is available to monitor at the nurse central station (a class IIb medical device according to the MDD classification) and question 3 is answered with "yes" because this can immediately harm the patient. This confirms our earlier assumption that network traffic is in this case a critical component of the medical system.

Table 1. Examples of the risk classification of data transfer applied to medical systems

Class 0	Class I	Class II	Class III
Registration of cleaning program scope disinfector	Echo images to database	Vital signs sent from medical device to Patient Data Management System (e.g. trend observation in OR)	Telemonitoring
Video connection OR to lecture room	History log of ECG signals	Radiology images to screens OR	Distributed alarm system

3   Conclusion and Discussion

We developed a new classification method to be able to classify the risks of data transfer in medical systems. Applying this method to designs of medical systems gives a first impression of the dependency on the IT network in the clinical setting and the accompanying risk levels. A more detailed risk analysis is needed to address all risks and to perform appropriate risk management. In the Leiden University Medical Center, we use a pragmatic prospective risk analysis (abbreviated as PRI) method to analyze medical systems with low risk classification (according to the classification method described above). Medical systems with high risk classified data transfer (class II and III) are analyzed in more detail using a template of a health Failure Mode Effect Analysis (hFMEA). In the pragmatic prospective risk analysis and hFMEA, all three key properties (Safety, Effectiveness and Data and system security) of medical systems are evaluated together with conventional criteria used for the individual components: medical devices and software.

The key property System and data security can be split up in three properties: Confidentiality, Integrity and Availability. For the developed classification method, we focused on the (un)availability of the IT network and the impact of interruptions in data transport on patient safety. All properties can have impact on the key property Safety. However, we assumed confidentiality of data to be equally important for all medical information concerning patient safety because the influence of confidentiality on patient safety is not direct. Consequently, other methods should be used to determine the confidentiality risks of the data. For instance, patient data that is directly linked to patient name and/or date of birth should be treated with special care.

Integrity of data can directly affect patient safety. An image stored in the patient record of the wrong patient can lead to wrong decisions in patient treatment. It could lead to misdiagnosis, wrong treatment and even death. In the developed classification method, no distinction concerning integrity is made for different medical information. The importance of integrity is only explicitly included in the method for data transport directly affecting the performance of a medical device class IIb or III. By example, integrity of data to a pacemaker/ICD is highly important because the performance of the pacemaker/ICD is directly influenced by this data. A hacker could possibly attack the confidentiality, integrity and availability of data. In case of integrity, reprogramming of the device could change the operation of a pacemaker/ICD which could directly lead to patient safety risks [6, 7, 10]. Therefore, data transport that can influence the performance of a medical device class IIb or III is classified as high risk data transport. Of course, the integrity of data transfer to a medical device class I or IIa could be of equally importance. Therefore, assigning these medical systems to a lower risk level does not mean the integrity of data automatically is of less importance. The demands on integrity of data should be discussed during both types of risk analysis: the pragmatic prospective risk analysis (pragmatic PRI) and the more detailed hFMEA.

In addition to assigning the appropriate risk analysis method (pragmatic PRI or a more detailed hFMEA) to the classification of data transfer, safety measures can be determined for the different classes. If network traffic is classified as class III data transfer, this will necessitate certain minimal requirements for the IT network. The availability and integrity must be high to secure patient safety. Medical systems with class II data transfer also have high requirements for availability and integrity but the necessary availability is lower than the requirements for class III data transfer. In the case of class I data transfer, availability is desirable for efficiency but not for patient safety while integrity demands might be the same as for higher classified data transfer to ensure patient safety.

Next to technical network requirements, measures should be taken for the operation (process of patient care) in case of high risk medical systems. In the Leiden University Medical Center, we are developing design rules for medical systems. These design rules are guidelines during the design phase of a medical system and are directly linked to the classification of data transfer in medical systems. The major and most important design rule is: "Only new technology in a high risk medical system (data transfer class II or III) when a risk analysis is done, a fallback scenario is made and distributed, and the medical system is tested in a representative test environment". Examples of the other design rules are the necessity for redundancy in a medical system, the need for monitoring of the whole system (chain) for at least class II en III medical systems, the appropriate method for risk analysis and the organization of system management for the use phase. Among other things, this system management includes an exclusive LUMC process flow for incident management of class II and III data transfer in medical systems, a troubleshoot tree for use during incident management and the need of a fallback scenario to ensure continuity of safe patient care.

Additionally, in the Leiden University Medical Center we use the classification as aid in improving the architecture of the medical IT network (network segregation, quality of service, etc.).

Nevertheless, it should be emphasized that the developed risk classification model is only a rough representation of the reality. The model can be used as a start of the risk management process to efficiently perform risk analysis and as a guideline to determine minimal network requirements and operational measures (e.g. fallback scenarios, system monitoring, incident management). Furthermore, it can be used for communication about risk management between engineers and medical professionals to increase awareness of risk levels. The tool can help in the discussion about necessary adjustments of patient care processes in case of network failures. However, the tool is only a start of the risk management process and risk analysis should be done with care to determine the adequate risk mitigations. For instance, it is crucial to pay attention to the influence low risk data transfer could have on high risk medical systems in the environment. A low risk classification still necessitates the pragmatic risk analysis including questions for instance about the impact of (loss of) data communication on the operation of the device/system itself or on its environment.

In conclusion, healthcare becomes increasingly dependent on network traffic between medical devices and IT systems. Unfortunately, a lot of examples of network failures exist. In addition, medical devices increasingly communicate by using the wireless network. For wireless network traffic no definite promises can be made about the availability of the network especially if no further measures are taken to establish a reliable connection. In the Leiden University Medical Center, we developed a new classification method to quickly determine the dependency on data transfer in the clinical setting of the medical system. The new method can be used as extension to the conventional classification of medical devices and software. It shifts the focus towards the medical system as a whole and the intended use of the entire system.

Subsequently, the tool can be used as communication tool and as the start of a risk management process to secure safe use of a medical system when the method of risk analysis and minimal safety measures are linked to the risk classification of a medical system. The practical experience with the classification method will give more inside in the need to expand the method with, for instance, more criteria for integrity and confidentiality of data.

References

1. Volkskrant (2014). http://www.volkskrant.nl/dossier-zorg/risico-uitval-draadloos-netwerk-in-zorginstellingen-onderschat ~ a3633074/
2. Hanuscak, T.L., Szeinback, S.L., Seoane-Vazquez, E., Reichert, B.J., McCluskey, C.F.: Evaluation of causes and frequency of medication errors during information technology downtime. Am. J. Health Syst. Pharm. **66**(12), 1119–1125 (2009)
3. Campbell, E.M., Sittig, D.N., Guappone, K.P., Dykstra, R.H., Ash, J.S.: Overdependence on technology: an unintended adverse consequence of computerized provider order entry. In: AMIA Annual Symposium Proceedings, pp. 94–98 (2007)
4. Sittig, D.F., Singh, H.: Defining health information technology-related errors: new developments since *to err is human*. Arch. Intern. Med. **171**(14), 1281–1284 (2011)
5. Skipr (2014). http://www.skipr.nl/actueel/id18982-ziekenhuis-weinig-alert-op-cybersecurity.html
6. Telegraph (2014). http://www.telegraph.co.uk/news/science/science-news/11212777/Terrorists-could-hack-pacemakers-like-in-Homeland-say-security-experts.html
7. Volkskrant (2013). http://www.volkskrant.nl/dossier-archief/hoe-hackers-ons-in-het-hart-raken ~ a3537587/
8. Austrian Times (2012). http://austriantimes.at/news/General_News/2012-12-01/45780/Patient%20hackers%20managed%20to%20dial%20a%20drug%20in%20hospital
9. The Economist (2014). http://www.economist.com/news/special-report/21606416-companies-markets-and-countries-are-increasingly-under-attack-cyber-criminals
10. Halperin, D., Heydt-Benjamin, T.S., Ransford, B., Clark, S., Defend, B., Morgan, W., Fu, K., Kohno, T., Maisel, W.H.: Pacemakers and implantable cardiac defibrillators: software radio attacks and zero-power defenses. Computer Science Department Faculty Publication Series. Paper 68 (2008)

11. Himss: Himss System Risk Analysis Survey Report (2012)
12. European Commission DG Health and Consumers: Medical Devices: Directive 93/42/EEC
13. European Parliament and Council of the European Union: Medical Devices: Guidance Document – Classification of Medical Devices MEDDEV 2.4/1 Rev. 9 (2010)
14. Ekker, A., van Rest, B.: Medische apps, is certificeren nodig? Nictiz (2013)
15. International Electrotechnical Commission (IEC): International Standard IEC 80001-1: Application of Risk Management for IT-networks Incorporating Medical Devices – Part 1: Roles, responsibilities and activities (2010)
16. NEderlandse Norm (NEN): NEN7510:2011 Medische Informatica – Informatiebeveiliging in de Zorg (2011)

Requirement Engineering for Functional Alarm System for Interoperable Medical Devices

Krishna K. Venkatasubramanian[1], Eugene Y. Vasserman[2], Vasiliki Sfyrla[3],
Oleg Sokolsky[4]([⊠]), and Insup Lee[4]

[1] Worcester Polytechnic Institute, Worcester, MA, USA
kven@wpi.edu
[2] Kansas State University, Manhattan, KS, USA
eyv@ksu.edu
[3] Grenoble, France
vasssiliki@gmail.com
[4] University of Pennsylvania, Philadelphia, PA, USA
{sokolsky,lee}@cis.upenn.edu

Abstract. This paper addresses the problem of high-assurance operation for medical cyber-physical systems built from interoperable medical devices. Such systems are different from most cyber-physical systems due to their "plug-and-play" nature: they are assembled as needed at a patient's bedside according to a specification that captures the clinical scenario and required device types. We need to ensure that such a system is assembled correctly and operates according to its specification. In this regard, we aim to develop an alarm system that would signal interoperability failures. We study how plug-and-play interoperable medical devices and systems can fail by means of hazard analysis that identify hazardous situations that are unique to interoperable systems. The requirements for the alarm system are formulated as the need to detect these hazardous situations. We instantiate the alarm requirement generation process through a case-study involving an interoperable medical device setup for airway-laser surgery.

Keywords: Interoperable medical devices · Alarms · Interoperability · Requirements engineering · Fault trees

1 Introduction

A recently emerging vision of dynamically composable and Interoperable Medical Device Systems (IMDS) will allow information integration from multiple clinical sources in a context-sensitive way to guide patient care and prevent common critical mistakes [12]. Various agencies and standards bodies, including the U.S. Food and Drug Administration, have signaled that the future of medical technology lies in medical device interoperability [12]. High-assurance device interoperability will be a critical requirement in realizing this vision.

This work was partially funded by NIH grant 1U01EB012470 and NSF grants CNS 1224007, CNS 1239543, and CNS 1253930.

© Springer International Publishing Switzerland 2015
F. Koornneef and C. van Gulijk (Eds.): SAFECOMP 2015, LNCS 9337, pp. 252–266, 2015.
DOI: 10.1007/978-3-319-24255-2_19

IMDS, while a subset of cyber-physical systems in general, are unique in that they are constructed as needed, i.e., *on demand*. An interoperability failure can lead to devastating consequences for the patients being treated e.g., sudden loss of closed-loop control. These systems are mission-critical — literally a matter of life and death — therefore we must ensure they are functioning (availability) and functioning properly (correctness) with high assurance. Risks in medical device interoperability arise due to its dynamic nature, meaning *the potential issues are emergent properties of the entire system* and therefore impossible to fully control ahead of time, so we need to monitor the "health" and proper functionality of the system itself at run-time. This means continually verifying that design-time assumptions hold at run-time and ensuring that faults, either natural or malicious, are detected.

IMDS typically consists of two main entity classes: medical devices for the treatment of patients, and software controller applications (referred to as *apps*) that coordinate these devices. An illustrative example is airway-laser surgery, in which a surgeon uses a laser to investigate or fix the patient's trachea or nearby organs. This carries the potential danger of a fire if the laser is active while oxygen is being delivered to the patient and the surgeon accidentally damages the oxygen delivery tube. Whenever the laser is being activated, a human operator must first block the air path. In a simplified patient model, brain damage may occur if oxygen is reduced for more than about 4.5 min or the blood oxygen saturation (SpO2) level drops below 40 % — both of these conditions must be avoided. In traditional operating room environments, nurses and surgeons are supposed to be aware of such potential fire and low-oxygen problems [10].

When an IMDS for Airway-Laser-Surgery (ALS-IMD) is deployed, it needs to ensure that interactions between constituent devices proceed according to the specification of the clinical scenario. Otherwise, the safety requirements of the system can be compromised, even if the controller itself is operating properly. If problematic interactions are detected, an alarm needs to be raised. Alarms are therefore a key component in ensuring safe operation of IMDS. Note that, these alarms are different from the clinical alarms in that they do not signal abnormal patient state, but rather the abnormal state of the entities that monitor and treat the patient. We refer to these as *technical alarms* (rather than *clinical alarms* which have to do with patient health).

In this paper, we explore the requirements to realize a robust yet flexible alarm system for IMDS. Henceforth, we refer to such a system as the *Interoperability Alarm System (IAS)*. The goal is to reliably alert clinicians to failures of the overall interoperability of the system. We use the term *fault* to mean cause(s) of *error* in the system, which may then eventually lead to loss of expected service from the system, or *failure* [3]. The main challenge in developing these requirements is that the IAS needs to support all IMDS that can be assembled from the available set of interoperable devices. (The full magnitude and variability of this set may not be known at IMDS design time.) Our approach to developing the requirements for IAS has three steps: (1) perform a hazard analysis for identifying interoperability failures within ICE, (2) identify the various faults that individual elements in the IMDS can manifest, (3) derive a set of fault trees that characterize how combining various faults may lead to identified hazards. Note that we do not claim that the use of hazard analysis or fault-trees to characterize the failures of IMDS is by itself novel. Novelty comes from applying existing and well-understood tools to the new and unique domain of IMDS.

In this regard, we consider an IAS that is decoupled from other entities in IMDS: although the controller app and medical devices are well-defined in terms of intended use and expected behavior, they cannot reliably monitor their own operation and trigger alarms. A key feature of the IAS is the flexibility of connection-time (i.e., system start-time) configuration, using specifications (required devices, information flows and their parameters) supplied by deployed apps and parameters of interoperability-compliant devices used to build the IMDS. Stand-alone medical devices already have built-in alarms, but in the interoperable context, augmenting device alarms with a high-level system alarm will not only simplify medical device design but will also increase their safety.

The **contributions** of this work are as follows: (1) a hazard analysis based requirements generation for IAS, and (2) a case study using the airway-laser surgery example to demonstrate the utility and expressiveness of our approach.

2   Background

Within the realm of healthcare interoperability, much work is done at the syntactic level (i.e., developing common formats for data exchange between medical systems [14]) in the form of standards such as 11073 [4], IHE [9] and HL7 [6]. However, we believe that realizing the full potential of IMDS needs a higher level of interoperability. Hence we make use of the ASTM 2761 Integrated Clinical Environment [2] standard, also known as MD PnP ICE, which aims to provide semantic interoperability (i.e., devices not only have a common data format, but they also understand the meaning of the data being exchanged). We adopt the ICE standard as the primary *system model* for our work. Logically, the ICE architecture is separated into three entities, which are illustrated in Fig. 1:

Supervisor (SUP): The Supervisor is responsible for executing clinical "scenarios" also referred to as *apps*, from common and easily scriptable tasks such as taking blood pressure at predefined intervals and recording the results, to more complex procedures like medication interaction monitoring and suppression of likely false alarms. The app thus encapsulates clinical knowledge about a particular treatment procedure that involves multiple devices. These clinical scenarios are viewed as control algorithms running on the Supervisor.

Medical Device (MDs): Medical devices in the ICE setup can be responsible for measuring the state of the patient or changing the state of the patient through some form of stimulus (e.g., electrical, mechanical) with the express object of causing a particular outcome (e.g., pace the heart, reduce blood glucose).

Network Controller (NC): ICE allows coordination between each medical device through the Network Controller, a sort of "medical router". It does not have any medical/clinical functionality itself, but facilitates communication

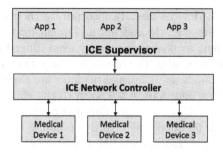

Fig. 1. Simplified diagram of the ICE architecture

between the medical devices and the Supervisor, with responsibilities including data routing, translation, and quality of service (QoS) enforcement.

In this architecture, the Supervisor and the NC are fixed, while MDs and apps are dynamic and change based on the clinical scenario. In [11], the authors describe a means for each medical device and each app to provide, during system instantiation, a model of its operation to the system. These models allow the Supervisor to ensure correct operation. We assume these models are also made available at system startup to the IAS, which can then use them to determine the presence of ICE failures. In addition the IAS is already assumed to possess a model for the Supervisor the NC, which is pre-supplied and does not change based on clinical scenarios. The availability of these models make it possible for the IAS to have a global view of the IMDS operation and therefore potentially detect failures that IMDS cannot detect by itself.

2.1 A Case for IMDS Alarms

Currently, medical systems are designed and deployed as monolithic, complete artifacts [5]. Only a small number of vertically-integrated systems permit any deviation from the original configuration. Integrators build systems for a specific clinical scenario out of a dedicated collection of devices, and then argue for the safety of this system. In this case, we can craft a monitoring subsystem that would raise alarms based on the requirements of the clinical scenario and failure modes of the devices involved. A fixed safety argument based on hazards of the clinical scenario can be built. A dynamically composed setup, on the other hand, is customized (usually by the appointed clinician) for each patient for whom it is deployed in terms of the included devices and applications that run on it, and **the monolithic system safety approach does not straightforwardly extend to the on-demand interoperability setting**, since the safety argument is no longer tied to a particular scenario, nor are the "safe" parameters known ahead of time. Crafting a safety argument ahead of deployment time for a system is challenging, to say the least. However, a high-assurance alarm subsystem can significantly simplify the task, if we can ensure that unsafe conditions reliably trigger an alarm and a failover-to-operator (manual, non-interoperating) mode.

Stand-alone medical devices already incorporate their own alarm systems. Indeed, alarm parameters, e.g., the concept and quantification of deviation from "safe," vary from patient to patient, and may even differ for the same patient for different treatment strategies. For instance, if a patient receives blood pressure reducing medication, "safe" / normal readings are expected to be outside a pre-defined range — this information is known to the clinician, but potentially not to the alarm system. Clinical logic (automatic reasoning about the condition of the patient) can be almost arbitrarily complex, with a large number of factors, from basic patient information like height, weight, and gender, to current medications and condition treated. ICE apps receive data about a patient from different sources, and perform a clinically useful function, for example, monitoring patient vital signs and predicting potential problems, which would be manifested as alarms. We call these *clinical alarms*. Since logic for clinical alarms is encapsulated within apps, we consider such alarms out of scope for this paper. However, apps rely on correct operation of medical devices and the underlying ICE platform. Which faults may lead to failures depends on which apps are deployed in the ICE instance. No single component within the system has all the relevant information to make informed decisions regarding which faults to detect and whether or not to raise an alarm in the event of a fault. Therefore, we focus on **technical alarms** that are the *result of a fault of the ICE instance* — emergent issues that arise because of the very fact that the system is interoperable and constructed as needed from units whose capabilities are limited.

3   IAS Requirements Generation

In this section we describe requirements generation for the Interoperability Alarm System (IAS) — the technical alarm system for IMDS. The IAS is responsible for detecting any interoperability failures within IMDS itself; in our case this is ICE. A well-designed ICE infrastructure should itself be capable of detecting technical issues with its operation, similar to exception handling in software engineering: if a medical device does not start when it is supposed to, or if the Supervisor crashes, such technical faults can be detected within ICE by e.g., the Supervisor or the device itself, respectively. Therefore the technical issues of ICE under the purview of IAS are those that cannot be reliably detected within ICE. Our main challenge is to determine when self-checks within ICE are insufficient.

Let us further consider our ongoing example of airway-laser surgery. A device, e.g., the pulse oximeter, sending valid but incorrect values is out of scope for the moment, since this does not constitute an interoperability problem. On other hand, sending values at a wrong rate is an interoperability problem that, presumably, can be detected by the ICE component receiving the values. However, because of the on-demand nature of ICE, the receiver may not know what the right rate is (since we may use different oximeters in different instantiations). Thus, whoever checks the value has to match the expected rate against the rate provided by the specific device used in a particular instance. If the check is performed incorrectly, we are in a situation that requires detection by IAS.

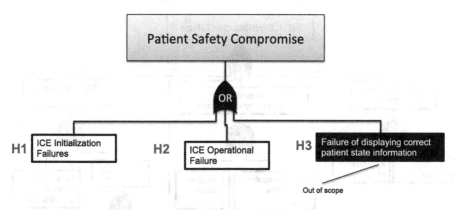

Fig. 2. Hazard causing patient safety

Our general approach to identify the (categories of) requirements for IAS has three steps: (1) identifying the principal hazards in ICE, (2) determining the high-level causes for these hazards, and (3) identifying the basis of the causes in the previous step. We build a fault-tree for each of these ICE failures to trace the origins of the fault. The output of the fault-tree analysis gives us a set of conditions within ICE operation that can eventually lead to hazards and **failure of ICE that IAS is responsible for detecting**, hence forming its requirements. In other words, the leaf nodes of this fault-tree essentially provide us with a category of IAS requirements.

We now present a categorization of the IAS requirements rather than list each of them one by one, i.e., we do not attempt to provide a comprehensive list of all possible sources of hazards within ICE. Further, IMDS hazards and the faults leading to them are also situation-specific. We prune the fault trees appropriately.

3.1   Hazard Analysis-Based Requirements Gathering

The goal of hazard analysis is to determine, based on the operational under-standing of a system, the various situations which can lead to hazardous condition for its users. In the case of ICE, hazardous conditions pertain to situations where the interoperability capability provided by ICE is not executed or executed incorrectly, leading to patient safety consequences. For IMDS we see that patient safety compromise appears from a set of three main hazards in ICE (see Fig. 2): (1) *Hazard H1:* ICE initialization failure, which prevents the interoperability platform from executing, leading to the patient not being able to receive its benefits; (2) *Hazard H2:* ICE operational failures, which occur during the executing of the interoperability by ICE, leading to sudden stoppage or incorrect interoperability; (3) *Hazard H3:* ICE status presentation failure, which leads to the wrong patient and ICE status being conveyed (e.g., through patient displays connected to ICE) to the caregiver and the patient, potentially leading to incorrect diagnosis and treatment. We consider H3 to be out of scope because if an

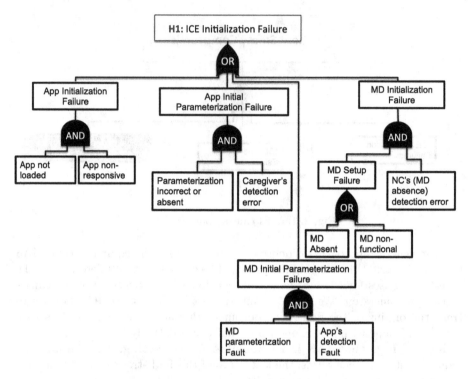

Fig. 3. Fault-tree for H1: Initialization failures

app is displaying the wrong information (but acting on correct information, as the hazard specifies) there is a problem only if a clinician observes the information and acts on it. If the display did not exist, everything would be operating normally. We now describe the causes of in-scope hazards H1 and H2 in detail:

Initialization Failures: H1 focuses on problems within ICE during the initialization of the interoperability setup around the patient. These manifest themselves when the various medical devices are integrated with ICE and the apps loaded onto the Supervisor within ICE and the interoperation is started. At this stage, failures can manifest themselves due to faults at all levels of ICE from the medical device to the Supervisor. For example, supervisory coordinator (i.e., app) initialization fault can occur if the Supervisor is not able to load the app. Similarly, the supervisor control algorithm can itself have initialization issues where it is not parameterized correctly or at all. Figure 3 illustrates the fault-tree for the initialization failures.

Operational Failures: H2 considers operational failures within the ICE, which happen after a successful (failure-less) initialization. The causes of H2 can again manifest themselves anywhere within ICE. An example of an operational failure is when a medical device sends corrupted data and the Network Controller does not check the CRC of the data received, failing to detect corruption. If either of the entities worked correctly, the fault would be detected within ICE and IAS

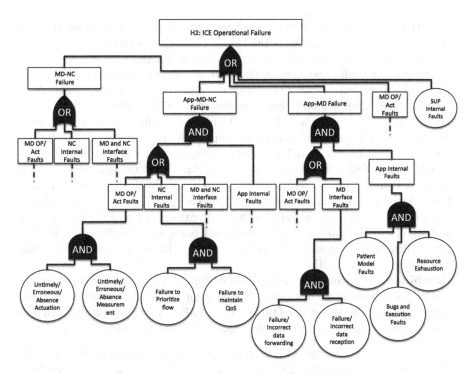

Fig. 4. Fault-tree for H2: Operational failures

would not be engaged. Other examples include: (1) a mismatch between actual medical device operation and operation expected by the app; (2) loss of device data or commands from the app due to insufficient bandwidth in the Network Controller; (3) software fault in the app crashing the Supervisor. Figure 4 illustrates the fault-tree for the operational failures. Some of the intermediate events appear more than once in the fault tree. For such events, we have expanded only one of the many occurrences into its constituent basic events. For the rest, we simply use a dashed line to denote that they should be expanded further.

As we can see from the fault-trees generated for the initialization and operational failures, failures of ICE that fall under the purview of IAS are those where one or more of the four components in the ICE fails to follow the prescribed protocol while at the same time the ICE entities fail to detect that the protocol is not being followed. For example, a medical device fault in measuring the patient's physiology is not by itself sufficient to involve the IAS. That is, IAS will be involved only if a fault in the data source ICE entity is accompanied by a fault in the data sink ICE entity (the entity ultimately receiving and processing the data). In general, there appear to be four types of failure scenarios in ICE operation that cannot be managed by ICE without the IAS:

– **Single-Entity Failures:** Certain entities within ICE are crucial for its operation, namely the Supervisor. Faults within the Supervisor and its control

algorithms are typically difficult to detect within ICE. Certain faults associated with the processing of patient data cannot be detected by any entity
within ICE and therefore fall under the purview of IAS.

- **Multi-Entity Failures:** During the flow of data or commands from apps
  to the medical device and vice-versa, a component $e1$ in ICE faults along
  with another component $e2$ that is responsible for detecting the fault of $e1$.
  For example, $e1$ is a medical device which fails to collect a measurement in
  response to an Supervisor's command, and $e2$ is the Supervisor, which does
  not detect that the requested data from the medical device is *not* received.
- **Entity-Link Failures:** During the flow of data or commands between two
  adjacent components $e1$ and $e2$ that share a communication link, the link
  faults (i.e., alters, delays, or loses data) and the receiver entity does not detect
  the fault. For example, the link between the Supervisor and the NC is noisy
  and results in the altering of the command being sent by the controller (to
  the medical device), and the NC does not detect this alteration as it does not
  correctly verify the CRC.
- **Combination Failures:** Finally, combination failures occur when more than
  one of the above three failures manifest simultaneously. As each of these
  instances are failures not detectable within ICE, a combination of them will
  also be undetectable, and would therefore fall under the purview of IAS.

Given the dynamic nature of ICE, many of the requirements may be difficult
to design for without making IAS arbitrarily complex. At this stage, however,
our goal is not to prune for detectability but to identify potential ICE failure
categories that can only be detected by a decoupled entity, such as IAS.

As note of caution, we stress that our goal is to design an alarm system
that is as generic and reusable as possible, and one that works for a variety of
apps and interoperability situations. Hence, we keep the description of our three
hazards as general as possible. It is therefore likely that some of the constituent
hazards may not apply fully in specific IMDS instances. For example, consider
a cardiac activity monitoring IMDS that collates sensing devices such electro-
cardiogram, photoplethysmogram, and continuous blood pressure to develop a
complete picture of the patient's cardiac process. This IMDS will not harm the
patient in any way through incorrect actuation. Therefore several sub-trees of
H1 and H2 will not be relevant for this particular IMDS. The alarm system can
be configured to ignore any faults reported from such sub-trees at run-time.

4   Case Study

Now we show how to apply our requirement generation approach to developing
the requirements for an alarm system for IMDS. Given the space constraints,
we do not provide an extensive fault-tree for the case study, but cover the four
types of failures presented earlier. The IMDS chosen for the purposes of this
case study is one that facilitates the clinical scenario of safe airway-laser surgery
(ALS-IMD) in the context of ICE by providing a safety interlock between the
ventilator and the laser. The ventilator supplies oxygen to an intubated patient,

and needs to be stopped when the laser is used to make an opening in or near the patient's throat. This has the potential danger of a fire if the laser is activated while high oxygen concentration is supplied by the ventilator. Whenever the laser is being activated, a human operator must block the air path from the oxygen concentrate while ensuring that the patient does not remain without oxygen for too long [10]. In traditional operating room environments, clinicians are supposed to be aware of potential fire and patient hypoxia problems. IMDS for safe airway-laser surgery must meet the following two safety invariants (requirements): (1) **R1:** The supply of oxygen from the ventilator must be blocked during the use of the laser to prevent surgical fire; (2) **R2:** The oxygen supply must be resumed within 4.5 min or if the patient's SpO2 level falls below 40 % [10].

In an ICE context, where safety properties are enforced not by dedicated hardware but by an app running on the supervisor, failure of ICE components to function correctly may jeopardize safety. In order to mitigate such situations, we need an external entity like IAS that can look at the IMDS holistically and detect failures with its operation. The rest of the section is divided into two parts: we begin with a description of the system model ASL-IMD, then discuss how an IAS would be used in an ICE-based implementation of ASL-IMD.

4.1 ALS-IMD System Model

The system model for interoperable medical device system aiding in the safe execution of airway-laser surgery is illustrated in Fig. 5. There are three medical devices in this interoperability setup — laser, SpO2, and ventilator. **Individual medical devices may have their own internal logic to detect conditions that affect patient safety.** An ASL app is responsible for making sure that the two safety constraints are satisfied at all times. As in [10], the app makes use of

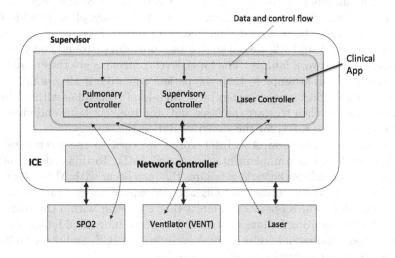

Fig. 5. Airway-laser surgery interoperable medical device system model

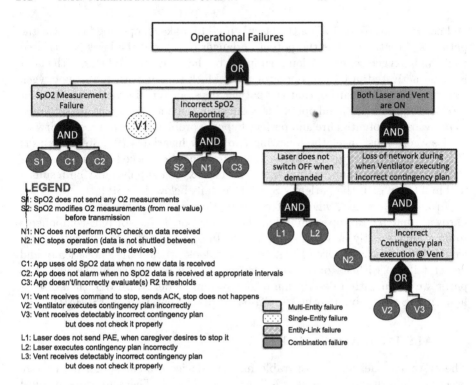

Fig. 6. Airway-laser surgery interoperable operational failures

two dedicated "low-level" controllers: a pulmonary controller for the SpO2 and the ventilator, and a therapeutic controller for the laser system. The pulmonary controller maintains a pulmonary model and generates a contingency plan for the ventilator and the laser to follow. These contingency plans provide hard limits for when the laser should stop and the ventilator switched back on in order to ensure R1 and R2 are never violated, providing patient safety even in the presence of network failures. The lower-level controllers are thus closed-loop themselves and will attempt to keep the patient safe even if all else fails. Each of low-level controllers is coordinated by a "high-level" controller within the app which determines when to start the laser and stop the ventilator and vice-versa depending upon the needs for the caregiver during the surgery.

Now that we know how ASL-IMD works, we turn to the interoperability hazards of an ICE-based implementation of ASL-IMD. To this end, we build a fault-tree that describes the various failures that can occur with ALS-IMD which cannot be detected by entities in ICE and so require an external/decoupled entity. Figure 6 captures operational faults that can occur within the ALS-IMD system and the resulting failures that arise from these individual faults. The leaf nodes represent individual faults in some entity within ICE, and these faults are combined to create operational failure scenarios.

From the perspective of the characterization given in Sect. 3, we can see that all of the identified faults fall within the four categories of faults that form the requirements for the IAS. The shading of nodes in Fig. 6 illustrates the categorization of the identified failures. This lets us conclude that an IAS module, built to satisfy these requirements, would successfully raise alarms to notify operators about failures in the ALS-IMD system. As mentioned before, the goal is not to be comprehensive with the fault-trees but to demonstrate how they are generated.

The IAS system will require various fault detection modules that detect the problems specified in the leaf nodes in our fault trees. Many of these detection modules may be IMDS-specific and need to be loaded at run-time when the IMDS is assembled. Our goal with IAS is to build a modular or parametric alarm system that can incorporate detection modules into a larger whole. An important consideration in integrating these detection modules into IAS is the resultant complexity of the alarm system, which can make any problems with IAS itself difficult to detect. One might even decide to leave out the detection modules for certain faults, thus rendering them undetectable, as long as they do not necessarily cause immediate harm to the patient.

5   Related Work

Integrated Modular Avionics: In aviation, Integrated Modular Avionics (IMA) describes an architecture fairly similar to ICE. The major difference, however, is that components are assembled and integrated beforehand, while, to extend the aviation analogy to ICE, we would be swapping equipment in and out while the aircraft is in flight. IMA describes a distributed real time network of computing platforms known as modules. Modules are networked to each other, to devices of the aircraft such as sensors/actuators and the environment. An IMA module is a layered architecture, described in the avionics standard ARINC 653 [13]. This standard is based on the concept of partitions. Each partition is an area separated from the operating system for scheduling and memory space purposes. Each partition contains an application of the avionics software. Applications have access to common services of the operating system. The operating system interacts with the supporting hardware via a hardware interface layer. Applications can have different levels of criticality and are executed independently. IMA consists of a health monitoring system for fault detection and reporting of application software, OS and hardware failures.

The role of apps in ICE, rather than performing a specific functionality, is to determine the medical devices used in each case and orchestrate their executions. ICE Supervisor is compared to an IMA platform which encapsulates several apps and interacts with the network. Concerning the IMA health monitoring system, it provides fault detection only of the IMA platform. Contrary to IAS that detects faults of the whole architecture, IMA health monitoring systems do not detect faults coming from the network, devices of the aircraft and the environment.

IEC 60601-2-8: The IEC 60601-1-8 standard [7] defines alarms for medical equipment, their associated problems, and provides some suggestions for risk mitigation strategies. Primary considerations are alarm source identification, distractions caused by alarms, and false positive alarms. The system being monitored is best described as a distributed system with associated components, so IAS fulfills the role of a *technical alarm* that ensures, as required by 60601-1-8, that the failure of a component of a distributed system must generate a technical alarm condition. Note that IAS *is not a primary alarm* — these are generated by devices and/or clinical applications. IAS is a secondary alarm which detects component failure when those components themselves either do not detect it or are acting maliciously. The IEC standard was not meant for use in the presence of malicious devices/actors. IAS is compliant with 60601-1-8, and is a step toward making the system being monitored compliant with 60601-1-8, assuming adequate documentation, and an external log, provided by the interoperable system being monitored, for alarm recording.

IEC 80001-2-5: The IEC 80001-2-5 standard [8] deals with *distributed* alarm systems (which are only briefly mentioned in IEC 60601-1-8). These systems handle *multiple medical devices simultaneously*, and their functionality may not be housed within one physical location, and therefore subject to additional safety issues such as transmission delays and lost messages within the medical IT-network. Types of systems include guaranteed delivery, guaranteed delivery with confirmation, and "informational" systems which do not guarantee delivery. Only those systems offering guaranteed delivery with confirmation are sufficiently safe to be used for primary notification. Once again, it is important to recall that IAS is not a primary alarm. Further, defining the means of communicating IAS-generated alarms are beyond the scope and space constraints of this work.

ICE Logging: In [1], the authors discuss the design of a data logging system for an Integrated Clinical Environment (ICE). The data logger is contained in the ICE Network Controller and logs data from all medical devices. Log data is useful for debugging network interactions, clinical event analysis, analyzing patient outcomes and developing advanced clinical algorithms. The data logger provides options to allow user decide the granularity of details of the logs, a suitable clock logic to establish causal ordering between events in cases where real-time clock is not available, special formats for interpreting data between connected devices, security options for ensuring trustworthiness of the log and methodologies for clinical log and debugging playback of the log data. Note that this is both a technical and a clinical data logger.

6   Conclusion

In this work, we develop requirements for a technical Interoperability Alarm System (IAS) for dynamically composable on-demand IMDS. As part of our work we define the scope of IAS as distinct from a clinical alarm. We use the ICE architecture as the basis of our IMDS for alarm requirements generation. Our approach is to use hazard analysis and fault-trees to systematically and comprehensively categorize the various faults within the ICE architecture that the IAS would be responsible for detecting. The faults thus identified have an important common characteristic — they are all problems that cannot be detected from within ICE by the various ICE entities because they are a result of the simultaneous faults in more than one ICE entity. This work can be generalized to other cyber-physical systems, but is particularly important (and indeed difficult) in the medical system space, where systems are expected to be assembled as needed, with no dedicated integrator or integration testing of a particular system configuration. While the described alarm system cannot detect all failures emergent from interoperability (failures which would not be possible in a non-interoperable system), it significantly increases our assurance that an interoperable medical system will function as intended, and that operators will be notified when it deviates from expected behavior.

As part of the future work, we plan to design the IAS architecture including the required monitors and the alarm logic blocks, develop the specification language and associated vocabulary for event descriptions, and implement IAS as part of an existing ICE implementation.

References

1. Arney, D., Weininger, S., Whitehead, S.F., Goldman, J.M.: Supporting medical device adverse event analysis in an interoperable clinical environment: design of a data logging and playback system. In: ICBO (2011)
2. ASTM 2761: Medical devices and medical systems – essential safety requirements for equipment comprising the patient-centric integrated clinical environment (ICE) (2013)
3. Avizienis, A., Laprie, J., Randell, B., Landwehr, C.: Basic concepts and taxonomy of dependable and secure computing. IEEE Trans. Dependable Secure Comput. 1(1), 11–33 (2004)
4. Clarke, M., Bogia, D., Hassing, K., Steubesand, L., Chan, T., Ayyagari, D.: Developing a standard for personal health devices based on 11073. In: EMBS (2007)
5. Hatcliff, J., King, A., Lee, I., Macdonald, A., Fernando, A., Robkin, M., Vasserman, E., Weininger, S., Goldman, J.M.: Rationale and architecture principles for medical application platforms. In: ICCPS (2012)
6. Health Level Seven International. http://www.hl7.org/
7. IEC. Medical electrical equipment - Part 1–8: General requirements for basic safety and essential performance - Collateral Standard: General requirements, tests and guidance for alarm systems in medical electrical equipment and medical electrical systems (2008)
8. IEC. Application of risk management for IT-networks incorporating medical devices - Part 2–5: Application guidance - Guidance for distributed alarm systems (2014)
9. Integrating the healthcare enterprise. http://www.ihe.net/
10. Kang, W., Wu, P., Rahmaniheris, M., Sha, L., Berlin, R., Goldman, J.: Towards organ-centric compositional development of safe networked supervisory medical systems. In: CBMS (2013)

11. King, A., Arney, D., Lee, I., Sokolsky, O., Hatcliff, J., Procter, S.: Prototyping closed loop physiologic control with the medical device coordination framework. In: SEHC (2010)
12. Lesh, K., Weininger, S., Goldman, J., Wilson, B., Himes, G.: Medical device inter-operability – assessing the environment. In: HCMDSS-MDPnP (2007)
13. Prisaznuk, P.J.: ARINC 653 role in integrated modular avionics (IMA). In: DASC (2008)
14. Tolk, A., Diallo, S., Turnitsa, C.: Applying the levels of conceptual interoperability model in support of integratability, interoperability, and composability for system-of-systems engineering. Journal of Systemics, Cybernetics and Informatics, vol. 5, no. 5 (2007)

Architectures and Testing

The Safety Requirements
Decomposition Pattern

Pablo Oliveira Antonino[1(✉)], Mario Trapp[1], Paulo Barbosa[2],
Edmar C. Gurjão[3], and Jeferson Rosário[4]

[1] Fraunhofer Institute for Experimental Software Engineering - IESE,
Kaiserslautern, Germany
{pablo.antonino,mario.trapp}@iese.fraunhofer.de
[2] Nucleus for Strategic Health Technologies - NUTES,
State University of Paraíba - UEPB, Campina Grande, Paraíba, Brazil
paulo.barbosa@nutes.uepb.edu.br
[3] Electrical Engineering Department,
Federal University of Campina Grande - UFCG,
Campina Grande, Paraíba, Brazil
ecandeia@dee.ufcg.edu.br
[4] Lifemed, Porto Alegre, Rio Grande do Sul, Brazil
jeferson.rosario@lifemed.com.br

Abstract. Safety requirement specifications usually have heterogeneous
structures, most likely based on the experience of the engineers involved in the
specification process. Consequently, it gets difficult to ensure that recommendations given in standards are considered, e.g., evidence that the requirements
are complete and consistent with other development artifacts. To address this
challenge, we present in this paper the Safety Requirements Decomposition
Pattern, which aims at supporting the decomposition of safety requirements that
are traceable to architecture and failure propagation models. The effectiveness of
the approach has been observed in its application in different domains, such as
automotive, avionics, and medical devices. In this paper, we present its usage in
the context of an industrial Automated External Defibrillator system.

Keywords: Safety requirement · Architecture · Failure propagation model ·
Traceability · Completeness · Consistency

1 Introduction

Safety requirements are fundamental artifacts in the specification of safety-critical
systems, since they often result from safety analysis of the architecture, and must
ultimately be addressed by elements of the architecture [1, 2].

Because of this key role of safety requirements in safety engineering activities, it is
important to assure that they meet certain quality attributes [3]. In particular, completeness and consistency of safety requirements have been widely discussed, as it has
been demonstrated that the lack of guidance on how to properly specify traceable safety
requirements is one of the main reasons for their incompleteness and inconsistency and,
consequently, a root cause of safety incidents [4].

© Springer International Publishing Switzerland 2015
F. Koornneef and C. van Gulijk (Eds.): SAFECOMP 2015, LNCS 9337, pp. 269–282, 2015.
DOI: 10.1007/978-3-319-24255-2_20

In this regard, the work described in this paper addresses this challenge by providing a hierarchical decomposition structure to support the systematic decomposition of safety requirements specifications that are explicitly traceable to failure propagation models (e.g., Markov Chains and Fault Trees Analysis) and to architecture specifications–the Safety Requirements Decomposition Pattern (SRDP).

The SRDP has been used in several projects in the automotive, avionics, and medical device industries in Europe and Brazil, and has proven to be effective in improving completeness and consistency of safety requirements. In this paper, we present the use of the approach in the safety requirements specification of an Automated External Defibrillator (AED) system, which is being specified in a technology transfer collaboration process between the Nucleus for Strategic Health Technologies (NUTES[1]), which is an initiative of the Brazilian Health Ministry for promoting the technological development of medical devices, and the medical device producer Lifemed[2], which has more than thirty years of activity in the area of production of equipment and consumption material destined to the medical-hospital sector.

The remainder of this paper is structured as follows: In Sect. 2, we discuss the state of the practice in safety requirements specifications. In Sect. 3, we present the main drivers for establishing the SRDP, and in Sect. 4 we present it in detail. In Sect. 5, we describe its usage in the context of the NUTES/Lifemed Automated External Defibrillator system and discuss the results. In Sect. 6 we present the related works, and, in Sect. 7 we present conclusions and discuss future work.

2 State of the Practice in Specifying Safety Requirements

Standards and regulations such as ISO 26262 [2], DO-178C [5], and ANSI/AAMI/IEC 62304 [6] describe strict recommendations to be considered during the specification of safety requirements. ISO 29148 [7], e.g., recommends providing evidences showing that the requirements are consistent, complete, validated, verified, and fully traceable to all system artifacts. Nevertheless, none of these norms specifies a defined structure for safety requirements specifications, nor guidelines to be followed during the specification process. In practice, each safety requirements specification has a different structure, most likely based on the understanding and experience of the engineers involved in the specification process. Furthermore, because of this lack of a structured definition, following the argumentation of safety requirements specifications is not a trivial task, especially if the reader is not the author [8]. As a consequence, it becomes difficult to ensure that the aspects recommended by standards and regulations are considered, such as completeness and consistency of safety requirements with respect to the results of the failure analysis and to the architecture specification [4, 9]. For instance, Maeder et al. [4] analyzed the traceability documents of a medical device submitted to the US Food and Drug Administration - FDA and found that the majority

---

[1] http://nutes.uepb.edu.br/.

[2] http://www.lifemed.com.br/.

of the safety requirements were incomplete and that many of their traces to safety analysis results and to the architecture were inconsistent.

In a sense, there is a lack of means for intelligently and efficiently reasoning about existing and missing traceability between artifacts, which includes, among other things, the types of artifacts and relationships that are permissible and the granularity level to which the different artifacts should be decomposed [1, 10].

3 Designing the Safety Requirements Decomposition Pattern

The architecture specification is one core artifact to be considered when specifying safety requirements, as these requirements often result from a safety analysis of the architecture [1, 2]. In this regard, to design the SRDP, we analyzed several mature model-based architecture specification methodologies, such as (i) Kruchten's "4 + 1" View Model [11], (ii) the Software Engineering Institute's Viewtypes [12], (iii) the Siemens Four View Models [13], and (iv) the SPES 2020 Methodology for Model-Based Engineering of Embedded Systems [14]. Additionally, we had fruitful discussions with practitioners from the automotive, avionics, and medical devices domains, and, compiling the results from both sources, we observed that at least two aspects are usually addressed when specifying the architecture of a safety-critical system: (i) *the functions of the system*; i.e., implementation-independent specification of what the system should provide in terms of services to its users [11]; and (ii) *description of the architectural elements that realize the functions*, either software resources, e.g., a scheduling slot, or hardware resources, e.g., a processor [14]. In a sense, both the state of the art and the state of the practice indicate that it is important to document at the architectural level at least the functions of the systems and how they are realized by software and hardware artifacts (cf. Architecture Design slot of Fig. 1).

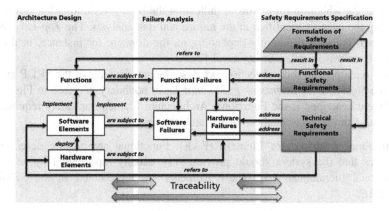

Fig. 1. Dependencies between development artifacts in safety-critical systems considering the functions and technical resources (software and hardware) that realize them.

In the development of safety-critical systems, portions of the architecture are subject to failure analysis, which, in turn, is performed using appropriate techniques, such as Markov Chains and Fault Trees Analysis, which aim at identifying and representing the logical relationships between software and hardware failures and how they cause functional failures (cf. Failure Analysis slot of Fig. 1) [1, 2].

Based on this context, we understand that it is also necessary to have a hierarchical decomposition of the safety requirements to ensure that failures associated with architecture elements of the different levels of abstraction (function, software, and hardware) are addressed with an adequate level of detail (cf. Safety Requirements Specification slot of Fig. 1). This is where the SRDP plays its role in guiding the construction of safety requirements specifications, enriching them semantically by considering hazard-contributing factors described in failure propagation models and risk control measures described in the architectural specification.

4   The Safety Requirements Decomposition Pattern

We split the description of the SRDP into three parts: first, in Subsect. 4.1, we present its decomposition structure for specifying functional safety requirements; then, in Subsect. 4.2, its decomposition structure for specifying technical safety requirements; and in Subsect. 4.3, the elements that are common to the functional and technical levels.

4.1   Safety Requirements Decomposition Pattern at the Functional Level

As illustrated in Fig. 1, we understand that it is necessary to specify safety requirements associated with architecture elements of different levels of abstraction. At the functional level, the safety requirements should describe how the elements of the functional architecture should collaborate to fulfill the *Top-Level Safety Requirement* (cf. top-most part of Fig. 2), which, in turn, aims at indicating the high-level mitigation strategy for addressing the hazards identified in the hazard and risk analysis. The *Top-Level Safety Requirement* is called differently depending on the domain; for instance, in the road vehicles domain it is called Safety Goal [2].

In the remainder of this subsection, we describe the elements of the SRDP grouped inside the *Safety Requirements @ Functional Level* boundary depicted in Fig. 2. The first element described is the Functional Architecture Element, as safety requirements often result from a safety analysis of the architecture:

- **Functional Architecture Element (FAE):** Functional architecture describes the services that the system should provide [11], usually represented by networked functional hierarchies [14]. These elements are represented in the SRDP by the *FAE*.

Next, we describe the elements identified during the Failure Analysis (cf. central part of Fig. 1), which are depicted in the left-most part of Fig. 2:

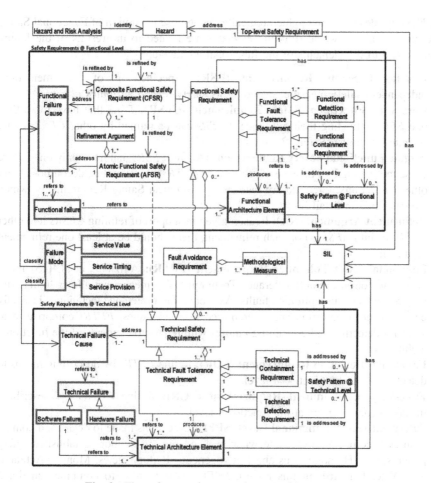

Fig. 2. The safety requirements decomposition pattern.

- **Functional Failure (FF):** ISO 26262 defines failure as the termination of the ability of an element to perform a function as required [2]. One of the reasons that might cause failures is the lack of compliance between the services delivered and the system specification at the functional and technical levels [1, 2]. At the functional level, we call this item Functional Failure (FF). It is about what might happen with elements of the functional architecture that can lead to the system failure. These failures are identified throughout the failure analysis using failure propagation models.

- **Functional Failure Cause (FFC):** Failure conditions associated with failures of elements of the functional architecture that lead to system malfunction. *FFCs* are classified according to Failure Modes, which, in turn, are described in Sect. 4.3.

Next, we describe how to hierarchically decompose the notion of Functional Safety Requirement and how the resulting elements are related to the results of the failure analysis and to the elements of the functional architecture.

- **Functional Safety Requirement (FSR):** Specification of implementation-independent safety measure, including its safety-related attributes [2].
- **Composite Functional Safety Requirement (CFSR):** *FSRs* that have more than one *FFC* motivating their existence. *CFSRs* can be refined by other *CFSRs* or by Atomic Functional Safety Requirements (AFSR).
- **Atomic Functional Safety Requirement (AFSR):** *FSRs* that have only one failure cause motivating its existence. *AFSRs* refine *CFSRs* that cannot be decomposed into other *CFSRs* anymore, and are realized by Technical Safety Requirements, which are described in detail in Sect. 4.2.
- **Refinement Argument (RA):** Reason given in support of refining *CFSRs* into other *CFSRs* or into *AFSRs*. For each refinement, there should be at least one refinement argument.
- **Functional Fault Tolerance Requirement (FFTR):** Avizienis et al. [15] introduced the notion of Fault Tolerance Techniques as a means that allows living with systems that are susceptible to faults. Avizienis' fault tolerance techniques basically consist of error detection and system recovery techniques. *FFTRs* comprise measures for detecting and containing failures with regard to elements of the functional architecture.
- **Functional Detection Requirement (FDR):** Refine *FFTRs* by describing means to detect errors at the functional level.
- **Functional Containment Requirement (FCR):** Refine *FFTRs* by describing means to handle errors at the functional level.
- **Safety Pattern @ Functional Level (SPFL):** Decisions made to detect and contain failures become more concrete when realized by one or more established safety patterns, e.g., Homogeneous and Heterogeneous Redundancies, Monitor-Actuator, and Watchdog [16]. In this regard, *SPFLs* indicate how to combine functional architecture elements to detect and contain functional failures.

4.2 Safety Requirements Decomposition Pattern at the Technical Level

At the technical level, the safety requirements should describe how the strategies specified at the functional level are realized using software and hardware resources. The artifacts used as inputs at this level are (i) the *AFSR*, as they are the most refined descriptions of the safety strategy at the functional level, and (ii) the technical architecture specification (i.e., software and hardware entities). In the remainder of this subsection, we describe the elements of the SRDP grouped inside the *Safety Requirements @ Technical Level* boundary depicted in Fig. 2.

- **Technical Architecture Element (TAE):** Software and hardware entities.

The following elements are identified during the Failure Analysis (cf. central part of Fig. 1):

- **Technical Failure (TF):** This is about what happened with technical architecture elements that led to functional failures. We adapted the convention proposed by Wu and Kelly [18] and categorize a technical failure according to one of the following two abstract types: (i) *Software Failure (SF)* - Incomplete or inaccurate specification, or incorrect design and implementation can cause unexpected behavior of the software; and (ii) *Hardware Failure (HF)* - Correct software can still misbehave due to unexpected behavior of the underlying hardware.
- **Technical Failure Cause (TFC):** Failure conditions associated with failures of elements of the technical architecture (hardware and software resources) that lead to functional misbehavior and finally result in a malfunction of the system. Technical failures are classified according to Failure Modes, which are described in Sect. 4.3.

The items listed below describe how to hierarchically decompose the notion of Technical Safety Requirement per se, and how the resulting elements are related to the results of the failure analysis and to the elements of the technical architecture.

- **Technical Safety Requirement (TSR):** ISO 26262 defines TSRs as *"requirements derived for implementation of associated functional safety requirement"* [2]. To follow this principle, in the scope of this paper *TSRs* comprise strategies for realizing an AFSR.
- **Technical Fault Tolerance Requirement (TFTR):** Specification for detecting and containing failures with regard to elements of the technical architecture. The measures described at this level should be consistent with those specified at the functional level with the FFTR.
- **Technical Detection Requirement (TDR):** Refine *FFTRs* by describing means to detect errors at the technical level.
- **Technical Containment Requirement (TCR):** Refine *FFTRs* by describing means to handle errors at the technical level.

The *TDRs* and *TCRs* as well as *FDRs* and *FCRs* (cf. Sect. 4.1) should refer to technical and functional architecture elements that concretize the safety measures. If these elements already exist in the architecture, they just need to be referenced in the requirement; if not, they have to be included according to the demands described in the requirement, as indicated by the *refers to* and *produces* relationships, respectively, between Functional and Technical Fault Tolerance Requirements and Functional and Technical Architecture Element shown in Fig. 2.

- **Safety Pattern @ Technical Level (SPTL):** At this abstraction level, elements of the technical architecture should be considered in order to realize the *SPFLs*.

4.3 Safety Requirements Decomposition Pattern Elements that are Common to the Functional and Technical Levels

In this section, we discuss the SRDP elements that are common to both functional and technical levels: *Failure Mode, Safety Integrity Level*, and the *Fault Avoidance Requirement*.

Failure Mode (FM) is the manner in which an element or item fails [15]. At the functional level, the Failure Mode is associated with the manner in which elements of the functional architecture fail. At the technical level, it is associated with the manner in which elements of the technical architecture fail. We adopted the failure mode classification proposed by Fenelon et al. [17, 18]: (i) *Service provision* - Omission, Commission; (ii) *Service timing* - Early, Late; and (iii) *Service value* - Coarse incorrect, Subtle incorrect.

Safety Integrity Levels (SIL) are discrete levels, corresponding to a range of safety integrity values, where SIL 4 has the highest level of safety integrity and SIL 1 has the lowest level [19]. In this regard, the SIL needs to be indicated explicitly throughout the specification of functional and technical safety requirements to ensure safety integrity compatibility between *Top-Level Safety Requirement, Functional Safety Requirements, Functional Architecture Elements, Technical Safety Requirements,* and *Technical Architecture Elements.*

Fault Avoidance Requirements (FAR) Descriptions of methodological measures to modify the development process (e.g. testing strategies and code conventions) in order to reduce the number of faults introduced during the development time of safety-critical systems [15]. As FARs are related to methodological measures, their demands affect system development as a whole, independent of how the system specification is abstracted.

5 Specifying the Safety Requirements of an Automated External Defibrillator with the Safety Requirements Decomposition Pattern

AED is a medical device used for ventricular fibrillation/tachycardia treatment, which are cardiac arrhythmias with the highest incidences of fatal cases. The AED is operated by a rescuer to deliver controlled energy to the patient's chest. The amount of energy delivered is based on an automated analysis of the Electrocardiography (ECG), which is also performed by the AED. Delays in the application of the defibrillator shock are safety-critical because every minute without the application of the shock implies a 7 % to 10 % decrease of the chance of survival [20]. In this regard, it is important to ensure optimized recharging to minimize discharge intervals. We explored the AED, which is being specified in a technology transfer collaboration process between the medical device producer Lifemed and the Brazilian Health Ministry initiative NUTES, to demonstrate how the SRDP contributed positively to improving the specification of traceable safety requirements.

5.1 Preliminary Specification of the Automated External Defibrillator

Figure 3 depicts the context diagram for the AED system. This diagram aims at showing each external entity, the main functional units, and their interactions. In simplified terms, the main input variable to be received is the patient's cardiac pulse. The Signal Analyzer employs algorithms for detecting the signal complexity and

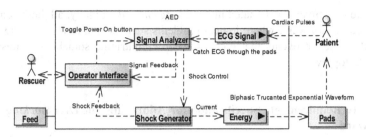

Fig. 3. Context diagram of the AED system.

determines whether a cardiac arrest has occurred. If this is the case, the Shock Generator provides controlled energy to the patient's chest through the cardiac pads.

In order to identify potentially safety-critical failures of the AED, we conducted quantitative and qualitative safety analysis considering heterogeneous artifacts of the system, such as those depicted in Fig. 3. An excerpt of the analysis is depicted in Fig. 4, where the failure paths leading to the *Overshocking* hazard can be seen. The information presented in this analysis will later be traced to elements of the safety requirements using the SRDP. As shown in Fig. 4, the *Overshocking* hazard occurs as a result of the combination of intermediate and basic events inside the *Shock Generator* (cf. Fig. 3), which is composed of *Charge* and *Discharge* hardware and software entities inside their controllers. In the *Charge module*, the main causes stem from the loss of ability of the *Charge Controller* to maintain the stability of the energy transfer process. In the *Discharge module*, the main causes stem from the wear of hardware components and the failure in detecting and mitigating problems due to the high level

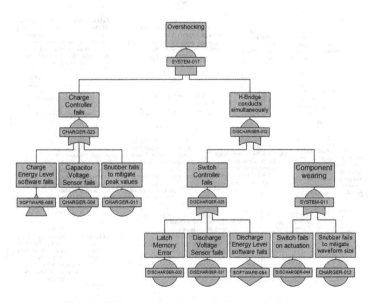

Fig. 4. Failure propagation analysis as a fault tree.

of energy to be delivered originated in the *Charge module*. Finally, all these controllers have embedded software, where logical problems such as data error or wrong control flow might generate events that could somehow contribute somehow to raising the undesirable top event.

5.2 Safety Requirements Specification for Addressing the *Overshocking* Hazard

We specified safety requirements for mitigating the hazard of *Overshocking* using the SRDP presented in this paper, and the result is summarized in Fig. 5.

One of the measures for mitigating AED overshocking is to ensure that the switching voltage of the shock generator (cf. Fig. 4) will not deliver energy above the

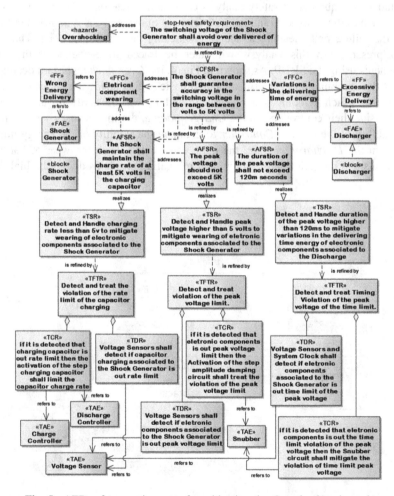

Fig. 5. AED safety requirements for mitigating the *Overshocking* hazard.

specified level. This aspect is represented by the *Top-level safety requirement* element in Fig. 5. The main causes that might lead to the occurrence of this hazard are (i) wear of electronic components or (ii) an unexpected loss of control by the software leading to unexpected values. This motivates new fine-grained specifications such as charging rates for capacitors, specific voltage peak values, or specific frequencies via semi-conductor switching. Therefore, three technical safety requirements were derived and matched perfectly to those defined in the SRDP. Two cases (the leftmost ones) refer to the architectural element Shock Generator module, and the other one (the rightmost one) refers to the architectural element Discharge module. This parameterization makes it easier to clearly define the goal of each subtree specification.

Going towards fine-grained specifications, the next refinements will be fault tolerance requirements such as indication of components wear; alerts indicating the need for maintenance and repair; coupling of new amortization circuits in order to deal with unexpected peak values; or coupling of new circuits for the management of periods to avoid extrapolation of time limits for issuing peak tensions. This generates technical containment requirements and technical detection requirements, which are also defined according to the parameterized templates. Finally, the last layer of specification will require specific sensors and actuators for efficient detections and actions over all hazardous conditions.

5.3 Brief Discussion

The proposed methodology applied to medical devices allows mapping internal risks from a possible hazard and is critical in AED design due to its crucial utilization. In addition, the analysis permits both software and hardware risk specification in an integrated way, which is difficult to perform. As engineers are usually not completely aware of how a failure in a small piece of internal circuits affects the whole system safety, we consider the developed traceability to be an important achievement regarding the challenge of introducing safety engineering practices into system engineering processes. Finally, the clear decomposition proposed in this approach constitutes a concrete tool for meeting the very abstract recommendations provided by ANSI/AAMI/IEC 62304 [6].

6 Related Works

Habli et al. [21], investigated how to hierarchically decompose safety concepts [4] using the Goal Structuring Notation (GSN) in such a way that the safety argumentation is traced to a set of SysML models. Nevertheless, they present no systematic means for instantiating the approach. Actually, there is no guideline on how to decompose from high-level safety requirements to software-/hardware-related safety requirements and no indication of the types of artifacts and relationships that are permissible, nor of the granularity level to which the different artifacts should be decomposed. These aspects are extremely important for precisely and intelligently decomposing complete and consistent safety requirements [1, 10], and are provided by our approach. The approach targets mainly inter-traceability (traceability among different artifacts) and neglects intra-traceability (traceability within the safety requirements decomposition). The SRDP improves both aspects: regarding intra-traceability, it provides a systematic hierarchical decomposition of the safety requirements that precisely indicate how top-level safety requirements as well as functional and technical safety requirements are related to each other; regarding inter-traceability, it requires matching the safety requirements decomposition to the hierarchical abstraction of the architecture elements and their respective failure propagations. Finally, our approach is not strictly tied to any particular modeling approach such as GSN or SysML because we understand that engineers should be free to use whichever approach and notation they are used to and should just have to consider the decomposition strategy described in the SRDP.

Katta and Stalhane [22] proposed a conceptual model of traceability for safety systems, which comprises a variety of artifacts and their traceability links. Their model includes elements from (i) the System Development Process, which comprises elements such as functional description, system and software requirements, and architectural components, and (ii) the Safety Assessment Process, which comprises elements such as hazards, risks, and common cause failures. Some of the intra-artifacts traceability inks proposed were considered during the elaboration of the SRDP. In this regard, we adapted their model by clearly separating safety requirements, architecture elements, and their associated failures at the functional and technical levels, and we provide systematic decomposition guidelines at each level. Moreover, we provide a clear execution path from the top-level safety requirements to the software and hardware requirements. Katta and Stalhane, on the other hand, do not provide any decomposition flow to be followed, which causes confusion and uncertainties when using their model. As for Habli et al. [21], Katta and Stalhane do not specify the granularity level to which the different artifacts should be decomposed, all of which is provided by our approach.

Birch et al. [23] analyzed the implicit safety argument structure of ISO 26262 and propose using GSN for structuring and logically decomposing the argumentation in order to justify "why" a safety requirement is indeed a Safety Requirement. The SRDP also handles justification of the existence of safety requirements, as it requires indicating the failure modes/failure paths that motivate the existence of each safety requirement. However, the SRDP requires referencing the failure propagation model that describes the failures being addressed in the safety requirement and the related architecture elements; it does not specify the level of detail to justify why a safety requirement is, indeed, a safety requirement.

Beckers et al. [24] proposed an approach centered in UML and GSN to breakdown safety goals into functional safety concepts [2]. The approach consists of seven steps that covers important aspects like, e.g., checking the completeness of a functional safety concept and ASIL decomposition, functional safety concepts allocation. Our approach differs from Beckers' as we also consider technical requirements and their synergies with functional requirements, contributing then for multi-level consistent specifications. Moreover, beyond explicitly referencing architecture elements of both levels, the SRDP offers basis for referencing failure models associated to these elements that triggered the creation of the safety requirements. Additionally, the global approach of which the SRDP is part supports not only completeness, but also consistency checks, as described in a previous work of ours [25]. Last, the SRDP improves Becker's approach in terms of context appropriateness as its current version results from intense use not only in the road vehicles, but also in the avionics and medical devices domains.

7 Conclusions and Future Works

In this paper, we presented the Safety Requirements Decomposition Pattern, which addresses the challenges regarding completeness and consistency of safety requirements by providing a hierarchical decomposition structure to support the systematic decomposition of safety requirements specifications that are explicitly traceable to failure propagation models and to architecture specifications.

We have seen that our approach offers a reasonable basis for ensuring that there is enough information at each abstraction level of a system specification describing how the appropriate safety measures should be considered in order to address the failure causes described in the failure propagation models.

As future work, we intend to define relationships between the Safety Requirements Decomposition Pattern and other safety analysis artifacts such as safety cases and customize controlled natural languages to support content elaboration of the elements that compose the Safety Requirements Decomposition Pattern.

Acknowledgements. This work is supported by the Fraunhofer Innovation Cluster Digitale Nutzfahrzeugtechnologie. We would also like to thank Sonnhild Namingha for proofreading, and to the head of NUTES Prof. Dr. Misael Morais.

References

1. Hatcliff, J., Wassyng, A., Kelly, T., Comar, C., Jones, P.: Certifiably safe software-dependent systems: challenges and directions. In: FOSE 2014, Hyderabad, India (2014)
2. International Organization for Standardization: ISO/DIS 26262 - Road Vehicles – Functional Safety. Technical Committee 22 (ISO/TC 22), Geneva, Switzerland (2011)
3. Adler, R.: Introducing quality attributes for a safety concept. SAE Technical Paper 2013-01-0194, Detroit, Michigan, USA (2013)
4. Maeder, P., Jones, P.L., Zhang, Y., Cleland-Huang, J.: Strategic traceability for safety-critical projects. IEEE Softw. **30**(3), 58–68 (2013)
5. DO-178C/ED-12C: Software Considerations in Airborne Systems and Equipment (2011)
6. ANSI/AAMI/IEC 62304:2006: Medical Device Software—Software Life Cycle (2006)
7. International Organization for Standardization: ISO/IEC/IEEE 29148:2011 Systems and software engineering - Life cycle processes - Requirements engineering. IEEE (2011)
8. Kaiser, B.: Approaches Towards reusable safety concepts. Presentation at the VDA Automotive SYS Conference, Berlin, Germany (2012)
9. Antonino, P.O., Trapp, M.: Improving consistency checks between safety concepts and view based. Architecture design. In: PSAM12, Honolulu, Hawaii, USA (2014)

10. Cleland-Huang, J., Goetel, O., Hayes, J.H., Maeder, P., Zisman, A.: Software traceability: trends and future directions. In: FOSE 2014, Hyderabad, India (2014)
11. Kruchten, P.: The 4+1 view model of architecture. IEEE Softw. **12**, 42–50 (1995)
12. Clements, P., Garlan, D., Bass, L., Stafford, J., Nord, R., Ivers, J., Little, R.: Documenting Software Architectures: Views and Beyond. Pearson Education, Upper Saddle River (2002)
13. Hofmeister, C., Nord, R., Soni, D.: Applied Software Architecture, 1st edn. Addison-Wesley Professional, Boston (2009)
14. Pohl, K., Hoenninger, H., Achatz, R., Broy, M.: Model-Based Engineering of Embedded Systems - The SPES 2020 Methodology. Springer, Heidelberg (2012)
15. Avizienis, A., Laprie, J.C., Randell, B., Landwehr, C.: Basic concepts and taxonomy of dependable and secure computing. IEEE Trans. Dependable Secure Comput. **1**(1), 11–33 (2004)
16. Douglass, B.P.: Real-Time Design Patterns: Robust Scalable Architecture for Real-Time Systems. Addison-Wesley Longman Publishing, Boston (2005)
17. Fenelon, P., McDermid, J.A., Nicolson, M., Pumfrey, D.J.: Towards integrated safety analysis and design. ACM SIGAPP Appl. Comput. Rev. - Special Issue on Safety-Critical Software **2**, 21–32 (1994)
18. Wu, W., Kelly, T.: Deriving safety requirements as part of system architecture definition. In: 24th International System Safety Conference, Albuquerque, USA (2006)
19. International Organization for Standardization: IEC 61508 - Functional safety of electrical/electronic/programmable electronic safety-related systems, Geneva, Switzerland (1998)
20. American Heart Association, ECC Guidelines. http://circ.ahajournals.org/content/102/suppl_1/I-60.full. Accessed March 2015
21. Habli, I., Ibarra, I., Rivett, R., Kelly, T.: Model-based assurance for justifying automotive functional safety. SAE Technical Paper 10AE-0181, Detroit, USA (2010)
22. Katta, V., Stålhane, T.: A conceptual model of traceability for safety systems. In: 2nd Complex Systems Design & Management Conference (CSD&M 2011), Paris, France (2011)
23. Birch, J., Rivett, R., Habli, I., Bradshaw, B., Higham, D., Jesty, P., Monkhouse, H., Palin, R.: Safety cases and their role in ISO 26262 functional safety assessment. In: Bitsch, F., Guiochet, J., Kaâniche, M. (eds.) SAFECOMP 2013. LNCS, vol. 8153, pp. 154–165. Springer, Heidelberg (2013)
24. Beckers, K., Côté, I., Frese, T., Hatebur, D., Heisel, M.: Systematic derivation of functional safety requirements for automotive systems. In: Bondavalli, A., Di Giandomenico, F. (eds.) SAFECOMP 2014. LNCS, vol. 8666, pp. 65–80. Springer, Heidelberg (2014)
25. Antonino, P.O., Trapp, M., Venugopal, A.: Automatic detection of incomplete and inconsistent safety requirements. SAE Technical Paper 2015-01-0268, Detroit, USA (2015)

Automatic Architecture Hardening Using Safety Patterns

Kevin Delmas$^{(\boxtimes)}$, Rémi Delmas, and Claire Pagetti

ONERA/DTIM, 2 Av. E. Belin, 31055 Toulouse, France
{Kevin.Delmas,Remi.Delmas,Claire.Pagetti}@onera.fr

Abstract. Safety critical systems or applications must satisfy safety requirements ensuring that catastrophic consequences of combined component failures are avoided or kept below a satisfying probability threshold. Therefore, designers must define a *hardened architecture* (or implementation) of each application, which fulfills the required level of safety by integrating redundancy and safety mechanisms. We propose a methodology which, given the nominal functional architecture, uses constraint solving to select automatically a subset of system components to update and appropriate safety patterns to apply to meet safety requirements. The proposed ideas are illustrated on an avionics flight controller case study.

1 Introduction

The design and development of safety critical applications must satisfy stringent dependability requirements. Certification authorities even request the correctness of embedded avionic applications to be proved using formal arguments.

Context. To help designers reaching that objective, several avionics standards are available. The aerospace recommended practices (ARP) 4754 [13] is a guideline for development processes under certification, with an emphasis on safety issues. Any avionics function is categorized according to the severity of its loss and subject to qualitative and quantitative safety requirements. For instance, a function categorized as CAT (catastrophic) shall not fail with strictly less than three basic failures and the probability of loss shall not exceed 10^{-9} per flight hour. High-level functions are then refined to a *preliminary functional architecture*, that is, their *implementation* is designed as a combination of sub-functions providing the expected functionality. This preliminary architecture is then analyzed to check whether the high level safety requirements are fulfilled assuming some properties (such as failure independence, failure modes and propagation rules). This design activity is iterative: in case the functional architecture does not satisfy the safety requirements, the designers must propose a new architecture with additional redundancies. We intervene at that level by automating the choice of *safety patterns* to use in order to tolerate hardware failures.

Contribution. Our work consists in helping the designer to define a *hardened architecture* (or implementation) of each application fulfilling the required safety requirements by integrating redundancy and safety mechanisms. The hardening

F. Koornneef and C. van Gulijk (Eds.): SAFECOMP 2015, LNCS 9337, pp. 283–296, 2015.
DOI: 10.1007/978-3-319-24255-2_21

mechanisms to be used are often chosen depending on the designer's expertise and by considering the impact on the design of non-functional criteria (such as CPU consumption, temporal performance, etc.). Usually, the experts rely on well-formed safety design patterns of proven efficiency [7,12]. To determine which design pattern to use, experts usually rely on guidelines or decision trees [2,11]. In this paper we propose a methodology to automate the hardening process with respect to qualitative safety requirements, whereby the minimum number of basic failure events required to trigger a failure condition shall be above a certain threshold. The main steps of the proposed design process are: (1) Safety assessment: the functional application architecture without any safety mechanism (nominal architecture) is first analyzed with regards to qualitative safety requirements. We use the ALTARICA language [3] to model the architecture's dysfunctional behaviour in a modular way. We use the graphical IDE Cecilia OCAS [4] developed by Dassault to generate all the failure sequences that lead to a failure condition. A sequence is a list of events of ALTARICA components leading the system to a given error state. (2) Hardening strategy: once the minimal sequence set is generated, a pseudo-Boolean optimization problem is generated and solved automatically. The solution indicates a subset of system components that invalidate the safety requirements (involved in a minimal event sequence the size of which is too small) and, for each component, indicates the safety pattern to apply in order to increase the size of the invalid event sequence. (3) Component Substitution: Each selected component is then replaced by its hardened version in the system. The new system has a necessarily improved minimal sequence set.

This *Assessment, Hardening, Substitution* process is repeated and the system is modified until an architecture satisfying the safety requirements is obtained. In practice very few iterations are needed, since all non-satisfying minimal event sequences are dealt with and improved in each iteration. In this work, we consider high level fault-tolerance mechanisms based on spatial or temporal redundancy, which can be implemented in several ways on many-core target architecture.

Related Work. Automatic architectural optimization of fault-tolerant systems, under qualitative constraints and with respect to multiple quantitative criteria has been addressed in several previous papers [1,5,10,14]. Most of these earlier approaches use genetic algorithms to explore the search space. Genetic algorithms breed numerous alternative evolutions of an initial architectural design while continuously assessing their fitness according to qualitative fault-tolerance properties and various other non-functional aspects encoded as criteria. They attempt to enumerate the Pareto-front of the solution space to propose all possible design trade-offs to the user.

The work presented in this paper pursues identical goals, however the modelling formalisms and most importantly the design optimization techniques differ. First, we use the ALTARICA language and tools to specify system models and perform the qualitative safety evaluation. HIP-HOPS could have been a viable option, but it is more anchored in the automotive domain, while ALTARICA is well established in the aerospace domain and enjoys very mature qualitative safety evaluation tools. ALTARICA however contains no specific means of specifying the design space to be explored for architecture optimization. As a consequence, the notions of *design pattern*, *pattern instantiation* and *component-pattern substitution* need to be handled externally. Modelling frameworks such as EAST-ADL, designed with product-line specification in mind, offers a built-in *implementation variability* notion, and our method could fairly easily be adapted in such frameworks. The most salient feature of our approach is the way in which the optimization problem is formalized and solved: In a quick preprocessing phase, we generate a local failure model for each possible safety pattern, and from them we derive an ordering of safety patterns representing the fault-tolerance increase they offer, in all cases. This pattern ordering is then embedded in the optimization problem given to the constraint solver. These preprocessing and embedding techniques allow to totally avoid the typical computational bottleneck of most (if not all) genetic approaches to design optimization: the thorough qualitative evaluation (minimal sequence or minimal cut set generation) of the numerous candidate solutions in each generation.

The rest of the paper is organized as follows: Sect. 2 presents the case study. Section 3 explains the general ideas of the proposed hardening approach. Section 4 details how to generate the pseudo-Boolean optimization instance which, when solved, yields a hardening strategy for the system and provides results obtained on the case study. Last, Sect. 5 concludes the paper and outlines perspectives to this work.

2   Case Study

In this section, we present a control-command application that is hosted on a multi/many-core platform and has to be hardened against hardware failures of the execution platform.

The ROSACE Case Study. We consider the open-source avionics control engineering case study ROSACE defined in [9], managing the longitudinal motion of a medium-range civil aircraft in *en-route* phase.

The Fig. 1(a) roughly depicts the functional development cycle for such a controller. The control engineers model the application with MATLAB/SIMULINK, analyze the model behaviour and synthesize controllers satisfying performance

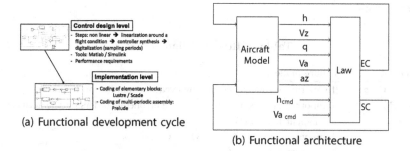

(a) Functional development cycle

(b) Functional architecture

Fig. 1. ROSACE overview

and robustness properties. The Fig. 1(b) details the functional interface between the controller (*Law*) and the *Aircraft model* that represents the system to be controlled (aircraft, engines and elevators). The controller must satisfy several properties, in particular control performance properties (*eg overshoot, settling time, . . .*), which are validated within SIMULINK by intensive simulation.

The MATLAB/SIMULINK specification is then translated (manually or automatically) to (1) a set of SCADE/LUSTRE programs and (2) a multi-periodic assembly expressed in a home made language or in PRELUDE, as proposed in the original ROSACE paper. The functional correctness of the implementation is validated via intensive simulation, compliant with the activities at the MATLAB/SIMULINK level, to verify the performance properties. The controller can then be ported on a real target.

Fault Model. The original implementation of ROSACE is nominal in the sense that no special fault-tolerance mechanisms is included to tolerate failures of the execution hardware. A first usual hardening is made at the functional level, *ie* in the MATLAB/SIMULINK specification. The purpose is to support external failures, of the sensors for instance. The specification is modified using standard methods such as analytic redundancy (exploiting mathematical invariants of the controller) or Kalman filters. We have modified the MATLAB/SIMULINK specification in that way with the help of David Saussié. In the sequel, we will use a version of the *Law* function that can tolerate the failure of either sensor V_z, h, a_z or q, in erroneous or loss mode, without being degraded. Indeed, thanks to analytic redundancy techniques, any missing or erroneous value of V_z, h, a_z or q can be reconstructed from the others. The details of these modifications are out of the scope of this paper.

We then want to generate a *hardened* version of the controller to support SEU-induced failures of the execution platform. We first detail our fault model, *ie* the possible effects of SEUs on the application. We applied a FMECA (Failure mode, effects and criticality analysis) to determine them (Table 1).

Both the erroneous behavior and total loss of the controller are classified as CAT (catastrophic), therefore the safety requirements on the execution on the multi/many-core platform are:

P1 No single or double error shall lead to the loss of the control function.
P2 No single, double or triple error shall lead to the erroneous control of the actuators.

Table 1. ROSACE failure modes

Element	Failure modes	Explanation
h, V_a, V_z, q, a_z	Temporary erroneous (*err*)	Involved in computation in law
EC, SC	Temporary erroneous (*err*)	Provide erroneous orders on the actuators
Law	Permanent loss (*lost*)	Run-time error
	Temporary loss (*lost*)	OP-CODE error
	Temporary erroneous (*err*)	False result
	Permanent erroneous (*err*)	Faults in integrator (*eg* when h.*err*)

Table 2. Minimal cut sets in the initial specification

Failure condition	Event sequence	
	1	2
Loss of the control	$\{V_a.err\}$; $\{Law.lost\}$; $\{Law.lost\}$	$\{S_1.err, S_2.err\}$ where $S_1, S_2 \in \{V_z, h, a_z, q\}$ and $S_1 \neq S_2$
Erroneous control	$\{Law.err\}$; $\{Law.err\}$; $\{V_a.err\}$; $\{EC.err\}$; $\{SC.err\}$	$\{S_1.err, S_2.err\}$ where $S_1, S_2 \in \{V_z, h, a_z, q\}$ and $S_1 \neq S_2$

The minimal event sequences leading to the failure conditions for the nominal design are given below (Table 2).

3   Overview of the Proposed Hardening Approach

Given an initial system architecture, we address the problem of automatically increasing its fault-tolerance level, while preserving its functionality. To do so, we propose to use safety design patterns and combinatorial optimization under pseudo-Boolean constraints. This section introduces notations used in the rest of the paper, and a synthetic overview of the proposed method.

3.1   Design Methodology Overview

A safety design pattern is an abstract design with known fault-tolerance properties, expressed in terms of one or more *component parameters* (place-holders). Such parameterized designs are noted $P\langle C\rangle$, where $\langle C\rangle$ denotes the parameter, which must be instantiated with an actual component to yield a concrete design. The main steps of the proposed design process are depicted in Fig. 2.

Safety Evaluation. The initial architecture is first analyzed with regards to qualitative safety requirements. We use the ALTARICA modelling language [3] to represent the architecture's dysfunctional behaviour. ALTARICA is based on extended finite automata which can exchange values of specific variables (named data-flow variables) and which can be synchronized (synchronized product or broadcast). The idea is to describe the failure modes of a component as different states of an automaton. Transitions between states are triggered by the occurrence of failure

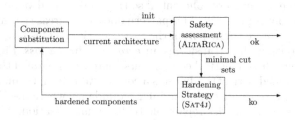

Fig. 2. Hardening process

events, and data-flow equations are used to define the propagation of failure modes through components, from input to output depending on their internal state.

Hardening Strategy. Once the minimal event sequences have been generated, either their cardinalities satisfy the safety requirements and the current architecture is good enough, or else we need to apply more safety patterns on some well chosen components. The hardening decisions are performed automatically in two steps: (1) **Component Selection**: a subset of components of the system is selected for pattern application based on the events present in the sequence needing a size improvement. (2) **Pattern Selection**: for each selected component, a single hardening pattern is selected from a library of applicable patterns. Pattern composition and multi components pattern are not allowed, which makes the analysis bounded yet possibly sub-optimal. However, in practice this restriction is not harmful. As will be seen in Sect. 4, the main novelty and strength of the proposed process with respect to traditional approaches is the simultaneous and automatic resolution of both the *component selection* and *pattern selection* problems using a combinatorial optimization technique: based on the system's minimal sequences set (or minimal cut sets) and on an ordering of safety patterns obtained through a preprocessing step, a pseudo-Boolean optimization problem is generated and solved using a state-of-the-art solver (for instance SAT4J [8], or any similar solver).

Component Substitution. Each selected component is then replaced by its hardened version in the system. This operation increases the size of at least one minimal event sequence in the set of unsatisfactory sequences, while not reducing the size of others. A new iteration is started on the modified system, beginning with a qualitative safety evaluation pass to determine if further improvement is needed.

3.2   Considered Safety Patterns

Many patterns exist in the literature. Figure 3 illustrates three of them. The graphical conventions are as follow: dashed rectangles represent safety mechanisms assumed to be fail-free and dotted rectangles represent safety mechanisms that can fail. Obviously, the pattern parameter C can fail. Figure 3(a) is a COM/MON (command and monitoring) pattern. Two redundant components work in hot redundancy, computing a same value. A comparator (assumed perfect) checks if the outputs are coherent, if so the consolidated value is forwarded, otherwise no output is provided. This pattern does not increase the minimal event sequence size for failure conditions of the *loss* type (if one C is lost the comparator blocks the output) but transforms an *erroneous* into a *loss*. Figure 3(b) is a triplication where three identical components compute in parallel the same value and a voter (assumed perfect) elaborates a correct value from them. Figure 3(c) is more complex: it is based on triple modular redundancy where the C components have permanent failure modes repairable by hot reinitialisation, M are memory components which errors are periodically repaired, and V are memory-less median

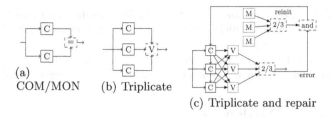

(a) COM/MON   (b) Triplicate

(c) Triplicate and repair

Fig. 3. Patterns

voters with transient failure modes (the whole voter state is refreshed at every execution of the function). Each of the three V receives a numerical value from each C, produces a consolidated output value and diagnoses which of the three C is currently failing (deviation from the median above a set threshold). The function '2/3' is a classic two thirds majority vote, assumed fail-free, which consolidates the V outputs, *ie* the pair *(output_value, failing_C)*. A single permanent C-error will be diagnosed coherently by all three V and pass the 2/3 vote. However, a single transient V-error will be filtered out by the 2/3 vote, so no false positive or negative C-error detection is possible. The state of each C is periodically saved to its corresponding M, as long as no C-error is diagnosed. A C reinitialisation is triggered when all three V identify a same failing C, and is achieved by replacing the failed C's internal state with a safe state elaborated from the M values using the 2/3 voting (so that any single permanent M-error is filtered out), and by resuming the component's operation in the *ok* state. Under the assumption that a C-error is always repaired before the next independent C-error, and that M-errors are periodically fixed by saving a valid C state in each M, this pattern has a better SEU fault-tolerance than a simple triplex.

We will mostly use the patterns based on triplication Fig. 3(b) and (c) since we need to detect and tolerate *erroneous* behaviours.

Let us consider a component C with two failure modes *lost* and *err*. We detail below the minimal event sequences obtained when applying each of the patterns proposed above. We denote by C^i the i-th instance of C in the pattern (Table 3).

The approach proposed in this paper is today restricted to patterns based on component replications and functionally neutral failure detection and recovery mechanisms (voter, comparator, switch), which preserve the component data-flow

Table 3. Patterns event sets

Pattern	Failure mode	Basic event sets (or sequences)
Figure 3(a)	$P\langle C\rangle.lost$	$\{\{C^1.lost\}, \{C^2.lost\}, \{C^1.err\}, \{C^2.err\}\}$
	$P\langle C\rangle.err$	$\{\{C^1.err, C^2.err\}\}$
Figure 3(b)	$P\langle C\rangle.lost$	$\{\{C^i.lost, C^j.lost\}, \{C^i.err, C^j.lost\}\}$ with $i \neq j$
	$P\langle C\rangle.err$	$\{\{C^i.err, C^j.err\}\}$ with $i \neq j$
Figure 3(c)	$P\langle C\rangle.lost$	$\{\{V^1.lost, V^2.lost, V^3.lost\}; \{C^1.lost, C^2.lost, C^3.lost\};$ $\{M^i.err, M^j.err, C^k.err, C^l.lost\}\}$
	$P\langle C\rangle.err$	$\{\{M^i.err, M^j.err, C^k.err, C^l.err\}; \{V^1.err, V^2.err, V^3.err\}\}$

interfaces. We will assume that these are sufficient arguments to allow us to say that pattern application, which consists in replacing a component C by $P\langle C \rangle$, preserves the original functionality.

Other, more complex patterns exist in the literature and are out of scope of the proposed approach for the moment, they will be considered in future work.

4   Automatic Hardening

After defining the notion of pseudo-Boolean constraint system, we detail notations and how to formalize the component and pattern selection problems as pseudo-Boolean constraints and optimization criteria. The ROSACE application used for illustration is a dynamic system so minimal event sequences are used to explain and illustrate the method, however the method works in the very same way for static models for which minimal cut sets are used.

4.1   Pseudo-Boolean Constraint Systems

A pseudo-Boolean constraint system expresses constraints over a set of pseudo-Boolean decision variables $\{x_i\}_i$, ie Boolean variables interpreted as $0/1$ integers. A *literal* l_i is a pseudo-Boolean variable x_i (positive literal) or its logical negation $\neg x_i$ (negative literal). Negative literals can be eliminated in favor of positive literals by rewriting $\neg x$ to the equivalent $(1-x)$. A *linear pseudo-Boolean constraint* has the following form: $[a_1.l_1 + \cdots + a_n.l_n \langle \text{rel} \rangle k$. Where the dot '.' represents scalar multiplication, $a_1, \ldots, a_n \in \mathbb{Z}$ are relative integers (and can be omitted when equal to 1), $l_1, \ldots, l_n$ are decision literals, with underlying variables $x_1, \ldots x_n$ and no repetition, $\langle \text{rel} \rangle \in \{<, \leq, =, \geq, >\}$, $k \in \mathbb{N}$ is a positive integer. An *interpretation* I for a pseudo-Boolean constraint system is a total mapping $I : \{x_i\} \mapsto \{0, 1\}$. An interpretation I is called a *model* of the constraint system if and only if each constraint is satisfied under I. In the remaining we will denote models with the letter M instead of I.

A model is qualitatively assessed by defining one or more numerical criteria over it. An *optimization criterion* is any linear pseudo-Boolean expression over the problem variables, of the form: $K \equiv a_1.l_1 + \cdots + a_n.l_n$, where: $a_i \in \mathbb{Z}$ and l_i are literals. A criterion is evaluated under an interpretation just as left hand sides of constraints are. Given a single criterion and a constraint set we define the notion *min-optimality*: M is *min-optimal* with respect to the criterion if and only if there exists no other model yielding a smaller value for the criterion.

4.2   System and Safety Pattern Characterization

System Model and Notations. A candidate system is characterized by the following sets and functions: (i) Comps: the set of system components; (ii) Events: the set of all basic failure events that can be fired in the system; (iii) Comp2Evt : Comps $\mapsto 2^{\text{Events}}$ returns for each component the subset of events belonging to that component (the set of events admits a partition indexed by the set of components); (iv) Evt2Comp : Events $\mapsto$ Comps returns for each event the component to which this event belongs.

Safety Pattern Model and Notations. Safety design patterns are abstract designs, parameterized by one or more *component parameters* with known fault-tolerance properties. Patterns are noted $P\langle C \rangle$, where $\langle C \rangle$ denotes the parameter. Parameters must be instantiated with actual components to yield a concrete design. The set of all patterns, in their abstract, parameterized form is noted Pat.

The interface of a component C consists of a list of typed input data-flow variables and a list of typed output data-flows: $\text{InFlows}(C) = [o_i : t_i | i \in [1, N_I]]$, $\text{OutFlows}(C) = [o_i : t_i | i \in [1, N_o]]$, where N_i, N_o are the numbers of input and output flows of the component, each t_i is an enumerated type of the form $\texttt{enum}\{\texttt{ok}, \texttt{fault}_1, \ldots, \texttt{fault}_n\}$, in which the value $\texttt{ok}$ is always present and represents the "no fault" state (imposed by design guidelines).

To be usable in our approach, in addition to providing the same functionality as the parameter component, a design pattern needs to preserve at least the output interface of the parameter component:

$$\text{OutFlows}(P\langle C \rangle) = \text{OutFlows}(C) \tag{1}$$

Since design patterns may have some restrictions which make them only applicable to certain components, we assume that for each component C the following function provides us with the subset of safety patterns applicable to C: $\text{CompPat} : \text{Comps} \mapsto 2^{\text{Pat}}$, such that $\text{CompPat}(C) \mapsto \{\text{Id}\} \cup \{P_1, \ldots, P_n\}$, where the distinguished element Id, the *identity pattern*, equal to the component itself without modification, is always available.

An Order Relation Over Safety Patterns. We now need to define a formal characterization of the effect, on the minimum size of minimal event sequences of a system, of applying a design pattern to a component. Intuitively, replacing a component C by $P\langle C \rangle$ should augment the number of failure events needed to reach a same faulty state, or even render that state unreachable, which should entail an improvement of the minimal event sequence set of the system hosting this hardened component, either by increasing the size of some sequences, or by removing sequences.

Due to the modeling guidelines used in the proposed approach, the fact that a component C enters a faulty state after firing an event e necessarily manifests itself at the output interface of the component, in which at least one the output flows takes a value different from the $\texttt{ok}$ value. So, a component is in a faulty state whenever the following logical formula evaluates to $\top$:

$$\text{Faulty}(C) \equiv \bigvee_{o \in \text{OutFlows}(C)} o \neq ok \tag{2}$$

In order to determine the general increase of fault tolerance level we can obtain from using a pattern $P \in \text{CompPat}(C)$ instead of C in the system, we will compute all combinations of events allowing to reach, in $P\langle C \rangle$, any fault state observationally equivalent[1] to some fault state of C with respect to the formula defined in (2).

---

[1] two components with matching output interfaces are in observationally equivalent states with respect to some formula expressed over their outputs flows if the formula evaluates to true for both components.

It is always possible to compare C and $P\langle C\rangle$ through the formula defined in (2) thanks to the output interface preservation property of patterns (cf. Eq. (1)). Reformulating a little bit, we can generate the minimal event sequences for the failure condition Faulty($P\langle C\rangle$) on the component $P\langle C\rangle$, in isolation, outside of the context of the system[2]. Such sets of minimal sequences are noted as follows: MSS($\underbrace{P\langle C\rangle}_{\text{component}}$, $\underbrace{\text{Faulty}(P\langle C\rangle)}_{\text{failure condition}}$) Once we have the minimal sequences for both C and $P\langle C\rangle$, we need to define some criterion that will allow us to soundly measure the increase of fault tolerance provided by the pattern. To do so we propose to compare the minimum cardinality of sequences present in each set. We first define the function which returns the size of the smallest sequence found in a set of minimal sequences: MinCard(MSS) $= min\{\text{card}(ms)|ms \in \text{MSS}\}$ Last, if the pattern $P\langle C\rangle$ satisfies the following relation:

$$\text{MinCard}(P\langle C\rangle, \text{Faulty}(P\langle C\rangle)) > \text{MinCard}(C, \text{Faulty}(C)) \tag{3}$$

it indeed provides an increase of fault tolerance level over C *in any situation*, since it takes strictly more events to reach a fault state in $P\langle C\rangle$ than it takes to reach any observationally equivalent fault state in C. We can generalize this idea and compare not only a pattern against a base component but also a pattern against a pattern, by defining an order relation $>_{\text{CompPat}(C)}$ over the set of patterns CompPat(C):

$$
\begin{aligned}
P >_{\text{CompPat}(C)} P' \equiv \ &\text{MinCard}(P\langle C\rangle, \text{Faulty}(P\langle C\rangle)) \\
&> \text{MinCard}(P'\langle C\rangle, \text{Faulty}(P'\langle C\rangle))
\end{aligned}
\tag{4}
$$

In our approach, this order relation must be computed *a priori* for each component, by instantiating each pattern available for this component and generating minimal sequences for the Faulty failure condition (cf. Eq. (2)).

Example 1. Let us consider a component Sensor with two failure events Sensor.*lost* and Sensor.*err* and the *Triplicate* pattern introduced earlier. Assuming that the Vote component itself has no failure mode, we get the following results, compliant with previous results given in Sect. 3.2.

So in conclusion *Triplicate*$\langle Sensor\rangle$ $>_{\text{CompPat}(Sensor)}$ *Sensor* (Table 4).

Table 4. Patterns characterisation

	Sensor	Triplicate$\langle$Sensor$\rangle \equiv$ Vote(Sensor^1, Sensor^2, Sensor^3)
MSS	{Sensor.*err*}	Triplicate$\langle$Sensor$\rangle$.*err* = {Sensor^i.*err*, Sensor^j.*err*} *with* $i \neq j$
	{Sensor.*lost*}	Triplicate$\langle$Sensor$\rangle$.*lost* = $\begin{cases} \{\text{Sensor}^i.err, \text{Sensor}^j.lost\} \\ \{\text{Sensor}^i.lost, \text{Sensor}^j.lost\} \end{cases}$ *with* $i \neq j$
MinCard(MSS)	1	2

---

[2] The minimal sequence set generation tool of the ALTARICA tool suite easily allows us to obtain the desired result.

Component Substitution Model. Last, we need to trace the system's evolution from one hardening iteration to the next. For that we define the function: PrevPattern : $C \in \text{Comps} \mapsto P \in \text{CompPat}(C)$ which returns for each component the pattern previously applied to that component, or the identity pattern if none was applied.

4.3   Component and Pattern Selection Constraints Generation

To model the component selection problem, we begin by introducing new a set of pseudo-Boolean variables.

Definition 1 (Component Selection Variables). *The set of* component selection variables *is defined as:* $\{\text{SelectComp}(C) | C \in \text{Comps}\}$, *where* $\text{SelectComp}(C) = \top$ *if and only if component C is selected for pattern application.*

We then consider a set MSS of minimal sequences, such that each element has a cardinality below the threshold required by the classification of some failure condition. We must make sure that at least one component involved in each minimal sequence will be selected for pattern application. We do so by generating a component selection constraint for each element of the set MSS using the following definition.

Definition 2 (Component Selection Constraint). *The component selection constraint for a minimal sequence* $ms = \{e_1, \ldots, e_n\}$ *is defined as:* $\text{SelectCompCtr}(ms) \equiv \sum_{e \in ms}(\text{SelectComp}(\text{Evt2Comp}(e))) \geq 1.$

The problem of selecting a minimal set of components allowing to cover a given set of minimal sequences (more exactly, cut sets) was previously addressed in [6], using a prime implicant calculus for formulas in disjunctive normal form. In the approach proposed here however, we use pseudo-Boolean constraints to achieve the same goal, because it allows us to integrate and solve the pattern selection constraints in a unified framework. Consequently, to model the pattern selection problem, we begin by introducing new a set of pseudo-Boolean variables.

Definition 3 (Pattern Selection Variables). *The set of* pattern selection variables *for a component* $C \in \text{Comps}$ *is defined as:* $\{\text{SelectPat}(C, P) | C \in \text{Comps}, P \in \text{CompPat}(C)\}$, *where* $\text{SelectPat}(C, P) = \top$ *if and only if pattern P must be applied to component C.*

For each component C, the following constraint is instantiated, to make that at most one applicable pattern is selected: $\text{AtMostOnePatternCtr}(C) \equiv \sum_{P \in \text{CompPat}(C)} \text{SelectPat}(C, P) \leq 1.$

Next, in order to ensure that a pattern gets selected for a component *if and only if the component itself is selected*, the following constraint is instantiated for each component $C \in \text{Comps}$ and each pattern $P \in \text{CompPat}(C)$: $\text{SelectCoherenceCtr}(C, P) \equiv \neg\text{SelectComp}(C) + \text{SelectPat}(C, P) \leq 1$

Furthermore, the pattern selected for a component must be better, according to the order relation $>_{\text{CompPat}(C)}$ defined in Eq. (4), than the previously selected pattern for that component, which is given through the function PrevPattern defined in page 11. The relevance of a pattern for a certain failure mode is guaranteed by the way we expressed and precomputed the pattern ordering relation: a pattern is ranked higher than a bare component or another pattern if all of its minimal cut sets are of greater cardinality for any failure mode. We assume that the pattern ordering relation is defined for each component C and each pair of applicable patterns $(P, P') \in componentPatternSet(C)^2$ through the following set of variables: $\{GT_C(P, P') | C \in \text{Comps}, (P, P') \in \text{CompPat}(C)^2\}$ such that $GT_C(P, P') = \top$ if and only if $P\langle C \rangle >_{\text{CompPat}(C)} P'\langle C \rangle$. The relation itself, ie the truth-values for these variables, can be encoded using a set of constraints of the form $\text{OrderRelationCtr}(C, P, P')$, where $GT_C(P, P') > 0$ if $P\langle C \rangle >_{\text{CompPat}(C)} P'\langle C \rangle$ and $\neg GT_C(P, P') > 0$ if $P\langle C \rangle \leq_{\text{CompPat}(C)} P'\langle C \rangle$. Last, we instantiate the following constraint for each $C \in$ Comps and each pattern $P \in \text{CompPat}(C)$: $\text{BetterThanPrevious}(C, P) \equiv \neg \text{SelectPat}(C, P) + GT_{\text{CompPat}(C)}(P, \text{PrevPattern}(C)) \leq 1$ in order to make sure that the selected pattern for C, if any, is better than the previous one according to the pattern ordering relation (the previous pattern chosen for C is available through the PrevPattern function).

Optimization Criterion. As explained in Sect. 4.1, when solving a constraint system it is possible to define one or more optimization criteria to guide the search towards solutions minimizing or maximizing some numerical quantitative ranking function(s). We chose to minimize the number of components selected for pattern instantiation: $\text{NofComponents} \equiv \sum_{C \in componentSet} \text{SelectComp}(C)$

4.4   Results

The hardened architecture for the case study is given in Fig. 4.

In order to validate our initial intuition that pattern-ordering and SAT-based constraint solving would sidestep the computational bottleneck of assessing the safety attributes of a system, its minimal cut sets in particular, we modelled the same case study inside the HIP-HOPS SIMULINK plugin, by annotating the functional architecture with fault behaviour information required by HIP-HOPS. This experiment is not strictly an apples-to-apples comparison, since HIP-HOPS was run in this case study in reliability optimization mode, while our optimization algorithm focuses on the cut set size. Nevertheless, we can perform some high level comparison of the computations performed by both tools: In the genetic approach, for each candidate, in order to evaluate the metric under optimization (reliability for instance) a fault-tree must be built from the modular system

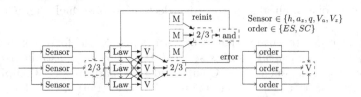

Fig. 4. Hardened Architecture for ROSACE

description, then minimal cut sets must be extracted and only then can the reliability be evaluated to see it if is better or worse than the previous best candidate design.

If we were trying to use genetic algorithms to optimize the size of the cut sets, in theory we also would need to generate the actual set of minimal cut sets of each candidate system, possibly from a fault-tree assembled from a modular description, before being able to asses if the cut sets are better or worse than the previous best we had with another candidate design. However the key of our optimization approach is to avoid building the sets of minimal cut sets explicitly for each candidate thanks to some preprocessing which yields an ordering relation of patterns that captures their effect on the size of cut sets, and is used by the SAT-solver to select appropriate patterns. So this comparison with HIP-HOPS can in a way indicate if we succeeded in reducing the computational cost of determining where the minimal cut sets of a candidate design stand with respect to the optimization goal.

After one hour of computation, the reliability optimization function of HIP-HOPS had not yet completed the first iteration of the genetic routine, which consists in producing, by component-to-pattern substitution, an initial candidate population, and in evaluating these candidates by generating their fault trees and extracting minimal cut sets from them. Other numerical metrics are evaluated by HIP-HOPS in this phase, such as reliability, whereas they are not in our method. However, once minimal cut sets are known, evaluating these metrics has a cost proportional to the size of the cut sets, which suggests that fault tree and minimal cut set generation probably constitutes most of the observed runtime of HIP-HOPS. Our experiments are still in an early and very incomplete state. Nevertheless, we believe that these results validate our initial intuition and motivate studying the SAT-based approach further.

5   Conclusion and Future Work

In this paper we presented an approach to automate the task of hardening a given candidate system which does not meet qualitative requirements. Starting from the minimal sequence set (or minimal cut sets) of the system for some failure condition and from a collection of safety design patterns applicable to system components, we proposed a detailed method to generate a pseudo-Boolean constraint system which, when solved, proposes a detailed strategy for hardening the system, consisting of a selection of components and of associated safety patterns. We performed a preliminary comparison of the proposed approach with another well-known design optimization tool based on genetic algorithm. The outcome of this experiment validated our initial intuition about the potential performance benefits of SAT-based optimization, and encouraged us to develop the approach further.

As of today, the proposed approach only handles qualitative safety requirements and can only deal with safety patterns based on redundancy and voting. Other, more complex patterns exist which, for instance, do not satisfy the interface preservation property we use in this paper. So, future work will consist in refining the logical safety patterns characterization to be able to deal with a greater variety of design patterns. We also would like to be able to handle the difference between design patterns appropriate for *erroneous* failure conditions and those appropriate for *lost* failure conditions. Our current patterns ranking criterion simply does not distinguish between these two cases. A possible solution could be to generate distinct minimal sequence sets (or minimal cut sets) for each possible failure mode of a component and corresponding pattern, not just for some failure mode, to be able to precisely characterize the effect of each pattern on each possible mode, and base pattern selection on these metrics. We also recently started working on extending the approach with quantitative safety indicators such as reliability or failure rate, our goal is to be able to optimize automatically a design with respect to both qualitative and quantitative safety indicators. Last, we will also evaluate the scalability of the approach on several larger systems.

References

1. Adachi, M., Papadopoulos, Y., Sharvia, S., Parker, D., Tohdo, T.: An approach to optimization of fault tolerant architectures using hip-hops. Softw. Pract. Exper. **41**(11), 1303–1327 (2011)
2. Armoush, A.:. Design patterns for safety-critical embedded systems. Ph.D. thesis (2010)
3. Arnold, A., Point, G., Griffault, A., Rauzy, A.: The altarica formalism for describing concurrent systems. Fundam. Inform. **40**(2–3), 109–124 (1999)
4. Dassault. Cecilia OCAS framework (2014)
5. Güdemann, M., Ortmeier, F.: Model-based multi-objective safety optimization. In: Flammini, F., Bologna, S., Vittorini, V. (eds.) SAFECOMP 2011. LNCS, vol. 6894, pp. 423–436. Springer, Heidelberg (2011)
6. Humbert, S., Seguin, C., Castel, C., Bosc, J.-M.: Deriving safety software requirements from an AltaRica system model. In: Harrison, M.D., Sujan, M.-A. (eds.) SAFECOMP 2008. LNCS, vol. 5219, pp. 320–331. Springer, Heidelberg (2008)
7. Kehren, C., Seguin, C., Bieber, P., Castel, C., Bougnol, C., Heckmann, J.P., Metge, S.: Architecture patterns for safe design. In: AAAF 1st Complex and Safe Systems Engineering Conference (2004)
8. Le Berre, D., Parrain, A.: The Sat4j library, release 2.2 system description. J. Satisf. Boolean Model. Comput. **7**, 59–64 (2010)
9. Pagetti, C., Saussié, D., Gratia, R., Noulard, E., Siron, P.: The ROSACE case study: from Simulink specification to multi/many-core execution. In: 20th IEEE Real-Time and Embedded Technology and Applications Symposium (RTAS 2014), April 2014
10. Papadopoulos, Y., Grante, C.: Evolving car designs using model-based automated safety analysis and optimisation techniques. J. Syst. Softw. **76**(1), 77–89 (2005)
11. Preschern, C., Kajtazovic, N., Kreiner, C., et al.: Catalog of safety tactics in the light of the IEC 61508 safety lifecycle. In: Proceedings of VikingPLoP 2013 Conference, p. 79 (2013)
12. Rugina, A.-E., Feiler, P.H., Kanoun, K., Kaâniche, M.: Software dependability modeling using an industry-standard architecture description language. In: Embedded Systems and Real-Time Systems (ERTS 2008) (2008)
13. SAE. Aerospace Recommended Practices 4754a - Development of Civil Aircraft and Systems (2010)
14. Walker, M., Reiser, M.-O., Piergiovanni, S.T., Papadopoulos, Y., Lönn, H., Mraidha, C., Parker, D., Chen, D.-J., Servat, D.: Automatic optimisation of system architectures using east-adl. J. Syst. Softw. **86**(10), 2467–2487 (2013)

Modeling the Impact of Testing on Diverse Programs

Peter Bishop$^{(\boxtimes)}$

City University and Adelard LLP, London, UK
pgb@csr.city.ac.uk, pgb@adelard.com

Abstract. This paper presents a model of diverse programs that assumes there are a common set of potential software faults that are more or less likely to exist in a specific program version. Testing is modeled as a specific ordering of the removal of faults from each program version. Different models of testing are examined where common and diverse test strategies are used for the diverse program versions. Under certain assumptions, theory suggests that a common test strategy could leave the proportion of common faults unchanged, while diverse test strategies are likely to reduce the proportion of common faults. A review of the available empirical evidence gives some support to the assumptions made in the fault-based model. We also consider how the proportion of common faults can be related to the expected reliability improvement.

Keywords: Software diversity · Multi-version programs · Diverse test strategies

1 Introduction

When diverse programs are developed, different software versions are developed and debugged by independent teams. Diversity seeking decisions (DSDs) can be used both in the development approach (languages, software design, etc.) and in the verification and testing used to debug the software. This paper focuses primarily on the impact of using similar or diverse test strategies.

The impact that testing has on single and diverse programs has been examined before [5, 7] but those models were based on the standard "difficulty function" approach, and evaluated testing strategies in terms of their impact on the probability of failure on demand (*pfd*). This paper takes a related but different approach to assessing the impact of different test strategies where the model is expressed in terms of a set of "characteristic faults" that might be introduced into the software. The diversity of the program versions is modeled by the proportion of faults that are common between the versions. Test strategies are modeled by different orderings of bug removal in the two versions and the impact of different test strategies on program diversity are examined. The effectiveness of alternative test strategies in reducing the common faults proportion is modeled, and we discuss how the common fault proportion can be related to the expected improvement in reliability.

© Springer International Publishing Switzerland 2015
F. Koornneef and C. van Gulijk (Eds.): SAFECOMP 2015, LNCS 9337, pp. 297–309, 2015.
DOI: 10.1007/978-3-319-24255-2_22

2 The Diverse Debug Model

Versions are developed and debugged by independent teams, and different approaches can be taken by both teams (whether by accident or design). So in general we need to consider the:

- Likelihood of inclusion of faults in development;
- Likelihood of removal by testing.

In this model we assume that:

1. There are "characteristic program faults", i.e. different developers can make identical mistakes. There is a finite pool of N possible faults available for selection;
2. Faults from this pool are independently selected by the two development teams, i.e. a given fault, i, is selected with probability $s(i)$ by both development teams;
3. The test strategies examined are equally effective at removing faults, i.e. remove the same proportion f of the faults present in the diverse programs.

2.1 Fault Inclusion Model

The fault selection probability $s(i)$ is assumed to be the same for both teams, so the probability that fault i is common to versions A and B is:

$$P_{AB}(i) = s(i)^2$$

This is similar to the Eckhardt and Lee difficulty function model [3] for modeling common mode failure where there is a probability that a given *input point* is faulty. The fault selection model could perhaps be generalized to have different selection probabilities for A and B (similar to the Littlewood and Miller difficulty model [4]), i.e.:

$$P_{AB}(i) = s_A(i)s_B(i)$$

However an assumption of common $s(i)$ values for both versions is the worst case, and will be taken to hold in the remainder of this paper.

If we now consider the whole set of N characteristic faults where $i = 1...N$, the mean number of single version faults is:

$$N_A = N_B = \sum s(i)$$

The mean number of common faults is:

$$N_{AB} = \sum s(i)^2$$

The mean proportion of common faults is:

$$\beta = \frac{N_{AB}}{N_A}$$

So substituting for N_A and N_{AB}:

$$\beta = \frac{\sum s(i)^2}{\sum s(i)} \tag{1}$$

2.2 Modeling Fault Removal

Testing changes the existence probability of the characteristic faults. We can model the impact of diverse testing by two test reduction probabilities, $t_A(i)$ and $t_B(i)$. The test reduction probability $t_A(i)$ is the probability that fault i will be removed after applying the test strategy used for version A. So the expected number of faults remaining in a program version is:

$$N'_A = \sum s(i)t_A(i), \ N'_B = \sum s(i)t_B(i) \tag{2}$$

The number of faults remaining can differ for versions A and B, as different test strategies may be deployed by the two teams, but we have made an assumption (see assumption 3) that the teams will choose equally effective test strategies, where there is similar reduction f in the proportion of faults in both versions, i.e.:

$$N'_A = N'_B = fN_A = fN_B \tag{3}$$

So after testing, the expected proportion of common faults, β', is:

$$\beta' = \frac{N'_{AB}}{N'_A} = \frac{N'_{AB}}{N'_B} = \frac{\sum s(i)^2 t_A(i) t_B(i)}{\sum s(i) t_A(i)} = \frac{\sum s(i)^2 t_A(i) t_B(i)}{\sum s(i) t_B(i)} \tag{4}$$

We can use this equation to model the impact of different test strategies by assigning different probability distributions to $t_A(i)$, $t_B(i)$.

3 Modeling Different Test Strategies

We can use the model to examine combinations of some extreme test strategies for the two versions, namely:

- Random removal, where faults are randomly removed from each version;
- Strictly ordered removal, with the same removal sequence in both versions;
- Strictly ordered removal with a sequence that depends on selection probability.

These test strategies may not necessarily be realistic, but they can help identify the best and worst cases achievable by different test strategies.

3.1 Random Removal Test Strategy

In the random removal strategy we assume that, for all faults $1\ldots N$:

$$t_A(i) = t_B(i) = f$$

From Eq. (2), it follows that:

$$N'_A = \sum s(i)f, \quad N'_{AB} = \sum (s(i)f)^2$$

So it follows the fault reduction factor is also f. From Eq. (4):

$$\beta' = \frac{\sum s(i)^2 f^2}{\sum s(i)f} = f\frac{\sum s(i)^2}{\sum s(i)} \tag{5}$$

From the original definition of β in Eq. (1):

$$\beta' = f\beta$$

As a result, the proportion of common faults decreases as the number of residual faults decreases, i.e.:

$$\beta' \to 0, \quad f \to 0$$

3.2 Ordered Removal Strategy (with Independence)

In an ordered removal test strategy all faults will be removed in a specific order in both versions. This would, for example, occur if both program versions were tested with a common test set. Without loss of generality we can assume that the removal order runs from N down to 1. With some fraction f of the N potential faults remaining:

$$t_A(j) = t_B(j) = 1, \quad j \le Nf$$
$$t_A(k) = t_B(k) = 0, \quad k > Nf$$

If we consider the case where the test effectiveness probability of defect $t(i)$ is independent of the defect inclusion probability $s(i)$, then:

$$\beta' = \frac{N'_{AB}}{N'_A} = \frac{\sum s(j)^2}{\sum s(j)} \approx \frac{f\sum s(i)^2}{f\sum s(i)} = \beta \tag{6}$$

Hence with exactly the same order of removal of common faults in the diverse programs, we expect the proportion of common defects to remain constant (on average) as testing proceeds, i.e.:

$$\beta' \approx \beta, \quad f \to 0$$

3.3 Ordered Plus Random Removal Strategies (with Independence)

In this scenario, one team follows a random removal strategy and the other team uses an ordered removal strategy and we assume the removal order is independent of the selection probability. Both tests reduce the number of faults by the same fraction f so only faults $j = 1\ldots fN$ remain in one version and all faults in the other version have a survival probability f. It follows that the proportion of common faults after testing is:

$$\beta' = \frac{N'_{AB}}{N'_A} = \frac{N'_{AB}}{N'_B} = \frac{\sum s(j) \cdot s(j)f}{\sum s(j)} \approx \frac{f \sum s(i)^2}{\sum s(i)} \tag{7}$$

For this combination of test strategies, it follows that:

$$\beta' \approx f\beta$$

And in the limit:

$$\beta' \to 0, \quad f \to 0$$

3.4 Ordering Dependent on Inclusion Probability

If the defects are removed in sequence from $j = N$ to $j = 1$ and the removal order is strictly dependent on the inclusion probability then:

$$\max s(i) = s(j = 1) \geq s(j = 2) \geq \ldots \geq s(j = N) = \min s(i)$$

So rare faults will be detected and removed first and faults that occur frequently in software will be removed last. With this ordering:

$$\beta' = \frac{\sum_{j=1}^{\Delta N} s(j)^2}{\sum_{j=1}^{\Delta N} s(j)} \leq \frac{\Delta N \max s(i)^2}{\Delta N \max s(i)} \leq \max s(i), \quad f = \frac{\sum_{j=1}^{\Delta N} s(j)}{\sum_{j=1}^{N} s(j)} \tag{8}$$

Where ΔN is the number of potential faults remaining. In the limit as $\Delta N \to 0$:

$$\beta' \to \max s(i), \quad f \to 0$$

Conversely, the reverse removal order where commonly occurring faults are removed first will leave the rarely occurring faults until last. So in the best case:

$$\beta' \rightarrow \min s(i), \quad f \rightarrow 0$$

3.5 Dependent Order Plus Random Removal Strategies

If one removal strategy is random with detection probability f and the other strategy is ordered with dependency between $s(i)$ and the removal order, it follows that the proportion of common faults is bounded by:

$$f\min s(i) \leq \beta' \leq f\max s(i)$$

Even in the worst case where $\beta' \leq f \max s(i)$, it follows that:

$$\beta' \leq \beta, \quad f < \frac{\text{mean } s(i)}{\text{max } s(i)}$$

So the proportion of common faults will still reduce when $f \rightarrow 0$.

4 Summary of the Model Results

The fault-based model results are summarized in Table 1 below, where:

f is the fraction of faults remaining after testing;
β is the expected proportion of common faults before testing starts;
β' is the expected proportion after testing.

Table 1. Common fault proportion after testing (different test assumptions)

Test strategy A	Test strategy B	Correlation with $s(i)$	Expected β'
Ordered	Same order	None	$\approx \beta$
Random	Random	None	$f\beta$
Ordered	Random	None	$\approx f\beta$
Ordered	Same order	Small s removed first	$\rightarrow \max s(i)$
Ordered	Random	Small s removed first	$\rightarrow f \max s(i)$
Ordered	Same order	Large s removed first	$\rightarrow \min s(i)$
Ordered	Random	Large s removed first	$\rightarrow f \min s(i)$

It can be seen that the overall proportion of common faults depends on the correlation between:

- The two test strategies;
- Each test strategy and the fault selection probability.

In practice, the test strategies are unlikely to correspond exactly with any of the specific cases shown in Table 1, but we can see that, even with the *same* test set, it is possible for β' to remain the same, and with differing test strategies, it is likely that the proportion of common faults will decrease.

This observation is however only valid if the model assumptions are valid. This will be considered in more detail in the next section.

5 Validity of Model Assumptions

5.1 Set of Characteristic Faults

There is some experimental evidence that programmers make similar mistakes that result in a set of characteristic faults. The "programming contest" programs [10] provide a useful research resource as there are many thousands of implementations of particular contest problems. Research studies [1, 11] have shown that many programmers can produce exactly the same characteristic faults.

On a smaller scale, but with more realistic programs, an analysis of faults found in the Knight and Leveson diversity experiment showed that similar faults existed in multiple versions [2] where (possibly) 7 out of 27 versions contained a similar fault.

There is therefore considerable support for the assumption that characteristic faults exist in programs (typically related to specific functions that are implemented by the program).

5.2 Independent Selection of Faults from the Pool

An analysis of the Knight and Leveson diversity experiment [2] found 45 faults in 27 versions. If we take these to be the characteristic set of N faults, we can use the data to test the independent selection assumption. With independent selection, the probability of a perfect version, p_p, is:

$$p_p = \prod_{i=1,N} (1 - s(i))$$

It should be noted that dependence in fault selection would actually *increase* the value of p_p. For example, if $s(1) = s(2) = 0.5$, then $p_p = 0.25$ but if the two faults were always selected together, then $p_p = 0.5$.

In the Knight and Leveson example, the number of faults found was $N = 45$, and the average faults per version is 1.67. With $s(i)$ assumed to be identical for all faults at $s = 1.67/45 = 0.037$. Assuming independent selection, $p_p = (1 - 0.037)^{45} = 0.183$, so $(27 \times 0.183) = 4.95$ versions are expected to be perfect. This is close to the actual figure of 6 perfect versions out of 27. Given the sampling uncertainties involved, the two numbers are in good agreement, which suggests the independent selection assumption is a reasonable approximation in this example.

5.3   Same Fault Selection Probabilities by Diverse Teams

The fault selection probabilities could differ in the diverse teams (e.g. due to different development techniques). It might even be the case that some faults, like array bound violations, are impossible in some technologies, i.e. $s_A(i) = 0$. In the most extreme case, the selection probabilities could be completely disjoint (i.e. complete negative correlation between s_A and s_B). So the assumption of similar detection probabilities (i.e. complete positive correlation between s_A and s_B) is the most pessimistic assumption as it maximizes β.

5.4   Independence of Fault Removal Order and Fault Selection Probability

The credibility of independence between fault selection probability and fault removal is difficult to determine empirically, but we do have some experimental evidence for cases where the removal is ordered by the fault "size" (where fault size is defined as the proportion of input space occupied by the fault). Typically we would expect faults detected by dynamic testing to fail more often if the faults are larger, so the removal order would be related to fault size. With independence, we would expect similar inclusion probabilities regardless of fault size. Unpublished data from research undertaken for [11] is shown in Fig. 1 below. This shows the distribution of failure region sizes as a proportion of the whole input space. It should be noted that an "equivalence class" can be a "basic fault" (where programmers make the same mistakes in different versions) or a combination of two or more "basic faults".

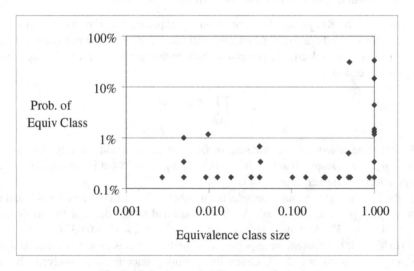

Fig. 1. Selection probability versus fault size

It can be seen that, apart from the very large equivalence class sizes, the inclusion probability varies between 0.1 % and 1 % for most classes. So with ordered removal we would expect β' to be 10^{-2} or less during fault removal.

A preliminary review of the distribution of failure rates in Knight and Leveson data (used as a surrogate for fault size) indicates that there is one case where 4 versions in 27 had faults with identical failure rates that were related to the same basic function. If this is due to the same characteristic fault i being present in 4 versions, then $s(i) \sim 15$ %. There are also 3 cases where faults in 2 versions out of 27 have similar rates (i.e. s $(i) \sim 7.5$ %). The remaining 35 faults only appear in one version ($s(i) \sim 3.7$ %). These fault selection probabilities appeared to have little correlation with their associated failure rates.

These limited results suggest, at least in some cases, a presumption of independence between fault inclusion and removal may be credible. However more empirical studies are needed to determine whether such independence is likely for test strategies in general.

6 Discussion

6.1 Relationship to Prior Research

Littlewood et al. [5] showed that diverse test strategies can be more effective at improving reliability than a single test strategy, but only in the context of a single program version. Popov and Strigini [8] proposed a fault-based model for diverse programs for modeling the improvement achievable by diversity, but did not explicitly consider the impact of testing or diverse test strategies. Popov and Littlewood [7] considered the impact of a range of test strategies on diverse program versions during development, but the model is constructed at the level of specific points in the input space (rather than the failure regions covered by a fault) so it is difficult to represent fault inclusion and fault removal explicitly.

Unlike these earlier models, the model presented in this paper has a more limited scope as there is no attempt to estimate the individual and joint *pfd*s of the diverse versions. The analysis in this paper only sought to estimate the *proportion* of faults that are likely to be common (β) and how this proportion is affected by testing (β'). The relationship of β' to individual and joint *pfd*s is indirect. We would expect that a smaller β' would result in a smaller joint *pfd*, but this might not be true for all usage profiles.

For the model to be applicable, we need to be confident that the underlying assumptions are valid and that the β model is a useful measure of the potential reliability improvement. The evidence presented in Sect. 5 provides some justification that the fault inclusion assumptions are credible and shows how an analysis of the number of common faults observed during the testing of diverse versions could provide an empirical estimate for β.

In the remainder of this discussion we consider the relationship of β to the expected reliability improvement and how this might be justified. We also consider how the reduction in β predicted for diverse strategies could be validated experimentally.

6.2   Relationship of β to *Pfd*

While our model indicates that the choice of testing strategies could either keep the proportion of common faults β constant or even decrease the proportion, it is difficult to relate the results directly to the expected improvement in reliability of a diverse pair of programs under a given choice of test strategies. To make a link with *pfd*, further modeling assumptions need to be made.

If there are n faults in versions A and B, and $n\beta$ are common faults then:

$$pfd_A = \sum_{i=1,n\beta} p_{AB}(i) + \sum_{j=n\beta+1,n} p_A(j), \quad pfd_B = \sum_{i=1,n\beta} p_{AB}(i) + \sum_{k=n\beta+1,n} p_B(k)$$

Where $p_{AB}(1..\beta n)$ are the probabilities of failure of the common faults, $p_A(\beta n + 1..n)$ are the probabilities of failure of the unique faults in version A, and $p_B(\beta n + 1..n)$ are the probabilities of failure of the unique faults in version B.

If we further assume that the failure probabilities are similar for common and unique faults, i.e. $Ep_{AB}(i) \approx Ep_A(j) \approx Ep_B(k)$, then the *pfd*s of A and B are similar, i.e.:

$$pfd_A \approx pfd_B = pfd$$

Where *pfd* is the average probability of failure on demand of a single version. It also follows that the probability of simultaneous failure due to the common faults is:

$$pfd_{common} \approx \beta \cdot pfd$$

If we further assume that the unique faults fail independently between versions, then the probability of coincident failure between versions due to the unique faults is:

$$pfd_{unique} = \sum_{j=n\beta+1,n} p_A(j) \cdot \sum_{k=n\beta+1,n} p_B(k) \approx ((1-\beta) \cdot pfd)^2$$

Combining these two contributions, the overall probability of coincident failure between the versions, pfd_{pair}, is:

$$pfd_{pair} = \beta \cdot pfd + (1-\beta)^2 pfd^2 \tag{9}$$

If we define a reliability improvement ratio R as pfd/pfd_{pair}, then from Eq. (9):

$$R = \frac{1}{\beta + (1-\beta)^2 \cdot pfd} \tag{10}$$

When *pfd* is small:

$$R \to \frac{1}{\beta}, \quad pfd \to 0$$

While for a large *pfd*, the second term in Eq. (10) is dominant, i.e.

$$R \to \frac{1}{(1 - \beta)^2 pfd}, \qquad pfd \to 1$$

So we would expect the improvement ratio R to be close to the independence assumption for large *pfd* values, where $R \approx 1/pfd$, and be asymptotic to a plateau value of $R = 1/\beta$ for small *pfd* values.

There is some empirical support for these predictions from experiments undertaken in [9, 12] using a large number of program versions produced in a programming contest [10]. The experimental analysis progressively removed the versions with the highest *pfd*s and, for the remaining versions, calculated the mean *pfd* of all single programs and program pairs (pfd_{pair}). An example of the resultant reliability improvement R ratio is shown in Fig. 2 below (similar graphs were obtained for the other program examples).

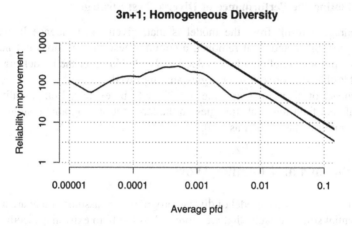

Fig. 2. Reliability improvement ratio vs. mean *pfd* of versions (van der Meulen et al. 2008)

It can be seen that for large mean *pfd* values, R is close to the reliability improvement expected when all failures are independent (the straight line). For small *pfd* values, the improvement reaches a plateau at around 100, which corresponds to a β value of around 0.01. Both these features are predicted by Eq. (9). The plateau at low *pfd* is expected for small *pfd* values where we expect R to remain constant at $1/\beta$. With strict removal ordering which is independent of inclusion probability $s(i)$, we would expect β' to be invariant, and we do see some evidence that a plateau has been reached. This would be consistent with inclusion probabilities $s(i)$ with a mean value of 0.01. The "ideal" behavior predicted by the model is shown in Fig. 3 below (where $\beta = 0.01$ is assumed).

The similarity of theory and experiment lends some support to the model proposed in Eq. (9). Note that this represents the improvement expected *on average*—not the actual improvement achieved for a specific program pair and usage profile.

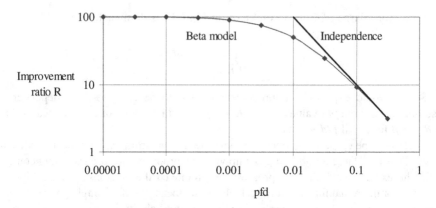

Fig. 3. Reliability improvement ratio (β model)

6.3   Validating the Performance of Diverse Test Strategies

One encouraging result from the model is that, given independence between fault inclusion probability and fault removal, a common test strategy does not necessarily increase the proportion of common faults, i.e. $\beta' = \beta$. However the model suggests that $\beta' < \beta$ is feasible if diverse test strategies are employed.

The impact of alternative strategies on β' could be evaluated empirically by simulating different fault removal strategies on the large set of program versions produced in programming contests such as [10].

7   Conclusions and Further Work

This paper has presented a model of diverse programs that assumes there are a common set of potential software faults that are more or less likely to exist in a specific program version.

Testing is modeled as a specific ordering of the removal of faults from each program version. Different models of testing were examined to derive the proportion of common faults as testing progresses.

Given the assumptions made, the theory suggests that a common test strategy (where common faults are removed in the same order in both program versions) could leave the proportion of common faults unchanged. So a common test strategy need not reduce the efficacy of diverse programs. We also show that diverse test strategies are likely to reduce the proportion of common faults. In the best case, where the test strategies are entirely uncorrelated, the common proportion after testing tends to zero.

We have also discussed how this proportion of common faults could be related to the expected reliability improvement.

Further work should be undertaken to:

- Validate the assumptions used in the model;
- Investigate the link between the proportion of common faults and the expected reliability improvement;
- Validate the testing strategy predictions in experimental research studies;
- Expand the theory to cover diverse development methods.

Acknowledgments. The author wishes to acknowledge the support of the UK Control and Instrumentation Nuclear Industry Forum (CINIF) who funded the research presented in this paper.

References

1. Bentley, J.G., Bishop, P.G., van der Meulen, M.J.: An empirical exploration of the difficulty function. In: Heisel, M., Liggesmeyer, P., Wittmann, S. (eds.) SAFECOMP 2004. LNCS, vol. 3219, pp. 60–71. Springer, Heidelberg (2004)
2. Brilliant, S.S., Knight, J.C., Leveson, N.G.: Analysis of faults in an N-version software experiment. IEEE Trans. Softw. Eng. **16**(2), 238–247 (1990)
3. Eckhardt, D.E., Lee, L.D.: A theoretical basis for the analysis of multiversion software subject to coincident errors. IEEE Trans. Softw. Eng. **12**, 1511–1517 (1985)
4. Littlewood, B., Miller, D.R.: Conceptual modeling of coincident failures in multi-version software. IEEE Trans. Softw. Eng. **15**(12), 1596–1614 (1989)
5. Littlewood, B., Popov, P.T., Strigini, L., Shryane, N.: Modeling the effects of combining diverse software fault detection techniques. IEEE Trans. Softw. Eng. **26**(12), 1157–1167 (2000)
6. Littlewood, B., Rushby, J.: Reasoning about the reliability of diverse two-channel systems in which one channel is "possibly perfect". IEEE Trans. Softw. Eng. **38**(5), 1178–1194 (2012)
7. Popov, P., Littlewood, B.: The effect of testing on reliability of fault-tolerant software. In: International Conference on Dependable Systems and Networks, DSN 2004, pp. 265–274. IEEE (2004)
8. Popov, P., Strigini, L.: The reliability of diverse systems: a contribution using modelling of the fault creation process. In: International Conference on Dependable Systems and Networks, DSN 2001, pp. 5–14). IEEE (2001)
9. Popov, P., Stankovic, V., Strigini, L.: An empirical study of the effectiveness of "forcing" diversity based on a large population of diverse programs. In International Conference on Software Reliability Engineering, ISSRE 2012, pp. 41–50. IEEE (2012)
10. Revilla, M., Skiena, S.: Programming Challenges: The Programming Contest Training Manual. Springer, New York (2003)
11. Van der Meulen, M.J.P., Bishop, P.G., Villa, R.: An exploration of software faults and failure behaviour in a large population of programs. In: International Symposium on Software Reliability Engineering, ISSRE 2004, pp. 101–112. IEEE (2004)
12. Van der Meulen, M.J., Revilla, M.A.: The effectiveness of software diversity in a large population of programs. IEEE Trans. Softw. Eng. **34**(6), 753–764 (2008)

Safety Cases

A Model for Safety Case Confidence Assessment

Jérémie Guiochet[1,2]([✉]), Quynh Anh Do Hoang[1,2], and Mohamed Kaaniche[1,2]

[1] LAAS-CNRS, 7 Avenue du Colonel Roche, 31031 Toulouse, France
[2] Université de Toulouse, Toulouse, France
{guiochet,qdohoang,kaaniche}@laas.fr

Abstract. Building a safety case is a common approach to make expert judgement explicit about safety of a system. The issue of confidence in such argumentation is still an open research field. Providing quantitative estimation of confidence is an interesting approach to manage complexity of arguments. This paper explores the main current approaches, and proposes a new model for quantitative confidence estimation based on Belief Theory for its definition, and on Bayesian Belief Networks for its propagation in safety case networks.

Keywords: Safety case · Confidence · Uncertainty · Quantitative estimation · Bayesian belief network · Belief theory

1 Introduction

Safety cases are used in several critical industrial sectors to justify safety of installations and operations. As defined in the standard [6]: "a Safety Case is a structured argument, supported by a body of evidence, that provides a compelling, comprehensible and valid case that a system is safe for a given application in a given environment". An important research work has also been initiated to deliver guidelines to document safety cases. An initial work developed at York University [19], based on an adaptation of Toulmin argumentation model [25], led to the proposal of the Goal Structuring Notation (GSN). Other proposals such as CAE for Claims-Argument-Evidence [3] and KAOS (Knowledge Acquisition and autOmated Specification) [5], but they did not reach the maturity of GSN [14]. The Object Management Group (OMG) has also delivered a meta-model for the argumentation approach [22]. The goal of these approaches is to make more explicit the supporting arguments for a top-level claim.

Given a claim and a supporting argument, an important and growing issue is to understand how much confidence one could have in the claim and how the different arguments contribute to such confidence. For instance, let us consider the classical example of the claim "{System X} is safe", supported by the evidence that all specific hazards have been eliminated as presented in Fig. 1. Main concepts of GSN are presented here: goals present claims forming part of the argument; Strategies describe the nature of inferences that exist between a goal and its supporting sub-goal(s); Solutions present a reference to an evidence

© Springer International Publishing Switzerland 2015
F. Koornneef and C. van Gulijk (Eds.): SAFECOMP 2015, LNCS 9337, pp. 313–327, 2015.
DOI: 10.1007/978-3-319-24255-2_23

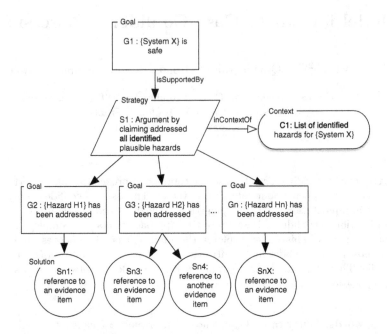

Fig. 1. GSN example adapted from Hazard Avoidance Pattern [20]

item (results of a fault tree analysis for instance); Contexts present contextual artifacts (they could be a reference to contextual information, or statements). Other elements are used in GSN but not presented here as our proposal focuses on these main components of GSN. Each element of such an argument may be subject of uncertainties, such as "do all the hazards have been identified?" or "is the treatment of hazard n effective?". Moreover, considering that argument structures tend to grow excessively, it may become too complex for third parties to analyse the argument. Therefore, appropriate methods to assess confidence in the argument structures and supporting evidence are required. Three main challenges are of particular interest: how confidence could be formally defined, how confidence could be quantitatively estimated, and how confidence in argument leaves could be propagated to assess the impact on the main claim confidence.

In this paper we mainly address the first and third issues by introducing a new method for defining and propagating a quantitative estimation of confidence of a safety case. After presenting related work in Sect. 2, we introduce our definition of confidence based on belief theory in Sect. 4. This definition is used in Sect. 5 where details about confidence propagation are given. Finally, in the conclusion we will discuss about first results and open issues in this area.

2   Related Work

The issue of confidence in argument structures has already been addressed by several works, with slightly different objectives and scopes. Table 1 presents a common framework to analyze some relevant related work considering the following dimensions:

- Argument modelling: construction of the "case" which may be based on GSN or other notations
- Argument uncertainties identification: uncertainties in inferences and arguments elements are identified
- Confidence modelling: construction of a confidence case, with explicit representation of dependencies between the uncertainties
- Confidence estimation: theoretical framework for quantitative estimation of the confidence
- Decision support: provide support based on the quantitative estimation in order to make a decision for the acceptability of the argument, or its improvement.

Qualitative Approaches

In [16], the inventors of GSN address the confidence issue, by proposing to split a traditional safety case in two pieces. The first is the safety argument, showing all evidences, and the second is a confidence argument that addresses confidence in evidences, contexts, and individual inferences. This confidence argument is also represented with GSN. It starts by adding to the safety case some possible

Table 1. Different approaches for managing confidence in safety case

	Argument modelling	Argument uncertainties identification	Confidence modelling	Confidence estimation	Decision support
[21]			Bayesian network	Probability law	
[26]	Argumentation Metamodel (ARM) based case	Based on Toulmin model	Bayesian network (with Hitchcock criteria)	Probability law (with basic logical gates)	
[7]	GSN		Bayesian network	Probability law and tool support with AgenaRisk	
[4]	Trust case based on Toulmin model			Dempster-Shafer Theory	Decision level associated to confidence level
[2]	GSN			Dempster-Shafer Theory	Decision based on the confidence value
[1]	GSN	Common Characteristic Map (CCM)	Confidence case based on GSN		
[13]	GSN	Based on Assurance Claim Points (ACP)	Confidence case in GSN	Baconian probability	
[16]	GSN	Based on Assurance Claim Points (ACP)	Assurance case in GSN		

uncertainty sources, which are called Assurance Claim Points (ACP), that are attached to inferences (the arrows connecting claims), contexts (explanatory information), or solutions. Then, for each ACP, an argumentation mainly focuses on demonstrating that the ACP is trustworthy and appropriate, which is built using GSN. Another proposal [1], is based on the ACP but only focuses on Context and Solution elements. The authors propose to use a map (Common Characteristic Map) as a check list to identify sources of uncertainties, with recursive dependencies. For instance, if a safety case includes a solution which is a "Process result", they propose the generic uncertainties related to "the use of a language", "the use of a tool", "the use of a mechanism", "the involved artifacts", etc. All those characteristics are then refined, with possible recursive dependencies.

The proposed approach in [12] is quite similar, adapting the defeater concept from Defeasible Reasoning theory introduced by [24]. These defeaters that could be compared to previous ACP, or weaknesses in the argumentation, are then analyzed to be reduced one by one.

Both previous proposals focus on the identification of the weaknesses in an argumentation, and present methods for a well structured approach. Nevertheless, such approaches may lead to complex confidence cases. Although controversial, we believe that quantitative estimation approaches may help to analyze the safety case confidence. For instance, it can support sensitivity analyses to identify the weak elements of an argumentation.

Quantitative Approaches

This group of approaches tries to apply mathematical formalism to capture lack of confidence in argument elements. Apart from some proposals based on simple mathematical models as in [13] where the number of uncertainties is estimated, two main ways of approaching the problem can be identified:

- Bayesian Belief Networks (BBNs): in this case the uncertainty is interpreted as a probability. BBNs are then applied to deduce the confidence in a goal from credibility of its backing arguments. Some authors directly use BBNs for modeling arguments and confidence. For instance, in [18], they only use BBNs and commercial tools to calculate "trustworthy", which is actually a conditional probability. With a similar approach, authors of [21] particularly focus on the diversification in argumentation, calculating how a "multilegged" argument (a claim is supported by two evidences) impacts the probability (interpreted as a confidence level) of achieving the main claim. However, they directly use BBNs, without any safety case. On the contrary, [26] propose to apply to each claim of a Toulmin model argument, a Bayesien network pattern showing relationships between uncertainties in the argumentation based on Hitchock criteria [17]. However, confidence propagation is not clearly analyzed and justified. In [7], the authors present an interesting approach to build a BBN from the safety case, and use the work of [11], to define a distribution of confidence for each argument element, but they do not propose transformation rules between safety case in GSN and the confidence BBN. The confidence propagation formulas are also not justified.

– Dempster–Shafer (D-S) theory of evidence. These approaches are based on the belief theory developed by P. Dempster in 1967, and extended by G. Shafer in 1976. A common justification for its use, is that probability theory does not make difference between epistemic and aleatory uncertainties [10]. In the D-S approach, belief, disbelief and epistemic uncertainty are explicitly quantified. An important work by [4] is based on this theory. The authors, propose to build "Trust cases" based on Toulmin concepts, and to directly associate levels for belief and uncertainties, linked with a decision to accept or not an argument element. In this case, they do not build a confidence case, but directly propose a method and a tool for decision support. As presented later, they do not explicitly take into account confidence in the inferences of the argument. Authors of [2], directly reuse the previous work, with a limited version, only considering that for each argument element it exists a level for "sufficiency".

In summary, defining and measuring confidence in assurance claims is an important and open issue. A framework for determining confidence is needed, and this paper presents some initial steps to fulfill this objective.

3 Proposed Approach Overview

Our objective is to propose a method to identify weaknesses in safety case, in order to improve it. Referring to Table 1, our contribution focuses on the following steps presented Fig. 2:

– Argument modelling: the safety case is built using GSN
– Confidence modelling: we propose to annotate the GSN models and transform them into a confidence network
– Confidence estimation: confidence in the network leaves are estimated and propagation formulas are used
– Sensitivity analysis: impact of confidence variations is analyzed to identify weaknesses of the safety case.

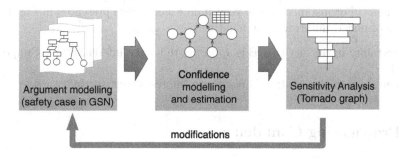

Fig. 2. Overview of the proposed method

4   Measuring Confidence

Confidence may be used as a common concept for different theories, including probability, and D-S. As in [1,4], we define confidence using the D-S approach. In this theory, a belief function is defined from the powerset $\mathcal{P}(\Omega)$ of possible events into $[0; 1]$. For instance, let ω be the state of an indicator light that can have two values on and off, then $\Omega = \{on, off\}$ and $\mathcal{P}(\Omega) = \{\{on\}, \{off\}, \{on, off\}, \varnothing\}$. In this example the belief function Bel, is defined as the mass m of belief such as $Bel(\{on\})$ represents the credibility of the light to be ON. As an example, a possible estimation would be $Bel(\{on\}) = m(\{on\}) = 0.2$, $Bel(\{off\}) = m(\{off\}) = 0.5$ et $m(\{on, off\}) = m(\Omega) = 0.3$. When events are Boolean, like in this example, we can sum-up the D-S concepts with the Fig. 3 (Plausibility is another D-S concept which will not be included in this paper).

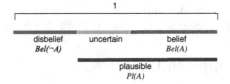

Fig. 3. D-S theory concepts, with a Boolean set

We will consider in a safety case that all elements leaves are observed, and that they cannot be false. Hence, for an element A, $Bel(\overline{A}) = 0$. This led us to define confidence and uncertainty as the belief functions:

$$\begin{cases} m(A) = Bel(A) = g(A) \in [0, 1] & : \quad confidence \\ m(A, \overline{A}) = 1 - g(A) \in [0, 1] & : \quad uncertainty \\ m(\overline{A}) = 0 \end{cases} \quad (1)$$

In the context of safety case, we consider two types of uncertainty sources, which are similar to those presented in [16] named "appropriateness" and "trustworthiness". For instance, in the very simple safety case presented in Fig. 4, two sources of uncertainties may be identified:

- uncertainty in the fact that B is appropriate for the inference "A is Supported by B"
- uncertainty in the solution B itself: are the tests trustworthy?

5   Propagating Confidence

5.1   Argument Types

The very basic inference is the simplest one, "A is Supported by B". Nevertheless, most of arguments are more complex than direct one-to-one inference. For

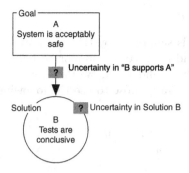

Fig. 4. Uncertainty points in a simple inference

instance, let us consider the example presented with the main claim "A: System is fit for use", supported by both "B: Tests are conclusive" and "C: Formal verification has been performed". In that case, we can expect that both evidences independently increase the level of confidence in A. This concept is presented as "alternative argument" in [4]: even if there is no confidence in B, the fact that C also independently supports A will preserve some level of confidence.

An another form of inference, is presented in the GSN "Hazard Avoidance Pattern" proposed in [20], presented Fig. 1. In that case, the main Goal "System is Safe", depends on all the sub goals together (we do not consider "Strategy" as a node, because it is only a descriptive element). Each of the premises covers a part of the goal. [4] propose to name such an argument a "complementary argument".

Figure 5 present those two types of arguments, with the inference "A supported by B and C". We also illustrate the fact that in both types of argument, the sub nodes may have a different weight in the overall confidence in the claim A. Other types of arguments may be included, as introduced in [2,4], but they are not included in this paper.

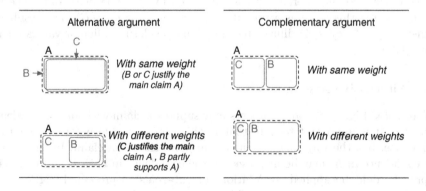

Fig. 5. Alternative and complementary arguments

5.2   Simple Argument

The basic inference, "A is supported by B" can apply to the cases (a) a goal is
refined into a subgoal and (b) a goal is supported by an evidence, as presented
in Fig. 6. In this case, the confidence network is represented like a BBN, using
two nodes and one edge. We propose to use the following table to describe the
confidence propagation:

g(B)	0	1
g(A)	0	p

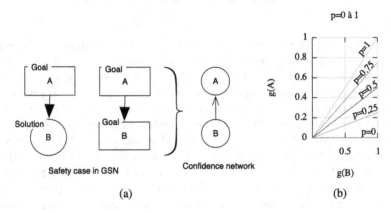

Fig. 6. (a) GSN Simple argument transformation into confidence network and (b) $g(A)$
in function of $g(B)$, for $p \in [0; 1]$

In this table, the confidence in A is estimated when there is no confidence in
B (i.e. when $g(B) = 0$), then $g(A) = 0$, and when there is a maximum confidence
in $g(B)$. In this case, the confidence in A depends on a factor p, which represents
the confidence in the inference "A is supported by B". The final confidence is
obtained using this table as a probability table: $g(A) = p * g(B)$. The result is
a linear dependency $g(A)$, illustrated in Fig. 6 considering different values for p
and g(B).

5.3   Alternative Arguments

As presented Fig. 5, several arguments may support a claim with an independent
influence. It is important to note that in this Figure, we do not represent the
confidence, but the way each argument supports the main claim. In this case,
the confidence in A, may be increased by the confidence in both B and C. Such
approach could be applied to Solutions or sub-goals as presented Fig. 7. The
Strategy node is not part of the confidence network, as it only gives explanations
on the choices made for argumentation.

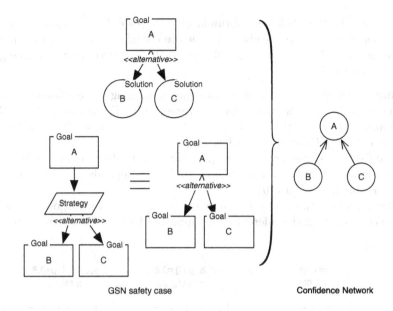

Fig. 7. Alternative argumentation transformation into confidence network

We chose for this argument type to use a *leaky noisy-or* as defined in probability theory [8]. It was originally introduced in [23], and it is based on a logical OR between parent nodes (Y_i) and a child node(X), but it includes the fact that the relationship between parents and the child node are not necessary deterministic. The *leaky* effect corresponds to the fact that even when both parents (B and C) have 0-value probability, there is still a "leaky" probability for the child node. For probabilities, the mathematical function is, with Y_v the set of Y_i in state $\{True\}$:

$$P(X = \{True\}|Y_i) = 1 - (1 - l) * \prod_{Y_i \in Y_v} (1 - p_i) \qquad (2)$$

with $p_i = P(X|Y_i, \{\overline{Y_i}\}_{j \neq i})$. In its application to confidence, we do not consider the leaky effect, it is indeed obvious that if there is no confidence in B and C $(g(B) = g(C) = 0)$, then the confidence in A is zero, i.e. $g(A) = 0$. Consequently, we obtain the following equation:

$$g(X|Y_i) = 1 - \prod_{Y_i \in Y_v} (1 - p_i) \qquad (3)$$

According to 3, the resulting table for two parents is:

g(B)		0		1
g(C)	0	1	0	1
g(A)	0	q	p	1-(1-p)(1-q)

This leads to the confidence formula $g(A) = p * g(B) + q * g(C) - g(B) *$ $g(C) * p * q$. p and q respectively represent the confidence in A in case one only has confidence in B or C. Figure 8 illustrates the evolution of confidence g(A) for different situations:

– Figure (a) where $p = q = 1$ illustrates that increasing the confidence in $g(B)$ alone or $g(C)$ alone, automatically increases $g(A)$. For instance, for $g(C) =$ 0.75 and $g(B) = 0.5$, the resulting confidence is 0.875. Confidence of 1 for A, occurs only if $g(B)$ or $g(C)$ reaches 1.
– Figure (b) shows influence of p on $g(A)$. For a low confidence p in the inference "A is supported by B", the confidence in A only depends on confidence in C ($g(A)$ is constant for $p = 0$).
– Figure (c) shows that for a low value of $g(C)$ (0.1), the variation of q, which is the confidence in the inference "A supported by C", has no effect on $g(A)$.

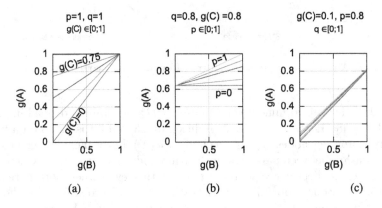

Fig. 8. Alternative argument: g(A), in function of g(B), g(C), p and q

5.4 Complementary Arguments

Complementary arguments are used when a set of solutions or subgoals are required simultaneously for supporting the main goal. However, a weight for each element is assigned to rate its relative importance. For instance, in the "Hazard Avoidance Pattern", some hazards may have a less impact on the overall safety, and the lack of confidence in their treatment, may induce less reduction in the main confidence, than for other more severe hazards. Several models are used in the literature for such arguments, such as simple And-gate [26], weighted mean [7], or Noisy-And [18]. In our case, after several simulations, we decided to define our own Noisy-And, to obtain the trends that are relevant for complementary argumentation. In this case, we based our calculation on the uncertainty as defined in Eq. 1 and using the leaky noisy-or defined in Eq. 2, but taking for the leak $v = 1 - l$. We then obtain the following confidence table:

$m(B,\overline{B})$		0		1	
$m(C,\overline{C})$	0	1	0	1
$m(A,\overline{A})$	$1-v$	$1-v.(1-q)$	$1-v.(1-p)$	$1-v.(1-p).(1-q)$

To calculate the confidence table, we apply the relation $g(X) = 1 - m(X,\overline{X})$, and we also decided to fix $g(A) = 0$ when $g(B) = g(A) = 0$ (which should be obtain for whatever weight of B and C). We thus obtain the following table:

$g(B)$		1		0	
$g(C)$	1	0	1	0
$g(A)$	v	$v.(1-q)$	$v.(1-p)$	0

One main difference with other research works, lies in the interpretation of the parameters. In our case, p and q represent the weight of B and C to decrease confidence (increase uncertainty). In the context of confidence calculation, we also propose to introduce a relation between leak value v, p, and q such as: $v = (p + q)/2$. Indeed, when p and q are lower than 1, it means that the confidence in the inference is less than one. The generalization of this constraint to a complementary argument with n parents is:

$$v = \frac{1}{n} \sum_{i=1}^{n} p_i \tag{4}$$

The values in the confidence table are:

$$g(X|\overline{Y_1}, ..., \overline{Y_k}) = v. \prod_{i=1}^{k}(1 - p_i)$$

where p_i represent the weight of Y_i in the argument. We consider in the following discussion that having a value of 0, for any confidence is not considered, has such an element (no confidence at all), will be removed from a safety argument. Figure 9 presents the result for 2 parents, B, and C, and one child, A. In (a) and (b) we illustrate that when q decreases (q=1, q=0.5) then the influence of $g(C)$ decreases. On the figure, the lines for different values of $g(C)$ are close depending only on $g(B)$ (with a value of 0.5, not presented here due to limitation space). We also illustrate in (b), that when p and q are less than 1, we obtain a residual confidence when $g(B) = 0$ and $g(C) > 0$. This is actually an expected result, because, when the weights are less than one, this means that the argument is not a perfect AND gate. In (c), p is low (0.1), which is interpreted as a low influence of $g(B)$, and characterized by the fact that all lines are nearly horizontals (i.e. with no influence of $g(B)$). A complete analysis of limits, which is not presented here, has demonstrated that the variations of $g(A)$ are compliant with a complementary argument [9].

5.5   Mixed Arguments

The previous arguments could be used also to integrate the confidence in the GSN "Context" element. Indeed, a context is actually a complementary ele-

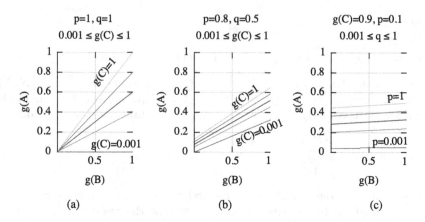

Fig. 9. Complementary argument: g(A) in function of g(B), p and q

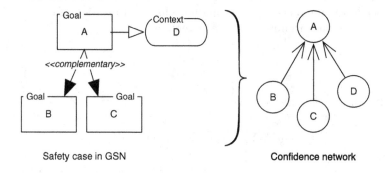

Fig. 10. Mixed argumentation 1

ment for the considered argument. Figure 10 presents a complementary argument, where a context has also been defined. In this case, the resulting network,
is a node A, with three parents (B, C, D), and a noisy-and table for node A.
When an alternative argument is used between B and C, then, an intermediate
node LBC is included, with an alternative table for B and C. The confidence
table in A is a noisy-and between D and LBC.

5.6   Sensitivity Analysis

We propose to perform a sensitivity analysis using a tornado graph. It is
a simple statistical tool, which shows the positive or negative influence of
basic elements on main function. Basically, considering a function $f(x_1, ...x_n)$,
where values $X_1, ..., X_n$ of the variables x_i have been estimated, the tornado
analysis consists in the estimation for each $x_i \in [X_{min}, X_{max}]$, of the values
$f(X_1, ..., X_{i-1}, X_{min}, X_{i+1}, ...X_n)$ and $f(X_1, ..., X_{i-1}, X_{max}, X_{i+1}, ...X_n)$, where
X_{min} and X_{max} the maximum and minimum admissible values of variables x_i.

Hence for each x_i, we get an interval of possible variations of function f. The tornado graph is a visual presentation with ordered intervals. In our case, we estimate the intervals of $g()$ with $X_{min} = 0$ and $X_{max} = 1$.

If we take the example of alternative argument, with arbitrary values $q = 0.7$ and $p = 0.9$, we get the following table:

g(B)	0		1	
g(C)	0	1	0	1
g(A)	0	0.7	0.9	0.97

If we choose the values of $g(B) = 0.8$ and $g(C) = 0.7$, the confidence table leads to the value $g(A) = 0.8572$, also computed with the tool AgenaRisk[1], presented Fig. 11. In this example, to determine the sensitivity to $g(B)$, we keep all the values for p, q, and $g(C)$, and only calculate the values $g(A)$ for $g(B) = 0$ and $g(B) = 1$ (we obtain the values 0.49 and 0.949).

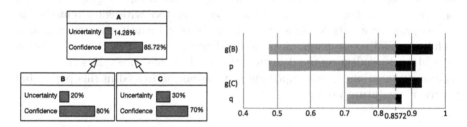

Fig. 11. (a) Example of an alternative argument with the tool Agenarisk and (b) Corresponding Tornado graph

The same approach is used for other variables p, q, and $g(C)$. The result is presented Fig. 11(b). In this tornado graph, g(B) appears to be the most influent parameter to decrease or increase the confidence in A. The left part is between 0.49 and 0.872, which means that if g(B) is equal to its lower limit, then the confidence in A could be reduced to 0.49. On the opposite, with a maximum value of g(B), then confidence in A could reach 0.949.

Such an analysis leads to identify some sensitive points in a confidence network. This could be used to increase the confidence focusing first on the most positive sensitive points, or to focus on the elements where confidence should never be decreased (to consolidate the safety case confidence). Nevertheless, two main limits appear: it is not possible to identify combination of confidence variations, and such a diagram does not identify which variables are the easiest to increase. For instance, even if $g(C)$ appears to be less influent, it may be easier to increase its confidence than the one in $g(B)$. Our approach does not focus on those aspects, but they are important points to study.

---

[1] http://www.agenarisk.com.

6   Conclusion

This paper proposed a new approach for the definition and estimation of confidence in a safety case. We argue that it is important to have a separation between the safety case and the confidence case. Our aim is to analyze uncertainties that may be present in a safety case, using a sensitivity analysis. Our approach is based on the Dempster-Shafer theory for the definitions of confidence and uncertainty. But the constraint $m(X, \overline{X}) = 0$, brings the main benefit of letting use mathematical tools, such as BBN. Hence, we proposed for most common safety case models in GSN, some transformation rules into a confidence network. We particularly introduce the use of noisy-or for alternative arguments, and an adapted version of noisy-and for complementary arguments. An experiment on a real case study of a rehabilitation robot [15] has been carried out [9]. A confidence graph of 65 nodes has been identified with only two alternative arguments (all the others were complementary). The complete analysis is still under development but, we were able to compute the complete graph and get a tornado graph in few minutes with the AgenaRisk tool with consistent results. In this paper, we only focus on the feasibility of a quantitative estimation of confidence, and its propagation in a confidence network. But this is obviously completely dependent on the determination of the confidence values themselves. As already mentioned, this important issue is not addressed in this paper, but is part of our future work.

References

1. Ayoub, A., Kim, B.G., Lee, I., Sokolsky, O.: A systematic approach to justifying sufficient confidence in software safety arguments. In: Ortmeier, F., Lipaczewski, M. (eds.) SAFECOMP 2012. LNCS, vol. 7612, pp. 305–316. Springer, Heidelberg (2012)
2. Anaheed, A., Jian, C., Oleg, S., Insup, L.: Assessing the overall sufficiency of safety arguments. In: 21st Safety-critical Systems Symposium (SSS'13), Bristol, United Kingdom (2013)
3. Bishop, P., Bloomfield, R., Guerra, S.: The future of goal-based assurance cases. In: DSN Workshop on Assurance Cases: Best Practices, Possibles Obstacles, and Future Opportunities. Florence, Italy, July 2004
4. Cyra, L., Górski, J.: Support for argument structures review and assessment. Reliab. Eng. Syst. Saf. **96**(1), 26–37 (2011)
5. Dardenne, A., Fickas, S., van Lamsweerde, A.: Goal-directed requirements acquisition. Sci. Comput. Program. **20**, 3–50 (1993)
6. DefStan 00–56: Defence standard 00–56 issue 3: Safety management requirements for defence systems. UK Ministry of Defence (2004)
7. Denney, E., Habli, I., Pai, G.: Towards measurements of confidence in safety cases. In: Proceedings of the 5th International Symposium on Empirical Software Engineering and Measurement (ESEM 2011). Banff, Canada, September 2011
8. Díez, F.J., Druzdzel, M.J.: Canonical probabilistic models for knowledge engineering. In: UNED Technical reports, Research Center on Intelligent Decision-Support Systems. Madrid, Spain (2007)

9. Do Hoang, Q.: Analyse et justification de la sécurité de systèmes robotiques en interaction physique avec l'humain (in French). Ph.D. thesis, INP Toulouse, LAAS-CNRS (2015)

10. Felipe, A., Mohamed, S., Walter, S., Siqi, Q.: On the distinction between aleatory and epistemic uncertainty and its implications on reliability and risk analysis. In: European Safety and Reliability Conference, ESREL 2013 (2013)

11. Fenton, N., Neil, M.: Risk Assessment and Decision Analysis with Bayesian Networks. CRC Press, Taylor and francis Group, Boca Raton (2012)

12. Goodenough, J., Weinstock, C., Klein, A.: Eliminative induction: A basis for arguing system confidence. In: 35th International Conference on Software Engineering (ICSE2013), pp. 1161–1164, May 2013

13. Goodenough, J.B., Weinstock, C.B., Klein, A.Z.: Toward a theory of assurance case confidence. In: Software Engineering Institute, Carnagie Mellon University (2012)

14. GSN-Standard: GSN COMMUNITY STANDARD VERSION 1 (2011). http://www.goalstructuringnotation.info. Accessed Decembre 18th 2014

15. Guiochet, J., Do Hoang, Q.A., Kaaniche, M., Powell, D.: Model-based safety analysis of human-robot interactions: The MIRAS walking assistance robot. In: 2013 IEEE International Conference on Rehabilitation Robotics (ICORR), pp. 1–7 (2013)

16. Hawkins, R., Kelly, T., Knight, J., Graydon, P.: A new approach to creating clear safety arguments. In: Proceedings of 19th Safety Critical Systems Symposium. Southampton, UK, February 2011

17. Hitchcock, D.: Good reasoning on the toulmin model. Argumentation 19(3), 373–391 (2005)

18. Hobbs, C., Lloyd, M.: The application of bayesian belief networks to assurance case preparation. In: Proceedings of the 20th Safety-Critical Systems Symposium, Bristol, UK. pp. 159–176. Springer London (2012)

19. Kelly, T.P.: Arguing safety - a systematic approach to managing safety cases. Ph.D. thesis, University of York (1998)

20. Kelly, T., McDermid, J.: Safety case construction and reuse using patterns. In: 16th International Conference on Computer Safety and Reliability (SAFECOMP97) (1997)

21. Littlewood, B., Wright, D.: The use of multilegged arguments to increase confidence in safety claims for software-based systems: A study based on a BBN analysis of an idealized example. IEEE Trans. Softw. Eng. 33(5), 347–365 (2007)

22. OMG-ARM: Structured assurance case metamodel (SACM), version 1. Object Management Group (2013)

23. Pearl, J.: Probabilistic reasoning in intelligent systems: networks of plausible inference. Morgan Kaufmann Publishers Inc., San Francisco (1988)

24. Pollock, J.: Defeasible reasoning. In: Reasoning: Studies of Human Inference and Its Foundations, pp. 451–469 (2008)

25. Toulmin, S.: The uses of argument. Cambridge University Press, Cambridge (1958)

26. Zhao, X., Zhang, D., Lu, M., Zeng, F.: A new approach to assessment of confidence in assurance cases. In: Ortmeier, F., Daniel, P. (eds.) SAFECOMP Workshops 2012. LNCS, vol. 7613, pp. 79–91. Springer, Heidelberg (2012)

Towards a Formal Basis for Modular Safety Cases

Ewen Denney and Ganesh Pai[✉]

SGT / NASA Ames Research Center, Moffett Field, CA, USA
{ewen.denney,ganesh.pai}@nasa.gov

Abstract. Safety assurance using argument-based safety cases is an accepted best-practice in many safety-critical sectors. Goal Structuring Notation (GSN), which is widely used for presenting safety arguments graphically, provides a notion of modular arguments to support the goal of incremental certification. Despite the efforts at standardization, GSN remains an informal notation whereas the GSN standard contains appreciable ambiguity especially concerning modular extensions. This, in turn, presents challenges when developing tools and methods to intelligently manipulate modular GSN arguments. This paper develops the elements of a theory of modular safety cases, leveraging our previous work on formalizing GSN arguments. Using example argument structures we highlight some ambiguities arising through the existing guidance, present the intuition underlying the theory, clarify syntax, and address *modular arguments*, *contracts*, *well-formedness* and *well-scopedness* of modules. Based on this theory, we have a preliminary implementation of modular arguments in our toolset, AdvoCATE.

Keywords: Safety cases · Argument structures · Modularity

1 Introduction

Modular safety arguments are desirable for a number of reasons: first, they can be useful to *manage safety case size*, and also to *improve comprehensibility*, by providing an abstract, architectural view of the argument that clarifies the relevant relationships between various argument components. Second, modularity is useful to *minimize and contain the impact of required changes* to a safety case, and, consequently, maintain the assurance provided [1]. Thirdly, they can support *distributed and concurrent development* of the different argument modules [2]. The vision is that a modular organization will facilitate module replacement during an *incremental certification* process [3], so that an argument module can be exchanged for another that meets the same safety properties whilst also protecting intellectual property, e.g., by exposing only the *public details* of arguments as appropriate. To support this vision, the Goal Structuring Notation (GSN) [4], a widely-used graphical notation for presenting safety arguments, provides a notion of modular arguments. Still, there has been limited experience with using

© Springer International Publishing Switzerland 2015
F. Koornneef and C. van Gulijk (Eds.): SAFECOMP 2015, LNCS 9337, pp. 328–343, 2015.
DOI: 10.1007/978-3-319-24255-2_24

modular safety cases (to our knowledge). We believe that this is due to, in part, insufficient tools and techniques supporting both a practical and correct use of the modular safety case concept.

Indeed, in a cost-benefit study of modular safety case development [5], the lack of adequate tool support was one of the concerns identified amongst the risks of using modular arguments. Additionally, although there have been various efforts at both formalizing the GSN, e.g., [6,7], and standardization [4,8], the GSN Standard [4] leaves many questions open (see Sect. 3 for details). This, in turn, presents challenges for tool development (e.g., to build well-formed modular arguments), with existing tools that implement modular GSN varying in how they handle modules. This paper is a first attempt at closing that gap. Our goal is to provide a formal basis for an implementation that will provide, to the extent possible, automation in creating and manipulating modular arguments. Another aim of this paper is to clarify the GSN Standard, i.e., to make explicit numerous constraints that were hitherto implicit rather than a critique, or radical replacement, of the existing notation. Specifically, our paper makes the following contributions: (*i*) a formal definition of *modular arguments* and *contracts*, clarifying their permissible interconnections; (*ii*) extending modules with a notion of hierarchy, giving a rigorous definition for *containment* and *scope*, and using these to formulate a notion of *well-formedness*; and (*iii*) foundations for implementing modular organization in tools supporting GSN, e.g., our toolset, AdvoCATE [9], or others such as ASCE[1].

2   Modular Extensions to Goal Structuring Notation

We use intra-module GSN (Fig. 1) in an argument (within a specific module) to refer to other modules, and/or invoke specific elements in other modules (using, respectively, so-called *module reference*, and *away* nodes). An away goal (context, or solution) in one module essentially repeats a *public* goal (context, or evidence item) present in another module, indicated by a '⊟' annotation placed at the top right of the node (e.g., Fig. 1, goal node G1). Thus, other modules can access (i.e., reference) a public node of a given type using the corresponding type of away node. Each away node additionally contains a reference to the module containing the public node (e.g., Fig. 1, away goal node AG1). As shown, we can link to away goals using both the *Is Supported By* (→) and *In Context Of* (⇢) relations. The former implies claim refinement (i.e., by a public claim in the referenced module). The latter is a substitution for a justification node, but where *more* justification is required than can be provided by a justification node alone, and where the additional justification is provided in a different module.

GSN also provides a concept of *contract module*, containing a definition and/or justification of the relationship between two or more modules, in particular how a claim in one (or more) module(s) support(s) the argument in the

---

[1] Assurance and Safety Case Environment, available at: http://www.adelard.com/asce/.

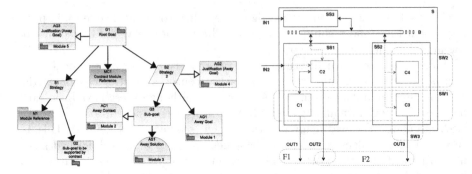

Fig. 1. Intra-module GSN   **Fig. 2.** Motivating example system.

other(s) [4]. As originally conceived, (argument) contracts were meant to represent relations between goals, context and evidence of modules participating in a composition, and were documented using *contract tables*. Currently, the GSN standard provides little guidance to specify the contents of a contract. However, to integrate and view a contract within a common framework, the use of GSN itself has been proposed to specify contracts within contract modules [10,11], which is the convention we will follow here. Thus, we use intra-module GSN to specify a contract, although away goals have a slightly different interpretation: as the link to the modules accessing the contract (see Fig. 3 for an example), in addition to a contextual use, i.e., to provide justification in the contract as appropriate.

When an argument is supported in an, as yet, unspecified module but the contract of support is available in a contract module, we show the reference to that contract using a *contract module reference* node (e.g., Fig. 1, node MC1). When the contract itself is unspecified, we use the '*to be supported by contract*' (⊟) annotation (e.g., Fig. 1, goal node G2). This annotation is analogous to, and mutually exclusive with, the '*to be developed*' (*tbd*) annotation (◇) in non-modular GSN.

Effectively, we use inter-module GSN to specify a *module view* that shows modules and their relationships. We can link modules to (*a*) other modules, using the → and/or ⇢ links, and (*b*) contract modules, using the → link. The contract module explicates the support relationship between the modules to which it is linked. In this paper, we primarily focus on intra-module GSN, deferring inter-module GSN to future work.

3   Motivating Example

We present an example to illustrate some of the ambiguities that arise when using the currently available guidance on modular structuring of GSN arguments [4]. Consider a system S comprising subsystems SS1, SS2, and SS3 communicating over a bus B, and providing the functions F1 and F2 by processing inputs IN1 and IN2 (Fig. 2). Subsystems SS1 and SS2 contain the components (C1, C2),

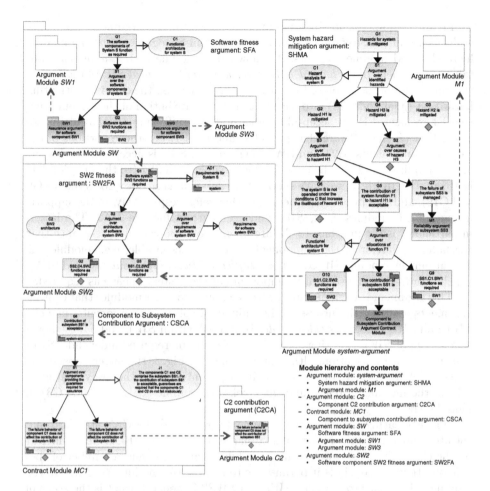

Fig. 3. Possible modularization of (fragments of) argument structures addressing different assurance concerns for the system S of Fig. 2. Note that module boundaries, cross-module linking, and containment, are only illustrative and not part of GSN.

and (C3, C4) respectively. The software operating on system S uses software components SW1, SW2, and SW3, deployed such they require the subsystem components (C1, C3), (C2, C4), and (C3, C4) respectively. The hazard analysis for system S indicates that there are three hazards H1, H2, and H3, to be managed for assuring system safety. In particular, it is determined that the function F1 and subsystem SS3 contribute to hazard H1. The system S can represent, for example, an idealized and abstract *integrated modular avionics* (IMA) system, where different software applications of varying safety-criticality operate on a number of COTS computing modules connected by a real-time computer network.

Figure 3 shows a possible modular organization of argument fragments addressing different assurance concerns for system S, together with the module hierarchy, and module contents. As shown, the module *system-argument* contains (a fragment of) a *hazard mitigation argument* (labeled SHMA) asserting the mitigation of the identified hazards. Here, we develop the claim of mitigating hazard H1 (goal node G2) into a claim that the contribution of the system function F1 to hazard H1 is acceptable (goal node G5). To support that claim, we assert that (*i*) the software that provides function F1, i.e., those portions of the software components SW1 and SW2 operating on SS1, is acceptable and operates as required, and (*ii*) the contribution of subsystem SS1 (to the function F1) is acceptable. In Fig. 3, we have shown those sub-claims as away goals (nodes G9 and G10), and as a public goal (node G8) that refer, respectively, to the supporting argument modules *SW1*, *SW2* and the contract module *MC1*. The latter, in particular, is the interface to the argument modules providing assurance that the failure behavior of the components of SS1 is acceptable, e.g., module *C2*. The argument module *SW* contains a *software fitness argument* (labeled SFA), which asserts that the software components of the system behave as required.

This argument is itself modular, with references to other modules that contain arguments assuring the fitness of the individual software components: namely, *SW1* and *SW3* (shown as *sub-modules* contained within *SW*), and *SW2* (shown as a *sibling* of *SW*). Assuring software fitness may be required independently of assuring hazard mitigation, although, as shown in Fig. 3, the latter depends on elements of the former. In particular, in argument SHMA, the away goal node G10 in the module *system-argument* invokes the public goal (i.e., node G3) in module *SW2*.

Whilst creating such modular arguments, we found the GSN standard and the literature on practical usage of modular arguments, e.g., [10,11] to be unclear on the characteristics of well-formed modular arguments, and a number of specific questions arose: (1) Is it permissible to include the module *SW2* within the module *SW*, similar to modules *SW1* and *SW3*? In general, what is the *scope* of public argument elements? (2) Can elements of the module *SW*, e.g., SFA, refer to elements of the module *system-argument*, e.g., SHMA, thus resulting in cyclic links between the two modules, and potentially in the overall argument? In general, what constraints apply across module boundaries? (3) If properties of the components of subsystem SS1 are known, can the hazard mitigation argument SHMA in the module *system-argument* additionally develop the claim in goal node G8? In general, can a claim be supported by multiple contracts, or can a claim be supported by both a contract and a local argument? (4) What are the valid elements of a contract argument represented using GSN, e.g., as proposed in [10]? In general, is a contract argument subject to the same constraints as any other (modular/non-modular and non-contract) argument structure? (5) What are the valid properties of the nodes specified with modular GSN, e.g., can away goals be undeveloped (i.e., annotated with ◊), as shown in Fig. 3? (6) Supposing module *SW* contained module *SW2*, but the latter offered no public goals (like module *SW1*), is it meaningful to construct and invoke a single contract (referencing the module SW), from multiple goal nodes of the hazard mitigation argument (containing different claims about the software)? In general, is it permissible for multiple claims in one (or more) module(s) to invoke a common contract? Towards addressing these issues, next (Sect. 4) we give rigorous definitions for modular GSN extensions, in particular intra-module GSN.

4   Formalization

First, we recall the (non-modular) definition of argument structure [6,7] (Definition 1), which we will extend to formalize the notion of a single modular argument structure, i.e., an individual diagram, to account for intra-module GSN (Definition 2). Then, we define *contracts* (Definition 3). Subsequently, we will extend the formalization to inter-connected collections of modules, clarifying containment (Definition 4), and scope (Definition 5). Thereafter, we will define the characteristics of a well-formed module hierarchy (Definition 6). Note that Definitions 2, 5 and 6 work together: Definition 2 gives structure on individual modules; Definition 5 gives the permissible and required connections between arguments, and Definition 6 gives additional constraints that must hold between linked arguments.

Definition 1 (Argument Structure). *An* argument structure S *is a tuple* $\langle N, l, \rightarrow \rangle$ *comprising: a set of nodes N; a family of labeling functions l_X, where $X \in \{t, d, m, s\}$, giving the node fields* type, description, metadata *(i.e., attributes), and* status; *and* $\rightarrow$ *is the connector relation between nodes. Let* $\{g, s, e, a, j, c\}$ *be the node types* goal, strategy, evidence, assumption, justification, *and* context *respectively. Then,* $l_t : N \rightarrow \{g, s, e, a, j, c\}$ *gives node types,* $l_d : N \rightarrow string$ *gives node descriptions,* $l_m : N \rightarrow \mathcal{P}(A)$ *(where A is an attribute set) gives node instance attributes, and* $l_s : N \rightarrow \mathcal{P}(\{tbd\})$ *gives node development status. We define the transitive closure,* $\rightarrow^* : \langle N, N \rangle$, *in the usual way, and require the connector relation to form a* finite forest *with the operation* root$(\rightarrow, r)$ *checking if the node r is a root of the forest. Furthermore, the following structural conditions must be met:*

1. root$(\rightarrow, r) \Rightarrow l_t(r) = g$, *i.e., each root of the argument structure is a goal;*
2. $n \rightarrow m \Rightarrow l_t(n) \in \{s, g\}$, *i.e., connectors only leave strategies or goals;*
3. $(n \rightarrow m) \wedge [l_t(n) = g] \Rightarrow l_t(m) \in \{s, e, a, j, c\}$, *i.e., goals do not connect to other goals;*
4. $(n \rightarrow m) \wedge [l_t(n) = s] \Rightarrow l_t(m) \in \{g, a, j, c\}$, *i.e., strategies do not connect to other strategies or evidence;*
5. $tbd \in l_s(n) \Rightarrow l_t(n) \in \{g, s\}$, *i.e., only goals and strategies can be undeveloped.*

Definition 1 gives a *strict* notion of argument—i.e., a tree, rather than a directed acyclic graph (DAG)—where separate goals cannot share evidence, and goals require intermediate strategies. Both these conditions, which are often violated in practice, can be captured by a more relaxed definition (not given here). Now, let *mr* and *cr* be two additional node types denoting, respectively, *module reference* and *contract module reference*, in addition to the node types given in Definition 1.

Definition 2 (Modular Argument Structure). *A modular argument struc-
ture, (or module, for short), M, is a tuple $\langle N, l, t, d, \rightarrow \rangle$, where N and $\rightarrow$ are
as in Definition 1; d is a module description string. Again, as in Definition 1, l
is the same family of functions where $l_t : N \rightarrow \{s, g, e, a, j, c, mr, cr\}$ gives node
types; $l_d : N \rightarrow$ string gives node descriptions; and $l_m : N \rightarrow \mathcal{P}(A)$ gives node
instance attributes. $l_s : N \rightarrow \mathcal{P}(\{tbd, tbsbc, public, away, contextual\})$ gives node
status, i.e., whether a node is, respectively, 'to be developed', 'to be supported
by contract', declared public, referencing an away node, or 'used in context'.
t is a family of functions that gives the target of the nodes referencing other
modules: for module reference, x, $t_r(x)$ gives the target module, and for an away
node, $t_a(x)$ gives the pair of module and public node. Let $\mathcal{I}_m$ and $\mathcal{I}_n$ be sets
of identifiers (IDs) distinct from N, representing modules (and contracts; see
Definition 3) and nodes external to M. Then, we have the maps $t_a : \{n \in N \mid
away \in l_s(n)\} \rightarrow \mathcal{I}_m \times \mathcal{I}_n$, and $t_r : \{n \in N \mid l_t(n) \in \{mr, cr\}\} \rightarrow \mathcal{I}_m$. We
require individual modular argument structures to form forests. Additionally, the
following structural conditions[2] must be met:*

1. *The conditions in items 1, 2, 4, and 5 of Definition 1 hold;*
2. *Only goal, evidence, and context nodes can be marked as public or away nodes:
   $public, away \in l_s(n) \Rightarrow l_t(n) \in \{g, e, c\};$*
3. *Only goals are marked as to be supported by contract: $tbsbc \in l_s(n) \Rightarrow
   l_t(n) = g;$*
4. *Nodes cannot be both public and away: $\nexists n \in N . \{public, away\} \subseteq l_s(n);$*
5. *Nodes with status tbd and tbsbc are mutually exclusive: $\nexists n \in
   N . \{tbsbc, tbd\} \subseteq l_s(n);$*
6. *Goals with status away or tbsbc, and (contract) module references have no
   outgoing links: $away \in l_s(n)$ or $tbsbc \in l_s(n)$ or $l_t(n) \in \{mr, cr\} \Rightarrow \nexists m \in
   N . n \rightarrow m;$*
7. *$contextual \in l_s(n) \Rightarrow ([away \in l_s(n) \wedge l_t(n) = g] \vee l_t(n) = mr) \wedge \exists m \in
   N.m \rightarrow n$, i.e., contextual nodes are away goals or module references, and are
   link targets;*
8. *$n \rightarrow m \wedge l_t(n) = l_t(m) = g \Rightarrow contextual \in l_s(m)$, i.e., goal-to-goal links are
   contextual;*
9. *Goals supported by contract module references must be public, with no other
   out-links: $n \rightarrow m \wedge l_t(n) = g \wedge l_t(m) = cr \Rightarrow (public \in l_s(n) \wedge n \rightarrow m' \Rightarrow
   m = m')$.*

The standard permits away goals and module references to be linked to by
both $\rightarrow$ and $\twoheadrightarrow$ relations, whereas contract module references can only be linked
to using the $\twoheadrightarrow$ relation (e.g., see Fig. 3). Since our definition contains a single connector relation $\rightarrow$ where we derive the link type from the types of source/target
nodes, we introduce an additional status 'contextual' to represent the situation when goals or module references are used contextually. As in Definition 1,
we require individual modular argument structures to form forests. However,
whereas a non-modular argument is expected to be a tree eventually (with a

---

[2] To save space, we consider free variables to be implicitly universally quantified.

single top-level claim), a completed modular argument can naturally consist of several trees (see Fig. 3). Also, note that all nodes have unique IDs, including away goals and the public goals that they reference. The forest condition rules out cycles in the non-modular equivalent of modular arguments (see Fig. 5) and multiple parents (i.e., DAGs). This, and the condition of item 8, reflect the strict notion of argument in Definition 1. Later (Definition 5), we will give a condition to constrain inter-module cycles. The standard implies that module references cannot have status *tbd*, since an undeveloped goal and a goal supported by a module reference are alternative ways of stating that "support (for the claim) is (yet) to be provided". However, from an implementation standpoint, it seems reasonable to have a user preference that a *tbd* status on module references be derived from the corresponding module body; we therefore do not prevent *tbd* status on nodes of type *mr*.

As mentioned earlier, we consider contracts to be represented also using GSN. The simplest form of a contract specified using GSN contains *(i)* an away goal referencing a public goal in the *consumer* (or source) module—i.e., the module that invokes the contract—which is *(ii)* developed using an appropriate strategy into *(iii)* one or more module references to, or away goals that reference public goals in, the *provider* (or target) module(s)—i.e., the module(s) that are the target of the contract (e.g., see contract module *MC1*, in Fig. 3, for an example). In a contract, we term the away goals referring to consumer modules as the *in*–nodes, whereas the *out*–nodes of the contract are the away goals, contexts, solutions and module references that refer to provider modules.

Formally, if $l_t(n) = g$, $away \in l_s(n)$, $\neg\texttt{leaf}(\rightarrow, n)$, and $\forall n' . [\texttt{leaf}(\rightarrow, n') \Rightarrow n \rightarrow^* n']$, then the node n is an *in*–node, $in(n)$. Similarly, it is an *out*–node, $out(n)$, if $\texttt{leaf}(\rightarrow, n)$ and $(l_t(n) = mr \lor away \in l_s(n))$. We give the target module of a node x as $tmod(x) = M$, if $l_t(x) \in \{g, c, e\}$, $away \in l_s(x)$, and $t_a(x) = \langle M, \_\rangle$, or $l_t(x) = mr$ and $t_r(x) = M$. Here, note that the notions of *in*– and *out*–node are defined on a single module diagram, and do not depend on the connections to other modules (which we characterize later in Definition 5, when we define module scope).

Next, we formalize contracts.

Definition 3 (Contractual Argument Structure). *A contractual argument structure (contract, for short) C, is a tuple $\langle N, l, d, t, \rightarrow\rangle$ that satisfies the same conditions as Definition 2, with the exception of condition (6) for away goals. That is, away goals are allowed to have outgoing links. The following additional conditions hold:*

1. *There exists at least one in–node (i.e., a non-leaf away node above all leaf nodes): $\exists n \in N . in(n)$;*
2. $\texttt{leaf}(n) \Rightarrow l_t(n) \notin \{s, cr\} \land [l_t(n) = g \Rightarrow away \in l_s(n)]$, *i.e., each leaf node is either an away goal, a module reference, an evidence node, or a contextual element (context, assumption, or justification node). Hence, out–nodes will either be away nodes (goals, contexts, evidence), or module references;*
3. *There exists at least one out–node: $\exists n \in N . out(n)$;*

4. Nodes cannot be public: public $\notin l_s(n)$;

5. All away nodes are either in– or out–nodes: away $\in l_s(n) \Rightarrow in(n) \vee out(n)$.

From Definition 3, we observe the following: first, since contracts do not satisfy item 6 of Definition 2, formally they are not modules. Informally, though, we can think of them as a special kind of module, and will write '*(non-)contract module*' when the difference needs emphasis. Next, item 2 permits *local*, i.e., non-away, evidence[3], and not all branches need have *out*–node leaves; hence we also require the condition of item 3. It is a matter of interpretation that non-leaf away nodes can be only *in*–nodes. This, combined with item 2 implies that *in*–nodes must be above *out*–nodes and, in particular, that a node cannot be both an *in*–node and an *out*–node. Additionally, since the intended role of a contract is to provide an interface between the assertions of provider modules and the guarantee(s) required by consumer modules, it seems reasonable to constrain the way in which the contract is accessed. Thus, by prohibiting public nodes, i.e., item 4, we preclude access to those elements of the contract, that are not *in*–nodes. For the same reason, *in*–nodes are necessarily above all *out*–nodes. So also, the latter must be necessarily leaves since the premises of a contract are developed externally by provider modules, rather than internally to a contract. However, note that item 5 does not restrict an *out*–node from being used contextually. Figure 4 illustrates some of the variety in contractual argument structures, arising from the conditions of Definition 3.

Our definition does not excessively constrain the type of GSN structures that may be used to specify a contract. Thus, we allow additional internal nodes, e.g., we do not require the root to be an away goal, although children of *out*–nodes are prohibited (Fig. 4a). We also permit contracts to contain multiple *in*–nodes, e.g., a chain of *in*–nodes (Fig. 4c), so that the away goals are still linked to consumer modules (also see Definition 5). Figure 4 additionally shows some of the permissible links to/from module contracts, which we will clarify when we formalize module *scope* (Definition 5).

Given a set of modular/contractual argument structures, intuitively, we can logically collect and organize them according to (domain-)specific concerns, which gives rise to *containers* for the collections (e.g., SW and SW2 in Fig. 3) and a hierarchy (e.g., see Fig. 3, bottom right).

Definition 4 (Module Hierarchy). *A module hierarchy, $\mathcal{H}$, is a tuple $\langle \mathcal{I}_m, \mathcal{I}_a, \mathcal{I}_c, \mathcal{A}, \mathcal{C}, \mathcal{M}_a, \mathcal{M}_c, < \rangle$, comprising distinct sets of module container IDs, $\mathcal{I}_m$; modular argument IDs, $\mathcal{I}_a$; contractual argument IDs, $\mathcal{I}_c$; modular arguments, $\mathcal{A}$; contractual arguments, $\mathcal{C}$; and mappings $\mathcal{M}_a : \mathcal{I}_a \rightarrow \mathcal{A}$, and $\mathcal{M}_c : \mathcal{I}_c \rightarrow \mathcal{C}$, along with a forest $\langle \mathcal{I}, < \rangle$, where $\mathcal{I} = \mathcal{I}_a \cup \mathcal{I}_c \cup \mathcal{I}_m$, such that $i \in \mathcal{I}_a \cup \mathcal{I}_c \Rightarrow \mathtt{leaf}(<, i)$, and $\mathtt{root}(<, i) \Rightarrow i \in \mathcal{I}_m$.*

The forest represents the *containment relation* between modules, for which there need be no single top-level module. For convenience, we will abuse notation

---

[3] The rationale is to directly resolve *auxiliary* subgoals internal to the contract, without needing to create an additional, external module.

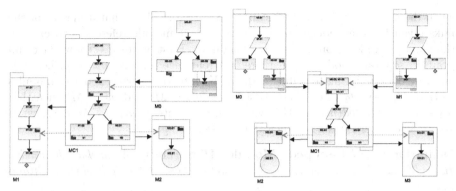

(a) Consumer module M0 invoking a non-root *in*–node in contract module MC1, linking to a non-root public goal in provider module M1.

(b) Common (root *in*–node in) contract module MC1 invoked from multiple consumer modules M0 and M1.

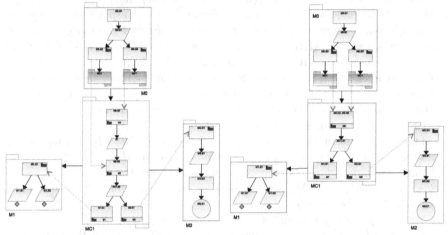

(c) Different argument legs in consumer module M0 (different claims) invoking different *in*–nodes of the same contract module MC1.

(d) Different argument legs in consumer module M0 (different claims) invoking common root *in*–node in same contract module MC1.

Fig. 4. Examples of constraints on contract modules showing internal/external links.

and write $M = \langle N, \ldots \rangle$ when we mean $\mathcal{M}_a(M) = \langle N, \ldots \rangle$, and $n \in M$ rather than $n \in N$.

A module hierarchy represents a snapshot of a possibly incomplete collection of safety arguments under development and, thus, although arguments must be leaves (and within a container), we do not require all leaves to be arguments. That is, during development, we allow a module leaf (with no argument within). We also allow a tree with a single node, i.e., an empty module. Since Definition 4 allows forests, we allow multiple arguments in a single module, and multiple argument fragments (with distinct roots) in a single argument. We will use *module* to refer to both modular arguments and contracts, as well as their containers, when the distinction is not significant. Next, we formalize what it means for the links given by away nodes and module/contract module references to exist in the appropriate location in a module hierarchy. First, write $x \dashrightarrow y$ when x and y are in separate modules and there is a reference link from x to y, i.e., x is an away node pointing to public node y. We extend $\dashrightarrow$ from nodes to modules so that $M_1 \dashrightarrow M_2$ when there exist nodes $m_1 \in M_1$ and $m_2 \in M_2$ such that $m_1 \dashrightarrow m_2$ or $tmod(m_1) = M_2$ (which we can write as $m_1 \dashrightarrow M_2$). We write $x \twoheadrightarrow y$ when there exists a z such that $x \dashrightarrow z \rightarrow^* y$.

Definition 5 (Well-scoped Module Hierarchy). *A module hierarchy,* $\mathcal{H} = \langle \mathcal{I}_m, \mathcal{I}_a, \mathcal{I}_c, \mathcal{A}, \mathcal{C}, \mathcal{M}_a, \mathcal{M}_c, < \rangle$, *is well-scoped if the following conditions hold:*

1. *For every away node in every non-contract module there is a corresponding public node in a separate non-contract module:* $\forall n_1 \in M_1 \,.\, away \in l_s(n_1) \Rightarrow \exists M_2 \in \mathcal{I}_a, m_2 \in M_2 \,.\, public \in l_s(m_2) \wedge t_r(n_1) = \langle M_2, m_2 \rangle$;
2. *For every module (contract module) reference, the corresponding appropriate type of module (contract module) exists, and is distinct from any of its container modules:* $n \in M, l_t(n) = mr \wedge t_r(n) = M' \Rightarrow M' \in \mathcal{I}_m \wedge M \not\leq M'$; *and* $n \in M, l_t(n) = cr \wedge t_r(n) = M' \Rightarrow M' \in \mathcal{I}_c \wedge M \not\leq M'$;
3. *If a goal node is supported by a contract module reference to a contract C, then the goal is a public node, and it corresponds to a non-leaf away node (i.e., an in–node) in C:* $l_t(n) = g \wedge l_t(c) = cr \wedge n \rightarrow c, t_r(c) = C \Rightarrow public \in l_s(n) \wedge \exists k \in C \,.\, away \in l_s(k) \wedge t_a(n) = \langle C, k \rangle$;
4. Anti-cycle condition: *If $n_1 \rightarrow_1^* m_1$ in argument module M_1 and $n_2 \twoheadrightarrow^* n_1$ and $m_1 \twoheadrightarrow^* m_2$, then $m_2 \not\twoheadrightarrow_2^* n_2$ in argument module M_2;*
5. Scope: *Inter-module links respect the module hierarchy, i.e., if $M_1 \dashrightarrow M_2$ then either M_1 and M_2 are siblings or M_2 is a child of M_1:* $\exists M_3 \in \mathcal{I}_a \,.\, M_1, M_2 < M_3$ *or* $M_2 < M_1$;

Additionally, for every contract, C, the following conditions hold:

6. *Out–nodes link to separate argument trees (which can be in the same module[4]), i.e.,* $out(n) \wedge out(n') \wedge t_a(n) = \langle M, g \rangle \wedge t_a(n') = \langle M', g' \rangle \Rightarrow \nexists m \,.\, m \rightarrow^* g, g'$; *and* $t_a(n) = \langle M, \_ \rangle \wedge t_r(n') = M' \wedge t_r(n'') = M'' \Rightarrow (M \neq M' \wedge M' \neq M'')$;
7. *In– and out–nodes link to different modules:* $in(x) \wedge out(y) \Rightarrow tmod(x) \neq tmod(y)$;
8. *At least one in–node is linked to a source:* $\exists n \in C \,.\, in(n) \wedge \exists m \in \mathcal{M}_a \,.\, public \in l_s(m) \wedge n \dashrightarrow m$;
9. *All out–nodes are linked to targets. Thus, if a leaf is an away node[5] then there exists a linked public node in the corresponding module[6]:* $\forall n \in C \,.\, away \in l_s(n) \Rightarrow \exists m \in \mathcal{M}_a \,.\, public \in l_s(m) \wedge n \dashrightarrow m$.

From Definition 5, our notion of scope (item 5) is that modules should only access those nodes of their siblings declared to be public, but not their siblings'

---

[4] Recall that (modular) argument structures are forests.

[5] Module references are handled by item 2 of Definition 5.

[6] Note that the public goal node need not be the root of module M (Fig. 4a).

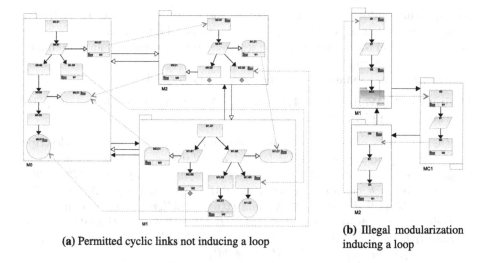

(a) Permitted cyclic links not inducing a loop

(b) Illegal modularization inducing a loop

Fig. 5. Examples of constraints on cyclic links between modules.

children modules nor their own grandchildren[7] based on the principle that to access a public node of a child module, the parent must itself use and then redeclare that node. Well-scoping forces the external sets of IDs in Definition 2 (i.e., $\mathcal{I}_m$ and $\mathcal{I}_n$) to be drawn appropriately from within the module hierarchy. Although we permit cycles between modules (Fig. 5a), we need to prevent cycles in the underlying 'unfolded' argument; thus, it is not sufficient to state the *anti-cycle condition* (item 4) for pairs of modules, i.e., we must consider arbitrary length chains. (Fig. 5b illustrates the underlying rationale).

Note that items 6–9 apply to contracts; thus, although item 1 seems to cover item 9, the former applies to *non-contract modules*. The intuition underlying the latter is that a contract may provide support to multiple consumer modules, e.g., via reuse. Thus, we permit an *in*–node to be invoked by multiple consumer modules (Fig. 4b), as well as by multiple claims in the same consumer module (Fig. 4d). This is useful in a scenario where a common contract provides support for multiple arguments, or for a claim that appears in related argument legs. Consequently, we require all *out*–nodes to be linked to provider modules, but not all *in*–nodes need be linked. Also, item 1 precludes referring to public nodes in a contract, by definition (Definition 3, item 4).

Items 8 and 9 prohibit nested contracts or references to other contracts, primarily to simplify formalization. In general, away nodes never point *into* a contract; rather, the *in*– and *out*–nodes (goals) of a contract refer *out* to the

---

[7] A possible relaxation of this condition would be that modules *can* access child modules of siblings, i.e., in $\mathcal{H}$, the module containing the target of an away node is ≤ the module containing the source node. Another possible relaxation is to allow a module access to its grandchildren. However, these alternatives limit the benefits of encapsulation.

corresponding public goals of the provider and consumer modules respectively. However, note that for contracts (Fig. 4) the → link between an away *in*–node of a contract and its referenced public leaf goal in the provider module points in the *opposite* direction.

Finally, we can define when a hierarchy is well-formed.

Definition 6 (Well-formed Hierarchy). *A well-scoped module hierarchy, $\mathcal{H}$, is a well-formed hierarchy if:*

1. *The properties of away–public node pairs are related, i.e., type and description are equal, status is equal for tbd and tbsbc (which can only apply to goals), while metadata of the away node are a superset of those of the public nodes: for each module/contract module $M = \langle N, l, t, d, \rightarrow \rangle \in \mathcal{M} \cup \mathcal{C} \in \mathcal{H}$, $M' = \langle N', l', t', d', \rightarrow' \rangle$, $n \in N$, and $t_a(n) = \langle M', n' \rangle$—i.e., n is an away node, n' is a public node—(and M, M' do not violate Definition 5), we have $l_t(n) = l'_t(n')$, $l_d(n) = l'_d(n')$, $l_m(n) \subseteq l'_m(n')$, $l_s(n) \cap \{tbd, tbsbc\} = l'_s(n') \cap \{tbd, tbsbc\}$, and $n' \in M', M \neq M'$;*

2. *Module/contract module reference descriptions equal those of the provider module/contract module (due to well-scoping, Definition 5, the diagram types are correct): if $t_r(n) = M = \langle N, l, t, d, \rightarrow \rangle$ then $l_d(n) = d$, and $l_t(n) = mr \Rightarrow M \in \mathcal{I}_a$ and $l_t(n) = cr \Rightarrow M \in \mathcal{I}_c$.*

Formally, away nodes also have a *description*, *metadata*, and *tbd* status, but not independently of the public goal node. Specifically, the *description*, and *tbd/tbsbc* status are the same as that of the public goal node. Moreover, the away node inherits the metadata of the public node, although we allow it to have additional attributes. Similarly, the description of a module/contract module reference is the same as that of the target module/contract module. The rationale for allowing additional metadata for away, module reference and contract module reference nodes, is that they are *private* to a module. A module user may augment such nodes with additional semantic information, local to the containing module, and specific to a user perspective and/or the context of usage, beyond what has been added to the target node (e.g., the intended use of the module, or other intellectual property). Alternatively, since the target of an away node is public, a reasonable assumption is that its metadata is also public and, therefore, inherited.

5   Discussion

Based on our formalization for modular arguments we now have a rigorous basis to distinguish modularity from hierarchy [12] in safety arguments. Informally, however, hierarchy can be considered as a *vertical* abstraction of structure, whereas modularity is useful when a *horizontal* abstraction is required (although it can be applied in both dimensions). We can now respond to the questions posed in Sect. 3 (in the same order): (1) In general, Definition 5, item 5, clarifies the scope of public nodes in a modular argument. In particular, in Fig. 3, we disallow module *SW* from containing module *SW2*, as it violates scope. Accordingly, module *SW1* also ought not to be contained in module *SW*. If such containment is required, the away goals of the argument SHMA, in module *system-argument*, should be replaced with equivalent public goals that either reference a contract offered by module *SW*, or are marked with status *tbsbc*; (2) Definition 5 also provides the constraints on links across module boundaries. In particular, the *anti-cycle* condition (item 4) allows cycles in modules but prohibits them in the underlying arguments. Thus, elements of the argument SFA in module *SW* can reference elements of the argument SHMA in module *system-argument*, subject to the constraints imposed by our formal definitions; (3) Definition 2, item 9 prohibits claim support though multiple contracts, since the presence of a contract module reference from a public goal precludes any other out links. However, we note that this condition indicates a conflict in the GSN standard guidance, which does not prohibit goals (in non-modular arguments) to be both supported directly by evidence, and also by other intermediate goals; (4) In general, contracts are subject to most of the same constraints as modular arguments (Definition 2), but must meet the specific constraints given by Definition 3; (5) Definition 6 clarifies the valid properties of modular GSN nodes. In particular, item 1 of Definition 6 permits away goals to have a *tbd* ($\lozenge$) status; (6) Finally, our formalization permits multiple claims in one module (or multiple modules) to invoke a common contract (Definition 3, Fig. 4), although the invocation of multiple contracts is prohibited (Definition 2).

6   Concluding Remarks

We have given the elements of a theory for formalizing modular safety arguments that provides a rigorous basis for tool implementation, and our focus has been mainly intra-module GSN. The current implementation of modules in our toolset, AdvoCATE [9], is preliminary and not all checks have yet been implemented. By formally defining modular arguments, contracts, scope, and well-formedness, we have clarified and made explicit many structural assumptions that were not previously described in the literature. We have also developed a theory of modular patterns (omitted here due to space limitations), which presents numerous design choices and subtleties. Though a lack of space has precluded our giving a correctness theorem, intuitively, all references are well-defined in a well-scoped and well-formed module hierarchy. To formalize this, we can interpret modules as non-modular arguments via a notion of *unfolding*, capturing the intuition behind inter-module links as denoting an underlying monolithic argument.

Many of the conditions that required formalization are quite intricate and the proscriptions of the standard often seem ad hoc. A more abstract approach to contracts, extended with a formal assume/guarantee language would be useful [13]. Various restrictions made through our formalization could be relaxed, e.g., nesting contracts, and references to other contracts seems to be reasonable. Our formalization is partly based on the guidance for modularity in the GSN standard [4] which, itself, is based upon the work in [2,14]. However, in general, the standard only provides limited guidance on the interconnections between modular arguments, contracts, the related constraints, and issues of scope. Moreover, it does not address hierarchy in (modular/non-modular) arguments. Earlier research on modular software safety arguments [11,15] has addressed scope and containment, albeit only informally, and is compatible with our formalizations (Sect. 4). Contemporary work on formalizing GSN modules [16] has not considered issues of well-formedness and scope, nor have (to our knowledge) notation agnostic meta-models of safety argumentation [8].

As future work, we will extend the theory to account for *module views*, i.e., inter-module GSN, and their relationship to the underlying modules. We also intend to look at additional aspects, e.g., how context shared by collaborating modules will be managed, and the relationship to modularization concepts in other modeling languages such as Unified Modeling Language (UML), etc. Elsewhere, we developed a notion of argument *query* [7] for individual argument structures. Extending this to modules would require a notion of multi-diagram view, which is another avenue for future work.

Acknowledgements. We thank Jane Fenn (BAE Systems), Ibrahim Habli, and Richard Hawkins (University of York) for earlier discussions on modular GSN. We also thank the anonymous reviewers for their helpful comments. This work was supported by the SASO project of the NASA ARMD Airspace Operations and Safety Program.

References

1. Despotou, G., Kelly, T.: Investigating the use of argument modularity to optimise through-life system safety assurance. In: 3rd IET International Conference on System Safety, pp. 1–6, October 2008
2. Kelly, T.: Managing complex safety cases. In: Redmill, F., Anderson, T. (eds.) Current Issues in Safety-Critical Systems, pp. 99–115. Springer, London (2003)
3. Fenn, J., Hawkins, R., Williams, P., Kelly, T., Banner, M., Oakshott, Y.: The who, where, how, why and when of modular and incremental certification. In: 2nd IET International Conference on System Safety, pp. 135–140, October 2007
4. Goal Structuring Notation Working Group: GSN Community Standard v1, November 2011
5. Kelly, T., Bates, S.: The costs, benefits, and risks associated with pattern-based and modular safety case development. In: Proceedings UK MoD Equipment Safety Assurance Symposium, October 2005
6. Denney, E., Pai, G.: A formal basis for safety case patterns. In: Bitsch, F., Guiochet, J., Kaâniche, M. (eds.) SAFECOMP. LNCS, vol. 8153, pp. 21–32. Springer, Heidelberg (2013)
7. Denney, E., Naylor, D., Pai, G.: Querying safety cases. In: Bondavalli, A., Di Giandomenico, F. (eds.) SAFECOMP 2014. LNCS, vol. 8666, pp. 294–309. Springer, Heidelberg (2014)
8. Object Management Group: Structured Assurance Case Metamodel (SACM) version 1.0. Formal/2013-02-01, February 2013

 9. Denney, E., Pai, G., Pohl, J.: AdvoCATE: an assurance case automation toolset. In: Ortmeier, F., Daniel, P. (eds.) SAFECOMP Workshops 2012. LNCS, vol. 7613, pp. 8–21. Springer, Heidelberg (2012)
10. Fenn, J., Hawkins, R., Williams, P., Kelly, T.: Safety case composition using contracts - refinements based on feedback from an industrial case study. In: Proceedings of the 15th Safety Critical Systems Symposium (SSS 2007), February 2007
11. Industrial Avionics Working Group: Modular Software Safety Case Process GSN - MSSC 203 Issue 1, November 2012
12. Denney, E., Pai, G., Whiteside, I.: Formal foundations for hierarchical safety cases. In: Proceedings of the 16th International Symposium on High Assurance System Engineering (HASE 2015), January 2015
13. Warg, F., Vedder, B., Skoglund, M., Söderberg, A.: SafetyADD: a tool for safety-contract based design. In: Proceedings of the 25th International Symposium on Software Reliability Engineering Workshops (ISSREW 2014) (2014)
14. Kelly, T.: Concepts and principles of compositional safety case construction. In: Technical report COMSA/2001/1/1, University of York (2001)
15. Industrial Avionics Working Group: Modular Software Safety Case Process Description - MSSC 201 Issue 1, November 2012
16. Matsuno, Y.: A design and implementation of an assurance case language. In: 44th International Conference on Dependable Systems and Networks (DSN 2014), pp. 630–641, June 2014

Security Attacks

Quantifying Risks to Data Assets Using Formal Metrics in Embedded System Design

Maria Vasilevskaya$^{(\boxtimes)}$ and Simin Nadjm-Tehrani

Department of Computer and Information Science,
Linköping University, Linköping, Sweden
{maria.vasilevskaya,simin.nadjm-tehrani}@liu.se

Abstract. This paper addresses quantifying security risks associated with data assets within design models of embedded systems. Attack and system behaviours are modelled as time-dependent stochastic processes. The presence of the time dimension allows accounting for dynamic aspects of potential attacks and a system: the probability of a successful attack changes as time progresses; and a system possesses different data assets as its execution unfolds. These models are used to quantify two important attributes of security: confidentiality and integrity. In particular, likelihood/consequence-based measures of confidentiality and integrity losses are proposed to characterise security risks to data assets. In our method, we consider attack and system behaviours as two separate models that are later elegantly combined for security analysis. This promotes knowledge reuse and avoids adding extra complexity in the system design process. We demonstrate the effectiveness of the proposed method and metrics on smart metering devices.

Keywords: Security risks · Confidentiality loss · Integrity loss · Data assets · Attack modelling · Stochastic modelling · Model-based · Embedded systems · Smart meter

1 Introduction

Concern for security issues in embedded systems is growing due to mass deployment of devices in a wide range of applications – from pace makers to critical infrastructures. Due to criticality of many such deployments and prevalent attacks, security should be an integral part of system development. Moreover, it should start already at an early design phase, because costs associated with security fixes grow steeply when progressing in the product life cycle. A serious obstacle to designing secure systems is that system engineers do not have suitable means to investigate how the decisions made at the design phase affect security. As a result, systems often remain unprotected. Our contribution to this research area is a method that enables analysing what security risks are inherent in a certain system model and how certain design decisions affect these risks. In particular, we address the risks related to data assets.

© Springer International Publishing Switzerland 2015
F. Koornneef and C. van Gulijk (Eds.): SAFECOMP 2015, LNCS 9337, pp. 347–361, 2015.
DOI: 10.1007/978-3-319-24255-2_25

The output provided by our method can be used by system engineers to reason about the protection needed for data assets in the context of a given design and to evaluate these needs with respect to other factors such as economical costs. In particular, the contributions of this paper are as follows:

– Formal definition of two probabilistic risk-based metrics to quantify confidentiality and integrity of data assets in the context of a given design model.
– Development of a formal method to calculate these metrics using three types of models: functional and platform models of a system, and attack models.
– Illustration of how these metrics can be used to show different risks to the assets of a metering device which is part of a smart grid.

We suggest that security analysis should treat attack behaviour and system design as two separate, though interrelated, elements. Both elements are usually highly complex constituents of security. Treating them separately provides their more accurate elaboration, while both of them are clearly interdependent. One is addressed in the research on methodologies for attack modelling, e.g. an attack tree technique introduced[1] by Weiss [24]. Another is supported by evaluating a system design and identifying relevant assets [21]. This paper combines the two ideas as components in a bigger picture: a generic engineering process that exploits domain-specific security knowledge captured from security experts [22].

Attack and system behaviours are modelled as time-dependent stochastic processes. The presence of the time dimension allows accounting for dynamic aspects of potential attacks and a considered system: the probability of a successful attack may change as time progresses, and a system may possess different valuable data assets as its execution unfolds. The use of probabilistic modelling, in turn, enables dealing with uncertainties that are present at the design phase.

One can potentially argue about difficulties of obtaining realistic data about the timing aspects of an attack and system at the design phase, and therefore, question reliability of results of the proposed security analysis. Nonetheless we propose that easier and more effective exploration of security threats and impacts is already a valuable input to design decisions, even when subject to some uncertainties. This enables asking 'what if' questions which help understanding the sensitivity of the system to potential attacks. Furthermore, the research that enables quantitative estimations of timing aspects of attacks and system at early design stages constantly progresses.

In Sect. 2, we discuss related works. Section 3 introduces two risk-based metrics by formalising the basic concepts and providing a method for their derivation. We illustrate the use of the proposed metrics in Sect. 4 on a real metering device in a smart grid, and conclude the paper in Sect. 5.

2   Related Work

There are general methods that cover main steps of risk analysis, e.g. CRAMM (CCTA Risk Analysis and Management Method) [1]. These methods prescribe

---

[1] The term, however, was coined by Schneier.

basic steps of risk analysis while leaving out details of their implementation. Security risk management is also addressed by a set of standards, e.g. NIST SP800-30 [20] and ISO 31010 [3]. NIST creates foundations of risk management and contains basic guidance that broadly covers conducting risk assessment on federal IT systems and organisations. As pointed out by Lund et al. [15], this guidance should be complemented with a risk analysis process and cannot be considered as a fully-fledged method. Similarly, ISO 31010 provides guidance for risk assessment, but does not specify methods or techniques to be used in a specific application domain. Our work can be considered as complementary to these guidelines and is specific for design phases of embedded system development.

Surveys of risk analysis methods and corresponding metrics are presented by Verendel [23], among others. Verendel [23] analyses more than 100 approaches and metrics to quantify security. The conclusion of the author, that is highly relevant for our work, is that CIA (Confidentiality, Integrity, Availability) quantification methods are under-represented.

Several models for risk evaluation exist that have slightly different ingredients. For example, risk for physical security is often modelled as $R = P \times V \times D$ [4,9] where P is the probability of threat occurrence, V is vulnerabilities of the system, and D is consequences. Another model represents security risks as $R = U \times C$ [15,20] where U is the likelihood of unwanted incidents and C is consequences. These models resemble each other, i.e. the unwanted incident component in the latter model combines the first two components in the former. We base our work on the second model and focus on evaluating the U component.

Model-based risk analysis encompasses methods such as CORAS [15] and CySeMoL [19]. While following the same basic structure of risk analysis, these methods provide richer support. CORAS [15] is a general approach for risk analysis (already applied in numerous domains) specified as 8 steps. It uses graphical notation to structure elicited assets and threat scenarios and is supported by formal calculus that enables calculation of risks. Sommestad et al. [19] propose the Cyber Security Modeling Language (CySeMoL) and framework for risk assessment of IT systems. CySeMoL captures dependencies among different elements of risk analysis and system architecture, so that a system engineer is aided in deriving risks associated with an architecture. Similar to such works we use formal models for deriving risks with a focus on the design phase.

Vasilevskaya et al. [21] provide a model-based method for security analysis (referred to as SEED [22]). SEED is described at two levels of abstraction: foundation and realisation. At the foundation level the method prescribes system modelling and domain-specific security modelling. At the realisation level, the method is refined to provide support for embedded systems by employing modelling languages specific for the domain. Risk estimation to support quantitative security analysis has yet to be elaborated in SEED [22]. This paper fills this gap applying and extending the ideas of the model-based risk analysis.

Another group of methods for security quantification is based on attack modelling. A comprehensive survey of these approaches based on direct acyclic graphs is presented by Kordy et al. [14]. We briefly mention some approaches that are not in the scope of this survey, but still relevant to our work. Almasizadeh and

Azgomi [5] define a state-based stochastic model to quantify different aspects of security. A system is abstracted away as a set of defender transitions, i.e. as backward transitions in an attack model. Madan et al. [16] propose a method to quantify security attributes of intrusion-tolerant systems. The analysis is done based on an interwoven model of the intrusion-tolerant system, encompassing both attack and system behaviours, as well as countermeasure reactions.

The novelty of our approach for quantification of risks is that it explicitly accounts for both elements (system and attacks), but avoids mixing them in a single model specifically created for security analysis. Such an approach has several benefits. A system engineer and a security expert can work separately on the artefacts belonging to their own fields of responsibility and professional expertise. In addition, the approach enables the reuse of self-contained attack models across several systems in one application domain (e.g. different designs of metering devices from the smart grid domain), because these systems can face the same attacks. To our knowledge this is the first method that aims to support system engineers in quantifying risks to data assets in the context of embedded system design models from multiple stakeholder perspectives.

In line with current attack-based analysis frameworks, our methodology deals with known attacks as opposed to unknown zero-day attacks. Preparing a system for zero-day attacks is also an important concern, but most embedded systems fail to resist even known attacks due to a lack of security considerations at the design phase. Bilge and Dumitras [7] demonstrate that the number of occurrences of an attack when it is transformed from a zero-day to a known attack only grows.

Acquiring quantitative estimations (e.g. execution time) already at the design phase in embedded systems is a recognised challenge. Model-based engineering provides methods for design-based estimations to support early design-space exploration, e.g. COMPLEX [11], among others. We capitalise on such methods in order to decorate our models with probability distributions for execution time.

Our approach rests on input data that may be uncertain to some degree. For example, this is the case due to incomplete knowledge about attacks or uncertainty connected to estimates given by experts. Today, there are methods and tools to deal with limited certainty of data used for decision making. A comprehensive classification of different kinds of imperfect information and tools to deal with it are discussed by Parsons [18]. In our work, we adopt probabilities and probability distributions to capture inherent uncertainty of used data.

3   Quantifying Risks to Data Assets

We start this section by introducing two probabilistic risk-based metrics to quantify confidentiality and integrity of data assets. Thereafter, we present a method to calculate these metrics using formal system and attack models as inputs.

3.1   Proposed Metrics and Risks

Risk is frequently modelled by the likelihood of a successful attack and the severity of its consequences. Different ways of handling assets within a particular system imply different exposure of these assets to confidentiality and integrity breaches associated with a certain attack vector. The likelihood of a successful disclosure and alteration of assets is, therefore, conditioned by the ways assets are handled (similar to [4]). Since assets are objects of value, their violation will imply different costs for different stakeholders [22]. As a result, confidentiality and integrity losses can be naturally defined as risk-based metrics parameterised by different stakeholders. Additionally, since both an attack and a system are dynamic entities, whose behaviour includes different exposure degrees at different states over time, the proposed metrics should be time-dependent.

We define *confidentiality loss* (*CL*) of a valuable data asset given an attack by time t as a risk metric that characterises the damage potentially caused by this attack on the asset. It is calculated as a product of the likelihood that the attack would disclose the asset by t and the cost of this breach for a stakeholder R. In turn, confidentiality loss of a system Y is a function (denoted by the symbol $\otimes$) of confidentiality losses for each data asset o_i that is subject to an attack A. The actual function will depend on the properties of the data assets in question and stakeholder's take on them.

$$CL(Y, A, R, t) = \otimes_i CL(o_i, A, R, t) \tag{1}$$

Similarly, *integrity loss* (*IL*) of a data asset from an attack by time t is a risk metric that characterises the effect from the potential alteration of the affected data asset. The notion is analogously extended to the system level. In the rest of this paper, we focus on confidentiality and integrity losses (*CL* and *IL*) for a single asset. Note that the definitions of confidentiality and integrity losses can be extended to the case when several attacks are present. However, for the sake of simplicity, we consider the case of one attack in this paper.

3.2 Basic Terms: Domain, Attack, and System

A domain is a notion that creates a common ground for system engineers and security experts. It is a broad concept in domain-specific modelling that includes many aspects. However, in this work, we say that a security expert and a system engineer work in the same application domain when they refer to a common set of components and objects while modelling respectively a system and attacks.

Definition 1. *A domain M is a tuple[2] (C, O) where C is a set of components and O is a set of data objects accessible in an application area. A set of assets is a subset of O, i.e. Assets $\subseteq O$.*

Attack modelling is a technique to capture behaviour of attacks. It can be formalised with attack trees or graphs. The basic elements of attack trees and graphs are attack steps and relations on them. Trees, additionally, have special elements such as gates, which are logical operations applied on attack steps (e.g.

---

[2] We use the term "tuple" as a finite ordered list (a sequence) of elements. Each element is addressed by its name in this paper.

AND and OR), and root, which represents the goal of an attack. Thus, attack trees resemble fault and event trees in other dependability analyses. An alternative language for modelling attacks is (classes of) Petri Nets. Quantitative time aspects of attack models can be captured by assigning a probability distribution of execution time to attack steps. In our work, we use the term *basic attack model* (which is neutral w.r.t. above languages) that captures the basic elements of an attack model needed for our analysis.

Definition 2. *A basic attack model is a tuple (AS, AR, l_{AS}) where: AS is a finite set of attack steps; $AR \subseteq AS \times AS$ is a relation between attack steps; and $l_{AS} : AS \to \mathcal{F}$ is a labelling function that associates execution time distributions from the set $\mathcal{F}$ to attack steps (AS).*

We extend this basic definition of an attack model with the *attack step annotation* concept. It enriches the definition of a basic attack model with *what, where,* and *how* information: *what* assets are targeted; *where* in a system (i.e. on which parts of a system platform); and *how* these assets are compromised, meaning which security attributes are violated.

Definition 3. *An attack step annotation is a tuple (TA, TC, AV) where: $TA \in 2^O$ is a set of targeted assets; $TC \in 2^C$ is a set of targeted components; $AV \in 2^{Attr}$ is a set of security attributes violated by the attack step where $Attr = \{Cnf, Int, Avl\}$. We denote a set of such annotations by N and we refer to each element x of the attack step annotation as by as.x (e.g. as. TA).*

For example, if an attack step reads message $m \in O$ from a network component $link \in C$ then an annotation for this step is $(\{m\}, \{link\}, \{Cnf\})$; if an attack step only connects to some $link$ then its annotation is $(\emptyset, \{link\}, \emptyset)$. These annotations allow relating an attack model to relevant elements of a system model. This enables combining attack models with system models. A basic attack model enriched with annotations is called an *annotated attack model*.

Definition 4. *An annotated attack model A is a tuple (AS, AR, l_{AS}, l_N) where (AS, AR, l_{AS}) is a basic attack model and $l_N : AS \to N$ is a labelling function that assigns an annotation to each attack step.*

For our analysis, we need to capture three aspects of a system: its functionality, execution platform and allocation information, and data object dependencies. These aspects are represented by *state model* and *data model*.

Definition 5. *A state model SM of a system is a tuple (S, s_0, P, H, l_O, l_S) where:*

- *S is the set of system states related to each other by a set of transitions;*
- *s_0 is the initial state;*
- *$P : S \times S \to [0, 1]$ associates a probability with a transition;*
- *$H : S \to \mathcal{F}$ associates a probability distribution with a state;*

- $l_O : S \rightarrow 2^O$ is a labelling function that associates a set of objects from domain M with each state;
- $l_C : S \rightarrow 2^C$ is a labelling function that associates a set of components from domain M with each state.

A state in S can be seen as a basic element of behaviour (e.g. an action) of a system. P and H formalise the probability of moving from one state to another and the probabilistic measure of execution time of each system state respectively. Thus, the first four elements of our state model form a semi-Markov chain [12] (SMC). The latter two elements extend a SMC with additional information that is utilised to automatically combine system and attack models. Function l_O allows capturing the information about data objects which exist at a certain state. Function l_C associates the states with components of an execution platform.

Definition 6. *A data model DM of a system is a tuple (D, l_D) where: $D \subseteq O \times O$ is a relation that captures immediate object dependency; $l_D : D \rightarrow 2^S \setminus \emptyset$ is a labelling function that associates a set of states from S with each tuple in D.*

The relation D represents dependencies between data objects in a system. In particular, $(o_i, o_j) \in D$ means that an asset o_j depends on an asset o_i, e.g. $o_j = f(o_i)$ where f is some function. In this paper, we omit the nature and strength of such dependencies, but this information can also be used. Function l_D captures at which system state the dependencies in D occur. Thus, if $l_D(o_i, o_j)$ returns state $\{s\}$ then it means that o_j is derived from o_i in s. Implicitly, a well-formed data model associates a non-empty state set to every element in D.

Finally, a system model is a combination of state and data models.

Definition 7. *A system model Y is a tuple (SM, DM) where SM is a state model and DM is a data model.*

Table 1 summarises the notation and terms used in this paper.

3.3 Metrics and Their Derivation

Confidentiality loss *(CL)* caused by an attack A to each valuable data asset o by time t is a product of the likelihood that A would disclose o by t, and the cost of this disclosure to stakeholder R. In our context, the likelihood is a probability.

$$CL(o, A, Y, R, t) = p(o, A, Y, t)\, cost(o, R) \qquad (2)$$

In Eq. (2), the cost of an asset, $cost(o, R)$, is a subjective estimate expressed by a stakeholder. In general case, the cost can also be time-dependent, but in this work we assume that it is time-agnostic. In turn, probability of a disclosure, $p(o, A, Y, t)$, can be broken down into a product of two events: (E_1) an attack A is in a step that can disclose o by time t; and (E_2) an asset o actually exists in system Y when it is attacked by time t.

$$p(o, A, Y, t) = p(E_1(o, A), t)\, p(E_2(o, Y), t) \qquad (3)$$

Table 1. Summary of the used notation

Sets and subsets	
C – components	AV – security **attributes violated**
O – objects	N – attack step annotations
$Assets$ – assets, $Assets \subseteq O$	S – system states
$\mathcal{F}$ – probability distributions	$\Omega_{o,o'}$ – all state sequences between o' and o
AS – attack steps	$S_{\langle o \rangle}$ – system states where object o exists
TA – targeted **assets**	C_{target} – system components targeted by an attack
TC – **targeted components**	$AS_{\langle Cnf,o \rangle}$ – attack steps violating confidentiality of an object o

Functions, dependencies and relations
l_{AS} – assigns execution time probability distributions to attack steps, $l_{AS} : AS \rightarrow \mathcal{F}$
l_N – assigns an annotation to an attack step, $l_{ASN} : AS \rightarrow \text{ASN}$
P – associates a probability with a transition, $P : S \times S \rightarrow [0,1]$
D – a dependency relation between data objects, $D \subseteq O \times O$
l_D – associates a set of system states with a data dependency, $l_D : D \rightarrow 2^S$
H – associates a probability distribution of execution time with a state, $H : S \rightarrow \mathcal{F}$
l_O – associates a set of existing objects with a state, $l_O : S \rightarrow 2^O$
l_C – associates a set of components with a system state, $l_C : S \rightarrow 2^C$
AR – a relation between attack steps, $AR \subseteq AS \times AS$
$cost$ – a cost of asset disclosure or alternation expressed by a stakeholder
κ – a function that checks whether there is a transitive dependency between two objects

Tuples	
$SM = (S, s_0, P, H, l_O, l_C)$ – a state model	$M = (C, O)$ – an application domain
$DM = (D, l_D)$ – a data model	$Y = (SM, DM)$ – a system model
$A = (AS, AR, l_{AS}, l_{ASN})$ – an annotated attack model	

Other		
R – a stakeholder	PE – propagation effect	ω – sequence of states
CL – confidentiality loss	DE – direct effect	γ – sequence of data objects
IL – integrity loss	ϕ – interval transition probability	

In other words, the E_1 event accounts for a subset of attack steps $AS_{\langle Cnf,o \rangle} \subseteq AS$ that compromise an asset o and violate its confidentiality; and the E_2 event accounts for a subset of system states $S_{\langle o \rangle} \subseteq S$ that are associated with asset o. Additionally, the attack steps from $AS_{\langle Cnf,o \rangle}$ should target a set of components that are used for allocation of system states from $S_{\langle o \rangle}$. This simply means that, for the attack to be successful, a system should have components with certain targeted vulnerabilities exploited by the attack steps from $AS_{\langle Cnf,o \rangle}$. We refer to this subset of targeted components as C_{target}.

Given a set of states S and a set of attack steps AS of an attack A, we define a set of targeted components (C_{target}), a set of attack steps disclosing an object o ($AS_{\langle Cnf,o \rangle}$), and a set of states where an object o is potentially compromised ($S_{\langle o \rangle}$):

$$C_{target} \qquad = \{c \mid s \in S, as \in AS, c \in l_C(s) \cap as.TC\} \qquad (4)$$

$$AS_{\langle Cnf,o \rangle} = \{as \mid as \in AS, as.TC \cap C_{target} \neq \emptyset, o \in as.TA, Cnf \in as.AV\} \qquad (5)$$

$$S_{\langle o \rangle} = \{s \mid s \in S, l_C(s) \cap C_{target} \neq \emptyset, o \in l_O(s)\} \tag{6}$$

To put it another way, execution of any attack step in $AS_{\langle Cnf,o \rangle}$ leads to disclosure of a given object o, which is essentially the E_1 event. This corresponds to construction of an attack tree with attack steps from $AS_{\langle Cnf,o \rangle}$ which are all connected by the OR gate. This is expressed in Eq. (7).

$$p(E_1(o, A), t) = 1 - \prod_{as \in AS_{\langle Cnf,o \rangle}} \left(1 - p(as, t)\right) \tag{7}$$

Finally, the probability of E_2 is the sum of probabilities that the system Y will transit to each state from $S_{\langle o \rangle}$ where asset o exists. Thus,

$$p(E_2(o, Y), t) = \sum_{s \in S_{\langle o \rangle}} \phi(s_0, s, t) \tag{8}$$

In Eq. (7), $p(as, t)$ is a probability of success of an attack step as by time t. It is returned by l_{AS} given t that is, in turn, calculated from a selected modelling formalism for attack step relations (e.g. attack trees or graphs). In Eq. (8), $\phi(s_0, s, t)$ is a so-called interval transition probability of the system Y transiting from a state s_0 to a state s in interval $(0, t)$ [12]. It is calculated from the system equation that describes the dynamics of an underlying SMC.

Integrity loss (IL) is a metric that defines the risk of alterations to an asset o, and should account for two aspects: the *direct effect* (DE) – the loss caused by the direct influence of an attack A on asset o; and the *propagation effect* (PE) – the loss caused by spreading corrupted data and further contaminating the computations dependent on asset o.

$$IL(o, A, Y, R, t) = DE(o, A, Y, R, t) + PE(o, A, Y, R, t) \tag{9}$$

The reason to include the propagation effect in the IL metric, but not in the CL metric can be explained with the following rationale. Whether a breach of confidentiality will propagate depends on specific attack capabilities, i.e. if an attack is capable of learning additional data when it has observed a part of it. This learning is a self-contained attack step and should be explicitly included in an attack model. For example, the sole fact that an attack compromises an encryption key does not directly imply that all data encrypted by this key is compromised; it is compromised if an attack actually reads this data. In contrast, a breach of integrity propagates independently from an attack, but it depends on the system behaviour. For example, if a public key is modified, then data signed by this key can not be decrypted if the decryption state is part of a system.

The direct effect DE is calculated in analogy to CL, where $AS_{\langle Int,o \rangle}$ is defined by Eq. 5 and $Int \in as.AV$ replaces $Cnf \in as.AV$.

The intuition for the propagation effect is as follows: if an object $o' \in O$ is computed in a state $s' \in S$ based on an object o that has already been corrupted in a state $s \in S_{\langle o \rangle}$ then o' is also considered corrupted. To derive this effect PE with respect to each such object o' we consider the four aspects described below.

First, we need to check whether o' immediately or transitively depends on o. The immediate dependency is already captured in the data model DM by $(o, o') \in D$. We say that transitive dependency exists, if it is possible to construct such a sequence of objects γ of length n that $\gamma = (\gamma_k \mid \gamma_1 = o, \gamma_n = o', 1 \leq k < n : (\gamma_k, \gamma_{k+1}) \in D)$. We formalise this test as a function $\kappa : O \times O \to \{0, 1\}$ that returns 1 if such a sequence γ exists, otherwise it returns 0.

The next two elements are the cost of o' as expressed by a stakeholder R and the probability that o will be actually attacked by time $\tau \leq t$.

Finally, the propagation effect occurs only when the system Y will transit from a state $s \in S_{(o)}$ to a state s' where o' is computed from o immediately or transitively. Such a state s' can be returned by the labelling function l_D, if immediate dependency between o and o' exists. However, if an immediate dependency does not exist, but a transitive dependency exists then we need to consider a sequence of states ω (of length $n - 1$) along which the transitive dependency, captured by a sequence of objects γ, occurs. We construct ω in such a way that $\omega = (\omega_k \mid 1 \leq k < n - 1 : \omega_k \in l_D((\gamma_k, \gamma_{k+1})))$. Since there can be several valid sequences of states relating o and o', we denote by $\Omega_{o,o'}$ the set of such state sequences. In other words, $\Omega_{o,o'}$ is the set of all state sequences along which o' can be compromised when o is attacked.

The propagation effect given the four elements above is calculated as follows:

$$PE(o, A, Y, R, t) = \sum_{o' \in O} \kappa(o, o') \, cost(o', R) \sum_{s \in S_{(o)}} p(E_1(o, A), \tau) \sum_{\omega \in \Omega_{o,o'}} P(s_0, s, \omega, t) \tag{10}$$

In Eq. (10), $P(s_0, s, \omega, t)$ is the interval transition probability that the system that starts at s_0 will first pass the state s (where asset o is attacked by A), and then will go through each state from (any possible) sequence ω. This probability can be computed recursively as follows:

$$P(s_0, s, \omega, t) = \phi(s_0, s, \tau) \, P(s, \omega_1, \omega_{[2..]}, t - \tau) \tag{11}$$

We denote by ω_1 the first element of the sequence ω and by $\omega_{[2..]}$ a suffix of this sequence starting from the 2nd element. The validity of Eq. (11) can be proven by induction (omitted due to space restrictions).

4   An Illustrative Example

In this section we apply our methodology on an open platform device developed based on the design from the European project SecFutur [2], where a Trusted Sensor Network (TSN) was a case study. We illustrate how confidentiality and integrity losses capture the security risks associated with data assets.

The TSN consists of a set of meters, servers, and a communication infrastructure. TSN collects measurements of energy consumption at households for billing purposes. This infrastructure has a range of diverse security considerations and data assets: measurements, user account data, a set of certificates, commands,

Table 2. Stakeholder costs expressed for measurements

	User	Utility provider	National regulatory agency
Confidentiality	Major	Minor	Insignificant
Integrity	Moderate	Major	Minor

etc. Here we study a *metering device* and, for simplicity, we focus on *measurements* as an asset under analysis.

We consider three stakeholders: user, utility provider, and national regulatory agency. The stakeholder costs of losing confidentiality or integrity for measurements are shown in Table 2. We adopt a common linguistic scale [15] {*insignificant, minor, moderate, major, catastrophic*} to encode these costs, which we further map to a numerical vector $\{0, 0.1, 0.5, 0.8, 1\}$. Note that we use this simplified numerical scale only for exemplification. In practice, one can use intervals or even continuous scales, as our methodology does not impose specific requirements on the form of the scale.

4.1 System and Attack Modelling

Figure 1(a) depicts a system model for a metering device from the TSN scenario. The system expects a command (*cmd*) from an administrator of a utility company. On receipt, it proceeds to registration, configuration, or calibration procedures. When the device is calibrated it starts collecting data (*raw_msr*), processing it into ready measurements (*msr*), writing them into the memory and creating a unique id (*id_msr*), sending them to the server, and waiting for an acknowledgement (*ack*). If *ack* has not arrived a meter continues to collect measurements; otherwise, it proceeds to the verification procedure. If verification succeeds the device searches for the measurement by id (*id_msr*), deletes this measurement from storage, and waits for the next command from the server. If verification fails, the device reads the measurement from storage and resends it.

Construction of state and data models (introduced in Sect. 3.2) can be accomplished by traversing and transforming control and data flows of the UML activity model. UML activity diagrams can be directly transformed into a state model [17]. Alternatively, UML activities can be first transformed into some variant of Stochastic Petri Nets (SPNs) [8]. They offer easier translation from UML activity diagrams and also provide great capabilities such as dealing with concurrency and various forms of dependency. These variants of SPNs can be further used to generate Markov and none-Markov models, i.e. SMC in our case. For the purpose of this illustration we directly move on to the state model and omit intermediate steps. A data model can be obtained by traversing the UML activity and utilising its built-in data flows. Note that we use the UML activity as an example. Our approach is not limited to this choice.

Figure 1(b) depicts the state model (*SM*). The numbers on arcs are probabilities of the transitions (*P*) and the numbers on states are mean state execution

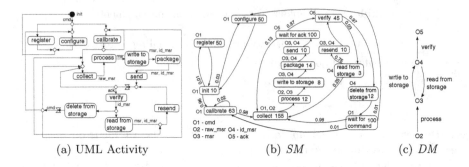

(a) UML Activity   (b) SM   (c) DM

Fig. 1. Illustration of the formalised system model for the metering device

times from normal distributions (H). To obtain this data, design phase estimation methods outlined in Sect. 2 exist, but we employ prototyping as a viable alternative. The object references next to each state correspond to the labelling function l_O. Our metering device model includes a simplified execution platform built of two components: a *link* and a *device*. The *link* is a communication network, and the *device* is the basic meter. The *init, package, send, wait for acknowledgement, resend,* and *wait for command* states are allocated on the *link*, and the rest of the states are executed on the *device*. This corresponds to the labelling function l_C. Figure 1(c) depicts the data model (DM), where the labels on dependency arcs are names of corresponding states from the state model (SM). This corresponds to the labelling function l_D.

Privacy and integrity of measurements are two serious concerns for smart meters [13]. Privacy can be violated by eavesdropping energy consumption measurements passed over the communication network. Integrity of measurements can be broken by spoofing the original data sent by a meter. Here we consider these two types of attack. Respective annotated attack models in the form of attack graphs are depicted in Figs. 2(a) and (b). To eavesdrop an attacker should intercept the data packets (pkt) sent over the network $(link)$, i.e. to sniff, filter and decode them. To perform a spoof attack the data packets should also be intercepted and then inserted back into the network in a modified form.

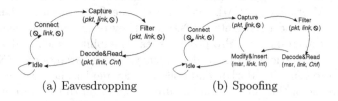

(a) Eavesdropping   (b) Spoofing

Fig. 2. Two attacks against measurements

In addition to annotations, each attack step is associated with a probability distribution (the labelling function l_{AS}). Arnold et al. [6] discuss two alternative approaches to obtain such distributions: (1) based on historical or empirical data; and (2) based on expert opinions. For our illustrative example, we employ the former approach by running experiments with the constructed prototype. We use kernel density estimations [10] to obtain the needed distribution functions.

4.2 Calculating Metrics

A combination of the attack and system models gives the following sets of compromising attack steps and system states (from Eqs. (4)–(6)): $AS_{\langle Cnf,msr \rangle} = \{Decode\&Read\}$, $AS_{\langle Int,msr \rangle} = \{Modify\&Insert\}$, and $S_{\langle msr \rangle} = \{package, send, resend\}$.

In this section we show only the values observed when confidentiality (CL) and integrity losses (IL) stabilise. In reality the risks can still change over time, which is also the case in our illustrative example, but for brevity we do not show the whole trend since the risks stabilise relatively fast.

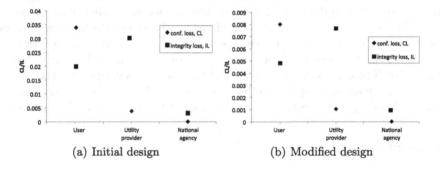

(a) Initial design   (b) Modified design

Fig. 3. CL and IL in the initial design and after mitigation by modification

Figure 3(a) shows that confidentiality loss for the user is about 9 times higher than for the utility provider (0.035 against 0.004), integrity loss is highest for the utility provider (0.031), and the national agency bears the lowest risk both in terms of confidentiality and integrity losses. It should be mentioned that due to a narrowed down set of considered assets (i.e. measurements only) in our example, stakeholder-wise comparison of the confidentiality and integrity loss metrics is not as informative as it could be in a general case with multiple assets. However, what our example demonstrates distinctly is how the proposed metrics reflect reduction of risks when mitigation measures are applied. That, in turn, indicates how each stakeholder benefits when the initial design is modified for strengthening its security aspects [22].

Now, we illustrate how a modification of a design can act as a mitigation against the two attacks. We modify the state "collect", so that the system in Fig. 1 sends measurements in chunks of 10 readings. By this, the mean execution time of this state is changed from 155 to 1550 ms. Figure 3(b) shows results for an improved system, and we observe a significant drop in original risks. In particular, confidentiality loss for the user and utility provider drops down by a factor 4 in comparison with the risks derived from the initial design. Similarly, a significant drop is observed for integrity loss, i.e. *IL* for all stakeholders is 3–4 times lower than in the original design.

Once the risks for the stakeholders are calculated as confidentiality and integrity losses, they should be assessed. This is an extensive decision problem that typically involves other criteria (e.g. resource footprint of countermeasures, quality of service requirements, etc.). The following steps in risk assessment are out of the scope of this paper and are treated elsewhere.

5   Conclusion and Future Work

In this paper we formalised confidentiality and integrity losses as two probabilistic metrics that quantify risks associated with data assets within embedded systems. Our proposed metrics account for system design, attack scenarios, and different stakeholder preferences regarding data assets. We applied the metrics on a smart metering device and showed their use for visualising of and reasoning about security risks. In addition, we illustrated how our methodology allows analysing the impact of design decisions on the risks in question, demonstrating their potential to increase security awareness of engineers within early design stages. For future work, we aim to extend the tool set developed for the SEED process [22] by integrating this methodology, and enable trading off risks against other criteria, e.g. resources efficiency, when selecting suitable security measures.

References

1. CCTA Risk Analysis and Management Method. www.cramm.com, October 2013
2. The SecFutur project: Design of Secure and Energy-efficient Embedded Systems for Future Internet Application. http://www.secfutur.eu
3. IEC/ISO 31010 - Risk Management - Risk Assessment Techniques (2009)
4. DHS Risk Lexicon. Technical report, DHS Risk Steering Committee (2010)
5. Almasizadeh, J., Azgomi, M.A.: A stochastic model of attack process for the evaluation of security metrics. J. Compt. Networks **57**(10), 2159–2180 (2013). (Elsevier)
6. Arnold, F., Hermanns, H., Pulungan, R., Stoelinga, M.: Time-dependent analysis of attacks. In: Abadi, M., Kremer, S. (eds.) POST 2014 (ETAPS 2014). LNCS, vol. 8414, pp. 285–305. Springer, Heidelberg (2014)
7. Bilge, L., Dumitras, T.: Before we knew it: an empirical study of zero-day attacks in the real world. In: ACM Conference on Computer and Communications Security (2012)
8. Ciardo, G., German, R., Lindemann, C.: A characterization of the stochastic process underlying a stochastic Petri net. IEEE Trans. Softw. Eng. **20**(7), 506–515 (1994)
9. Flammini, F., Marrone, S., Mazzocca, N., Vittorini, V.: Petri net modelling of physical vulnerability. In: Bologna, S., Hämmerli, B., Gritzalis, D., Wolthusen, S. (eds.) CRITIS 2011. LNCS, vol. 6983, pp. 128–139. Springer, Heidelberg (2013)
10. Hastie, T., Tibshirani, R., Friedman, J.: The Elements of Statistical Learning: Data Mining, Inference, and Prediction. Springer, New York (2009)

11. Herrera, F., Posadas, H., Peñil, P., Villar, E., Ferrero, F., Valencia, R., Palermo, G.: The COMPLEX methodology for UML/MARTE modeling and sesign space exploration of embedded systems. J. Syst. Archit. **60**(1), 55–78 (2014). (Elsevier)
12. Howard, R.A.: Dynamic Probabilistic Systems. Wiley, New York (1971)
13. Jobst, M.E.: Security and privacy in the smart energy grid. In: Smart Grid Security Workshop at CSS. ACM (2014)
14. Kordy, B., Piètre-Cambacédès, L., Schweitzer, P.: DAG-based attack and defense modeling: don't miss the forest for the attack trees. Comput. Sci. Rev. **13–14**, 1–38 (2014). (Elsevier)
15. Lund, M.S., Solhaug, B., Stølen, K.: Model-Driven Risk Analysis: The CORAS Approach. Springer, Heidelberg (2010)
16. Madan, B.B., Goševa-Popstojanova, K., Vaidyanathan, K., Trivedi, K.S.: A method for modeling and quantifying the security attributes of intrusion tolerant systems. Perform. Eval. **56**(1–4), 167–186 (2004). (Elsevier)
17. Ouchani, S., Mohamed, O., Debbabi, M.: A formal verification framework for SysML activity diagrams. J. Expert Syst. Appl. **41**(6), 2713–2728 (2014)
18. Parsons, S.: Current approaches to handling imperfect information in data and knowledge bases. IEEE Trans. Knowl. Data Eng. **8**(3), 353–372 (1996)
19. Sommestad, T., Ekstedt, M., Johnson, P.: A probabilistic relational model for security risk analysis. Comput. Secur. **29**(6), 659–679 (2010). (Elsevier)
20. Stoneburner, G., Goguen, A.Y., Feringa, A.: SP 800–30. Risk Management Guide for Information Technology Systems. In: NIST (2002)
21. Vasilevskaya, M., Gunawan, L.A., Nadjm-Tehrani, S., Herrmann, P.: Integrating security mechanisms into embedded systems by domain-specific modelling. J. Secur. Commun. Networks **7**(12), 2815–2832 (2013). (Wiley)
22. Vasilevskaya, M., Nadjm-Tehrani, S.: Model-based security risk analysis for networked embedded systems. In: Conference on Critical Information Infrastructures Security. Springer (2014)
23. Verendel, V.: Quantified security is a weak hypothesis: a critical survey of results and assumptions. In: New Security Paradigms Workshop. ACM (2009)
24. Weiss, J.: A system security engineering process. In: National Computer Security Conference. National Institute of Standards and Technology/National Computer Security Center, pp. 572–581 (1991)

ISA²R: Improving Software Attack and Analysis Resilience via Compiler-Level Software Diversity

Rafael Fedler, Sebastian Banescu ^(✉), and Alexander Pretschner

Technische Universität München, Boltzmannstr. 3, 85748
Garching Bei München, Germany
{fedler,banescu,pretschn}@cs.tum.edu

Abstract. The current IT landscape is characterized by *software mono-culture*: All installations of one program version are identical. This leads to a huge return of investment for attackers who can develop a single attack once to compromise millions of hosts worldwide. Software diversity has been proposed as an alternative to software monoculture. In this paper we present a collection of diversification transformations called ISA²R, developed for the low-level virtual machine (LLVM). By diversifying the properties crucial to successful exploitation of a vulnerability, we render exploits that work on one installation of a software ineffective against others. Through this we enable developers to add protective measures automatically during compilation. In contrast to similar existing tools, ISA²R provides protection against a wider range of attacks and is applicable to all programming languages supported by LLVM.

Keywords: Software diversity · Software protection · Code obfuscation

1 Introduction

Security can be considered a matter of economics: If the effort or investment required to develop and deploy an attack surpass its promised yields, the attack will not be carried out [11], which holds for all attackers that act rationally in the economical sense. This notion is especially useful as the modern attacker model is increasingly characterized by financial motivation, e.g. monetization of compromised hosts' resources, or indirect economical and political intentions.

Nowadays, malicious adversaries can reverse engineer a program and develop an exploit or patch for it once, then successfully launch it against potentially hundreds of millions of systems, e.g. in the case of widespread vulnerable target software such as browsers, Adobe Reader and Flash Player, or Oracle's Java Runtime Environment, which can be found on almost all private and many commercial computer systems. Thus, by only developing one exploit, millions of systems can be compromised by the attacker. This leads to a big return of investment for many attackers, e.g. exploit developers, software crackers, malware authors and buyers [1]. If the incentive for attack development is lowered, many attacks might not be developed in the first place.

© Springer International Publishing Switzerland 2015
F. Koornneef and C. van Gulijk (Eds.): SAFECOMP 2015, LNCS 9337, pp. 362–371, 2015.
DOI: 10.1007/978-3-319-24255-2_26

Contributions: In this paper, we present ISA^{2}R, short for *Improving Software Attack and Analysis Resilience*, a collection of diversification transformations for the LLVM compiler infrastructure. ISA^{2}R currently includes 12 transformations diversifying both the process memory layout and executable code of program being compiled. ISA^{2}R generates different program code in each compilation run, which has the same input-output behavior as its input program code. The output programs automatically gain protection against exploits with different aims than availability (e.g., code execution). After transformation, an exploit developed to work on one instance of this program will fail with high likelihood and at most cause an availability issue by making other instances crash. However, the exploit does not achieve its original goal of compromising confidentiality or integrity of the program, e.g. injected code execution. Unlike previous similar work, ISA^{2}R offers protection against a broad range of attacks and supports all programming languages which have an LLVM front-end: C/C++, Java bytecode, C#, Python, Ruby, Objective-C, Go, Swift, Fortran, ActionScript, etc.

This paper is organized as follows: Sect. 2, presents related work. Section 3 describes the transformations offered by ISA^{2}R. Section 4 covers the evaluation of ISA^{2}R. Conclusions and future work ideas are presented in Sect. 5.

2   Related Work

Software diversity as a concept to increase fault tolerance has been an active research area since the 1970s [10]. Software diversity for security purposes, however, has gained momentum only rather recently [2,5]. *Obfuscator-LLVM*[1] is a tool similar to ISA^{2}R. However, *Obfuscator-LLVM*'s 3 transformations aim to protect intellectual property (IP) against *manual reverse engineering*, while ISA^{2}R offers 12 transformations hampering *automatic reverse engineering*, a pre-requisite for developing effective buffer overflow and code patching exploits. Nevertheless, the transformations of these two tools can be merged into one tool since they both operate on LLVM code. *Sandmark*[2] and *Tigress*[3] are two obfuscation and diversification tools. They offer transformations similar to those of ISA^{2}R. However, they are applicable to Java, respectively C source code whereas ISA^{2}R supports all languages with an LLVM front-end. These tools that leverage software diversity concepts in order to increase security have the following drawbacks: Some are limited to specific program languages, while others are limited with regard to attacks they defend against (e.g. reverse engineering, buffer overflow exploits). With ISA^{2}R, we provide one single tool (for all languages supported by LLVM), which offers protection against most attacks aiming to compromise a large user-base of an application by reusing the same attack, and which can be extended to satisfy a wide range of security-enhancing transformation needs.

---

[1] https://github.com/obfuscator-llvm/obfuscator.
[2] http://sandmark.cs.arizona.edu/.
[3] http://tigress.cs.arizona.edu/.

3   Implemented Transformations

This section presents all ISA^{2}R transformations, which provide protection against each attack category from the taxonomy of Larsen *et al.* [9], i.e.: information leaks, reverse engineering, memory corruption, code injection, code reuse, program tampering. We make ISA^{2}R available to anyone from academia and industry upon request. Most can be controlled by a set of parameters, which we do not describe in detail for the sake of brevity, however, they are described in ISA^{2}R's user manual. One of these parameters is called the transformation probability and specifies the likelihood that a potential target function will be transformed.

Instruction Reordering: By determining the happened-before relation on code and thus the temporal dependencies of instructions, one also determines which statements are independent of each other and can thus be randomized in regards to their execution order. This transformation was created to help against code reuse attacks, as it diversifies the location of instructions relative to the base address of the program similar to Instruction Location Randomization (ILR) [6].

Insertion of Loops with Randomized Iteration Count: This transformation inserts loops into conditional branches (`if/else` statements as well as loop entry/exit conditions). These loops calculate the Collatz series, which, until it converges, greatly varies in the number of iterations until convergence depending on its input character. This transformation is intended to automatically counter timing and, to some extent, power side channel attacks [7,8].

Opaque Predicate Insertion: Opaque predicates are logical predicates whose evaluation is known a priori to the party performing the transformation, but whose evaluation is hard to perform statically [4]. In some cases, as in well implemented pointer arithmetic-based opaque predicates, evaluation may be close to practically infeasible. They can be used to obscure control flow. Often, opaque predicates are used to strengthen other transformations.

Insertion of Bogus Code: This transformation inserts random instructions which do not interfere with the original instructions of a method. It is protected against static analysis using opaque predicates in the condition of `if/else`-statements that either lead to correct instructions or to incorrect ones. This transformation obfuscates the logic of a method, which make reverse engineering harder. However, the added instructions also influence the location of pre-existing program instructions, having a positive effect against code reuse attacks.

Stack Frame Size Diversification: This transformation adds an odd random number of bytes to each stack frame of a binary, being a more fine-grained version of ASLR. This makes buffer overflow exploits applicable to only a fraction of binary instances of a program. Therefore, if the attacker uses the same code injection exploit code that writes a fixed number of bytes to the vulnerable buffer on a diversified program instance, it overwrites the stack pointer (ESP) and the return address (EIP) on the stack with values which will very likely lead to a crash, not achieving the attacker's goal of capturing the control flow of the program. This happens because the offset of ESP and EIP will vary for each diversified binary instance.

Stack Variable Order Randomization: The order of the variables on the stack are randomized, in order to diversify the distance from a vulnerable buffer to important target values such as the copies of ESP and EIP on the stack. This decreases the applicability of a buffer overflow exploit which assumes a fixed variable layout. Additionally, this transformations places all buffers/arrays above all non-buffer variables on the stack, to prevent pointers or variables (used in branch-condition evaluation), from being overwritten if a buffer overflow occurs.

Addition of Bogus Method Arguments: This transformation inserts random arguments in method definitions, removing part of the logical abstractions of the program. The bogus arguments are used by bogus code added to the corresponding method and are finally secured with opaque predicates which make it seem as though the bogus argument actually contributes to the return value.

Method Merging: This transformation breaks the abstraction created by developers (i.e. methods) by merging two unconnected methods into one. The only requirement is that the return type of the two methods is identical. An additional selection parameter is appended to the argument list and all call sites are adjusted accordingly. This makes reverse engineering harder, but also diversifies the location of instructions relative to the base address of the program, breaking certain code reuse exploits.

Shuffling of Method Arguments: This transformation randomly permutes the arguments of a method. It is very useful in combination with the method merging transformation, as it always appends an additional indicator variable to determine which of the contained methods should be executed in the merged version.

Method Cloning: To confuse an adversary, methods are cloned and some – but not all – call sites are adjusted to call the clone. It is advisable to run transformations which diversify the code in order to protect the clone from being identified as a clone of another method.

Randomization of Symbolic Method Names: Symbolic method names provide a reverse engineer with useful information about the functionality of a method. They must sometimes be retained in programs and often so in libraries for linking. This transformation assigns random names to methods and provides a textual mapping to assist in automatic name adjustment.

Proceduralization of Static Data: This transformation removes static buffers in a program, which are never written to. For each of them it creates (1) a key and (2) a keyed generator function. At runtime, before each access to such a buffer, the generator function using the correct key recreates the buffer dynamically. Generator function and key can be protected using other transformations such as bogus code insertion. This transformation protects static data such as passwords, host names, etc. from extraction through static analysis attacks – in order to see such data, the adversary must perform dynamic analysis.

4   Preliminary Evaluation

In order to evaluate the ISA²R collection of transformations described in Sect. 3, we want to answer two questions: (1) Are ISA²R's transformations practical to use, or is the impact on binary file size, runtime performance, or compilation process duration too costly to justify the benefits (if any)? and (2) Are

ISA^{2}R's transformations effective at achieving the formulated goal of diversifying a program such that attacks are not applicable on all instances of that program due to the introduced diversity? We performed a preliminary evaluation to start answering these questions. This includes an efficiency and effectiveness evaluation, detailed in the following. As test compilation targets we used the well-known ls utility from the GNU core utilities (version 8.23) and our own implementation of the Sieve of Eratosthenes, as they cover very different code profiles. ls was chosen as a non-trivial application (over 3000 lines of C code), which is I/O- and user-interaction centric, with lots of branching and special case treatment. Though lacking a GUI, it is comparable to end-user productivity and web software. As such, we used ls to determine compilation time and binary file size overhead. The Sieve of Eratosthenes was selected as our implementation is CPU intensive and heavy on memory operations without any blocking or other interruptions. It represents software with high CPU performance needs and thus was used to measure runtime overhead of ISA^{2}R's transformations.

4.1 Efficiency

Compilation Time: When compared to GCC, the ISA^{2}R transformations each added about 20 to 30 % compilation time overhead on average.Comparing to a pure LLVM build, which is significantly faster than a pure GCC build, the median relative overhead was 16 % higher. The overhead for all single transformations can be found in Table 1. Significant penalties occur when chaining multiple transformations, as the effect stacks. If all transformations are performed, compilation time increases by more than 200 %. We assume, however, that optimizing the implementation of ISA^{2}R can lead to a 50 % reduction of the compilation overhead through caching results of currently redundant calls.

Table 1. Median ($n = 500$) increase in build time, binary size by single transformations

Transformation	ls build-time relative increase		ls binary file size relative increase				
	GCC	LLVM	O0	O1	O2	O3	Os
AddBogusArguments	30.7 %	48.4 %	0.27 %	0.27 %	0.02 %	0.25 %	0.02 %
CloneFunctions	33.3 %	52.6 %	2.75 %	2.49 %	2.06 %	2.05 %	1.56 %
InsertBogusCode	20.5 %	32.4 %	0.27 %	0.00 %	0.25 %	0.25 %	0.02 %
InsertRandomLoops	81.0 %	127.9 %	7.49 %	3.76 %	4.54 %	4.82 %	2.40 %
MergeMethods	29.7 %	46.8 %	2.00 %	0.60 %	0.30 %	0.03 %	0.91 %
OpaquePredicateGenerator	32.8 %	51.8 %	0.80 %	0.00 %	0.25 %	0.02 %	0.02 %
ReorderInstructions	23.3 %	36.8 %	0.00 %	0.00 %	0.25 %	0.02 %	0.02 %
ScrambleFunctionNames	16.7 %	26.3 %	0.13 %	0.41 %	0.31 %	0.31 %	0.06 %
ShuffleArguments	25.0 %	39.5 %	0.00 %	0.28 %	0.37 %	0.65 %	0.30 %
StackOrderDiversify	17.3 %	27.4 %	0.00 %	0.00 %	0.25 %	0.02 %	0.02 %
StackSizeDiversify	17.2 %	27.1 %	0.00 %	0.00 %	0.00 %	0.00 %	0.00 %
StaticToProceduralData	153.0 %	241.6 %	17.87 %	7.72 %	11.52 %	11.55 %	11.84 %

Binary File Size Overhead: Most transformations did not add significantly to the size of the diversified binary, as can be seen in the right part of Table 1, which presents the median value taken over 500 repeated measurements for each of the follow 5 different optimization levels of LLVM: O0, O1, O2, O3 and Os. Values range from 0 % to a maximum of 17 %, with the average below 5 %.

Runtime Overhead: As stated above, we used an implementation of the Sieve of Eratosthenes which is heavy on memory and CPU processing to measure runtime overhead. The maximum runtime overhead measured was 5 %, except for recursive calls which suffered from a 116 % increase in runtime when the transformation to remove static data and have it recreated dynamically at runtime is applied. All in all, however, runtime penalties where usually below 1 %, except for InsertRandomLoops and StaticToProceduralData, which are affected by recursion in the sieve of Eratosthenes.

4.2 Effectiveness

To demonstrate the effectiveness of ISA^{2}R we chose to design one scenario and corresponding vulnerable program from each attack category in [9]. Figure 1 provides a condensed and simplified version of these programs combined into one. If the user executing this program is the administrator (line 34), then top secret information is printed (lines 35-36). Otherwise, the program takes an input argument which is copied into a statically allocated buffer called `key` (line 32), which is passed as an argument to an ad-hoc string hashing function called `hs()` (lines 14-20), which in turn makes calls to an integer hashing function called `h` (lines 1-12). If the hash of the input argument is equal to a hard-coded constant (line 37) then secret information is displayed to the authenticated user (lines 38-39). To enable a ROP attack [9] the program uses a function that prints a new line in a strange way (lines 21-26). We use this program as a running example for all attack categories presented below, except information leaks described next.

```
 1  unsigned int h(unsigned int v){
 2    uint32_t x = v;
 3    uint32_t y = rotl(v, 8);
 4    uint32_t z = rotl(v, 16);
 5    uint32_t w = rotl(v, 24);
 6
 7    uint32_t t = x ^ (x << 11);
 8    x = y; y = z; z = w;
 9    w ^= (w >> 19) ^ t ^ (t >> 8);
10
11    return w;
12  }
13
14  unsigned int hs(char str[]){
15    int sum = 0;
16    for (int i = 0; i < strlen(str
         ); ++i){
17      sum += h(str[i]);
18    }
19    return sum;
20  }
```

```
21  void strangeWayToPrintNewLine(){
22    const char path[] = "/bin/echo";
23    char *const myArgv[] = {path, NULL};
24    char *const myEnvp[] = {NULL};
25    execve(myArgv[0], myArgv, myEnvp);
26  }
27
28  int main(int argc, char* argv[]){
29    register uid_t uid;
30    char key[20];
31    uid = geteuid();
32    strcpy(key, argv[1]);
33
34    if (uid == ADMIN) {
35      printf("crown jewels");
36      strangeWayToPrintNewLine();
37    } else if (hs(key) == 0xCAFE){
38      printf("here's your cup");
39      strangeWayToPrintNewLine();
40    }
41    return 0;
42  }
```

Fig. 1. Running example illustrating a vulnerable C program

Information Leaks: To assess effectiveness against information leaks, we chose an RSA implementation using a left-to-right square-and-multiply Montgomery multiplication for exponentiation (pseudo-code in Fig. 2) as our transformation target, where m is the plaintext and n is the length of the key in bits. Before transformation, it is vulnerable to a timing side channel attack due to the if-statement inside the for loop, which allows an

```
x = m
for i = n - 2 downto 0
  x = x * x
  if (key[i] == 1) then
    x = x * m
endfor
return x
```

Fig. 2. Square and multiply

attacker to extract a private RSA key. We add perturbations to this timing side channel, by adding a loop with a random number of iterations on every conditional branch. The previous dependency of execution time on key bits is distorted. Before transformation, the implementation will exhibit longer timing in 50 % of multiplications, and in 30 % of squaring operations. As multiplication and squaring operations depend on key bits, this is a statistical prediction model for these key bits. After transformation, however, the bit prediction model is altered because of adding instructions (and thus execution time) randomly to either the case where the current key bit is 0, 1, or to branches independent of key bits at all. As long as the attacker has no access to the diversified implementation, it is hard to predict which behavior is induced by which branches. Quantifying the number of bits leaked by a program after transformation is out of the scope of this paper. However, intuitively timing side channel attacks are harder to perform due to this transformation [7].

Reverse Engineering Attacks: Typically imply extracting the key verification algorithm (line 37, Fig. 1) or hard-coded secrets (lines 35, 38, Fig. 1). To protect against reverse engineering, we applied transformations to merge methods, add bogus operands, obscure control flow through opaque predicates, insert bogus code, and replace static data (i.e. hard-coded secrets) through dynamic generator functions. For lack of objective metrics measuring obfuscation strength and to illustrate ISA^{2}R's transformations, we choose to present an example of effects by ISA^{2}R on the program described above. The left part of Fig. 3 shows the control-flow graphs of two functions h() (a single basic block at the top) and hs() (four basic blocks at the bottom) before transformation. The right part of Fig. 3 shows the resulting control-flow graph after the application of the aforementioned transformations. The gain in complexity is evident: Two disjoint functions are merged into one, and statically an attacker cannot easily determine which basic block will be the one to return the correct value, thanks to the opaque predicates and bogus code. Moreover, the hard-coded values on lines 35 and 38 in Fig. 1 were transformed into encoded strings by the StaticTo-ProceduralData transformation, which eliminates low-hanging-fruit that could be extracted using the Linux `strings` command-line utility.

Memory Corruption Attacks: We constructed a buffer overflow exploit code tailored for the program in Fig. 1. The exploit assumed that the variables on the stack frame of the main function are `key` above `uid` with sizes of 20 bytes, respectively 4 bytes. By giving a 24 byte argument to the program, the call to `strcpy()` on line 32 in Fig. 1 overwrites the value of variable `uid` with the last 4 bytes of the input argument. If these 4 bytes are equal to the value of `ADMIN`

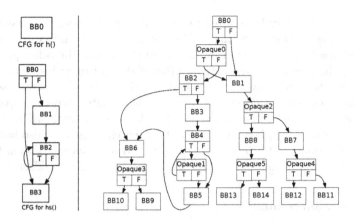

Fig. 3. Control-flow graph of h() (top-left), hs() (bottom-left) and their merger (right)

the check on line 34 is bypassed and the "crown jewels" are disclosed (line 35). After performing the transformations to randomize stack size and stack variable order of the program from Fig. 1, the same exploit code failed on the diversified instances of the same program, i.e. uid would no longer be overwritten because it is placed below key and a random size buffer would be placed above key. If the size of the inserted buffer was higher than the size of uid, the program continued functioning correctly, otherwise a crash occurred. This works reliably for exploit buffers crafted to fit certain byte boundaries. For exploit buffers that consist of repeatedly sprayed return addresses, however, the attacker can still correctly overwrite the EIP on the stack with a probability of 1 divided by the memory address width in bytes. Again, the attacker loses precision in predicting the stack layout which increases the difficulty to construct effective exploits.

Code Injection Attacks: Similar to memory corruption attacks, code injection attacks on the stack fail for the program in Fig. 1. The reason is that due to randomized stack layout and stack frame sizes, it becomes harder for the attacker to predict target address for the injected code. While stack frame size diversification adds a random number of bytes within a certain range to the stack frame, the diversification of the order of variables leads to NOP slides being ineffective, i.e. the execution might try to commence too low in memory, before the buffer holding the NOP slide and the code to be executed. Again, exploits working on the program from Fig. 1 failed in a similar way as for memory corruption attacks, on its diversified instances compiled to allow executable stacks, i.e. the code was placed on the stack but it was not executed successfully.

Code Reuse Attacks: The application from Fig. 1 can be leveraged by ROP exploits, as it calls *libc* functions such as execve on line 25. Therefore, we constructed a ROP exploit against this program that bypasses ASLR. By applying transformations to reorder instructions, insert bogus code, insert random loops, and opaque predicates, we randomized code locality as much as possible. Previous gadget addresses were invalidated and the ROP exploit failed with a crash as some gadget addresses now pointed elsewhere, leading to invalid opcodes.

Program Tampering: We crafted two patches for the compiled version of the program in Fig. 1. One rewriting its binary at a specific offset to patch the equality comparison represented by line 37 in Fig. 1, and the other performing pattern matching to locate the correct offset of the call to hs inside the binary. By applying the same transformations as in the code reuse attack scenario, we diversified the code section and the fixed offset patch overwrote parts of 2 instructions in the binary program, which failed with a crash when executed. This was not surprising; however, the pattern matching exploit also failed with a crash, as the operand to the call opcode it tried to patch was altered through diversification transformations, i.e. hs was transformed and its offset displaced.

4.3   Evaluation Summary

As shown in Sect. 4, ISA^{2}R was effective at fending off attacks from each attack category presented by Larsen *et al.* [9] for our example programs. However, this does not mean that ISA^{2}R is effective against all attacks from each category and it may also be ineffective if applied to particular target programs. To further investigate effectiveness we are performing similar case studies using ISA^{2}R on various open source projects. Efficiency measurements showed that most ISA^{2}R transformations have little impact on program file size and execution time which, however, stacks when multiple transformations are applied on the same program. The party who compiles the software bares a significant relative increase since each single transformation takes between 20 % and 30 % more compilation time on average, also resulting in much higher compilation times when multiple (or all) transformations are combined. However, we expect to lower these numbers by around 50 % in the future by eliminating recurring instructions through caching.

5   Conclusion and Future Work

In this work, we presented ISA^{2}R, a collection of software diversification transformations to harden software against attacks. Since ISA^{2}R is based on LLVM it can be applied to programs written in any language supported by LLVM. We have shown through examples that ISA^{2}R is effective at fending off attacks from all software attack categories presented by Larsen *et al.* [9]. Nevertheless, this does not mean that it defends against all attacks.

In our experiments we have constructed attacks which work against one program instance and fail against other diversified instances. Although our evaluation is based on case studies we believe that exploit resilience for the attacks mentioned in our evaluation section generalizes for the majority of programs. It is important to note that vulnerabilities are not removed, but unified exploitation through identical attack vectors is hindered. The more instances exist, the smaller the likelihood of a successful attack for adversaries. This decreases the return of investment for attackers, as one exploit no longer suffices to successfully attack and compromise all installations of a software. This is achieved without prohibitive runtime or file size overhead. However, one significant impact lies in the diversification process, which increases the costs of the software compilation and their distribution to end-users. Usability for software developers is considered high, as they only need to plug in ISA²R into the compilation process.

ISA²R offers 12 transformations for improving resilience against various attacks presented in [9] in a unified way, whereas existing specialized tools support only specific programming languages and are usually commercial or focused on a particular attack. To cover more attacks types, we will add further transformations in the future. ISA²R is available to interested parties upon request.

We intend to add more transformations to protect against further attacks and strengthen existing protections. For example, we plan on integrating *simulation* [3] to further complicate code injection attacks and runtime diversification (also known as *build and execute* [3]) to hamper reverse engineering. More importantly, we plan to assess the resilience of such diversification transformations to adaptable exploits, which are aware of the transformations that can be employed.

We are currently conducting work in the field of *transformation semantics and correctness*. Some transformations presented above can be easily verified to produce valid and semantically equivalent code, e.g. stack size and order diversification, instruction order randomization, etc. Others, however, cannot be trivially verified. As it is of utter importance that diversity transformations do not change functionality or introduce bugs into diversified instances, we are exploring ways to maintain specification semantics and correctness, while changing attack semantics; and to describe formal requirements to ensure these properties.

References

1. Allodi, L., Shim, W., Massacci. F.: Quantitative assessment of risk reduction with cybercrime black market monitoring. IEEE Sec. Priv. Workshops (2013)
2. Banescu, S., Pretschner, A., Battré, D., Cazzulani, S., Shield, R., Thompson, G.: Software-based protection against changeware. In: Proceedings of the 5th ACM Conference on Data and Application Security and Privacy, pp. 231–242 (2015)
3. Cohen, F.B.: Operating system protection through program evolution. Comput. Secur. **12**(6), 565–584 (1993)
4. Collberg, C., Thomborson, C., Low, D.: Manufacturing cheap, resilient, stealthy opaque constructs. In: 25th ACM SIGPLAN-SIGACT, pp. 184–196 (1998)
5. Forrest, S., Somayaji, A., Ackley, D.: Building diverse computer systems. In: 6th Workshop on Hot Topics in Operating Systems, pp. 67–72, May 1997
6. Hiser, J., Nguyen-Tuong, A., Co, M., Hall, M., Davidson, J.: ILR: where'd my gadgets go? In: IEEE Symposium on Security and Privacy, May 2012
7. Kocher, P.C.: Timing attacks on implementations of diffie-hellman, RSA, DSS, and other systems. In: Koblitz, N. (ed.) CRYPTO 1996. LNCS, vol. 1109, pp. 104–113. Springer, Heidelberg (1996)
8. Kocher, P.C., Jaffe, J., Jun, B.: Differential power analysis. In: Wiener, M. (ed.) CRYPTO 1999. LNCS, vol. 1666, pp. 388–397. Springer, Heidelberg (1999)
9. Larsen, P., Homescu, A., Brunthaler, S., Franz, M.: SoK: automated software diversity. In: IEEE Symposium on Security & Privacy (2014)
10. Randell, B.: System structure for software fault tolerance. IEEE Trans. Softw. Eng. **1**, 220–232 (1975)
11. Schechter, S.E.: Computer security strength & risk: a quantitative approach. Ph.D. thesis, Harvard University, Cambridge, Massachusetts, May 2004

Cyber Security and Integration

Barriers to the Use of Intrusion Detection Systems in Safety-Critical Applications

Chris W. Johnson[✉]

School of Computing Science, University of Glasgow,
Glasgow G12 8RZ, Scotland, UK
johnson@dcs.gla.ac.uk
http://www.dcs.gla.ac.uk/~johnson

Abstract. Intrusion detection systems (IDS) provide valuable tools to monitor for, and militate against, the impact of cyber-attacks. However, this paper identifies a range of theoretical and practical concerns when these software systems are integrated into safety-critical applications. Whitelist approaches enumerate the processes that can legitimately exploit system resources. Any other access requests are interpreted to indicate the presence of malware. Whitelist approaches cannot easily be integrated into safety-related systems where the use of legacy applications and Intellectual Property (IP) barriers associated with the extensive use of sub-contracting make it different to enumerate the resource requirements for all valid processes. These concerns can lead to a high number of false positives. In contrast, blacklist intrusion detection systems characterize the behavior of known malware. In order to be effective, blacklist IDS must be updated at regular intervals as new forms of attack are identified. This raises enormous concerns in safety-critical environments where extensive validation and verification requirements ensure that software updates must be rigorously tested. In other words, there is a concern that the IDS update might itself introduce bugs into a safety-related system. Isolation between an IDS and a safety related application minimizes this threat. For instance, information diodes limit interference by ensuring that an IDS is restricted to read-only access on a safety related network. Further problems arise in determining what to do when an IDS identifies a possible attack, given that false positives can increase risks to the public during an emergency shutdown.

Keywords: SCADA · Intrusion detection · Safety · Cyber-security

1 Introduction

Intrusion detection systems (IDS) provide valuable tools for detecting potential cyber-attacks. Aldenstein [1] stresses the need for protective monitoring over Supervisory Control and Data Acquisition (SCADA) systems – based on the capability of operating systems to monitor running processes and to examine the raw memory of a machine. Sutherland et al. [2], have also explored the use of protective monitoring tools to identify requirements for better access to information on memory, network and system activity to inform intrusion detection.

© Springer International Publishing Switzerland 2015
F. Koornneef and C. van Gulijk (Eds.): SAFECOMP 2015, LNCS 9337, pp. 375–384, 2015.
DOI: 10.1007/978-3-319-24255-2_27

Most previous work in this area has focused on intrusion detection for UNIX and Windows platforms. However, problems arise when control systems are hosted as applications on top of these mass-market operating systems. Changes are often made by suppliers– for instance to customise file handling. This can frustrate attempts to use existing IDS when operating system modifications undermine existing authentication and security mechanisms. For instance, role-based file access mechanisms are typically used to implement security policies. Unauthorized users can then be locked out of a system while authorized users can continue to access system resources. However, many safety-related control systems use ad hoc or absolute permission techniques. System processes are not sufficiently distinguished to trace potential access violations – especially in legacy SCADA implementations.

This paper identifies a range of theoretical and practical concerns when intrusion detection systems are integrated into safety-critical applications. Some of these barriers stem from the technical difficulty of distinguishing valid behaviours from the symptoms of a potential attack. Many safety-related industries make extensive use of sub-contracting. Suppliers often have IP concerns in disclosing detailed information about the behaviour and performance of their products. This is compounded by the use of Commercial Off The Shelf (COTS) software, where the supplier may have little idea that their products are being used within a critical application. It can be costly and time consuming to profile the behaviour of systems that were developed many years ago and for which there may only exist incomplete documentation. Further problems stem from the manner in which conventional IDS operate on conventional IP stacks rather than the lower level protocols used in many SCADA systems.

More theoretical barriers include the sensitivity of IDS in safety-related applications. It is important not to miss malware within a safety related application. However, if an IDS is too sensitive then it may trigger false alarms halting the operation of an otherwise 'healthy' system. The closing sections of this paper argue that it can be difficult to determine appropriate actions after an IDS has correctly identified the presence of malware in safety-critical systems. It may be difficult to reach a safe state following an attack, given that we cannot be certain about the extent of a cyber-attack. There are few guidelines about appropriate forensic activities. Preserving safety may involve the continued operation of a compromised process until it can be shutdown. This can overwrite the data needed to diagnose the causes of an incident. It may also imply an increased level of risk while a compromised process is closed down before any forensic analysis can be completed. Finally, we argue that many regulators lack both the technical insight and the political motivation necessary to guide the deployment of IDS. In consequence very few detection systems have been implemented within safety-critical control applications. We remain extremely vulnerable to a host of persistent threats.

2   Manual Approaches to Intrusion Detection

National and international organisations warn against an increasing threat to safety-critical systems from malware [3, 4]. However, it is hard to quantify the extent of this threat. Organisations can be reluctant to disclose information about previous incidents when they might motivate further attacks. This prevents other companies from determining whether or not they have been subject to similar attacks.

Technical and organisational barriers frustrate attempts to detect potential intrusions. Malware is often identified as part of the normal fault detection processes that support the operation of complex infrastructures [5]. System logs and network-monitoring tools provide the evidence necessary to identify an intrusion [6]. However, a number of factors combine to undermine cyber-Situation Awareness in safety-critical systems:

- *Legacy systems.* Many safety-related applications combine layers of software that were gradually developed over many years. This complicates the manual detection of malware. Legacy systems were seldom designed with cyber-security as a primary concern. It can be difficult for engineers to distinguish normal behaviour from the symptoms of an attack when there is a limited understanding of the proprietary code that was written many decades before by companies that are no longer in business.
- *IPR concerns and out sourcing.* The manual detection of malware is complicated because many safety-critical industries now make extensive use of out-sourcing. This can include the provision of network services. Unfortunately, outsourcing a service does not outsource the risk to safety-related companies [3]. In contrast, it can create vulnerabilities when malware propagates from sub-contractors that lack the security culture of the companies that employ them. Out-sourcing complicates the manual detection of malware using standard debugging techniques. Safety-critical organisations may identify the symptoms of an attack but lack the detailed understanding of sub-contractors' code to unambiguously diagnose the causes of an intrusion. It is hard for end users who experience the safety-related consequences of a security breach to trace the technical causes of particular violations.
- *Failure of incident reporting.* There are many barriers to the reporting of security violations throughout the supply chain. Contracting companies have significant concerns about the legal and commercial implications of admitting cyber incidents [3]. Some organisations have responded by creating legal requirements to share information about cyber-attacks. The members of the United States Security and Exchange Commission are required to report cyber incidents. Article 13a of the Telecoms Directive (2009/140/EC) requires network service providers report significant security breaches to competent national authorities. The proposed EC Network and Information Security Directive (COM2013/48) extends Article 13a's reporting obligations across European critical infrastructures. Without such requirements, it is hard for safety-critical service providers to use information about previous incidents to guide the detection of future attacks.
- *Lack of competency.* Few safety-critical organisations have the technical capacity to diagnose and combat a broad range of attacks on their own infrastructures [7, 8]. It is for this reason that the US government has established their Industrial Control System Computer Emergency Response Team (ICS-CERT, https://ics-cert.us-cert. gov). They have the specialist expertise that is required to identify malware without undermining the safety of complex application processes. Many European industries lack this support and instead have to rely on external security service providers

who have little understanding of the critical nature of the underlying software architectures [8]. In particular, few security companies have experience of working under regulatory agencies in safety related industries.

- *Lack of appropriate guidance.* Both ENISA [3] and NIST [11] provide valuable guidance on how to improve the detection and reporting of potential incidents. Neither considers the complexities that can arise in safety-critical applications, for example when malware is potentially detected in software that has gone through a formal certification process. This is an important omission; lives may depend on the timely provision of information about the scope and extent of any violation [10].
- *Lack of forensic tools.* The manual detection of an intrusion is complicated because safety-related systems can be very different from the office-based systems that are the focus of most forensic analysis. While there are significant monitoring and analysis tools available for conventional IP networks and devices, very few are available for Supervisory Control And Data Acquisition (SCADA) environments that employ protocols such as HART for communication between field devices [9].

The factors that complicate the detection of malware using conventional network and systems analysis tools motivate attempts to support automated intrusion detection in safety-critical systems.

3 Blacklist Approaches to Intrusion Detection

NIST [12] advocate the use of several different intrusion detection systems to automatically identify potential incidents. The intention is to increase cyber situation awareness. However, the use of diverse monitoring systems further complicates safety-critical software engineering. In order to obtain regulatory approval, companies must demonstrate the reliability of their code within its intended context of use. They must show that intrusion detection and prevention systems, antivirus software, and file integrity systems do not undermine the safety of application processes.

Blacklisting relies on detecting the characteristics of malware in contrast to whitelisting, discussed in subsequent sections, which compiles lists of approved code. All processes/requests are approved unless they are explicitly mentioned on the blacklist. In contrast, whitelist approaches to intrusion detection block everything by default unless they are explicitly approved. Greylist approaches enable the temporary suspension of access rights.

Blacklist techniques can be applied across a range of resources. They can be used to filter email addresses – for example, to prevent phishing attacks. They can also be applied to IP addresses and Domain Name Servers to throttle back denial of service attacks. Most typically, however, blacklists are used to record characteristics of malware including file names, types, sizes, content patterns etc. Control software is needed to implement the blacklist, blocking attempts to execute the files associated with known malware.

A number of concerns limit the application of blacklist approaches in safety-related systems. Most IDS are deployed to protect office-based systems. Existing systems cannot easily protect industrial automation protocols, such as HART. There have, however, been initial attempts to develop IDS for control systems, including Modbus, which have been embedded within commercial, open source tools [16]. Without further work to improve incident reporting and exchange, significant doubts remain about whether the malware signatures that are embedded within these tools can accurately characterise the range of threats being deployed against safety-critical applications [5].

Process components in safety-related systems are seldom connected to the Internet. The Programmable Logic Controllers (PLCs) that are widely used in industrial applications are often not connected to any local area network. This improves security because the 'air gap' between the device and any network in theory limits the opportunities for remote attacks. However, the 'air gap' also limits opportunities to use blacklist approaches. There is no easy way for system administrators to automatically update nodes with the lists of known attacks. This limitation can be addressed by manually uploading malware signatures. Operators must physically go to each device to update their software. However, this leads to a paradox. It is hard for any attacker to compromise these isolated devices. However, the more often an operator hooks up a laptop or other device to update the blacklist on an IDS then the more likely it is that the update process will lead to cross-contamination. There are also significant resource implications from implementing this policy across the thousands of low level devices used in complex, distributed control systems.

There are further concerns. In safety environments, it is important to ensure that a blacklist IDS does not erroneously block critical software. Other concerns centre on the reliability of the IDS itself. Uploading a corrupted blacklist could cause the failure of a detection system with knock-on consequences for safety-related processes. In such circumstances, safety engineers would continually be engaged in a test and re-test cycle to ensure that new versions of protection and detection systems could safely be integrated into critical operating environments. There is a trade-off between the time required to verify that new malware signatures would not affect the reliability of an IDS and the imperative to quickly upload new definitions to protect safety-related applications from new threats.

4 Whitelist Approaches to Intrusion Detection

Whitelist approaches provide an alternative to blacklist intrusion detection in safety-critical applications. Whitelisting aims to ensure that only approved programs and software libraries can be executed. All others are denied system resources. Whitelists profile 'normal behaviour' and report any deviations. A deep knowledge of normal operation can be gained by reviewing logs and by the routine analysis of system behaviour. In order to be successful, this approach relies on the following measures:

- Identifying specific executables and software libraries, which should be permitted to execute on a given system. This cannot rely on file names or directory structures because malware can then masquerade as a legitimate application;
- Preventing any other executable files and software libraries from running on that system. This can be implemented by creating a hash digest of all software applications. If the hash of an executable does not match what is contained in the list, it will trigger a security event.

– Preventing unauthorised users from changing the lists indicating which files can be executed [17].

Application whitelisting depends on software that maintains the lists of approved executable and library files. It also depends on the maintenance of Access Control Lists that prevent unauthorised users from manipulating these lists. In a safety related environment, the software used to implement a whitelist approach must pass the relevant regulatory requirements. In addition, the approved lists may themselves be subject to safety assessments given the implications of denying resources to critical executable files. A host of commercial tools exist to support whitelisting – including Microsoft's AppLocker, the Bit9 Parity Suite, McAfee Application Control etc.

A small number of attempts have been made to extend this approach to safety-critical infrastructures [18]. The proponents of this technique argue that it has significant benefits over alternate approaches, including blacklisting. Whitelist approaches provide a degree of protection again zero-day exploits – even if the signature of an attack is unknown, the malicious code will not be included on the approved hash list. Protection against zero-day exploits is extremely important for SCADA systems. The Human Machine Interfaces (HMIs) that control local processes are, typically, connected to data historians and servers. The relative stability of the software running on these systems provides considerable opportunities for the use of whitelist techniques. Locking down the data historian and HMI can block zero-day exploits and notify security managers of potential attacks.

Whitelist IDS have significant benefits over blacklist approaches for safety-related systems when infrastructure components are isolated from standard network connections. Recall that there are significant resource implications when administrators have to manually update blacklist malware signatures across complex, distributed control systems. Whitelisting avoids these overheads as the approved process list is likely to be more stable than the blacklist malware signatures for these 'air gapped' control systems.

There are some complications – for instance, the same attack across multiple instances of a control system will simultaneously lead to a large number of distributed security events. These can overwhelm an organisation's ability to respond in a timely fashion and may also be triggered by non-malicious causes. In particular, software updates that are not reflected by changes in the whitelist can lead to a large number of false positives. It, therefore, becomes imperative that staff and sub-contractors follow agreed security update procedures during all software installations.

The impact of false alarms can be reduced in safety-related systems by logging a warning rather than automatically closing down critical applications. This creates problems because security staff and system administrators must then monitor the alarm logs that can be maintained by the thousands of devices distributed across complex control systems. Recall that the use of 'air gapping' means that many components will not be connected to a local area network and that connecting a laptop to a PLC or controller to examine a whitelist alarm log will increase the risk of cross-contamination.

System administration is further complicated by the need to periodically update the hash tables that record the list of approved executable files, for example when an application needs to be patched. The whitelist software must be disabled without exposing the system to a synchronised attack. Recall that other application processes will still be running to support safety-related functions during the update process. Recalculating the hash tables for approved software can take several hours for even relatively simple control applications.

Hybrid approaches use blacklist software to scan for malware both before and after the whitelist update process. This still creates vulnerabilities – for instance, from zero day exploits that would not be identified during the scan. Further concerns arise when an attacker obtains physical access to a control system – potentially enabling them to reboot the workstation without accessing the whitelist software.

As mentioned before, it can be hard to coordinate the activities of many different sub-contractors to ensure that they do not trigger security events by installing unrecognised executable files. This creates particular concerns when the time required to re-computed the whitelist hash values might delay necessary safety updates. Further problems can arise in ensuring that engineering teams support the policy when they may have grown accustomed to making ad hoc updates to the systems they support. In consequence, whitelisting techniques may be restricted to a safety kernel within more complex applications.

Previous sections have focussed on application white listing. Alternative approaches focus on the resources used by processes rather than on executable file structures. Each recognised process on a whitelist is granted finite access to network, memory and processing resources. If the approved process exceeds these limits then a security event will be generated.

Resource-based whitelisting raises further concerns for safety-critical systems. Systems administrators are, typically, concerned to avoid resource starvation rather than to accurately model the dynamic behaviour of processes over time. Networks that have experienced few operational problems will often not be analysed to any significant extent. There are numerous reasons for this. The most obvious is that safety-related engineering is guided by risk-based techniques – resources are focussed on those applications that are most likely to have a significant impact on safe and successful operation. Attention tends to focus on those areas that cause the greatest problems for operations rather than on areas that might be the most vulnerable to cyber-attacks.

5   Information Diodes and the Threat from False Positives

Naedele [5] argues that IDS can undermine cyber situation awareness by increasing "confusion and operator stress in critical situations, for example if a malfunction in the plant causes a storm of alarm messages in the automation system which then again are interpreted as unusual by the IDS, causing additional alerts from the IDS". This is particularly important for whitelist approaches – where any unusual activity may be interpreted as a potential threat leading to a cascade of false positives. This 'alarm storm' is less of a concern for blacklist approaches; where degraded modes of behaviour are unlikely to match the signatures used to characterise existing forms of malware. As we have seen, however, blacklist approaches create significant concerns for validation and verification. In particular, it can be difficult to convince safety regulators that updates to a signature-based IDS will not introduce new failure modes or create vectors for the transmission of malware to isolated PLCs, controllers etc.

Data diodes can address some of the concerns that arise when introducing IDS into safety-critical control systems. These only allow data to travel in one direction. They are most often implemented by removing the send and receive transceivers from one direction of a fibre-optic cable. ISA 99 and IEC 62443 advocate the use of these devices to implement zoning throughout Industrial Control Systems. In this case, process data can flow from the operational zone to business and management systems. However, any threats resident on the business systems cannot spread to the real time arena.

Data diodes support intrusion detection. A one-way flow of data from the operational system is monitored for signs of malware using either a white or black list approach. This data can include information about file and process structures as well as resource usage. The isolation of the IDS from the control system reduces concerns that the detection system will have an adverse effect on safety-related processes and that IDS updates may themselves provide an attack vector. The IDS is separated from control applications by the one-way diode. Unfortunately, this approach cannot easily be deployed across air gap architectures. There are significant overheads in monitoring thousands of distributed, standalone devices even if each one is protected by a data diode and associated IDS. In the future it is likely that production pressures combined with the difficulty of sourcing devices that can operate without connectivity will increase the networking of safety-related control systems. Until then there will remain major logistic barriers to the use of IDS across many of our most critical infrastructures.

There are further issues. Greater levels of monitoring may lead to an increasing number of false alarms, whereas raising tolerance thresholds increase missed positives. Further work is urgently required to determine whether advanced visualisation techniques can be combined with, for instance, machine learning algorithms to ensure that IDS enhance rather than undermine the cyber-situation awareness of operators in complex safety-critical environments.

Other concerns remain at the nexus between safety and security. In particular, it is far from clear what measures should be taken once an intrusion has been detected. Existing guidance from the US Department of Justice and the UK Association of Chief Police Officers suggests that computational infrastructures should be treated as a crime scene [7]. Equipment should be switched off and no redundant or secondary systems should be enabled in case they destroy forensic evidence or extend an infection. In many industries this creates significant concerns that safety will be undermined in the aftermath of an incident.

There is an urgent need to develop forensic guidelines for SCADA systems, where extensive logs are not usually retained for thousands of isolated PLCs distributed across production facilities. In the same way that existing intrusion detection systems provide greatest support for office systems, we need appropriate forensic tools that can be applied at the lower levels of many safety-critical infrastructures.

6   Conclusions

Intrusion detection systems help to detect malware in a range of software systems. Whitelist approaches enumerate the processes that can legitimately exploit system resources. This paper has argued that whitelist techniques cannot easily be used in safety-related applications. Intellectual Property (IP) barriers associated with the extensive use of sub-contracting make it different to enumerate the resource requirements for all valid processes. Further concerns stem from the widespread use of legacy systems, where users have limited access to source code. It is difficult to characterise legitimate behaviours under a range of operating conditions when system developers are no longer available. Subsequent sections summarised the vulnerabilities that arise during the re-computation of hash tables that implement whitelist techniques. We have also identified concerns over a loss of situation awareness when large numbers of unwarranted security alarms are triggered by degraded modes of operation.

In contrast, blacklist intrusion detection systems characterize the behaviour of known malware. In order to be effective, blacklist IDS must be updated at regular intervals. Otherwise, application processes will be vulnerable to known attacks. We have argued that blacklist updates raise enormous concerns in safety-critical systems where extensive validation and verification requirements ensure that software patches must be rigorously tested. In other words, there is a concern that an IDS signature update might itself introduce bugs into a safety-related system. Further concern stem from the difficulty of updating malware signatures in distributed control systems where airgaps are deliberately introduced to isolate low-level components.

Data diodes limit the impact of IDS on safety related applications. These devices ensure that data only flows in one direction, for example using modified fibre optic cables. Data diodes reduce the likelihood that signature updates will cause the failure of a blacklist IDS or will cross-contaminate SCADA systems. They can also be used in whitelist approaches to ensure that the computational overhead of checking process permissions does not rob critical applications of critical processing resources.

We have argued that data diodes do not provide a panacea for intrusion detection in safety-related systems. Problems arise when IDS false positives compromise the reliability of safety-related applications. Greater levels of monitoring may lead to an increasing number of false alarms, whereas increased tolerances increase the potential for missed positives. These concerns can be addressed through, for example, machine learning techniques that adjust the tolerances of the IDS to anomalous behaviour. It remains to be seen whether such techniques can meet regulatory requirements across a range of safety-related industries.

Over the last decade we have seen a host of valuable guidelines, from organisations including NIST and ENISA, which enable organisations to establish security management systems. These have been backed by more detailed technical support – for example in incident response and forensic analysis that can be used to implement these high level guidelines. This paper has focussed more narrowly on intrusion detection and argued that significant problems remain before these techniques can be successfully applied in safety-critical applications. There are political and organisational barriers between the regulatory agencies responsible for safety and for information security. In consequence, the government bodies that provide support for more general forms of information security often do not consider the impact of threats in transportation, energy production and manufacturing. These sectors are typically the responsibility of other agencies. Unless we can remove these barriers, safety-related control systems will remain vulnerable to a growing range of cyber attacks.

References

1. Adelstein, F.: Live forensics: diagnosing your system without killing it first. Commun. ACM **49**(2), 63–66 (2006)
2. Sutherland, I., Evans, J., Tryfonas, T., Blyth, A.: Acquiring volatile operating system data tools and techniques. SIGOPS Oper. Syst. Rev. **42**(3), 65–73 (2008)
3. European Network and Information Security Agency (ENISA): Technical Guidelines on Reporting Incidents: Article 13a Implementation, Heraklion, Greece, December 2011
4. US Government Auditors Office: Information Security: FAA Needs to Address Weaknesses in Air Traffic Control Systems, GAO-15-221, 29 January 2015
5. Naedele, M.: Addressing IT security for critical control systems. In: Proceedings of the 40th Hawaii International Conference on System Sciences. IEEE Computer Society (2007)
6. Johnson, C.W.: Anti-social networking: crowdsourcing and the cyber defence of national critical infrastructures. Ergonomics **57**(3), 419–433 (2014)
7. Johnson, C.W.: Inadequate legal, regulatory and technical guidance for the forensic analysis of cyber-attacks on safety-critical software. In: Swallom, D. (ed.) Proceedings of the 32nd International Systems Safety Society, Louisville, USA. International Systems Safety Society, Unionville (2014)
8. Garfinkel, S.L.: Digital forensics research: the next 10 years. Digital Invest. **7**, 64–73 (2010)
9. Nilsson, D.K., Larson, U.E.: Conducting forensic investigations of cyber attacks on automobile in-vehicle networks. In: Proceedings of eForensics 2008, Proceedings of the 1st International Conference in Forensic Applications. ACM (2008)
10. Jones, R.A., Horowitz, B.: A system-aware cyber security architecture. Syst. Eng. **15**(2), 225–240 (2012)
11. U.S. National Institute of Standards and Technology (NIST): Computer Security Incident Handling Guide (Draft), Special Publication 800-61 Revision 2 (Draft), Gaithersburg, Maryland (2012)
12. U.S. National Institute of Standards and Technology (NIST): Guide to Integrating Forensic Techniques into Incident Response, Special Publication 800-86, Gaithersburg, Maryland (2006)
13. DigitalBond SCADA intrusion detection forum. http://www.digitalbond.com/support-center/. Accessed March 2015
14. Australian Signals Directorate: Application Whitelisting Explained. Australian Government, Department of Defense (2012)
15. Anderson, D., Khiabani, H.: Protect critical infrastructure computer systems with whitelisting. The SANS Institute, Bethesda (2014)

Stochastic Modeling of Safety and Security of the e-Motor, an ASIL-D Device

Peter T. Popov[✉]

Centre for Software Reliability, City University London,
Northampton Square, London EC1V 0HB, UK
p.t.popov@city.ac.uk

Abstract. This paper offers a stochastic model and a combined analysis of safety and security of the e-Motor, an ASIL D (ISO 26262) compliant device designed for use with AUTOSAR CAN bus.

The paper argues that in the absence of credible data on the likelihood and payload of cyber attacks on newly developed devices a sensible approach would be to separate the concerns: (i) the payloads that may affect the device's safety can be identified using standard hazard analysis techniques; (ii) the difficulty with the parameterization of a stochastic model can be alleviated by applying sensitivity analysis for a plausible range of model parameter values.

Keywords: Stochastic modeling · Adversary · Safe state · Cyber attack · ISO 26262

1 Introduction

Cyber security of industrial electronics is becoming increasingly important as the Internet of things is becoming a reality. High profile vulnerabilities of embedded safety critical devices have been revealed, e.g. of insulin pumps, of pacemakers, etc. Researchers have developed exploits for these devices which demonstrate that patients' safety can be compromised remotely via cyber attacks.

Attention to cyber security has increased in automotive industry, too. Several demonstrations revealed that the CAN bus can be accessed remotely, e.g. via the entertainment (Bluetooth) system. CAN bus was designed as part of a "trusted" environment for which no authentication and authorization mechanisms were developed to protect the embedded devices connected to the CAN bus from malicious activities.

The good news is that despite the demonstrated vulnerabilities of automotive devices, the risk from exploiting these seems still relatively low and no significant accidents caused by cyber attacks have been recorded. The chip manufacturers, however, are taking proactive measures to create chips with built-in capabilities for enhanced security, e.g. the chips for automotive applications by Infineon and Freescale are manufactured with built-in *security processors*. Security analysis is increasingly taken seriously by the car manufacturers, too. Several research projects in the USA and in Europe are looking at the issue and attempt to lay down sound principles for future cyber security standardization. For example, the forthcoming extension of ISO 26262 is

© Springer International Publishing Switzerland 2015
F. Koornneef and C. van Gulijk (Eds.): SAFECOMP 2015, LNCS 9337, pp. 385–399, 2015.
DOI: 10.1007/978-3-319-24255-2_28

expected to at least acknowledge the importance of cyber security. Other safety standards, e.g. IEC/ISO 61508 (in v. 2010, clause 7.4.2.3), already acknowledge that cyber security must be an essential part of software safety analysis.

Cyber security for industrial control systems (ICS) has been discussed in a number of reports from various standardization bodies both in the US and in Europe. There is an essential difference between how cyber security is dealt within the ICT and in ICS in that the *reactive* approach, which dominates the ICT (patch as soon as a noteworthy vulnerability is discovered), may be inappropriate in the ICS. High availability and real-time requirements make patching difficult to implement and in many cases - simply inadequate.

Research effort has been allocated on demonstrating the benefits of proactive approaches to defending against cyber threats, e.g. using fault–tolerance, but this author is not aware of commercial solutions based on this approach.

2 Problem Statement and Related Research

Models of cyber attacks (including malicious software) have been proposed by many in the past. Cyber attacks broadly consist of a *delivery* mechanism, i.e. a mechanism of accessing the target, and a *payload*, the particular mechanism via which the attacker gains their rewards. These two can be seen as orthogonal: the same payload can be delivered via different mechanisms and the same delivery may be used to deploy different payloads. Conflicker worm, for examples used an aggressive delivery mechanism, but no particular payload for it has been identified [1]. At the other extreme, there are examples of a complex set of delivery mechanisms contained in a single malware. Stuxnet, for instance, is known to include among the delivery mechanisms 4 zero-day exploits and several different delivery mechanisms [1], some of which were known before Stuxnet, but have not been reported/fixed by the vendors.

Probabilistic models of cyber attacks have been used in the past ranging from very detailed models of a *particular attack* to models which operate at a relatively high level of abstraction suitable for exploratory analysis. An example of the first approach is [2] which models Stuxnet. An example of abstract models is the ADVISE formalism [3] and the various models of cyber economics. In between are models, which take a detailed look at the delivery mechanisms, e.g. [4] and make "pessimistic" assumptions about the payload. The same approach is quite common in ICT when getting an access to protected assets is seen as a "game over" event, as once the Adversary gains an access to the target they can do anything they please. Concentrating on delivery mechanisms and assuming the "worst" for the payload has been applied in ICS, too. For instance, [5] studied the impact of cyber attacks on a sub-station of a power transmission network and assumed that once the Adversary passes a substation firewall (s)he would switch off *all assets* controlled by the sub-station: generators, loads and bus-bars.

Given the wide range of delivery/payload combinations observed in cyber attacks and malware it is somewhat unclear how one should build *useful stochastic models* for security. My view is that attempts to model the delivery mechanisms in detail are unlikely to be useful. Models which rely on detailed knowledge of a particular combination of delivery mechanisms, e.g. [2], provide a probabilistic *explanation* of what is already known, hardly a useful insight. One is usually, interested in studying the risk from attacks that have *not been seen before*. In my view modeling the delivery mechanisms should be done at a high level of abstraction, e.g. as a stochastic state machine with a small number of states which allow one to express the time (and effort) needed for a successful attack. The effect of the envisaged defense mechanisms on the likelihood of a successful attack must be modeled, too. A small number of parameters, characterizing the transitions between the states (that capture the possible multi-step paths of successful attacks) should allow a modeler to capture various scenarios and defense policies. This approach has been tried in the past [6].

While the delivery mechanisms should be modeled at relatively high level of abstraction, modeling the payload should be *as detailed as possible* and tailored to the specifics of the particular system. For safety critical systems enumerating the pertinent "failure modes" which can be caused by cyber attacks seems an essential starting point. Such an enumeration is typically a result of a *safety analysis*, which will produce the important hazards specific for the modeled safety critical system.

An essential problem for a useful probabilistic model is model parameterization. While with software reliability and safety putting in place a credible measurement program is usually sufficient for eliciting accurately the needed probabilistic parameters, for cyber security the feasibility of a measurement program is *questionable*. The international effort in this regard, e.g. with honey pots, provides plenty of evidence. Some colleagues seriously consider rethinking the concept of cyber risk in the light of this difficulty. The very idea of probabilistic security analysis is in doubt. Indeed if I cannot credibly parameterize a model how can I trust the findings from such a model about the risk from an unknown attack? The issue here is what we expect to learn from a probabilistic model? If the expectation is that we will be able to make predictions similar to those that we are able to make today about software reliability of a *specific* software system in its *specific operational environment* I do not believe that the problem can be solved! The issue is the Adversary profile, which can only be hypothesized, but is generally unknown and little can be learned from past observations about the next attack. Every new noteworthy attack looks like a "Black Swan" [7]. And yet, declaring that no meaningful probabilistic security analysis is possible will be in my opinion wrong, especially for those safety critical systems in which the primary concern is system availability and integrity. In such systems serious safety analysis is undertaken and the important hazards and failure modes are not merely identified but measures for error and failure detection, containment and recovery are provided. A good probabilistic security model will include two groups of parameters:

- *knowable*, i.e. with *low* epistemic uncertainty. Examples of such parameters would be the parameters related to accidental failures, their repairs, of the coverage of various detection mechanisms, etc., and
- *unknowable*, i.e. with *high* epistemic uncertainty. The parameters related to the behavior of an Adversary and even the Adversary models themselves fall into this category. For these parameters, however, one might be able to identify a range, possibly a large one, of *credible values*.

Epistemic uncertainty has been dealt with in the past, e.g. using the Bayesian analysis. Bayesian analysis asks for explicit quantification of epistemic uncertainty (in the form of a prior distribution), which may be problematic, and in the absence of a significant number of observations, the significant epistemic uncertainty may produce predictions, which are "too imprecise" to be useful. A reasonable alternative to a Bayesian assessment would be sensitivity analysis on the model parameters of the modeled safety critical system. Such an analysis would allow one to explore the space of *plausible* parameter values (without stating explicitly the epistemic uncertainty over this space) and to determine the range, for which the modeled system behaves *acceptably* and those for which the system behaves unacceptably (i.e. the cyber risk is too high). Sensitivity analysis can also be extended to the parameters of the mechanisms of cyber defense and help establish the parameter values, for which these mechanisms reduce the risk from cyber attacks to an acceptable level. Consider for example an intrusion detection/prevention system (IDS/IPS). In sensitivity analysis one can analyze the frequency of cyber attacks (subject to high epistemic uncertainty), for which cyber attacks pose too high a risk for the safety critical systems and "play" with IDS/IPS *coverage* to establish the coverage values, for which the risk from cyber attacks is reduced to a tolerable level. As a side effect "sensitivity analysis" may reveal that some (unknowable) parameters have low/negligible impact on system risk.

In this paper sensitivity analysis is demonstrated on a non-trivial case study.

3   The Model

The e-Motor case study was developed in the SESAMO (Artemis JU) project [8, 9] and is intended to be an ASIL-D[1] device. As a measure of safety assurance the device is designed to consist of *two diverse software channels*. The device is connected to the CAN bus of a car and is supplied by a torque request processed by the two channels independently. The control stimuli to the actual electric motor are provided by one of the two channels after adjudication of the outputs from the channels. The model presented in this paper is built under a number of assumptions about the architecture and the fault tolerant mechanisms used in the e-Motor, which are summarized below:

1 Each of the two channels is *self-checking*, capable to detect its own failures with some probability (coverage);
2 Each channel is provided with a *safe state*, e.g. a piece of code/data which can be used by the channel to move the device to a safe state, if instructed to do so by the "higher authority" (see below).
3 Each of the channels can be in one of the following states:

   – working correctly;
   – failed detected, which is further split into:

---

[1] ASIL-D is the highest safety integrity level defined in ISO 26262 and requires the highest degree of rigor in development.

- "safe failure state", if the *safe state* for the device has not been compromised. While in a safe failure state the channel can on its own complete a transition of the entire device to a safe state, i.e. irrespective of whether the other channel works correctly or has failed.
- "Unsafe failure state 2" – if the safe state has been compromised. In this case, if the channel is instructed to move the device to a safe state, the device will find itself in an unsafe state.
- Unsafe failure state" – if the channel has failed, but did not detect its failure.

4 The decision about which of the two channels controls the electric motor and executes a safe function (e.g. moves the device to a safe state) is taken by a "higher authority", which is outside the e-Motor itself. We assume that the higher authority is acting always *correctly*, i.e. if there is a channel that can to perform a control/safety function correctly (e.g. to move the device to a safe state) such as channel is always selected to do so. The e-Motor is essentially a 1-out-of-2 system with self-checking channels and a perfect adjudicator.

The system state is established from the channel states as follows:

- If at least one of the channels is OK, then the system is OK;
- If none of the channels is OK, but at least one is in "safe failure state", then the system itself is in a safe failure state. If this situation occurs, the assumption is that the higher authority will instruct a channel in a "safe failure state" to move the e-Motor to a safe state. Further we assume that the transition to the safe system state occurs *instantaneously* and once it is started it is always completed successfully.
- If both channels are neither in OK nor in "safe failure state", then the system enters (instantaneously) the unsafe system state.

The initial idea for combined analysis of safety and security of the e-Motor is shown in Fig. 1 using the SAN formalism (Stochastic Activity Networks).

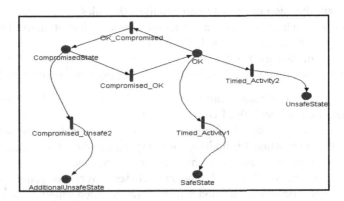

Fig. 1. A simplified SAN model of a channel of the e-motor

The "places" represent the states of the device: OK – represents the normal operation, CompromisedState – the state in which the safe state configuration is tampered with, SafeState – the state when proper reaction to a safety related event is taken,

UnsafeState – represents a unsafe failure state (either the failure is not detected at all or it is detected but has been handled correctly) and the AdditionalUnsafeState (unsafe operation due to calling upon the safe state, which in fact has become unsafe due to a successful tampering with of the safe state of the e-Motor device). The "stochastic activities" model the distribution of time a transition between two states takes. For instance, the activity "OK_Compromised" represents a transition (and the probability distribution of the duration of this transition) from OK state to the CompromisedState. Similarly, the activity "Compromised_OK" represents a transition to OK state from CompromisedState.

"CompromisedState" state models the fact that, due to a data integrity violation, the *safe state* of an e-Motor channel has been altered. The safe state definition (code and data) is stored in *safe state configuration file*. One of the configuration files is *active* at a time and should the e-Motor fail to perform correctly, the active safe state will be invoked by the higher authority logic built in the e-Motor. An alteration of the e-Motor's safe state will place the channel in a ***compromised state***, i.e. will create a ***new hazard*** and will have no consequence until the device needs to enter its safe state. Should the safe state be called upon while the device is in the "compromised" state, then the e-Motor instead of entering the designated safe state will enter an unsafe state (AdditionalUnsafeState), as shown in Fig. 1.

If the incorrect (e.g. the tampered with) safe state configuration file is detected before a transition to the "safe" state is called upon and there is a mechanism to restore the correct configuration (i.e. the compromised state is 'fixed' by a return to the state OK), then the "compromised" state will have no effect on device safety.

3.1   Simplifications Made

Type of attacks. The model considers three types of attacks as listed below of which only the first type is discussed in detail in the paper[2]:

1. A malicious alteration of the safe state configuration files.
2. A malicious modification of the requested torque (information coming to the e-Motor as an input, i.e. over the CAN Bus).
3. A malicious modification of the channels' control loop parameters. These do not affect immediately the device's safe operation, but may cause a channel failure.

Common cause accidental failures are modeled simplistically. It is based on the Marshall and Olkin model [10] of common stress.

Limited knowledge about stochastic properties of the modeled cyber attacks. As discussed in the introduction this limitation is not specific to the e-Motor case study and applies to most attempts to model stochastically cyber attacks.

Detection of attacks. The SAN model includes several techniques of attack detection: (i) a generic attack detection capability (represented simply by a probability of detecting an attack), (ii) plausibility checks on the values of torque requests. Plausibility checks are among the mechanisms considered by the vendors for the real

---

[2] This attack type was missed in the initial safety analysis.

e-Motor device, and iii) timing checks, e.g. torque requests should not occur more frequently than a predefined timing constraints. This paper, however, uses only the first of the three detection techniques.

3.2   The SAN Model

Model Description. The Mobius (SAN) project is shown in Fig. 2.

The project consists of several atomic models: Adjudicator, Adversary, Control_configuration_channel, SW_channel, T_config_channel and configuration_channel.
The model also includes a composed model, Div_SW.

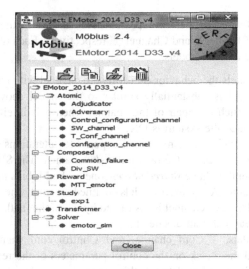

Fig. 2. The SAN project, e-Motor_2014_D33.

The Reward, Study and Solver components are parts of project, too.
The model is solved via Monte Carlo simulation.

The Composed Model, Div_SW. Figure 3 presents the composed model of the e-Motor.

It consists of a number of other models:

- Channel 1 – represents the behavior of the first s/w channel;
- Channel 2 – represents the behavior of the second s/w channel;
- Adjudicator – offers the functionality, necessary to deal with the redundant channels. It implements a 1-out-of-2 architecture with two self-checking channels.
- Adversary – models the behavior of an adversary who might attempt one of 3 possible attacks described above. The adversary model allows for implementing a single attack or multiple attacks.

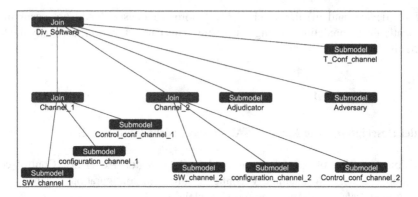

Fig. 3. The structure of the composed model, Div_SW

Each of the software channels is represented by a Join in the composed model Div_SW. These are Channel_1 and Channel_2, respectively. Each of these, in turn, is a composition of three atomic models:

- SW channel – models the behavior of a software channel with respect to accidental failures. This model is substantially similar to the model shown in Fig. 1. with various additions such as repair of the channel when it is in either safe or unsafe failure state provided the system is OK;
- Configuration_channel_1/2 – models the possible alterations of the safe state configurations (files) used by the respective s/w channel. The SW_channel and the respective configuration have *shared places* (one of the Mobius mechanism used for linking various atomic/composed models) defined, so that when the configuration file is altered and the sw_channel is instructed by the higher authority to enter a safe state, it will instead enter an unsafe state.
- The atomic models, T_Conf_channel and Control_conf_channel_1/2, model a torque attack and the attack on the control parameters of the respective s/w channels. Neither is discussed in detail in this paper.

The many models listed above communicate with each other via the mechanism of *shared places*. The interested reader can get further details about the model from the author (including the SAN model itself).

Using pairs of configuration files in the model (safe states and control_conf, respectively) – one per channel – is dictated by the requirement in ISO 26262 to eliminate any *single point of failure* in the e-Motor design.

The Atomic Models. *SW_channel.* The model is shown in Fig. 4.

This model includes a model of common failures, captured by the place CCF_active (a shared place for both SW_channel atomic models) and the activity CCF_propagate. The common failure is enabled only when both channels are OK (Input_Gate). The place CCF_active is shared with the respective place in the atomic model Adjudicator and triggers a common failure event. The intervals between the

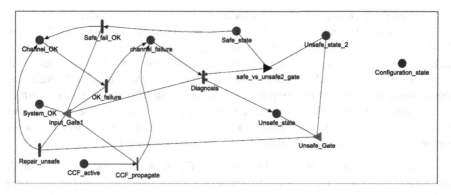

Fig. 4. Model of a SW channel

simultaneous failures are specified in the Adjudicator atomic model. More specifically, the model offers four distinct states for a software channel as defined in Fig. 1 above: Channel_OK, Channel_failure, Safe_state – this is the state where the channel will end up, if the diagnosis determines successfully the need for a safe state AND the safe state at this moment in time is not compromised. If, however, the safe state is compromised, then the channel will end up in Unsafe_state_2; the decision logic which state to move to is captured by the output gate safe_vs_unsafe2_gate. The probabilities of successful diagnosis are defined explicitly as global variables.

From Safe_state a channel can be returned back to Channel_OK. Similarly, a channel after unsafe failure (Unsafe_state or Unsafe_state_2) can be repaired. Both repairs are conditional on the system being in OK state, i.e. at least one of the channels is OK, achieved via the place System_OK and the input gate, Input_Gate_1.

Adversary. This model is shown in Fig. 5.

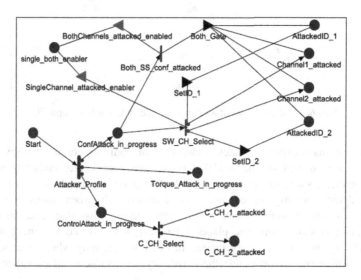

Fig. 5. A SAN model of the adversary

It consists of several places: Start, where one can place a number of tokens to simulate attacks. The number of tokens determines how many attacks will be simulated. Each attack (a token being passed from Start place to either ConfAttack_in_progress, Torque_attack_in_progress or Control_Attack_in_progress will trigger a scenario of an attack of one of the three types. For the attacks on the safe state the scenarios may involve attacking a single channel or attacking both channels. Which of the options will be used in a study is controlled by the token in Single_both_enabler place (and the two input gates linked to this place). The other two attacks – on the torque and on the control loop parameters – are not discussed in this paper.

Configuration_channel. This model is shown in Fig. 6. A state model of a channel's safe state configuration file. This model defines the states associated with the safe states as follows:

- Correct (default) – the safe state is not tampered with.
- Incorrect_1, Incorrect_2 – model two other states for the safe states, both valid as safe states for other contexts (i.e. modes of operation of a SW channel), but inadequate for the currently active mode of operation of the e-Motor. The use of two states to model the consequences of tampering with the safe state configuration file is motivated by the description of the device provided by the vendor in [8].

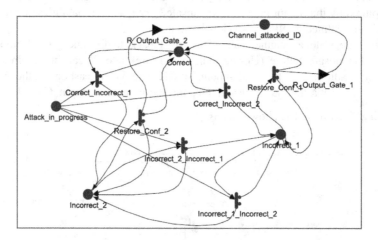

Fig. 6. A state model of a channel's safe state configuration file.

- The transitions between the states of the safe state configuration file are governed by the activities in this atomic model (Correct_Incorrect_1, etc. including restoring from incorrect states to the correct one, Restore_conf_1), which are enabled by the place Attack_in_progress enabler. The transitions between states (i.e. tokens between places) are only possible when Attack_in_progress place contains a token. This place is shared with the places, Channel1_attacked and Channel2_attacked, respectively, of the Adversary model. In other words, only when an attacker has chosen which channel to attack (the Adversary can choose to attack either a single channel or both simultaneously) is a transition of the respective configuration_channel enabled.

- Channel_attacked_ID place is shared with the places AttackedID_X of the Adversary model. The tokens in it are used in the predicates of the activities, which drive the transitions of tokens between the other places of this model.

Adjudicator. The model is omitted here for lack of space, but is described in [11]. It implements the logic summarized above and uses the mechanisms of shared places.

Studies. Sensitivity analysis was completed to establish how model behavior is affected by the values of model parameters documented in [11]. Here a small sample is presented to illustrate the work and comment on some outcomes which at first looked surprising.

Sensitivity analysis has been applied to a number of parameters. In the model these parameters are defined as *global variables*. Global variables can be used for defining the properties of activities (e.g. the parameters of the probability distributions used) and to define the initial marking of the places used in the SAN models. SAN allows for defining "studies". A study in SAN terms corresponds to a particular set of values assigned to global parameters. Further details are provided in [11].

4   Findings

A number of studies have been completed via Monte Carlo simulation. Full details are available from the author. The results consist of the probabilities of e-Motor (as a system) being in one of the 3 possible system states – "Success" (mission completed without a failure), "Safe failure" (device moved to safe state) and "Unsafe failure" (failure occurred, but the device failed to reach safe state) – at the end of *missions of fixed lengths*. The results are provided for missions of length in the range of 1000... 12000 h (slightly over a month to more than an year). These were derived from simulation traces of length 200,000 h, i.e. 22 years of operation, likely to exceed the typical lifetime of a car.

An example of sensitivity analysis is provided in Table 1.

Table 1. A sensitivity analysis example.

Global variable name	Exp 1	Exp 2	Exp 3	Exp 4
AttackRate	0.001			
CC_failure_rate	1.00E-04			
Config_repair_success	0.6			
SS_repair_rate	36	360	3.6	36
USF_repair_rate	36	36	36	360
attack_CH1_success_pr	0.2			
attack_CH2_success_pr	0.1			
attack_count	10			
channel_failure_rate	0.001			
failure_coverage	0.8			

The four studies are parameterized identically except for the values of two parameters, **SS_repair_rate** and **USF_repair_rate**, the rates of repair of a channel from safe and unsafe failure, respectively. Common accidental failure is allowed with rate an order of magnitude lower than the rate of channel failure. Accidental failures are assumed to have the same rate as the attacks on the safe state. All probabilities of success (of attacks, of repairs, restoring the safe state and of failure detection) used in the studies are provided in Table 1.

The model behavior under the four parameterizations is summarized in Table 2 in which the probabilities of success, safe failure and unsafe failure at the end of missions of fixed length are computed.

Table 2. Effect of repair time rates on the probabilities of how missions of fixed length will end (Success, Safe failure or Unsafe failure).

Mission duration [hours]	Probability of mission ending in	Probability of mission Success/Safe failure/Unsafe failure			
		Exp 1	Exp 2	Exp 3	Exp 4
1000	Success	0.999120	0.999245	0.999660	0.999175
	Safe failure	0.000880	0.000755	0.000340	0.000825
	Unsafe failure	0	0	0	0
2000	Success	0.998290	0.998415	0.009525	0.998405
	Safe failure	0.001710	0.001585	0.990475	0.001595
	Unsafe failure	0	0	0	0
7000	Success	0.994180	0.995060	0.008180	0.995015
	Safe failure	0.005815	0.004940	0.991820	0.004985
	Unsafe failure	5.00E-06	0	0	0
8000	Success	0.993410	0.019340	0.007930	0.019285
	Safe failure	0.006585	0.980660	0.992070	0.980715
	Unsafe failure	5.00E-06	0	0	0
11,000	Success	0.991455	0.017560	0.007290	0.017650
	Safe failure	0.008540	0.982440	0.992710	0.982350
	Unsafe failure	5.00E-06	0	0	0
12,000	Success	0.020310	0.017005	0.007100	0.017070
	Safe failure	0.979685	0.982995	0.992900	0.982930
	Unsafe failure	5.00E-06	0	0	0

Note that the sum of the probabilities shown in Table 2 per selected mission duration equal to 1 as each individual mission will end up in one and only one of the three alternatives.

5   Discussion

The studies have been chosen so that one can systematically trace the impact of a single parameter on the behavior of the model. It is somewhat surprising that when the rates of repair from both safe state and unsafe state of a channel are the *same* (Exp 1) the mission is likely to survive longest without a failure. The probability of failure of the mission is very low until missions of 12,000 h. Increasing one of the repair rates by an order of magnitude (Exp 2 or Exp 4, respectively) does not improve the chances of mission survival. For these two experiments the probability of a mission failure drops dramatically at around 8,000 h. At first this may seem counterintuitive. Fast recovery must be a good thing. But somehow the improvement of the repair rates *asymmetrically* does not improve the mission chances to survive without a failure. The good news is that this drop is due to safe failures, which one would consider acceptable, although availability is reduced.

Looking at the probability of unsafe failure, we notice that for both Exp 2 and Exp 4 the probability of unsafe system failure the first 12,000 h is 0. In fact after inspecting the entire distribution (up to the simulated 200,000 h per simulation run) we observed that no unsafe failure was recorded for Exp 4 at all. For Exp 2 the first mission length for which unsafe system failure was recorded was 24,000 h[3]. For Exp 1, on the other hand, we did observed unsafe system failures starting from mission duration of 5,000 h. In other words, the improvement of the repairs seems to indicate that the chances of unsafe failures are reduced, which is what one would expect/want.

Exp 3 is not surprising. Reducing the repair rate for channels in safe failed state does reduce the chances of a mission survival. Missions without a failure are very unlikely for missions longer than 2000 h. On the other hand, unsafe failures were first recorded for missions of 13,000 h. This is better than for Exp 1, but the confidence in the computed probabilities is very low for us to draw any conclusions.

The dependent accidental failures of the two channels are modeled using the model of common stress of Marshal and Olkin [10]. It is worth pointing out, that while the adequacy of the model for software failure may be questioned, it clearly models adequately hardware failures – both channels are executed on the same hardware. The model of common mode can be replaced by suitable alternatives, e.g. [12, 13] or [14] and may impact availability .

6   Conclusions and Future Work

In this paper an approach to stochastic modeling of a safety critical device is presented which accounts for both – accidental failures and cyber attacks affecting safety. The study is centered upon one particular attack type: an attack which may lead to eliminating the safe state of the device. The device being specified as an ASIL-D device

---

[3] For all probabilities lower that 10^{-4} the relative confidence in the particular number was lower than 10 %. Thus, for small probabilities (including values of 0) the numbers should be treated as statistically insignificant.

must be built using design diversity and the model accounts for the two-channel architecture of the device.

The paper demonstrates that probabilistic modeling may be useful in quantifying the risk from cyber attacks. The approach advocated in the paper is that a probabilistic model should be detailed enough to account for *all hazards* identified in the safety analysis (in the presented model three hazards have been included and one of them studied in detail) while the epistemic uncertainty with model parameters (i.e. in deciding the values of the parameters related to the attacks) should be addressed by sensitivity analysis exploring the space of *plausible* parameters.

For lack of space the paper could not demonstrate sensitivity analysis more extensively, e.g. varying the rates and probabilities of success of the attacks; the impact of these on model behavior will be studied in the future:

- The model of accidental dependent failures is simplistic, possibly unrealistic and in the future will be replaced with alternatives;
- In the particular context of AUTOSAR an interesting design trade-off exists between protecting the individual devices against cyber attacks specific to a device vs. using a generic intrusion detection/protection system (IDS). Probabilistic modeling seems particularly suitable for addressing this problem and we intend to study the trade-off it in the future.

Acknowledgement. The work was supported by the Artemis JU SESAMO project (grant agreement number 295354). The author would like to thank the anonymous reviewers and Dr Kizito Salako for their thorough reviews of earlier drafts of the paper.

References

1. Zetter, K.: Countdown to Zero Day: Stuxnet and the Lunch of the World's First Digital Weapon. Crown Publishers, New York (2014)
2. Kriaa, S., Bouissou, M., Pietre-Cambacedes, L.: Modeling the stuxnet attack with BDMP: towards more formal risk assessments. In: 7th International Conference on Risk and Security of Internet and Systems (CRiSIS). IEEE, Ireland (2012)
3. Ford, M.D., et al.: Implementing the ADVISE security modeling formalism in Möbius. In: The 43rd Annual IEEE/IFIP International Conference on Dependable Systems and Networks (DSN). IEEE, Budapest (2013)
4. Wang, L., et al.: k-zero day safety: a network security metric for measuring the risk of unknown vulnerabilities. IEEE Trans. Dependable Secure Comput. **11**(1), 30–44 (2014)
5. Ten, C.-W., Liu, C.-C., Manimaran, G.: Vulnerability assessment of cybersecurity for SCADA systems. IEEE Trans. Power Syst. **23**(4), 1836–1846 (2008)
6. Netkachov, O., Popov, P.T., Salako, K.: Model-based evaluation of the resilience of critical infrastructures under cyber attacks. In: The 9th International Conference on Critical Information Infrastructures Security (CRITIS). Springer, Limassol (2014)
7. Taleb, N.N.: The Black Swan: The Impact of the Highly Improbable, p. 394. Penguin, UK (2008)
8. SESAMO: Use Case Specification (Deliverable D1.2), SESAMO Consortium, p. 105 (2013)
9. SESAMO: E-motor (2014). http://sesamo-project.eu/content/e-motor

10. Marshall, A.W., Olkin, I.: A generalised bivariate exponential distribution. J. Appl. Probab. **4**, 291–302 (1967)
11. SESAMO: Integration of Safety and Security Analysis and Assessment Techniques (Deliverable D3.3), SESAMO Consortium, p. 250 (2013)
12. Ammann, P.E., Knight, J.C.: Data diversity: an approach to software fault tolerance. IEEE Trans. Comput. **C-37**(4), 418–425 (1988)
13. Bondavalli, A., et al.: Modelling the effects of input correlation in iterative software. Reliab. Eng. Syst. Saf. **57**(3), 189–202 (1997)
14. Popov, P., Manno, G.: The effect of correlated failure rates on reliability of continuous time 1-out-of-2 software. In: Flammini, F., Bologna, S., Vittorini, V. (eds.) SAFECOMP 2011. LNCS, vol. 6894, pp. 1–14. Springer, Heidelberg (2011)

Organisational, Political and Technical Barriers to the Integration of Safety and Cyber-Security Incident Reporting Systems

Chris W. Johnson[✉]

School of Computing Science, University of Glasgow,
Glasgow G12 8RZ, Scotland, UK
Johnson@dcs.gla.ac.uk

Abstract. Many companies must report cyber-incidents to regulatory organisations, including the US Securities and Exchange Commission and the European Network and Information Security Agency. Unfortunately, these security systems have not been integrated with safety reporting schemes. This leads to confusion and inconsistency when, for example a cyber-attack undermines the safe operation of critical infrastructures. The following pages explain this lack of integration. One reason is a clash of reporting cultures when safety related systems are intended to communicate lessons as widely as possible to avoid any recurrence of previous accidents. In contrast, disclosing the details of a security incident might motivate further attacks. There are political differences between the organisations that conventionally gather data on cyber-security incidents, national telecoms regulators, and those that have responsibility for the safety of application processes, including transportation and energy regulators. At a more technical level, the counterfactual arguments that identify root causes in safety-related accidents cannot easily be used to reason about the malicious causes of future security incidents. Preventing the cause of a previous attack provides little assurance that a motivated adversary will not succeed with another potential vector. The closing sections argue that we must address these political, organisational and technical barriers to integration given the growing threat that cyber-attacks pose for a host of complex, safety-critical applications.

Keywords: Incident reporting · Safety · Cyber-security · Accident analysis · Organisational resilience

1 Introduction

The EU Telecoms directive (2009/140/EC) places an obligation on the providers of networks and services to manage security risks. In particular, Article 13a requires that providers report significant security breaches and losses of integrity to competent national authorities. The proposed Network and Information Security Directive extends this obligation to 'market operators' responsible for critical national infrastructures, across the energy, banking, health, transport, financial services and food sectors. These initiatives mirror trends in the United States, where for example the Security and

© Springer International Publishing Switzerland 2015
F. Koornneef and C. van Gulijk (Eds.): SAFECOMP 2015, LNCS 9337, pp. 400–409, 2015.
DOI: 10.1007/978-3-319-24255-2_29

Exchange Commission already expects its members to file information about cyber incidents. In consequence, many organizations are establishing reporting systems for gathering information about cyber-incidents. These initiatives typically build on reconstruction, causal analysis and pattern matching techniques that were initially intended to support existing Safety Management Systems. There are further similarities. In particular, both safety and security reporting systems must operate across increasingly complex supply chains. Many companies find it difficult to obtain reliable information about safety-concerns and near-miss incidents from sub-contractors, including those working on their sites. Similarly, it is increasingly important for organisations to secure their supply chain, especially where they may not know about the COTS products being used by sub-contractors within their own facilities. This is difficult when the response to security related incidents is often to deny responsibility and avoid blame [2]. This compromises the utility of incident reporting when commercial confidentiality and IP barriers frustrate attempts to diagnose the vulnerabilities that compromise cyber-security.

Given these common concerns it is, therefore, surprising that safety and security reporting systems often run in isolation to each other [1]. Companies report safety-related incidents to their industry regulators. Information about cyber events go to local and national law enforcement, to Computer Emergency Response Teams (CERTs), to national infrastructure protection agencies etc. This lack of integration leads to inconsistent data and disclosure requirements between security and safety reporting systems. Their utility is further undermined by the lack of data mining or other information retrieval tools that might be used to identify common patterns across the different reporting applications.

Section 2 explains the genesis of security-related incident reporting in safety management. Section 3 identifies the benefits that might be gained from the integration of safety and security reporting. Section 4 then enumerates barriers that prevent integration. These include an imbalance between the numbers of safety and security related incidents reported each year. The strong-reporting culture in many safety-related systems contrasts sharply with the routine under-reporting of security violations. We also identify the political barriers to integration. For example, the government bodies dealing with cyber-security and national critical infrastructure protection are very different from those dealing with the safety regulation of individual industries. Finally, we identify technical barriers to integration. In safety-critical systems, counterfactual arguments identify causes by determining that an incident would have been avoided if a number of recommendations had been implemented. It is far harder to sustain these arguments in security incidents when a motivated adversary will actively improvise new methods of attack. Section 5 summarises the conclusions from our analysis and identifies areas for further work.

2   From Safety Management to Cyber Incident Reporting

Incident reporting systems provide information about hazards that were not identified during the early stages of design [3]. They can also provide important insights into hazards that were identified but that were not adequately mitigated during the implementation of safety-critical software. These schemes have been used to improve safety across many industries – include the UK Confidential Reporting Programme for Aviation and Maritime (CHIRP), the European Railway Agency harmonised reporting systems and the Safe Work Australia tools for the process industries. International safety-reporting systems also support information exchange between different stake-holders including operators, suppliers, regulators, safety managers, accident investigators etc. These include EUROCONTROL's Skybrary on http://www.skybrary.aero.

The success of safety incident reporting schemes has inspired a number of organisations, including the US National Institute for Standards and Technology (NIST) and the European Network and Information Security Agency (ENISA) [4], to recommend similar infrastructures for gathering information about cyber-security incidents. Both safety and security reporting systems gather data on historic incidents that can inform the probability and consequence estimates that drive prospective risk assessment. Incident information is also important for the nascent cyber-insurance industry where actuaries require probability and consequence data in order to assess appropriate premiums. Without reliable data about cyber incidents the Obama administration has recently considered tax breaks to encourage companies to invest more in cyber-security. A limit on liability has also been proposed; this reduces the cost of cyber-insurance because under-writers can be sure of the upper limit of their exposure for each claim based on the existing Terrorism Risk Insurance Act (TRIA).

Incident reporting systems provide important feedback on the strengths and weaknesses of security measures in the same way that they can be used to improve the design of safety-related infrastructures. In consequence, the US Department of Homeland Security (DHS) has developed the National Cyber security and Communications Integration Center (NCCIC) to coordinate the collection and dissemination of incident information. This is intended to improve situation awareness, increase national resilience and inform longer-term threat assessments.

3   Integrating Safety and Cyber Security Reporting Systems

Safety-critical systems are subject to a growing range of cyber attacks [5, 6]. In the past, these applications were hard to attack because few people had the technical skills necessary to identify vulnerabilities in bespoke operating systems and network protocols. In contrast, many safety industries now rely on Commercial Off-The Shelf (COTS) infrastructures, including Linux and the IP stack.

There are at least three main cyber threats to safety-critical infrastructures. The first stems from disaffected insiders. Companies rely on a wider range of sub-contractors with correspondingly less knowledge of their underlying technical infrastructures. Incident reporting is important because it can help national security agencies and regulators to determine the extent of vulnerabilities stemming from the use of service oriented outsourcing.

A second source of attack is from the creators of mass-market malware. The perpetrators typically have little interest in safety-related applications. Their focus is on intercepting credit-card details or account passwords, not trying to halt electricity generation or aviation operations. These attackers have little idea of the impact their code can have on safety-related systems.

Finally, state sponsored agencies have developed a range of more advanced, persistent threats. The detection of W32.Stuxnet and its predecessors has shown what is possible. Sniffers exfiltrate network data. They have been found in national critical infrastructures. It is, therefore, important to learn as much as possible about cyber-attacks that are intended to inflict deliberate damage as well as those that disclose sensitive information and compromise longer-term safety.

In previous work, with support from ENISA, we have identified a range of techniques that can be used to integrate safety and security incident reporting [2]. There are a number of motivations for this. The most obvious is to reduce the complexity of maintaining two orthogonal reporting architectures, especially when individuals are unsure where they should report an incident.

4 Differences between Safety and Cyber Security Reporting

This section identifies the barriers that have prevented the integration of safety and security reporting schemes.

4.1 Under-reporting and an Imbalance between Safety and Security Incidents

Many organisations receive far more reports about safety incidents than they do security concerns [2]. One interpretation is that safety-related organisations suffer a comparatively low level of security incidents. Alternatively, it can be argued that the imbalance reflects a reporting bias – with staff either failing to detect or deliberately not submitting cyber security reports. Further work is required to investigate these different hypotheses. Until then, it seems likely that the reporting imbalance stems from a mixture of concerns. Management implicitly improve many security violations, for example the use of USB devices by sub-contractors, because they are anxious to maintain operations. Such incidents are seldom reported even though they threaten the integrity of an infrastructure. At the same time, many safety-related systems lack automated intrusion detection that might identify potential malware – this is particularly true for SCADA systems using Programmable Logic Controllers with very limited forensic support.

The relatively low frequency of cyber-security incidents in safety-related industries has knock-on consequences for security management systems. Many companies lack the specialist forensic resources to identify the causes of a cyber attack. Internal resources must be supplemented by external expertise from national Computer Emergency Response Teams (CERTs), regulatory agencies or industry associations. In practice, this implies a loss of control and an admission that the company cannot cope on its own. The loss of control and the reliance on external agencies can also compromise intellectual property where investigators must be familiar with commercially sensitive information in order to diagnose the causes of an attack. In consequence, there are significant disincentives for companies to report cyber-security concerns. In contrast, standard internal debugging and maintenance processes are sufficient to address most mainstream safety concerns.

A key conclusion of our work in this area is that the public-private partnerships that have been in-place to encourage cyber-incident reporting in recent years have failed to address concerns about under-reporting. It is time for legislation to ensure companies seek external support when potential attacks are identified against national critical infrastructures. The US Federal Communications Commission has levied punitive fines on those companies that have been shown not to report similar incidents through their NORS and DIRS reporting infrastructures [2].

4.2   The Threats from Dissemination

The exchange of information about safety-related incidents helps prevent any future recurrence. A strong safety culture ensures that recommendations are widely distributed. In contrast, reports about the causes of a security breach can expose the vulnerability of other systems that remain to be patched. Information about the remedial actions taken after a security incident can also provide insights into continued vulnerabilities that remain unaddressed. It is for this reason that many organisations operate closed or internal reporting architectures; where information is only shared with others inside that company. There can also be concerns about helping competitors by disclosing information about previous attacks. Disseminating cyber-reports might undermine market confidence and trigger litigation. Without legal protection, many companies only provide anonymous summaries about security incidents, especially those that impact safety.

The need to protect victim confidentiality and to prevent 'copy cat' attacks has justified the publication of summary reports that omit the technical details necessary to replicate an attack. Unfortunately, these reports often omit the technical detail necessary for others to prepare an adequate defence against future attacks. This can leave Chief Information Security Officers frustrated when trying to learn from the generic lessons published by security reporting systems. Further work is urgently required to identify appropriate levels of abstraction that can be used to protect future systems without publicising existing vulnerabilities to potential attackers.

4.3   Political Conflicts of Notification

One of the most immediate concerns from the integration of safety and cyber-security reporting systems is to determine who must be notified about an incident. It can be unclear whether reports should be sent to an industry regulator, such as the US Federal Aviation Administration or Nuclear Regulatory Commission, to a security agency, such as the Department of Homeland Security or the US CERT, or to telecoms regulators who have responsibility for collating information about wider cyber-security concerns, such as the Federal Communications Commission. In some cases, a single incident must be reported to more than one agency. For example, in the UK a cyber-attack with safety related consequences must be reported to the national industry safety regulator and potentially also to a subset of the National Crime Agency, the National Cyber Crime Unit, GOVCERT, the UK Information Commissioner as well as the CESG/Centre for the Protection of National Critical Infrastructure via providers registered under the Cyber Incident Response (CIR) or the Cyber Security Incident Response Scheme (CSIR).

The lack of integration across safety and security reporting systems has a number of adverse consequences. Some of the agencies that run these systems understand the safety-related domain in which an incident occurs but have little cyber security competence. Others have little or no safety-related competence but do understand the general class of cyber-threats. These concerns have been recognised, for example in recent reports from the US Government Accountability Office: "A Better Defined and Implemented National Strategy Is Needed to Address Persistent Challenges" [8] and "Cyber security: National Strategy, Roles, and Responsibilities Need to Be Better Defined and More Effectively Implemented" [9]. Letters of agreement can clarify roles and responsibilities between regulatory and security agencies in the aftermath of a cyber-attack. They help to avoid "turf wars" when engineers are working to ensure the safety of compromised systems. However, these agreements need to be drafted before an incident occurs rather than negotiated in an ad hoc manner following a major incident.

The problems of multiple safety and security reporting systems are compounded for companies that operate across national borders. There are different reporting mechanisms between different countries. For example, there are no UK organisations that can be directly compared to the United States Department of Homeland Security. In Europe, there is increasing pressure to share incident information across member states using consistent reporting mechanisms but without infringing national sovereignty. Appropriate means of achieving this remain the subject of heated debate within the European Commission [9].

4.4 Different Legal Contexts

Arguably, there are differences in the degree of forensic rigour that is required in response to safety and cyber-security investigations. In aviation safety, forensic investigations are governed by the ICAO International Standards and Recommended Practices (SARPS) contained in the 19 Technical Annexes to the Convention on International Civil Aviation. In particular, investigators must notify state security agencies if they believe that material has been tampered with. In contrast, a host of more detailed judicial and legal requirements govern the forensic investigation of security incidents [7, 10]. The systems and networks that are affected by a suspected cyber-attack represent a crime scene. Evidence must be preserved according to legal principles preserving the chain of evidence. It is necessary to uncover normal, hidden, deleted, encrypted and password-protected files to gain as much information as possible about the nature and scope of any attack.

The legal and regulatory framework for the investigation of cyber incidents is likely to become more and more complex with the increasing cross-border integration of national critical infrastructures. The European Commission has encouraged the interoperability of national rail networks. They have promoted the development and integration of smart grids and the creation of the single European skies network. The US Department of Justice makes it clear that the web of international interdependencies is far more complex in cyber incidents, for example when a company in one country is attacked through the exfiltration of operational data on servers in a second state that are attacked by systems in a third nation remotely controlled by attackers in a fourth state [11].

The US Department of Justice [11] suggest that forensic investigators must:

- "Immediately secure all electronic devices, including personal or portable devices.
- Ensure that no unauthorized person has access to any electronic devices at the crime scene.
- Refuse offers of help or technical assistance from any unauthorized persons.
- Remove all persons from the crime scene or the immediate area from which evidence is to be collected.
- Ensure that the condition of any electronic device is not altered.
- STOP! Leave a computer or electronic device off if it is already turned off".

These principles were drafted to support cyber incidents in office-based systems. It would be hard to enforce such requirements in safety-critical applications. Removing "all persons from the crime scene" could be catastrophic in a crowded Air Traffic Control centre or nuclear control room. To "leave a computer or electronic device off if it is already turned off" would prevent the use of redundant protection systems. Forensic security investigators must work closely with systems safety engineers. We urgently need guidance on roles and responsibilities for the forensic analysis of cyber incidents affecting safety-critical infrastructures [2].

4.5 Concerns over Causal Analysis

There has been a growing focus on the systemic factors that create the context in which an incident or accident is likely to undermine the safety of application processes. In contrast, security investigations tend to focus more narrowly on the policies and procedures that have been violated. There is often a disciplinary aspect to the causal analysis. These differences can partly be explained by the different legal context. There are other potential interpretations. The differences in causal analysis and in recommendations between safety and security incidents but they may also stem from different levels of maturity. The focus on the direct human causes of security incidents is similar to the 'perfective approach' to safety-related accident and incident reporting more than a decade ago. We might, therefore, expect that the focus of security investigations to shift towards systemic factors in the future.

Further questions remain about the tools and techniques that investigators might use to improve the coherence and consistency of causal analysis in the aftermath of cyber incidents. In particular, it is unclear whether existing safety-related root cause analysis techniques, including those using counter-factual reasoning, support the analysis of cyber-attacks [3]. Previous paragraphs have raised concerns over counter factual approaches. It is hard to argue that particular changes would have prevented a security incident given that adversaries often launch multiple, simultaneous lines of attack and that some of these will not always be detected.

4.6 Conflicting Recommendations in Security and Safety Reporting Systems

A final area of concern illustrates both the need for integration between safety and cyber-security incident reporting as well as the technical problems in achieving integration. Many existing safety recommendations create security vulnerabilities and vice versa. As a specific example, redundancy is typically used to increase the dependability of critical systems. However, this provides few benefits in software related systems without some level of diversity. Leaving aside the issue of common requirements failure, two redundant versions of the same code are likely to contain the same bugs and hence will fail in the same way. In consequence, N-version programming techniques rely on using two or more contractors to develop redundant versions of the same program. In the event that one fails, the other will not. It is assumed that the use of a diverse supply chain will ensure that both programs do not share common bugs. Unfortunately, such techniques create immediate problems for security management. Companies must devote considerable expense to securing two diverse supply chains – increasingly this involves audit processes to ensure that sub-contractors meet agreed security policies during the development of redundant code. These security concerns are seldom factored into the costs associated with safety-critical software development practices. The meta-level point is that integrating safety and security reveals a host of tensions, which can only be addressed through integration. Without this, we cannot assume that two isolated communities will deliver viable solutions to the problems identified in this paper.

5   Conclusions and Further Work

It is important to collate and disseminate information about previous cyber attacks so that organisations can protect themselves by removing existing vulnerabilities. Unless we aggregate data about the number and consequences of previous incidents then it is hard to assess the risks of future cyber attacks. In consequence, regulatory organisations, including the US Securities and Exchange Commission and the European Network and Information Security Agency, require that organisations provide confidential information in the aftermath of cyber-incidents. Unfortunately, these security-related reporting systems have not been integrated into existing schemes for gathering information with safety-reporting mechanisms. This leads to confusion and to inconsistency when, for example a cyber-attack undermines the safe operation of critical infrastructures.

This paper has identified organisational, political and technical barriers to the integration of security and safety incident reporting. For instance, the benefits from rapid and widespread dissemination of safety recommendations contrast with the dangers of warning adversaries about previous security vulnerabilities and potential attack vectors. There are political barriers to integration. Different government bodies deal with cyber-security, national critical infrastructure protection and the safety regulation of individual industries. Further differences stem from the legal context surrounding safety and security related incidents. It can be hard to sustain the 'no blame' or 'proportionate blame' culture established in safety-critical industries with the direct legal consequences of deliberate security violations.

Technical barriers to integration arise from the need to preserve a chain of evidence in forensic investigations. This is arguably less critical in safety related incidents when evidence is unlikely to be used in legal proceedings, although this may happen in cases of negligence. Further technical barriers arise from the difficulty of identifying common approaches to root cause analysis. Counterfactual arguments help determine causation; a safety-related incident would have been avoided if the root causes did not occur. These counterfactual arguments are harder to sustain in security incidents when motivated adversaries will actively improvise multiple concurrent forms of attack. Tensions can also arise from different recommendations made in the aftermath of safety and security incidents. For example, a safety incident might motivate the use of backup software from multiple suppliers. This creates enormous security overheads; analysts must now audit the security policies and practices across multiple supply chains. These tensions reinforce the need to overcome organisational, political and technical barriers to the integrated reporting of safety and security incidents.

References

1. Johnson, C.W.: Supporting the exchange of lessons learned from cyber-security incidents in safety-critical systems. In: Swallom, D. (ed.) Proceedings of the 32nd International Systems Safety Society, Louisville. International Systems Safety Society, Unionville (2013)
2. Johnson, C.W.: Inadequate legal, regulatory and technical guidance for the forensic analysis of cyber-attacks on safety-critical software. In: Swallom, D. (ed.) Proceedings of the 32nd International Systems Safety Society, Louisville. International Systems Safety Society, Unionville (2014)
3. Johnson, C.W.: Failure in Safety-Critical Systems: A Handbook of Accident and Incident Reporting. University of Glasgow Press, Glasgow (2003)
4. NIST: Computer Security Incident Handling Guide: Recommendations of the National Institute of Standards and Technology, NIST Special Publication 800-61 Revision 2, August 2012
5. Johnson, C.W.: CyberSafety: on the interactions between cybersecurity and the software engineering of safety-critical systems. In: Dale, C., Anderson, T. (eds.) Achieving System Safety, pp. 85–96. Springer Verlag, London (2012). Paper to accompany a keynote address, 20th Annual Conference of the UK Safety-Critical Systems Club. ISBN: 978-1-4471-2493-1
6. Johnson, C.W.: The telecoms inclusion principle: the missing link between critical infrastructure protection and critical information infrastructure protection. In: Theron, P., Bologna, S. (eds.) Critical Information Infrastructure Protection and Resilience in the ICT Sector. IGI Global, Pennsylvania (2013)
7. U.S. National Institute of Standards and Technology (NIST): Guide to Integrating Forensic Techniques into Incident Response, Special Publication 800-86, Gaithersburg, Maryland (2006). http://csrc.nist.gov/publications/nistpubs/800-86/SP800-86.pdf

8. US Government Accountability Office: A Better Defined and Implemented National Strategy Is Needed to Address Persistent Challenges, GAO-13-462T, Washington, DC, USA, 7 March 2013

9. US Government Accountability Office: Cybersecurity: National Strategy, Roles, and Responsibilities Need to Be Better Defined and More Effectively Implemented, Washington, DC, USA, GAO-13-187, 14 February 2013

10. U.S. National Institute of Standards and Technology (NIST): Computer Security Incident Handling Guide (Draft), Special Publication 800-61 Revision 2 (Draft), Gaithersburg, Maryland (2012). http://csrc.nist.gov/publications/drafts/800-61-rev2/draft-sp800-61rev2.pdf

11. U.S. Department of Justice: Forensic Examination of Digital Evidence: A Guide for Law Enforcement (2004)

12. Association of Chief Police Officers: Managers Guide: Good Practice and Advice Guide for Managers of e- Crime Investigation ACPO (2011). http://www.acpo.police.uk/documents/crime/2011/201103CRIECI14.pdf

A Comprehensive Safety, Security, and Serviceability Assessment Method

Georg Macher[1,2]([⊠]), Andrea Höller[1], Harald Sporer[1], Eric Armengaud[2],
and Christian Kreiner[1]

[1] Institute for Technical Informatics, Graz University of Technology, Graz, Austria
{georg.macher,andrea.hoeller,sporer,christian.kreiner}@tugraz.at
[2] AVL List GmbH, Graz, Austria
{georg.macher,eric.armengaud}@avl.com

Abstract. Dependability is a superordinate concept regrouping different system attributes such as reliability, safety, security, or availability and non-functional requirements for modern embedded systems. These different attributes, however, might lead to different targets. Furthermore, the non-unified methods to manage these different attributes might lead to inconsistencies, which are identified in late development phases. The aim of the paper is to present a combined approach for system dependability analysis to be applied in early development phases. This approach regroups state-of-the-art methods for safety, security, and reliability analysis, thus enabling consistent dependability targets identification across the three attributes. This, in turn, is a pre-requisite for consistent dependability engineering along the development lifecycle. In the second part of the document the experiences of this combined dependability system analysis method are discussed based on an automotive application.

Keywords: HARA · Automotive · System analysis · Reliability quantification

1 Introduction

Embedded systems are already integrated into our everyday lives and play a central role in all domains including automotive, aerospace, healthcare, industry, energy, or consumer electronics. In 2010, the embedded systems market accounted for a turnover of almost 852 billion dollars and is expected to reach 1.5 trillion by 2015 (assuming an annual growth rate of 12 %) [21]. For the automotive industry embedded systems components are responsible for 25 % of vehicle costs, while the added value from electronics components range between 40 % for traditional vehicle up to 75 % for electric and hybrid vehicles [27].

The trend of replacing traditional mechanical systems with modern embedded systems enables the deployment of more advanced control strategies, such as reduced fuel consumption and better driveability, but at the same time the higher

© Springer International Publishing Switzerland 2015
F. Koornneef and C. van Gulijk (Eds.): SAFECOMP 2015, LNCS 9337, pp. 410–424, 2015.
DOI: 10.1007/978-3-319-24255-2_30

degree of integration and criticality of the control application bring new challenges. Future automotive systems will require appropriate systematic approaches to support dependable system engineering, rather than traditional engineering approaches managing safety, security, or reliability features separated. System dependability features have mutual impacts, similarities, and interdisciplinary values in common and a considerable overlap among existing methods. Further to this, standards, such as ISO 26262 [16] in safety and Common Criteria [17] in the security domain, have been established to provide guidance during the development of dependable systems and are currently being reviewed for similarities and alignment. System dependability attributes have a major impact on product development and product release as well as for company brand reputation. Hence, incomplete dependability argumentation might be a show-stopper for the development of the entire system. On the other hand, smart counter-measures might represent unique selling points by reducing development costs and improving the quality of the system developed. In this document we define dependability according to [7] as an integrating concept that encompasses the following attributes:

a safety: absence of catastrophic consequences on the users and environment.
b security: the concurrent existence of availability for authorized users only, confidentiality, and integrity with improper meaning of unauthorized.
c serviceability: the combination of reliability (continuity of correct service) and maintainability (ability to undergo modifications and repairs).

This paper presents a combined approach for analysis of dependability features in early design phases of an embedded automotive system. We employed an approach which classifies the probability and impact of security threats using the STRIDE approach [20] and safety hazards using hazard analysis and risk assessment (HARA). This approach, described as the SAHARA approach in [19], quantifies the security impact on dependable safety-related system development at system level. We further extended the inductive analysis methods HARA and SAHARA to also enable the quantification of additional dependability features (such as reliability and availability). This service deterioration analysis (SDA), described in [18] gives further information about the deterioration resistance level (DRL) required for a specific system reliability/availability.

In the course of this document, a description of the state of the art analysis techniques and related works is given in Sect. 2. In Sect. 3 a description of the combination of methods and information handover for system dependability feature analysis is provided. Section 4 assesses an experience report of a system dependability analysis method for safety, security, and reliability attributes during the early development phases of an automotive battery management system (BMS) use-case. Section 5 concludes this work.

2   Related Work and Background

Dependability and security are superordinate concepts regrouping different system attributes such as reliability, safety, confidentiality, integrity, or availability.

Systems dependability and security are thus challenging research domains inheriting a continuous development process and currently of growing importance. Dependable systems rely on mature quality management and development methods such as requirements/systems engineering, system analyses (e.g., FMEA), design and validation plans. For the automotive domain legacy (e.g., emission), liability (e.g., safety and security), and reputation (e.g., reliability and availability) aspects have been identified as key aspects for sustainability in the market.

2.1 State-of-the-Art

Although safety standards only exist in the automotive domain (road vehicles functional safety norm ISO 26262 [16] and its basic norm IEC 61508 [13]), several safety and security norms and guidelines have been established in the avionic domain. In addition to DO-178C [28] for aerospace software safety, ARP4754 [24] gives guidance for system level development and defines steps for adequate refinement and implementation of requirements. Safety assessment techniques, such as failure mode and effects analysis (FMEA), and functional hazard assessment (FHA) among others, are specified by ARP4761 [23]. Security concerns in avionic domain are tackled e.g. by common criteria [31] approach and ED202 [9] specification.

Reliability and availability standards mainly originate from railways and the armaments industry. DIN EN 50126 [6] focuses on specification and demonstration of reliability, availability, maintainability, and safety (RAMS) of the railway system. In 1980 the US Department of Defense defined a standard reliability program for systems and equipment development and production (MIL-STD-785B [2]). Additionally, the military handbooks 338B [5] and 781A [4] assist with guidelines for electronic reliability design and reliability test methods, plans and environment for engineering. Nevertheless, most standards and guidelines, like the military handbook 217F [3] and the technical report TR 62380 [11] rely on reliability prediction of electronic equipment based on mathematical reliability models of the system components. Only a few works focus on quantification of dependability features (other than safety or security) in early stages of the development process.

Most reliability measures and work focus on estimation of probabilities and stochastic processes. All of this work requires detailed design information of the SuD and is therefore not applicable for an early design phase evaluation. Nevertheless, the process improvement techniques of Six Sigma [12,30] aims at improving the quality of process outputs by identifying and removing the causes of defects (errors). The Six Sigma approach uses a set of quality management methods, including statistical methods. One of the Six Sigma methods CTQ trees (critical-to-quality trees) are the key measurable characteristics of a product or process and are used to decompose broad customer requirements into more easily quantified elements. These elements are then converted to measurable terms, this approach is also the basis for Service Deterioration Analysis [18] described later in this section.

The work of Gashi et al. [10] focuses on redundancy, diversity, and their effects on safety and security of embedded systems. This work is part of SeSaMo (Security and Safety Modeling for Embedded Systems) project, which focuses on synergies and trade-offs between security and safety through concrete use-cases. In contrast to this, the work of Macher et al. [19] proposes an approach involving a security-informed hazard analysis and describes an assessment process determining the impact of security attacks on safety features.

Some recent publications in the automotive domain also focus on security in automotive systems. On the one hand, the work of Schmidt et al. [25] presents a security analysis approach to identify and prioritize security issues, but provides only an analysis approach for networked connectivity. The work of Ward et al. [32], on the other hand, also mentions a risk assessment method for security risk in the automotive domain termed threat analysis and risk assessment, based on the HARA.

The works of Roth and Liggesmeyer [22] and Steiner and Liggesmeyer [29] also deal with safety and security analysis, but focus on state/event fault trees for modeling of the system under development. Schmittner et al. [26] presents a failure mode and failure effect model for safety and security cause-effect analysis. This work categorizes threats by using the STRIDE threat model, but focusing on IEC60812 conform FMEA.

Finally, the STRIDE threat model approach [20] developed by the Microsoft Corporation can be used to expose security design flaws. This approach uses a technique termed threat modeling. With this approach the system design is reviewed in a methodical way, which makes it applicable for integration into the HARA approach. Threat models, like STRIDE approach, may often not prove that a given design is secure, but they help to learn from mistakes and avoid repeating them, which is another commonality with HARA in safety domain.

To recap, there are approaches addressing safety, security, and reliability in early development stages. However, these methods are often performed independently and cross-dependencies and mutual impacts are often not considered. Our contribution here is a step towards filling this gap by presenting an approach for addressing safety, security, and reliability issues in early phases and on an interdisciplinary basis.

2.2   Dependability Analysis Methods

Each phase of the development process has a number of analysis methods for the different system features (e.g. safety, security or reliability) in place. In this work we focus solely on the system level rather than software or hardware development stages. The most commonly used analysis methods are hazard analysis and risk assessment (HARA), failure mode and effects analysis (FMEA), and fault tree analysis (FTA) in different variations for safety, security, or reliability/availability. FMEA [1,14] and FTA [15] variation are common for all system features. Nevertheless a method is standardized for initial design assessment exclusively for safety analysis (HARA [16]). The proposed contribution of this work is to combine a security-aware hazard analysis and risk assessment

(SAHARA) [19] and service deterioration analysis (SDA) [18] in a common approach. In the rest of this section both approaches are summarized (for standard hazard analysis and risk assessment as in use in the automotive domain please refer to [16]).

Table 1. Classification examples of knowledge 'K', resources 'R', and threat 'T' value of security threats

Level	Knowledge example	Resources example	Threat criticality example
0	Average driver, unknown internals	No tools required	No impact
1	Basic understanding of internals	Standard tools, screwdriver	Annoying, partial reduced service
2	Internals disclose, focused interests	Non-standard tools, sniffer, oscilloscope	Damage of goods, invoice manipulation, privacy
3		Advanced tools, simulator, flasher	Life-threatening possible

Safety-Aware Hazard Analysis and Risk Assessment (SAHARA). The objective of SAHARA [19] is, analog to HARA, the systematic identification of possible attacks having a possible impact on the correctness of the system (protecting the system against the human). Security attacks are identified and categorized according to their threat criticality (T), know-how (K), and resources (R) required to violate security barriers. The threat criticality (T) relates to the possible effects on the system, the know-how (K) relates to the required know-how to perform the attack, and the resources (R) relates to the required resources to perform the attack. Table 1 contains examples of resources, know-how, and threat levels for each quantification level of K, R, and T values. The three factors define a security level (SecL), as shown in Table 2 which is used to determine the appropriate number of countermeasures needed to be considered. Furthermore, a threat criticality of the highest level implies an impact on safety, has a SecL of minimum 1, and is added to the safety analysis.

Service Deterioration Analysis (SDA). In analogy to the two previously mentioned analysis methods, the service deterioration analysis (SDA) [18] systematically analyzes the impact of component malfunction on the system availability. The deterioration resistance level (DRL) is categorized by the deterioration impact (I) on the system's dependability, the component's repair aggravation (A), and the operation profile (O). The deterioration impact (I) relates to the availability impact on the system, the component's repair aggravation (A) to the capability and easiness to undergo a repair, and the operation profile

Table 2. SecL determination matrix - determination of the security level from R, K, and T values [19]

Required Resources 'R'	Required Know-How 'K'	Threat Level 'T'			
		0	1	2	3
0	0	0	3	4	4
	1	0	2	3	4
	2	0	1	2	3
1	0	0	2	3	4
	1	0	1	2	3
	2	0	0	1	2
2	0	0	1	2	3
	1	0	0	1	2
	2	0	0	0	1
3	0	0	0	1	2
	1	0	0	0	1
	2	0	0	0	1

(O) to the intended harshness of the environment (and therefore the probability for break-down). The repair aggravation factor is determined aligned with the definition of inspection frequency and reliability life cycle degradation control of military handbook 338B [5]. The A factor is therefore the sum of the system's complexity ($high \rightarrow 1, low \rightarrow 0$), accessibility for maintenance ($hard \rightarrow 1, easy \rightarrow 0$), and diagnostic capability ($complex \rightarrow 1, manageable \rightarrow 0$). Table 3 shows the DRL determination matrix used to establish a quantitative indicator determining the impact on system's dependability. A description of the classification of deterioration impact (I), repair aggravation (A), and operation profile (O) values can be seen in Table 4.

3   Combined Approach for Dependable System Development

In the automotive industry, dependability engineering is currently moving its center of gravity from mainly mechanical reliability towards functional safety and security of the control system. While the target is still to provide a convincing argumentation that the system can justifiably be trusted [7], the hazards to consider as well as the development methods must be adapted accordingly. Hence, dependability is seen according to [7,8], as an integrating concept that encompasses more different attributes. Fig. 1 provides an overview of the attributes (aspects) of dependability, the analysis methods available for each attribute, and a common dependable development block indicating the fact that each aspect needs to be addressed within a consistent engineering framework.

Table 3. DRL determination matrix - determination of DRL via I, O, and A values [18]

Operation Profile 'O'	Repair Aggravation 'A'	Deterioration Impact 'I'		
		0	1	2
0	0	0	0	1
	1	0	1	2
	2	0	2	3
	3	0	3	4
1	0	0	0	0
	1	0	0	1
	2	0	1	2
	3	0	2	3
2	0	0	0	0
	1	0	0	0
	2	0	0	1
	3	0	1	2

Table 4. Classification examples of deterioration impact ('I'), repair aggravation ('A'), and operation profile ('O') value

Level	'I' Example	'A' Example	'O' Example
0	No impact	Can be performed by end-user	Normal/intended operation environment
1	Minor impacts	Can be performed at any workshop (trained skills required)	Unplanned/harsh environment
2	Major impacts/reputation compromised	Need to be performed at the production center (specialized skills required)	Misuse
3		No repair possible (repair action not foreseen, product not useable anymore)	

Indeed, a common analysis method delivering consistent dependability targets over the different attributes is the basis to perform consistent dependability engineering during the entire product development. It can also be seen that security is a composition of the attributes of confidentiality, integrity, and availability. Security is the combination of confidentiality, the prevention of unauthorized

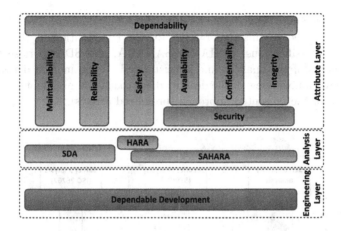

Fig. 1. General overview of dependability attributes and analysis methods

Table 5. Mapping of safety, security, and service oriented engineering terms

	Safety Engineering	Security Engineering	Service-Oriented Engineering
Analysis Subjects risk	hazard	threat	warranty claim, unplanned maintenance
system inherent deficiency	malfunction	vulnerability	service loss or degradation
external enabling condition	hazardous situation	attack	(mis)usage profile
Analysis Categories impact analysis	severity	threat criticality	reputation loss, deterioration impact
external risk control analysis	controllability	attacker skills, know-how	repair efforts, repair aggravation
occurrence analysis	exposure	point of attack, attack resources	operation condition spectrum
Analysis Results design goal	safety goal	security target	dependability target
design goal criticality	ASIL	SecL	DRL

information disclosure and amendment or deletion of information, plus availability and also the prevention of unauthorized withholding of information [7].

The common engineering basis for all dependability aspects raises the requirement for a combination of the different analysis methods and targets, thus a mutual understanding of focuses and language concepts. Table 5 shows a mapping of safety, security, and service oriented engineering terms.

Combining the different dependability feature analysis methods and dependability targets is of high importance. The SAHARA approach [19] already implies an identification of security threats having a possible impact on safety and an information exchange between the security and safety domain. Nevertheless, the approach described in this paper relies on the combination of the outcomes (targets and classifications) of HARA, SAHARA, and SDA to raise the level of completeness of the analysis and consistency between mutual dependencies. Figure 2 shows an overview of the described approach and highlights the distinctive features of the presented approach (broad red arrows).

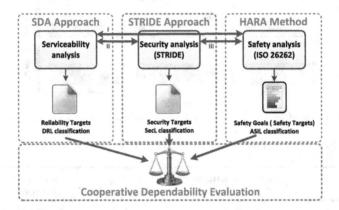

Fig. 2. Overview of the described approach with highlighting of distinctive features (Color figure online)

The mutual impact of serviceability analysis considerations and safety considerations (see Fig. 2 - arrow I) exists between safe states and reliability targets of the system. A tradeoff between higher availability and higher safety of the system impacts the design of safe states (e.g. a system shutdown in case of uncertainty of the actual system state can be a good option from a safety or cost point of view, but has negative effects on system availability). The targets and target classifications found in SDA, therefore have an impact on the design of safe states (e.g. fail-silent vs. fail operational). On the other hand, higher safety levels (ASIL) require higher reliability of the related components. This affects the design and quality requirements of components which might have not been in focus of SDA. Formulating these mutual dependencies between serviceability and safety leads to two regulations:

$DRL \geq 3 \rightarrow$ component related safe states need to be reviewed, eventual adaptation of degradation concept required
$ASIL > QM \rightarrow$ specific component reliability required, eventual adaptation of DRL of neglected component required

Preventing unauthorized access to control interfaces by security password affects the system security positively, beside this, it reduces the availability and controllability of the whole system (see Fig. 2 - arrow II). Requiring authentication of each system component positively affects the overall security, but simultaneously increases the maintenance effort and time requirement, which further impacts system availability. On the other hand easing the maintenance burden by reducing security authentication discloses attack vectors probably not considered during security analysis (e.g. the simple replacement of encryption chip). The regulation of the mutual dependencies between serviceability and security leads to the following:

$DRL \geq 3 \rightarrow$ component related security targets need to be reviewed
$SecL \geq 3 \rightarrow$ serviceability might be affected, review required to determine impact on operational readiness

The third mutual impact (see Fig. 2 - arrow III) exists between safety and security. Safety and security features frequently appear to be in total contradiction to the overall system features. An example of this contradiction can be shown by the electrical steering column lock system. In the security context the system locks the steering column when in doubt, because this doubt area might result from an attack. From the safety perspective, however, it might not be the best approach to lock the steering column as a fallback, since the issue involved might well be an occurrence directly before a high speed corner turn. Mutual dependencies between safety and security can be prescribed as:

$ASIL > QM \rightarrow$ safe state need to be reviewed for possible deactivation of security
$T = 3 \rightarrow$ safety might be affected, a review is required to determine impact on operational readiness

These regulations of the mutual dependencies, the required information handover, and the mapping of the different engineering domain terms allow a cooperative dependability evaluation by cross-domain expert teams and provide traceable measures for early design decisions.

Security Risk description			Security Risk classification				Security Risk related Safety goal description					
Security Hazard ID	STRIDE Function	attacker generated malfunction	Required Resources 'R'	Required Know-How 'K'	Threat Level 'T'	Resulting SecL	Severity 'S'	Exposure 'E'	Controlability 'C'	Resulting ASIL	Safety Goal	Safe State
SH_4	Spoofing	extending safe operation areas of HV battery (temp, cell current, cell voltages)	1	1	5	3	3	4	2	ASIL C	Estimate correct cell status information	assume worst case, No torque provided, driver warning
SH_5	Denial of service	communication with charger jammed	2	2	3	1	3	2	3	ASIL B	Battery outgasing and fire shall be prevented	Disconnect HV battery, driver warning
SH_6	Denial of service	immobilizing of driving functionality	1	0	2	3	0	0	0	QM	--- no safety impact ---	--- no safety impact ---
SH_7	Denial of service	emergency kill switch without limiting element	1	2	3	2	3	2	3	ASIL B	Manual main switch off must be possible	Disconnect HV battery, driver warning
SH_8	Denial of service	replace fuse with non current limiting element	1	1	3	3	3	4	3	ASIL D	Battery outgasing and fire shall be prevented	Disconnect HV battery, driver warning
SH_9	Spoofing	HV system ready without ensured overall system safety	2	2	3	1	3	2	3	ASIL B	Detect short circuit and isolation faults, Prevent from electric shock	Disconnect HV battery, driver warning
SH_10	Tampering	extending safe operation areas of HV battery (temp, cell current, cell voltages)	3	3	3	0	3	4	3	ASIL D	Battery outgasing and fire shall be prevented	Disconnect HV battery, driver warning
SH_11	Spoofing	extending safe operation areas of HV battery (temp, cell current, cell voltages)	1	2	3	2	3	4	2	ASIL C	Correct amount of power shall be maintained	No torque provided, driver warning
SH_12	Denial of service	bypass HVIL	1	2	3	2				ASIL A	Detect short circuit and isolation faults, Prevent from electric shock	Disconnect HV battery, driver warning

Fig. 3. Excerpt of the application of the SAHARA analysis of the BMS use-case

4   Application of the Approach

This section describes the application of the approach as described above for an automotive battery management system (BMS). The BMS use-case is an illustrative material, reduced for training purpose of both students and engineers. The technology-specific details have thus been abstracted for commercial sensitivity and the analysis results presented are not intended to be exhaustive.

Battery management systems are control systems inside of high-voltage battery systems used to power electric or hybrid vehicles. The BMS consists of several input sensors, sensing e.g., cell voltages, cell temperatures, output current, output voltage, and actuators (the battery main contactors).

For the scope of this work the focus is set on early design decision evaluation. This evaluation includes an ISO 26262 [16] aligned HARA safety analysis, a security analysis based on the SAHARA approach, and a serviceability analysis based on the SDA approach. An excerpt of the SAHARA analysis of the BMS use-case is shown in Fig. 3. The excerpt highlights (a) the threat level classification 'T' triggering further analysis of the threat for safety impact and (b) a security hazard aiming on denial of service of the HV fuse. The HARA of the BMS use-case covers 52 hazardous situations, quantifies the respective ASIL and assigns safety goals fully in line with the ISO 26262 standard. Additionally, 37 security threats have been identified using the SAHARA approach, 18 of these security threats have been classified as having possible impacts on safety concepts. Furthermore, 63 service deterioration scenarios have been analyzed using the SDA approach.

Figure 4 shows an excerpt of the SDA for normal operation modes of the BMS use- case also highlighting the HV fuse data. The overlaid excerpt show the impact of the security countermeasure against the threat 'replace fuse with non current limiting element'. As can be seen in the overlay, using corrugated-head screws for the fuse cover decreases the security risk of 'replace fuse with non current limiting element', but increases the repair aggravation value of the HV fuse, which also results in a higher DRL.

Table 6 shows the analysis results related to the three focused elements for this application example (HV fuse, BMS controller, and interlock circuit). The HV fuse related part of Table 6 highlights how a security threat countermeasure which has not affected the ASIL nevertheless affects the DRL of the system, as already shown in Fig. 4. Part two of the table, related to the interlock circuit, indicates that a component of less importance from the safety or service perspective can have huge impact on the system's safety. The BMS controller related part of the table, highlights on one hand the opposite. The data encryption chip does not affect the system's safety, but is related to system's security and also the reputation of the system. On the other hand the table also indicates, that components (such as the BMS controller) which have major impact on the system's safety commonly also demand higher security and serviceability requirements.

ID	Part	System Service	Effect on System Service	Deterioration Impact 'I' Deterioration Impact 'I'	Repair Aggravation 'A' Part Complexity	Part Accessibility	Diagnostic Capability	Resulting 'A'	Operation Profile 'O' Operation Profile 'O'	Operation Profile Description	DRL DRL
8	HV Fuse	provide electric energy	required for system service	2	0	1	0	1	0	normal operation	2
10	BMS controller	provide electric energy	required for system service	2	1	1	1	3	0	normal operation	4
12	Interlock Contactor	store electric energy	reduced service can be provided	1	0	0	1	1	0	normal operation	1
18	HV Fuse	store electric energy	required for system service	2	0	1	0	1	0	normal operation	2
20	BMS controller	store electric energy	required for system service	2	1		1	3	0	normal operation	
8	HV Fuse	provide electric energy	required for system service	2	0	0	0	0	0	normal operation	1
10	BMS controller	provide electric energy	required for system service	2	1	1	1	3	0	normal operation	4
12	Interlock Contactor	store electric energy	reduced service can be provided	1	0	0	1	1	0	normal operation	1
18	HV Fuse	store electric energy	required for system service	2	0	0	0	0	0	normal operation	1
20	BMS controller	store electric energy	required for system service	2	1		1	3	0	normal operation	

Fig. 4. Excerpt of the SDA application of the BMS use-case

Table 6. Component related analysis results of BMS examples

Component	ASIL	SecL	DRL
HV Fuse	B(D)	3	1
		2	2
Interlock circuit	D	2	2
BMS controller	D	3	4
Data encryption chip	QM	4	4

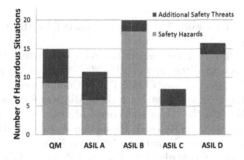

Fig. 5. Safety analysis of the BMS use-case (using SAHARA approach) [19]

Figure 5 additionally presents the number of hazardous situations which have been analyzed and quantified with ASILs and highlights the additional portion of safety hazards derived from security threats.

5 Conclusion

Dependability engineering aims at providing a convincing and explicit argumentation that the system under development has achieved an appropriate level of maturity. Dependability engineering in the automotive domain, while relying on a strong and long-term body of experience, is still an emerging trend. Although, several approaches exist for addressing safety, security and reliability in early development stages, many of these methods are often performed independently and cross-dependencies and mutual impacts are often not considered. This paper presents a concept for a cooperative dependability analysis in early development phases and an application of this analysis for an automotive battery management use-case. The approach conjointly combines security, safety, and serviceability analysis concepts (SAHARA, HARA, and SDA) to enable a common analysis and language base enabling dependable system development. In the course of this study document, (a) a mapping of safety, security, and service oriented engineering terms, (b) a combination of the different analysis methods and targets, and (c) regulations of the mutual dependencies and the required information handover between the different dependability aspect analysis have been presented.

The application of the approach presented has been demonstrated utilizing a simplified automotive BMS use-case. While the authors does not claim completeness of the analysis (due to confidentiality issues), the benefits of the approach are already evident. First, the dependencies between safety/security and reliability analysis are made explicit and can be handed over from one domain to the other according to identified rules. Second, and this is possibly the most important issue, the proposed cooperative dependability evaluation enables consolidation of the different dependability targets in a consistent and at an early design phase, thus providing a single source of dependability targets for the rest of the development.

Acknowledgments. This work is partially supported by the INCOBAT and the MEMCONS projects.

The research leading to these results has received funding from the European Unions Seventh Framework Programme (FP7/2007-2013) under grant agreement n 608988 and financial support of the "COMET K2 - Competence Centers for Excellent Technologies Programme" of the Austrian Federal Ministry for Transport, Innovation and Technology (BMVIT), the Austrian Federal Ministry of Economy, Family and Youth (BMWFJ), the Austrian Research Promotion Agency (FFG), the Province of Styria, and the Styrian Business Promotion Agency (SFG).

We are grateful for the contribution of the SOQRATES Safety AK experts and the expertise gained in SafEUr professional trainings.

Furthermore, we would like to express our thanks to our supporting project partners, AVL List GmbH, Virtual Vehicle Research Center, and Graz University of Technology.

References

1. Military Standard Procedures for Performing a Failure Mode, Effects and Criticality Analysis, November 1980
2. Military Standard Reliabilty Program for Systems and Equipment Development and Production, September 1980
3. Military Handbook Reliability Prediction of Electronic Equipment, December 1991
4. Department of Defense Handbook for Reliability Test Methods, Plans, and Environments for Engineering, Development Qualification, and Production, April 1996

5. Military Handbook Electronic Reliability Design Handbook, October 1998
6. Railway Applications: The specification and demonstration of reliability, availability, maintainability and safety (RAMS), March 2000
7. Avizienis, A., Laprie, J.-C., Randell, B.: Dependability and its threats - a taxonomy. In: Jacquart, R. (ed.) IFIP Congress Topical Sessions, pp. 91–120. Kluwer, Dordrecht (2004)
8. Avizienis, A., Laprie, J.-C., Randell, B., Landwehr, C.: Basic concepts and taxonomy of dependable and secure computing. IEEE Trans. Dependable and Secure Comput. 1(1), 11–33 (2004)
9. European Organization for Civil Aviation Equipment (EUROCAE WG-72) and Radio Technical Commission for Aeronautics (RTCA SC-216): Airworthiness security process specification, ED-202 (2010)
10. Gashi, I., Povyakalo, A., Strigini, L., Matschnig, M., Hinterstoisser, T., Fischer, B.: Diversity for safety and security in embedded systems. In: International Conference on Dependable Systems and Networks, 26 June 2014
11. International Electrotechnical Commission: Reliability data handbook - universal model for reliability prediction of electronics components, PCBs and equipment. Technical report IEC TR 62380, International Electrotechnical Commission (2004)
12. International Organization for Standardization: ISO 13053 quantitative methods in process improvment - Six Sigma (2011)
13. ISO - International Organization for Standardization: IEC 61508 functional safety of electrical/electronic/programmable electronic safety-related systems
14. ISO - International Organization for Standardization: IEC 60812 analysis techniques for system reliability - procedure for failure mode and effects analysis (FMEA) (2006)
15. ISO - International Organization for Standardization: IEC 61025 fault tree analysis (FTA), December 2006
16. ISO - International Organization for Standardization: ISO 26262 road vehicles functional safety, Part 1–10 (2011)
17. van Tilborg, H.C.A., Jajodia, S. (eds.): Encyclopedia of Cryptography and Security. ISO/IEC 15408, 2nd edn. Springer, US (2011). doi:10.1007/978-1-4419-5906-5_1338
18. Macher, G., Hoeller, A., Sporer, H., Armengaud, E., Kreiner, C.: Service deterioration analysis (SDA): an early development phase reliability analysis method. In: Review at 45th Annual International Conference on Dependable Systems and Networks (DSN) - RADIANCE Workshop (2015)
19. Macher, G., Sporer, H., Berlach, R., Armengaud, E., Kreiner, C.: SAHARA: a security-aware hazard and risk analysis method. In: Design, Automation Test in Europe Conference Exhibition (DATE 2015), pp. 621–624, March 2015
20. Microsoft Corporation: The stride threat model (2005)
21. Petrissans, A., Krawczyk, S., Veronesi, L., Cattaneo, G., Feeney, N., Meunier, C.: Design of future embedded systems toward system of systems - trends and challenges. European Commission, May 2012
22. Roth, M., Liggesmeyer, P.: Modeling and analysis of safety-critical cyber physical systems using state/event fault trees. In: SAFECOMP 2013 - Workshop DECS (ERCIM/EWICS Workshop on Dependable Embedded and Cyber-physical Systems) of the 32nd International Conference on Computer Safety, Reliability and Security (2013)
23. SAE International: Guidelines and Methods for Conductiong the Safety Assessment Process on Civil Airborne Systems and Equipment (1996)

24. SAE International: Guidelines for Development of Civil Aircraft and Systems (2010)
25. Schmidt, K., Troeger, P., Kroll, H., Buenger, T.: Adapted development process for security in networked automotive systems. In: SAE 2014 World Congress and Exhibition Proceedings, (SAE 2014–01-0334), pp. 516–526 (2014)
26. Schmittner, C., Gruber, T., Puschner, P., Schoitsch, E.: Security application of failure mode and effect analysis (FMEA). In: Bondavalli, A., Di Giandomenico, F. (eds.) SAFECOMP 2014. LNCS, vol. 8666, pp. 310–325. Springer, Heidelberg (2014)
27. Scuro, G.: Automotive industry: Innovation driven by electronics (2012). http://embedded-computing.com/articles/automotive-industry-innovation-driven-electronics/
28. Special Committee 205 of RTCA: DO-178C Software Considerations in Airborne Systems and Equipment Certification (2011)
29. Steiner, M., Liggesmeyer, P.: Combination of safety and security analysis - finding security problems that threaten the safety of a system. In: SAFECOMP 2013 - Workshop DECS (ERCIM/EWICS Workshop on Dependable Embedded and Cyber-physical Systems) of the 32nd International Conference on Computer Safety, Reliability and Security (2013)
30. Tennant, G.: Six Sigma SPC and TQM in Manufacturing and Services. Gower Publishing Ltd, Aldershot (2001)
31. The Common Criteria Recognition Agreement Members: Common Criteria for Information Technology Security Evaluation (2014). http://www.commoncriteriaportal.org/
32. Ward, D., Ibara, I., Ruddle, A.: Threat analysis and risk assessment in automotive cyber security. In: SAE 2013 World Congress and Exhibition Proceedings, pp. 507–513 (2013)

Programming and Compiling

Source-Code-to-Object-Code Traceability Analysis for Avionics Software: Don't Trust Your Compiler

Jörg Brauer[1]([envelope]), Markus Dahlweid[1], Tobias Pankrath[1], and Jan Peleska[2]

[1] Verified Systems International GmbH, Bremen, Germany
{brauer,dahlweid,panke}@verified.de
http://www.verified.de
[2] Department of Mathematics and Computer Science,
University of Bremen, Bremen, Germany
jp@informatik.uni-bremen.de
http://www.informatik.uni-bremen.de/agbs

Abstract. One objective of structural coverage analysis according to RTCA DO-178C for avionic software of development assurance level A (DAL-A) is to either identify object code that was not exercised during testing, or to provide evidence that all code has been tested in an adequate way. Therefore comprehensive tracing information from source code to object code is required, which is typically derived using a manual source-code-to-object-code (STO) traceability analysis. This paper presents a set of techniques to perform automatic STO traceability analysis using abstract interpretation, which we have implemented in a toolsuite called RTT-STO. At its core, the tool tries to prove that the control flow graphs of the object code and the source are isomorphic. Further analyses, such as memory allocation analysis and store analysis are then performed on top. Our approach has been applied during low-level verification for DAL-A avionics software, where the effort for STO analysis was significantly reduced due to a high degree of automation. Importantly, the associated analysis process was accepted by the responsible certification authorities.

Keywords: DO-178C · Source-code-to-object-code traceability · Static analysis · Abstract interpretation

1 Introduction

Background. For safety-critical systems software verification, many activities are performed on source code level.[1] As a consequence, the validity of these verification results depends on the consistency between source code and object code.

---

[1] In this paper, the term *source code* is used to denote code written in a high-level programming language, such as Ada or C/C++.

© Springer International Publishing Switzerland 2015
F. Koornneef and C. van Gulijk (Eds.): SAFECOMP 2015, LNCS 9337, pp. 427–440, 2015.
DOI: 10.1007/978-3-319-24255-2_31

In some application domains, this issue is addressed by utilising validated compilers [16,23]. This approach, however, is not accepted in the avionics domain. The current standard for software development for airborne systems, RTCA DO-178C [19], states clearly that any automation tool applied in the development or verification process can only be qualified for the specific target system under consideration [20, Chap. B-1]. For compilers, the standard requires an approach where the object code produced is verified by means of tests and analyses, so that a qualification of compilers is not necessary; [19, Chap. 4.4.2] states that

> "*Upon successful completion of verification of the software product, the compiler is considered acceptable for that product.*"

To support this approach, the standard requires to perform various testing activities which show that the executable object code complies with the high-level and low-level requirements, that it is robust with respect to these requirements, and that it is compatible with the target computer [19, Chap. 6.4].[2] In order to show that the requirements-driven tests performed during the verification activities suffice, a *structural coverage analysis* has to be performed [19, Chap. 6.4.4.2]. Structural coverage analysis detects whether some code structures or interfaces have not been exercised during testing. This code has to be removed if it does not contribute to the realisation of the requirements, or it may lead to refined tests or analyses, if the requirements-driven tests performed so far had been too coarse-grained to exercise all case distinctions reflected by the uncovered code.

For less critical applications, the structural coverage analysis may be performed on source code level alone. This means, that the code coverage achieved with the requirements-driven tests is analysed, and the tests may be considered as complete, if (1) all requirements are covered by at least one test case, and (2) the code coverage achieved is 100 %.[3] For software of the highest criticality – this is *Development Assurance Level A (DAL-A)* – however, additional analyses have to be performed on object code level; this activity is called *Source-Code-to-Object-Code (STO) Traceability Analysis*. Its main objective is to verify that any additional object code which has been generated by the compiler but is not directly traceable to the source code does not introduce any errors and has been adequately covered by tests and/or analyses [19, Chap. 6.4.4.2 b.].[4] STO

---

[2] The latter objective addresses the problem that formally correct code may produce errors at runtime due to hardware/software incompatibilities, such as insufficient register sizes for certain arithmetic operations.

[3] For software of criticality level DAL-C, the standard requires statement coverage, for DAL-B software decision coverage has to be achieved, and MC/DC coverage is required for DAL-A [19, Table A-7].

[4] STO traceability analysis was already required for DAL-A software by the DO-178B [22]. However, the text has often been misunderstood, and clarifications have been published [7,8]. These clarifications have been incorporated into the DO-178C, which now explicitly mentions that STO traceability not only involves the branching structure of the program, but also the identification of untraceable side-effects in linear code blocks, such as memory accesses or function invocations.

traceability analysis certainly is a non-trivial task, because in principle, compilers may (1) add, (2) delete, or (3) morph code during compilation. As analysed in [21, Chap. 4.12] and [18, Chap. 9.7.4.4], situation (1) can occur due to stack initialisation, branch optimisation, addition of compiler generated checks, built in error detection, or hidden library routines.[5] (2) may be caused again by branch optimisation or removal of unreachable source code introduced due to defensive programming.[6] (3) may be caused by register tracking[7] or instruction scheduling.[8] While the situations listed above are the legal variants of (1), (2), and (3), an erroneous compiler may also add, remove, or morph code in an illegal way, so that the consistency between source code and object code is violated.

Objectives and Main Contributions. In this paper, we present an automated approach to STO traceability analysis. We show that the variants of adding, removing, or morphing code described above can all be detected by static analysis and abstract interpretation techniques [9], which are structured into four analysis passes: (a) branching analysis, (b) memory allocation analysis, (c) hidden call detection, and (d) store analysis. Pass (a) detects all variants of branches added or removed during compilation, (b) identifies data structures allocated with insufficient memory, (c) detects untraceable function calls, and (d) finds untraceable accesses to memory and registers.

Importantly, the analysis method is associated with a verification workflow that has been approved by certification authorities for the verification of DAL-A software. The method has been implemented in the industrial-strength tool RT-Tester Source-Code-to-Object-Code Traceability Analyser (RTT-STO) and effectively applied in the STO traceability analysis of DAL-A code for an Airbus avionics control system. The key purpose of the tool is to *soundly detect traceability issues*[9], rather than verify them, and leave the *verification* of these situations to verification engineers. Therefore, its performance is suitable for the analysis of fair-sized real-world systems. In some situations, however, additional branching inserted by the compiler for optimisation purposes can be already verified as legal, and untraceable writes or reads and illegal register copies can be identified as compiler flaws. A tool qualification kit according to RTCA DO-178C is available, so that target-specific qualification can be performed with low effort. To our best knowledge, there are currently no other tool-based approaches to STO traceability analysis offering the same degree of automation.

---

[5] For example, the compiler may call built-in library functions for fast memory copy or for arithmetic operations; these function calls are invisible on source code level.

[6] Think of a switch statement containing all possible switch cases and an additional (superfluous) default-branch.

[7] The compiler tracks the contents of registers to avoid reloading values if they are used again soon. Variables, constants, and structure references such as (a.b) are tracked through linear code blocks.

[8] Move/load/store/branch operations may be re-grouped by the compiler in order to optimise the parallelisation options offered by the RISC processor.

[9] Soundness means that no untraceable object code remains undetected.

Overview. In the following, Sect. 2 first discusses the branching analysis and presents its core steps by means of a worked example. Next, Sect. 3 discusses the remaining three analysis passes. Then Sect. 4 presents performance values and other evaluation results from the application of RTT-STO in the aforementioned DAL-A low-level verification project, before the paper closes with a presentation of related in work in Sect. 5 and a discussion in Sect. 6.

2   Branching Analysis Using Graph Isomorphisms

As discussed before, STO-analysis using RTT-STO is structured into four successive analysis passes. The base of these analysis passes is the branching analysis, the purpose of which is to associate branches on source code and object code level. If successful, control flow in both program representations is indistinguishable, and the control flow graphs (CFGs) can be considered *isomorphic*.[10] The key idea of branching analysis in the context of STO-analysis is thus to provide a technique that derives an *isomorphism* between the CFGs, a technique that is familiar when comparing different versions of the same executable program [10,11,13]. This section thus addresses the question of how isomorphisms between source and object code CFGs can be established.

In order to detect whether two CFGs are isomorphic, we turn to a representation using deterministic finite automata (DFAs). The DFAs are derived from a CFG so as to represent the control flow of the underlying CFG. Then, two or more CFGs can be considered isomorphic if their DFAs accept the same languages, an observation that can be used as a criterion for isomorphism. Recall that a DFA $\mathcal{A}$ is defined as a tuple $(Q, \Sigma, \delta, q_0, F)$, where

- Q is a finite set of states,
- Σ is a finite input alphabet whose elements are called symbols,
- $\delta : Q \times (\Sigma \cup \{\varepsilon\}) \to Q$ is a transition function,
- $q_0 \in Q$ is an initial state, and
- $F \subseteq Q$ is a set of accepting states.

Here, ε is used to denote the empty label. An intuitive choice is to associate with each basic block in the CFG a state $q \in Q$ and to define the input alphabet of $\mathcal{A}$ as the set of edges of the CFG. We sketch the DFA construction and the decision procedure for isomorphism by means of a worked example.

From CFGs to Finite Automata. Figure 2 depicts the C code for a function f() that serves as the running example. This function is part of a simple state machine, where the current state is evaluated using a `switch` statement, and the respective handlers are called in sub-functions. The CFG generated from the above source code is shown in Fig. 1. It consists of an entry node and 12 basic

---

[10] CFG reconstruction from source code and object code is not the scope of the paper, and we thus assume that CFGs for both representations are readily available; see Sect. 5 for further details on this issue.

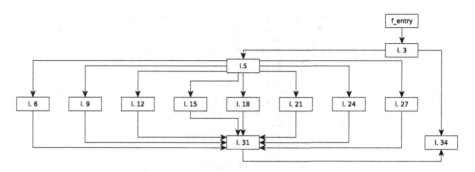

Fig. 1. Control flow graph extracted from the code of a function that uses a `switch` statement with seven `case` branches and one `default` branch, see Fig. 2.

blocks[11], each of which is represented by a single node. The exit node $\boxed{\text{l. 34}}$ corresponds to the `return` statement in line 34. Note that the `if`-statement represented by $\boxed{\text{l. 3}}$ induces an explicit **then**-branch to the `switch`-statement in $\boxed{\text{l. 5}}$ as well as an implicit **else**-branch that targets the `return`-statement represented by $\boxed{\text{l. 34}}$.

As sketched before, a DFA $\mathcal{A}$ can be extracted by adding a state for each basic block and then labelling the edges with unique descriptions of their role. In the running example, we choose labels IfThen and IfElse for the edges induced by the `if` statement in line 3 and Case_i with $i \in \{0, \ldots 7\}$ for the edges from the `switch` statement to the `case` and `default` branches. All other edges receive the empty label ε. As accepting state, we additionally introduce a distinguished exit-node _end, whose incoming edge is labelled with E. We likewise add an initial state _start. This way, we obtain the DFA $\mathcal{A}$ given in Fig. 3, where the fresh nodes are highlighted using dashed lines. Likewise, we obtain a CFG and a DFA from the object code of the function in Fig. 2. The DFA is depicted in Fig. 4. Whilst this DFA looks quite similar to the one generated from source code, it is yet to decide whether both DFAs implement isomorphic control flow.

Deciding CFG Isomorphism. The final step is thus a decision procedure for isomorphism of two or more CFGs represented by their DFAs. The comparison of two DFAs $\mathcal{A}_1$ and $\mathcal{A}_2$ is implemented using a variant of Hopcroft's algorithm [14], which ensures that two DFAs which accept the same language are equal up to isomorphism. Minimised DFAs can thus be compared using graph traversal. In the worked example, the verdict is that the control flow of the CFGs differs because the resulting DFAs are not isomorphic due to the transition from b0 to L236 in Fig. 4 labelled by Case_8.

---

[11] In the example, nodes are labelled with their line numbers from the listing. However, the choice of a labelling is inconsequential as long as the node labels are unique.

```
1  ReturnType f(const State_t state) {
2    ReturnType status = SUCCESS;
3    if (state != currentState) {
4      previousState = currentState;
5      switch(state) {
6      case STATE_INIT:
7        status = toInit();
8        break;
9      case STATE_PREACTIVE:
10        status = toPreactive();
11        break;
12      case STATE_PROCESSING:
13        status = toProcessing();
14        break;
15      case STATE_UPLOADING:
16        status = toUploading();
17        break;
18      case STATE_ERROR:
19        status = toError();
20        break;
21      case STATE_FAILED:
22        status = toFailed();
23        break;
24      case STATE_DEBUG:
25        status = toDebug();
26        break;
27      default:
28        status = ERR_PARAM;
29        break;
30      }
31      stateTime = getTimeStamp();
32      performEntryAction = TRUE;
33    }
34    return status;
35  }
```

Fig. 2. C code for the worked example.

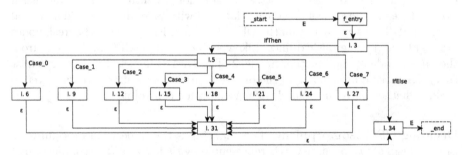

Fig. 3. DFA derived from the CFG in Fig. 1.

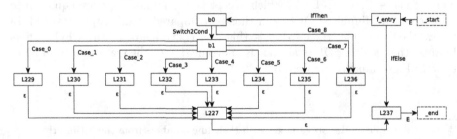

Fig. 4. DFA derived from the object code generated from the source code in Fig. 2.

Is the Code Legitimate? Now that the branching analyser has shown that the source code and the object code implementation of function f() implement a differing branching structure, additional effort has to be put into understanding the reason for this deviation. It turns out that the least value handled in the switch-statement, STATE_INIT is defined as holding the integer value 1. The compiler — even though it has been configured to perform no optimisations at all — thus produces code that preventively checks whether the value of parameter state is at least 1; if not so, control is passed directly to the default-branch without exercising all the possible branches in the switch-statement itself (in the DFA in Fig. 4, this branch is represented by the transition b0 $\xrightarrow{\text{Case\_8}}$ L236, for which no counterpart is found on source code level). This form of control flow is invisible from source code level. However, the branch is reachable and legitimate, and thus two distinguished test cases are required: one that passes value 0 for parameter state and thus triggers the additional branch, and another one that passes another unhandled value so as to trigger the actual default-branch.

Limitations of Automata-Based Branching Analysis. The alert reader will have observed that the chosen representations of the control flow using CFGs and DFAs are not equivalent. Indeed, the described transformation from CFGs to DFAs inevitably leads to a loss in precision. As an example, let us return to Fig. 4. Suppose the compiler has by mistake generated code that gives a transition b0 $\xrightarrow{\text{Case\_8}}$ L235 instead of b0 $\xrightarrow{\text{Case\_8}}$ L236. The branching analysis based on comparison of automata does not uncover this flaw, which may appear to be a serious problem of the approach; it is not. Branching analysis in the context of DO-178C is not a stand-alone analysis, but *complements* requirements-based testing activities. Such erroneous edges would thus have been uncovered using requirements-based tests beforehand.

3   Beyond Branching Analysis

As argued before, one of the key aspects of STO analysis is to provide evidence that the branching structure of the compiled object code of a program correctly models the branching structure induced by the source code. However, tracing branches in both representations is only the first step required to receive certification credit. This section focuses on further subtleties that need to be analysed.

Hidden Call Detection. Even if the branching structure of the object code matches the source code, this does not imply that the compiler has not introduced additional function calls. Naively, one could argue that the compiler is not allowed to do so. This is not true. For example, suppose a program on a 32-bit PPC platform uses a 64-bit integer division, which is not natively supported by the processor. The compiler then *should* replace this operation by a call to a built-in function, which in turn leads to a different calling structure and stack layout compared to what is expected from source code. The identification of such *hidden calls* is straightforward, given the information about the program structure that has been derived during branching analysis.

Recall that for branching analysis, we have determined a mapping between basic blocks in both source code and object code. Hence, it suffices to check whether all basic blocks invoke the same sub-functions in exactly the same order in both program representations. If this is not the case, a traceability issue has been detected, thereby requiring additional verification.

As an example, consider the following assembly fragment generated by a PPC compiler, which contains calls to two functions `getMsgTime()` and `__udiv64()`. The function `getMsgTime()` returns an unsigned 64-bit integer value.

```
1: bl    getMsgTime           7: addi  r6, r6, 16960
2: mr    r12, r4              8: li    r5, 0
3: mr    r11, r3              9: bl    __udiv64
4: mr    r4, r12             10: mr    r12, r4
5: mr    r3, r11             11: mr    r11, r3
6: lis   r6, 15              12: stw   r12, 16(r31)
```

This basic block could directly be traced to the following C block, which contains just one call:

```
msg->timestamp = (uint32) (getMsgTime() / MILLI_TO_NANO);
```

The function `__udiv64()` called in the assembly has been inserted by the compiler to implement the unsigned 64-bit division. The code is thus not traceable, yet correct, and additional verification measures have to be taken. With the traceability data for basic blocks, it is straightforward to point verification engineers to program locations that need to be examined.

Memory Allocation Analysis. The memory allocation analysis checks whether the object code contains data allocations (on the heap, on the stack, or in form of registers) where the size of the allocated memory region does not conform to the size expected from the type declarations in the source code. The concept behind this analysis is thus simple: Sound expectations have to be derived from the source code, and an object code analysis has to determine whether the object code meets these expectations. The size-allocation strategies for data structures are usually laid out in the application binary interface (ABI) of the target processor, cf. [24], and can thus be "mimicked" by the STO traceability analyser to infer the expected values. Moreover, compilers typically provide information as to how they set up stack frames. For the example from Fig. 2, for instance, we obtain the following information:

```
#function:                  f
#stack frame size:          16
#link area offset:          0
#local storage area offset: 12
#gpr save area offset:      12
```

```
#status                        r31    local
#state                         r11    param
```

These outputs indicate that the overall size of the stack frame of f() is 16, that parameter state is passed via register r11, and that status is stored locally in register r31. Along with the declarations of global data in the .data respectively .rodata sections the object code, these information need to be analysed. Of course, one also has to check whether the object code correctly allocates the data regions, in particular the setup of the stack frame. However, such an analysis comes for free when performing a dedicated store analysis, which is discussed in the following section.

Store Analysis. A quite subtle observation is that an erroneous compiler may have inserted undesired store operations targeting some memory addresses. Since requirements-based tests typically only examine the effects of desired store operations in the expected results — but not all possible alterations of the memory state — such malicious behaviour is likely to be missed during testing.

On RISC processors, all accesses to memory are implemented using explicit load and store operations such as stw r12, 4(r31), which stores the contents of register r12 in the memory cell addressed in r31 with an offset of 4. It is therefore important that the store analysis traces the values of those registers that are used as sources respectively targets in the load and store operations. The abstract interpretation is thus implemented as an intraprocedural fixed-point iteration on assembly code [1,6] with an abstract domain specifically designed to trace variable addresses. We thus build on the side-effect analysis for PPC assembly of Flexeder et al. [12], which infers side-effects of procedure calls onto the runtime stack, and straightforwardly extend it to heap-based data.

A noteworthy characteristic of PPC assembly is that loading addresses of variables into registers is distributed over multiple instructions. Suppose that label .L42 in the assembly refers to a global variable x. Then, the code fragment

```
lis r4, %hiadj(.L42)
addi r4, r4, %lo(.L42)
```

loads the address of x into register r4, that is, it corresponds to the C-expression &x: first, the upper half word of the address is loaded into r4, and then its lower half word is added. This address handling pattern has to be tracked during abstract interpretation.

4 Evaluation

In the introduction, we have stated that we have applied RTT-STO – which implements the different techniques discussed in this paper – during the low-level verification activities of DAL-A code for an Airbus avionic control system. This section discusses our experiences from this project. The software itself was written in C and compiled for a 32-bit PPC platform using a compiler that has been developed specifically for the avionics domain. As required for DAL-A software, all compiler optimisations were disabled. The overall codebase consisted of 298 C-functions, with some additional low-level code written directly in assembly language (the assembly code was not analysed during the STO-related verification activities).

4.1 Branching Analysis

In the branching analysis pass, RTT-STO could prove that the control matches for 270 out of 298 functions, which is a success rate slightly above 90%. The overall runtime was in the order of a few minutes, where most time was actually spent parsing the codebase. Those situations in which the automatic analysis failed to prove traceability can roughly be classified as follows:

switch statements. The compiler provides two different strategies for generating object code from switch statements: it either implements a binary decision tree to compare the switch variable with the specified cases (including the default case), or produces a jump table. In both cases, the compiler may produce untraceable object code. If the different cases refer to integer values $c_1, \ldots, c_n$ and there exists a value $c_0 < c_1$, the object code may contain an additional branch for handling this situation in addition to the implementation of the default branch. We have seen this situation in Sect. 2. Additional tests may thus be necessary to ensure that this situation is properly exercised during testing activities.

64-bit arithmetic. As a 32-bit platform, the PPC target naturally has to emulate 64-bit arithmetic using a sequence of operations that may contain additional branching. For example, if a 64-bit unsigned integer x is compared to a 32-bit unsigned integer variable y, the compiler emits code to first compare the most significant 32 bits of x to 0 and subsequently compare the least significant 32 bits of x to y. The compiler thus generates branches that are not directly traceable to source code. For these situations, additional tests had to be designed which carefully trigger the low-level branching behaviour.

4.2 Hidden Call Detection

The tool produced zero false positives and has identified all calls to built-in library functions. All calls could be traced directly to the source code that has legitimately induced the code. The overall runtime was below one minute, where again most time was spent parsing the codebase.

4.3 Memory Allocation Analysis

The analysed codebase contains 1477 variable and constant declarations. Correctness of memory allocation could automatically be shown for 1360 of these declarations, and the analysis failed for 117 cases. All warnings turned out to be false positives. About 30 % of those situations in which the tool failed are declarations of string constants, which were not supported in the RTT-STO version used in the project. The remaining 70 % of false positives directly follow from these warnings; if the compiler places a variable on stack and the allocation analysis fails, all variables allocated in the same stack frame have to be marked as potentially corrupted, which explains the relatively high number of warnings.

4.4 Store Analysis

Overall, the object code contains 2296 instructions that access memory (recall that RISC processors have explicit load and store operations for memory access, unlike CISC; intermediate computations are thus always stored in registers before written into memory). Tracing between the accesses in the object code and the source code could automatically be established for approximately 80 %. The overall runtime of the tool for this pass was below five minutes. Most warnings generated by RTT-STO stem from two different cases. First, the abstract interpretation implemented in RTT-STO loses precision in case of pointer arithmetic that models accesses to multi-dimensional arrays in the object code. Hence, for all write-accesses to multi-dimensional arrays, a warning was emitted. Second, suppose that the codebase contains the code fragment given in Fig. 5, where Data_t is a structure. For such situations, the PowerPC application binary interface [24] states the following behaviour:

> *"Functions that return structures or unions which do not conform to the requirements of being returned in registers shall place the results in a storage buffer that has been pre-allocated by the caller. The address of this storage buffer shall be passed as the first argument [...]"*

Hence, the compiler has to generate untraceable code to be compliant to the ABI, since the assignment to variable t in line 7 of Fig. 5 is implemented by means of memcpy()-like code fragment. It is not the object code of function exec() that stores globalData in t, but the assignment is instead implemented in the object code that implements getData(). Hence the generated code is untraceable and thus warrants additional verification measures to be taken.

```
1 Data_t getData() {
2   return globalData;
3 }
4
5 ...
6 void exec() {
7   Data_t t = getData();
8 }
```

Fig. 5. Simple C code fragment that leads to untraceable object code.

5   Related Work

According to the DO-178C standard [19, Table A-7], STO traceability analysis is part of structural coverage analysis. It is important to note that structural coverage analysis is performed to identify any functionality that was not exercised during the requirements-based testing activities [18, Chap. 9.7.4]. Structural coverage analysis must thus not be confused with structural testing (which is inadequate for DO-178C-related projects), the purpose of which is to systematically exercise a program based on the structure of its code.

Little effort has so far been put into the automation of the very time-consuming STO traceability analysis process. The tool COUVERTURE [5] uses QEMU [4] — which performs dynamic binary translation — to provide a virtualised execution environment for the target software on a host rather than the actual target. The software is then executed and coverage is measured. Their work can thus be seen as diametrically opposed to our approach, which is based on static analysis in the abstract interpretation framework rather than dynamic measurements. However, it is doubtful whether the dynamic binary translation used by COUVERTURE would be accepted by certification authorities for DAL-A software. Other tools, such as OSMOSE [2] use dynamic symbolic execution to generate test cases directly on the level of object code. An interesting aspect of OSMOSE is that it identifies potentially infeasible branches directly in the binary [2, Chap. C], and the authors argue that tools such as OSMOSE are useful to complement to source-level testing activities [2, Chap. D].

From a technical perspective, our work builds on several topics related to program analysis and abstract interpretation. Control flow graph reconstruction from object code — which is the groundwork for STO traceability analysis — using abstract interpretation techniques has widely been studied in the past [3,15,17]. In our setting, control flow reconstruction is much simpler since indirect control which frequently occurs in x86-software (for example, through virtual functions in C++) barely occurs in DAL-A code. Further, certification authorities accept object code analysis to be performed on top of the assembly output of the compiler rather than the bare object code [7,8], which eliminates the need for proper disassembly of binaries. Graph-based algorithms have been applied to the comparison of binaries, they are also based on the idea of finding isomorphic CFGs [10]. Their work, however, focuses on finding differences between different versions of the same binary for malware analysis.

6   Concluding Discussion

This paper advocates using static program analysis techniques to ease the challenging issue of STO traceability analysis for certification of DAL-A software according to RTCA DO-178C. The RTT-STO tool-chain described in this paper is not new in terms of theoretical contributions. It builds upon well-understood techniques from the areas of program analysis, abstract interpretation and automata theory. However, the combination of these techniques has a significant impact on STO analysis in practise. Rierson [18, Chap. 9.7.4.4] describes the way STO analysis is usually performed in practise as follows:

> *"The analysis is usually applied using a sample of the actual code, rather than 100 % of the code. The sample used should include all constructs that are allowed in the source code and comprise at least 10 % of the actual code base. [...] The analysis requires an engineer with knowledge of the specific language, assembly, machine code, and compilers."*

Her brief summary of STO analysis in practise directly exposes the contributions of our work compared to the state-of-the-art. By way of contrast, our technique

- performs the analysis on the entire code base rather than on a sample, and, consequently,
- covers all constructs used in the source code, and
- requires less engineering man-power with expertise in assembly language, due to a high degree of automation.

We have discussed our experiences with this approach in an industrial avionic project, and the savings in terms of workload — and thus, cost — are significant. There are certain situations in which RTT-STO fails to detect traceability even though the code is traceable, as we have discussed in Chap. 4. In practise, discussions with certification authorities often circle around the question how completeness of the verification activities can be proven. A simple but very valuable side-effect of tool-supported STO analysis, even if the tools produce some false positive warnings, is that it guides verification engineers to locations that warrant additional verification.

References

1. Balakrishnan, G., Reps, T.W.: WYSINWYX: what you see is not what you execute. ACM Trans. Program. Lang. Syst. **32**(6), 23:1–23:84 (2010)
2. Bardin, S., Baufreton, P., Cornuet, N., Herrmann, P., Labbé, S.: Binary-level testing of embedded programs. In: QSIC, pp. 11–20. IEEE (2013)
3. Bardin, S., Herrmann, P., Védrine, F.: Refinement-based CFG reconstruction from unstructured programs. In: Jhala, R., Schmidt, D. (eds.) VMCAI 2011. LNCS, vol. 6538, pp. 54–69. Springer, Heidelberg (2011)
4. Bartholomew, D.: Qemu: a multihost, multitarget emulator. Linux J. **2006**(145), 3 (2006)
5. Bordin, M., Comar, C., Gingold, T., Guitton, J., Hainque, O., Quinot, T.: Object and source coverage for critical applications with the couverture open analysis framework. In: ERTS (2010)
6. Brauer, J., Noll, T., Schlich, B.: Interval analysis of microcontroller code using abstract interpretation of hardware and software. In: SCOPES. ACM (2010)
7. Certification Authorities Software Team (CAST): Guidelines for Approving Source Code to Object Code Traceability - Position Paper CAST-12. CAST (2002)
8. Certification Authorities Software Team (CAST): Structural Coverage of Object Code - Position Paper CAST-17. CAST (2003)

9. Cousot, P., Cousot, R.: Abstract interpretation: a unified lattice model for static analysis of programs by construction or approximation of fixpoints. In: POPL, pp. 238–252. ACM (1977)

10. Dullien, T., Rolles, R.: Graph-based comparison of executable objects. SSTIC **5**, 1–13 (2005)

11. Flake, H.: Structural comparison of executable objects (2004)

12. Flexeder, A., Petter, M., Seidl, H.: Side-effect analysis of assembly code. In: Yahav, E. (ed.) SAS 2011. LNCS, vol. 6887, pp. 77–94. Springer, Heidelberg (2011)

13. Gao, D., Reiter, M.K., Song, D.: BinHunt: automatically finding semantic differences in binary programs. In: Chen, L., Ryan, M.D., Wang, G. (eds.) ICICS 2008. LNCS, vol. 5308, pp. 238–255. Springer, Heidelberg (2008)

14. Hopcroft, J.: An n log n algorithm for minimizing states in a finite automaton. Technical report, DTIC Document (1971)

15. Kinder, J., Zuleger, F., Veith, H.: An abstract interpretation-based framework for control flow reconstruction from binaries. In: Jones, N.D., Müller-Olm, M. (eds.) VMCAI 2009. LNCS, vol. 5403, pp. 214–228. Springer, Heidelberg (2009)

16. Leroy, X.: Formal verification of a realistic compiler. Commun. ACM **52**(7), 107–115 (2009)

17. Reinbacher, T., Brauer, J.: Precise control flow reconstruction using boolean logic. In: EMSOFT, pp. 117–126. ACM (2011)

18. Rierson, A.: Developing Safety-Critical Software. CRC Press, Boca Raton (2013)

19. RTCA SC-205/EUROCAE WG-71: Software Considerations in Airborne Systems and Equipment Certification. No. RTCA DO-178C, RTCA Inc. 1140 Connecticut Avenue, N.W., Suite 1020, Washington, D.C., 20036, December 2011

20. RTCA SC-205/EUROCAE WG-71: Software Tool Qualification Considerations. No. RTCA DO-330, RTCA, Inc., December 2011

21. RTCA SC-205/EUROCAE WG-71: Supporting Information for DO-178C and DO-278A. No. RTCA DO-248C, RTCA, Inc., December 2011

22. RTCA, SC-167: Software Considerations in Airborne Systems and Equipment Certification, RTCA/DO-178B. RTCA (1992)

23. European Committee for Electrotechnical Standardization: EN 50128:2011 - Railway applications - Communications, signalling and processing systems - Software for railway control and protection systems. CENELEC, Brussels (2001)

24. Sobek, S.,Burke, K.: Power PC Embedded Application Binary Interface (EABI): 32-Bit Implementation. Freescale Semiconductor Inc. (2004)

Automated Generation of Buffer Overflow Quick Fixes Using Symbolic Execution and SMT

Paul Muntean[(⊠)], Vasantha Kommanapalli, Andreas Ibing,
and Claudia Eckert

Department of Informatics, Technical University Munich, Munich, Germany
{paul,kommana,ibing,eckert}@sec.in.tum.de

Abstract. In many C programs, debugging requires significant effort and can consume a lot of time. Even if the bug's cause is known, detecting a bug in such programs and generating a bug fix patch manually is a tedious task. In this paper, we present a novel approach used to generate bug fixes for buffer overflow automatically using static execution, code patch patterns, quick fix locations, user input saturation and Satisfiability Modulo Theories (SMT). The generated patches are syntactically correct, can be semi-automatically inserted into code and do not need additional human refinement. We evaluated our approach on 58 C open source programs contained in the Juliet test suite and measured an overhead of 0.59 % with respect to the bug detection time. We think that our approach is generalizable and can be applied with other bug checkers that we developed.

Keywords: Program repair · Symbolic execution · Software bugs

1 Introduction

"If one tries to put or to retrieve data from a non existing place/index he is going to make a mess" *Mother Nature Law.*

According to the 2011 CWE/SANS top 25 of most dangerous software errors [23] which can lead to serious vulnerabilities in software, buffer overflows are ranked on 3rd place after SQL injection and OS command injection. Buffer overflows can generate risky resource management vulnerabilities as the recent Heartbleed bug [24] confirms. This bug generates a buffer over-read in the OpenSSL library by leaking sensitive information to the outside world without the need for the attacker to have root access on the attacked system and without leaving any trace on the attacked system. This proves that buffer overflows can lie undiscovered in software for many years and can lead to extremely dangerous information leaks in highly used open source software.

In this paper we focus on fault localization and repairing of buffer overflow bugs by leveraging precise information (failure detection, bug diagnosis, buggy variables (program variables which are directly responsible for bug appearance),

© Springer International Publishing Switzerland 2015
F. Koornneef and C. van Gulijk (Eds.): SAFECOMP 2015, LNCS 9337, pp. 441–456, 2015.
DOI: 10.1007/978-3-319-24255-2_32

e.g., buffer index or buffer size) provided by our buffer overflow checker [13]. The failure detection and bug diagnosis data is used to generate quick fixes for buffer overflows and to support the repair process of removing the bug with a refactoring wizard. A novel algorithm is used to detect possible insertion locations in code for the generated code patches ((a) "in-place"—directly before the statement which contains the bug and (b) by searching for other, not "in-place" locations where the bug can be fixed). Our approach for generating program repairs is based on: code patch patterns, SMT solving and possible quick fix locations searching in program execution paths which could affect the program behavior by inserting a patch at a not "in-place" location. The generated patches are sound (e.g., do not change the behavior of the program for input which does not trigger the bug), final (no further human refinement needed), human readable (no alien code), syntactically correct and compilable.

We address offline behavioral repair [25] (by modifying the source code). Others have addressed state [8] or test-suite based program repair such as GenProg [19] and PAR [18]. The defect class which we address is inappropriate index variable assignment which results in an incorrect usage of the buffer index range. The fix defect class consists of input checks based on semi-defined patch patterns. The aim of the quick-fix is fail-secure error mitigation (e.g., to prevent that an attacker exploits the error in order to gain system access). The final version of the patch is determined using SMT solving.

Program repair lies at the conjunction of two dimensions (first, an *oracle* is needed to decide what is incorrect in order to detect the bug (first dimension) and another *oracle* to tell what should be kept correct for sake of non-regression (second dimension)) of software correctness [25]. We used the same SMT constraint system which was used to trigger the bug for defining what is incorrect in the program. Additionally, we created a second SMTLib (constraint system definition language used by the Z3 [5] solver) constraint system consisting of the previously mentioned constraint system and new SMTLib constraints used to impose input saturation constraints on the buggy variable.

Our patches are generated automatically and inserted semi-automatically offline with the possibility to insert them also online.

Our problem statement: Provide code patches ("in-place" or not "in-place") which can be used independently to remove a buffer overflow bug using a bug detector (checker).

In summary we make the following contributions:

- An algorithm for generation of "in-place" and not "in-place" bug fixes, Sect. 4.1.
- A novel approach for bug fix generation based on input saturation, Sect. 4.2.
- Semi-automated patch insertion based on source files differential views, Sect. 4.3.
- Automated check for behavior preserving of the patched program, Sect. 6.4.

Further we present related work in Sect. 2 and a motivating example of a buffer overflow bug and why automated bug repair merits future research in Sect. 3. We present the algorithm used to search for quick fix locations and generation of quick fixes in "in-place" (at the location where the bug was detected) and not "in-place" in Sect. 4. We discuss implementation details of our tool in Sect. 5 and present experimental results and the evaluation in Sect. 6. Finally, we conclude in Sect. 7.

2 Related Work

Source code patches for quick fixing bugs can be generated in different repairing ways [12], from free form bug reports [1,2,33], from statically defined patch patterns [11,18], from test suite using SMT solver [7,28], from test suite and genetic programming [19,34], by replacing the unsafe *libc* [29,32], functions with safe functions [3]. Hafiz et al. [30] addressed **buffer overflows quick fixing** by replacing unsafe library functions with safe alternatives. Cowan et al. [4] have used **static analysis for generating code patches** based on four approaches in which the buffer overflow vulnerabilities can be *defended*. Jacobs [16] has proposed to use **buffer overflow refactoring patterns** as an extension for the C language called SMART C. In recent years, many **quick fix generation tools for buffer overflows** have been proposed: AutoPaG [21], SafeStack [17], DYBOC [31], TIED [6], LibsafePlus [6], LibsafeXP [20], HeapShield [9].

To the best of our knowledge the AutoPAG [21] tool developed by Lin an colleagues is most similar to our approach from the backward visiting of program statements perspective. Our tool can not be compared with AutoPAG from the point of view of computation time and quick fix quality at this stage of development since AutoPAG has several limitations which we will briefly list. Our algorithm stops the search after encountering the first not "in-place" bug fix location whereas AutoPAG tries to detect all possible not "in-place" bug fix location by running a repeated inefficient data flow analysis (no program execution paths used). AutoPAG is not aware of program execution paths and uses a rudimentary backward information flow propagation approach based on the sequential ordering of program statements. The analysis (no SMT solver used) is repeated until there are no visited variables in the previously constructed set of tainted variables. This set can contain all program variables and can generate a significant overhead as already mentioned in the AutoPAG paper.

3 Motivating Example

In this section we present two real-world bug fixes as an example to highlight the fact that bug patch generation is not a trivial task. It needs deep insights into the functionality of the program and merits further study. There are typically an endless number of programs who adhere to a formal specification. As such, a bug can be fixed with infinite number of functionally correct patches. The automatically generated patches will change the behavior of the program or not. We present two distinctive patches depicted in Listing 1 on lines 5–6 and 11–13 with "+" and by using an italic font. Note, that these two fixes do not change program behavior for program input which does not trigger the bug. Listing 1 contains on line 6 code comments we present other possible quick fixes usable to remove the buffer overflow bug located at line 12 which most likely will change program behavior.

Listing 1 displays a C code snippet extracted from the test case CWE-121 [22] which is contained in [27]. The code snippet contains a buffer overflow bug at line 12 which can be removed by using one of the two patches depicted in Listing 1 on lines 5–6 and 11–13. Note, that the patch structure, the used constraint variables and the bug fix insertion locations are different for each buggy C program.

Listing 1. Buffer overflow bug due to missing input checks

```
0. void foo_bad(){
1.  int data = -1;
2.  char input_buf[CHAR_ARRAY_SIZE] = "";
3.  if (fgets(input_buf,CHAR_ARRAY_SIZE,stdin) != NULL){
4.     data = atoi(input_buf);
5. + if (data > 9 || data < 0)
6. + exit(EXIT_FAILURE); // data = 9; or data = rand() % 9; or return 0;
7.  }else{
8.     printLine("fgets() failed.");}
9.  int i, buffer[10] = { 0 };
10. if (data >= 0){
11. + if (data <= 9 &&data >= 0){
12.       buffer[data] = 1;   // Buffer overflow bug, index out of range
13. +}else{exit(EXIT_FAILURE);} // stop program execution
14.    for(i = 0; i < 10; i++){printIntLine(buffer[i]);}
15. }else{
16.    printLine("ERROR: Array index is negative.");}
17. }
```

Finding the *right* program variables in order to impose a constraint through a patch is a hard task because, in the worse case the values selection depends on all the other program variables. Determining not "in-place" bug fix locations is not a trivial task and this should be based on correct bug detection and on a kind of backward program execution technique on all program execution paths which contain the bug. In general, the insertion location and structural form of the quick fix patch can influence the overall program behavior. Thus, care should be taken that a patch is syntactically correct, compilable and does not change program behavior for program input which does not trigger the bug.

4   Quick Fixes Generation

In this section we present our quick fix locations search algorithm, the steps needed to automatically generate buffer overflow fixes and the mechanism for inserting the patches semi-automatically into the buggy program.

4.1   Quick Fix Locations Search Algorithm

The Algorithm 1 contains two phases as follows: (a) Finding the first program execution path which contains the buggy statement and generating the "in-place" quick fix. This quick fix will be suggested to the user in the GUI only if it is sound (e.g., the buffer size is equal on all buggy program executions paths).

Note, that the buffer index and size are context-sensitive. In case there are different buffer sizes on different paths then in order to preserve the soundness of the patched program a complex "in-place" patch can be generated containing one "if" branch and N "if else" branches (N represents the number of different buffer sizes on each buggy path). Furthermore, the size (LOC) of this patch grows exponentially with the number of paths containing different buffer sizes which renders such a quick fix to be not always practical (*). (b) Traversing the current selected path in backward program execution order from the location where the bug was found until a not "in-place" fix location is detected and generating a new quick fix at that location. At this program location the program execution can be safely finished (e.g., exit(EXIT_FAILURE);) (this will not change the program behavior for input which does not trigger the bug) if the buffer index is out of bounds or a numeric value can be set if desired (this will not terminate program execution and most likely will change program behavior). The second quick fix is sound as it can be observed that it does not change program behavior for program input which does not trigger the bug—similar to the first "in-place" quick fix. Quick fix (b) represents an alternative for the first quick fix which is not always feasible (e.g., (*)) and will be suggested in the GUI only if it does not change program behavior for input which does not trigger the bug and for each buggy program execution path at least one not "in-place" quick fix was successfully generated. This is assessed with the counters $countBP$ and $countGQF$ indicated in Algorithm 1 which must be equal (each buggy path has a not "in-place" quick fix associated) when the algorithm finishes the search. If the counters are not equal when the search algorithm finishes then there is at least one path where a not "in-place" bug fix location was not found. Thus, the whole quick fix will be not offered in the GUI since there could exist one program execution path on which the bug was not fixed.

Phases (a) and (b) are repeated for all program execution paths which contain the buggy statement (line number and file name) where the bug was detected as follows: first, the algorithm searches for possible insertion locations (e.g., "in-place" and not "in-place") for buffer overflow quick fixes and second, it generates bug fixes. The algorithm uses: $startIndex()$ to set the start index from where to search on the initial path, $setWorkList()$, to initialize the buggy first path, $initNode()$, to initialize the node at which the bug was found and $refact()$, to create a new refactoring. We now extend the notation, S_{paths}, consisting of all program execution paths, W_{set}, used to hold the current selected execution path, N_{set}, is a set of nodes used to store "in-place" and not "in-place" path nodes (these represent program locations where refactorings will be later on inserted) and R_{set}, is the set of refactorings. In line 3, N_{set}, and, W_{set} are initialized to empty set. In line 6, the algorithm picks a new path from the, S_{paths}, in each new iteration. Upon verifying that the chosen path contains the buffer overflow bug (previously detected), $hasBug(s_k)$, the start index, i, and the initial buggy path, w_k, are initialized. In line 11 and 12, the number of quick fix locations, $NLocs$, is initialised to 1 and the quick fix location counter, C, to 0 respectively. On encountering the condition statement, getLength(w_k) > 0, the algorithm

---

Algorithm 1. Quick fix locations searching and patches generation

---

Input: Satisfiable program execution paths set $S_{Paths} := \{s_k | \ 0 \leq k \leq n, \ \forall \ n \geq 0\}$
Output: Refactorings set $R_{set} := \{r_j | \ 0 \leq j < 2\}$

```
 1  W_set := {w_k| 0 ≤ k ≤ n, ∀ n ≥ 0}; // set of working lists, k'th list
 2  N_set := {n_t| 0 ≤ t ≤ n, ∀ n ≥ 0}; // set of nodes
 3  N_set := ∅; W_set := ∅; // initializing both nodes set and working list set to empty set
 4  countBP :=0; countGQF :=0; // init. counters, count buggy paths and generated fixes
 5  R_set :=∅;
 6  while ((Sat_paths.hasNext)) do
 7  │   if (hasBug(s_k)) then
 8  │   │   countBP := countBP + 1; // count the buggy paths
 9  │   │   i := startIndex(s_k); // set the start index of the path
10  │   │   w_k := setWorkList(s_k); // set the detected buggy path into the work list
11  │   │   NLocs := 1; // number of quick fix locations
12  │   │   C := 0; // quick fix locations counter
13  │   │   // if the work list length greater than 0 else skip path
14  │   │   if (getLength(w_k) > 0) then
15  │   │   │   n_t := initNode(w_k); // the node at which the bug was detected
16  │   │   │   N_set :=N_set ∪ {n_t}; // add a node for the in-place fix
17  │   │   │   r_j := refact(n_t); // create a new bug refactoring
18  │   │   │   R_set :=R_set ∪ {r_j}; // add new refactoring to the set R
19  │   │   │   while (i >0 ∧ C <NLocs) do
20  │   │   │   │   fNode := {w_{k,i}}; // get next node from work list located at index i
21  │   │   │   │   if (isQuickFixNode(fNode)) then
22  │   │   │   │   │   n_{t+1} := fNode; // store current node
23  │   │   │   │   │   N_set:=N_set ∪ {n_{t+1}}; // add the node for a not in-place fix
24  │   │   │   │   │   setConsObject(w_k); // store constraint
25  │   │   │   │   │   if (notAffectedPaths(S_Paths, n_{t+1})) then
26  │   │   │   │   │   │   pLoc := probLoc(n_{t+1});
27  │   │   │   │   │   │   putMarker(pLoc); // put new marker
28  │   │   │   │   │   │   r_{j+1} := refact(n_{t+1}); // create a new bug refactoring
29  │   │   │   │   │   │   R_set :=R_set ∪ {r_{j+1}}; // add refactoring
30  │   │   │   │   │   │   countGQF := countGQF + 1; // count the generated fixes
31  │   │   │   │   │   end
32  │   │   │   │   │   C := C + 1; // increase not in-place quick fix locations counter
33  │   │   │   │   end
34  │   │   │   │   i := i - 1; // go one step backwards on the path
35  │   │   │   end
36  │   │   end
37  │   │   k := k + 1; // get next satisfiable program execution path
38  │   end
39  end
```

---

checks the working list, w_k, length if it is greater than 0 and then initializes the node where the bug was found updating the nodes set, N_{set}. In line 17 a new refactoring is created updating the refactorings list in line 18. From line 19 to line 35, the algorithm traverses the path backwards in order to find a not "in-place" fix location of the bug until the index value, i, is greater than 0 and the counter value, C, is less than number of quick fix locations, $NLocs = 1$. While visiting each path node it checks for potential not "in-place" locations, $isQuickFixNode(fNode)$. Upon encountering a not "in-place" location, it stores the current node, n_{t+1}, and then N_{set} is updated. This node is used for generating the bug patches. In line 24 the constraint object is set at the index, k. The algorithm traverses the current selected program execution path to check if there are any influenced paths using, $notAffectedPaths(S_{Paths}, n_{t+1})$. At this stage of development a simple check is performed in order to see if the context-sensitive buggy variable appears on the right hand side of an expression (e.g., var = expr.; e.g. expr. = a binary expression, expr. contains our buggy variable which will be constrained with the patch). Furthermore, it is needed to be checked if the other influenced variables (e.g., var) are dead or live variables along a program path. In future we plan to compute a *distance-bounded weakest precondition* [10] (our engine supports the weakest precondition computation; loop and recursion invariants are not supported) in order to check if program behavior is preserved or not.

In case the algorithm finds no influenced paths then a new refactoring is created and added to R_{set}, line 29. Note, that in case of using "exit(EXIT_FAILURE)" in the not "in-place" quick fix than no check for influenced paths is needed. In line 32 the counter, C, is incremented by 1 which indicates that a second refactoring was created and the index value, i, is decremented by 1 so that the algorithm proceeds one step backwards on the current path in line 34. Note, that the algorithm can accommodate the search for more than one not "in-place" location by increasing the value of *NLocs* and updating the detection rules.

4.2   Bug Detection with SMT

Our contribution lies in bridging the gap between a buffer overflow bug report provided by an existing buffer overflow checker and automated generation of one or more quick fixes (quick fix structure, insertion location and values used inside the patches) which remove (automatically assessed by re-running the bug detector on the patched program) the buffer overflow bug.

The bug localization is based on the buffer overflow checker contained in our static analysis engine [13]. The buffer overflow checker returns the location of the bug containing the file name, line number and a unique ID which defines the type of the bug. Based on the bug report ID the following steps are performed automatically. The SMTLib constraint system which was used to detect the bug (from the buffer overflow checker) is selected. After obtaining the system a SMTConstraintObject object is instantiated containing the following attributes: the buffer size, the offset and the previous mentioned SMTLib constraint system. Next, we introduce the patch creation process consisting of the following 7 steps.

Step 1. Input Saturation: Listing 1 contains at line 4 a not "in-place" quick fix location for the buffer overflow bug which can be addressed with a missing input check, lines 5–6. Due to the missing input check the values of the index variable data used in buffer[data] can take values outside the buffer index interval [0, 9] which leads to a buffer overflow or underflow. In order to determine if the index variable data can take values outside the allowed interval [0, 9] a SMT constraint system is generated. The SMT constraint system is provided as input to the Z3 [5] SMT solver which will output the message SAT if data can take values outside the allowed interval. In order to remove the buffer overflow bug we decided to generate two types of quick fixes ("in-place" and not "in-place") which are based on the input saturation principle. The input saturation principle consists of basically limiting the possible values which the index variable data can take to only values which are contained in the buffer index range. The generated quick fixes represent additional checks which limit the upper and lower values of data (see Listing 1). The upper allowed value for `data` should not be larger than the allowed `buffer[data]` upper index bound value, 9, and not smaller than 0.

Step 2. SMT Constraint System used for Bug Detection: The original SMT constraint system used to detect the buffer overflow bug (excerpt presented in Listing 2) had 317 LOC. We depict only the SMTLib statements which matter most in our context and changed the names of the symbolic variables for brevity. During buffer overflow/underflow detection the checker uses SMTLib statements which represent path constraints and other specific statements for buffer overflow or underflow checking. The statement in bold font located on line 5 in Listing 2 represents the constraint which we get from the our checker (`assert (>= data bufferSize)`) in case of checking for an buffer overflow. In the case of an buffer underflow check the checker adds to the constraint system the statement (`assert (< data 0)`). If one of these two constraints are satisfied then this means that the variable `data` can take values outside the range of the buffer. Thus, a buffer overflow or underflow bug report will be issued.

The value of `data` depicted in Listing 2 with b is constraint to be greater or equal 10. The solver answers to this constraint system from Listing 2 as **SAT**. Thus, the set of possible solutions for b is contained in the set $[10, +\infty)$. This means

Listing 2. First oracle

```
0. (set-logic AUFNIRA)
1. (declare-fun b () Int)
2. (declare-fun c () Int)
3. % c is the buffer size
4. (assert (= c 10 ))
5. (assert (>= b c))
6. (check-sat)
7. (exit)
```

Listing 3. Second oracle

```
0.  (set-logic AUFNIRA)
1.  (set-option:produce-models true)
2.  (declare-fun saturation () Int)
3.  (declare-fun b () Int)
4.  % c is the buffer size
5.  (declare-fun c () Int)
6.  (assert (= c 10 ))
7.  (assert (>= b c))
8.  (assert (< saturation c))
9.  (assert (>=(saturation (c-1)))
10. (check-sat)
11. (get-value (saturation))
12. (exit)
```

that if the program variable `data` takes any value greater or equal to 10 than a buffer overflow bug will be detected. The checker is checking each possible execution path by asking the Z3 solver if the SMT constraint system is satisfiable or not. If a bug report is issued then a `SMTConstraintObject` will be instantiated. The buffer size, buggy variable and the SMT constraint system used to trigger the bug are added as attributes to the previously generated `SMTConstraintObject` object.

Step 3. Bug Type Classification: The bug type classification is based on the checker which was used to detect the bug. The bug checker generates a report containing a unique identifier for each type of bug detected. Currently we have other checkers (information flow checker [26], infinite loop checker [15], integer overflow checker and race condition checker [14]) which can run in parallel and have unique checker identifiers. We used for our checkers a unique ID which was saved in the checker bug report. Based on the generated bug identifier we can decide which type of bug we are dealing with. After obtaining the unique bug identifier the bug patch pattern is selected which will be used for bug fixing.

Step 4. Patch Pattern Selection: Based on the bug type classification we select the patch pattern(s) which can be used to fix this type of bug. Our patch patterns consist of empty C code skeletons where certain values have to be computed based on the used SMT solver (e.g., (1) +if (buff_size > N || buff_size < 0); e.g., (2) +if (buff_size < = N && buff_size > = 0);). N represents the buffer size determined during static analysis. Note, that N can have different values on different program execution paths.

Step 5. Constraint Values Selection: We construct our SMT constraint system based on the attributes stored in the SMTConstrintObject object. These attributes have to be added to the SMT constraint system which was used to detect the bug. After solving the SMT constraint system we will obtain the numeric values which will be inserted into the previous selected patch patterns.

Step 6. Generating SMT Constraint Values: The generation of the constraint values is based on the previously stored SMTLib system as an attribute of the SMTConstraintObject. The new SMT constraint system (see Listing 3) contains the same SMT statements presented in Listing 2 plus some new SMTLib statements used to perform the calculation of the needed value which will be later on used inside our selected patch(es). Note, that the newly added SMTLib statements are marked with bold font in Listing 3. The added SMTLib statements are used to perform input saturation on the variable **data**. The solver answers to this constraint system from Listing 3 as **SAT**. After solving the generated SMT system we obtain the value 9 for **data**. This value will be used later when we generate our final code patches. **b** represents the symbolic variable **data** and the symbolic variable **saturation** represents our constraint variable used to constrain the variable **data**. The symbolic variable **saturation** is used to constrain the solution space of the real variable (source code variable) **data**. The symbolic variable **saturation** can have as solution only the numeric value 9.

Step 7. Generating Final Code Patches: After solving the constraint system from Listing 3 we obtain the numeric value **9** as solution for the symbolic variable **saturation**. The value 9 will be inserted in the previously selected patch patterns in order to constrain the possible values which **data** can take. After this step, we obtain code patches which are syntactically correct, can be compiled and could be further on edited after insertion if desired.

4.3 Semi-automatic Patch Insertion Wizard

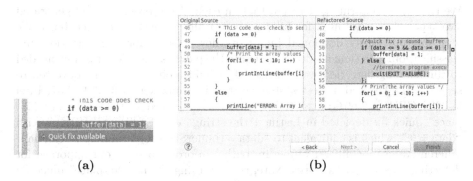

(a)   (b)

Fig. 1. Patch insertion wizard (Color figure online)

The buffer overflow checker places a bug marker depicted in the Fig. 1(a) with a yellow bug icon, on the left of the C statement if the statement contains a buffer overflow bug. By pressing on this bug marker the user can start the code refactoring wizard. The code refactoring wizard is composed of two user pages. The first user page is used to make patches selections (in-place or not in-place fix, only one can be selected at a time). The second page depicted in the Fig. 1(b) contains a differential files view presenting the differences between the original file containing the bug and the modified file with the selected patch(es) inserted. The user has the possibility to navigate between this two pages using the buttons "<Back", "Next>" and "Cancel" in order to compare the results of applying the in-place or the not in-place quick fix. Finally, by pressing on the "Finish" button the user accepts the selected quick fix, the patch will be written in the file and the wizard will be stopped.

5   Implementation

We have integrated our bug fixing tool into our existing Static Analysis Engine (SAE) [13] which is developed as an Eclipse IDE plug-in. We implemented a refactoring wizard based on the Eclipse Language Tool Kit (LTK), JFace and CDT in order to introduce semi-automatically the generated bug patches into the buggy program. Our bug patching technique is composed of two steps. First, the bug detection analysis is performed. If the bug is detected then this will be marked with a marker. Second, the bug fixing algorithm starts to search backwards on the buggy path until it detects a first not "in-place" location. If such a bug fix location is found then our tool marks visually the location in code with another marker. The backward searching algorithm can be easily updated in order to accommodate the suggestion of multiple quick fixing locations which can be addressed with other techniques than input saturation.

6   Evaluation

6.1   Methodology

We ran our refactoring generation tool on each of the programs and generated two types of patches used for fully automatically fixing the detected bugs. We used our previously developed buffer overflow checker for bug detection and classification. The time needed to generate the patches and the total time needed to run the bug detection were measured in milliseconds and then converted to seconds [s]. We used as test system an 64-bit Linux kernel 3.13.0-32.57, Intel i5-3230 CPU @ 2.60 GHz × 4. Note, that we replaced in the sound not "in-place" quick fix depicted in Listing 1 the string "exit(EXIT_FAILURE);" with "data = 9;", which is equivalent to "data = (bufferSize − 1);" (bufferSize can have different values for different program paths) in order to see if our apporach for detecting affected paths works. Note, that by using the not "in-place" quick fix depicted in Listing 1 (contains "exit(EXIT_FAILURE);" instead of "data = 9;")

the program behavior is preserved w.r.t. program input which does not trigger the bug. We evaluated our approach by addressing three research questions:

RQ1: What is the overall computational overhead of our tool? We wanted to find out what was the overhead introduced by our patch generation tool with respect to the bug detection time.

RQ2: Are the generated patches useful for bug fixing? We wanted to find out if the final generated patches containing the values obtained from the Z3 solver are useful for the bug fixing.

RQ3: Is the behaviour of the patched program preserved? We wanted to find out if the generated patches change the program behaviour. Finally, we addressed threats to validity of our approach.

6.2   RQ1: Performance of Our Tool

We addressed RQ1 by measuring the performance of our tool in terms of the patch generation overhead compared with the bug detection time.

Figure 2(a) presents the results of running our tool on 19 memcpy programs contained in CWE-121. The introduced overhead is calculated by comparing the times represented with black bars (patch generation time) located on top of the yellow bars (bug detection time). The total overhead of 1.97 % was obtained by comparing the bug detection time, 21.030 [s] $(21.454[s] - 0.424[s])$, and the patch generation time, 0.424 [s], column 7 of Table 1.

Figure 2(b) contains the results obtained during patch generation for the 39 fgets programs contained in CWE-121. We used the same index enumeration which was used in the open source Juliet test suite [27] in order to have a clear mapping between analyzed programs and programs extracted from the test suite. In comparison with the Fig. 2(a) we used in Fig. 2(b) a logarithmic

Table 1. Bug detection and patches generation results

Test programs	#LOCS	# Paths	# Affected paths	# Nodes	# Not "in-place" locations	Patches generation [s]	Prevented
CWE-121 memcpy	1980	39	0	2918	18	0.424	✓
CWE-121 fgets	8771	641	20	231337	38	0.755	✓
Total	10751	680	20	234255	56	1.197	✓

Table 2. Comparison of time cost between our system and GCC

Test programs	Bug detection + Patch generation [s]	GCC recompile time [s]	Total [s]	GCC compilation [s]	Ratio
CWE-121 memcpy	21.454	2.813	24.267	2.813	8.6x
CWE-121 fgets	178.276	6.713	184.989	6.713	27.5x
Total	199.730	9.526	209.256	9.526	36.1x

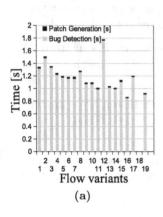 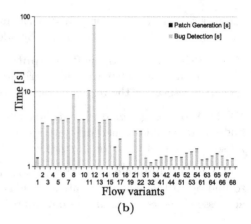

(a)   (b)

Fig. 2. Quick fix generation for memcpy and fgets programs (Color figure online)

scale in order to make the results better readable. From Fig. 2(b) we observe that the patch generation times indicated with black bars on top of the yellow bars are considerably lower than the bug detection times indicated with yellow bars. The total overhead of 0.4 % was obtained by comparing the bug detection time, 17.7521 [s], (17.8276[s] − 0.755[s]) and the patch generation time (0.755 [s]) contained in column 7 of Table 1.

The obtained results show that the patch generation time grows by a factor less than 2 (from 0.424 [s] to 0.755[s]) if the number of execution paths increases by a factor of 16.4x (641/39, see Table 1 3rd column) and the number of nodes by a factor of 79.2x (231337/2918, see Table 1, 5th column). We demonstrated that our approach is applicable to open source C programs and the induced overhead is under 1 %.

Figure 3 presents the overall overhead with yellow bars (the bug detection time) for the fgets and memcpy programs. The black bars on top of the yellow bars represent the overhead introduced by the patch generation algorithm for the fgets and memcpy programs. The patch generation overhead is 1.197 [s] which represents 0.59 % from the bug detection time of 199.730 [s] indicated in column 7 of Table 1 and in column 2 of Table 2.

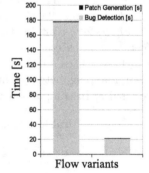

Fig. 3. Total overhead (Color figure online)

Table 2 shows that there is no compilation difference between the patched programs and the un-patched programs. This is because our patches have a small size and introduce no compilation overhead. We observed an overhead decrease from 1.97 % (memcpy programs) to 0.4 % (fgets programs) for 79.27 times (231337/2918, see Table 1, 5'th column) more nodes and for 16.4 times (641/39, see Table 1, 3'rd column) more paths. With regard to RQ1, the results confirm that the patch generation overhead is 0.59 % when compared to the bug detection time.

6.3 RQ2: Usefulness of the Generated Fixes

We addressed RQ2 by considering following scenarios: First, the syntactical correctness of our generated patches and if the code can be recompiled after the patch was inserted. Second, if the bug patch was useful for removing the detected bug. Third, the usefulness of the not "in-place" patch which is depicted in Table 3, column 4. Table 3, column 2 shows if the resulted program after the insertion of the "in-place" or the not "in-place" patches remained compilable. Columns 3 and 4 depicted in Table 3 indicate if the bug was removed by inserting the patch "in-place" (bug location) or at the not "in-place" location.

Table 3, column 3 shows that all the bug could be removed by inserting the patch at the place where the bug was detected. Table 3, column 4 shows that all the bugs were removed by inserting the patch at the

Table 3. Bug fixing results

Test programs	Recompile	"in-place" Fix	Not "in-place" Fix
CWE-121 memcpy	✓	✓	✓
CWE-121 fgets	✓	✓	✓*

not "in-place" location except the ones indicated with ✓*. The notation "N (M)" was used to denote the control flow variant "N" and the number of detected affeted paths, "M" contained in the Juliet test case CWE_121_fgets [27]. In total 8 C programs: 42 (3), 45 (2), 61 (1), 63 (4), 64 (5), 66 (2), 67 (1), 68 (2) contained 20 $((3) + (2) + (1) + (4) + (5) + (2) + (1) + (2))$ affected paths. An affected path contained at least one usage of the constrained variable (e.g., "data") in another statement as the path was traversed in program execution order. Thus, the program behavior can be in this way influenced by the set of values that the constraint variable can take after it was constrained. Note, that this is not a sufficient condition to guarantee soundness. Thus, the results presented in Table 3 confirm RQ2, that the generated bug patches were useful for removing the bugs.

6.4 RQ3: Program Behavior Preserved After Patch Insertion

We addressed RQ3 by checking if the inserted patch at the not "in-place" location influences other existing program paths. The abbreviations in Table 4 mean: Total

Table 4. Programs behavior preserving

Test programs	# Programs	# IPrograms	# IPaths	% Ratio
CWE-121 memcpy	18	0	0	0
CWE-121 fgets	38	8	20	14.2
Total	56	8	20	14.2

number of programs containing influenciable paths (IPrograms), Influenciable Paths (IPaths), % Ratio represents the ratio between the total number of programs to the total number of programs containing at least one influenced path. Our Algorithm 1 visits not "in-place" candidate nodes in backward program execution manner in order to find bug fixing locations. Next, it checks if by patching the found node contained in the affected path the behavior of the program will change. If the algorithm finds an affected path then the not "in-place" quick fix will be not generated since it could influence other variables contained in the affected paths. We successfully avoided changing the behavior of all the analyzed programs by proposing the fix at the bug location which is indicated in column 3 of Table 3. For 14.2 % of the programs (56/8, **# Programs/# IPrograms** presented in Table 4 in columns 2 and 3) we avoided changing the behaviour by not proposing the not "in-place" quick fix. Thus, we can confirm that for 85.8 % (100 % − 14.2 %) of the analyzed programs the program behaviour did not changed with regard to RQ3.

6.5   Threats to Validity

Internal Validity: In case we did not interpret the results of our execution measurements right then the overhead of 0.59 % could not be achievable. To avoid time measurement mistakes we carefully designed our time measuring mechanism and measured for all the 58 programs three times. Some of the decisions we make are static (select type of patch patterns for a bug type) and some are dynamic (SMT constraint system solving). Thus, only the dynamic decisions can influence the overhead introduced by our tool. We are aware that in case the bug checker cannot detect or diagnose the bug type then our approach would suffer from imprecision or does not work at all.

External Validity: We are aware that there are some threats which could hinder our approach from being generalizable for large programs. We think that our patch generation approach can be generalized since we followed the basic automatic program repair steps (failure detection, bug diagnosis, bug cause localization and repair inference). We think that 0.59 % overall overhead is negligible and by addressing other types of checks than input saturation or by using other bug patterns no major time increase would be noticeable. Thus, programs containing long execution paths would not increase the overhead significantly with respect to the bug detection time.

7   Conclusion and Future Work

We presented a novel approach which can be used to automatically fix buffer overflow bugs by generating bug patches using static execution and SMT solving. Our automatically generated patches do not need any human refinement, are compilable and can be semi-automatically inserted into buggy programs with the help of our refactoring wizard. Our experimental results show that our tool is efficient and successfully removed all bugs. We think that our approach can be applied to high quality projects since the generated quick fixes remove the bug and preserve program behavior.

We are confident to say that our approach can be applied in future in conjunction with other types of bug checkers [14, 15, 26] which we developed.

Acknowledgments. This research is funded by the German Ministry for Education and Research (BMBF) under grant number 01IS13020.

References

1. Aho, A.V., et al.: A minimum-distance error-correcting parser for context-free languages. SIAM J. Comput. **1**(4), 305–312 (1972)
2. Chen, L., et al.: R2Fix: automatically generating bug fixes from bug reports. In: Proceedings of the 2013 IEEE 6th ICST
3. Crispin, C., et al.: StackGuard: automatic adaptive detection and prevention of buffer-overflow attacks. In: Proceedings of the 7th USENIX SSYM 1998
4. Crispin, C., et al.: Buffer overflows: attacks and defenses for the vulnerability of the decade*. In: DARPA Discex 2000
5. de Moura, L., Bjørner, N.S.: Z3: an efficient SMT solver. In: Ramakrishnan, C.R., Rehof, J. (eds.) TACAS 2008. LNCS, vol. 4963, pp. 337–340. Springer, Heidelberg (2008)
6. Deepak, G., et al.: TIED, LibsafePlus: tools for runtime buffer overflow protection. In: Proceedings of the 13th Conference on USENIX Security Symposium, SSYM 2004
7. DeMarco, F., et al.: Automatic repair of buggy if conditions and missing preconditions with SMT. In: Proceedings of the CSTVA 2014
8. Demsky, B., Rinard, M.: Automatic detection and repair of errors in data structures. In: Proceedings of the ACM SIGPLAN OOPSLA 2003
9. Emery, D.B.: HeapShield: library-based heap overflow protection for free. UMass CS TR 06-28 (2006)
10. Gu, Z., et al.: Has the bug really been fixed? In: Proceedings of the ICSE 2010
11. Haddad, H.M., Shahriar, H.: Rule-based source level patching of buffer overflow vulnerabilities. In: Proceedings of the 10th ITNG 2013
12. Harrold, M.J., et al.: Fault prediction, localization, and repair. Dagstuhl Seminar 13061, February 2013
13. Ibing, A.: SMT-constrained symbolic execution for eclipse CDT/Codan. In: Proceedings of the 3th WS-FMDS 2013
14. Ibing, A.: Path-sensitive race detection with partial order reduced symbolic execution. In: Canal, C., Idani, A. (eds.) SEFM 2014 Workshops. LNCS, vol. 8938, pp. 311–322. Springer, Heidelberg (2015)
15. Ibing, A., Mai, A.: A fixed-point algorithm for automated static detection of infinite loops. In: Proceedings of the 16th IEEE HASE 2015
16. Jacobs, M., Lewis, E.C.: SMART C: a semantic macro replacement translator for C. In: Proceedings of the Sixth IEEE SCAM 2006
17. Jin, H., et al.: SafeStack: automatically patching stack-based buffer overflow vulnerabilities. IEEE Trans. Dependable Secure Comput. **10**(6), 368–379 (2013)
18. Kim, D., et al.: Automatic patch generation learned from human-written patches. In: Proceedings of the International Conference on Software Engineering, ICSE 2013
19. Le Goues, C., et al.: Genprog: a generic method for automatic software repair. IEEE Trans. Softw. Eng. **38**(1), 54–72 (2012)
20. Lin, Z.: LibsafeXP: a practical and transparent tool for run-time buffer overflow preventions. In: Proceedings of the 7th Annual IEEE Information Assurance Workshop, IAW 2006
21. Lin, Z., et al.: AutoPaG: towards automated software patch generation with source code root cause identification and repair. In: Proceedings of the 2nd ACM Symposium on Information, Computer and Communications Security, ASIACCS 2007
22. Mitre: CWE-121. http://cwe.mitre.org/data/definitions/121.html

23. Mitre: 2011 CWE/SANS Top 25. http://cwe.mitre.org/top25/
24. Mitre: Heartbleed Bug. https://cve.mitre.org/cgi-bin/cvename.cgi?name=CVE-2014-0160
25. Monperrus, M.: A critical review of automatic patch generation learned from human-written patches: essay on the problem statement and the evaluation of automatic software repair. In: Proceedings of the 36th International Conference on Software Engineering, ICSE 2014
26. Muntean, P., et al.: Context-sensitive detection of information exposure bugs with symbolic execution. In: Innovative Software Development Methodologies and Practices, InnoSWDev 2014
27. NIST: Juliet Test Suite v1.2 for C/C++
28. Satish, C., et al.: SemFix: program repair via semantic analysis. In: Proceedings of the International Conference on Software Engineering, ICSE 2013, pp. 772–781
29. Sauciuc, R., Necula, G.: Reverse execution with constraint solving. Technical report No. UCB/EECS-2011-67, May 2011
30. Shaw, A., et al.: Automatically fixing C buffer overflows using program transformations. In: Proceedings of the IEEE/IFIP Conference on Dependable Systems and Networks, DSN 2013
31. Sidiroglou, S., Giovanidis, G., Keromytis, A.D.: A dynamic mechanism for recovering from buffer overflow attacks. In: Zhou, J., López, J., Deng, R.H., Bao, F. (eds.) ISC 2005. LNCS, vol. 3650, pp. 1–15. Springer, Heidelberg (2005)
32. Smirnov, A., et al.: Automatic patch generation for buffer overflow attacks. In: Proceedings of the Third International Symposium on Information Assurance and Security, IAS 2007, pp. 165–170
33. Westley, W.: Patches as better bug reports. In: International Conference on Generative Programming and Component Engineering, GPCE 2006
34. Westley, W., et al.: Automatically finding patches using genetic programming*. In: International Conference on Software Engineering, ICSE 2009

A Software-Based Error Detection Technique for Monitoring the Program Execution of RTUs in SCADA

Navid Rajabpour and Yasser Sedaghat$^{(\boxtimes)}$

Dependable Distributed Embedded Systems (DDEmS) Laboratory,
Computer Engineering Department,
Ferdowsi University of Mashhad, Mashhad, Iran
n_rajabpour@stu.um.ac.ir, y_sedaghat@um.ac.ir

Abstract. A Supervisory Control and Data Acquisition (SCADA) system is an Industrial Control System (ICS) which controls large scale industrial processes including several sites over long distances and consists of some Remote Terminal Units (RTUs) and a Master Terminal Unit (MTU). RTUs collect data from sensors and control actuators situated at remote sites and send data to the MTU through a network. Since RTUs operate in a harsh industrial environment, fault tolerance is a key requirement particularly for safety-critical industrial processes. Studies show that a significant number of transient faults due to a harsh environment result in control flow errors in the RTU's processors. A software error detection technique has been proposed to detect control flow errors in several RTUs. For experimental evaluation 30,000 faults injected on network; the average performance and memory overheads are about 33.20 % and 36.79 %, respectively and this technique detected more than 96.32 % of injected faults.

Keywords: SCADA · RTU · Transient fault · Fault tolerance · Fault injection · Software-based error detection

1 Introduction

The most critical infrastructures, such as major electrical and mechanical system and industrial networks are controlled by industrial control systems (ICSs). These systems are typically employed to monitor and control the plants and industrial environments such as oil and natural gas pipeline, water distribution, electrical power grids and transportation [1]. In these applications, which are commonly safety-critical, a system failure may lead to significant risks to the health and the safety of human's life, serious damages to the environment, or serious financial and economical issues [2].

A Supervisory Control and Data Acquisition (SCADA) system is an ICS which controls large scale industrial processes included several sites over long distances [3]. A SCADA system is a distributed system typically comprised of a Master Terminal Unit (MTU) and several Remote Terminal Units (RTUs). MTU gathers data from RTUs, provides an operator interface to display information, and controls the remote sites. RTU interfaces with field sensing devices, local control switchboxes, and valve actuators. To transfer data between MTU and RTUs, a communication network based

© Springer International Publishing Switzerland 2015
F. Koornneef and C. van Gulijk (Eds.): SAFECOMP 2015, LNCS 9337, pp. 457–470, 2015.
DOI: 10.1007/978-3-319-24255-2_33

on the client/server over the communication protocols, such as TCP/IP or Ethernet/IP protocols, is commonly used [4, 23].

RTUs operate in an industrial environment, which is commonly a harsh environment [5]. In a harsh environment, transient faults may occur in electronic devices (i.e. microprocessors and microcontrollers, memory, internal bus) due to Electromagnetic Interferences (EMI), Power Supply Disturbances (PSD), radiations and high operating temperature [19] in RTUs. This fault resulting in an inversion of a bit state [24] (i.e. single bit flip). Presented studies in [6] show that transient faults in the electronic devices can cause control flow errors and data errors. Control flow errors refer to deviations from the normal instruction execution flow of the software program and data errors refer to alter the contents of memory variables or in a register. It has been shown that about 33 %–77 % of transient faults are converted to control flow errors [6] and the remaining are converted to data error. Monitoring the execution of program in RTU by MTU is very important and a CFE error would prevent the program from performing properly. Therefore, RTUs should be equipped with a technique in order to be able to detect such errors, and Control Flow Checking (CFC) is one of the best techniques to detect the occurrence of control flow errors.

Several CFC techniques have been presented since 1980s [6–17] that can be divided into three categories of hardware-based, software-based, and hybrid. Hardware-based techniques use an extra hardware such as a watchdog processor to monitor state performance and state of the master processor [7]. Software-based techniques employ software redundancy to detect deviations in software program execution flow by signature monitoring mechanisms [8, 9]. These techniques have software code and performance overheads. In comparison with hardware-based techniques, software-based techniques are more flexible, less costly and being easily updated and they have also a better maintenance facility [6]. In hybrid techniques, a software technique would be merged with a hardware-based technique, in order to make balance between overheads and costs and have advantages of both software-based and hardware-based techniques.

In this study, a software control flow checking technique, called PLC-CFC, is proposed in order to detect control flow errors in RTUs. This technique is employed to monitor the program execution flows of some RTUs in a SCADA system and composes of two parts. A software-based control flow checking technique has been embedded in each RTU and the MTU processor, along with doing its tasks, is employed to monitor the program execution flow of all RTUs. The ICS-CFC technique can be applied in all industrial control systems which employ microcontrollers, microprocessors, PLCs, or personal computers. As a case study, the proposed technique has been applied on a real ICS in Parin Beton Amood Company, manufacturing "Autoclaved Aerated Concrete" in Mashhad, Iran. The mentioned ICS includes eight personal computers as its RTUs and a main server as its MTU. The experimental results showed that among a total of 30,000 injected faults on distributed network and the presented technique detects more than 96.32 % of them.

The organization of this paper is as follows. Section 2, several related studies are reviewed. In Sect. 3 the proposed technique explained. The experimental results of different technique are given in Sect. 4. Finally Sect. 5 concluded the paper.

2 Related Works

Control flow checking techniques are typically employed signature monitoring mechanisms to check the execution flow of a program. Before the system's run-time, an abstract of the program for the correct program execution is extracted. Afterward, several signatures, representing the chosen abstract, are assigned to the program. During the run-time, signatures are again generated in real-time and are compared with the stored, expected signatures. If a disagreement occurs, the occurrence of a control flow error is detected and reported [10].

As mentioned before, control flow checking techniques can be divided into three main types. In software-based techniques such as CFCSS [14, 15], ECCA [13], RSCFC [16], I2BCFC [25], and SCFC [17], several redundant instructions are inserted into a program to check the execution flow of the program. These techniques do not have any hardware overhead. The main advantages of software-based techniques are low cost and flexibility (easily changeable). However, these techniques impose significant performance and memory overheads due to the redundant instructions. Moreover, since the monitoring is done by inserted instructions into the program, these techniques cannot detect the program crash failure.

In hardware-based techniques, to detect control flow errors a hardware device like Watchdog timer [11] and Lock stepping [12], is utilized to check the execution flow of a program or to trace memory accesses. In these techniques, the behavior of the main processor is monitored using only redundant hardware devices. Therefore, these techniques, commonly designed for a special purpose, cannot be easily changed or updated, and have considerable costs due to redundant hardware. In the hybrid control flow checking techniques, redundant instructions are inserted into a program. These instructions produce some signatures and send them to a redundant hardware device as an external monitor. In these techniques, the control flow checking is done partly in the program (employing software-based techniques) and partly in the redundant hardware. CFCBTE [18], SWTES [10], PECFC [24], are the samples of hybrid techniques. In the SWTES technique, a hybrid-base technique using encoded signatures monitors the behavior of a program and an on-chip microcontroller timer has been exploited as a watchdog timer to detect the program crashes. This technique is experimentally evaluated on an ATMEL MCS51 microcontroller. The CFCBTE is a hybrid control flow checking technique for the PowerPC processors. In this technique, beside redundant software codes which are employed to compare signatures, three hardware-based mechanisms, i.e., Machine Check Exception, watchdog timer, and Branch Trace Exception, have been utilized.

To the best of our knowledge, almost all control flow checking techniques have been proposed to protect a single processor from control flow errors; while, SCADA is a distributed system composed of several RTUs and a MTU connected to a communication network. RTUs and MTU include a microcontroller, a microprocessor, a PLC, or a personal computer as their main processor. To protect SCADA from control flow errors it is necessary to employ a control flow checking technique. In this paper a software control flow checking is proposed for industrial control systems.

3 The Proposed Technique: ICS-CFC

As mentioned before, SCADA system is a distributed industrial control system composed of several RTUs and a server as a MTU. RTUs interface with field sensors and local control devices provide an operator interface to control remote sites. These units execute their configuration and software control programs and send their control and sensing data to MTU through a client/server communication network. The MTU gathers data from RTUs to process and control the remote sites [5].

In the proposed control flow checking technique, called ICS-CFC technique, monitoring of the program execution is being done partly on the MTU and partly on each RTU. Employing this technique, the MTU ensures that the execution flow of the programs in all RTUs is correct, by online monitoring the received signatures from RTUs through the communication network. Local signature monitoring mechanism has been implemented in RTUs to reduce the number of transmitted signatures through the network.

3.1 ICS-CFC Technique Implementation in RTUs

To implement the local checking the control flow of an RTU's program, three steps should be taken as follows: Step 1: Partitioning the program into several basic blocks, Step 2: Assigning a unique signature to each basic block, and Step 3: Inserting control flow checking instructions to the program.

Partitioning the Program Code. The RTU's program code is first divided into several basic blocks. The basic block is a maximal set of ordered instructions such that its execution begins from the first instruction and terminates with the last instruction. There is no jumping or branching instruction in a basic block except for the last one [14]. A program can be represented by a directed graph, called Control Flow Graph (CFG) [20]; nodes are the basic blocks and the arcs represent a control flow transfer between the basic blocks. A simple program and its related CFG are shown in Fig. 1.

Assigning a Unique Signature. After indicating the basic blocks and extracting the CFG of the program, a unique signature should be assigned to each basic block, called Detection Signature (DS). The DS of each basic block demonstrates the successor blocks of the current basic block. Bits related to successor blocks of the present block equal 1. As shown in Fig. 2(a), the DS contains two fields. The first field (T) represents the type of the signature. The value of the T field for a Detection Signature is 1. If the number of basic blocks is N, then the second field of the DS (DS_{BN}), which represents the signature's value, have N bits. This field contains the assigned signature of the related basic block. If there are many basic blocks, then the number of signature bits can be equaled Log_2 N. For example, if N = 512, then the number of bits can be 9 lengths.

In addition to the Detection Signature (DS), two other types of signature are employed in the ICS-CFC technique: Alive Signatures and Error Signatures. An Alive Signature (AS) would be sent from RTUs to the MTU in certain periods of time. These periods are determined by the MTU in the configuration time of RTUs. Receiving an

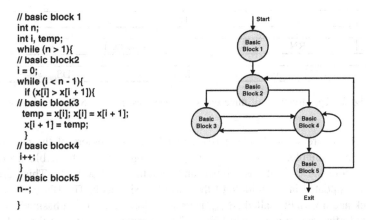

```
// basic block 1
int n;
int i, temp;
while (n > 1){
  // basic block2
  i = 0;
  while (i < n - 1){
    if (x[i] > x[i + 1]){
      // basic block3
      temp = x[i]; x[i] = x[i + 1];
      x[i + 1] = temp;
    }
    // basic block4
    i++;
  }
  // basic block5
  n--;
}
```

Fig. 1. A simple code and its related CFG of a bubble sort program

AS from an RTU informs the MTU that the sender RTU has not been crashed. As shown in Fig. 2(b) the signature has three fields. The first field (T) represents the type of the signature. The value of the T field for an Alive Signature is 2. The second field represents number of an RTU which has sent the signature. The third field shows the time of sending the AS in the RTU.

An Error Signature (ES) is sent when a control flow error being detected in an RTU by its local monitoring mechanism. Therefore, when an error occurs, *Send()* procedure would be run and this would be send ES to a function called CFE-Handler. Then programs control would be transferred to this function, which has two tasks. First, finding the basic block in which errors occurred by checking the value of the fields in ES. Second, sending an ES to MTU to handle error in RTU by checking the value of ES fields, in case that RTU crashes or cannot execute the program. Meanwhile, the technique has been designed in a way that if an error occurs in each basic block, it would be detected in next basic block and detection latency [20] would be reduced. Therefore, CFE-handler function needs ES signature fields.

As shown in Fig. 2(c), the ES has five fields. The first field (T) represents the type of the signature. The value of the T field for an error signature is 3. The second field (RN) represents number of an RTU which has been encountered a control flow error. The third field (BN) and the fourth field (DS_{BN}) represent number and assigned signature of a basic block, respectively, which a control flow error has occurred in it. Assessing these fields, the MTU discovers that a control flow error has occurred in which RTU and which basic block of that RTU's program (current basic block in that RTU). The last field (DS_{curr}) represents the signature of the preceding basic block of the current basic block in the faulty RTU.

Inserting Control Flow Checking Instructions. To check the control flow of an RTU's program, some control flow checking instructions are inserted in each basic block of the program. In Fig. 3(a), the structure of a basic block after applying the ICS-CFC technique has been presented.

The DS_{BN} variable contains the signature of a basic block and is composed of N bits, if the program has N basic blocks. In this variable, the ith ($DS_{BN}[i-1]$) and j^{th}

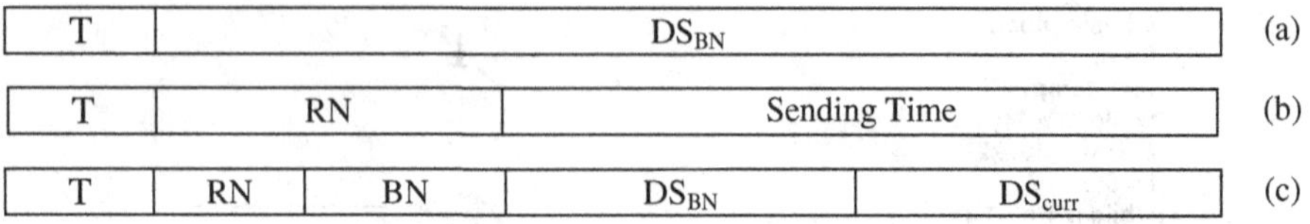

| T | DS_{BN} | | (a) |

| T | RN | Sending Time | (b) |

| T | RN | BN | DS_{BN} | DS_{curr} | (c) |

Fig. 2. The structures of three types of signatures in the ICS-CFC technique

($DS_{BN}[j-1]$) bits are set to 1, if the BB_i and BB_j are successors of the current basic block. Another variable, called DS_{curr} contains the signature of a basic block should be executed before the current basic block and initialize to '0000...1'. This variable is checked and updated in the middle of the current basic block. The BN is number of a basic block and a variable called BN_{curr} is used to store number of a basic block should be executed after the current basic block. This variable is updated at the end of each basic block. In the ICS-CFC technique, if a basic block has more than one successor, a unique number is assigned to each successor, called SN. The SN variable is set at the end of a basic block with more than one successor basic block and is checked in the middle of the executed successor basic block.

As shown in Fig. 3(a), in the beginning of each basic block, the flow upon its entrance into the basic block is checked by comparing the BN_{curr} with BN. If a mismatch is detected, due to an illegal jump to the beginning of the current basic block, an ES is sent to the CFE-Handler function.

In the middle of each basic block, DS_{curr} is checked. If the execution flow of the program is correct, n^{th} bit of DS_{curr} ($DS_{curr}[BN-1]$) in basic block BB_n should be '1'. In this situation, DS_{curr} is updated with the value of DS_{BN}. Otherwise, if that bit was '0', a control flow error is detected and an ES sent to the CFE-Handler function. In addition to this check, the value of SN should be assessed in the middle of each basic block by *check()* procedure. If the current basic block is one of the more successors of its predecessor basic block, SN value should be compared with successor number of the current basic block. If there a mismatch is detected, a control flow error is detected and an ES sent to the CFE-Handler function.

At the end of each basic block, BN_{curr} is updated with number of next basic block which should be executed after the current basic block. Moreover, if the current basic block has more than one successor blocks, SN is also updated with number of successor basic blocks by *set()* procedure, which should be run after the current basic block. In order to reduce detection latency, it is possible to insert the instructions, which have been added at the beginning, to the end as well. So, the error detection would be occurred in the basic block and *send()* procedure would be run.

The ICS-CFC technique divides a basic block into two parts. Analyses show that this technique can detect almost all illegal branches to a basic block from another basic block, even for branches from the first part of a basic block to its second part. Despite the software-based techniques, the proposed technique is able to detect the program crash, employing by the MTU.

Figure 3(b) illustrates the control flow graph of the bubble sort benchmark (presented in Fig. 1), after applying the ICS-CFC technique on it.

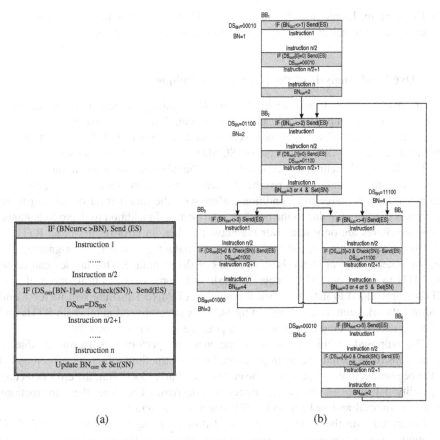

Fig. 3. The structures of basic blocks in the proposed technique

3.2   ICS-CFC Technique Implementation in the MTU

As mentioned before, an Alive Signature (AS) is sent to the MTU by each RTU in a certain period of time. Receiving an AS from an RTU shows that the RTU has not been crashed. In the configuration time of an ICS, the MTU configures and programs each RTU. In this technique, at the configuration time, the time period of sending AS is set for each RTU and a profile for each of them is created in the MTU.

After receiving a signature from an RTU, the MTU recognizes the type of the signature. If the received signature is an AS, the MTU checks the "sending time" field of the signature and compares it with the "sending time" of the last received AS stored in the RTU's profile. The MTU detects a control flow error in that RTU, if the time between two received Alive Signatures is more than the predetermined time period, which is also stored in that RTU's profile. Inserting "sending time" into an Alive Signature ensures that network latencies cannot affect the correctness of the technique. In this situation, the network latency can only cause to detect a control flow error, later.

Moreover, if a received signature from an RTU is an ES, the content of the signature show that a control flow error has been occurred in which basic block of the

RTU's program. Employing this feature, the MTU can display the information to its human operator to select the best strategy to encounter the problem.

3.3   Overhead Analysis of the ICS-CFC Technique

When error detecting technique implemented on main program, there are different parameters which impose overheads on a system. Thus, to improve the proposed technique, the trade-off between parameters should be considered. In this section, the overhead of the ICS-CFC technique on SCADA system will be presented.

The ICS-CFC technique proposed in a client/server communication network. Therefore, network traffic is an overhead, because only Alive Signatures are sent over the network in the error free conditions. Moreover, the time period of sending these signatures is adjustable due to the network's properties. In addition to Alive Signatures, Error Signatures are only sent over the network when an error occurs in an RTU. In addition, since the sending time of an Alive Signature is stored in the signature, the network latency cannot affect the correctness of the technique. This latency can cause the MTU to detect an RTU's program crash with some delays. Furthermore, if new RTUs being added to network, then the number of Alive Signature will increase and lead to network latency. Thus, regarding SCADA structure and number on RTUs and Alive Signature sending time it would be possible to make a trade off.

The proposed technique has some memory and performance overheads due to inserted instructions into the main program. Some instructions which have been added at the beginning, in the middle or at the end of each basic block; But, the error detecting capability will increase and detect latency will decrease. Therefore, these instructions being customized and make a trade-off between parameters.

Compared with the other typical control flow checking techniques, the ICS-CFC technique does not impose any hardware redundancy. In this technique, the existed MTU is also employed as a hardware monitor. And for monitoring there is no need to add a watchdog for each RTU and therefore it would cause cost decrease in system.

4   Experimental Results

In this section, the setup environment is explained and the experimental results are given. In order to analyze proposed technique, first the fault models determined, then the technique applied to two following environment: (1) A distributed local network compose of some PC, (2) A real ICS network compose of some industrial PLCs. Thus, based on fault models, the faults in these two environments injected and results evaluated accordingly.

4.1   The Models of Fault

A fault can occur in a system memory, system bus and Internal CPU in RTUs. The errors which may occur due to these faults can be modeled as CPU Crash, Data errors and CFE. CPU Crash happens when the processor does not work and can be detected by MTU, which is used in proposed technique. Data error is detectable by some techniques like assertion. CFE may occur either in memory content or processor internal registers.

Fault injection approach is used that has three kinds: (1) Random Branch Insertion: replacing a non-control instruction with a control instruction. (2) Random Branch Deletion: deleting some branches of the program randomly. (3) Random Branch Modification: the target address of a control instruction is being modified.

By use of the mentioned fault models, the behavior of a CFE in memory can be exactly modeled. These models are not capable to represent the CFE behavior due to an error occurred in processor internal registers. In these cases, the behavior of such errors can be modeled by manipulating Programs Counter (PC) and Status Register (SR). The control flow errors will be produced and also the efficiency of different techniques can be compared with each other by applying above mentioned fault models. The faults are randomly injected to the assembly code of benchmarks. By changing registers and program counter of the program, control flow errors would occur in the program. Thus, the efficiency of different techniques can be evaluated.

4.2 ICS-CFC Technique Execution in a Local Network

To evaluate the proposed technique, the ICS-CFC technique was applied to a local network composed of eight personal computers as RTUs connected to a main server as a MTU through a client/server communication network. Each RTU had an Intel Core i5 as its CPU, 4 GB RAM, and Windows 7 as its operating system. MTU had an Intel Core i7 as its CPU, 8 GB RAM, and Windows server 2008 as its operating system. The communication protocol was the TCP/IP and the Microsoft Visual Studio 2008 was employed to implement the benchmark programs. To communicate between RTUs and MTU over network and send signature, socket programming was employed [21]. Four benchmark programs, i.e. Bubble Sort (BS), Matrix Multiplication (MM), Quick Sort (QS), and Linked List Insertion (LLI), which are typical benchmarks employed in previous researches, were implemented on each RTU and ICS-CFC technique was applied to them.

For experimental evaluation the ICS-CFC technique was applied to a personal computer as an RTU and 30,000 faults were injected, based on fault models, into the mentioned benchmarks. Seven versions are considered for each benchmark. First is the original code (the code of the benchmark), to which other six techniques being applied. For each version, the fault injection randomly executed, based on fault models. According to the effects of the injected faults in the RTU's program, five different cases occur: (1) Correct Result (CR): injected fault does not change the final result of the program and no control flow error is detected. (2) Wrong Result (WR): fault results in a wrong output and is not detected by the ICS-CFC technique. (3) Time Out (TO): injected fault caused the program execution time to change and it does not finish in a specified time. This type of errors is detected by the MTU in the ICS-CFC technique. (4) Os Exception (OS): These faults cause the operating system exception. Generally, this percentage of faults is regarded as being detected by the operating system. (5) Single Detection (SD): injected fault results in a control flow error and is detected by techniques in the RTU. The fault injection results into the four benchmarks for some software techniques running on the RTU have been presented in Table 1.

Table 1. Experimental evaluation average results of CFCSS [14, 15], ECCA [13], RSCFC [16], I2BCFC [25], SCFC [17], and ICS-CFC

Techniques	CR %	WR %	TO %	OS %	SD %	Memory overhead %	Performance overhead %	Fault coverage %	Evaluation result %
No CFC	38.10	42.20	07.01	12.69	00.00	00.00	00.00	31.83	31.83
CFCSS	40.48	12.01	08.30	08.59	30.62	31.30	25.00	79.82	43.49
ECCA	38.96	09.50	06.50	10.15	34.89	33.00	27.80	84.43	44.51
RSCFC	37.11	11.02	06.20	11.13	34.54	35.00	28.10	82.48	42.71
I2BCFC	32.37	06.05	08.15	07.70	45.73	35.80	31.00	91.05	45.51
SCFC	31.95	05.36	08.35	05.40	48.94	36.10	32.50	92.12	45.56
ICS-CFC	27.37	02.67	07.50	04.15	58.31	36.79	33.20	96.32	47.42

As presented in Table 1, among all 30,000 injected faults, 27.37 % faults lead to correct output results. Among all the remaining injected faults, only 02.67 % injected faults, which result in wrong output results, were not detected by the ICS-CFC technique. Therefore, the fault coverage of the proposed technique is about 96.32 %.

Table 1 presents average fault coverage for some techniques and also shows the memory and the performance overheads in average for the above mentioned techniques. The performance overhead of the ICS-CFC technique, due to execution of the redundant instructions, is about 33.20 %. The memory overhead of the proposed technique, due to insertion of redundant instructions into basic blocks of a program and signature variables, is about 36.79 %.

Moreover, the new parameter Evaluation Result (ER), which has been defined, would cover fault coverage, memory and performance overheads concurrently. This technique should be able to balance these parameters with each other. The ER is defined as follows:

$$ER = \frac{Fault\ Coverage}{Memory\ Overhead * Performance\ Overhead} * 100 \qquad (1)$$

Table 1 shows ER for some techniques, in which ICS-CFC has greater ER than other techniques and is more appropriated for employing in safety-critical systems.

The ICS-CFC technique does not have any hardware redundancy, compared to other typical hybrid-based control flow checking techniques. The existed MTU is also employed as a hardware monitor. It should be noted that in ICS-CFC technique, RTUs send the signatures to the MTU over the network without any effect on the performance of the RTUs.

4.3   Case Study: Execution ICS-CFC Technique in a Real ICS

The mentioned benchmarks are small and limited and their confidence level is too low and just used for different techniques comparison. Therefore, in order to clarify technique better, it has been tested precisely and which high confidence level in case study [22]. So, it has been implemented on some big benchmarks and program's robustness in industrial environment.

The ICS-CFC technique applied to a real ICS distributed network comprise of three Steam Boiler (Steam boiler is basically a closed vessel into which water is heated until the water is converted into steam at required pressure) devices and three RO (Reverse osmosis is a process in which dissolved inorganic solids like salts are removed from a solution like water) devices and an HP server. There have been 3 PLC modules set up above mentioned machines, and are being monitored by HP server through the wireless network. SIMATIC S7 software installed on the server and some benchmarks, with STEP7 programming language, implemented on PLCs. Benchmarks specifications have been shown in Table 2.

Table 2. Benchmark programs used in the experiments

Benchmarks	Devices	PLC models	#Basic blocks	Memory overhead	Performance overhead
SB200E	Steam Boiler1	SIMATIC ET200	39	13.00 %	28.34 %
SB300S	Steam Boiler2	SIMATIC S7-300	41	15.67 %	27.10 %
SB400S	Steam Boiler3	SIMATIC S7-400	42	14.10 %	25.85 %
R200E	RO1	SIMATIC ET200	26	15.25 %	26.09 %
R300S	RO2	SIMATIC S7-300	29	16.30 %	24.10 %
R400S	RO3	SIMATIC S7-400	33	16.45 %	23.50 %

For experimental evaluation the ICS-CFC technique was applied to PLCs and 30,000 faults were injected into the mentioned benchmarks. Two versions are considered for each benchmark. The first is the original code, to which ICS-CFC technique is being applied. Table 3 shows the experimental results of the original program and ICS-CFC programs, respectively. For each version, according to the effects of the injected faults in the PLC's programs, five different cases occur: Correct Result, Wrong Result, Time Out, Os Exception and Single Detection. The occurrence percentages of these cases are shown in Table 3.

Table 3. Experimental evaluation average results of NO-CFC and ICS-CFC

Benchmarks	No CFC					ICS-CFC				
	CR %	WR %	TO %	OS %	SD %	CR %	WR %	TO %	OS %	SD %
R400S	14.20	64.45	11.60	09.75	0.00	11.00	04.30	08.90	07.60	68.20
R300S	13.80	64.15	12.09	09.96	0.00	12.30	05.90	09.10	07.90	64.80
R200E	15.00	63.80	10.67	10.53	0.00	12.80	05.20	09.90	08.50	63.60
SB400S	12.90	65.10	12.90	09.10	0.00	09.10	06.30	10.80	07.10	66.70
SB300S	13.80	62.90	11.45	11.85	0.00	10.10	05.28	08.60	06.98	69.04
SB200E	11.65	59.20	09.60	19.55	0.00	08.30	06.10	08.90	07.20	69.50

Table 2 presents the memory and the performance overhead of 6 benchmarks. The average memory overhead of the ICS-CFC technique, due to insertion of redundant instructions into basic blocks of a program and signature variables, is about 15.13 %. The average performance overhead of the technique, due to execution of the redundant instructions, is about 28.83 %.

5 Conclusions

Industrial Control Systems (ICS) are essential factors to ensure execution of an industrial process safe and successfully. SCADA system, a type of an ICS, is a widely distributed system primarily used to remotely control and monitor of industrial processes from a central location. SCADA covers the transfer of data between a server as MTU and a number of remote sites as RTUs. Since an RTU works in a harsh environment, fault tolerance is one of the most significant among many challenges in industrial networks. In this paper, a hybrid control flow checking technique, called ICS-CFC, was proposed in order to detect control flow errors in RTUs. This technique is employed to monitor the program execution flows of several RTUs in a SCADA system as a distributed system. The proposed technique can be applied to all ICSs which employ microcontrollers, microprocessors, PLCs, or personal computers as their RTUs. To evaluate the fault coverage of ICS-CFC technique, 30,000 faults were injected on distributed system. Among all injected faults, the ICS-CFC technique detects more than 96.32 % of faults resulted.

Acknowledgement. The authors would like to appreciate Parin Beton Amood Company for providing the opportunity of field work and evaluation of the ICS-CFC technique in a real Industrial Control System.

References

1. Mollah, M.B., Islam, S.S.: Towards IEEE 802.22 based SCADA system for future distributed system. In: Proceedings of IEEE International Conference on Informatics, Electronics & Vision, pp. 1075–1080. Dhaka, Bangladesh, 18–19 May 2012
2. Atlagic, B., Milinkov, D., Sagi, M., Bogovac, B.: High-performance networked SCADA architecture for safety-critical systems. In: Proceedings of the Second Eastern European Regional Conference on the Engineering of Computer Based Systems, pp. 147–148, Bratislava, Slovakia, 5–6 September 2011
3. Avhad, M., Divekar, V., Golatkar, H., Joshi, S.: Microcontroller based automation system using industry standard SCADA. In: Proceedings of Annual IEEE India Conference, pp. 1–6. Mumbai, India, 13–15 December 2013
4. Qiang, Z., Danyan, C.: Design and implementation of distribution network SCADA system based on J2EE Framework. In: Proceedings of International Forum on Information Technology and Applications, pp. 633–636. Chengdu, China, 15–17 May 2009
5. Misbahuddin, S.: Fault tolerant remote terminal units (RTUs) in SCADA systems. In: Proceedings of International Symposium on Collaborative Technologies and Systems (CTS), pp. 440–446. Chicago, USA, 17–21 May 2010

6. Tan, L., Tan, Y., Xu, J.: CFEDR: control-flow error detection and recovery using encoded signatures monitoring. In: Proceedings of IEEE International Symposium on Defect and Fault Tolerance in VLSI and Nanotechnology Systems (DFT), pp. 25–32. New York, USA, 2–4 October 2013

7. Mahmood, A., McCluskey, E.J.: Concurrent error detection using watchdog processors-a survey. J. IEEE Trans. Comput. **37**(2), 160–174 (2002)

8. Makoto, S.: A dynamic continuous signature monitoring technique for reliable microprocessors. J. IEICE Trans. Electron. **94**(4), 477–486 (2011)

9. Chen, Y.Y., Leu, K.L.: Signature-monitoring technique based on instruction-bit grouping. IET Proc. Comput. Digital Tech. **152**(4), 527–536 (2005)

10. Sedaghat, Y., Miremadi, S.G., Fazeli, M.: A software-based error detection technique using encoded signatures. In: Proceedings of the 21st IEEE International Symposium on Fault-Tolerance in VLSI Systems (DFT 2006), pp. 389–400. Arlington, USA, 4–6 October 2006

11. Benso, A., Carlo, S.D., Natale, G.D., Prinetto, P.: A watchdog processor to detect data and control flow errors. In: Proceedings of the 9th IEEE On-line Testing Symposium, pp. 144–148, 9–7 July 2003

12. Horst, R.W., Harris, R.L., Jardine, R.L.: Multiple instruction issue in the nonstop cyclone processor. In: Proceedings of the 17th International Symposium on Computer Architecture, pp. 216–226. Seattle, Washington, USA, 28–31 May 1990

13. Nicolescu, B., Velazco, R.: Detecting soft errors by a purely software approach: method, tools and experimental results. In: Proceedings of the Design, Automation and Test in Europe Conference and Exhibition (DATE 2003), pp. 57–62. Munich, 3–7 March 2003

14. Oh, N., Shirvani, P.P., McCluskey, E.J.: Control-flow checking by software signatures. J. IEEE Trans. Reliab. **51**(1), 111–122 (2002)

15. Yu, J., Garzaran, M.J., Sni, M.: Techniques for efficient software checking. In: Proceedings of the 20th International Workshop on Languages and Compilers for Parallel Computing (LCPC 2007), pp. 16–31. Urbana, Illinois, USA, 11–13 October 2007

16. Li, A., Hong, B.: On-line control flow error detection using relationship signatures among basic blocks. J. Comput. Electr. Eng. **36**(1), 132–141 (2010). Elsevier

17. Asghari, S.A., Taheri, H., Pedram, H., Kaynak, O.: Software-based control flow checking against transient faults in industrial environments. J. IEEE Trans. Indus. Inform. **10**(1), 481–490 (2014). IEEE

18. Fazeli, M., Farivar, R., Miremadi, S.G.: Error detection enhancement in powerpc architecture-based embedded processors. J. Electron. Test. Theory Appl. (JETTA) **24**(1–3), 21–33 (2008). Springer

19. Koren, I., Krishna, C.M.: Fault-Tolerant Systems. Elsevier, San Francisco (2007)

20. Chaudhari, A., Park, J., Abraham, J.: A framework for low overhead hardware based runtime control flow error detection and recovery. In: 2013 IEEE 31st VLSI Test Symposium (VTS), pp. 1–6. Berekley, CA, April 2013

21. Xue, M., Zhu, C.: The socket programming and software design for communication based on client/server. In: Proceedings of Pacific-Asia Conference on Circuits Communications and System (PACCS), pp. 775–777. Chengdu, China, 16–17 May 2009

22. Leveugle, R., Calvez, A., Maistri, P.: Statistical fault injection: quantified error and confidence. In: Design, Automation and Test in Europe Conference and Exhibition, DATE 2009, pp. 502–506. Nice, 20–24 April 2009

23. Rysavy, O., Rab, J., Halfar, P.: A formal authorization framework for networked SCADA systems. In: Proceedings of the 19th International Conference and Workshops on Engineering of Computer Based Systems (ECBS), pp. 298–302. Serbia, 11–13 April 2012

24. Regel, R.G., Parameswaran, S.: Hardware assisted pre-emptive control flow checking for embedded processors to improve reliability. In: Proceedings of the 4th International Conference hardware/software codesign and system synthesis, pp. 100–105, Seoul, Korea, 22–25 October 2006
25. Asghari, S.A., Taheri, H., Pedram, H., Abdi, A.: An effective intra-inter block control flow checking method against single event upsets. Res. J. Appl. Sci. Eng. Tech. 4, 4367–4379 (2012)

Real-World Types and Their Application

Jian Xiang, John Knight[⊠], and Kevin Sullivan

University of Virginia,
85, Engineers Way, PO Box 400740, Charlottesville, VA 22904, USA
{Jian,Knight,Sullivan}@cs.virginia.edu

Abstract. Software systems sense and affect real world objects and processes in order to realize important real-world systems. For these systems to function correctly, such software should obey constraints inherited from the real world. Typically, neither important characteristics of real-world entities nor the relationships between such entities and their machine-world representations are specified explicitly in code, and important opportunities for detecting errors due to mismatches are lost. To address this problem we introduce real-world types to document in software both relevant characteristics of real-world entities and the relationships between real-world entities and machine-level representations. These constructs support specification and automated static detection of such mismatches in programs written in ordinary languages. We present a prototype implementation of our approach for Java and case studies in which previously unrecognized real-world type errors in several real systems were detected.

Keywords: Real-world types · Dependability · Static analysis

1 Introduction

Software systems, especially cyber-physical systems, interact with the real world in order to sense and affect it. Such software should obey rules inherited from the real world that it senses, models, and affects, as well as from the machine world in which the software executes. For example, software that computes physical quantities should respect units and physical dimensions, and many analysis systems have been built to perform units and dimensions checking on software.

Frequently, however, important characteristics of real-world entities are undocumented or are documented incompletely, informally, and implicitly in code. As a result, constraints inherited from the real world are stated and enforced either in ad-hoc ways or not at all. Crucial relationships between machine-world representations and real-world entities remain under-specified, and programs treat machine-world representations as if they were the real-world entities themselves. As a result, faults are introduced into systems due to unrecognized discrepancies, and executions end up violating constraints inherited from the real world. The results are software and system failures and adverse downstream consequences.

The failure of software to represent real-world entities with sufficient fidelity has been a causal factor in various accidents and incidents. In 1999, the Mars Climate Orbiter was lost because different parts of the software system used different units of

© Springer International Publishing Switzerland 2015
F. Koornneef and C. van Gulijk (Eds.): SAFECOMP 2015, LNCS 9337, pp. 471–484, 2015.
DOI: 10.1007/978-3-319-24255-2_34

measurement [1]. More recently, in 2013 a delay in berthing Orbital's Cygnus spacecraft with the International Space Station (ISS) occurred because Cygnus and the ISS used different forms of GPS time data; one based on the original 1980 ephemeris, and the other based on an ephemeris designed in 1999 [2]. In both cases, different real-world entities were represented using the same machine-world types, allowing machine-world operations to be applied in ways that made no real-world sense.

In this paper, we introduce the concept of *real-world types* and *type checking*. For entities of a given real-world type, the type definition documents the real-world specification, the machine representation, and the relation between the two. The specification of a real-world type defines relevant, observable properties of real-world entities of that type. The machine representation defines how a real-world entity is represented in the machine and thus becomes accessible by software. The relationship defines the connection between real-world entities and associated machine elements.

The goal of real-world types is to enable reasoning about and automated checking of the logic of a program based on the real-world entities with which the program has to interact. To exploit real-world types, we introduce the concept of connecting them with entities in programs such as variables, constants and functions so as to extend the programmer designated type. The explicit, formal documentation of real-world types supports analysis and enforcement of real-world constraints on programs in a systematic way, thereby enabling new classes of software fault prevention and detection, without requiring programmers to adopt new machine-level programming languages. Among other things, real-world types can be used in effect to annotate uses of machine-level values in ways that enable prevention of the kind of real-world type mismatches that led to such failures as that of the Mars Climate Orbiter.

If real-world types are to be used in the development of realistic software systems, an approach to integrating them into widely used languages and development methods is needed. We have developed a prototype demonstrating the integration of real-world types with the Java language. The implementation connects real-world type definitions to Java entities without modifying the Java source program and provides type checking of Java code against real-world type rules defined by system experts. We present case studies in which real-world types were applied to a set of pertinent projects including a project with 14,000 LOC. The real-world type checking revealed both unreported faults and faults that had previously been reported as bugs.

In the next section, we discuss the role of real-world entities in software, and in Sect. 3 we present the real-world type system concept. In Sect. 4 we discuss our prototype implementation for Java. Our evaluation of real-world types is presented in Sect. 5. Related work is summarized in Sect. 6 and we conclude in Sect. 7.

2 From the Real World to the Machine

Frequently, software systems are developed with an emphasis on the machine, focusing on the machine context rather than the real-world entities that the machine has to manipulate. We refer to this as the *machine-world* viewpoint. Variables, values, or instances, i.e., machine-world entities, are introduced to represent real-world entities, thereby also introducing uncertainties and assumptions about the real-world entities in those representations.

That real-world entities are what the computer ultimately is *intended* to manipulate is often forgotten. The problem is that machine-world entities are not the same as real-world entities. The relationships between them are usually incomplete because of: (a) the absence of much of the real-world semantic information in the machine world, (b) the approximations inherent in finite-precision representations in the machine world and in the sensing of values from the real world, (c) noisy and mis-calibrated sensors, and (d) sensor and related failures. However, by focusing on the real-world context and documenting comprehensively the relationship between the real-world entities and the associated machine-world entities, i.e., taking a *real-world* viewpoint, the incompleteness and other limitations in the relationships become explicit and analyzable. Software design and analysis should be fully informed by the real-world context if it is to be rigorous and complete. The contrast between the real-world and the machine-world viewpoints is illustrated in Fig. 1.

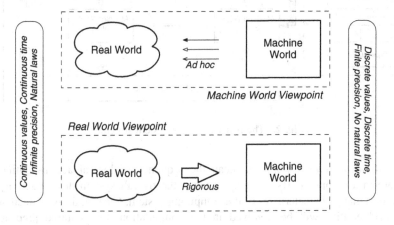

Fig. 1. From a machine-world viewpoint to a real-world viewpoint

This real-world viewpoint has several benefits: (a) the precise semantics of the real world including all relevant attributes and invariants are clear; (b) the rules and relationships between real-world entities are explicit and can be used to check the software for violations of the rules and relationships; (c) the differences between real-world entities and their machine-world realizations can be documented and analyzed; (d) specific analysis techniques derived from the real-world context can be developed.

Real-world types are designed to document real-world entities, and to document and leverage the relationship between real-world entities and programs. They provide a pragmatic and robust infrastructure for error analyses. Many characteristics of real-world entities define constraints that are unlikely to change yet should be observed in any applications that access the pertinent real-world entities. Therefore, a library of generic real-world types and rules could be established for use in various different applications.

3   The Real World Type System

3.1   Overall Structure

The overall structure of the real-world type system and its interfaces with: (a) the real world, (b) the computation of the associated system, and (c) overall system design are shown in Fig. 2.

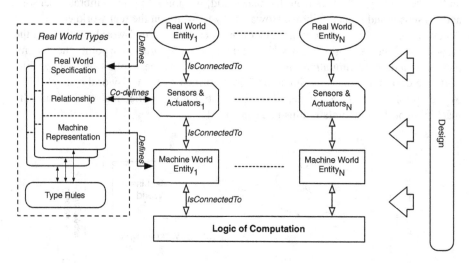

Fig. 2. The real-world type system structure

By *logic of computation*, we mean the sequence of logical actions defined by software in a computer. By *design*, we mean the overall system design activity that determines many characteristics of the computing system. Clearly, design affects which real-world entities will be involved in the computation, the required precision of computations, details of timing, and so on.

In the overall structure, system designers define the specifications of the real world types based on real-world entities of interest. The representations of real-world types are determined by design and are used to define the machine-world entities that will represent real-world entities in the computation. The relationships between the specifications and representations are determined by design and analysis, including details of the sensing and actuation needed to interface the computation to the real world. Sensing and actuation can contribute to the definition of the relationships because of limitations inherent in the associated equipment such as sensing precision and rate of update. Finally, the type rules associated with the real-world types are determined by the semantics of the operations that are required for the entities being manipulated.

3.2   The Definition of Real-World Types

A real-world type has a name and a definition that consist of three parts:

- The specification of the type derived from the associated real world entities.
- The machine representation of instances of the type.
- The relationship between the specification and the representation.

We present details of these three parts in the remainder of this section.

Real-World Specification. The first part of the specification is an explication of the type intended for humans. An explication is a detailed explanation of the meaning of something, and explications are required for real-world types so as to ensure that a single source of meaning is provided for all the entities with which the computing system interacts. The explication could be in natural language, one or more formal languages, or a combination. The explication is the means by which interpretation is given to the real-world type.

As an example, consider the notion of altitude in an avionics system. Altitude could mean height above local ground level or height above mean sea level, and could be determined by radar, barometric pressure, or GPS. Exactly how each semantic concept is used for this type needs to be explained in an explication for altitude.

The second part of the specification is a set of real-world semantics. A real-world semantic concept can be any real-world property of interest. Every semantic concept is defined through: (a) an explication of the concept, (b) the set of values that the concept can take, and (c) reference sources such as an ontology or a dictionary.

Returning to the example of an aircraft's altitude, a semantic concept is the measurement reference level. This concept could be either sea level or local ground level. Documentation for the specification of such a concept is shown in Table 1.

Table 1. Example real-world semantic concept

Concept	Reference level
Explication	Reference datum from which altitude value is measured
Possible values	Mean sea level; local ground level
References	Basic Geo Vocabulary; DAML's location ontology

A complete set of semantics for altitude would include reference level, frame of reference (surface location, Earth center, etc.), units of measurement, etc.

Units and physical dimensions are examples of real-world semantics, and their introduction into programming languages along with analysis techniques to perform type correctness checks have been explored previously [3–5]. In our theory of real-world types, units and dimensions are just special case semantics and are predefined because of their widespread use and importance in real-world properties.

Units can be enumerated as needed by an application. The dimensions semantic concept consists of the seven basic dimensions of physics (mass, length, time, electric current, temperature, luminosity, and amount of substance) [6]. The existence of this semantic concept allows the standard dimensional analysis of physics to be applied. For simplicity, in our own use of dimensional analysis we added *angle* to the set for a vector length of eight. Thus, a semantic value of dimensions is an eight-element vector of integers defining the real-world dimensions of the associated variable. Some example dimensions are:

- Speed: (0,1,-1,0,0,0,0,0)
- Acceleration: (0,1,-2,0,0,0,0,0)
- Energy: (1,2,-2,0,0,0,0,0)

Machine Representation. The machine representation of a type is characterized by a set of semantics that describe the properties derived from the machine context. Machine-world semantics in the representation use a similar format to that used for the real-world semantics in the specification.

Some examples of machine-world semantics and the associated values that they can take are:

- encoding: integer, floating point, double
- mutability: mutable, non-mutable

The mutability semantic concept indicates whether objects of the type are constant, thereby allowing for detection of unintended assignments.

Relationship. The relationship that connects the specification to the machine representation of a real-world type is defined as a logical expression. The expression typically has the form of a conjunction of predicates where each predicate indicates one dimension of imprecision. In the altitude example, the mapping might take the form:

```
value: error < delta and delay < tau
```

The first predicate documents the maximum difference between the actual altitude and the value supplied by the sensing system, and the second documents the maximum delay between sensing the altitude and the associated value being available in the machine world.

3.3 Real-World Type Rules

Real-world type safety is determined by rules derived from real-world entities. All necessary checking of the predefined semantics (units and physical dimensions) are included by default. Such analysis is limited though useful, and the general notion of real-world types presented here provides a broad basis for defining type safety rules. Any relevant limitation, expectation or invariant that arises in the real world can be encoded as type rules provided it can be expressed using real-world type semantics.

Developers define type rules based on the semantics of types and the desired effect on semantics of operations by programs. In arithmetic expressions, for example, units must match, the dimensionality rules of physics must be observed, arithmetic operations can only be applied to types for which they are defined, and the results of arithmetic operations must have the correct real-world type.

Example type rules that detect operations which are probably erroneous include:

- The units of an angle and a latitude must match if they are added. The result is of type latitude measured in the same units.
- A velocity, dimensions (0, 1, −1, 0, 0, 0, 0, 0), cannot be added to a distance, dimensions (0, 1, 0, 0, 0, 0, 0, 0).
- A latitude or a longitude cannot be added to a latitude or a longitude.
- An x coordinate in one frame of reference cannot be used in any arithmetic operation with a coordinate from a different frame of reference.

- A variable of type *magnetic* heading cannot be used in an expression expecting a variable of type *true* heading, even if both are represented as integers and are commensurable.
- A variable of type *geodetic* latitude cannot be used in an expression expecting a variable of type *geocentric* latitude, even if both are represented as floating point and are commensurable.

As an example of type-rule definition, consider the semantics of the result of subtracting two operands of type `vertical_cartesian_axis`, e.g., for calculating the altitude difference between two points in the same Cartesian coordinate system. The definition is illustrated in Fig. 3.

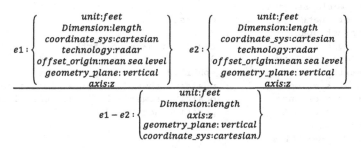

Fig. 3. Example type rule definition. The notation e:T denotes a type judgment (e is of type T), and the overall construct defines an inference rule defining the type of the result of applying a specific operator, here subtraction, to operands, e1 and e2, of the specified types

3.4 Real-World Types and Program Structures

The notion of type in programming languages includes structures such as arrays and records. An array of integers and a record with multiple fields are types with various associated usage and equivalence rules.

Real-world types do not have any structure beyond that discussed so far. The reason is that including all of the structures that arise in programming languages is neither possible nor necessary. Defining real-world types as presented above and using them as building blocks in language structures provides the necessary structure. For a record, for example, a real-world type would be defined for the record as a whole and separate real-world types could be defined for each field. The type for a given field is then the *union* of the type information for the record and the type information for that field. Nested records accumulate type in the union as each level is progressed.

This approach raises an issue with structured types, because different instances of a user-defined type might have different real-world types. A record structure might be instantiated more than once to hold information with different real-world semantics but identical structures. This issue is dealt with in our present theory of real-world types by associating different type information with different instances of a structure but requiring that the components of a structure have the same type information in all instances. This restriction might be relaxed in future to allow more flexibility.

3.5   Real-World Type Example

An example of a real-world type is a point in three-dimensional space, 3Dloc. Measurements designed to locate a point are only relevant if the associated coordinate system is defined completely. If multiple coordinate systems are in use in a program they must be distinguished. Thus, the real-world type information associated with an instance of the class needs to document the different aspects of the coordinate system.

The type definition for the coordinate system of 3Dloc could be:

```
geographic_cartesian_coord_sys:
  Specification
    explication          : <text>
    real_world_semantics
      coordinate_sys_type : cartesian
      target_space        : Earth
      origin              : center of mass of Earth
      dimensionality      : 3
      earth_model         : spheroid
      x_axis_orientn      : positive toward 0 degrees longitude
      y_axis_orientn      : positive toward 90 degrees east longitude
      z_axis_orientn      : positive northward
  Representation
    machine_semantics
      representation      : record structure - (float, float, float)
  Relationship            : <null>
```

Note that this type definition is created just to *distinguish* coordinate systems. Separately, we need the types of the three fields that will be used for a point in the coordinate system. For this, one, two, or three different type definitions might be needed. For this example, we assume that the x and y variables can share a type definition and a second definition is used for z. For x and y, we define the following type:

```
horizontal_cartesian_axis:
  Specification           : <text>
    real_world_semantics
      linear_units        : mile
      dimensions          : (1, 0, 0, 0, 0, 0, 0, 0)
      technology          : GPS
      geometry_plane      : horizontal
  Representation
    machine_semantics
      representation      : float
      mutable             : no
  Relationship
      value_error < delta1 and delay < tau1
```

In this example, altitude is part of a complete reference frame with origin at the center of mass of the Earth but with a presumed offset to mean sea level:

```
vertical_cartesian_axis:
  Specification
    explication              : <text>
    real_world_semantics
      linear_units           : feet
      dimensions             : (1, 0, 0, 0, 0, 0, 0, 0)
      technology             : radar
      geometry_plane         : vertical
      offset_origin          : mean sea level
  Representation
    machine_semantics
      representation         : float
      mutable                : no
  Relationship
    value_error< delta2 and delay < tau2
```

Such a type might be used to hold data in any space of interest. For example, the type could be used to hold location information for aircraft, climbers, balloons, etc.

4 An Implementation for Java

We have developed a prototype implementation of real-world types for Java. A choice made for the overall approach was that the system should operate without requiring changes to the subject Java program. This choice provides three major advantages:

1. Real-world type information does not obscure the basic structure of the Java program.
2. Real-world type information can be added to existing Java programs without having to modify (and possibly break) the original source text.
3. Real-world type information can be added to a Java program without impeding development of the Java program itself.

Motivated by this design choice, the prototype operates separately from the compiler via its own user interface.

4.1 Operation of the Prototype

The subject Java program is parsed, and real-world type definitions and type rules are either loaded from a file or entered via the user interface. Using the type-checking system requires that relevant Java program variables be annotated with appropriate real-world types. Entities just in the machine world, such as loop counters, are not annotated. Annotations are established by clicking on the type and then on the variable. Various displays are available to allow the real-world types and their use to be viewed, e.g., all of the Java variables of a given real-world type can be displayed, all of the type rules associated with a given real-world type can be displayed, etc.

Annotations can be limited to subsets of variables that are of interest. Entities with no annotation are assumed to be type correct in all circumstances. This permits incremental introduction of annotations as use of real-world types increases.

Real-world type checking involves examination of the Java program looking for violations of the type rules. The system provides for subsets of the type rules to be checked separately if desired. For example, separate checking of just the rules for units might be useful. This mechanism is also useful in debugging type rules.

Running the type checker yields diagnostics if type rules are violated. Diagnostics are presented with details of the type rule and the associated text is highlighted.

4.2 Type Conversion

An important issue in the type system is type *conversion*. For example, a conversion from feet to inches requires multiplying a variable storing a value in feet by 12. Explicit type conversion is dealt with simply by including type rules associated with whatever special operator or function is used. Implicit type conversion is more difficult. Conversions between real-world types can be syntactically simple. The difficulty is locating such conversions automatically without generating false negatives.

We deal with implicit type conversion by requiring that the programmer mark implicit type conversions as such. Thus, diagnostics generated for type conversions of which the type system was unaware require that the programmer suppress the diagnostic by indicating that there is an expected type conversion thereby indicating that the diagnostic has been investigated and the code found to be as desired.

5 Evaluation

We conducted a two-part study in which we developed real-world types for several open-source projects with which we have no association. In the first part, a complete set of real-world types were defined for a project called the *Kelpie Flight Planner* [7]. Various elements of the software were given real-world types, a set of type rules defined, and type checking was performed.

In the second part, we reused real-world types and type rules created in part one on a set of projects that access the same real-world entities. For these projects, type checking has only been applied to pertinent packages and files to detect errors.

5.1 Kelpie Flight Planner

The Kelpie Flight Planner is an open-source Java project based on Flightgear [8]. The program uses the airport and navaid databases of Flightgear to determine routes between airports based on user inputs. The program is 13,884 lines long, is organized as 10 packages, and is contained in 126 source files.

A critical element of the data used by the Kelpie Flight Planner in modeling aircraft movement, the *velocity surface,* is a two-element vector consisting of the horizontal velocity (motion across the Earth's surface) and the vertical velocity (climb or sink rate) of the aircraft. The details of the velocity surface are shown in Fig. 4.

Various models of the Earth's geometry have been created, including a sphere and an ellipsoid. For the ellipsoid, different models have been developed for special

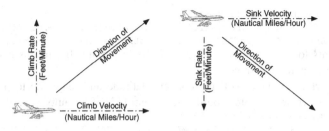

Fig. 4. The velocity surface

purposes; for example, the International Geomagnetic Reference Field IGRF [9] and the World Magnetic Model WMM [10]. In order to undertake useful calculations, programs like the Kelpie Flight Planner have to operate with a model of the Earth's geometry, and details of the model need to be included in the real-world type system in order to allow appropriate checking.

For the Kelpie Flight Planner, 35 different real-world types were defined along with 97 type rules. The total number of type links for the project was 255. For illustration, we summarize three of six faults that were identified by the real-world type analysis. None of these faults had been reported in the project error log.

The source code containing the first fault is:

```
alt -= legTime * plan.getAircraft().getSinkSpeed()/60;
```

The expression references the wrong data. `getSinkSpeed()` returns a quantity measured horizontally and `alt` is measured vertically.

The source code containing the second fault is:

```
alt += legTime * plan.getAircraft().getClimbRate()/60;
```

`plan.getAircraft().getClimbRate()` returns the climb rate in feet/minute, the variable `legTime` is time in hours, and `alt` is altitude in feet. The conversion factor is 60, but the conversion requires multiplication by 60, not division.

The source code containing the third fault is:

```
alt -= legTime * plan.getAircraft().getSinkSpeed()/60;
```

The expression references the wrong data. As in the first fault, `getSinkSpeed()` returns a quantity measured horizontally and `alt` is measured vertically. Correcting this fault yields code with the same units issue as arose in the second fault requiring an additional fix.

5.2   Other Java Applications

We reused the real-world types and type rules created for the Kelpie Flight Planner project to check packages and source files in other applications with pertinent functions. We chose applications for which a log was available for defects reported from the field after release. We include examples here for illustration.

OpenMap is a Java Beans based toolkit for building applications and applets that access geographic information [11]. The code for the first fault we detected is:

```
lon2 = l12.getY();
```

The variable `lon2` is a longitude, but the method `getY()` returns a latitude.

The code for the second fault is:

```
double[] llpoints = GreatCircle.greatCircle(startLLP.getY(),
    startLLP.getX(), endLLP.getY(), endLLP.getX(), numPoints, true);
```

The arguments to `greatCircle()` should be in radians, but in this call the arguments are measured in degrees.

Geoconvertor is a Java API that converts latitude and longitude to points in the Universal Transverse Mercator coordinate system [12]. The faulty code detected is:

```
if (datum.name().equals("WGS84")) {
    e1=eccentricityOne(WGS84.MAJOR_AXIS, SAD69.MINOR_AXIS);
    e2=eccentricityTwo(WGS84.MAJOR_AXIS, SAD69.MINOR_AXIS)};}
```

The constructors `eccentricityOne()` and `eccentricityTwo()` each expect two arguments of the same Earth model, SAD69 for the first and WGS84 for the second. The code has the argument Earth models confused.

6 Related Work

Research efforts on requirements and specification have modeled the connections between the real world and the machine world [13–16]. Parnas and Madey introduced the 4-variable model that describes the relationship between real-world entities and machine world primarily as mathematically relations [16]. Miller and Tribble extended the original 4-variable model that isolated the virtual versions of the monitored and controlled values in subsystems [15].

Zave and Jackson characterized phenomena of interest to the system and separate world phenomena from machine phenomena [14]. The reference model of Gunter et al. gives a detailed explanation of different classes of phenomena and relationship between environment and system [13].

Other research efforts extend type systems to support additional checking capabilities [17–19]. These frameworks refine the built-in type system so as to allow additional types to be defined. By contrast, real-world types urge programmers to think from the perspective of the real world.

Ait-Ameur et al. [20] propose bringing more system information into the development of software. They emphasize the separation of implicit and explicit semantics.

Dimensional analysis and units checking have been explored in many programming languages [21, 22]. Previous research focused on extending programming languages to allow checking dimensions of equations. Some researchers focused on validating unit correctness [3–5].

Researchers have attempted to improve program understanding by linking structured semantic information in real-world contexts to formalisms [23]. Ratiu et al. have developed techniques to improve the understanding of formalism elements by making explicit mappings between ontology classes and the program elements [23].

7 Conclusion

We have presented a general notion of type based upon the real-world properties of entities with which a computer system operates and the mapping from those entities onto their representations in the computer system. Real-world types allow the definition and enforcement of type rules derived from the real world, as well the machine world. This enables a new range of analyses including automatic detection of real-world type violations, and inspections targeted at error prone software practices.

Future work in this area includes development of libraries of real-world types, additional empirical studies, the mining of system documentation for real-world type information, and the further clarification, for software engineering applications, of the representational correspondences between symbolic references and their referents.

Acknowledgements. This work was supported in part by Dependable Computing LLC, in part by the National Science Foundation grant number 1400294, and in part by the U.S. Department of Defense under Contract H98230-08-D- 0171. Any opinions, findings and conclusions or recommendations are those of the authors and do not necessarily reflect the views of the United States Department of Defense.

References

1. Mars Climate Orbiter Mishap Investigation Board Phase I Report. National Aeronautics and Space Administration, Washington DC (1999)
2. Bergin, C. Harding, P.: Cygnus Delays ISS Berthing Following GPS Discrepancy. http://www.nasaspaceflight.com/2013/09/cygnus-cots-graduation-iss-berthing/
3. Antoniu, T., Steckler, P.A., Krishnamurthi, S., Neuwirth, E., Felleisen, M.: Validating the unit correctness of spreadsheet programs. In: 26th International Conference on Software Engineering, pp. 439–448. IEEE Press, New York (2004)
4. Grein, C., Kazakov, D.A., Wilson, D.B.: A survey of physical unit handling techniques in ada. In: Rosen, J.-P., Strohmeier, A. (eds.) Ada-Europe 2003. LNCS, vol. 2655, pp. 258–270. Springer, Heidelberg (2003)
5. Kennedy, A.: Dimension types. In: 5th European Symposium on Programming, pp. 348–362. ACM Press, New York (1994)
6. International System of Units. National Institution of Standards Technology, Washington, DC
7. Kelpie Flight Planner for Flightgear. http://sourceforge.net/projects/fgflightplanner/
8. FlightGear. http://www.flightgear.org/
9. International Association of Geomagnetism and Aeronomy: International geomagnetic reference field: the eleventh generation. Geophys. J. Int. **183**(3), 1216–1230 (2010)
10. World Magnetic Model. http://www.ngdc.noaa.gov/geomag/WMM/DoDWMM.shtml
11. OpenMap. https://code.google.com/p/openmap/
12. Geoconvertor. https://code.google.com/p/geoconvertor/
13. Gunter, C.A., Gunter, E.L., Jackson, M., Zave, P.: A reference model for requirements and specifications. IEEE Softw. **17**(3), 37–43 (2000)
14. Jackson, M., Zave, P.: Deriving specifications from requirements: an example. In: 17th International Conference on Software Engineering, pp. 15–24. ACM, New York (1995)
15. Miller, S.P., Tribble, A.C.: Extending the four-variable model to bridge the system-software gap. In: 20th Digital Avionics System Conference, pp. 1–5. IEEE Press, New York (2001)
16. Parnas, D.L., Madey, L.: Functional documents for computer systems. Sci. Comput. Program. **25**(1), 41–61 (1995)

17. Papi, M., Ali, M., Correr, Jr., T.L., Perkins, J.H., Ernst, M.D.: Practical pluggable types for Java. In: SIGSOFT International Symposium on Software Testing and Analysis, pp. 201–212. ACM Press, New York (2008)
18. Markstrum, S., Marino, D., Esquivel, M., Millstein, T., Andreae, C., Noble, J.: JavaCOP: declarative pluggable types for java. ACM Trans. Program. Lang. Syst. **32**(2), 41–437 (2010)
19. Dietl, W., Dietzel, S., Ernst, M.D., Muşlu, K., Schiller, T.W.: Building and using pluggable type-checkers. In: 33rd International Conference on Software Engineering, pp. 681–690. ACM, New York (2011)
20. Ait-Ameur, Y., Gibson, J.P., Méry, D.: On implicit and explicit semantics: integration issues in proof-based development of systems. In: Margaria, T., Steffen, B. (eds.) ISoLA 2014, Part II. LNCS, vol. 8803, pp. 604–618. Springer, Heidelberg (2014)
21. Chen, F., Rosu, G., Venkatesan, R.P.: Rule-based analysis of dimensional safety. In: Nieuwenhuis, R. (ed.) RTA 2003. LNCS, vol. 2706, pp. 197–207. Springer, Heidelberg (2003)
22. Jiang, L., Su, Z.: Osprey: a practical type system for validating dimensional unit correctness of C programs. In: 28th International Conference on Software Engineering, pp. 262–271. ACM, New York (2006)
23. Ratiu, D., Deissenboeck, F.: From reality to programs and (not quite) back again. In: 15th IEEE International Conference on Program Comprehension, pp. 91–102. IEEE Press, New York (2007)

Author Index

Abdulkhaleq, Asim 121
Alemzadeh, Homa 213
Altschaffel, Robert 47
Antonino, Pablo Oliveira 269
Armengaud, Eric 410
Arts, Thomas 74
Ayatolahi, Fatemeh 135

Baalbergen, Jan Jaap 243
Banescu, Sebastian 362
Barbosa, Paulo 183, 269
Beckers, Kristian 90
Bezerra, Juliana M. 19
Bishop, Peter 297
Bondavalli, Andrea 166
Bothe, Lex 243
Brauer, Jörg 427

Ceccarelli, Andrea 166
Chen, Daniel 213
Chen, Sanjian 228
Cintra, Marcelo 151
Côté, Isabelle 90

Dahlweid, Markus 427
de Weerd, Rob 243
Delmas, Kevin 283
Delmas, Rémi 283
Denney, Ewen 328
Dittmann, Jana 47
Do Hoang, Quynh Anh 313

Eckert, Claudia 441
Espinoza, Huascar 183

Fedler, Rafael 362
Feng, Lu 228
Finnegan, Anita 197
Folkesson, Peter 135
Frese, Thomas 90

Guiochet, Jérémie 313
Gulan, Stefan 111
Gurjão, Edmar C. 269

Harnisch, Jens 111
Hatcliff, John 228
Hatebur, Denis 90
Heisel, Maritta 90
Höller, Andrea 410
Hoppe, Tobias 47

Ibing, Andreas 441
Islam, Mafijul 135
Itria, Massimiliano 166
Iyer, Ravishankar 213

Johnson, Chris W. 375, 400
Johr, Sven 111

Kaaniche, Mohamed 313
Kalbarczyk, Zbigniew 213
Kalkman, Cor J. 3
Karlsson, Johan 135
King, Andrew L. 228
Knight, John 471
Kommanapalli, Vasantha 441
Kreiner, Christian 410
Kretschmer, Roberto 111
Kuhlmann, Sven 47

Latvala, Timo 29
Lee, Insup 228, 252
Lettner, Martin 59
Leveson, Nancy 213
Lewis, Andrew 213
Luiijf, Eric 7

Macher, Georg 410
McCaffery, Fergal 197
Medeiros, Yang 183
Mehmed, Ayhan 59
Muntean, Paul 441

Nadjm-Tehrani, Simin 347
Nagarajan, Vijay 151

Pagetti, Claire 283
Pai, Ganesh 328

Pankrath, Tobias   427
Peleska, Jan   427
Pereverzeva, Inna   29
Popov, Peter T.   385
Pretschner, Alexander   362
Procter, Sam   228
Punnekkat, Sasikumar   59

Rajabpour, Navid   457
Raman, Jaishankar   213
Rieger, Stefan   111
Rosário, Jeferson   269
Rosenbrand, Dagmar   243
Ruiz, Alejandra   183

Sangchoolie, Behrooz   135
Sano, Humberto H.   19
Sedaghat, Yasser   457
Sfyrla, Vasiliki   252
Sokolsky, Oleg   228, 252
Spampinato, Giacomo   59
Sporer, Harald   410

Stefanakis, Georgios   151
Steiner, Wilfried   59
Sullivan, Kevin   471

Tarasyuk, Anton   29
Tonetta, Stefano   74
Trapp, Mario   269
Troubitsyna, Elena   29

Vasilevskaya, Maria   347
Vasserman, Eugene Y.   252
Venkatasubramanian, Krishna K.   252
Villela, Carolina D.   19
Vinter, Jonny   135

Wagner, Stefan   121

Xiang, Jian   471

Zalman, Rafael   111
Zoppi, Tommaso   166

Printed in the United States
By Bookmasters